W9-AZC-062

Greenberg's GUIDES®

LIONEL® TRAINS

1987 - 1995

Motive Power and Rolling Stock

RICHARD KUGHN ERA

Michael Solly

 Published by Kalmbach Publishing Co., 21027 Crossroads Circle, Waukesha, WI 53187.

Printed in China

02 03 04 05 06 07 08 09 10 11 10 9 8 7 6 5 4 3 2 1

Visit our website at
http://kalmbachbooks.com
Secure online ordering available

Publisher's Cataloging-in-Publication
(Provided by Quality Books, Inc.)

Solly, Michael A.
Greenberg's guide to Lionel trains 1987-1995 : the Richard Kughn era / Michael Solly. — 1st ed.
p. cm.
Includes index.
ISBN 0-89778-517-7 (softbound)
ISBN 0-89778-518-5 (hardbound)

1. Railroads—Models. 2. Lionel Corporation.
I. Title. II. Title: Guide to Lionel trains 1987-1995

TF197.S65 2002 625.1'9
QBI01-201476

Art director: Kristi Ludwig
Book design: Sabine Beaupré

Table of Contents

ACKNOWLEDGEMENTS

The readers of our text are always happy to keep your intrepid editors on the straight and narrow, and so it is with this volume. A special thanks to our two longtime readers and commentators—Lou Bohn and Chris Rohlfing—who lent countless wonderful details to our sometimes-dry chapters. Chris was the "color man"—making sure all those shades of colors were properly described! Lou sees many uncataloged and unexpected Lionel items in his business and keeps better notes on them than anyone around. George Brown from Texas contributed our chapter on TrainMaster Command Control, and also reviewed all the chapters. Dave Kris from Michigan and LOTS Director Cris Matuszak from Chicago lent their considerable Lionel expertise as well. Dave helped with some uncataloged sets information. We were assisted greatly in those hard-to-find pieces by Mark Salce, Donald Eberly, Ralph Taylor, and John O'Neill as well. Also deserving of mention is the detailed work of our Lionel experts and friends in the collector clubs, particularly Bill Schmeelk, whose series on the trains in LCCA's *The Lion Roars* is legendary. Thanks to all.

The photos of the beautiful trains wouldn't have been possible without the superb assistance and collection of Al Rudman, owner of Sidetrack Hobbies in Leonardtown, Maryland. Al put up with the author, editor, and photographer over two marathon weekends and lent his support and experience to the entire production. Most of the trains you see here are from his store, and we encourage any visitors to the Washington, D.C., area to give Al a call and visit. Not only is he a Lionel expert, he always manages to give buyers a terrific deal. LOTS compatriot Dave Przyborski donated his Department 56 and Christmas items for photography; likewise, our great friends Al Schwartz and Rich Williams of the Nassau Lionel Operating Engineers graciously allowed us to photograph pieces of their collection.

Lionel, of course, provided much excellent information needed for the organization of the book. Our thanks go to Mike Braga, Lisa Stanko, Todd Wagner, and Ken Silvestri.

Finally, we hope all of the readers who have sent kind letters and notes to the Greenberg Guides over the past eight years will find their efforts rewarded herein. There were too many to list here, but we are very grateful to all of them for their excellent contributions to this work.

Mike Solly
December 2001

CHAPTER 1

Introduction

Kalmbach Publishing Co. is proud to bring you *Greenberg's Guide to Lionel Trains, 1987–1995*—the most comprehensive report on this era of the modern Lionel train marketplace yet produced. This book is intended to be an encyclopedia of Lionel Trains for this period, telling the full story of the trains, and goes far beyond the one-line listings of a pocket guide.

USING THIS GUIDE

WHAT'S INCLUDED, WHAT ISN'T

The listings in this book cover Lionel production from 1987 through the latter part of 1995, the period we have designated "The Kughn Era." The years covered align with the period during which real-estate developer Richard Kughn owned Lionel (Lionel Trains Inc., also known as Lionel LTI).

Our original intent was to include trains produced through 2000; however, Lionel's product output during the late 1990s increased greatly, and it became impossible to include everything in a single volume that the market would support. Hence, our projected Volume II will begin with 1996 production, the year Wellspring Associates acquired the company from Mr. Kughn. No delivery date on Volume II had been determined when this book went to press.

The period preceding the Kughn Era and following the Postwar Era (the Fundimensions Era—1970–1985), is well treated in earlier volumes, known as the "Big Red" books: *Greenberg's Guide to Lionel, 1970–1991, Vols. 1 and 2* [out of print]. Most of the Fundimensions-period data in those books, with the possible exception of some prices, is still relevant.

Richard Kughn

The breakpoint between Fundimensions and LTI (Kughn Era) is a logical place to divide the volumes. Not only does it mark Richard Kughn's purchase of the company from Fundimensions (a whole new era for Lionel in many ways), but also at that time Lionel changed the catalog numbers for the trains from four digits to five. Thus, a modern piece can usually be located in the Fundimensions era if it has four digits and in the Lionel LTI/LLC period if it has five.

The photographs, included directly above the listings for easier reference, cover roughly half of all the production and include some of the rarest and most unusual of Lionel's products. Nearly all of the special convention cars for the national train clubs are included, along with most club division or anniversary pieces.

Even with the restricted time period of this volume, the quantity of pieces manufactured by Lionel LTI made it such that we could not cover related products other than the O gauge motive power and rolling stock, and still produce a book of manageable size. This means that such related topics as sets, trucks, boxes, accessories, Large Scale, American Flyer, Standard Gauge, and "Classics" could not be included. (In appropriate listings we do show the set numbers in which the pieces were included.) Sincere apologies to our hobbyist friends who are interested in those subjects we were unable to address; our intention is to include them in later volumes. Note that Lionel's Modern Era (1970–1997) accessories were covered in Roland Lavoie's Greenberg Guide from 1997.

We are happy to report that all of the "Special Production" club cars, department store specials, and factory errors described in Volume II in the 1991 series have been "re-absorbed" into this book. In addition, our index for this volume is more comprehensive than in the past. This has enabled us to make this volume as all-inclusive as possible, within the size restrictions imposed.

DETERMINING VALUES

Toy train values vary for a number of reasons:

• The "relative knowledge" of the buyer and seller. A seller may be unaware that he has a rare variation and sell it for the price of a common piece.

• Short-term fluctuation, which depends on what is being offered at a given train meet on a given day. If, for example, four 18620s are for sale at a small meet, one would expect that supply would outpace demand and lead to a reduction in price.

• Another important source of price variation is the relative strength of the seller's desire to sell and the buyer's eagerness to buy. Clearly a seller in economic distress will be more eager to strike a bargain. Personalities will enter into it too. Some sellers like to move items quickly and price their pieces accordingly. Others will stick to a higher price and keep the item on the table at meets until it finds a willing buyer.

• Another source of price variation is regional. Not only are trains generally less plentiful in the South and West than they are in the Northeast, but there are regional road name preferences as well. For example, Union Pacific items may be hard to find and expensive in the West due to high collector interest in that road name; yet Reading and Erie, which are more in demand in the East, may be somewhat easier to find in Western regions.

• Any reconditioning done by the dealer will affect the price. Some dealers take great pains to clean and service their pieces so that they look their best and operate properly. Others sell their items just as they received them, dust and all. Naturally, the more effort the dealer expends in preparing his pieces for sale, the more he can expect to charge for them. This factor may account for significant price differences among dealers selling the same equipment.

• In today's market, the influence of on-line trading has had a strong competitive impact on prices for many Lionel trains. It has also widened the gap in pricing between old, unusual "one-of-a-kind" items and the more run-of-the-mill regular production. On-line prices for the former are skyrocketing, while prices for the regular production are well below what might be expected, sometimes below dealer cost.

Overall, our observations have been that train prices since our last edition in 1991 have been level or dropping (for the majority of items) by as much as 20 to 30 percent.

Train values in this book are based on obtained prices, rather than asking prices. The prices represent a ready sale, that is, prices most likely to affect a quick sale at most large train meets. They may sometimes appear lower than those seen on trains at meets.

From our studies of train prices, it appears that mail-order prices for used trains are generally higher than those obtained at train meets. This is appropriate, considering the costs and efforts of producing and distributing a price list and packing and shipping items. Mail-order items do sell at prices above those listed in this book.

This book does not use devices such as "trend arrows" or "price arrows." We do not presume to dictate, in a market where things change day by day and region by region, whether the price or desirability of an item is going up or down. That is an issue best left to individual buyers and sellers.

On some items, we have indicated No Reported Sales (NRS) in the value column. This does not necessarily indicate that an item is particularly rare. It simply indicates that inadequate information is available for pricing these items.

CONDITION

For this edition, covering only the very recent Lionel products, we have provided two categories: **Excellent (EXC),** and **Mint (MT).**

EXCELLENT—Minute scratches or nicks, no dents or rust

MINT—Brand new, absolutely unmarred with no visible signs of handling, in original box

There is little market for Good or Very Good condition trains of the recent vintages. Such conditions are more prevalent in Lionel trains from the Postwar or Fundimensions periods. Typically one might expect deductions of about 30 percent from the Excellent price for trains in Very Good condition, or 50 to 60 percent off the Excellent price for items listed as Good. As the trains listed here get older, there may be more of a market for items in Very Good or Good condition.

In the toy train field there is a great deal of concern with exterior appearance and less concern with operation. If operation is important to you, ask the seller if the train runs. If the seller indicates that he does not know whether the equipment operates, you should test it. Most train meets have test tracks for that purpose.

However, there is substantial confusion in the minds of both sellers and buyers as to what constitutes Mint condition. How do we define "Mint"? Among experienced train enthusiasts, "Mint" means that the piece is brand new, in its original box, never run, and extremely bright and clean (and the box is, too). An item may have been removed from the box and replaced in it, but it should show no evidence of handling. A piece is not Mint if it shows any scratches, fingerprints, or evidence of discoloration. It is the nature of a market for the seller to see his item in a very positive light and to seek to obtain a Mint price for an Excellent piece. By contrast, a buyer will see the same item in a less favorable light and will attempt to buy a Mint piece for the price of one in Excellent condition. Buyers and sellers will need to settle or negotiate their different perspectives.

We receive many inquiries as to whether or not a particular piece is a "good value." This book will help answer that question, but there is no substitute for experience in the marketplace.

We strongly recommend that novices do not make major purchases without the assistance of friends who have experience in buying and selling trains. If you are buying a train and do not know whom to ask about its value, look for the people running the meet or show and discuss with them your need for assistance. Usually they can refer you to an experienced collector who will be willing to examine the piece and offer his opinion.

CATALOGED OR UNCATALOGED?

The Lionel train hobby has its own terminology. Two terms—"cataloged" and "uncataloged"—deserve particular attention.

A "cataloged" item is one that appears in one of Lionel's principal annual consumer catalogs. In the 1980s and 1990s, Lionel produced one or two medium-size catalogs each year. By 1995 the book had reached 88 pages, and after that the company produced multiple smaller ones each year. It is clear from this that the amount of Lionel production has accelerated greatly in the 1990s—not necessarily in the total number of items made, but in the quantity of individual different trains.

An "uncataloged" item is one that either appears in special Lionel publications, such as a single-page dealer flyer or Stocking Stuffers brochures, or does not appear in any Lionel publication. Uncataloged items produced for clubs, such as TCA or LCCA, are not publicized in Lionel's advertising, but are actively promoted in the respective club's publications.

In our listings, an item is assumed cataloged unless otherwise stated. The dates provided for a cataloged item are the period of years in which the item appeared in the Lionel consumer catalogs. Usually this period corresponds to the item's availability from the Lionel factory to its dealers. However, in some cases, an item cataloged by Lionel in the first year listed did not become available until the second year. On the other hand, Lionel may have made an item only in its first cataloged year, but continued to list and sell remaining inventory of that item in subsequent years. The years noted for cataloged items, therefore, may not necessarily be the years in which the item was actually manufactured. Furthermore, many Lionel pieces are marked with built dates, causing confusion for the collector. For example, a car may be marked, "BLT 1-92" indicating the car was built in January of 1992, though that might not be the actual date of production. Collectors should be cautious of accepting these dates as true indicators of production, as they may or may not correspond to fact.

For uncataloged items, the years reported are the years in which the item appeared in special Lionel publications, club publications, or other advertisements.

Examples also exist in which an item was uncataloged in its first year (such as a department store set piece), but appeared in the consumer catalog later. Our listings provide both years for these items, with a note indicating where and when the item was advertised.

The pricing of uncataloged items can be a tricky proposition. Some uncataloged items are hard to find, while others are quite common. The fact that an item is uncataloged does not in itself determine the item's value, and many uncataloged items sell for the same price as similar cataloged items. Collectors should apply the same criteria for determining the value of an uncataloged item as is used for determining the value of a cataloged item.

SPECIAL PRODUCTION

"Special Production" is a loosely defined term that generally refers to particular uncataloged items, which appear unannounced. These are generally understood to be the major club cars from such organizations as the Train Collectors Association (TCA), Lionel Collectors Club of America (LCCA), the Lionel Operating Train Society (LOTS), and the Toy Train Operating Society (TTOS). Our friends from the Lionel Collectors Association of Canada (LCAC) will find their production listed here, as will the more regional organizations such as the Chicagoland Railroader Club, their cousins from St. Louis and Milwaukee, and the Nassau Lionel Operating Engineers in New York. The TCA and TTOS have divisions that have produced many cars. Other groups like Artrain, Knoebels amusement park, and Department 56 have had specials produced by Lionel. And the company continues its long tradition of producing special sets—and cars—for stores like Sears, J. C. Penney, and Bloomingdale's.

These pieces will have internal Lionel catalog numbers (most often in the 52000-series of numbers) even though Lionel doesn't actually show them in their catalogs. Most of the time, Lionel will make the entire car for the club. In some cases, however, it will provide blank unpainted bodies and trucks/motors, with the club contracting to have the finished decoration done by an outside firm, such as the artisans at Crown Model Products, NGS, or Pleasant Valley Process. This occurs where the number produced is too small for Lionel to expend the costs of the painting and paint masks.

The special pieces in sets will generally be made entirely by Lionel, as will the whole set. Some sets have all unique pieces made for it. Examples are the Quaker Oats, Little League Baseball, or Monopoly sets. In other cases one will find a special production car inserted in an otherwise regular Lionel set.

Pieces made for special events or organizations have become a more prominent area of Lionel production in recent years. The 52082 Steamtown boxcar is an example of this. Some collectors believe anything made for a particular club, group or department store is special production, since it is not cataloged. Other railroad purists feel that all non-prototypical cars (such as the entire "I Love" set) should be labeled as special production!

In the interest of assembling as much information as possible under one cover, we have elected to include in this volume all the Special Production items (the club cars, Toy Fair and Season Greetings cars, cars commemorating special events, store specials) which were in the previous Volume II edition. Since all these pieces are available on the open train market and elicit considerable interest from Lionel fans, they have been listed in this volume to complete the story.

AN AMERICAN ICON

The history of Lionel trains is a wonderful story of tremendous highs and saddening lows, of incredible innovation and laughable errors, of business insight and near-fatal management decisions. Through it all stands the magic name "Lionel"—the term that invokes one image in the minds of the general public: big, rugged toy trains.

One of the most ironic aspects of the story today is that the origin point of it all—the Lionel Corporation—is no longer with us, having declared bankruptcy in the middle of the 1990s. The Lionel Corporation had reached the pinnacle of the toy industry in the 1950s—the biggest toy company in the world—with the guiding hand of its legendary founder, Joshua Lionel Cowen. Cowen had worked hard to build his company from nothing in 1900, starting with a few 2⅞-inch gauge trolleys and gondolas, eventually to an O gauge colossus that dominated the model train world. In the interim he guided the company through two world wars and a depression. The mass-market Mickey Mouse handcar helped get the company through the Depression, and the manufacture of military equipment helped it through World War II, when no trains were in production. But after Çowen retired the company suffered reversal after reversal in the 1960s as the public turned from model trains to other means of entertainment, with many of the model railroaders who remained in the hobby reverting to the smaller, cheaper "Half-O" (HO) size. Lionel's O gauge empire crumbled in the hands of successive managers who tried manifold different ways to stem the hemorrhaging but could ultimately not stop it.

A Timeline of Lionel's History

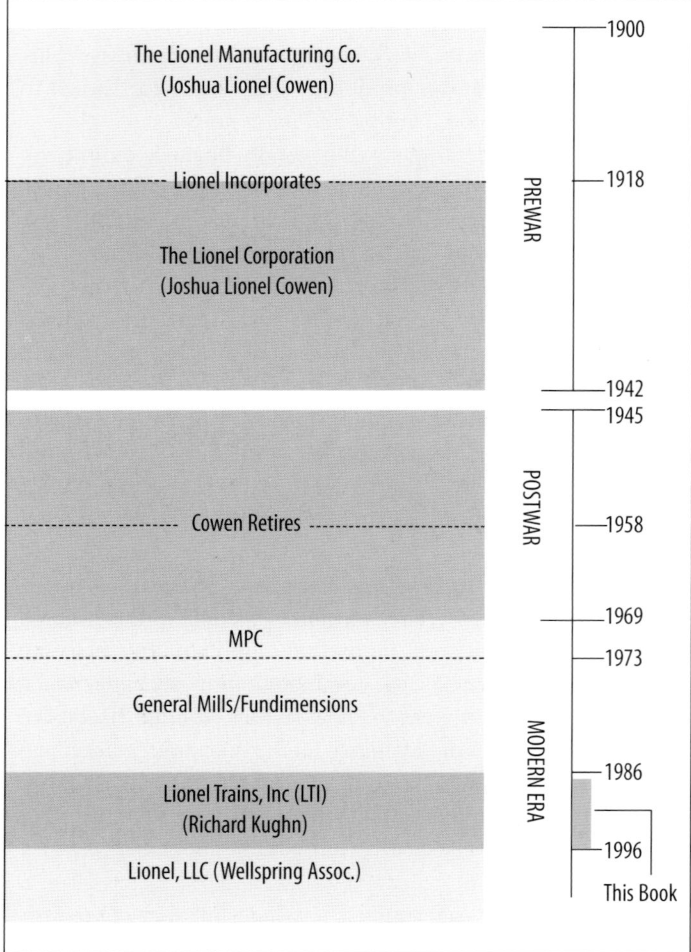

The original Lionel sold the rights and tools to the trains in 1969 to the Model Products Corporation (MPC) Division of General Mills in 1969. This event, also marked by Lionel's move to Detroit from its longtime home in New York City, is denoted by most Lionel aficionados as the dividing point between Lionel's "postwar" era and the "modern era."

It took a courageous leap of faith by the General Mills management to even consider continuing production of the trains in a market that was perhaps one-tenth (or less) the size it was in the 1950s. Despite frequent quality problems which stemmed from MPC's (later renamed "Fundimensions") efforts at cost control, General Mills kept train production going, and the hobby moved slowly from the realm of toys to one principally of collectibles. And General Mills recognized the critical importance of the name—there would have been no market for "General Mills" trains. But even then a market remained for Lionel trains. Meantime the original Lionel Corporation devoted its limited energy to marketing toys via the Kiddie City chain, an endeavor that ended in bankruptcy in 1995. Thus the original Lionel Corporation is no more. General Mills struggled to continue the train line through the 1980s and slowly improved the quality and volume of the items. But in 1983 Fundimensions made a near-fatal error by attempting to move production to Mexico. By 1986 this decision was having far-reaching effects, as General Mills tried to reverse it and bring production back to Detroit. The 1986 catalogs were the smallest since the postwar company's final years, and the company was up for sale.

After a very brief period of ownership by Kenner-Parker, developer Richard Kughn rode to the rescue and purchased the entire train-making operation. The new company was called Lionel Trains, Inc (LTI). Kughn's new era brought Lionel back to life, and by the mid-1990s the company had brought out many new engines and cars, had reestablished itself as a force in the model train hobby. Perhaps most important, with the help of rock star Neil Young, Lionel had incorporated new technology into the trains—especially by the development of the TrainMaster Command Control system.

The story continues today. In early 1996 Mr. Kughn retired to the position of Chairman Emeritus and sold Lionel to Wellspring Associates, a group of investors based in New York. The new company is referred to as Lionel, LLC. In mid-2001, the new company, under the direction of former Bachmann director Richard Maddox, announced another stunning change for the American icon—that all its production and factory operations, in a major cost-cutting move, was to move from Michigan to the Far East. After 100 years, Lionel Trains were no longer to be "Made in the U.S.A." The long-term impacts of this move have yet to be seen.

TOY TRAINS TODAY

There are several basic facts about the Lionel train hobby today which our readers should understand:

• The market for O gauge trains is much smaller (by ten or so times) than it was in the 1950s. This means that corporate decisions about the trains—what is made and how much—are drastically different. Where Lionel might have made 500,000 milk cars in the early 1950s, 25,000 of them in the 1990s would be a long production run. Lionel is walking a tightrope here. Its factory setup and subcontractors force real limitations on how many pieces it can produce in one run. On the other hand, it knows that if runs are too limited hobbyists will be driven away entirely. For better or worse, the era of "limited editions" is with us.

• The decorating and art capabilities of modern Lionel are far superior to what the postwar company could produce. Thus Lionel today can make five individual brightly colored boxcars where postwar would make only one. Indeed, there are far more individual pieces in the modern era than at any time before, though a much-reduced quantity of each one is made.

• The same improvements in decoration have reduced the number of factory errors substantially. Most of the factory errors we encounter now are in the form of skipped paint steps.

• The competitive and development pressures on Lionel are stronger today than at any time in its history, at least since Lionel fought Ives for preeminence in the field just before the Depression. Lionel today has been forced to make important decisions to move much of its production overseas, as its competitors had already done in order to keep prices under control.

• The electronic control and sound technology that has appeared in the 1990s has come to dominate much of Lionel's production. This is the area in which Lionel has managed to keep a leadership position relative to most of its competitors.

• The period under Richard Kughn and also now under Lionel LLC has seen a very clear progression toward scale and ever-larger motive power and rolling stock. The growing field of "hi-rail" modeling (scale-detailed trains operating on the out-of-scale three-rail track) is a major portion of Lionel's constituency. Yet the company must maintain its presence as well in the low-cost starter set arena, and many people, restricted in budget and layout space, still operate the O27 variety of trains. So the catalogs continue to show a mixture of the high-end and low-end trains.

• As production was reduced in the 1970s and 1980s, and as the desirability of the nostalgic postwar pieces virtually exploded, prices for all types of Lionel trains increased dramatically in the Fundimensions era and in the early years of the Lionel LTI period. During this period, the hobby attracted the attention of investors who may or may not have been Lionel hobbyists. The process made life difficult for everyday middle-class hobbyists. Fortunately, the inflation has eased in the last five years (matching the time when competition increased), and prices on some items have come down. Still, times have not changed so much as our relative wealth and our perception of what is expensive. The $100 New York Central starter sets of today are not (relatively) more costly than the same $11 train sets of the 1950s.

LIONEL'S NUMBERING SYSTEM

When the changeover occurred in 1986 from Fundimensions to Kenner-Parker and then to Richard Kughn's LTI, Lionel started a new five-digit numbering system. The Fundimensions period used four-digit numbers, and so it is relatively easy to distinguish Lionel trains from these respective eras by the number of digits in the catalog number. Some carryover pieces from Fundimensions were produced/released in the early years of LTI.

Actually the numbering system (see the table on page 10) is really six digits, with a "6" preceding the five numbers. But most hobbyists and dealers ignore the "6".

Lionel used various terms to denote its starter-type lower-priced trains from its high-end collector pieces. The former go by "Traditional" (and later "Classic") designations, while the higher-end trains are called "Collector" (and later "Heritage"). The term "O27" is still used interchangeably to denote the smaller-than-scale, inexpensive trains intended for the mass toy market—usually "Traditional"-type pieces. The full "O" and "Standard O" near-scale items occupy the other end of the spectrum. With the move toward scale in the last 20 years, it is not surprising that several of the number sequences outlined in our table are reserved specially for the Standard O and Collector items.

With the change to Lionel LLC in 1996, more number sequences were opened up; the older ones were running out because of the exceptional number of products being made.

The numbering system further distinguishes the motive power and rolling stock by type. At the premium end of the line, collectors will find the actual catalog number nowhere on the body of the car—instead prototypical or "nostalgic" numbers (referring back to postwar originals) will be shown, or none at all. In any case, all these pieces have internal catalog numbers based on the system. In many of these cases the catalog number is on the box.

There are, as always, exceptions to the rules shown in the table, along with some odd-numbered pieces that do not fall into the category. Gaps still remain in the number sequences. We cover these pieces in numerical order within their applicable chapters.

We have tailored this new edition especially for the Lionel collector/operator who wishes to learn about and have fun with his or her trains, on the shelf and on the layout. We hope the thousands of facts and stories related here will help make your collections "come alive" for you.

Mention must also be made of the practical impossibility of actually seeing, photographing, and evaluating each of the thousands of pieces Lionel has manufactured through this period. Some of the items are very rare or made in such quantities as to be simply impossible to find. In such cases, we encourage comments from our readers to fill out the story. In the long Greenberg tradition, we of course encourage our readers to send in their notes about factory errors they may have in their possession, or to add more details to the listings that may not be fully complete, or even any interesting stories they can relate about one of the items.

The collecting of Lionel trains is a rewarding and fascinating experience. We consider the documentation of Lionel's continuing evolution to be of extreme importance to the hobby, as well as our enjoyable service to the enthusiast. As the saga of Lionel reaches its hundredth year, the importance of maintaining its history comes into greater focus. Join us for a look at a critical ten years of modern Lionel's production, even as we anticipate an exciting and expanding future of Lionel trains.

LIONEL'S NUMBERING SYSTEM (1987–PRESENT)

117XX -119XX	Set designators	87-99	185XX	Diesels, GP-type, switchers (Collector)	87-99
127XX- 129XX	Accessories	87-99	186XX	Steam engines (Traditional)	87-99
13XXX	Standard gauge (not covered in this book)	88-92	187XX	Plastic steam engines/General (Traditional)	87-99
151XX	Small passenger cars (Traditional)	95-99	188XX-189XX	Diesels, all types (Traditional)	87-01
160XX	Small passenger cars (Traditional)	88-97	190XX	Passenger cars (Madison/Heavyweight)	91-98
161XX	Tank cars/reefers/stock cars (Traditional)	87-98	191XX	Aluminum passenger cars (Collector)	89-99
162XX	Boxcars, reefers, Autocarriers (Traditional)	87-98	192XX	Boxcars (Collector), including 6464-series	87-97
163XX	Flatcars, gons, TOFCs, ore, barrel (Traditional)	87-94	193XX	Hoppers and ore cars (Collector)	87-99
164XX	Hoppers (Traditional)	87-99	194XX	Flats/gondolas/crane/other cars (Collector)	87-01
165XX	Cabooses (Traditional)	87-98	195XX	Reefers and stock cars (Collector)	87-97
166XX	Operating cars (Traditional)	87-95	196XX	Tank cars/bunk-tool/bullion cars (Collector)	87-99
167XX	Bunk/tool and later operating cars (Traditional)	95-99	197XX	Cabooses (Collector)	87-99
168XX	Special production club cars	87-97	198XX	Operating cars of all types (Collector)	87-99
169XX	Flatcars with loads (Traditional)	94-99	199XX	Special series cars (Christmas/Toy Fair/I Love)	87-99
170XX-171XX	ACF and Standard O hoppers (Collector)	87-99	217XX	Set designators	98-01
172XX	Standard O and 50-foot boxcars (Collector)	87-99	262XX	Boxcars (Traditional)	98-01
173XX	Standard O reefers (Collector)	87-99	265XX	Cabooses (Traditional)	97-01
174XX	Standard O gondolas (Collector)	87-99	269XX	Collector cars of various types, including die-cast	97-01
175XX	Standard O flatcars (Collector)	87-99	280XX	Steam engines (Collector)	99-01
176XX	Standard O cabooses (Collector)	87-99	290XX	Passenger cars (Madison/heavyweight)	98-01
178XX	Club cars, TTOS, TCA, LCCA, LOTS, Artrain	87-93	291XX/391XX	Aluminum passenger cars (Collector)	99-01
179XX	Standard O tank cars (Collector)	90-98	292XX/392XX	Boxcars (Collector)	97-01
180XX	Steam engines (Collector)	87-01	330XX	Railscope items	88
181XX	Diesel engines F-type (Collector)	87-99	360XX	Flatcars (Traditional)	98-01
182XX	Diesel engines SD-type, Dash 8(Collector)	87-01	381XX	Diesel engines F-type (Collector)	99-01
183XX	Electric, FM-type diesels (Collector)	87-99	51XXX	O gauge classics (not all in this book)	91-96
184XX	Motorized Units	87-99	52XXX	Special production and club cars	92-01

CHAPTER 2

TrainMaster Command Control

By George Brown

Lionel Trains Incorporated introduced their benchmark digital electronic control system for three-rail O gauge electric trains in 1995: TrainMaster Command Control, which is often referred to by its abbreviation: TMCC, or even TCC. Electronic control of three-rail O gauge trains is not entirely new—the original Lionel Corporation produced an Electronic Control train set in 1948. Although the Electronic Control set was a technical marvel in its time (perhaps oddity is a better description) it was rather short-lived as an expensive and unreliable product.

TrainMaster is a remote-controlled, modular control system for Lionel and Lionel-compatible trains and accessories. It integrates digital microprocessor technology into model train equipment that has been using AC motors and solenoids for more than half a century, as well as the more recent generation of locomotives equipped with DC can motors and on-board AC-to-DC control electronics. Modular components allow control of a variety of layout types—from one as simple as a single loop of track running one train with no switches or accessories, to a complex three-rail empire with multiple trains and a multitude of switches and accessories.

TrainMaster provides walkaround control of as many as 100 locomotives as well as up to ten individual tracks, divisions, or blocks, while giving more-realistic speed/direction and sound effect control over each train than is possible with conventional transformers (such as the ZW). The use of a handheld ("cab") controller with the system was a revolutionary departure from the past fixed-transformer convention, and certainly was new to Lionel and O gauge. Other manufacturers and smaller scales had been using RF-remote control of layouts for several years.

Layout control possibilities with TMCC include selecting and throwing individual switches, grouping switches to throw simultaneously to change train routes, turning on or off action accessories and lights, powering up or down track blocks, just to name a few.

In a full-featured system, TrainMaster controls locomotives using one of two modes: Command or conventional. Command mode is for Command-equipped locomotives only. Conventional mode controls Lionel and Lionel-compatible locomotives that do not have Command electronics—including products from the original Lionel Corporation as well as modern-era trains from MPC/Fundimensions, LTI, and Lionel LLC. In other words, Lionel logically did not want to prevent its new system from operating the older equipment.

In Command mode, the TMCC system transmits electronic messages called "commands," in the form of digital electrical signals, over the outside rails of tinplate or hi-rail track to control locomotive motion and on-board sound effects. The track acts as the system's antenna, radiating the commands to all locomotives on the layout. In turn, each Command-equipped locomotive has an on-board receiver and microcomputer that receives every command sent out, but reacts only to the ones meant for it. Each engine is assigned an engine number or a train number between 0 and 99, and you can change it to fit whatever numbering scheme you use. With the handheld remote-control pad, you can select the engine you want and give it a command to do something such as speed up or slow down, slow down to the sound of squealing brakes and then automatically return to its former speed and change direction. You can also uncouple it from its train anywhere on the track (if the engine is equipped with an "Electrocoupler"), blow its horn or whistle, raise or lower the volume of its on-board digital RailSounds system, initiate sounds of two-way radio chatter with the train crew, and more.

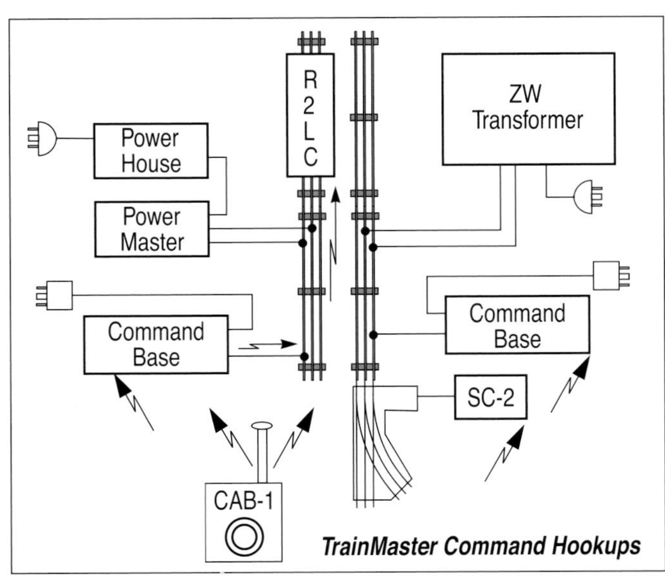

TrainMaster Command Hookups

In "conventional" mode, the TMCC system varies AC power to the track to control locomotives that have traditional mechanical E-units or electronic reverse units. Control of locomotive motion and sound activation is achieved by varying or interrupting the power to the track, similar to that achieved by conventional transformers, but using slightly different AC power principles (described later in this chapter). To simplify the discussions, the term "conventional transformer" refers to any 100-watt or larger AC transformer, such as the Lionel ZW, KW, LW, 1033, and so forth.

Beginning with the 1998 catalog year, Lionel sold Command-ready and Command-equipped versions of the same engine with the Command-ready models being less expensive than the ones equipped with the full Command electronic package factory installed. A Command-ready engine can be upgraded later to a full Command-equipped model with a line of upgrade kits that Lionel sells through its dealers.

Lionel Command-equipped locomotives also include a sophisticated, microprocessor-controlled digital sound system, RailSounds, that very realistically reproduces sounds made from actual recordings of diesel, electric, or steam locomotives in action. RailSounds is an integrated part of the TrainMaster system with volume control and actuation of specific sounds commanded through the CAB-1 remote control handheld unit. RailSounds for each release of a Lionel locomotive, like the 2328 Burlington GP-7 or 2373 Canadian Pacific F-3, has its own set of features. Depending on the engine, these features can include air compressors, steam blow-down, unique multichime horns, air-operated bell clapper, two-way radio chatter from the "crew," brake shoe squeal, operating couplers, and so forth.

Some Command-equipped engines and all the Command-ready ones have SignalSounds, which typically reproduce only diesel horn or steam whistle sounds, plus a warning bell. But if you want to later upgrade a SignalSounds engine to RailSounds, Lionel also offers generic steam or diesel RailSounds upgrade kits for those engines listed in the 1998 or later catalog years.

TRAINMASTER SYSTEM COMPONENTS

Any TrainMaster Command Control system includes components that are essential for TMCC operation, power components, and those that are optional:

Essential train control components

- CAB-1 wireless remote control
- Command Base
- Command-equipped locomotive

Power supply and power distribution components

- PowerHouse 135-watt or 190-watt transformer (or a conventional transformer)
- Type ZW "Multi-Control" TrainMaster controller
- PowerMaster power controller

Optional components

- SC-1 or SC-2 switch and accessory controller
- Big Red Switch control button

We'll briefly describe each of these components, beginning with the CAB-1 remote.

12868 CAB-1 Remote (1995–present) is the wireless handheld remote control panel for the complete system. Basically, you use the CAB-1 Remote to control a layout in much the same way as you use a remote control to control your video or audio home electronics. CAB-1 transmits radio signals to the Command Base, or to the PowerMaster, that tells it what you want the system to do, such as speed up or slow down a specific locomotive, apply the locomotive's brakes, throw a switch, start the log loader running, and so forth.

12911 Command Base (1995–present) is the digital electronic message (signal) generator for all commands sent out to the layout. Command Base is absolutely essential for experiencing the full control features of the TrainMaster Command system and RailSounds. Without a Command Base, the system will control trains but without many of the motion and RailSounds features.

Command Base receives the radio signals from the CAB-1 Remote and translates them into the electronic commands for the Command-equipped locomotives, as well as any SC-1 or SC-2 Switch and Accessory Controller(s) installed on the layout. Red and green visual indicators on the top of the Command Base light to indicate that its power is on and that it is transmitting message signals to the layout.

When Command Base is connected to a PowerMaster that is set to command mode, it directs each command to a designated Command-equipped engine or switch/accessory controller you select using the CAB-1. For conventional locomotives that do not recognize digital signals, the PowerMaster is set to conventional mode where the Command Base is not necessary for train control functions.

If the Command Base is connected directly to the layout without a PowerMaster in the system, and it is powered up, all Command-equipped locomotives and switch and accessory controllers are always in Command mode. To run conventional locomotives using only a conventional transformer, simply use its controls as normal since the Command Base has no effect on conventional locomotives.

Command-equipped locomotive (1995–present) which includes the Command electronics plus either the RailSounds or SignalSounds sound system. Either the initial-release Lionel Command Reverse Unit, called the LCRU, or the later-released modular R2LC is the in-locomotive microcomputer-based brain of each Command-equipped Lionel locomotive. Each version of the Command electronics receives and monitors all command signals sent over the tracks but accepts only those that the operator intends for the specific locomotive. Both the LCRU and the R2LC use, or process, the Command signals to control the locomotive's motion, audio and visual effects such as smoke or directional lighting, and the specific RailSounds or SignalSounds effect, all on command from the operator. A version of the LCRU, the LCRX, controls the sound effects from a RailSounds system that resides remotely in a diesel B unit or in a steam engine tender.

When a Command-equipped locomotive is running in Command mode, its electronics take a constant voltage from the track and vary the AC power supplied to the locomotive's motor(s), according to operator command. Normally this constant power is 18 volts, but a lower voltage, such as 14 or even 12 volts, works well with a lower top speed for the locomotive and cooler light bulbs. When a Command Base is connected to the track and is powered up, it automatically sends signals telling any Command-equipped locomotive on the track to run in Command mode.

If a Command-equipped locomotive is being run on a non-Command layout using a conventional AC transformer with no Command Base, the command and RailSounds or SignalSounds electronics sense this fact and control the locomotive's motor(s) like any conventional basic electronic reversing unit and sound system. However, several of the Command and sound features that are available from the CAB-1 in Command mode will not operate in conventional mode.

12866 (135-watt, 1995), **22983** (190-watt, 1999) **PowerHouse** is a fixed-voltage AC transformer specifically designed for the TrainMaster system. A PowerHouse is required if there is no conventional transformer providing the AC power supply for the system. Two models of the PowerHouse are available, rated at either 135 watts or 190 watts and supply 18 volts AC to either the four-channel electronic ZW Controller or to the earlier single-channel PowerMaster. Controls for the PowerHouse are an illuminated power on/off switch and resettable 7-amp circuit breaker.

For conventional transformer power, Lionel recommends the original ZW, but just about any 100-watt or greater transformer or electronic power supply will work. If a conventional transformer supplies the system power, a PowerHouse transformer is not needed.

22982 (w/135-watt PowerHouses) (1998), **32930** (w/190-watt PowerHouses) **Type ZW "Multi-Control" TrainMaster Controller** (1999) is an electronic train controller that has four variable voltage controls and outputs, or channels, plus controls for direction, whistle, and bell for two of the channels. It is styled almost identically to the classic ZW transformer from the postwar era but is a sophisticated electronic power controller with external power supplies. Two 135- or 190-watt PowerHouse transformers are included with the new ZW; any combination of up to four 135- or 190-watt PowerHouses can be connected to it giving the "modern ZW" a potential maximum power capacity of 760 watts, far more than the old postwar standby. With the four-channel Lionel Type ZW controller, you can remotely address and control track power from each individual channel or all four channels using the CAB-1 remote.

Switching between conventional and Command operating modes is automatic on the Lionel Type ZW controller; it senses if you have a Command Base connected to it for Command operation. If not, the ZW controller runs your trains as a conventional transformer, just like the original ZW.

12867 PowerMaster (1995) is a single-channel power controller and requires either a PowerHouse or a conventional transformer as a front-end power supply. Using a conventional transformer as the power source requires Lionel's PowerMaster adapter cable. Upon command from the CAB-1, the PowerMaster controls power to a track, block, or even a division within your three-rail layout. When multiple tracks, blocks, or divisions exist on a layout, Lionel recommends that a PowerMaster control each one with a maximum of up to ten per layout.

A switch on the PowerMaster lets you manually select either Command or conventional mode. In Command mode, PowerMaster puts a constant effective power of 18 volts on track; in conventional mode, it puts variable voltage on the track on command from the CAB-1 remote. As with the Command Base, red and green indicators on the top indicate whether or not power is applied to it and whether or not it is receiving a signal from the CAB-1 remote.

As a side note, if you are running your PowerMaster in conventional mode and you have a Command Base also powered up on your layout, you may notice that your locomotives are slow in responding to changes in speed, as directed from your CAB-1. Basically, the Command Base receives every signal sent from a CAB-1 and transmits commands, regardless of whether the PowerMaster is in Command or conventional mode. These command signals from the Command Base interfere with the track control signals that the CAB-1 is sending to the PowerMaster. The cure for the problems is simple; unplug the AC power from the Command Base so it will not interfere with PowerMaster operation in conventional mode. Of course, this anomaly does not exist when the system is operating in Command mode since the PowerMaster outputs continuous full power to the track.

12914 SC-1 (1995), **22980 SC-2** (1998) switch and accessory controllers are optional components that receive signals from CAB-1 to control track switches, either singular or in groups, and action accessories such as a log loader, coaling station, or coal loader. SC-1 can control up to four switches plus two selected accessories. SC-2 is a 15-watt controller for up to six switches or 12 accessories, in any combination.

12890 Big Red (1995) control switch is an optional component that connects to the CAB-1 and gives "kids" of all ages (especially very young children) and the physically challenged the fun of having the train do something when they press the button. Pressing the Big Red switch causes the CAB-1 to repeat the last command issued.

TRAINMASTER'S AC POWER

PowerMaster uses a constant voltage, nominally 18 volts or less, from the PowerHouse or conventional transformer and generates variable-duration electrical pulses that it then outputs to the track. These pulses switch on and back off at 60 times per second, which relates directly to the 60 cycles per second of AC power supplied in North America. The pulse duration, or the length of time that each pulse lasts, determines the effective AC power being produced. This type of power is often called "chopped sine wave" or in engineering terms, "phase-modulated AC." For simplicity, you can consider chopped sine wave current as a form of AC pulse power.

In contrast, an original ZW and other conventional transformers produce a continuous stream of AC power, often called "pure sine wave" AC. If you view a pure sine wave on an oscilloscope, it appears as an "S" turned horizontally. A chopped sine wave displays this horizontal "S" as a regularly spaced series of dashes signifying the power pulses rather than one continuous wave form.

Varying the duration of chopped sine wave pulses causes the effective AC power on the track to vary accordingly, similar in overall electrical behavior to varying the track voltage from a conventional AC transformer. Longer duration pulses increase the effective AC power and make the motor, and thereby the locomotive, run faster; shorter duration pulses do just the opposite, and the loco runs slower.

This pulsed AC power also causes the motor to provide considerably more torque at a given armature speed than it can develop from a conventional transformer's pure sine wave. Most three-rail locomotive motors begin to run, at around 6 to 8 volts. Motor speed and torque, which translates to pulling power through the gear mechanism, increases dramatically as its electrical power rises toward 18 volts. When an electrical pulse that is derived from 18 volts is applied to a motor, its armature reacts and turns quite quickly, and with high torque. When that pulse is removed, the armature starts to coast on its own momentum, losing revolutions and torque, but at a much slower rate. Applying another pulse of power to it again causes the armature to turn sharply for another moment, and then coast when the pulse disappears. With this increased torque available at slow armature speeds, the Command-equipped or conventional locomotive can literally crawl without stalling as well as run at a very precise and constant rate for more normal speeds.

However, with a nominal track power at 16 to 18 volts, some of the earlier TMCC locomotives with can motors exhibited jerky movement in a slow startup and at low speeds. Can motors are more efficient than the traditional three-pole open-frame Pullmor motors; their armatures react more quickly to high power pulses, even those equipped with flywheels. These fast-acting armatures cause their locomotives to lunge and jerk with no apparent reason of defect. However, with a reduced track voltage of 12 to 14 volts, startup and low speed operation is smooth and predictable. Also, because can motors are inherently more efficient than the classic Pullmor motors, top speed for the locomotives is still high enough to cause the locomotive to leave the rails in sharp turns, such as O31. In the later TMCC locomotives with can motors, Lionel revised the power control software in the R2LC locomotive controller to give smooth performance at any track voltage.

With a PowerMaster running in Command mode, pulses are at their maximum duration of almost ⅟₆₀ second and supply an effective power of approximately 18 volts to the track. An LCRU or R2LC running in Command mode further modulates or varies duration of these long pulses supplied to the track, and thereby varies the effective AC power to its locomotive motor(s). Of course, varying the AC power to the motors makes the locomotive do what the operator commands it to do via the CAB-1 remote—start, run faster, run slower, and stop.

Similarly, a PowerMaster running in conventional mode varies pulse duration to the track and thereby varies the effective AC power to the locomotive(s) running on that track; again, to start, run faster, run slower, or stop on command from the CAB-1.

PowerMaster in conventional mode will run just about any three-rail locomotive with the exception of locomotives made by MTH Electric Trains and equipped with the MTH Proto-Sounds train control system. These locomotives are not compatible with the PowerMaster's chopped sine wave power. This incompatibility shows up in a variety of ways, including the locomotive not running at all, running erratically with inconsistent sounds and unpredictable sound control, or running satisfactorily but without any sounds.

RAILSOUNDS

RailSounds is a microprocessor-based, digital sound system that reproduces locomotive and other train-related sounds. Operators command sound functions at will through the CAB-1 remote such as brake squeal, diesel rev up and down, two-way radio cab crew conversations, coupler clank, and sound volume. A number of other sounds are automatic, such as air pumps, steam let-off, and diesel start-up with battery-supported shutdown.

Lionel audio engineers recorded these sounds from actual steam, diesel, or electric locomotives or in specialized surroundings, such as a railway passenger station. Several iterations and versions of RailSounds have been released over the past decade, including the original RailSounds, RailSounds-II, and Railsounds 2.5 or 4.0, with these cryptic numbers referring primarily to the version of the sound-producing microcomputer software.

The initial RailSounds of 1990 was independent of the locomotive's power or reverse unit with limited features of diesel roar or steam chuff, air horn or steam whistle, and bell. Electronic printed circuit boards and the speaker were carried in the dummy diesel A unit or the steam engine tender with a speed sensor on one of the trucks triggering one of three speed rates. Sounds were generic recordings of diesel or steam engines and were the same in all of the respective models that featured them; primarily the premium diesels such as the 11711 Santa Fe F-3, 11737 TCA 40th Anniversary F-3, 18107 D&RGW

Alcos or top-of-the-line steamers like the 18005 700-E Hudson, 18009 Mohawk, 18018 Southern Mikado, and others.

RailSounds-II was offered in high-end locomotives in conjunction with TrainMaster Command Control beginning with the 1995 catalog. For operators of earlier traditional-sized steam engines such as the 736, 2046, 2056, and their modern era successors, add-on tenders such as the 2671RS and 2426RS equipped with RailSounds-II or 2.5 were also offered. See the listings in the Steam Engines chapter.

RailSounds-II and RailSounds 2.5 are recorded from the appropriate types of diesel such as the early GM F-3 or GP-7/9 and the Alcos or late GM and GE as well as steam engines such as BC Rail's *Royal Hudson* and Union Pacific's Challenger. The recording for each model is uniquely mixed so it has a slightly different portion of the recording from other models. For example, the early GM 567 diesel prime mover sounds from the NYC and SP 2380 GP-9s are slightly different from those of the Postwar Celebration Burlington 2328 GP-7. And the SD-60 features sounds of the later and correct GM 643 prime mover. Of course the Warhorse Hudson has to reproduce sounds made from a real Hudson that runs today on BC Rail. Additionally, several different recordings of the horn or whistle are reproduced at random when actuated, giving a different sound each time.

RailSounds 2.5 features significant technical enhancements over the original RailSounds in the amplifier electronics and the microcomputer software that reproduces the sounds. Plus, on later diesel or steam engines, beginning with those released in 1998, the sound system is installed in an acoustically-sealed B unit or tender, which gives a much improved base reflex response similar to that produced by fine audio entertainment systems.

RailSounds 4.0 uses a modular approach to the system's electronics, plus an even more powerful amplifier and enhanced software. For steam engines, a new feature for RailSounds 4 is "DynaChuff," which gives a louder exhaust report when you increase power to the engine via the CAB-1. When you decrease the power, the steam exhaust chuff gets softer. In several of the larger steamers that use a large tender, such as the 2-6-6-6 Allegheny, two speakers are mounted in the acoustically sealed tender for increased sound volume capabilities and sound reproduction.

From the old electromechanical E-unit and motor-driven air whistles, Lionel's modern Command Control and Railsounds have taken train control and sound into the 21st century, with microcomputer controlled electronics. Even J. L. Cowen could not have envisioned contemporary turn-of-the-century electronic train controls, but he would most assuredly have been pleased with TMCC and RailSounds.

CHAPTER 3

Steam Engines

The molds for steam engines tend to be more detailed and expensive than those for diesel engines. In the first place, the boilers are rounded instead of square-sided, resulting in a more intricate mold-creating process. Additionally, the molds must be made strong enough to withstand die-casting with metal, even though the same mold can be (and has been) used with plastic. Tooling costs can be enormous. For example, when Fundimensions issued its American Flyer passenger cars, it found that key pieces of the observation car molds were missing. It cost Fundimensions well over $30,000 just to obtain those pieces and change the molds.

Imagine, if you will, the enormous cost of creating a steam engine mold from scratch, and you will understand why Lionel-Fundimensions chose not to be creative with new steam engine designs, at least during the first few years of its post-1970 recovery. Instead, the company used the steam engine molds it inherited from the original Lionel Corporation and modified them as needed. Now, if you want to put out a product that at least seems to be new, what would you do? The most cost-effective strategy would be to modify currently existing molds and issue new paint schemes; and in that sense, Fundimensions was exceptionally creative.

Of course, there is a price to be paid—dies and molds eventually wear out with use. By the mid- to late 1980s Lionel had reached the time when it had to invest in retooling with entirely new steam engine dies or updated versions of the old ones. Either way involved considerable expense. The changes since 1986 reflect this new approach.

For example, consider the two basic molds for the Hudson 4-6-4 steam engine—the smaller Baldwin boiler and the larger Alco boiler. The Baldwin mold was used until 1979 for the small Hudsons, but for more than a decade afterward, every Hudson made by Lionel used the larger Alco boiler. The probable reason is wear and tear on the Baldwin boiler mold. Compare a Fundimensions locomotive with an original 665 or 2065 Lionel Hudson from the 1950s and 1960s, and you will see the advance of fuzziness of detail as the die has worn. The Wabash 4-6-2 Pacific issued in 1986 used the Baldwin mold once again. It is obvious that the die had been cleaned and reworked, most likely by a new plating of chrome on the inside of the die surface. This, of course, accounts for the slow variation in steam engines, prior to Lionel LTI's takeover, relative to the rapid expansion of the diesel engines.

In 1970 Fundimensions began its production of steamers with simple 2-4-2 Columbia locomotives in plastic. In 1972 Fundimensions issued the 8206 Hudson steamer, the only large steamer made until 1976, when the 8600 and 8603 Hudsons appeared. After that the story gets much more complicated, probably because Fundimensions had built its market to sufficient numbers to justify the issue of many new steamers.

Establishing why Lionel/Fundimensions produced so few variations of the medium and large steamers in its first decade or so helps us understand the magnitude of the revolution now occurring at Lionel LTI and LLC. Since 1987, the company has produced no less than 13 entirely new die-cast steam bodies (which we will describe in more detail) and reintroduced two other classics (the 700E scale Hudson and the B-6), all of which required heavy investment in new tools and dies. Making the process doubly complex and expensive, each of the new engines released also brought along an entirely new tender design. Many more new engines are anticipated as the new century gets underway. Lionel has even recently updated the dies of the smaller steamers too. By making such risky moves, Lionel is stating that it trusts the train-collecting hobbyists for their support. The explosive growth of the hobby in recent years appears to be paying off for Lionel so far, as well as for its competitors. Lionel's bold moves to relocate its major locomotive die-making to the Far East in recent years has motivations both in competitive pressures (other manufacturers were already using the resources of the Orient to produce never-before-created die-cast steam engines) and in cost pressures—there would be no way Lionel could economically create massive steam locomotive dies in the United States.

Lionel Trains, Inc., and Lionel LLC have succeeded in carrying on the great tradition of tinplate steam engines with some of the most appealing and best-made products imaginable—even though the cost of these locomotives has proven prohibitive for some collectors. The lower-priced Lionel steamers run reasonably well, are highly collectable, and, as a group, offer the chance for a fine collection. It took a while to achieve the variety, but it was worth the wait.

This chapter categorizes the steam engines into three sections: "large" (or Collector-level) steam engines, including the big six- and eight-drive-wheel locomotives), "small" (four drive wheels and some smaller six-wheelers—generally translated into the Traditional Line engines), and the unique "Generals." A short section at the end itemizes Lionel's stand-alone tenders, made to add sounds to older steam engines that did not have them.

But before we discuss these individual engine types, a few notes on wheel arrangements, motor types, and tender types.

Steam Engine Wheel Arrangements

Wheel arrangements on steam locomotives (based on number of pilot truck wheels, driving wheels, and trailing truck wheels) have been assigned certain descriptive names by the prototype railroads and rail watchers over the years. For example, a 4-6-4 is called a "Hudson" because the New York Central made that arrangement famous with the *20th Century Limited,* pulling it along the banks of the Hudson. Other boiler types and railroads used the 4-6-4, of course, but "Hudson" is the descriptive name that stuck.

Other names have been given by the railroads or the manufacturers to the most prominent engines that used the wheel types, loosely based on "Whyte's Classification."

Unhappily, things are not so neat that we can identify one body type with one wheel arrangement, either on the prototype roads or in Lionelville. In many cases Lionel placed a body style on a wheel arrangement on which it was not normally found in real life. For example, many different body styles were placed on the 4-6-4 wheel arrangement—the Alco small Hudson boiler; the Baldwin small Hudson boiler; and, of course, the semi-scale Hudsons themselves. Berkshire, "J"-class, Northern, and T-1 bodies have been placed on 4-8-4 wheel sets.

It is relatively easy for Lionel to change pilot and trailing trucks, whether it produces a prototypically correct body/wheel combination or not. The names included in our listings—and in Lionel's catalog descriptions, merely reflect the way the bodies and wheel sets are "usually" related.

A Note About Reverse Units

One important terminology note on the reverse units: Prior to the development of the circuit board reverse unit in 1980, Lionel used a gravity-operated mechanical plunger-drum device known as the "E-unit" to reverse its locomotives. The E-unit has become familiar to millions of Lionel operators, along with the unmistakable buzz of its internal solenoid. E-units came in two varieties: two-position (forward/reverse) and three-position (forward/neutral/reverse).

The micro circuit board reverse device that made its appearance in 1980 is absolutely silent and not mechanical in function at all. It is really not appropriate to call it an E-unit (although Lionel sometimes did), because the only thing it has in common with a mechanical E-unit is its ability to reverse the motor. The circuit is also used to rectify AC into DC for the can motor, so it can run on both types of power. The older mechanical E-unit does not do this. As a result, the more versatile electronic reverse is now installed in the bigger engines that still use the traditional "Pullmor" AC motor, and the old mechanical E-unit has been phased out of the production line.

To avoid confusion, this Guide refers to the older devices as the "E-unit" (or mechanical E-unit) and to the circuit board as the "electronic reverse unit." There are several versions of the latter, one called "Liontech," as the company progressed toward what eventually became the Trainmaster Command Control system. The reverse function is only one of many segments of TMCC, which will function with AC or DC motors.

The same discussion applies to the diesels as well.

Steam Engine Motor Types

In terms of the motors, Lionel concerned itself principally with the drive wheels; so it had one motor frame for the four-wheelers (Columbias and switchers), one for the six-wheelers, and one for the scale Hudsons. It used several variations for the big eight-drivered monsters. One is for the Berkshires—also used for the J-1 class and the Northerns. Another was made for the Mikados. Another even larger chassis was created in 1989 for the huge Reading T-1. It has since been used for the Mohawks and the one-and-only scale Pennsylvania Turbine. Unique frame/motor assemblies have been made for the *General,* the Shay, the B-6 scale switcher, the Camelbacks, and most recently the gigantic Allegheny and Big Boy articulated locomotives, manufactured in Korea. Each of the four- and small six-wheel motor frames has a variation to accommodate an AC brush or DC can motor. There are many subvariations of the major designs, depending on what features each locomotive has. This section will outline only the major types, some of which are illustrated in fig. 3-1 (next page).

TYPE I: The "four-wheel AC brush motor" was the most common steam engine type made by Lionel prior to the development of the can motor. Its armature and field are mounted transversely (horizontally) in a frame consisting of two parallel metal plates. The metal frame is fitted with spacers which keep the plates a specified distance apart; they sandwich the motor field windings. To this structure literally everything else on the engine is attached—the wheels, pickup rollers, E-units (when present), smoke units, and the boiler body itself. The motor is a standard carbon-brush type, although the brushplate is a lighter-weight plastic than the older postwar versions. A pinion gear, mounted to the end of the armature shaft, transmits torque through cluster gears and idler gears to the drive wheels. Reversing this motor requires the mechanical E-unit to be wired in series to the motor. Except for the very inexpensive DC-only engines, this motor was used on most of the Fundimensions small steam engines before approximately 1979. In the next decade, the Type II DC motor was phased in, but the Type I is still used on occasion.

TYPE II: The "four-wheel DC can motor" is now by far the most common type of steam locomotive motor. It has been used in the small steam locomotives since about 1979. It consists of the same type of frame as the Type I motor, except that a DC can motor replaces the brushes, armature, brushplate, and field of the older AC design. The motor is completely self-contained, with only the shaft and pinion gear protruding. The remaining gearing and wheel arrangement are similar to Type I, since the structure was intended to fit inside the same boiler designs. The can motor represents a major technical innovation on the part of Lionel, important to nearly every form of motive power it has made. The can itself operates on DC power. This feature means it is silent, smooth, and able to move on very low voltages that would stall an AC motor. Direction can be reversed by simply changing the polarity of the current. The signature buzz of the mechanical E-unit has become history.

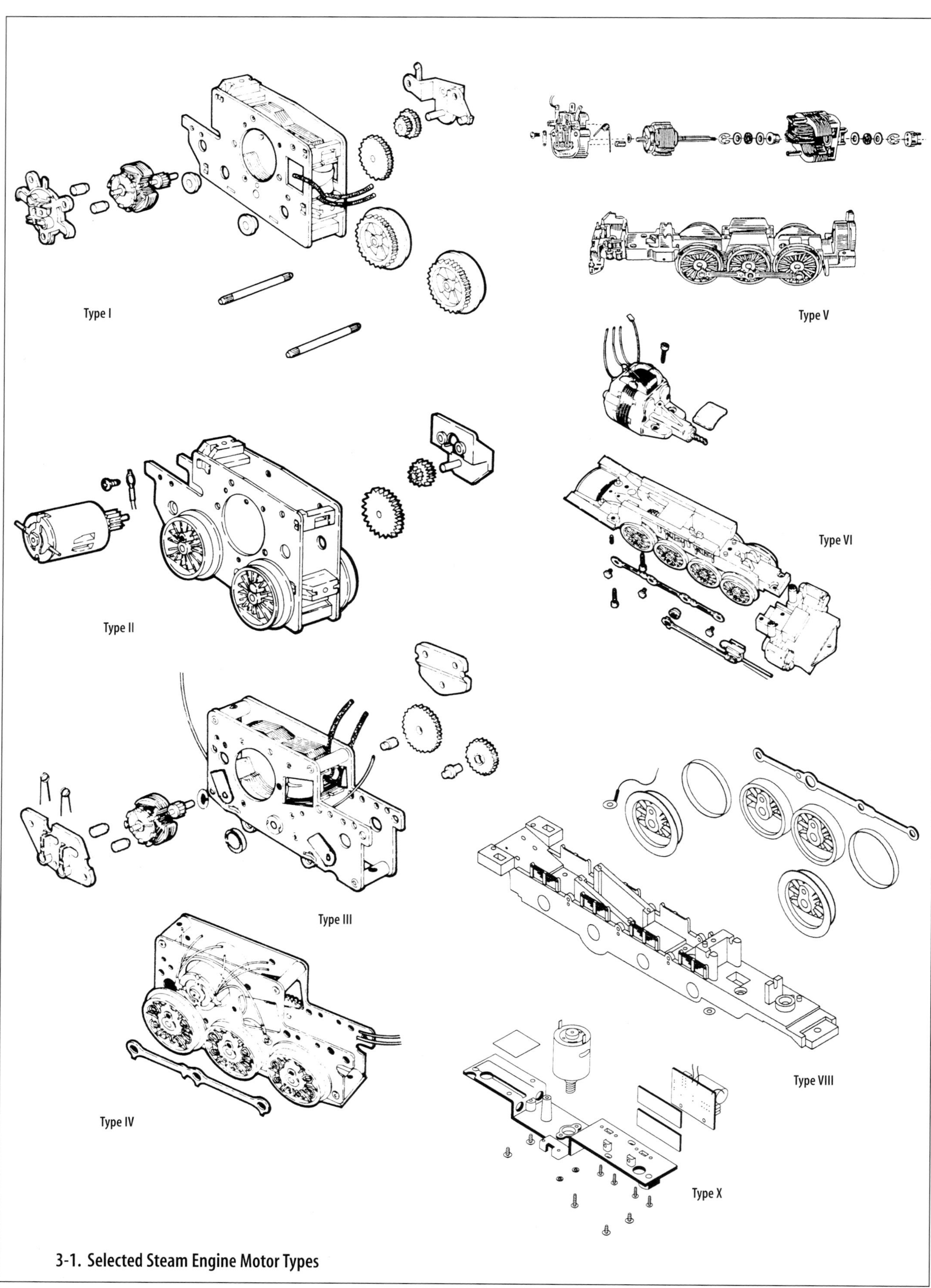

3-1. Selected Steam Engine Motor Types

Lionel has used this configuration on most of its lower-end steam engines. The first steam engine to use this frame and DC motor was the 8903 Rio Grande Columbia in 1979. In the 1980s and during the first five years of the Lionel LTI era, the company used the DC-only version of this motor, without the electronic circuit card, for several of the very small steam engines such as the Dockside and Porter. Operating them inadvertently on AC current will burn out the motor. It is fun to read the stern, no-nonsense warnings to this effect directed at the purchaser of such trains. Sometime in the late 1970s, microcircuit technology had advanced to the point where Lionel could create an electronic equivalent of the E-unit that rectified the power so that the can-motored engines could operate on AC-power. There is no difference in the motor itself. The difference between an AC/DC can motor and a DC-only can motor is the presence or absence of the reverse circuit board. The circuit board and its components still took up volume, which required some maneuvering to fit inside the smaller steamers. The board also functioned to create a standard three-position forward/neutral/reverse sequencing to which Lionel hobbyists have become accustomed over the years.

TYPE III: The "six-wheel AC brush motor" appears today as the standard for the six-wheeled medium-sized steam engines and the smaller Hudsons. It is mechanically similar in form to the Type I motor, except that the frame is somewhat larger to support the six drive wheels and the larger boilers associated with these models.

TYPE IV: The "six-wheel can motor" is a version of the Type III six-wheel engine. It bears the same relationship to Type III as the four-wheel can does to its AC Type I equivalent. An interesting note is that this motor was used in its DC-only form on only two engines, the 8001 and 8007 in 1980, which were apparently issued just before the electronic reverse unit was perfected. These two curious engines are the only K-4 engines and the only six-wheel plastic locomotives Lionel has made. Slow sellers because of the plastic mold and the DC-only restriction, the 8001 and 8007 were not repeated and are now somewhat hard to find. The Type IV motor reappeared (with the electronic reverse enabling AC/DC operation) on the 18606-18609 Atlantic steam engines, starting in 1989.

TYPE V: The "scale Hudson" motor is a massive engine consisting of a die-cast chassis to which the six drive wheels (larger than on the Type III and IV motors) are fitted with all their attendant rods and cranks. The motor itself is of the "Pullmor" type (described in the diesel section). It rests horizontally near the cab and is connected via a complex set of flexible universal joint couplings and bearings to a worm shaft, which in turn drives the wheels. One attractive feature of this design is its lack of unsightly external gearing, thereby enhancing the scale model appearance. It has been used for the scale Hudsons as well as the streamlined Hudsons made in the mid-1990s. The 785 and the 1-700E feature an upgrade of the armature bearings to reduce binding on the brushplate. Another feature worth noting is the center drive axle, which actually utilizes the rods and cranks to drive the rear and front wheels.

TYPE VI: The "eight-wheel Berkshire" is used on the big eight-drivered monsters of the Lionel Line—the Berkshires, bullet-nosed J-types, and Northerns. In each case, the front and rear trucks vary. This motor is similar in concept to the scale Hudson with its Pullmor motor mounted lengthwise to the rear of a long die-cast chassis, long enough here for eight main wheels. Again, the side rods actually assist the motor in driving all the wheels. This style engine, but with smaller wheels, was used for the Pennsylvania 6-8-6 steam turbine.

TYPE VII: *"General"* (not illustrated). Up until 1979, the unique *General* engines used a small Pullmor motor mounted vertically in the cab, attached to a worm wheel—sort of a miniature version of the Hudson motors. Later the design was changed drastically, with the can motor assembly mounted transversely on the small frame, and with a spur gear arrangement driving the back set of main wheels. This arrangement and the light weight of the engine itself produce an unusually powerful locomotive. Early Fundimensions-era *Generals* with the can motor were DC-only, but since 1986 all have been AC-DC. The General engine listings are at the end of this chapter.

TYPE VIII: In 1989, Lionel introduced the Reading "T-1" with an eight-drivered chassis, even bigger and more massive than the Hudsons and Berkshires. It uses the same concept as the scale Hudsons and Berkshires—a Pullmor motor driving the rear main axles, but applied on a new frame design. Like the scale Hudsons, the assembly uses a universal-joint coupling concept for smoother operation. Lionel introduced a new type of large, spoked wheel for this engine, with holes machined directly in the casting. The motor appeared again in 1990 for the 18009 4-8-2 Mohawk, for the 18011 Chessie T-1 in 1991, and for the large Pennsylvania Turbine that year, as well. A slightly modified frame (TYPE VIIIA) was applied for the Mikado introduced in 1992.

TYPE IX: The "B-6" (not illustrated) is essentially a shortened version of the Hudson engine—die-cast frame with a Pullmor-type motor mounted horizontally in the cab. Because of its size, this engine is quite unusual and in a category of its own. Also because of its size, weight, and low center of gravity, the B-6 is an excellent puller. Two new "Torpedo"-type engines also used this frame in 1997 and 1998.

TYPE X refers to the unique Shay steam engine. Everything about the Shay is a departure from the more traditional steam engines. Its bent metal frame has a large Pittman-type can motor sitting vertically in the center. The gearing to get the motor torque to the drive wheels on the rear truck is easily more complicated than any previous Lionel engine. Multiple worm gears are attached to an intricately machined pinion drive shaft which reaches both the wheels and the vertical steam chests mounted prominently on the side of the engine. With all this the motor appears to drive the steam pistons—as well as actually driving the wheels. The complexity of it all would have made Joshua Cowen proud. The complexity also has a major impact on the price!

Steam Engine Tender Types

The descriptions of steam engine tenders can be confusing, even for experienced Lionel collectors. This section attempts to clarify the listings of the tenders, with a short introduction to help keep them straight.

Descriptive names (such as "slope-back") are used for the listings, as well as a prewar or postwar number when applicable (such as 1130 or 243), which some readers will recognize as the original engine on which the tender type was introduced.

The many new die-cast tenders introduced by Lionel in the 1980s and 1990s—in conjunction with the steamers—obviously have no postwar equivalents, and so are named simply by the modern engines with which they are associated, such as Northern, T-1, or Vanderbilt. They are given numbers consistent with the first engines with which they were released. The number of Lionel's entirely new tenders and the speed with which they have been introduced in the last decade have been startling.

Tenders are unique pieces of rolling stock in model railroading because they are always associated with their engines, and therefore are not usually numbered themselves, although exceptions do exist. Lionel itself causes endless confusion by often assigning the tender a catalog number identical to the engine number (without actually printing it on the tender itself). This practice gives no clue to the tender's basic body style. Listings reflect the basic styles. There are many minor variations in types of trucks, back-up lights, handrails, and interior electronics. Because of the ease with which tenders can be mixed and matched, accurate documentation of the factory-produced combinations is essential. Most engines display their road names only on the tenders. To make matters worse, some engines used the same number, but different road names (as evidenced by the tender): the (1)8632 4-4-2 Columbia is a good example. A tender with another road name can easily be substituted and claimed as a variation, unless properly documented as original production.

There have even been tenders released alone—without an engine—each with a sound system. They are intended as replacements on older steam engines that had no sound system. These unique tenders, which do have their own catalog numbers, are outlined at the end of the chapter.

There are more types of steam engine tenders than even the most expert hobbyists realize. See fig. 3-2 for illustrations of some (not all) of these tenders.

SHORT STREAMLINED (1130 or 6066) is probably the most prevalent tender, along with the square-back, used on the low- to medium-end steam engines in the Lionel line. Do not confuse it with its longer 2046 cousin, which looks the same but is about an inch longer. The 1130's "streamlined" moniker is due to the smooth, rounded side and rear top edges, contrasted with the 243 square-back type. It came in many subvariations and with a variety of freight truck types. Some had a molded coal load and others had the top closed off with a simulated oil tank and hatch. During the Fundimensions period this tender was fitted with the odd "Mechanical Sound of Steam"—a plastic cylinder filled with ball bearings that rolled along the center rail, rattling the bearings in a rather rackety simulation of a steam chug.

The 1130 traces back to the 1130 engine in 1953 but did not appear in the prewar era. It was used on many postwar engines. Those familiar with the current Lionel Service Manual will recognize this one as the "Small Round Top."

LONG STREAMLINED (2046 or 2671) represents the longer version of the 1130 tender used on some of the higher-end and larger steam engines. It can be discerned from its smaller brother by the spacing between the wheelsets, and more easily by the prominent front platform on the smaller 1130. They were always coal-type tenders, except on the Southern Pacific *Daylight* 8307, for which collector pressure forced a change to the prototypical oil-type. All have a water scoop under the body. The long 2046 is found with four-wheel trucks of the plastic or metal variety, or with six-wheel die-cast passenger-type trucks. This tender was first created for the postwar 2046 in 1950. It is found with a "2671W" plate on the rear on a few recent modern era versions. It is also sometimes referred to as a "Pennsy"-style and as the "Large Round Top" (in the Lionel Service Manual). Today it will be often found with modern "RailSounds." The 2046 has no prewar counterpart.

SLOPE-BACK (1615 or 1050) defines a very recognizable small tender that first appeared for the prewar 201 switcher in 1940 and the postwar 1615. It is used on many small steam engines in the modern era, including such excellent pieces as the 18610 Rock Island and the 18054 New York Central switcher engines. All of these tenders have at least a simulated backup light, that operates only on the higher-end versions. Wire handrails have also been added on some of the higher-end tenders. Because of its smallish size the 1615 always uses four-wheel trucks—Symington-Wayne, ASF, or the metal modular type. Its signature down-sloped coal load looks very realistic behind some of Lionel's small steam engines. A newer, scale-length die-cast model of this tender was produced for the long-awaited reissue of the B-6 scale 0-6-0 switcher (18000) in 1989.

SQUARE-BACK SANTA FE (243 or 6026) tender has embodied all these names since its initial appearance on the postwar 243. Approximately the same length as the 1130, the square-back tender consists of flat, angled top edges and a multitude of boxes attached to the top and front—it is decidedly unstreamlined! The "Santa Fe" designation does not mean it always came in that road name, only that it first appeared in the postwar era behind a small Hudson using the Santa Fe–style boiler. Once again, this type of tender became known as the 243/6026 only because the 243 engine happened to have the number stamped visibly on the tender side.

The square-back uses plastic four-wheel trucks—Symington-Wayne initially and later the ASF style. This tender also

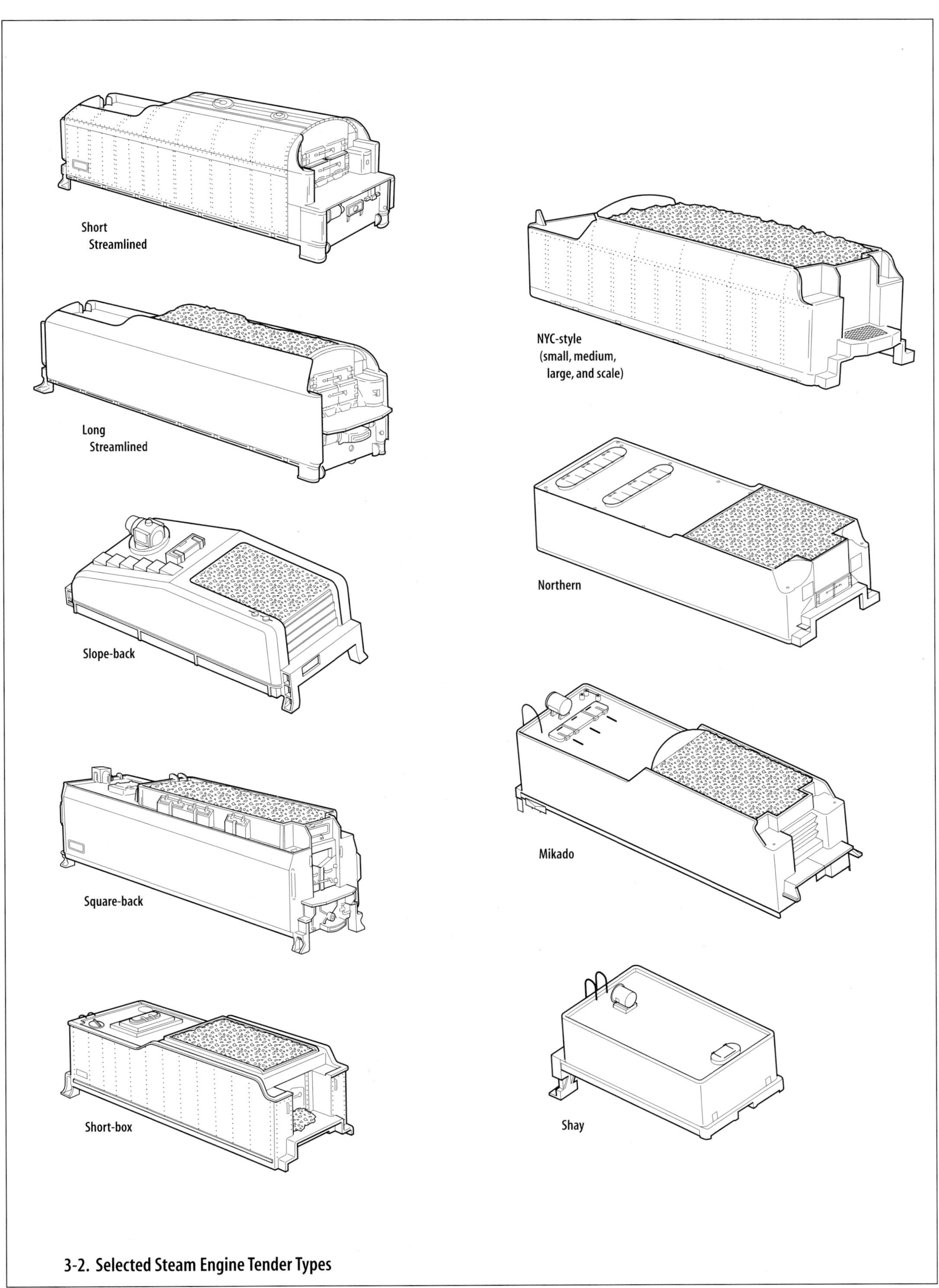

3-2. Selected Steam Engine Tender Types

received the strange mechanical Sound of Steam on some models, as did the 1130. Recently, Lionel produced an upgraded model with wire handrails—which it has lately added to almost all its tenders. Readers of Lionel's Service Manual will find this tender also called "Large Square-Top."

SHORT BOX (8040) tender is an infrequently used short, square-back piece that appeared first with the 8040 Nickel Plate Road 2-4-2 in 1972, and not again until the 18602 Pennsylvania 4-4-2 in 1987. It has not been used since. The latter sported handrails on the deck. Both versions used Symington-Wayne trucks. This strange, stubby tender is an early Fundimensions product—it was not produced in either the prewar or postwar eras. The Service Manual refers to it as a "Small Square-Top."

NEW YORK CENTRAL–STYLE represents a series of handsome tenders that have graced the Hudsons and larger steam engines through the years since 1938. Four different versions of this tender exist, looking generally the same, but each slightly different in length and detail. This book designates them as "small," "medium," "large," and "scale." The last is the granddaddy of them all, which came with the prewar 700E scale Hudson and did not appear again until 1990. Lionel derived the other smaller ones from this style, notable for a long, detailed coal load and a flat rear water tank deck, which may or may not come with railings. Possibly the most recognizable feature of this tender style is the semicircular plate that protrudes from the tender top at a 30-degree angle and separates the coal bin from the water tank. The body has somewhat streamlined shoulders like the Pennsy (streamlined), but they are not as pronounced. The flat rear deck is more evident on this tender. The small and medium styles have come into more prominence in the late modern era than under Fundimensions management. The four major variations are as follows:

A. Small New York Central (2466, 6466, or 2666) was resurrected in 1989 after a long absence. This tender is a simplified plastic version of the 2224 (medium New York Central) without the die-cast six-wheel trucks. The coal load is less detailed than its 2224 cousin and is missing the latter's rear steps and front wire handrails. Although popular in the early postwar period, it had not appeared again until it was included in the Desert King Service Station Special set in 1989. It was fitted then with postwar bar-end trucks, an unusual usage so far after the postwar period. Since 1989 it can be found with ASF or plastic arch-bar trucks. It has roots all the way back to the prewar-era 225 and 229 engines. This smaller NYC type is used with the smaller Atlantics and Pacifics in Lionel's Traditional Line, permitting reduced cost while retaining the classic lines of the NYC tender

The 2466 is actually very difficult to differentiate from the 2224 because it is only approximately ½ inch shorter. The other major difference is that this tender is plastic.

B. Medium Die-cast New York Central (2224) tender was a surprise resurrection on the 8101 Chicago & Alton in 1981; it had not appeared since the prewar era. This wonderfully detailed tender features a die-cast body with grab-rails on the front and rear, a high molded coal pile, which is prototypically higher than the engine cab, and a flat-topped water tank at the rear. This tender is somewhat less streamlined than the 2046 and 1130, but should not be considered square like the 243. It comes with die-cast six-wheel trucks and is used with some of the small Hudsons and several of the Berkshires. The 2224 tender is only slightly longer than its less detailed plastic 2466 brother and is often mistaken for it.

C. Large Die-cast New York Central Hudson (2426 or 2226) is the top-of-the-line tender, designed to be close to scale length to match the magnificent scale Hudsons. It features all the detailing described above for the 2224, but is approximately ¾ inch longer. This is often hard to tell unless two are placed together, but can be discerned by the difference in spacing of the trucks. Both the medium and large die-cast New York Central tenders come with many of Lionel's top features. Dating from the prewar 763 Hudson of 1940, a stepped-down version of the 700E, known in the prewar period as the 2226.

For some time this tender was used only with the semi-scale Hudsons, but it has since branched out into other big engines as well, most notably the 1997 Century Club Berkshire. To be precise, just as the 763 was a slightly stripped version of the 700E original Hudson (but still magnificent!), so too this tender is a slightly stripped and shorter version of the actual scale Hudson tender, the 700.

D. Scale New York Central Hudson (700) represents the big brother of all steam engine tenders. Until 1990 it had appeared only once in the history of Lionel, on the 700E Hudson of 1937. This tender sparked the famous "rivet debate" between Joshua Cowen and several hard-nosed scale model railroaders who claimed that the Lionel version did not have exactly the same number of rivets as the real-life prototype. (For a more complete accounting of this story, see the 1991 book *All Aboard,* by Ron Hollander.) In 1990 Lionel revived this tender with the reissue of the 700E—the 18005 Hudson. Modern technology enabled new Lionel to add a refinement not possible in 1937—the RailSounds system. Both versions are die-cast, with die-cast six-wheel trucks and complete piping and rivet detail. An interesting, unique feature is that they come with both NMRA scale couplers and Lionel standard couplers, which can be interchanged. This holds true for the engine as well. The only non-scale element of the 700E Hudsons is the oversized wheel flanges needed to operate on the tubular track. If scale wheel flanges were used, the engine would become airborne as soon as it hit a curve!

NORTHERN (18001) is a long, square-back die-cast tender (much longer than its 243 predecessor) with a stamped-metal frame. It has perfectly straight sides with excellent rivet detail. The engine and tender were the first major new steam engines made by modern Lionel, after a long period of resting on the designs inherited from the postwar company. This tender bears a shorter coal load and longer water tank than most other tenders. It continues Lionel's recent trend toward scale and detail with six-wheel die-cast trucks and chromed handrails on front and rear. The coal load reaches above the cab roof, as on prototypical engines. The tender also was plenty large enough for Lionel to install its best RailSounds systems.

T-1 (18006), yet another brand-new tender body mold, introduced for the much-hyped Reading T-1 in 1989. Incredibly, Lionel built a longer tender for this engine than the Northern or scale Hudsons! It not only features the same detailing and sounds those pieces featured, but also is one of the first recipients (along with the B-6 tender) of the RailSounds innovation. The tender is entirely smooth-sided. In addition, Lionel developed an amazingly detailed new six-wheel die-cast truck for this tender, complete with molded-in brake pads. Together, this die-cast tender and its engine produce a model 25 inches long, far longer than anything else Lionel had ever produced in O gauge! But the march continued, and it would not hold the distinction for long.

MOHAWK (18009) is still another huge tender released for the 18009 New York Central Mohawk in 1990. This phenomenal tender is a streamlined type resembling the 2046, but is almost 50 percent longer. It has the Type XI full-scale die-cast six-wheel trucks introduced on the T-1 tender. Other features include RailSounds, a small scale-size water scoop on the bottom, and an operating backup light. It is interesting to note that while most Lionel tenders were under-scale in length, the water scoops under them were over-scale. Not this time, though! This tender has outstanding rivet detail rivaling that of the 700, but its most recognizable characteristic is the gray-tinted long coal load—made much longer than on other tenders.

The **TURBINE** (18010) brought along its own long scale tender in 1991. This huge piece took the next step in tender realism—a nice RailSounds system mounted in a die-cast body with six-wheel metal trucks. It was the longest tender made thus far but would not hold the record for long. Interestingly, since only one prototype of the Pennsy turbine exists, and Lionel has modeled it, it is not likely that this engine and tender will be reproduced soon—a fact that has already had an impact on its price.

The Southern **MIKADO** (18018) in 1992 brought out another long tender style, similar in appearance to the other long ones. The Mikado tender has a prominent rear backup light housing, and the coal and water sections share about half the body length. It also has a small rounded coal bin separator similar to the NYC styles. It is of course die-cast, as are all the larger tenders, and rides on die-cast four-wheel trucks.

SHAY (18023) 1992 was a big year for new steam engine styles. The Shay is arguably the most unusual of all steamers made by Lionel before or since. The tender made for it is also quite unusual. It has the distinction of being the only tender in the modern era that rides on a single four-wheel truck. This is possible because it is short enough to do so and rides close to the back of the engine, which has its rear truck pretty far aft. The truck—unique to the Shay—is the same for both engine and tender. The box-like body has a sound board and directional lighting circuit board sandwiched inside.

STREAMLINE HUDSON tenders were created—individually, for the uncataloged Dreyfuss Hudsons in 1992, the C&O streamline Hudson in 1995, and the *Commodore Vanderbilt* in 1996. They are each different, tailored to their engine designs, but all are huge (compared to other tenders), and each of them has smooth metal streamlined sides and gorgeous six-wheel die-cast trucks. The Dreyfuss and C&O are both very long designs, similar in length to the T-1 and Mohawk models. Only 500 of the Dreyfuss engines exist, but the C&O was regularly cataloged. Of the three, the *Commodore Vanderbilt's* tender is the shortest, though still gigantic when compared to the more traditional ones—it is fully covered, with no coal load. All these tenders have RailSounds.

B-6 SLOPE-BACK (18000) switcher tender was created in 1989 for the scale die-cast Pennsylvania B-6, re-creating the classic B-6 of 1939–42, also known as the 701. This die-cast tender is slightly longer (i.e., closer to scale) than its 1615 predecessor, and came with four-wheel die-cast arch-bar trucks. It came with metal handrails and an operating backup light. It is one of the first pieces to receive the important Lionel innovation known as RailSounds.

GENERAL-style tenders are easy to recognize because they appear only with the unique 4-4-0 *General* engines and are the only tenders to carry a simulated wood load. They're normally plastic, come with arch-bar trucks, and are decorated in colorful schemes to match the old-time style of the engine. The General engines and their tenders first appeared in the mid-1950s.

LARGE STEAM ENGINES

For most people, the name "Lionel" conjures images of huge puffing steam engines roaring down the track, rods and cranks a spinning blur. This is the essence of Lionel trains, the heart of the Lionel hobby. It does not require much imagination to picture these glorious engines, although motionless in the photographs, speeding down the straightaway on our own layouts. The photographs here represent the top-of-the-line engines Lionel has produced in the modern era (with price tags to match). We'll provide a brief overview of the main types prior to the listings. The largest of these locomotives are restricted to the wider-radius O-gauge track—O-54 or O-72 as a minimum.

All of Lionel's top-of-the-line steam locomotives are numbered in the 18000-series.

HUDSON

The name "Hudson" is legendary in both the real world and, especially, in Lionel history. Its classic lines are almost the definition of a steam locomotive. The Hudsons have always commanded the greatest interest, and greatest collector demand, of any locomotive, steam or diesel. Lionel continues to capitalize on this fact, going back to its celebrated release of the first scale Hudson, the 700E, in 1937. Since then, many small and scale Hudsons have appeared—all good sellers—and the production continues today.

Lionel produces five principal types of Hudsons in the modern period. Three are scale (semi-scale) size. The primary one is the classic Hudson based on the 700 and its later incarnations through postwar and modern Lionel. The fantastic detail on the huge boiler of the scale Hudson is unmistakable. In the 1990s Lionel created new beautiful streamlined types of Hudson bodies, running on the frame of the standard model. These were the Dreyfuss bullet-nosed Hudson in 1992, the C&O Streamlined Hudson in 1995 (a body design similar to the Dreyfuss), and the *Commodore Vanderbilt* in 1996. All these engines have smooth sheets of metal covering the bumps, pipes, and indentations normally visible on a Hudson boiler.

Over the years Lionel has also made two types of small (a.k.a. "baby") Hudsons. The smaller of the two is the Baldwin boiler, with horizontally shaded windows on its cab. The larger one, with an Alco boiler, has square windows on the cab, cross-hatched into four smaller windows. These engines use a smaller six-wheel frame and a version of the Pullmor open-frame motor. On occasion one will find the larger Pittman can-motor-flywheel combination in them.

The small Hudsons were the only style available between the early 1960s and 1985. In that year, Fundimensions finally re-created the magnificent scale 8406 New York Central Hudson, followed by two others in quick succession, and culminating in the 1990 reissue of the granddaddy of them all—the 1-700E Hudson.

But the small Hudsons have a collector following all their own. Fundimensions put out a beautiful *Southern Crescent* Hudson in Southern green and gold livery with five matching passenger cars in 1977.

So well received was this Hudson that the next year Fundimensions revived one of the most revered names in Lionel history—the *Blue Comet.* This locomotive (8801), produced in two shades of glossy blue with gold trim, sported a feedwater heater on its boiler front. It too had its own set of matching passenger cars in a rich two-tone blue. Collectors snapped up this locomotive and its cars even more eagerly than they had the *Southern Crescent.*

Other baby Hudsons headed sets that have proven favorites among Fundimensions' production—the Santa Fe Famous American Railroad (FARR) set in 1979; the Chicago & Alton set from 1981, in which the die-cast 2224W tender reappeared after more than 40 years; another was 1982's Joshua Lionel Cowen Commemorative locomotive in bronze, black, and gold.

For whatever reason, Lionel ceased production of the "baby Hudsons" at that point, perhaps anticipating the renewed effort on the scale versions. The Alco and Baldwin boilers continued to appear on other wheel arrangements—notably the 4-6-2 Pacifics, but not as the Hudson. The baby Hudson was not revived again until 1995, when a handsome Boston & Albany model was made with the Alco boiler. Since then the baby Hudson has reasserted its rightful place in the Lionel line, fitted most recently with Lionel's latest sound and control technology.

Development of the semi-scale Hudsons has continued since the 8406 (actually numbered "783" on the boiler cab) became such a big collector favorite. Unfortunately, scale Hudsons are rather difficult and expensive to acquire.

In 1986 the 8606 ("784") Boston & Albany came out as part of a mail-order offer available only from Lionel itself and not the usual dealer network. This arrangement, as one may guess, did not sit well with the dealers. The B&A is somewhat dressier than its New York Central predecessor with its white-painted smokebox and white-edged driver wheels. A third scale Hudson, released in late 1988, was one collectors eagerly awaited. This is the 18002 New York Central (numbered "785" on the cab) in gunmetal gray—with spoked driver wheels, which had not been seen since the prewar 763E of 1938–42! This locomotive commemorated the 50th anniversary of the New York Central's proud thoroughbred steamer.

In 1990 Lionel finally committed the resources necessary to re-create the legendary king of all Lionel engines—the 700E scale Hudson of 1937. As the 1990 catalog stated, it was "equipped with every extra feature we could load in." To be accurate, it should be pointed out that the 763-, 773-, 783-, 784- and 785-series Hudsons are really semi-scale. This means that although they are correct in size, their couplers and wheel flanges are somewhat larger than scale in order to run on the tubular three-rail track with standard Lionel rolling stock. Also, the 2426 tender is slightly smaller than scale length, and the boiler piping detail is not as complete as on the original 700E. These slight downgrades were made on the 763 and 773 in the 1940s and 1950s to make the engine a bit more affordable. The 700E, and now its "1-700E" modern reincarnation (actually cataloged 18005, and with a cab number "5340"), have taken those extra steps to scale.

This super-detailed engine has greater boiler piping and handrail detail than the 783-, 784-, and 785-series semi-scale engines, along with many more details on the chassis, rods, and cranks. It also features a National Model Railroad Association (NMRA) scale coupler on the front, which can be changed to a regular Lionel coupler if desired. The tender, a remake of the original scale 700W in all its riveted glory, also comes with both scale and Lionel couplers. Only the wheel flanges remain non-scale, so that it can be run on standard Lionel track.

More changes were in store. 1992 saw a spectacular Dreyfuss Hudson model made for the Lionel Smithsonian Collection. This all-new body, using the same Hudson motor frame, was a bullet-nose streamlined die-cast mold made of brass and modeled after the 1930s prototype design by Henry Dreyfuss. With the brass somewhat more delicate than the usual zinc used in Lionel's die-cast models, the engine was not intended for regular release and was restricted to subscribers only. Just 500 of them exist.

Next, in 1995 Lionel created another streamlined model, the 18043 C&O. The gorgeous yellow and silver of this locomotive has a bullet design very similar to the Dreyfuss. For the first time, Lionel's Trainmaster Command electronics made their appearance on the scale Hudson. This engine, like many previous scale Hudsons, has proved to be a collector favorite. Among its many features are a new trailing truck bolster design and yet another long streamlined tender.

It didn't stop there. In 1996 Lionel released the scale *Commodore Vanderbilt,* second in what it called the Streamlined Hudson series. This model has smooth sheets of metal covering the bumps and indentations found on the Hudson boiler. With it came yet another large scale die-cast tender—a more box-like car than other tenders. This was quite an appropriate model for Lionel to make. The New York Central had created the real *Commodore Vanderbilt* in the same way by retooling its classic 5340. Lionel, however, ran into some controversy over the accuracy of the color of the engine and has since come out with several more of varying colors!

BERKSHIRE

The postwar Lionel 736 2-8-4 Berkshire was one of the great locomotives in all of model railroading. Its popularity rivaled that of the Hudson, due mainly to its huge die-cast body and sleek lines and details and to its powerful frame with eight drive wheels pushed by the premium Pullmor motor. The Berk has never failed Lionel, and collectors continue to cherish it even today.

In 1980 Fundimensions revived the Berkshire locomotive with several colorful models. One was a Union Pacific in a two-tone gray with smoke deflectors; another was the Chessie System Steam Special locomotive with a bright paint scheme of blue, gray, yellow, and vermilion. Another beautiful Berkshire, the 8615 Louisville & Nashville from the L&N's "Big Emma" series, came in 1986 as a special issue for J. C. Penney. The Berkshire boiler (the same Alco-style used on the small Hudsons) is often used for offshoots, as it was for example in 1983 for a 2-8-2 Southern Mikado in green, tuscan, and gold, and a Great Northern 4-8-4 locomotive in green and tuscan, made in 1981. Lionel did this again in 1994 with the 18034 Santa Fe, which it labeled a Mikado, but only because of the wheel arrangement—the body remains that of the beautiful Berkshire. Lionel made some "real" Mikados in 1992 using a prototypically correct body, but still riding on the sturdy Berkshire frame.

Lionel has maintained collector interest, and values, in the Berkshires by releasing only a few in the entire period covered by this book. One was a handsome Pere Marquette model in 1993, and the most recent was a revival of the 736 postwar Berkshire—this time with all the modern electronic wizardry—as part of the Century Club.

"J"-CLASS

In 1981 Fundimensions revived the beautiful Norfolk & Western "J"-class streamlined bullet-nosed 4-8-4 locomotive, and Lionel LTI did so again in 1995 with the 18040 model. The original postwar engine was numbered 746. The modern ones are numbered in the 600s after the prototype. Both modern locomotives headed a matched set of maroon and black *Powhatan Arrow* aluminum passenger cars to form a spectacular train well over 10 feet long, which many collectors consider among the handsomest trains Lionel has produced. Lionel used leftover 18040s in 1996, adding simulated weathering to it and placing it at the front of a new "Warhorse" set. The J includes all the deluxe Lionel characteristics, such as smoke from the cylinders, a feature which would have been viewed with displeasure by maintenance crews. The "J" boiler and frame were used again in 1991 for the 18007 Southern Pacific *Daylight* locomotive (a fine model of the original), which also pulled matching passenger cars. This colorful engine is a collector favorite. It is a Gs2, versus the Gs4 of the 1983 version, and came with RailSounds. Another one appeared in 1998. The *Daylight* differs mainly from the Norfolk & Western by the presence of the rounded bullet nose on the latter, versus a more traditional hinged boiler front door on the former.

TURBINE

In 1985 Lionel revived one of the great favorites of all its steamers—the Pennsylvania 6-8-6 S-2 steam Turbine. The original 671, 2020, 681, and 682 versions of this locomotive sold by the tens of thousands in the postwar era. Modern Lionel issued the locomotive in a handsome gray, Brunswick green, and black color scheme with a streamlined tender, whistle, Sound of Steam, smoke, and even the delicate boiler linkage from the old 682. Despite its smaller-than-scale wheels, this locomotive became a collector favorite very rapidly.

But that is not half the story. In 1991 Lionel did this engine true justice by making a full-scale model (30 inches long) that competed with the scale Hudson, Mohawk, and T-1 in mass, size, and quantity of detail. The new semi-scale Turbine (18010), unlike its earlier smaller brother, has RailSounds, firebox glow, and a huge scale-length tender.

NORTHERN

Remember that Lionel placed many body (boiler) styles on the 4-8-4 (Northern) wheel arrangement. Until 1987 none were actual models of the real Northern steam engine prototype. An entirely new Rock Island 4-8-4 Northern steam locomotive, in gunmetal gray with a die-cast tender and all the deluxe features of the Hudson, surprised the collecting world in 1987. The 18001 (actually numbered "5100" on the cab) used an all-new boiler and tender design with the proper chunky look of the real Northerns. It rode on a tried and true chassis, that of the Norfolk & Western "J"-class model of 1981. Collectors lined up for this engine, which was delayed in production due either to delays in parts or trouble with the boiler castings. When the engine came out, some examples had defective armatures, which caused serious running problems. The problem can be corrected (it involves replacing the armature bearings) but doing so is not simple, and so unrepaired originals have stayed in their boxes. A Lackawanna version followed in 1988, as did a Northern Pacific model in 1992, but disappointing sales, due mostly to the motor problems, have led Lionel to forego producing any further models.

T-1

Still another surprise stunned the collector world in mid-1989, when Lionel unveiled the gigantic scale 4-8-4 Reading T-1. This engine established a previously inconceivable milestone—it is considerably larger than the scale Hudson. It was literally new from front to back: a new pilot truck, new scale-size chassis with large wheels machined with lightening holes, a beautiful streamlined boiler with smooth lines, and a brand-new long tender with newly designed Type XI die-cast six-wheel trucks. The engine, needless to say, was an instant hit upon its release. A Chessie model followed in 1991. The reason Lionel took the time to make this engine, other than competitive pressures, was that it is one of the favorites of then-Lionel owner Richard Kughn, who championed its development and was part owner of the restored real locomotive!

MOHAWK

Any doubts regarding Lionel's future direction in the hobby were laid to rest with the introduction of this handsome steam model. Lionel was clearly taking the scale-minded collector very seriously and was responding more rapidly to collector concerns and competitors' innovations. The release of five completely new major types of large steam engines in quick succession in three years (the Northern, T-1, scale Hudson, B-6, and Mohawk) would have been unimaginable as little as ten years before. But apparently the direction of the company had been altered significantly by Mr. Kughn and the team at Lionel LTI: it was aware of its growing competition, the clamor of the growing number of collectors for top-of-the-line new engines, and the ability of those pieces to sell. Still, the cost of new tools and dies for these major engines was enormous, and Lionel was taking risks by introducing so many new ones. Lionel must have concluded that the risk merits the cost.

The 4-8-2 Mohawk continued the new design trend. Another all-new boiler style, it rides on the chassis introduced on the T-1 with a two-wheel trailing truck. This engine also pulled a new-design extra-long tender. An interesting controversy ensued when Lionel introduced the Mohawk with New York, Ontario & Western markings, as shown in the 1990 Holiday brochure. It was an attempt to generate interest in railroads other than the usual NYC, Pennsy, and Santa Fe. But collectors complained that the engine was properly a New York Central in the prototype, so Lionel relented and lettered it NYC for production.

A very nice Texas & Pacific engine followed as an uncataloged special for Sears in 1992. It didn't show up again until 1998 when another New York Central model appeared, this time with all the electronic wizardry. But by this time the Mohawk was competing for collectors' dollars with the other larger steamers.

MIKADO

The beautiful 2-8-2 Mikado (a.k.a. "Mike") had never been created by Lionel until 1992, when a spectacular Southern version in green and gold was spread across two pages of the catalog. Collectors reacted with enthusiasm to the new design—another example of Lionel's march toward scale, and a wonderful example of the artisan's craft of boiler casting. The Mikado uses the four-wheel "Berkshire" frame, with the added detail of a retractable front coupler. It introduced yet another style of long tender, with a stamped-metal frame riding on four-wheel trucks. Steel and brass accents, such as ornamental bells, wire handrails, and finely detailed headlights abound on Lionel's Mike, as do the electronic gadgets like RailSounds, backup lights, and a firebox glow light. Lionel added considerable detail to the new cab (with two engineer figures), a trend it was following on many steam engines in the 1990s. An uncataloged Frisco model followed in 1993, with a Santa Fe in 1994. These were the only models of the engine until a New York Central appeared in 1999. All have been quite desirable.

PACIFIC

Perhaps one of Lionel's most overlooked steam locomotives is the 4-6-2 Pacific. Most Pacifics made in the early part of the modern era used the handsome Baldwin-type boiler also sometimes found on the small Hudsons. The engine is recognizable by several features—divided cab windows with a distinctive shade; decorative bell and whistle on top, long headlight housing and prominent marker lights, and most of all its sleek, smooth lines. Fundimensions paid little attention to this engine in the 1970s and 1980s, using the boiler primarily on the 4-6-4 Hudson frames. But in 1993 and 1994, two handsome higher-end Pacifics lettered for the Chicago & North Western and the Baltimore & Ohio were very successful, and started a trend that would see quite a few colorful models made in the last part of the decade. In 1995 Lionel released a new modified casting made from the older Atlantic style (see the small-engine section below). It plunked this body on the six-wheel motor frame and called it a Pacific (see the 18639 and 18640 listings). This enabled the company to price the engine slightly lower than the models with the Alco and Baldwin boilers. The latter are noticeably longer and more expensive. Although Lionel numbers a few of them in the 18600-series with the small steam engines, these hefty steamers can properly be called large as well, and recently Lionel has included them at the collector level, in the 18000-series.

In 1997 Lionel tried something new—a "Torpedo"-shaped bullet-nose Pacific model which borrowed the B-6 frame as its basis. Two of these were made, in Pennsylvania and Lionel Lines lettering, but have not been repeated.

SHAY

The creative trend with steam engines continued in 1992, when Lionel produced this quirky but fascinating model of the Shay, a powerful compact steam locomotive designed for use in mountainous areas with tight turns and narrow gauge track, where the larger standard steamers could never venture. It achieves this convenience by rotating its pistons and drive linkage vertically on the side of the engine and connecting the drive wheels to the drive rods via a series of universal joints. All the drive wheels on the Shay are powered in real life anyway. Lionel developed new four-wheel truck frames and a new tender (naturally) to go with its new Shay. There are three trucks under the engine, two under the main body and one under the tender. There are no real pilot or trailing "trucks." You could take your pick as to whether it could be called a 4-4-4 or an 0-12-0, or even an 0-8-0 with a four-wheel tender! Despite its narrow intentions, Lionel's model is a scale engine, fully die-cast and quite massive.

The WM has appreciated considerably since 1992, even though it does not have TrainMaster Command.

18002 New York Central Hudson

B-6

This handsome switcher, revived in 1989, represents one of the most revered engines in Lionel history—the scale 0-6-0 B-6 switcher last seen in 1939. An extended-version big brother of the 1665 (see our small engine section), the B-6 is a near-true-scale model of the Pennsylvania workhorse; and Lionel's version (18000) even comes with an extended slope-back tender to enhance the scale appearance. This tender marked the first appearance of the new RailSounds system. The engine rode on a remake of the original six-driver chassis, complete with spoked wheels and a top-of-the-line Pullmor AC brush motor mounted horizontally under the cab. Despite its small size, this eagerly awaited engine had a steep price, so is rightfully considered a "big" steamer after all! It is also a one-and-only to date.

LARGE STEAM ENGINE LISTINGS

Exc Mt

18000 PENNSYLVANIA: 1989, 1991, 0-6-0 scale B-6 Switcher; black die-cast body; gold "8977" on cab and "PENNSYLVANIA" on new scale-length die-cast slope-back tender (catalog incorrectly shows lettering in white); smoke; headlight; metal handrails on engine and tender. Spoked whitewall drivers; three-position E-unit. The tender is a die-cast stretched version of the 1615 slope-back. This one features die-cast four-wheel leaf-spring (or arch-bar) trucks. This B-6 was the first Lionel engine with RailSounds. This locomotive further dramatizes Lionel's move toward scale and greater detail. Reissue of classic postwar 227/701 from 1939. Although the 18610 and 18662 engines are a similar style, this engine is a scale version placed on the correct 0-6-0 wheel arrangement, using a shorter variation of the Hudson motor. **500 650**

18001 ROCK ISLAND: 1987, 4-8-4 Northern; completely new die-cast scale design using new boiler on Berkshire (Type VI) motor and chassis; dark gunmetal gray die-cast boiler, faithfully reproducing the class R67 Northern owned by the Rock Island; graphite-gray smokebox; headlight with number boards centered in boiler front (actually numbered 5100 after prototype); top-mounted metal bell on boiler front; eight-paneled cab windows; white "5100" on cab; electronic Sound of Steam and whistle; MagneTraction; smoke with cylinder emissions; headlight; three-position E-unit. New long die-cast square-back

Exc Mt

Northern tender painted gunmetal gray with white Rock Island logo, detailed side riveting and coal load (made of molded rubber); six-wheel die-cast passenger trucks. Collectors objected again (as they did on the 783 Hudson) to the plastic tender coupler, which was finally fixed on the next Northern, the 18003. The prototype casting for this locomotive was too rough for production, but it illustrated the proper chunky look of the real locomotive. This engine is unlike any steam locomotive ever produced by Lionel. Despite initial casting and parts supply problems, the locomotive received considerable collector praise when it was finally issued. However, many units surfaced with defective armature bearings, which quickly failed and caused the engine to stop running. LTI was very attentive to the problem and repaired it quickly on those items returned to it. When in proper operating condition, it is an excellent runner. Buyers should verify running condition prior to purchase. The bearings can be repaired, but it is a difficult job. **300 450**

18002 NEW YORK CENTRAL: 1988, scale 773-type Hudson; uncataloged; gunmetal gray die-cast boiler; black pilot and lower frame; spoked drivers with chromed metal rims (the first appearance of these drivers since the 763E of 1938); locomotive lacks MagneTraction because of these wheels; white "785" on cab; smoke with cylinder emissions; headlight; Type V scale Hudson motor; three-position E-unit. 2426-type die-cast gunmetal tender with six-wheel die-cast passenger trucks and electronic Sound of Steam and whistle. This locomotive was offered in a 1987 year-end package to commemorate the 50th anniversary of the introduction of the Lionel New York Central Hudson in 1937, but was not released until 1988. It comes with a ⅝" x ⅜" commemorative metal plaque with an adhesive backing. The engine has climbed in price because it is modeled after the highly desirable 763E of prewar years. At one time, rumors were afoot that this locomotive would even be issued with the round Vanderbilt tender, but this proved untrue. This locomotive featured an improved motor design over its two predecessors. To prevent binding of the armature against the brushplate, a specially slotted armature and an additional retaining clip (671M-22) were used. This design uses four thrust washers (671M-23), two thrust bearings (681-12), and two retaining clips (671M-22) instead of the old design, which had a single-slotted armature shaft, two thrust washers (671M-23), and one thrust bearing (681-121). All armatures are interchangeable, but if an earlier type is used in a revised motor, it must be properly spaced. M. Sabatelle comments. **600 750**

18006 Reading T-1

Exc Mt

18003 LACKAWANNA: 1988, 4-8-4 Northern; semi-gloss black-painted die-cast boiler with graphite gray-painted smokebox; white prototype "1501" below cab window and on sand dome; white stripe along boiler and white-striped drivers; number in white alongside and below headlight; silver-plated ornamental bell on boiler front; green marker light; smoke from stack and steam chests; headlight; MagneTraction; Type VI Berkshire motor; three-position E-unit. Large die-cast Northern tender with coal load, white "Lackawanna" lettering, die-cast six-wheel passenger trucks and electronic Sound of Steam and steam whistle. The tender has a stronger die-cast coupler than its 18001 predecessor. Note: When the Rock Island predecessor to this engine came out in 1987 after delays in production, collectors noted that its boiler casting was made in Taiwan. This bears explanation. The original domestically produced castings for the Rock Island engine were extremely rough and unacceptable to Lionel. They were rejected, and a hurried call to the Orient found a source for properly made castings. The Lackawanna casting is significantly improved over the Rock Island casting; however, we do not know if the casting on this version was made domestically or abroad. The Lackawanna also suffered from the improper bearing problem that plagued the Rock Island. Many units have been repaired, many have not. Buyers should check operation before purchasing. **400 550**

18004 READING: 1989, 4-6-2 Pacific; die-cast Baldwin-type black boiler, using a reworked die to add piping detail; decorative steam whistle and bell; gold "8004" on cab; gold stripes on running board; white-wall drive wheels; electronic Sound of Steam and whistle; MagneTraction; smoke; headlight; Type III AC six-wheel motor; three-position E-unit. Die-cast 2046-type tender with six-wheel die-cast trucks; gold rectangle with "READING" in gold on tender sides. This engine was a slow seller because of the simultaneous release of the Reading T-1.

(A) As described. **250 350**

(B) Factory Error. "READING" missing from tender, both sides. Englehart Collection. **NRS**

Exc Mt

18005 NEW YORK CENTRAL: 1990, scale 4-6-4 Hudson; black Hudson die-cast boiler with "5340" on cab, prototypically correct for the J-series Hudsons; the catalog shows "5390" on the cab, but this was changed for production; headlight; smoke from stack and steam chests; without MagneTraction because of its spoked wheels; improved Type V scale Hudson motor; three-position E-unit. The casting of this engine body is reportedly better and smoother than any previous Hudson, similar in quality to the T-1 casting. Revival of full-scale 700W tender—die-cast body and trucks. Unlike the original, this tender includes RailSounds. Tender is lettered in white for "NEW YORK CENTRAL". Molded coal load was modified to add extra detailing. The number sequence indicates that it may have been planned before the T-1 came out the year before. This engine quickly sold out when announced and is hard to obtain. This locomotive is a reissue of the most famous Lionel engine of all time—the 700E Hudson of 1937. This new version is referred to by modern Lionel as "1-700E." Unlike the 783-, 784-, and 785-series, this engine is a complete scale model including full boiler piping and riveting detail, and both engine and tender have NMRA-standard couplers. Includes Lionel standard couplers, which can be changed if desired (the instructions for doing so are complicated, however). **1000 1200**

18006 READING: 1989, 4-8-4 T-1; black body; yellow "2100" on cab, after the prototype; yellow stripe on running board; Reading Line diamond logo on front; "2100" number plate under headlight; wire handrails and white-wall drive wheels are a new casting with round lightening holes molded in; smoke from stack and steam chests, three-position E-unit and RailSounds—first appearance of this system on a large steam engine. Tender is a new, very long, squared-off model using die-cast body, wire handrails, and newly designed Type XI six-wheel die-cast trucks. It even has snap-in water tank covers under the coal load. Base of tender is a sheet-metal frame stamped "LTI"; large yellow rectangle on tender sides with "READING" inside; "2100" on tender rear, along with operating backup lights. Perhaps a measure of Lionel's health and willingness to take risks, the T-1 represents new designs from front to back and has been a brisk seller. Engine is an all-new die-cast boiler casting using a Northern wheel arrangement. Chassis is larger with larger-diameter wheels and Pullmor motor attached to universal joint drive train in the style of the Hudson (Type VIII T-1 motor). This huge (27-inch) engine is larger than anything Lionel had made in O gauge to date. Reportedly it was a personal project of Lionel owner Richard Kughn. Offered in 1989 year-end Holiday Collection flyer. **600 750**

18007 Southern Pacific Gs2

	Exc	Mt

18007 SOUTHERN PACIFIC: 1991, 4-8-4 Gs2 "J"-class; the *Daylight;* die-cast "J"- series boiler first seen on the 8100 Norfolk & Western; *Daylight* orange, dark red-orange, white and black paint scheme; "4410" below cab window in white; "Daylight" in white script on orange stripe near front; "98" on boiler top number boards; silver boiler front with "4410" number board; single front headlight; MagneTraction; smoke from stack and cylinder chest; white sidewall drivers; Type VI Berkshire motor; three-position E-unit. 2046-type long streamlined oil tender has RailSounds, six-wheel die-cast trucks and operating coupler. Essentially a reissue of the 8307 from 1983, but with a modified boiler front with single headlight. There are other minor differences between the boilers of these two engines. **400 525**

18009 NEW YORK CENTRAL: 1990–91, 4-8-2 L-3a-class Mohawk; black die-cast body with white lettering, derived from the T-1 but with many differences; new boiler style represents the third major steam engine style brought out by Lionel in four years; scale model of L-3/L-4-class Mountain engine produced at Lima; engine rides on a Type VIII motor and chassis like the T-1; two-wheel rear trucks; three-position E-unit. "3000" and "L3A" in white on cab sides; "3000" on number board under front headlight with red NYC emblem below that; Lionel builder's plate under stack; engine has smoke through stack and steam chests; headlight; firebox light; retractable front coupler (a first on a regular-issue engine); wire handrails; spoked drive wheels. Yet another new extra-long tender with RailSounds, die-cast six-wheel trucks, operating coupler, and small water scoop on the underside. This tender has a detailed gray-tinted coal load longer than loads on other tenders, and is lettered on the rear with a large "3000" and capacity data. Tender also has a backup light. A good seller, despite its price tag. (Collectors in 1990 were probably reeling from the prices of the 700E!) Shown in 1990 Holiday flyer as New York, Ontario & Western, but collector pressure forced a change to the more prototypical New York Central. The change also deleted the silver boiler front shown in the flyer. This engine is pictured correctly in the 1991 Book 2 catalog. **700 850**

18010 PENNSYLVANIA: 1991–92, 6-8-6 S-2 steam turbine; semi-scale big brother to the 8404 turbine from 1984; brand new and expertly detailed die-cast Brunswick green metal body with silver smokebox; "6200" (a prototypical number) in gold on the cab and on the tuscan keystone on the boiler front; four different smoke units are piped to two stacks—unique in the Lionel line; Type VIII T-1 motor with eight polished-steel spoked wheels; three-position mechanical E-unit; finely detailed six-wheel pilot and trailing trucks; Baldwin builder's plate; operating headlight and backup light on tender, wired to constant-voltage circuit; firebox light; wire handrails; extra long tender lettered "PENNSYLVANIA" with die-cast six-wheel trucks and RailSounds. Together, engine and tender are 30 inches long (120 scale feet!) and are intended to run only on wide-radius track. The massive locomotive weighs 16 pounds. This engine is a good example of modern Lionel's strong move toward scale railroading since 1987. Many collectors consider this engine Lionel's best yet. A matching scale die-cast zinc Pennsylvania N-8 caboose was offered. See 51702. Somewhat hard to find now. **1100 1400**

18011 CHESSIE SYSTEM: 1991, 4-8-4 T-1; long die-cast T-1 boiler in black with silver smokebox; yellow and vermilion running board and tender sides; large-diameter drive wheels with lightening holes; yellow "2101" under cab window; 2101 number boards on front around operating headlight; smoke from stack and steam chests; firebox light; Type VIII T-1 motor and chassis; three-position E-unit. Long T-1-style die-cast tender with six-wheel die-cast trucks, backup light, steam RailSounds and operating coupler; large blue "Chessie System" lettering on tender. Follow-up to the successful Reading T-1 released in 1984; it did not sell as well as expected. This engine is a more accurate model of the actual Chessie Steam Special than the earlier 8003 Chessie Berkshire.

(A) As described. **650 800**

(B) Carail/Artrain versions. Approximately 30 exist. Specials made for Lionel (and Carail) owner Richard Kughn, These are 18011s repainted in white and blue (in the case of Carail), with the stylized Carail logo and "1994" on the cab. A similar few were made for the traveling Artrain art museum on rails, in dark gray with the Artrain logo. **NRS**

18014 LIONEL LINES: 1991, 2-6-4 Atlantic steam locomotive on Prairie wheel arrangement; die-cast boiler; all-pink body and tender; blue lettering and "8014" on cab; headlight; smoke unit; MagneTraction; Type IV six-wheel can motor; three-position electronic reverse; short streamlined 1130 tender with plastic arch-bar trucks. The catalog lists MagneTraction for this piece, but it is not made with it—includes traction tires instead. This engine is a revival of the famous 2037-500 Girls' Set engine from 1957. The original engine and set are scarce today. Lionel reissued both in 1991 with identical pastel colors but new numbers. Although the Atlantic engine type is normally used in the Traditional Line, this one is considered a Collector engine because it headed the Collector Line 11722 Girls' Train set. **150 200**

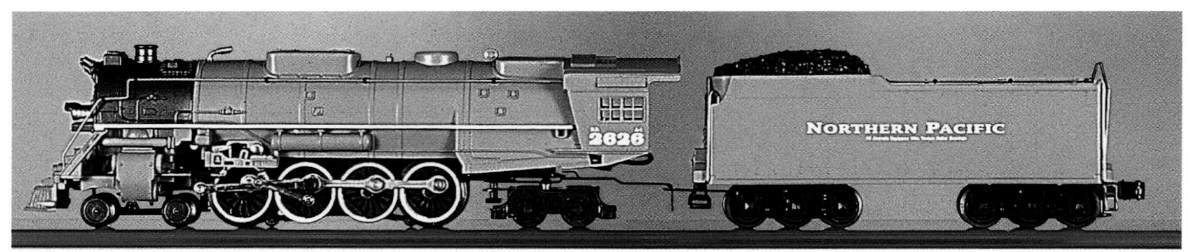

18016 Northern Pacific 4-8-4

Exc Mt

18016 NORTHERN PACIFIC: 1992, 4-8-4 Northern; light gray-painted die-cast boiler with graphite gray-painted smokebox; white prototype "2626" below cab window; red cab roof; cab has new "firebox glow" light; silver-plated ornamental bell on boiler front; smoke from stack and steam chests; constant-voltage headlight; MagneTraction; Type VI Berkshire frame using Pullmor motor; three-position E-unit. Diecast Northern tender with coal load, white "NORTHERN PACIFIC" lettering, die-cast six-wheel passenger trucks; backup light, operating coupler, and electronic steam RailSounds. **450 530**

18018 SOUTHERN: 1992, 2-8-2 Mikado; entirely new large steam engine model from Lionel; dark green die-cast boiler with excellent detail; silver-painted smokebox; steam cylinders, running board, and ashpan are also painted silver; gold accent lines on cab and domes; number is "4501" under windows and on domes, with SRR circle logo on cab; red cab roof; steel-rimmed drive wheels on frame (Type VIIA) derived from the T-1 models; large vertical can motor known as the "Pittman"—one of the first uses of this powerful new design; three-position electronic reverse; wire handrails; smoke from stack and steam chests; firebox light; operating headlight and marker lights; retractable front coupler; new cab interior with engineer and fireman figures. New style Mikado tender with steam RailSounds is painted matching green with "SOUTHERN" in gold; die-cast arch-bar four-wheel trucks; wire handrails; operating coupler; backup light. The engine is picture on our cover. It has proved very popular among collectors and is somewhat hard to find. **825 950**

18022 PERE MARQUETTE: 1993, 2-8-4 Berkshire; black die-cast Berkshire body, same as the classic postwar models; white "1201" on cab and also on front marker boards; roadname also in small white letters on sand dome; white-rimmed drivers; Type VI Berkshire frame with Pullmor motor; MagneTraction; electronic reverse unit (which Lionel was calling "Liontech" at the time); wire handrails; headlight; smoke unit; long streamlined (2046-style) plastic tender in black with "PERE MARQUETTE" in white; water scoop under tender; tender has six-wheel die-cast passenger trucks, and steam RailSounds. Reportedly a good runner. Intended to pull the matching set of Pere Marquette heavyweight Madison cars made in 1993. This is one of the rare releases of the Berkshire during the Lionel LTI/LLC period and its first appearance since 1986. In the interim, Lionel had retooled the engine, and the new casting has excellent refurbished details. It also marks another first for the Berkshire: the Liontech reverse unit meant that at long last the annoying E-unit lever and the slot for it in the top of the engine were gone. **500 575**

18023 WESTERN MARYLAND: 1992, Shay; entirely new Lionel steam engine model, accurately representing the logging industry's vertical-piston design created by Ephraim Shay and produced by Lima; black die-cast body and tender; silver smokebox with gold "Lima" Builder's plate; white-edged multiple-layer running board; gold "6" on cab and marking plate on front; gold "WESTERN MARYLAND" on tender; this engine cannot be categorized in the usual manner, as it has no pilot or trailing trucks; but rides on unique four-wheel assemblies fitted under the body—the rear one supporting the coal tender, and the forward two on either side of the vertical steam chests/pistons; even the wheels are different—their integral gear teeth mesh directly with the drive shaft; large vertical Pittman can motor in the center truck; three-position electronic reverse; headlight and backup light; smoke; synchronized RailSounds in tender; cab with firebox light, control details, and two figures; operating couplers at front and rear; additional brass detailing. Intended for wide-radius track. It is geared to run more slowly than road engines. **1600 2000**

18024 TEXAS & PACIFIC: 1992, 4-8-2 Mountain (Mohawk); uncataloged; second release of the Mohawk model; royal blue die-cast body, silver-painted smokebox; light gray ashpan and lower cab; "907" in dark gray lettering on cab; engine rides on a Type VIII motor and chassis like the T-1; three-position electronic reverse. "907" also on front numberboard; Lionel builder's plate under stack; engine has smoke through stack and steam chests; headlight; firebox light; retractable front coupler; wire handrails; spoked drive wheels painted blue; long Mohawk tender (also in blue) with RailSounds, die-cast six-wheel trucks, operating coupler, and small water scoop on undersides; tender has wide gray and white stripe through center of sides, and "TEXAS & PACIFIC" in gray above this. Tender also has a backup light. This engine was made specially for Sears (their catalog number 49N 95230) and was shown in the 1992 Sears Wishbook—the last one printed by Sears). The 18024 came with a wood-grained base and track, and a display case. It was available without the case as 18025. This engine may mark the pinnacle of Lionel's long relationship with Sears and certainly ranks as the nicest model ever made by Lionel for Sears. **750 900**

18025 see 18024

18034 Santa Fe Mikado

Exc Mt

18026 NEW YORK CENTRAL: 1992, streamlined 4-6-4 Hudson; uncataloged; new scale Hudson based on the J3a streamliner designed by Henry Dreyfuss; part of a special made in concert with the Smithsonian; 500 produced; gray-painted brass (not die-cast) streamlined body and tender; white number reading "5450"; operating headlight and smoke units; Type V scale Hudson frame and Pittman can motor; NYC nameplate on front skirt; silver-plated spoked wheels; die-cast NYC tender with six-wheel trucks; body is gray with a darker gray center stripe and "NEW YORK CENTRAL" in white; stripe has blue highlight lines; RailSounds in tender. Came with an oak display base and acrylic case. This was the two-rail O gauge version of the engine, with no roller pickups. The three-rail version is cataloged as 18027. These engines were the first in several releases in the "Lionel Smithsonian Collection"—a set of matching scale passenger cars for the *Twentieth Century Limited* would follow in 1993. They were available only through special subscription to Lionel and described initially in ads in the *Smithsonian* magazine. Each engine is serialized. **— 2500**

18027 NEW YORK CENTRAL: 1992, three-rail version of Dreyfuss Hudson; number on the engine is "5454"; otherwise same as previous entry. See 18026 for details. Reportedly 750 exist. **— 2500**

18028 PENNSYLVANIA: 1993, two-rail 4-6-2 K-4 Pacific; uncataloged; special release as part of Lionel's Smithsonian Collection; bullet-nose streamlined brass body (not die-cast) based on the Raymond Loewy prototype; silver-painted boiler and tender with gold highlights; number on cab is "3768"; silver Pennsy wing nameplate on nose; separate wire handrails on nose; engine uses the long Hudson frame with a Pittman can motor, with two-wheel leading truck; smoke, operating headlight; tender is lettered "PENNSYLVANIA" with the red keystone; tender also has RailSounds. Came with an oak display base and acrylic case. Available by subscription only through Lionel. 500 produced, each with individual serial numbers. **— 2500**

18029 same as 18027, except with operating roller base.

18030 FRISCO: 1993, 2-8-2 Mikado; uncataloged; second release of this new style engine; special available only to Lionel dealers; black Mikado body with gray-painted smokebox and red cab roof; number large white "4100" lettering on tender; steel-rimmed drive wheels on new style frame; Pullmor motor; three-position electronic reverse; wire handrails; smoke from stack and steam chests; firebox light; operating headlight and marker lights; detailed cab interior with engineer and fireman figures; Mikado tender with steam RailSounds; die-cast arch-bar four-wheel trucks; wire handrails; operating coupler; backup light. **600 700**

18034 SANTA FE: 1994, 2-8-2 Mikado using Berkshire boiler; black die-cast body; silver boiler front; "AT&SF" in small white lettering on cab; "3158" in large white letters on tender; Type VI Berkshire frame with Pullmor motor; MagneTraction; electronic reverse unit (which Lionel called "Liontech"); headlight; smoke unit synchronized with wheel speed; long streamlined (2046-style) tender in black; water scoop under tender; tender has six-wheel die-cast passenger trucks, and steam RailSounds; wire handrails on engine and tender. Though a handsome engine, its catalog price was very high (probably because it came with the new Liontech-Trainmaster system), and this locomotive has sold at roughly half that in most markets. **400 500**

18040 NORFOLK & WESTERN: 1995, 4-8-4 "J"-class; satin-black-painted streamlined boiler with broad maroon stripe edged in yellow; remake of postwar classic 746, and the 8100 from 1981; plastic bullet boiler front with lighted "612" numberboard; number also in yellow on stripe at center of sides; single front headlight; MagneTraction; smoke from stack and cylinder chest is synchronized to the sounds; Type VI Berkshire frame with Pullmor motor; three-position electronic reverse; trailing truck is die-cast—it was plastic on previous models; 2046-type long streamlined oil tender has RailSounds II, six-wheel die-cast trucks and operating coupler; tender body is die-cast, also an improvement from previous; maroon and yellow stripe continues on tender with "NORFOLK & WESTERN" in yellow block letters. Note the engine number is one off the 1981 model, which was "611". Apparently as a result of sluggish sales of this piece, Lionel rereleased it again the next year, at the head of a set, in a "weathered" paint scheme. Still the "J" at the head of the matching maroon *Powhatan Arrow* streamlined aluminum cars (also made in 1995) makes one of the most impressive trains ever. And this one was one of Lionel's first steamers to be Command-ready. Lionel had made many improvements in this engine since the 1981 model—the elimination of the E-unit and its obtrusive lever out the top of the boiler was a significant one. **750 850**

18043 Chesapeake & Ohio Streamlined Hudson

	Exc	Mt

18041 BOSTON & ALBANY: 1995, 4-6-4 small Hudson; steam whistle. This piece was intended as a lower-cost alternative to the 18042 below, but was never made. **Not Manufactured**

18042 BOSTON & ALBANY: 1995, 4-6-4 small Hudson using Alco boiler; black die-cast body; white boiler front; white lettering "618" on cab and "BOSTON & ALBANY" on tender; white running board stripe; white-rimmed drive wheels; numberboards on front read "618"; Type III six-wheel AC-Pullmor motor frame; MagneTraction; electronic reverse unit; headlight; smoke unit; die-cast 2224-style tender with die-cast six-wheel trucks; tender features RailSounds. The electronic "Liontech" reverse unit makes this one of Lionel's first steam engines to be Command-equipped. A model without the RailSounds was planned as the 18041, but was not made. **— 500**

18043 CHESAPEAKE & OHIO: 1995, 4-6-4 Streamlined semi-scale Hudson; all-new design for Lionel; new-style long silver body resembling the aluminum passenger cars; yellow upper section of sides and bullet-shaped boiler front; dark blue lettering with "C AND O" toward front; "490" on cab and in lighted numberboards, also on rear of tender; yellow stripe with blue accents continues aft from cab around tender body; Type V scale Hudson motor frame with heavy-duty Pullmor motor; drivers are spoked wheels painted silver; trailing truck is also a new design (wheels closer than on other Hudsons) with truck sides also painted silver; MagneTraction; electronic reverse unit; operating headlight; synchronized smoke unit; all new long streamlined coal tender with silver die-cast six-wheel trucks; tender features RailSounds II. This entirely new all-die-cast steam engine is 26 inches long and weighs 12.5 pounds. It was the first in what Lionel advertised as a new Streamliner series and is based on the 18026 Dreyfuss model. Lionel offered a scale (small) coupler for the rear of the tender. The only concession to tinplate "non-scale" are the flanges on the wheels—oversized to accommodate Lionel's tubular track. Hence the term "semi-scale." With its "Liontech" reverse unit circuit card, this was also one of Lionel's earliest steam engines to be made ready for the new TrainMaster system. The engine also looks good in front of the C&O heavyweight Pullman cars. It must operate on O54 or wider-radius track. **700 900**

	Exc	Mt

18090 DENVER & RIO GRANDE WESTERN: 1990, 4-6-2 Pacific; uncataloged 20th anniversary commemorative engine for the Lionel Collectors Club of America (LCCA); black Baldwin-style die-cast boiler; white "1990" lettering on cab with small "LCCA" underneath; white running board stripe and wheel rims; silver-painted smokebox and "1990" numberplate under headlight; 2224-type die-cast tender in black with "DENVER & RIO GRANDE WESTERN" in white; first use of this type tender with a Pacific loco; pad-printed "Scenic Line / Royal Gorge Route" logo on tender rear; tender has steam RailSounds; smoke; headlight; MagneTraction; Type III AC six-wheel motor; three-position E-unit. Intended as a match for the 17880 wood-side caboose also released that year. 1,866 made. The number assigned by Lionel was a special for LCCA as well—obviously out of date sequence with the other engines. **300 400**

SMALL STEAM ENGINES

The small steam engines issued by modern Lionel range from very inexpensive 0-4-0 switchers made almost entirely of plastic, to die-cast 4-4-2 and 2-6-4 mainline locomotives.

This subsection categorizes the body and motor types for easier reference.

Note that the larger die-cast 2-6-4 engines (for which Lionel uses Atlantic-type bodies on a 2-6-4 drive train) are really medium-sized "bridges" between the small and large (or Collector) steam engines. We include them here because Lionel still refers to them as "Traditional" pieces. The same statement applies to some of the Pacific models. A few of these are numbered in the 18600-series of steamers. The principal types are described below:

Small Steam Engine Body Styles

COLUMBIA

The Columbia-type represents by far the most prevalent body style Lionel has used for its smaller steam engines. It can be discerned most easily by its thick running board, often painted; by a two-paned window (window types are good indicators of the body styles); and by an inverted "V" pattern of piping under a relatively flat sand dome. In the early Fundimensions years, it rode on a 2-4-2 wheel arrangement.

ELONGATED COLUMBIA

The Elongated Columbia uses the same basic boiler style, except that the front is extended about ¾ inch, which can be discerned by the greater distance between the smokestack and the front. The die change was made around 1983 to allow a change to a four-wheel pilot truck. So its more recent incarnations are on a 4-4-2 arrangement, which is in real life an Atlantic style! This design is still in use, but the older, shorter model has been phased out. Many Columbias were made in the 1970s and 1980s, in both plastic and die-cast versions. The trend continues today, but with all the engines made of metal. Before 1979, the motor was a standard AC brush motor on a four-wheel chassis. After that it changed to a transverse-mounted can motor. In the postwar era these engines were made by the tens of thousands in the 200-series and were considered near the bottom-of-the-line. Modern Lionel has raised them in status a bit with desirable extra features and by creating even smaller steam styles for the very low-priced sets.

As Roland LaVoie stated in his excellent treatise on Columbias in the 1988 edition of this guide, this little engine bore the "corporate risk" of Lionel in the early days of its 1970s recovery, much more than the high-priced Collector engines. No other locomotive, diesel or steamer, has been so versatile or served Lionel so well for so long. Yet because of its mundane and unimpressive appearance, it has never raised much collector attention.

In 1990 Lionel modified the casting again to add a prominent feedwater tank to the top of the boiler front. This tank is rarely used on other steam engine styles, and so easily distinguishes the Columbia. In the 1990s Lionel's assembly line was churning out Columbia steam engines to head inexpensive starter sets and as stand-alone models. They were easy to change into new roads—simply by changing the number, painting the running board another color, or placing a different tender in back.

Lionel once again modified the tooling—perhaps it was beginning to wear excessively—in 1998. This step removed the feedwater tank once again. The bell was moved to a different spot on the top of the boiler. Otherwise the body is the same as the earlier Columbias.

ATLANTIC

The Atlantic-style, the second most-frequently used steam body for Lionel since 1970, appeared on many engines during the Fundimensions period, but has been quietly phased out of the line in favor of the larger Pacific-style boiler, in recent years. This may have to do with wear and tear on the die. It started on the 8142 in 1971 with an AC brush motor on the (correct) 4-4-2 wheel arrangement. Afterwards, the Atlantic body was converted to a 2-6-4, using the can motor with electronic reverse unit. The 2-6-4 drive train matched the way it first appeared in the postwar era as the 2026/2036. Note that a 2-6-4 is not correct for an Atlantic. The 2-6-4 wheel arrangement is used on the real railroads mostly in Europe, not in America. But postwar and modern Lionel have used it rather frequently on their model engines. Lionel has also used the same Atlantic boiler on a 2-6-2 Prairie wheel arrangement.

The Atlantic boiler is slightly larger and more massive than the Columbia, distinguished by its quartered window, condenser box on the pilot, larger sand dome, and large feedwater heaters on the left side. So far these engines are all die-cast with smoke and headlight.

After frequent appearances in the 1970s, '80s, and early '90s, including its one foray into the Collector realm at the head of 1991's revived Girls' Set, the Atlantic has not been produced by Lionel since 1994, though the body has reappeared on a 4-6-2 arrangement and called a "Pacific"!

PORTER

The Porter, a smaller boiler than the Columbia or Atlantic, features higher rounded domes on top and a distinctive shade over the windows. This is the same as the Scout (or 1060) locomotive of postwar fame, but has been produced only in plastic by modern era Lionel. It has appeared on seven engines in the post-1986 era, always on a 2-4-0 chassis, though it had appeared as an 0-4-0 during the Fundimensions era. The most unusual and hard-to-obtain model is one made for the Lionel Learning Center in 1993, given only to employees who had completed certain technical courses.

SWITCHER

The 1665 Switcher is another short steamer derived from the 1665 engine of 1948. The modern one retains the die-cast boiler of the original. It is recognized by the unsupported length of boiler in front of the steam chest and by the operating front coupler on later modern era versions. No other small steam engine has this feature, nor do most of the larger ones. The style appeared first on the 8310 in 1973, without the coupler but with a front axle (i.e., a 2-4-0) for some reason. It came back in its original 0-4-0 form with the coupler, heading an excellent NYC Yard Chief set and the ATSF Service Station Special in 1985–86. This time Lionel outfitted it with the can motor, three-position reverse, and a smoke unit (the first for any switcher), which emitted copious amounts of smoke. Since 1986 it has appeared only three times, most recently in nice New York Central and Pennsylvania models. This piece might be considered an under-appreciated "sleeper."

DOCKSIDE

The Dockside is a strange but whimsical locomotive that first appeared in an odd 1972 set called the "Dockside," from which it took its name. It is hard to imagine an engine body getting any smaller. It barely covers the frame on which it sits, which is otherwise a standard 0-4-0 steam chassis. It used a Type I brush motor initially, and switched to a Type II DC can in 1979. Needless to say, it features none of the higher-end goodies such as smoke, reverse units, or headlights. But since it can be purchased (and built) for next to nothing, it is perfect for the lowest end of Lionel's starter line. Lionel has even managed some rather standout color schemes for it, such as on the 1990 Badlands set, which also featured several other interesting cars. The Dockside's profile is unmistakable, with its *General*-type bulbous smokestack and prominent side number plate. In the Fundimensions period, it pulled a tender that resembled a stubby gondola. Lately it has not been accompanied by a tender.

SMALL STEAM ENGINE LISTINGS

Exc Mt

18600 ATLANTIC COAST LINE: 1987, 4-4-2 Elongated Columbia; uncataloged; die-cast boiler; smoke; headlight; Type II AC-DC can motor; three-position electronic reverse. Slope- back tender with Symington-Wayne trucks. Part of 11752 Timberline Freight set sold through J. C. Penney. **80 95**

18601 GREAT NORTHERN: 1988, 4-4-2 Elongated Columbia; die-cast boiler painted dark green with silver-painted smokebox and front; white "8601" on cab; headlight; smoke unit; Type II AC-DC can motor; three-position electronic reverse. Santa Fe 243-type square-back tender painted dark green with black coal load; red, white, and green circular "goat" logo; Symington-Wayne trucks; operating coupler. Does not have mechanical Sound of Steam feature as on previous locomotives of its type; wire handrails on boiler—an unusual feature for a Columbia. **80 95**

18602 PENNSYLVANIA: 1987, 4-4-2 Elongated Columbia; flat-front die-cast boiler; gold "8602" on cab (shown in white in catalog); smoke; headlight; Type II AC-DC can motor; three-position electronic reverse. Short box tender not issued since an 8040 model of 1972 carried it. This engine's tender differs from the earlier model in that it has a railing added to the tender's back deck; also has small, compressed "PENNSYLVANIA" lettering (very true to prototype), and Symington-Wayne trucks. Advertised in catalog as match for 16000-series Pennsylvania passenger cars, but sold separately in Type II box. **75 90**

18604 WABASH: 1988–91, 4-4-2 Elongated Columbia; die-cast boiler; headlight; smoke; wide white stripe along boiler; "8604" on cab; Type II AC-DC can motor; electronic three-position reverse; 243 Santa Fe–style square-back tender with Symington-Wayne trucks, "WABASH" lettering on white stripe and operating coupler. Essentially an updated version of the 8904 Wabash steamer produced in 1979, but with the extended Columbia boiler and new tender. Part of 11703 Iron Horse freight set. This engine came without the feedwater heater in 1988-90, then in 1991 it was rerun, with the feedwater heater, for the sets produced that year. L. Hippensteele comment.

(A) Without feedwater tank. 1988–90. **60 80**

(B) With feedwater tank. 1991. **70 90**

18605 MOPAR EXPRESS: 1987–88, 4-4-2 Elongated Columbia; uncataloged; black die-cast boiler; white "1987" on cab and black "ME" inside white rectangle on steam chest; white stripe on running board; headlight; smoke; green jewels on front marker lights; rubber tires on rear drivers; AC-DC Type II can motor; three-position electronic reverse. Black plastic square-back 243-type tender with mechanical Sound of Steam, three white stripes and "MOPAR EXPRESS" on sides; Symington-Wayne trucks. This engine headed an uncataloged Chrysler set

Exc Mt

in 1987 and 1988 (11757). The 1988 set came with an additional tank car. This engine is based on the 8617 Nickel Plate Special, but was offered only through a special Chrysler dealer promotion for its "Chrysler Motors Genuine Parts"—MOPAR. Reportedly 1,500 made. **60 80**

18606 NEW YORK CENTRAL: 1989, 2-6-4 with Atlantic boiler; black die-cast boiler; white "8606" on cab and "NEW YORK CENTRAL" on tender; smoke; headlight; Type IV AC-DC can motor with six wheels; three-position electronic reverse unit. First reuse of this motor since 8001/8007 in 1980. 6466-type tender with wire handrails and bar-end trucks. (See comments on tender under 18608.) Engine is similar to 18607, 18608, 18609, and 18611. Frequent reports of off-center axle mounting causing engine to wobble down track. Purchasers should test before buying. Six companion passenger cars (16016-16021) issued separately. **120 150**

18607 UNION PACIFIC: 1989, 2-6-4 with Atlantic boiler; light gray die-cast boiler; yellow-striped running board; yellow "8607" on cab and "UNION PACIFIC" on matching gray tender; smoke; headlight; Type IV AC-DC can motor on six-wheel chassis; three-position electronic reverse. Tender is 6466-type with die-cast postwar bar-end trucks and wire handrails. Engine is similar to 18606 and 18608. See comment under 18608. See 18606 for operating cautions. **130 165**

18608 RIO GRANDE: 1989, 2-6-4 with Atlantic boiler; uncataloged; black die-cast boiler; white "8608" and "Rio Grande" on tender; smoke; headlight; ornamental bell; Type IV AC-DC can motor on six-wheel chassis; three-position electronic reverse unit. 6466-type tender with wire railings and postwar die-cast bar-end trucks; no whistle. This is the first appearance of this style tender since the postwar era. Engine is similar to the old postwar 2037 and headed the 1989 Service Station Special set 11758, the Desert King. See comments on 18606 for operating cautions. **120 150**

18609 NORTHERN PACIFIC: 1990, 2-6-4 with Atlantic boiler; black die-cast body similar to 18606-18608; white "8609" on cab; smoke; headlight; Type IV AC-DC can motor on six-wheel chassis; three-position electronic reverse. "NORTHERN PACIFIC" in white on the 243-type square-back tender, which features new ASF strong-arm trucks and wire railings—an unusual addition for this tender; no sound effects. Six companion passenger cars (16034-16039) were issued separately. **140 180**

18610 ROCK ISLAND: 1990, 0-4-0, 1665 Switcher; black die-cast boiler with white "8610" on cab. Same construction details as for the 8516 and 8635 switchers: smoke, headlight, three-position electronic reverse, Type II AC-DC can motor. Operating front and rear couplers. Slope-back tender has wire railings, "ROCK ISLAND" lettering, ASF trucks, and a diode-controlled operating backup light. **125 150**

	Exc	Mt

18611 LIONEL LINES: 1990, 2-6-4 with Atlantic boiler; uncataloged; die-cast boiler in smoke-gray; white "8611" on cab; white stripe on running board; white "LL" in stylized rectangle on steam chest; headlight; smoke; Type IV AC-DC six-wheel can motor; three-position electronic reverse; body is same as 18606-18609 engines. Tender is a plastic 1130-type small streamlined oil version with first-class trim, such as die-cast leaf spring trucks and wire railings, yet without sound system. Apparently, Lionel planned a variety of tender types for this engine style. Came with 1990 Service Station Special set 11712, the Great Lakes Express. Four O27 passenger cars came with set. **120 150**

18612 CHICAGO & NORTH WESTERN: 1989, 4-4-2 Elongated Columbia; black die-cast body with silver-painted boiler front; white "8612" on cab; steel driver rims; wire handrails on boiler; headlight; smoke; Type II AC-DC can motor; three-position electronic reverse unit. 243-type square-back tender with red, white and black CNW logo and Symington-Wayne trucks. Engine is the same as 18601. **80 95**

18613 ATLANTIC COAST LINE: 1989, 4-4-2 Elongated Columbia; uncataloged; same engine as 18602 Pennsylvania, but came with Atlantic Coast Line slope-back tender as found on 8902 and 18600; white lettering; smoke; headlight; Type II AC-DC can motor; three-position electronic reverse unit. This engine was issued for an uncataloged Sears set 11773 that came with three of the regular production NYC O27 passenger cars (the Pullman, baggage and observation cars). The Sears catalog shows a photo of the 18602, but the engine was made as the 18613. **70 90**

18614 SEARS CIRCUS TRAIN: 1989, 4-4-2 Elongated Columbia; uncataloged; die-cast boiler painted light blue; "1989" on cab; headlight; smoke; Type II AC-DC can motor; three-position electronic reverse. Plastic 243-type square-back tender in matching blue with white "CIRCUS TRAIN" lettering, and clown and tent electrocal. This engine was part of an uncataloged 11770 Sears Circus Train set in 1989. **55 75**

18615 GRAND TRUNK WESTERN: 1990, 4-4-2 Elongated Columbia; black die-cast boiler; new boiler style with feedwater heater added to the front; wire handrails; white stripe on running board; white "8615" under cab; headlight; smoke unit; Type II AC-DC can motor; three-position electronic reverse; bright steel rims on drive wheels. Engine is similar to 18612 from 1989, except for added feedwater tank. 243-type square-back tender with G T W white and blue logo, and ASF trucks. **75 90**

18616 NORTHERN PACIFIC: 1990, 4-4-2 Elongated Columbia; uncataloged; black die-cast boiler; white "8616" on cab; white "NORTHERN PACIFIC" lettering on slope-back tender; headlight; smoke; Type II AC-DC can motor; three-position electronic reverse. Tender has ASF trucks. Engine was made for an uncataloged 1990 Sears set (49N95266) pulling three regular-issue Northern Pacific O27 streamlined passenger cars (the combo, vista dome, and observation). The regularly cataloged engine for the passenger set was 18609. **75 90**

18617 ADOLPHUS III: 1989, 4-4-2 Elongated Columbia; uncataloged; black die-cast boiler with no number; 1615-type slope-back tender; smoke; headlight; only lettering on cab is white "ADOLPHUS / III"; wire handrails on engine and tender; AC-DC can motor; three-position electronic reverse. Black plastic tender with white "ANHEUSER-BUSCH" and red and gold "A"-eagle logo; Symington-Wayne trucks. 18617 is its catalog number, but this is not mentioned in any Lionel literature. Part of uncataloged Anheuser Busch Budweiser set 11775. Reportedly only 2,500 made. Available only through an Anheuser-Busch gift catalog. It was made with and without the feedwater heater on the front of the boiler.

(A) With feedwater tank. **130 160**

(B) Without feedwater tank. **130 160**

18618 BALTIMORE AND OHIO: 1991, 4-4-2 Elongated Columbia. Announced in Lionel's 1991 Book 1 catalog, not manufactured. **Not Manufactured**

18620 ILLINOIS CENTRAL: 1991, 2-6-2 Atlantic steam locomotive; Atlantic boiler body on a Prairie-style wheel arrangement; black die-cast boiler; yellow lettering on tender and yellow running board on engine; "8620" on cab; headlight; smoke unit; Type IV six-wheel can motor; three-position electronic reverse unit; small New York Central-style tender (2466 type) with plastic arch bar trucks. Intended as a match for the Illinois Central O27 streamlined passenger cars (16042-16047) released the same year. Strangely enough, this is the first steam engine lettered for the Illinois Central Lionel has ever made. **150 195**

18621 WESTERN PACIFIC: 1992, 0-4-0 1665-style switcher; announced in the 1992 catalog, but never made **Not Manufactured**

18622 UNION PACIFIC: 1990–91, 4-4-2 Elongated Columbia; uncataloged; black die-cast boiler with feedwater tank; yellow running stripe; number "8622" in black on yellow stripe below cab windows; square-back tender has "UNION PACIFIC" lettering and shield in yellow; smoke and headlight; mechanical Sound of Steam; Type II AC-DC can motor; three-position electronic reverse. Engine is part of the 11785 UP Costco set, made specially for the wholesale chain. Not individually boxed. Most set cartons are misspelled "COSCO". Lionel later released the same engine, with the number changed, in 1993's UP Express set. **75 90**

18623 TEXAS & PACIFIC: 1992, 4-4-2 Elongated Columbia; black die-cast boiler with feedwater tank; gunmetal gray-painted smokebox; wire handrails; number on cab is "8623"; headlight and smoke;

18636 Baltimore & Ohio Pacific

	Exc	Mt

Type II AC-DC can motor; three-position electronic reverse; square-back tender with "TEXAS & PACIFIC" in white; whistle in tender. A matching T&P caboose was available. **75** **90**

18625 ILLINOIS CENTRAL: 1991, 4-4-2 Elongated Columbia; uncataloged; black die-cast boiler with feedwater tank; wire handrails; yellow running board stripe; number "8625" in yellow on cab; slope-back tender with two yellow stripes and "ILLINOIS CENTRAL" lettering; headlight and smoke; Type II AC-DC can motor; three-position electronic reverse. This engine was part of the Sears Illinois Central set from 1991 (Sears no. 49C95724), in which this engine pulled three of the regular-issue O27 Illinois Central passenger cars. Decoration is similar to the 18620, but on a different body. **90** **110**

18626 DELAWARE & HUDSON: 1992, 2-6-2 Atlantic steam locomotive; Atlantic boiler body on a Prairie-style wheel arrangement; black die-cast boiler; yellow lettering on tender and on engine; "8626" on cab; headlight; smoke unit; Type IV six-wheel can motor; white-edged drive wheels; three-position electronic reverse unit; small New York Central-style tender (2466 type) with plastic arch-bar trucks. Listed with a matching SP caboose. The catalog lists this engine with sounds, but it wasn't made with them. **150** **180**

18627 CHESAPEAKE & OHIO: 1992, 4-4-2 Elongated Columbia; black die-cast boiler with feedwater tank; number on cab is "8627" in yellow; yellow-painted running board; headlight and smoke; Type II AC-DC can motor; three-position electronic reverse; square-back tender with "CHESAPEAKE & OHIO" in yellow. Part of 11727 Coastal Limited set. By 1992 Lionel was regularly issuing this Columbia at the head of various sets and on occasion alone. **75** **90**

18628 MKT: 1992–93, 4-4-2 Elongated Columbia; black die-cast boiler with feedwater tank; number on cab is "8628" in white; white-painted running board; headlight and smoke; Type II AC-DC can motor; three-position electronic reverse; square-back tender with Missouri-Kansas-Texas shield in white. Part of 11728 High Plains Runner set. **75** **90**

18630 CHICAGO & NORTH WESTERN: 1993, 4-6-2 Pacific; die-cast Baldwin-type black boiler; decorative steam whistle and bell; white "2903" on cab and on sand dome; MagneTraction; smoke; headlight; Type III Pullmor AC six-wheel motor; three-position reverse; 2466 NYC-style small tender with die-cast arch-bar trucks; CNW logo in red and white on tender; steam whistle in tender. This engine was the first release of the Pacific since 1989's Reading model (18004), but the first of many which would follow, in both the Traditional (18600-) and Collector (18000-) lines. The engine was intended to pull the C&NW Madison cars also made in 1993. **300** **350**

18632 NEW YORK CENTRAL: 1993–99, 4-4-2 Elongated Columbia; black die-cast boiler with feedwater tank; white edging on running board; white "8632" on cab; headlight and smoke; Type II AC-DC can motor; three-position electronic reverse; square-back tender with "NEW YORK CENTRAL" in white, under- and overscored; steam whistle in tender. This engine headed the 11735 New York Central Flyer set, one of the longest-running starter sets in Lionel's history. An interesting footnote—its first appearance in the 1993 catalog shows it gray and with a streamlined tender, but the production engine is made black with a square-back tender. The other rolling stock in the set also changed colors from the prototypes to the production pieces. The correct colors and consist are shown in 1994 and subsequent catalogs. The engine also appeared in quite a few other uncataloged sets (with differing tenders) in the following years. See also the following entry.

(A) As described. 1993–98. **75** **90**

(B) Retooled Columbia with no feedwater tank. **—** **90**

18633 UNION PACIFIC: 1993–95, 4-4-2 Elongated Columbia; black die-cast boiler with feedwater tank; yellow running stripe and number, which is "8633" on cab in black on the yellow stripe, which is continuous through the cab side here, not interrupted as it is on other engines; headlight and smoke; Type II AC-DC can motor; three-position electronic reverse; square-back tender with "UNION PACIFIC" and UP shield logo in yellow; whistle in tender. The tender has "BLT 1-93", an unusual marking for a steam loco. This engine headed the 11736 Union Pacific Express set.

(A) Black number on yellow stripe. **75** **90**

(B) Yellow number on black background. Yellow stripe ends before meeting cab. 1995 version. **75** **90**

18638 Norfolk & Western Atlantic

Exc Mt

18633 CHESAPEAKE & OHIO: 1994–95, 4-4-2 Elongated Columbia; same description as 18633 UP above, except number, which is also "8633" in yellow on the black body of the cab, and the square-back tender reads "CHESAPEAKE & OHIO". See other details in the previous listing. This engine headed the 11746 Seaboard Freight set starting in 1994, the least expensive of Lionel's starter sets. Boxed in the set, not individually. **75 90**

18635 SANTA FE: 1993, 2-6-4 Atlantic locomotive body on a Prairie-style wheel arrangement; black die-cast boiler; white lettering "A.T.&S.F" on cab and "8625" on tender; headlight; smoke unit; Type IV six-wheel can motor; three-position electronic reverse unit; small New York Central-style tender (2466 type) with plastic arch-bar trucks, wire handrails and steam whistle. It is not clear why the number—in this case on the tender—is off by one digit from the usual scheme of including the catalog number less the initial "1". **150 180**

18636 BALTIMORE & OHIO: 1994, 4-6-2 Pacific; body is the Baldwin-type boiler painted dark green; smokebox painted graphite gray; gold lettering on engine reads "PRESIDENT WASHINGTON" with gold outline; number plates on front read "5300"; Type III Pullmor AC six-wheel motor; MagneTraction; smoke unit with synchronizing mechanism; headlight; three-position E-unit; small NYC-style tender is a matching green with gold "BALTIMORE & OHIO" and accent lines; tender has wire handrails, green-painted die-cast arch-bar trucks, and an operating steam whistle. This piece is a close re-creation of the Class P-7 "Presidential" engines used by the B&O in the 1920s and was a popular Lionel release. **300 350**

18637 UNITED AUTO WORKERS: 1993, 4-4-2 Elongated Columbia; uncataloged; black die-cast boiler with feedwater tank; yellow running stripe and number, which is "8633" on cab; headlight and smoke; Type II AC-DC can motor; three-position electronic reverse; square-back tender with "UAW EXPRESS" in yellow; ASF trucks on tender. This engine headed the special 11811 UAW Express set. It is precisely the same as the "8633" Chessie version used in the Seaboard Freight (see 18633), except the tender was replaced with a unique UAW one. **75 90**

18638 NORFOLK & WESTERN: 1994, 2-6-4 Atlantic; black die-cast boiler; yellow running board stripe and number, which is "638"; catalog shows white lettering; headlight; smoke unit; Type IV six-wheel can motor; three-position electronic reverse unit; small New York Central-style tender (2466 type) with die-cast arch-bar trucks, "NORFOLK & WESTERN" in white; steam whistle; wire handrails on engine and tender. This engine introduced a modified smoke unit with a piston activator that pushed smoke out as the wheels rotated. The engine was intended to pull the N&W Madison cars also released that year. **150 200**

18639 READING: 1995, 4-6-2 Pacific; new smaller boiler design different and shorter than the Baldwin boiler used before; black die-cast body; gold number on cab is "639" outlined in a box; Type IV six-wheel can motor frame; electronic reverse unit; headlight; synchronized smoke unit; small NYC (2466-style) tender lettered in gold for "READING"; operating steam whistle; ASF trucks on tender. This engine has a newly tooled boiler different from any others produced before. It is similar to the older "Atlantic" boilers used on some of the engines described earlier, but has a smoother main casting and somewhat less piping detail, as well as an additional relief valve fitting on top. It has wire handrails and the decorative bell and whistle, but in this case Lionel at last managed to delete the intrusive E-unit handle (and the slot for it in the top of the cab), since the electronic reverse had fully supplanted the old mechanical E-unit. Note there are slight body differences also (notably the addition of side feedwater heaters) between the 1995 catalog pictures and the production engines. The body is shorter than the Alco and

18641 Ford
Elongated Columbia

Exc Mt

Baldwin styles used on earlier Pacifics, as can be seen in the photos, and Lionel evidently intended to use this new version in its middle-range steam series. **125 150**

18640 UNION PACIFIC: 1995, 4-6-2 Pacific; new "Pacific" boiler design introduced in 1995 (see 18639); black die-cast body; white "8640" on cab; Type IV six-wheel can motor frame; three-position reverse unit; headlight; synchronized smoke unit; small NYC 2466-type tender lettered for "UNION PACIFIC" in white; operating steam whistle; ASF trucks on tender. **125 150**

18641 FORD: 1994, 4-4-2 Elongated Columbia; uncataloged; black die-cast boiler with feedwater tank; white running stripe and number, which is "8641" on cab in black on the white stripe, which is continuous through the cab side here; headlight and smoke; Type II AC-DC can motor; three-position electronic reverse; square-back tender with "Ford" in white script; whistle in tender. This engine headed a special 11814 Ford set. **75 90**

18642 LIONEL LINES: 1995, 4-6-2 Pacific; new "Pacific" boiler design introduced in 1995 (see 18639); black die-cast body; white running board stripe; number is "8642" on cab; Type IV six-wheel can motor frame; three-position reverse unit; headlight; synchronized smoke unit; square-back tender lettered for "LIONEL LINES" in white; operating steam whistle; ASF trucks on tender. This engine headed Lionel's top-of-the line Traditional (starter) set in 1995, the 11747 Lionel Lines Steam set. The set featured a variety of other classy, and now hard-to-find, rolling stock. **125 150**

Number TBS LIONEL LINES: 1995, 4-4-2 Elongated Columbia; black die-cast boiler with feedwater tank; no lettering on cab; Type II AC-DC can motor; headlight; smoke unit; square-back tender has white "LIONEL LINES"; no whistle. The engine headed a strange uncataloged set called the "Factory Selection Set," which was given number 11906. The name implied variations in the contents. A reefer, bulkhead flat, and Lionel Lines SP caboose were in this set, but other rolling stock could have been used. Reader Lou Bohn suggests it was an attempt by Lionel to get rid of excess stock, as well as its low-performing 12849 transformer. If it had a catalog number, based on the timing, the engine would have been something in the 1864X range. **40 60**

Exc Mt

18700 ROCK ISLAND: 1987–88, 0-4-0 Dockside; bright red plastic body; silver-painted smokebox, stack and steam chests; white "8700" and Rock Island logo; Type II DC-only can motor (running on AC will burn out motor). No tender. Part of the 11701 Rail Blazer set. **20 35**

18704 LIONEL LINES: 1989, (Microracers) 2-4-0 Porter; uncataloged; black plastic body; headlight; white "8704" on cab; Type II DC-only can motor (running on AC will burn out motor). White "LIONEL LINES" on slope-back tender; Symington-Wayne trucks. Part of unusual uncataloged Microracers set 11771 made for K-Mart. **40 60**

18705 NEPTUNE: 1990–91, (Badlands Express) 0-4-0 Dockside; black plastic body; gold trim and drive rods; red boiler front; gold "8705" and "NEPTUNE" on cab; Type II DC-only can motor (running on AC will burn out motor). No tender. Part of 11714 Badlands Express set. **25 35**

18706 ATSF: 1991, 2-4-0 Porter steam locomotive; black plastic body; white lettering; "8706" in large numbers on the tender; headlight; Type II DC-only can motor (running on AC will burn out motor); polarity reverse at transformer; 243-type square-back tender with ASF strong-arm trucks. Part of 11720 Santa Fe Special set. **25 40**

18707 MICKEY'S WORLD TOUR: 1991, 2-4-0 Porter steam locomotive; black plastic body; red lettering and running board stripe; "MICKEY'S WORLD TOUR '92" printed on cab roof (an unusual feature) and on the Santa Fe type slope-back tender; "8707" in red on cab; multicolor Mickey tour logo on tender side; headlight; Type II DC-only can motor (running on AC will burn out motor); ASF strong-arm trucks on tender. Part of 11721 Mickey's World Tour train set. The 1991 catalog boldly advertised the engine with smoke, but it was not made that way—it is close to impossible to fit a smoke unit inside this small engine. **40 55**

18709 LIONEL EMPLOYEE LEARNING CENTER: 1992, 0-4-0 Dockside; uncataloged; specially made for employees who completed various Lionel training classes (see also boxcar 19925); light blue

18702 Virginia & Truckee *General*

	Exc	Mt

plastic body; smiling image on smokestack; no lettering anywhere visible on body, but the piece is marked "8240-45" on the bottom; no tender; Type II DC-only can motor. Quite hard to find, as very few were made. The employees at Lionel fondly call it the "Little Blue Engine." — 150

18710 SOUTHERN PACIFIC: 1993, 2-4-0 Porter; black plastic body; white lettering; "2000" on cab; white running board edge; headlight; steel-rimmed drive wheels with traction tires; ornamental bell; Type II DC can motor with rectifier circuit to allow AC operation; electronic reverse unit; slope-back tender with white road name and ASF trucks. Lionel offered this and the 18711-18712 units as low-cost alternatives to prepackaged set engines. 35 45

18711 SOUTHERN: 1993, 2-4-0 Porter; dark green plastic body; white lettering; "2000" on cab; white running board edge; headlight; steel-rimmed drive wheels with traction tires; ornamental bell; Type II DC can motor with rectifier circuit to allow AC operation; electronic reverse unit; slope-back tender with white road name and ASF trucks. 35 45

18712 JERSEY CENTRAL: 1993, 2-4-0 Porter; medium blue plastic body; white lettering; "2000" on cab; white running board edge; headlight; steel-rimmed drive wheels with traction tires; ornamental bell; Type II DC can motor with rectifier circuit to allow AC operation; electronic reverse unit; slope-back tender with white road name and ASF trucks. 35 45

18713 CHESSIE SYSTEM: 1994–95, 2-4-0 Porter; black plastic body; yellow lettering; "1993" on cab; yellow running board

	Exc	Mt

edge; headlight; steel-rimmed drive wheels with traction tires; ornamental bell; Type II DC can motor with rectifier circuit to allow AC operation; electronic reverse unit; slope-back tender with white road name and ASF trucks. 35 45

GENERAL STEAM ENGINES

In 1977, Lionel resurrected another old favorite—the "General"—an old-time 4-4-0 locomotive first made by Lionel in the late 1950s. The Western & Atlantic no. 3 (8701) met with great success that year, especially after the old-time cars were issued for it. Since then, the General locomotive has been used in chromed Rock Island, blue and black B&O, and other color schemes. One version of this locomotive was part of the unusual 1988 Service Station set. A more recent one has achieved a new status in the Collector Line—a Disneyland 35th anniversary commemorative for 1990.

However, for unknown reasons, Lionel did not produce more of these handsome engines after 1991, until two terrific Union and Confederate Generals were placed at the head of the Civil War sets in 1999.

The Generals listed in this volume rest on a frame similar to that used for the Columbias and are powered by the same DC can motor with rectifier. They all have the electronic reverse unit. All of them pull a wood-toting tender, the only such tender Lionel makes in O Gauge.

GENERAL STEAM ENGINE LISTINGS

	Exc	Mt

18008 DISNEYLAND RAILROAD: 1990, 4-4-0 *General;* dark gray boiler with light gray front section and black boiler front; red cab, wheels and pilot; gold and brass trim; wire handrails on boiler; intricate decals in several locations; white "4" on cab; polished-steel wheels; smoke; headlight; Type VII General-style can motor; three-position electronic reverse. Tender bears Disney 35th anniversary herald and "DISNEYLAND RAILROAD" inside gold accents; die-cast arch-bar trucks on tender. Engine came with oak display base, Gargraves track, acrylic cover and silver nameplate. Issued to mark the 35th anniversary of Disneyland. Without the display case, it is cataloged as 18013. 250 300

18702 V. & T. R. R.: 1988 (Virginia & Truckee Railroad), 4-4-0 *General;* uncataloged; black boiler and cab; gold trim; gold "8702" and "RENO"; smoke; headlight; Type VII can motor; three-position electronic reverse. Tender with black body, gold outlining and "V & T R R"; plastic arch-bar trucks, brown

Exc Mt

simulated woodpile, and operating coupler. Part of "Dry Gulch Line" Service Station set 11706 for 1988. The previous Guide listed the base color of this engine as maroon. It is in fact black.

(A) As described. **110 140**

(B) Factory Error. Tender lettered on one side only. F. B. Collins, Jr. Collection. **NRS**

18716 LIONELVILLE CIRCUS: 1990–91, 4-4-0 *General;* red boiler; green cab; black frame and smokestack; yellow "8716" on cab; gold "LCS" on boiler nameplate; gold trim and drive rods; wire handrails; operating headlight; Type VII AC-DC can motor; three-position electronic reverse. Woodpile tender painted green with yellow "Lionelville Circus" and plastic arch-bar trucks; operating coupler. Part of the popular Lionelville Circus Special Traditional Line set 11716. Note: Lionel's 1990 catalog shows this engine correctly, with "8716" on the cab. The 1991 catalog, for some reason, has it incorrectly numbered as "8616"

(A) As described. **140 175**

(B) Factory Error. Missing the word "CIRCUS" on tender. J. Hirschmans Collection. **NRS**

TENDERS WITH SOUNDS

Once it had fully developed its state-of-the-art RailSounds technology in the early 1990s, Lionel naturally sought ways to market it and expand its application, as well as the rolling stock in which it could be found. Starting in boxcars, Lionel eventually managed to install the system in diesels, accessories, and of course steam engine tenders. By 1993 one of the marketers hit on the idea that a stand-alone tender with the sound system in it could be used with a variety of different engines, saving the consumer the cost of buying the expensive locomotive as well. Thus was born the basic black—and seemingly somewhat forlorn—steam engine tender with sounds.

Exc Mt

16655 STEAM TENDER WITH RAILSOUNDS: 1993, basic black long streamlined (2046 style) tender; no lettering; no engine; black body rides on die-cast six-wheel trucks; operating coupler. Steam RailSounds circuitry inside body. First of several similar releases of unmarked tenders that can be included behind any steam engine to inexpensively add RailSounds system to a collection. **120 140**

16673 LIONEL LINES: 1994–97, square-back tender with electronically activated air whistle; no engine; black body; ASF trucks; white lettering; no number; operating coupler; fixed coupler at front (removable); intended as an add-on or replacement for tenders/engines with no sound systems. **25 35**

19820 STEAM TENDER WITH RAILSOUNDS II: 1995–96, die-cast black 2046 long streamlined tender; unmarked; die-cast six-wheel trucks; fitted with RailSounds II circuitry inside; fixed coupler at front (removable); operating rear coupler. This larger tender, with the more advanced RailSounds II, is intended as a replacement for the older tenders on Lionel's previous large steam engines, to add RailSounds to the sets. **140 175**

52060 VIRGINIA TRAIN COLLECTORS: 1994, tender only; uncataloged; black long 2046-style tender with whistle; number on the body is "7694"; special for the Virginia Train Collectors group—one of its last specials. **— NRS**

CHAPTER 4

Diesel Locomotives

When General Mills' Fundimensions toy division took over production of trains from the Lionel Corporation in 1970, its managers realized that a whole new generation awaited the production and rediscovery of Lionel trains. The firm realized that this new generation did not necessarily share the nostalgia of its elders. Therefore, Fundimensions decided to market its locomotives not just to people with actual memories of steam locomotives, but also to those who would look for imitations of the contemporary world around them. That meant diesel engines, not steamers. The rapid proliferation of diesel engines made economic sense in the early years of Fundimensions, even if it might have been at the expense of the steamers—a new market for toy trains had to be developed.

There were two other highly significant economic advantages to the rapid marketing of many types of diesels. First, diesels had fewer parts and were less costly than steamers and faster to produce. Second, Fundimensions could take advantage of new decorating processes much more easily on the flat plastic surfaces of the diesel cabs than it could on the rounded boilers of the steam locomotives. The postwar decorating techniques were limited to decals, heat stamping, rubber stamping, and some silk-screening. As a subsidiary of General Mills, Fundimensions had access to people knowledgeable in the new and versatile decorating processes known as "electrocal" and "tampo." By these means, colorful contemporary railroad paint schemes could be applied to Fundimensions' trains—and color sells trains to the public.

Right from the start, Fundimensions made its policy apparent. In its 1970 catalog only a couple of 2-4-2 Columbia steamers were actually produced. However, the catalog featured an exceptionally colorful orange and white Illinois Central GP-9, a bright blue Santa Fe NW-2 switcher, and an Alco AA pair of Santa Fe diesels in the famous "warbonnet" paint scheme.

As the years went by, Fundimensions issued many different styles of diesels. Most of these styles have continued under the Lionel Trains, Inc (LTI) and Lionel LLC management. This chapter describes and lists them by major styles, including entirely new diesel types brought out by LTI in recent years.

Engine Numbering System

In its five-digit numbering system adopted after 1987, Lionel placed all of the powered units (diesels, steam engines, electrics, and small motorized units) in the 18000- series of numbers, with the third digit after the "18" indicating the major subcategory of engine. For the diesels, the categories can be found in the accompanying table.

In some cases the number on the cab of the engine (or its number board) will be the 18000-series number less the initial "1". This can lead to some confusion with engines from the Fundimensions era, which also had four digits starting with "8". It is not uncommon to find two entirely different engines with the same number on their cabs. For example, the 18903 Amtrak Alco bears the same "8903" cab number as a small Rio Grande steam engine from 1978!

In other cases, particularly where scale accuracy and realism is of primary concern, the piece will bear a prototypically correct number that has no relation to the cataloged number.

We should also point out that in some cases, sets or groups of engines were produced, or engines were part of cataloged sets, such that the 18000-series number is not actually listed in the catalog. The numbers we include here are the internal catalog numbers Lionel uses to track every individual piece of rolling stock.

Diesel Motor Types

Lionel has produced three basic motor types for its modern era diesels. Types I and II are carryovers from the hardy postwar motors that have seen so much use and abuse at the hands of Lionel operators for more than four decades. Type III is the "can motor," widely used since its 1982 inception. Actually, there are many sub-variations of the motor, gear, and truck assemblies because of the large variety of ways Lionel arranged the gearing to get one, two, or more drive axles. This was also determined by how much space was available and how the motor had to fit within the cab.

Each motor type was developed to achieve a long lifespan, able to withstand tremendous levels of shock, heat, and vibration. They are remarkable feats of model engineering.

Diesel Type	Pages	Number Ranges (1987–)
GM's F-3 and "FT" diesels	43-47	18100- and 38100-
Alco FA- and PA-diesels	47-50	18100- and 18900-
Alco RS-3 diesels	50-54	18800-
GM EMD's GP-series diesels	54-59	18500- and 18800-
GE U36B diesels	59-60	18800
GM EMD's SD-series diesels	60-64	18200-, 18500-, and 18800-
GM's NW-2 Switchers	64-66	18900-
FM TrainMasters	66-67	18300- and 18800-
GE's Dash 8 and Dash 9s	67-70	18200-
GE 44-ton Switchers	70	18900- and 28800-

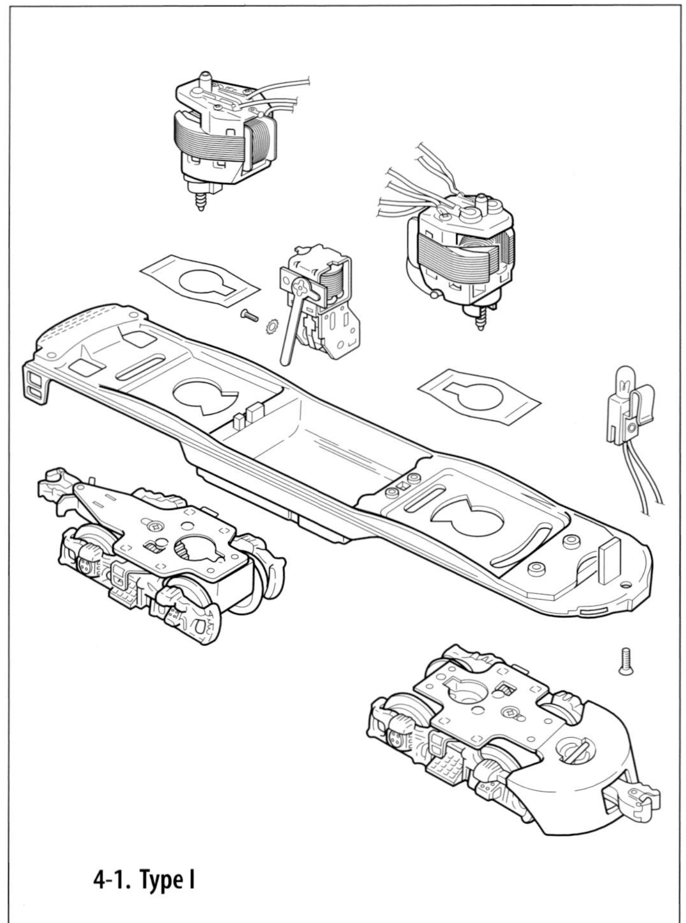
4-1. Type I

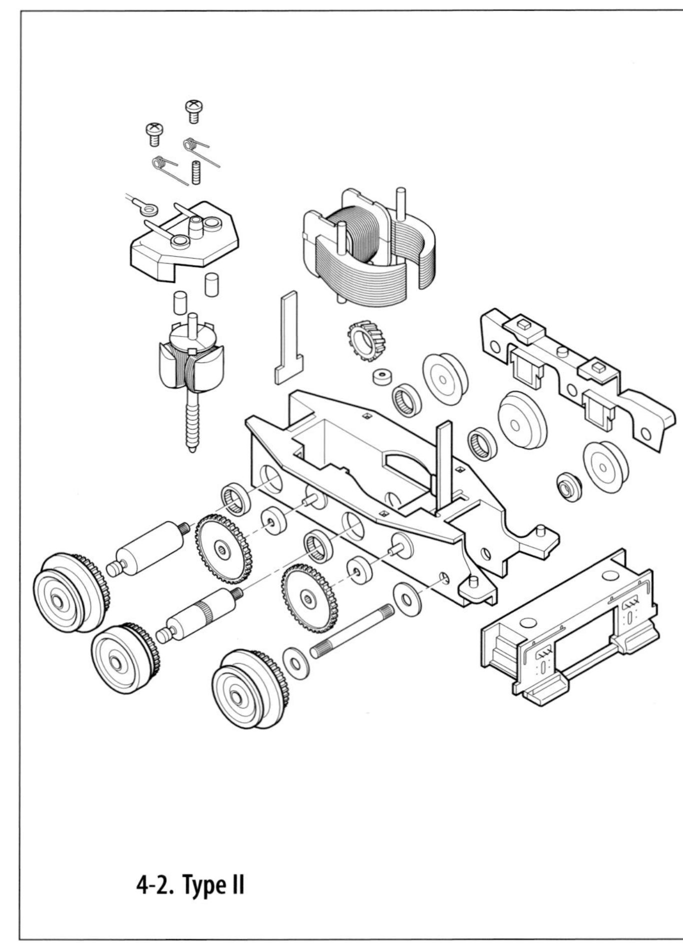
4-2. Type II

TYPE I: This is diversely known as a separate motor and truck assembly, or the "Pullmor motor" (a description found in the catalogs). This motor type (see fig. 4-1) consists of a single- or double-wound field, depending on the E-unit type, surrounding an armature with a worm gear. The worm gear fits down into the top of the power truck, where it drives either a gear on the main drive axle, or internal spur gearing in the truck which transmits power to more than one geared axle. The motor is mounted to the truck via a single mounting screw and pivots in a keyhole-shaped opening in the frame.

This arrangement provides excellent pulling power and track operation, since the free-pivoting trucks and wheels can round tight radii and switches more easily than the Type II motor. This drive system is a direct descendant of the system developed for the Fairbanks-Morse TrainMaster in 1954, and modern Lionel has used it in its "premium" diesels and electrics: the F-3s, FMs, EP-5s, and GG-1s. Interestingly, postwar Lionel used this motor in its GP models, but Fundimensions chose the less expensive Type II for the majority of its "Geeps." Happily the new Lionel has restored this nice feature to the GP engines it has made. When mounted in twin-motor configurations (especially with MagneTraction), as in the FMs, the GG-1s, and later F-3s, these motors can outpull anything else on tinplate rails.

TYPE II: Known as the "integral truck and motor assembly" (intended to differentiate it from Type I), this drive system (see fig. 4-2) was originally developed during Lionel's downsizing period in 1955 in response to cost-cutting demands. In this system the motor field, drive gears, and axle-mounting frame (i.e., the main body of the truck) are all one piece. The spur gears are mounted on one side of this piece, driving geared wheels. This drive system rides in a large hole in the frame, suspended from spring-loaded bushings traveling in curved slots fore and aft of the large hole. The integral motor/truck system does not perform as well on switches as its Type I counterpart, because its more rigid wheelbase does not conform to the curves as easily. Type II motors are found on modern era Lionel road switchers—GP-7s, GP-9s, GP-20s, Alcos, U36s, and smaller SD units. A larger modified version was created for use on the large SD-40 diesels and has migrated to other types of diesels in the late 1990s. It has a pulling power comparable to the Type I Pullmor. Because the field windings are of similar size, and the operation is essentially the same, Lionel has lately come to call this a Pullmor motor as well, leading to some confusion. Lionel owns the copyright to the term "Pullmor."

TYPE III: This is the "can motor," introduced by Lionel in 1982 (see fig. 4-3). More precisely, it originated on the low-end DC-powered switchers in 1974. The motor itself is DC-powered. In the early 1980s, Lionel was inspired to add a rectifier circuit, thereby allowing it to be used for AC operation as well. Since then, the can motor (and its rectifier) has moved into the higher-end Traditional diesels (those for separate-sale), and even a few Collector engines.

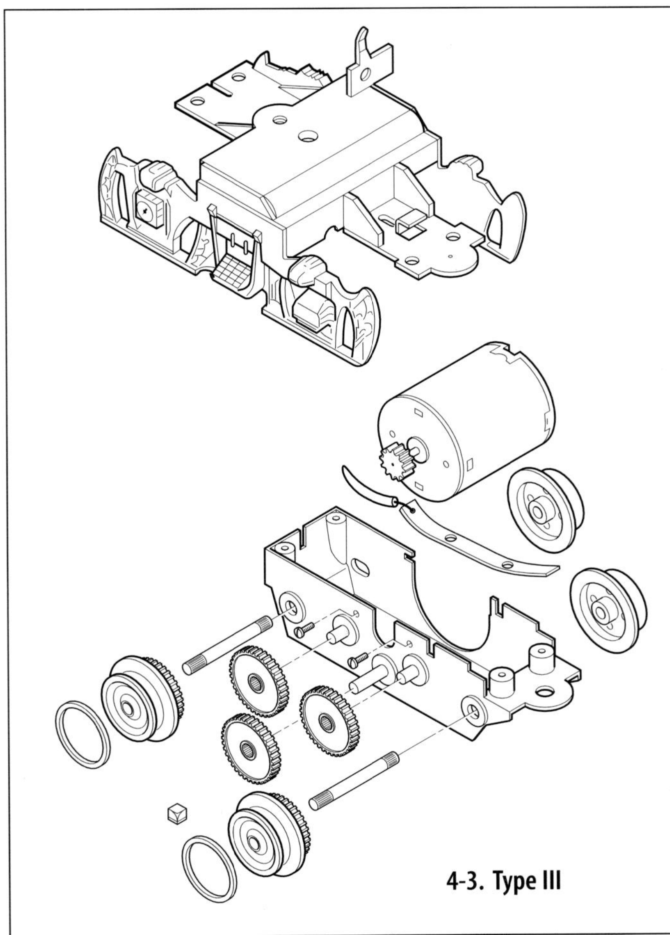
4-3. Type III

The principal feature of this motor is that it is small and completely enclosed, so maintenance is practically eliminated. In fact, Lionel advises that whenever maintenance is needed, the simplest solution is simply to discard the motor entirely and replace it with another one. The only protrusion is the armature shaft to which the pinion drive gear is attached. The remainder of the truck and geared wheel assemblies are similar to the Type II truck designs. However, in this case, the motor fits down into the truck body rather than riding above inside the cab (which, by the way, is the configuration used in real diesels). This has the additional advantage of permitting more room in the cab for such niceties as the electronic E-Unit, an electronic horn, or RailSounds.

The can motor is so small and lightweight that the first engines using it were too light to operate well and would jump the track at switches. This problem was solved by adding a weight in the cab, for which there was ample room. Lionel did this on models after 1984 and added a second can motor in the other truck for many newer engines. Engines with these motors run well at the lower voltages that cause the Type I and II motors to stall. The enclosed motor requires little or no lubrication, although the gears do. For all these reasons, and because of the reliability demonstrated by them so far, the Type III motors have been a hit with most Lionel operators—even the die-hard traditionalists. The Type III motors have proved to be excellent runners. Recent SD-series and GP-series diesels have used a larger variation on the motor (called the "Pittman") in which it is mounted vertically in the truck, not horizontally. Often this motor is fitted with a flywheel for realistic coasting and acceleration, overcoming the objectionable jackrabbit starts and stops. The larger can is capable of much greater pulling power than the smaller version. We will refer to it for the moment as a modified Type III can motor, or "Pittman," but it is really another major motor style.

The can motors are clearly less expensive for Lionel to produce (or subcontract) and have contributed to lower costs for manufacturer and consumer alike.

GENERAL MOTORS' F-3 DIESELS

In the late 1930s the Electro-Motive Division of General Motors startled the real train world with its FT diesel demonstrator engines. These streamlined locomotives piled up mile after maintenance-free mile, and they routinely pulled trains of six thousand tons, whereas the biggest steam engines could handle only half that much. Following World War II, these freight diesels and their sister passenger units, the E Series, rapidly replaced steam engines all over the country. In 1947 General Motors introduced the F-3 Series, the first truly successful freight diesels.

Despite some personal doubts on the part of Joshua Lionel Cowen, a die-hard steam fan, the Lionel Corporation was quick to start planning for O gauge models of these streamlined beauties. In 1948, just one year after the real locomotives emerged, Lionel produced its Santa Fe and New York Central F-3 locomotives. The Santa Fe model eventually became the best-selling locomotive in Lionel's history because of its dependable performance and its spectacular Santa Fe "warbonnet" paint scheme of red, silver, yellow, and black. Many, like the 1957 Canadian Pacifics, are true classic collector items today.

By 1978 Lionel's successor, Fundimensions, had reissued many of the scarcest Lionel models. Some of them, like the 1973 models of the Canadian Pacific and the Southern F-3s from 1975, would become just as scarce as their postwar forebears. In 1976 Fundimensions even reissued the Santa Fe model (8652 and 8653), expecting slow sales because of the presence of so many of the older locomotives within collections. However, the paint scheme was so appealing the firm could not make the Santa Fe locomotives fast enough, and today this model is harder to find than any of its postwar predecessors!

All of the F-3 models produced until 1978 were single-motor locomotives without MagneTraction, horns, or some of the intricate trim of the older Lionel pieces. In 1979 a Brunswick green Pennsylvania twin-motored pair restored the deluxe trim. The New York Central F-3 was revived in 1983, along with an attractive set of passenger cars to create a modern *Twentieth Century Limited.* Booster (or "B") units (no cabs) have been available for most of the F-3 locomotives produced, and in many cases two B units were made.

As it turned out, Lionel had something up its sleeve regarding this engine. After a gap in F-3 production following the 1985 and 1987 runs of the Illinois Central, Lionel (now LTI) announced the third revival of the Santa Fe F-3 in 1991—this time with RailSounds. It featured a brand-new body type with screened roof vents, new separate metal ladders, and perhaps most significant, a new all-die-cast heavy frame, which made for better running and accommodated much of Lionel's new electronic wizardry.

The 1990s saw new sets of beautiful F-3 engines that had not seen the light of day either with the old Lionel Corp. or with Fundimensions. An ABA set in the spectacular orange and green of the Great Northern appeared in 1992 and another in Santa Fe's blue and yellow freight colors in 1993. A good-looking, if underappreciated, set from 1996 sported the Atlantic Coast Line silver-purple-black scheme. This set also happened to be the first F-3s equipped with Command Control, as well as with the new RailSounds.

The F-3 diesels are excellent runners, thanks to the use of the separate (Type I) Pullmor motor and power truck instead of the integral (Type II) motor and power truck used on the GP-series diesels. They are usually brisk sellers that command a good premium. Strangely enough, the older postwar Lionel F-3 locomotives have also increased in value, even though they have been reissued. The probable reason for this is the strong appeal of this locomotive as both an operating unit and a historic locomotive. Many operators also say the massive look of the engine gives it a more scale appearance than other diesels.

The numbering system assigned to the F-3s was relatively straightforward—all in the 18100-series—until 1999, when Lionel appears to have discarded the previous numbering scheme. The new numbers are found in the 38100-series. Some pieces are released as sets of AA or AB units, or even as full sets with passenger cars. The individual piece numbers are not cataloged. We include the individual numbers in our listings where known.

The values of the popular F-3 diesels have moderated considerably in recent years after a sharp increase in pricing in the late 1980s and early 1990s. This may be good news for new members of the Lionel hobby. However, F-3 collectors still must have deep pockets. They remain among the most expensive of Lionel's diesels and run a higher price tag than anything in Lionel's line except the biggest of the steam locomotives.

F-3 Body Types

A series of body style variations (called Type I through Type V—see the previous edition of our Guide from 1991) was used on the F-3 A units from 1973 through 1980. The progressive changes involved the number of louvers on the sides and a series of ridges on the lower flanks. All of the body styles were notable for their molded-in (sealed) porthole windows, painted with the rest of the body.

In 1980 Lionel settled on the body style for all the entries it would make in that decade—Type VI. This style featured two welcome detailing additions—nose grab-irons and snap-in, clear plastic lenses in the now-opened portholes.

With the gap in production after 1987, Lionel LTI spent its time upgrading the body again with two more nice details. This Type VII variation has opened vents in the roof covered with screens on the inside (a detail found on most postwar production) and also has a separate metal door ladder on the side, rather than the older molded-in one. This too was a feature long since dropped from the Lionel line, even in the later postwar years. The Type VII body returned to four side louver vents, as was the case with Type I. The production between 1991 and 1998, starting with the 18100 Santa Fe set, used the Type VII body.

The Fundimensions era saw two B unit styles—the earlier one with closed portholes and one side louver, and the later one (associated with the Type VI A unit) with open portholes fitted with plastic lenses and two side louvers. When the company upgraded the F-3 in 1991, it did so with the B unit as well, changing the vents in the top to the opened screened type and went back to one side louver. Another minor modification was made in 1996 when directional lighting was added, with a bulb placed at one end of the B unit. For some interesting reason, Lionel's B units have never had the three ridges running along the lower sides, which the A units have.

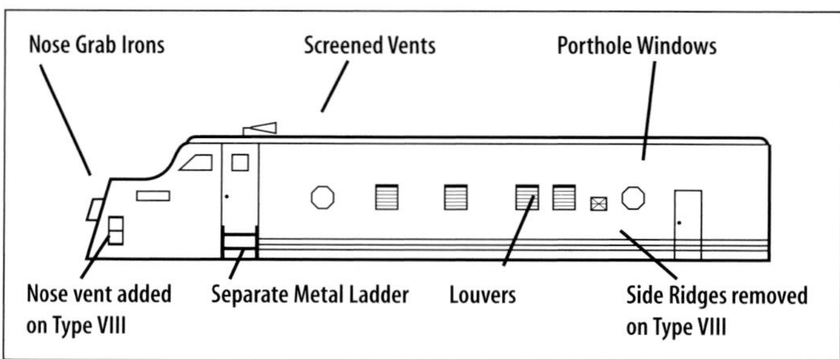

The F-3s in this book are powered by dual Type I "Pullmor" motors, one mounted to each truck. All have a solid die-cast metal frame, which serves not only to give weight traction to the unit but also to heat-sink the motors and the myriad electronics added as the decade went on. All modern F-3 A units have a nose lightbulb that illuminates the cab, number boards, and headlight. The couplers on the front of the A units are operating (sometimes magnetic, sometimes Electro-coupler style), while the couplers on the rear of the A units and often on the B units would be spring-centered and die-cast, but non-operating.

A NOTE ON F-3 DIESEL PRICING: The pricing of the F-3 diesels in this section follows usual sales practices. These engines (unlike most other diesels) were often boxed and sold together in AA, AB, or ABA combinations. It is extremely rare to find one component of these sets for sale separately. In such cases, this book lists a price as "priced as a set with . . .". A few add-on pieces were sold separately and boxed separately. Quantities varied. For example, the dummy 18103 Santa Fe B unit is far more difficult to find than its powered 18100 counterpart. In such instances this book shows individual prices.

18104 Great Northern F-3 A unit

F-3 LISTINGS

Exc Mt

11711 SANTA FE: see 18100.
11724 GREAT NORTHERN: see 18104.
11737 TCA: see 18112.

18100 SANTA FE: 1991, dual-motored F-3 A unit; red, silver, black, and yellow "war bonnet" paint scheme; Type VII body; MagneTraction; nose grab-irons; metal silver ladders; three-position E-unit; lighted; printed number boards read "8100"; die-cast silver-painted trucks; clear plastic portholes; operating couplers at both ends. This engine and its dummy A units feature a new die-cast frame—previous F-3s had stamped-metal frames. Lionel LTI billed this first F-3 engine made during its administration as a return to the detail design of the original 2333 postwar Santa Fe from 1948, including the mesh screen in the roof vents. Five matching passenger cars sold separately. The set was quite popular. Priced as a set (set no. 11711) with 18101 and 18102. **600 750**

18101 SANTA FE: 1991, unpowered F-3 B unit; this unit, unlike earlier B units, has screened roof vents; silver-painted trucks and operating couplers at both ends; no number; stamped-metal frame, otherwise matches 18100 and 18102. The catalog says metal ladders, but there are none on the body (as with the A unit)—the ladders are on the frame itself. Priced as a set with 18100 and 18102. An additional B unit (making a full ABBA combination) was released later in 1991, but was made in very limited quantities, to the consternation of many collectors who had purchased the '91 set.

(A) As described. **See 18100**

(B) Factory Error. Black outline paint around chief's head and logo missing. C. MacDonell collection. **NRS**

18102 SANTA FE: 1991, dummy F-3 A unit with RailSounds; lighted; screened roof vents; metal ladders; silver-painted trucks; matches 18100. Priced as a set with 18100 and 18101. **See 18100**

18103 SANTA FE: 1991, unpowered F-3 B unit; uncataloged; matches 18101 above and the '91 Santa Fe set; sold individually. It was made in far fewer numbers than the 18100 set; the restrained production of this piece angered collectors who had purchased the set. There was a spike in asking price initially, but it has since moderated, partly because of the follow-on 18115 piece made in 1993. Announced in the 1991 Stocking Stuffers brochure. **150 200**

Exc Mt

18104 GREAT NORTHERN: 1992, dual-motored F-3 A unit; orange and forest green body with yellow highlight stripes; "GREAT NORTHERN" in yellow on sides; GN goat logo decal on nose in red, white, and yellow; Type VII body; MagneTraction; nose grab-irons; metal ladders; three-position E-unit; lighted; illuminated number boards with "366-A" in small black lettering below windows; die-cast trucks; new die-cast frame; screened vents on roof; clear plastic portholes; operating coupler in front. This was the first-ever Lionel release of an F-3 in the Great Northern colors. Five matching passenger cars sold separately (19116 through 19120). The set was in good demand initially, but prices have moderated. Priced as a set (set no. 11724) with 18105 and 18106. Another B unit (18108) appeared the next year. **600 700**

18105 GREAT NORTHERN: 1992, unpowered F-3 B unit; orange and forest green body with yellow highlights; matches 18104 above except there is no "GREAT NORTHERN" name on the side; "370-B" is in small yellow lettering on sides; stamped-metal frame; die-cast F3 trucks; operating couplers both ends; screened vents on roof; open portholes with plastic lenses. Priced as a set with 18104 and 18106. An identical unit (18108) was made in 1993. Part of set no. 11724. **See 18104**

18106 GREAT NORTHERN: 1992, dummy F-3 A unit with RailSounds; matches 18104, except number on sides and in number boards is "351-C"; illuminated; Type VII body with screened vents. Priced as a set with 18104 and 18105 (set 11724). **See 18104**

18108 GREAT NORTHERN: 1993, unpowered F-3 B unit; matches 18105 above; number on sides is "371-B"; released individually as an add-on to the 11724 Great Northern set from 1992.

(A) As described. **100 125**

(B) Factory Error. "371-B" printed twice on one side of car, at each end, and not at all on the other. C. Lambe Collection. **NRS**

18117 Santa Fe F-3 A unit

Exc Mt

18112 TRAIN COLLECTORS ASSOCIATION: 1994, dual-motored F-3 A unit; uncataloged; orange body; black roof and lower sides delineated by silver stripes; "TRAIN COLLECTORS ASSOCIATION" in silver lettering on black section; black TCA logo on nose; Type VII body with plastic portholes and nose grab-irons; screened roof vents; black metal ladders; MagneTraction; die-cast silver-painted frame; die-cast F3 trucks; three-position E-unit; illuminated with lighted number boards reading "40"; "BUILT BY LIONEL" in smaller silver lettering at rear of body. This piece, sold as a set with the following entries, marked the TCA's 40th anniversary in 1994. The F-3 set has been followed by a matching set of identically decorated aluminum passenger cars every year since. Priced as a set with 18113 and 18114. The ABA set was given number 11737. **500 600**

18113 TRAIN COLLECTORS ASSOCIATION: 1994, unpowered F-3 B unit; uncataloged; decor matches 18112 above; operating couplers both ends; part of 40th anniversary TCA set no. 11737. Priced as a set with 18112 and 18114. **See 18112**

18114 TRAIN COLLECTORS ASSOCIATION: 1994, dummy F-3 A unit; uncataloged; matches 18112 above; includes diesel RailSounds; part of 40th anniversary TCA set no. 11737 with 18112 and 18113. Priced as a set with those two pieces. **See 18112**

18115 SANTA FE: 1993, unpowered F-3 B unit; matches 18101 and 18103 above; no number; released individually as an add-on to the 11711 Santa Fe set from 1991. This is in fact the third B unit for the set, and the production of this unit was intended to assuage collector concerns about the extremely limited number of 18103 units made.

(A) As described. **100 125**

(B) Factory Error. Missing Indianhead logo entirely on one side. C. Kuzminski collection. **NRS**

18117 SANTA FE: 1993, dual-motored F-3 A unit; blue and yellow Santa Fe freight color scheme; blue Type VII body with yellow cab roof section; yellow highlight lines and lettering; "200" on nose decal with Santa Fe cross logo; MagneTraction; nose grab-irons; black metal ladders; three-position mechanical E-unit; lighted; illuminated number boards read "200"; die-cast trucks; clear plastic portholes; operating couplers at both ends. This was the first time Lionel had made F-3s in the railway's "freight" colors of blue and yellow, not the passenger "warbonnet" scheme. Part of a set with 18118 below. B units were added in 1994 and 1995. Price for both units together. Shown only in the 1993 Stocking stuffer/1994 Spring release catalog. **350 400**

18118 SANTA FE: 1993, dummy F-3 A unit; matches 18117 above; sold as set with 18117; contains diesel horn; illuminated; number boards also read "200". Shown in the 1993 Stocking stuffer catalog. Collectors by now used to sophisticated audio systems were disappointed in the simple diesel horn unit in this set, and demanded more from Lionel. B unit was added to this set in 1995 with more a capable RailSounds system. **See 18117**

18121 SANTA FE: 1994, unpowered F-3 B unit; matches 18117 and 18118 above, except with small "200A" number in yellow at one end; no "SANTA FE" name on sides; die-cast F3 trucks; operating couplers both ends; screened vents on roof; open portholes with plastic lenses; sold separately as an add-on to the 18117-118 set from 1993; shown in the 1994 Stocking stuffer catalog. There is no sound system in this unit. **100 125**

18122 SANTA FE: 1995, unpowered F-3 B unit with RailSounds II; matches 18117 and 18118 above, except with small "200B" number in yellow at one end; no "SANTA FE" name on sides; die-cast F3 trucks; operating couplers both ends; screened vents on roof; open portholes with plastic lenses; sold separately as an add-on to the 18117-118 set from 1993; shown in the 1995 Stocking stuffer catalog. **200 220**

52005 CANADIAN NATIONAL: 1993, F-3 B unit shell only; uncataloged; special made by the Lionel Collectors Association of Canada (LCAC); intended as a match for the F-3 AA shells made in 1985; green body; gold stripe with black highlights; gold, black, and white lettering and CNR Maple leaf logo; number is "9517". These were unpainted Lionel blank F-3 shells decorated by PVP. Reportedly only enough were made (approximately 125) to match the number of A units existing, and members were allowed to order it only if they had also ordered the A units. Many of these will now be found on B unit frames and wheelsets in order to run on layouts. — **300**

AMERICAN LOCOMOTIVE COMPANY (ALCO) UNITS

FA-2 Freight Model

Among the first diesel locomotives revived by Fundimensions in 1970 was the little Alco streamlined diesel. The prototype of this locomotive is considered by diesel enthusiasts to be one of the most beautiful locomotives ever made, especially in its six-wheel PA passenger service configuration. Unfortunately, Lionel's much-shortened freight (FA) model is not to true scale and is not nearly as impressive as the F-3 diesel. However, Lionel needed an inexpensive diesel to head the low-cost sets of the late postwar and early Fundimensions eras, and the little locomotive was perfect in the role. Most of the early Fundimensions ones had two-position reversing units and were somewhat cheaply made.

In 1975 and 1976 Fundimensions tested the waters to see what reception a deluxe version of the Alco might get. The firm issued a triple Southern Pacific Alco ABA set in one box in "Daylight" colors. Unlike their stablemates, these Alcos had die-cast trucks, three-position reversing units, and two operating couplers. In 1976 Fundimensions issued three Canadian National units in brilliant orange and black with white zebra stripes, like the prototype. Sales of these triple units were disappointing, so Fundimensions proceeded no further along these marketing lines. Since that time, the small (freight) Alco has been limited to the lower end of the market.

There was a hiatus in new Alco FA issues after the popular Texas & Pacific Quicksilver Express set in 1982. In 1988 Amtrak (18903 and 18904) and Pennsylvania (18901 and 18902) Alcos with twin can motors were introduced. These came with matching O27-style short passenger cars, even though the FA-2 is a freight engine! The same applied to several Santa Fe small FA Alcos made through the '90s, found in Traditional Line sets pulling red-stripe short O27 passenger cars. It seems that Lionel just can't resist painting everything and anything in that warbonnet scheme. Lionel did the same with FA Alcos in such colors as Reading, New Haven, and Union Pacific. Despite the incongruity of the engine type, the sets looked reasonably good and were inexpensive means to build passenger sets. In 1995 Lionel improved the situation considerably (the Reading and Amtrak models) by replacing the old stamped-metal frame with a new lower plastic frame, so that the cab rode lower down. The new models look considerably better.

In 1993 Lionel LTI upgraded this small engine considerably, starting with the Erie Fallen Flags no. 7 set, and later with a nice UP set. With these Lionel changed to a heavy die-cast metal frame and to new die-cast truck frames, resulting in improved operation and handling of the small Alco. This change was tied to the replacement of the smaller can motor with a Pullmor model and MagneTraction. The set even went to die-cast metal couplers, another improvement over the earlier plastic couplers. One wonders why Lionel did not make these changes earlier. Cost, of course—which prompted LTI to continue the use of the cheaper model in its lower end Traditional sets well beyond that time.

In the 1970s Lionel made a series of minor changes to the body style of the small Alco, as described in the previous volume, *Greenberg's Guide to Lionel Trains, 1970–1991, Vol. I.* These involved whether the front of the engine had a coupler or not (i.e., with the pilot open or closed), whether a builder's plate reading "Lionel" appeared behind the door, and whether the number board slot was open (with a separate number piece) or simply closed off by the molded plastic. Most of the less-expensive postwar Alcos had the slot closed by the plastic, but a few (notably the UP anniversary set) had a lighted numberboard. All of the modern ones depicted in this volume have lighted numberboards (except the Santa Fe's from the 1993 Super Chief set), a front coupler, and no Lionel builder's plate.

The FA Alco is a great piece for the beginning locomotive collector to explore. There aren't a great number of them, and most are low priced and readily available. A reasonably complete collection of modern era (or even postwar) Alcos can be acquired in a short time without exorbitant expense.

PA (Passenger) Alco Model

The big news in 1992 was a totally new diesel model for the Lionel line—a huge near-scale model of the six-wheel Alco PA-1, in both A and B units. The first version was the 18107 Rio Grande in magnificent yellow and silver colors. These engines closely resemble the S gauge American Flyers Lionel had been making for years, but now finally scaled up to O gauge. Everything about the tooling for this piece was new—from its 16-inch length (almost twice that of its short FA cousin!) to the new incredibly detailed die-cast trucks, to intricate gridwork over the side vents to separate wire grab rails at the doors to the roof piece with fan detailing. Even the combined numberboard-MARS light is a new feature. The engine is powered by the larger Pittman heavy-duty can motors in each truck, with a rectifier circuit to permit AC or DC operation. The traction tires and weight enable this engine to pull and run well. After 1997 the Pittman motor was fitted with a flywheel for more realistic starts and stops.

After an initial surge of great interest in the Rio Grande and Erie-Lackawanna sets, there was a gap in production until 1997, and the prices have moderated somewhat recently.

The numbering system for the Alcos has been relatively consistent so far—the large Alco PAs are found in the 18100-series along with the big F-3 diesels, and the smaller Alco FA freight engines are in the 18900-series.

18109 Erie Alco FA-2 A unit

ALCO LISTINGS

	Exc	Mt

11734 ERIE: set of three; see 18109-18111.

18107 DENVER & RIO GRANDE: 1992, Alco PA-1 ABA set; first release of the new PA-1 Alco model by Lionel; silver and yellow body with black highlight stripes and "Rio Grande" script lettering; number on powered unit is "6001" and on dummy A is "6002"—catalog shows "600" and "601"; also on lighted side numberboards; heavy-duty Pittman can motors mounted into each die-cast truck of powered A unit; trucks are a new six-wheel version true to the prototype; 16-inch-long A unit body features exceptional detail—wire rails near operating doors; extensive grillwork on upper sides; operating intake fans on roof—a new detail for Lionel; porthole windows with clear lenses; number boards with integral MARS light; die-cast metal frame; constant lighting; illuminated interior with engineer figures in each A unit; electronic three-position reverse unit; traction tires; operating coupler at front of A units; dummy A has digital diesel RailSounds; B unit has no number. A group of *California Zephyr* aluminum passenger cars for this engine was produced later. This engine, made in Korea, is an excellent puller. The full set stretches nearly 50 inches! Price for ABA set. A photo of the engine graces our cover. **700 900**

18109 ERIE: 1993, powered Alco FA-2 A unit; black body; yellow-cream striping, number and Erie diamond logo; Erie wing herald in yellow on nose; number is "725A"; upgraded Alco FA model—new die-cast metal frame, which permits engine to ride lower than the earlier cheaper models; Type I Pullmor motor on new die-cast trucks; also a change from previous Alco models; MagneTraction; mechanical three-position E-unit; operating die-cast coupler at front, which protrudes rather far out; separate metal ladder piece at rear; illuminated cab and numberplate; headlight; priced as a set with 18110 and 18111 below. The three were part of the Erie Fallen Flags set no. 7 from 1993, (set no. 11734) whose components were sold separately. **225 275**

18110 ERIE: 1993, non-powered Alco FB-2 B unit; matches 18109 above, except number is "725B", no Erie logo; has a stamped-metal frame, not die-cast as on A unit. Priced as a set with 18109 and 18111. Part of set no. 11734, the Erie Fallen Flags no. 7. Lionel advertised it as the "first time an Alco B unit had been included in an Alco set." **See 18109**

18111 ERIE: 1993, non-powered Alco FA-2 A unit; matches 18109 above, except number is "736A", die-cast metal frame, illuminated cab and numberplate; includes electronic diesel horn. Priced as a set with 18109 and 18110. Part of set no. 11734, the Erie Fallen Flags no. 7. **See 18109**

18116 ERIE LACKAWANNA: 1993, Alco PA-1 AA set; second release of the new PA-1 Alco model by Lionel; gray and maroon body; black roof; yellow lettering and highlight stripes; Erie diamond in maroon on nose; number on powered unit is "858" and on dummy A is "859"—also on lighted numberboards; heavy-duty Pittman can motors (no flywheels) mounted into each six-wheel die-cast truck of powered A unit; wire rails near operating doors; extensive grillwork on upper sides; fan detail on roof, porthole windows with clear lenses; number boards with integral MARS light; die-cast metal frame; constant lighting; illuminated interior with engineer figures in both units; electronic three-position reverse unit; operating coupler at front of A units; dummy A has digital diesel RailSounds. A group of matching aluminum passenger cars for this engine was produced the next year. Lionel reported a problem with retaining track contact at slow speeds, a condition remedied by adding a shoulder screw and washer to each truck. Price for AA set. **450 575**

18119 UNION PACIFIC: 1994, powered Alco FA-2 A unit; yellow body; gray roof and nose hood; red lettering, number, and roof edge stripe; red, white. and blue UP shield logo on nose with dark blue wings; number is "8119"; upgraded Alco FA model—gray-painted die-cast metal frame; Type I Pullmor motor on gray-painted die-cast trucks; MagneTraction; electronic ("Liontech") three-position reverse unit; non-operating die-cast coupler at front, which is recessed to allow for a new apron design; separate metal ladder piece at rear; illuminated cab and numberplate; headlight; intended as a set with 18120 below. A matching set of passenger cars was

18120 Union Pacific Alco FA-2 unit (non-powered)

Exc Mt

also made in 1994. Second release of the "upgraded" Alco FA engine, after the Erie set in 1993. Usually found as a set with 18120, but can be found separately. **225 250**

18120 UNION PACIFIC: 1994, non-powered Alco FA-2 A unit; matches 18119 above, except number is "8120", die-cast metal frame, illuminated cab, and numberplate; includes electronic diesel horn. **60 80**

18901 PENNSYLVANIA: 1988, powered Alco FA-2 A unit; dark tuscan-painted body; gold striping along cab sides and front; gold "PENNSYLVANIA" and "8901"; stamped-metal chassis; lighted; twin Type III can motors mounted on trucks; electronic three-position reverse; weight in cab; plastic truck side frames and couplers. Separate-sale item made to match 16000-series Pennsylvania O27 short passenger cars introduced in 1987. Priced as a set with 18902 dummy unit. **100 125**

18902 PENNSYLVANIA: 1988, dummy Alco FA-2 A unit; numbered "8902"; lighted; matches 18901. Priced as a set with 18901. **See 18901**

18903 AMTRAK: 1988, powered Alco FA-2 A unit; silver-painted body; black roof; red nose; blue "8903"; red and blue Amtrak arrow logo; blue Amtrak lettering; stamped-metal chassis; lighted; twin Type III can motors mounted on trucks; weight in cab; electronic three-position reverse; plastic truck side frames. Essentially an updated version of the 8664 Amtrak Alco produced in 1976. Part of the top-of-the-line Traditional 11707 Silver Spike passenger set. Priced as a set with 18904 dummy unit.

(A) Regular production. **100 125**

(B) Overstamped with "Mopar Express" lettering and logo. This 1989 version of the Silver Spike set was made in very limited quantities (reportedly less than 100) as a special Chrysler promotion. The added stamping was done by Chrysler. The set included the three Amtrak O27 streamlined Silver Spike cars, also with a "Mopar" overstamp. It was won as a prize for

Exc Mt

matching a ten-digit number. Very hard to find. M. Salce and S. Troski comments. Priced as a set with cars and 18904(B). **— 500**

18904 AMTRAK: 1988, dummy Alco FA-2 A unit; blue "8904"; lighted; matches 18903. Priced as a set with 18903.

(A) Regular production. 11707 Silver Spike set. **See 18903**

(B) 1989 Mopar Express Special. Priced as a set with cars and 18903(B). See description above. **See 18903(B)**

18908 NEW YORK CENTRAL: 1993, powered Alco FA-2 A unit; black body; white lettering and number "8908"; NYC oval logo in red and white on nose; stamped-metal chassis; lighted; twin Type III can motors mounted on plastic trucks; electronic three-position reverse; weight in cab; traction tires; plastic couplers. Priced as a set with 18909 dummy unit. Interestingly, Lionel had never before made Alco FA-2 units in the New York Central colors, even though the NYC owned more of the real engines than any other railroad. **90 115**

18909 NEW YORK CENTRAL: 1993, dummy FA-2 A unit; matches 18908 above and priced as a set with it. **See 18908**

18913 SANTA FE: 1993–94, powered Alco FA-2 A unit; silver body; red warbonnet scheme on front; yellow and black Santa Fe cross logo on nose; black lettering and number, which is "8913"; stamped-metal chassis; twin type III can motors in plastic trucks; electronic three-position reverse; lighted; numberplate is closed off; weight in cab; traction tires; operating front coupler, dummy rear coupler. The warbonnet on this engine lacks the yellow and black edging lines of other similar engines—obviously to save paint steps. Some collectors did not care for the idea. Came as part of set no. 11739, the *Super Chief*, with three red-stripe Santa Fe O27 passenger cars. Boxed together, not individually. An 18919 dummy A unit was available separately. This set continued Lionel's odd tradition of heading an O27 passenger set with a freight (FA) engine. **60 75**

18915 Western Maryland Alco FA-2 A unit

	Exc	Mt

18915 WESTERN MARYLAND: 1993, powered Alco FA-2 A unit; black body; yellow stripes, lettering and number "8915"; WM circle logo in yellow on nose; WM "ball-of-fire" insignia under cab window; stamped-metal chassis; illuminated cab and number boards, which read "18915"; twin Type III can motors mounted on plastic trucks; electronic three-position reverse; weight in cab; traction tires; plastic couplers. Matching dummy A unit was made as 18916. **55 70**

18916 WESTERN MARYLAND: 1993, dummy Alco FA-2 A unit; matches 18915 above, except number is "8916"; illuminated with numberboards reading "18916"; electronic diesel horn. **30 40**

18919 SANTA FE: 1993–94, dummy Alco FA-2 A unit; intended as a match for the 18913 above, but available separately; matches 18913 except for number, which is "8919"; illuminated; numberboard closed off; electronic diesel horn; operating plastic coupler at front. **35 45**

18922 NEW HAVEN: 1994, powered Alco FA-2 A unit; black body; orange lower section and nose; white lettering and number "8922"; large serifed "N" over "H" on sides and on nose; stamped-metal chassis; lighted; twin Type III can motors mounted on plastic trucks; electronic three-position reverse; weight in cab; traction tires; plastic couplers. Intended as a set with 18923 dummy unit. O27 passenger cars were added to this set in 1995. **65 80**

18923 NEW HAVEN: 1994, dummy FA-2 A unit; matches 18922 above; except number is "8923" on sides and in number board; electronic diesel horn. **40 50**

18934 READING: 1995, powered Alco FA-2 A unit; black body; green lower side stripe; yellow highlight lines and lettering; number is "300" in yellow on sides and in white on nose; a new model frame in which Lionel replaced the older stamped-metal frame with a detailed plastic one which rides lower; lighted with engineer figure in cab (a first for the small Alcos); twin Type III can motors mounted on plastic trucks; electronic three-position reverse; traction tires; plastic couplers. Released as a set with 18934 dummy unit and priced with it. O27 passenger cars were added to this set in 1996. **85 110**

18935 READING: 1995, dummy FA-2 A unit; matches 18935 above; except number is "304" on sides and in number board; illuminated; new plastic frame replaces stamped-metal one and rides lower; electronic diesel horn. **See 18934**

18936 AMTRAK: 1995–96, powered Alco FA-2 A unit; silver-painted body; red, white, and blue stripes run around entire body below windows; black lettering and number, which is "8936"; uses new lower-riding plastic frame in place of the older stamped-metal frame; lighted with engineer figure in cab; twin Type III can motors mounted on plastic trucks; electronic three-position reverse; traction tires; plastic couplers. Part of 11748 Amtrak Passenger set, pulling three similarly decorated O27 passenger cars. Matching dummy A unit sold separately—see 18937. **— 75**

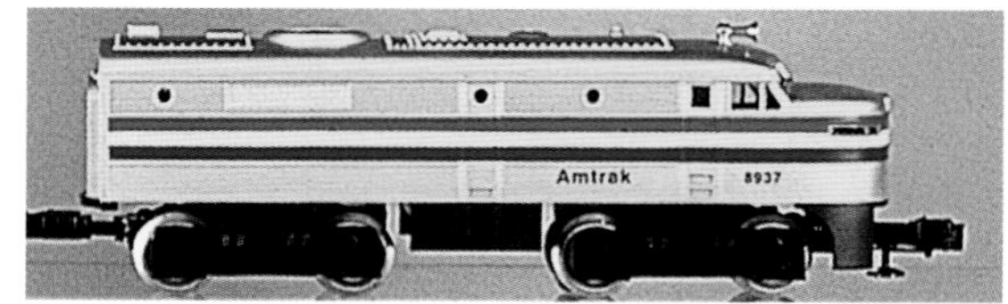

18937 AMTRAK: 1995–96, dummy FA-2 A unit; matches 18936 above; except number is "8937"; illuminated; new plastic frame replaces stamped-metal one and rides lower; electronic diesel horn. **— 40**

AMERICAN LOCOMOTIVE CO. ALCO RS-3 SERIES

This O scale model of the sleek Alco RS-3 diesel switcher is a creation of Lionel LTI—neither postwar Lionel nor Fundimensions had produced it. The real RS-3 was a 1600-horsepower locomotive that saw extensive service on many American railroads, particularly in the East, for both freight and passenger service. Lionel's model represented the prototype faithfully. It operates on a twin can-motor chassis. The stamped-metal chassis is the same as the one used on the GPs, with similar integral railings. The trucks are also the same as those on the GPs. These money-saving commonalities have allowed Lionel to produce the RS-3 quite inexpensively.

With its Type III can motor mounted in the trucks and tiny

18809 Susquehanna Alco RS-3

	Exc	Mt

electronic reverse circuit board, it is somewhat disconcerting to lift the cab of this engine to find little underneath. The attachment to the cab is a problem with the early models of this engine. Bent-up tabs from the frame do not always fit tightly to the plastic cab shell, and overtightening the screws can crack the shell. The matter was solved after about 1993, when screws up from the bottom were devised.

However, the RS-3 is a good runner, if somewhat light on the pulling capacity. These engines became a new anchor in the lower-end Traditional diesel lines and sets by the early 1990s, displacing some of the older GPs.

There have been several upgrades to the nice-looking and underappreciated RS-3 in the 1990s. In 1995 Lionel made new bodies (which it called RSD and RSC types) with heavier six-wheel trucks, which forced some rearranging of the underbody tanks and boxes. These two models (Seaboard and Pennsylvania) used a single larger can motor mounted vertically in one of the trucks, much like the SD diesels. They have not been repeated since—the company returned to the four-wheel can design with the Great Northern in 1996.

There has been an occasional hidden special in this series, as some of the train clubs have found the inexpensive engine a natural for club anniversary models. LOTS and the NLOE have done so, and J.C. Penney made two RS-3s as part of its special locomotive series in 1989 and 1992.

All RS-3s have featured twin Type III can motors (except the two Pittman-powered ones mentioned) and operating couplers. The lighting in the RS-3 diesels is unique. There are two grain-of-wheat headlight bulbs at each end of the engine and one standard bulb mounted near the top of the cab. This bulb, if not properly positioned, can burn a hole in the cab roof. Operators are advised to check the position of the lamp. A piece of aluminum foil between the bulb and the cab surface can prevent melting.

RS-3 LISTINGS

	Exc	Mt

18551 SUSQUEHANNA: see 18809

18554 GULF, MOBILE & OHIO: see 18822

18803 SANTA FE: 1988, dual-motored Alco RS-3 diesel; dark blue cab; yellow-painted ends, stripe along upper edge of cab and Santa Fe emblem and cross logo; "8803" on number boards but not on cab; brakewheel directly mounted on cab front end; large crew cab with four windows on each end and two windows on sides; large exhaust stack atop cab; large simulated fan shroud at one end; stamped-steel frame and railings, same as the GP's; twin Type III can motors mounted on trucks; electronic three-position reverse; weight in cab; plastic truck side frames; operating couplers. This is the first of Lionel's RS-3 models. **80 110**

18804 SOO LINE: 1988, dual-motored Alco RS-3 diesel; has a black plastic cab; yellow-painted ends with black safety striping; yellow lettering and "8804" on cab; stamped-metal frame and railings; lighted at front end; twin Type III can motors mounted on trucks; electronic three-position reverse; weight in cab; plastic truck side frames; operating couplers. **90 110**

18805 UNION PACIFIC: 1989, dual-motored Alco RS-3 diesel; yellow body with red stripe at top of cab beneath light gray roof; red lettering and painted number board; "The Streamliners" in red on cab; "8805" on sides and on numberboards; rubber tires on drive wheels; stamped-metal frame; twin Type III can motors; electronic three-position reverse; operating couplers. Due to bent-up tabs on the metal frame, the attachment of the body to the frame is often not tight, leaving a noticeable gap. A variation of this engine was made as a LOTS special in 1989. See 18890.

(A) As described. **90 120**

(B) Factory Error. Missing "UNION PACIFIC" on side and number "8805" under it. M. Lespznasse collection. **NRS**

18807 LEHIGH VALLEY: 1990, dual-motored Alco RS-3 diesel; red body; yellow lettering and stripe on lower section of cab; white safety stripes on front and rear; Lehigh Valley diamond logo; painted number boards; "8807" on cab; stamped-metal frame and railings; twin Type III can motors in plastic truck frames; three-position electronic reverse; operating couplers.

(A) As described. **90 110**

(B) Factory Error. No steps on front truck. **NRS**

18809 SUSQUEHANNA: 1989, dual-motored Alco RS-3 diesel; uncataloged; gray body; maroon stripe along cab top; gold lettering "SUSQUEHANNA" on stripe; gray and maroon "NYSW" and "8809" on cab; stamped-metal frame and handrails; twin Type III can motors; three-position electronic reverse; operating couplers. Came with Plexiglas display case, wood base and track section. Special issue for J.C. Penney in its

18822 Gulf, Mobile & Ohio Alco RS-3

Exc Mt

limited-edition engine series. Reportedly less than 3,000 made. The engine box is cataloged 18809. The engine and case together are listed as 18551.

(A) As described. **170 200**

(B) Factory error. Missing "NYSW" and "8809" on cab. R. Cole collection. The photo above shows this example—the missing lettering is on the other side. **NRS**

18814 DELAWARE & HUDSON: 1991, dual-motored Alco RS-3 diesel; gray body with blue roof; yellow "lightning" stripe separating gray and blue areas; blue and yellow lettering; D&H shield below cab window and on nose; yellow "8814" on nose and on number boards; illuminated cab; operating front and rear headlights; gray-painted stamped-metal frame; gray truck side frames; twin Type III can motors; three-position electronic reverse unit; diesel horn; two operating couplers. This engine headed the 1991 Service Station Special set, the 11719 Coastal Freight, which was the first Service Station set to be cataloged. **100 130**

18815 AMTRAK: 1992, dual-motored Alco RS-3 diesel; silver body with black roof; Amtrak red, white, and blue stripes run completely around body; black lettering outlined in white; "1815" on body and number boards; black stamped-metal frame; twin Type III can motors; three-position electronic reverse unit; diesel horn; illuminated cab; operating front and rear headlights; two operating couplers. This engine headed the unusual 11723 Amtrak Maintenance Train set, the top-of-the-line Traditional set in 1991. The set was initially announced in the 1991 catalog but was changed entirely prior to its actual release late in 1992. The set as made is shown properly in the 1992 Stocking Stuffers brochure. This piece also introduced the new RS-3 body, which attaches to the frame via screws up from the bottom, not with a single screw through the front, which had a tendency to crack the shell. **110 140**

18822 GULF, MOBILE & OHIO: 1992–93, dual motored Alco RS-3; uncataloged special made for J.C. Penney; red body with lighter red-orange central stripe; yellow lettering and lines; "GM&O" on ends; number on cab is "721"; dual can motors in stamped-metal chassis; electronic reverse; plastic trucks; operating couplers; illuminated cab and headlight. One of a very few GM&O pieces made by Lionel. This was a special for J.C. Penney and listed in their Christmas catalogs in 1992 and 1993,

Exc Mt

part of Penney's ongoing special engine series with Lionel. Reportedly less than 3000 made. It came with a Plexiglas display case and base. With the case, it is listed as 18554. The engine alone is cataloged as 18822. **170 200**

18827 HAPPY HOLIDAYS: 1993, dual-motor Alco RS-3; white body with green roof and accent lines; green "8827" on cab; "HAPPY HOLIDAYS" in red at center of sides with holly; twin Type III can motors; three-position electronic reverse unit; traction tires; stamped-metal chassis; diesel horn; illuminated cab; plastic trucks; operating front and rear headlights; two operating couplers. With the interest in Christmas items expanding, the value of this piece has increased. Many collectors have taken to selling it (with the matching 16457 caboose) and a group of Lionel's Christmas boxcars as a set. A similar red model was made in 1994. **140 180**

18832 PENNSYLVANIA: 1995, single-motor Alco RSD-4 diesel; body the same as RS-3 except frame is fitted with six-wheel (SD-style) trucks, and only one has a vertically mounted (Pittman) can motor; same stamped chassis as RS-3 but with rearranged underbody details to accommodate larger trucks; dark green body; yellow roadname and number, which is "8446" on cab and numberboards; three-position electronic reverse unit; traction tires; diesel horn; illuminated cab; plastic trucks; operating front and rear headlights; two operating couplers. This and the 18838 Seaboard are the only six-wheel Alco RS models made to date. They are listed as RSD-4 and RSC-3, though the body is identical to the regular RS-3s. **120 140**

18833 MILWAUKEE ROAD: 1994, dual-motor Alco RS-3; orange body with black roof and upper section of sides; small red and

18890 Union Pacific Alco RS-3

Exc Mt

white Milwaukee Road rectangle insignia on cab; white "2487" on numberboards; twin Type III can motors; three-position electronic reverse unit; traction tires; stamped-metal chassis; diesel horn; illuminated cab; plastic trucks; operating front and rear headlights; two operating couplers. The body on this piece has been corrected to remove the front-screw-tab mounting arrangement, in favor of screws inserted from the bottom into bosses in the body shell. **120 150**

18835 NEW YORK CENTRAL: 1994, dual-motor Alco RS-3; dark gray body with light gray and white "lightning stripe"; white roadname and number, which is "8223"; white "8223" on numberboards; twin Type III can motors; three-position electronic reverse unit; traction tires; stamped-metal chassis; diesel horn; illuminated cab; plastic trucks; operating front and rear headlights; two operating couplers. This unit headed the 1994 Service Station set, no. 11744, the New Yorker Passenger Freight. The set was unique (and popular) because of its mixed consist and the beautiful matching NYC short Madison cars included. Four more cars were added later to match this engine, and the RS-3 will now often be found for sale with the passenger cars. **— 150**

18837 HAPPY HOLIDAYS: 1994, dual-motor Alco RS-3; white body with red roof; red "8837" on cab and in black on numberboards; "HAPPY HOLIDAYS from LIONEL" in red at center of sides with holly; twin Type III can motors; three-position electronic reverse unit; traction tires; stamped-metal chassis; diesel horn; illuminated cab; plastic trucks; operating front and rear head lights; two operating couplers. The body on this piece has been corrected to remove the front-screw-tab mounting arrangement, in favor of screws inserted from the bottom into bosses in the body shell. Note similarity to 18827 from the year before, except this engine has red as its primary color. Also lacks the horizontal green lines of the earlier piece. **— 170**

18838 SEABOARD: 1995, single-motor Alco RSC-3 diesel; body the same as RS-3 except frame is fitted with six-wheel (SD-style) trucks, and only one has a vertically mounted (Pittman) can motor; same stamped chassis as RS-3; dark green body (catalog shows it brown); cream-yellow center section with red accent lines, cream-yellow lettering and number which is "1538" on cab and numberboards; red and white Seaboard heart decal on cab; three-position electronic reverse unit; traction tires; diesel horn; illuminated cab; plastic trucks; operating front and rear headlights; two operating couplers. This and the 18832 Pennsy are the only six-wheel Alco RS models made to date. **— 140**

18890 UNION PACIFIC: 1989, dual-motored Alco RS-3 diesel; uncataloged special for the 10th anniversary of the Lionel Operating Train Society (LOTS); description matches 18805, except with added red warning signs on cab reading "10th Anniv / LOTS". 400 made. **150 200**

18906 ERIE LACKAWANNA: 1991, dual-motor Alco RS-3; uncataloged; gray body; maroon center stripe on sides, accented with yellow lines; yellow nose; yellow lettering and number, which is "8906"; "8906" painted on number boards; "Radio Equipped" in red on cab; dual can motors; stamped-metal chassis; three-position electronic reverse; plastic trucks; illuminated cab and headlights; operating couplers. Headed the 11726 Erie Lackawanna Freight set, which is shown in the 1991 Stocking Stuffer brochure. It is not clear why this engine was given an 18900-series number, and not 18800-, where the other RS-3s are listed. **120 150**

52007 Long Island
NLOE Alco RS-3

	Exc	Mt
52007 LONG ISLAND NLOE: 1992, dual-motor Alco RS-3; uncataloged special for the Nassau Lionel Operating Engineers' 10th anniversary; gray body painted gray; orange ends; chassis railings and pilots/steps painted orange; plastic trucks painted gray; white lettering "LONG ISLAND" and number "1552" underscored; white "1983" and "1993" on numberboards; 10th anniversary logo; LIRR "Route of the Dashing Commuter" decal on short hood end; illuminated; electronic reverse unit and diesel horn. These were Lionel blank bodies supplied to NLOE and decorated by PVP. Only 65 produced.	—	350

GENERAL MOTORS' "GENERAL PURPOSE" (GP) DIESELS

General Motors' "General Purpose" ("GP" or Geep) series of diesel road switchers were among the most commonly encountered locomotives on American railroads; so it is not surprising that the GPs also represent the largest group of Lionel's diesels. GM's Electro-Motive Division (EMD) produced more than 6,500 diesels in the GP series in the 1950s and 1960s. Some units were equipped with steam generators, enabling them to act as both passenger and freight engines.

The only difference between Lionel's GP-7 and GP-9 models is the presence of a snap-on dynamic brake unit and fan atop the roof of the GP-9. Real GP-7 and GP-9 locomotives came both ways. Lionel held to that convention until 1997, when the catalogs confused matters by calling the engines GP-9s, whether or not they had the brake unit. Over the years Lionel has issued hundreds of GP diesels. Some have been entirely original in design, while others have been direct reissues of famous GP-7 and GP-9 locomotives previously issued by the Lionel Corporation in the 1950s. Most of these engines are common, and all levels of collectors can appreciate their relatively low prices. On the whole, the GPs give little trouble and are reliable runners that will pull a medium-sized train well.

The GP-series has seen two Lionel innovations. The first was the use of an AC/DC Type III can motor mounted directly into the power truck. This arrangement was very close to the one found on the prototype. Lionel's first locomotive with this motor, the Santa Fe GP-7 of 1982, was not entirely successful. The engine was too light and had sliding contact shoes instead of the better roller pickups.

Fundimensions quickly improved the design by adding a weight inside the cab and a second can motor, one on each power truck. The can motor has since been a staple in many Lionel engines, diesel and steam alike. The DC power in the can motor means very quiet running, and it was a simple matter to create the electronic reverse (circuit cards) for it. It is also easier to maintain because the motor never needs lubrication (although the gears do). The twin-motored performance proved a successful formula for the GPs, one which Lionel has followed since then.

The Geep was upgraded in late 1984 with extra detailing such as hand-inserted grab-irons on the front and rear, and the larger Type I Pullmor motor and power truck, instead of the integral Type II motor found in most Geeps up to that point. It was also fitted with twin-axle MagneTraction, lighted number boards, and an electronic horn. The locomotive was painted in the eye-catching black, gray, and white New York Central "lightning bolt" colors. All these premium features were met with collector enthusiasm. Since then the locomotive has been made in both the deluxe and standard versions, depending on whether it was planned to be a Collector (later called Heritage) or Traditional (later referred to as Classic) model.

In 1973 one of Fundimensions' mold and die experts invented a clever die insert for the GP-7 and GP-9 molds. By placing this insert into the die, which "chopped down" the nose of the model, Fundimensions created a new engine—the GP-20. Although this locomotive has not been issued in the large quantities like the GP-7s and GP-9s, it does have the distinction of being the locomotive responsible for the introduction of another Fundimensions innovation—the electronic diesel horn.

A surprise introduction for 1991 was a new GP-38 model in Kansas City Southern markings. This engine altered the GP mold again by adding clear plastic side vent details on the body and altering the roof fan arrangement. The cab design was also modified—the window arrangement changed, and the horn and headlight moved to the top front of the cab. It had a much larger fuel tank under the chassis than the other GPs. Unfortunately, Lionel decided to continue to use the primary body shell and frame, even though the real GP-38 is about 3 feet longer than the GP-7s and -9s. Still, the new diesel is a reasonable representation of the prototype. Lionel modified the design to a "GP-38-2" by placing a dynamic brake "blister" on the hood roof.

The earlier (Fundimensions and very early Lionel LTI period) GP-series diesels used the Type II integral motor, except for the "deluxe" engines discussed earlier, which used the premium Type I separate motor and also featured MagneTraction. Most of the more recent GPs were made with single or dual Type III can motors.

The body style variations in the GP models (GP-7, GP-9, GP-20, GP-38) are shown at right. The bodies and the frames of the GPs and the smaller SD models are very similar (in fact the stamped-metal frames are identical), the difference being that the SD engines always have six-wheel trucks, whereas the GPs have four-wheel trucks.

Several minor variations in the body styles of the GPs appeared during the early Fundimensions period. These involved the inscription on the builder's plate, the presence of printed numbers on the number boards, details on a hatch on the cab, and the relation of the cab to the railing ends. For the modern period, these changes have ended, with the only significant variation being whether the clear plastic numberboard inserts have the engine number printed on them or not. These inserts are illuminated by the bulbs in the front and rear of the engine. In the case of the GP-38, the railings were modified to accommodate the changed cab.

The trucks on the GPs come in identical plastic and die-cast versions, depending on whether the engine was a deluxe or a standard style. They are realistic copies of the prototype truck, which goes by the name "Blomberg."

Lighting in the GP diesels varies with the body style, motor type, and year produced. The earlier single-motored GP-7s and GP-9s have one or two nose lights that illuminate the headlights and the cab. The chopped-nose GP-20 forced the lightbulb into the cab itself, where it is fitted into a retainer in the window shell. In this way it illuminates both the cab and numberboards. When Lionel converted the GPs (all styles) to can motors, it retained this arrangement and left the lightbulb in the cab. Most GPs have headlights at both ends. One other small but interesting difference exists between the postwar and modern versions of the GP diesels: postwar models had three steps on the front and back, while the modern versions have two.

In the last three years of the 1990s, Lionel LLC released GPs by the boatload, creating multiple-unit lash-ups and reissuing many old favorites with the new electronics. In 1996 the deluxe GP-9 was upgraded even more with the new TrainMaster system, and then by adding RailSounds, directional lighting, and even a flashing warning light on the roof. Lionel also brought out many more dummy units, after only making one (a Nickel Plate) from 1987 through 1995. The year 1998 also saw the introduction of the GP "B unit," which uses the same basic body as the A unit, except the cab is nonexistent, although a porthole window lens remains. The frame is also modified so that the railing is continuous. These, like the A units, can be made into (Lionel's versions of) the GP-9 or GP-7 by adding or removing the dynamic brake piece.

In its numbering scheme, Lionel has assigned the 18500-series numbers to its "deluxe" versions of these diesels, and the 18800-series to the others. After 1996 even the GPs in this series had Pullmor motors and many of the deluxe features.

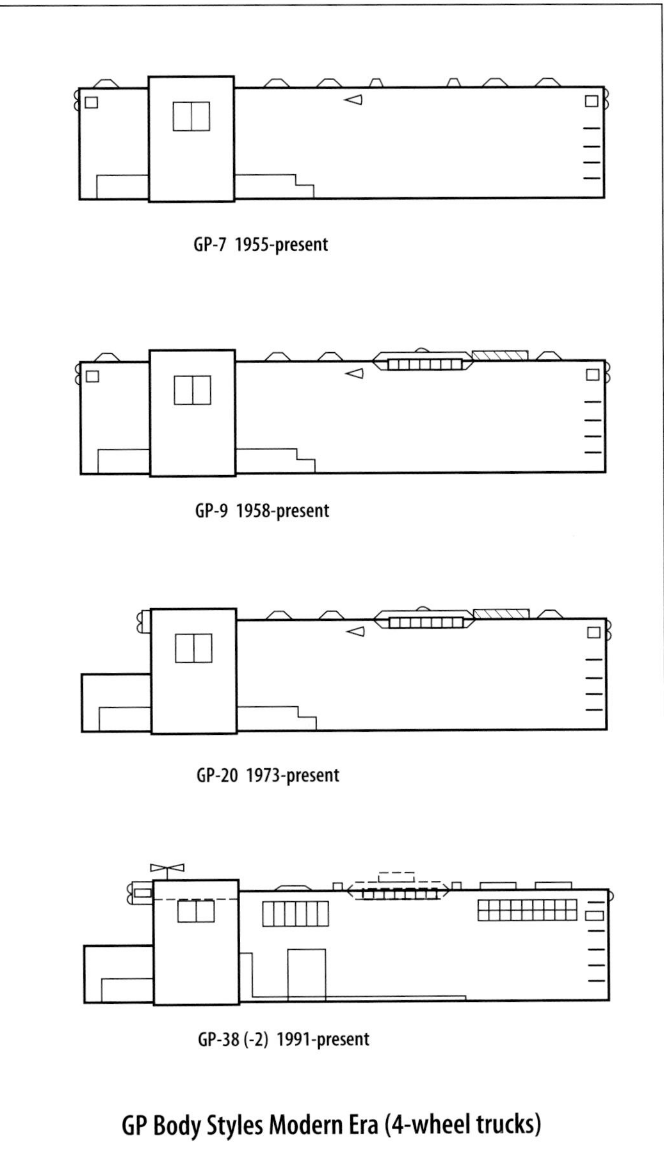

GP Body Styles Modern Era (4-wheel trucks)

GP SERIES LISTINGS

	Exc	Mt

18500 MILWAUKEE ROAD: 1987, GP-9 diesel; orange and black body shell (orange color continuous through cab as in scarce postwar version); white "8500" on black part of cab; black lettering on sides and ends; red and white Milwaukee logo on cab; MagneTraction; premium Type I motor; black frame; stamped-metal frame; plastic steps attached to both trucks; three-position E-unit; two operating couplers. Deluxe version GP, which came with separate-sale Fallen Flags set no. 2. This engine was also offered, without modification but with a display case, as a special purchase from J.C. Penney in 1987 as part of its continuing Special Engine series.

(A) As described, no display case. **160** **200**

(B) Factory Error. Missing Milwaukee Road decal from one side; motor truck not magnetized. G. Ligon Collection. **NRS**

18502 LIONEL LINES: 1990, GP-9 diesel; cream body; orange roof; blue cab; gold lettering and "90 YEARS" logo on main

18558 MKT GP-7

Exc Mt

body; number on cab is "1900", commemorating Lionel's beginning. Part of 11715 Lionel 90th Anniversary set. This engine continues the deluxe GP-series started by the NYC 8477: separate nose grab-irons; MagneTraction; Type I Pullmor motor; electronic horn/bell; three-position reverse unit; and headlights at front and rear. Catalog states the engine has RailSounds, but it is not made that way. RailSounds circuitry for the set was included in the 19219 boxcar. **140 160**

18504 FRISCO: 1991, GP-7 diesel; red body; broad white stripe completely around cab; red lettering and "504" below cab window. Continues deluxe GP-series: Type I motor; MagneTraction; separately installed nose grab-irons; lighted at both ends; stamped-metal frame; die-cast trucks; and three-position mechanical E-unit. Paint scheme similar to 8571/8572 U36 pair made in 1975. Part of Frisco Fallen Flags Series no. 5, whose components were all sold separately. **150 180**

18505 NICKEL PLATE ROAD: 1992, GP-7 powered and dummy set; deluxe model with Type I Pullmor motor and MagneTraction; black body; three yellow stripes surround entire shell; yellow roadname and "400" on cab; ("401" on dummy unit); lighted numberboards with "400"; black stamped-metal frame with iyellow edging; die-cast four-wheel GP trucks; electronic reverse; operating headlights both ends; separate grab-iron pieces on both ends; dummy unit contains RailSounds. These units headed the Nickel Plate Fallen Flags set no. 6, whose components were sold separately. The engines, however, were only sold together—neither piece has an individual catalog number. **250 300**

18513 NEW YORK CENTRAL: 1994, GP-7 diesel; next in the series of "deluxe" GP's; black body; white roadname and number, which

Exc Mt

is "7420" on cab and on lighted numberboards; red, white, and black NYC oval on ends; has deluxe features: Type I Pullmor motor; MagneTraction; separately installed nose grab-irons; operating headlights at both ends; stamped-metal frame with white edge; die-cast trucks; electronic reverse unit; electronic diesel horn; operating die-cast couplers. **140 160**

18514 MISSOURI PACIFIC: 1995, GP-7 diesel; next in the series of "deluxe" GP's; dark blue body; gray stripe ⅔ up sides, highlighted in yellow; gray nose and rear sections; roadname in blue on gray stripe; number on cab in gray is "4124", "4124" also on lighted numberboards; has deluxe features: Type I Pullmor motor; MagneTraction; separately-installed nose grab- irons; operating headlights at both ends; stamped-metal frame; die-cast trucks; "Liontech" electronic reverse unit—new feature for the GPs in 1994, allows multiple powered units to be run together without locking out the reverse unit; electronic diesel horn; operating die-cast couplers. Matching short Madison cars were also released in 1995. **175 200**

18550 MILWAUKEE ROAD: 1987, GP-9 diesel; uncataloged; same as 18500 except with display case. Made as a special for J.C. Penney in their ongoing special engine series. See 18500 for details. **180 230**

18553 UNION PACIFIC: see 18817

18558 MKT: 1994, GP-7 diesel; uncataloged special for J.C. Penney in its continuing special engine series; green body; yellow safety striping on cab, short hood, nose and rear; large "MKT" in yellow on sides; small number "91" on upper sides; dual Type III can motors in four-wheel plastic trucks; stamped-metal frame painted gray; illuminated cab and numberboards; electronic reverse; diesel horn; operating headlights; operating couplers. Unit came with a display case. Available only through J.C. Penney catalog. The store has been making special-release Lionel engines since 1980. The complicated striping on this engine would have required difficult paint masking by Lionel.

Exc Mt

It is likely this engine has an 18800-series number, without the display case, but if so it is not known. **200 230**

18800 LEHIGH VALLEY: 1987, GP-9 diesel; gray plastic body shell painted brick red; yellow "8800", lettering and striping; black and white safety stripes on cab ends; black frame; headlight; twin Type III can motors mounted in trucks; stamped-metal frame; electronic three-position reverse unit; two operating couplers. Came with 11702 Black Diamond freight set, which was one of the more popular Traditional Line sets. **100 125**

18802 SOUTHERN: 1987, GP-9 diesel; uncataloged; green- and white-painted body; gold stripe separates green and white colors; gold lettering and "8802"; black frame; twin Type III can motors mounted in trucks; stamped-metal frame; plastic steps attached to both trucks; electronic three-position reverse unit; two operating couplers. Came with 11704 Southern Freight Runner Service Station set for 1987, which is described only in a one-page Lionel flyer. **100 125**

18812 KANSAS CITY SOUTHERN: 1991, GP-38 diesel; pale-white body; red lettering; "4000" on cab; large "KCS" centered on body; black stamped-metal frame; modified railing arrangement to accommodate changed cab; ornamental horn moved to roof of cab; Type III can motor; three-position electronic reverse unit; diesel horn; single bulb illuminates cab, number boards and headlight; two operating couplers. This is a new GP-series body design introduced in 1991. It differs from earlier GP engines by its added side vent detail and altered fan arrangement on the roof. The nose detail has been modified as well. Lionel had never before used Kansas City Southern as a road name for an engine. Came as separate-sale only with a matching 16526 KCS SP-type caboose. **110 140**

18816 CHICAGO & NORTH WESTERN: 1992, GP-38-2 diesel; second in a series of new GP-38 models; this one differs from the KCS from 1991 by the addition of the dynamic brake blister on top; yellow body; Brunswick green cab and roof; CNW logo on cab; "4600" in black on side; clear plastic vent inserts; black stamped-metal frame and railings; twin Type III can motor in four-wheel plastic GP trucks; electronic reverse; diesel horn; illuminated cab and numberboards with "4600"; headlight; operating couplers. In addition to the blister, Lionel added a second can motor to the engine for this release, improving the tractive power. **130 160**

Exc Mt

18817 UNION PACIFIC: 1991, GP-9 diesel; uncataloged special for Sears; yellow body with gray roof and top third of sides; red highlight stripe between yellow and gray areas; red "UNION PACIFIC" and "150" on sides; "DEPENDABLE TRANSPORTATION" on cab side; dual Type III can motors in four-wheel plastic trucks; trucks painted gray; stamped-metal frame; numberboards read "150"; operating headlights both ends; illuminated cab; electronic reverse; electronic horn; operating couplers. This limited edition was produced for Sears and shown only in the 1991 Sears Wishbook. It is also the first Lionel GP ever made in the Union Pacific name, though the postwar company had planned one. D. Sliger comment. The engine itself is cataloged as 18817, and the engine with display case is listed as 18553. **160 200**

18818 LIONEL RAILROADER CLUB: 1992, GP-38 diesel; uncataloged; red-painted body; gold stripe through center of sides with white outlines; gray roof; white "1992 SPECIAL EDITION" and "LIONEL Railroader Club" lettering on sides; "THE INSIDE TRACK" in black on the gold stripe; steam engine outline on cab side; dual Type III can motors in four-wheel plastic trucks; stamped-metal frame painted gray; clear plastic vent inserts; no blister unit; illuminated cab and numberboards; electronic reverse; diesel horn; operating headlights; operating couplers. Special available only to LRRC members—"THE INSIDE TRACK" is the LRRC's newsletter. This engine is not, according to Lionel's lexicon, a GP-38-2 model—it has no dynamic brake unit. **120 140**

18819 LOUISVILLE & NASHVILLE: 1992, GP-38-2 diesel; gray body; yellow short nose hood; large "L&N" in yellow on sides; number on cab and numberboards is "4136"; red and white "L&N decal on nose; dual Type III can motors in four-wheel plastic trucks; stamped-metal frame painted gray; clear plastic vent inserts; dynamic brake unit; illuminated cab and numberboards; electronic reverse; diesel horn; operating headlights; operating couplers. This engine headed the Louisville & Nashville set, which changed character entirely between the 1992 Book 2 catalog and the 1992 Stocking Stuffer brochure. The latter shows the set as made. **135 175**

18820 WESTERN PACIFIC: 1992, GP-9 diesel; light gray body with orange circumferential stripe; black lettering; WP feather logo on cab; orange ends with black safety stripes; "8820" is in numberboards; dual Type III can motors in four-wheel plastic trucks; stamped-metal frame painted gray; illuminated cab and

18836 CN/GTW GP-38

Exc Mt

numberboards; electronic reverse; diesel horn; operating headlights; operating couplers. Headed the 11733 Feather River Service Station Special set for 1992. **140 165**

18821 CLINCHFIELD: 1993, GP-38-2 diesel; black body; yellow lettering and number, which is "6005"; "6005" is in numberboards; dual Type III can motors in four-wheel plastic trucks; stamped-metal frame with yellow edge stripe; clear plastic vent inserts; illuminated cab and numberboards; dynamic brake unit; operating headlights; electronic reverse; diesel horn; operating couplers. **110 140**

18825 SOO LINE: 1993, GP-38-2 diesel; red body; white lettering and number, which is "4000"; "4000" is in numberboards; white accent stripes; dual Type III can motors in four-wheel plastic trucks; stamped-metal frame; clear plastic vent inserts; illuminated cab and numberboards; dynamic brake unit; electronic reverse; diesel horn; operating headlights; operating couplers. Headed 11738 Soo Line Service Station Special set for 1993. **110 140**

18826 CONRAIL: 1993, GP-7 diesel; blue body; white lettering and Conrail wheel logo; number on cab is "5808" in white; lighted numberboards also have "5808"; dual Type III can motors in four-wheel plastic trucks; stamped-metal frame; illuminated cab and numberboards; headlights; electronic reverse; diesel horn; operating couplers. Headed the 11740 Conrail Consolidated—the top-of-the-line Traditional set for 1993. There are several SD engines made later in this same color scheme. **110 140**

Exc Mt

18830 BUDWEISER: 1993–94, GP-9 diesel; uncataloged; white body; blue cab section; red and white "Budweiser" herald on side, over "KING OF BEERS" in black; Anheuser Eagle-A and number "1947" on cab; dual Type III can motors in four-wheel plastic trucks; stamped-metal frame; illuminated cab and numberboards; headlights; electronic reverse; diesel horn; operating couplers. Headed the uncataloged 11810 Budweiser set—available only though the Budweiser catalog. **120 160**

18831 SOUTHERN PACIFIC: 1994, GP-20 diesel; gray body; red nose and rear; red wing logo with "SP" in white on nose; white lettering and number, which is "4060" on cab; "4060" on numberboards; dual Type III can motors in four-wheel plastic trucks; stamped-metal frame; illuminated cab and numberboards; headlights; electronic reverse; diesel horn; operating couplers. **110 140**

18836 CN/GTW: 1994, GP-38 diesel; red and black body with red nose section and black rear section, divided by a diagonal white stripe; black roof, cab roof, and short hood roof; white CN lettering on main body, white "GTW" and number on cab, which is "5800"; "5800" is in numberboards; dual Type III can motors in four-wheel plastic trucks; stamped-metal frame; clear plastic vent inserts; illuminated cab and numberboards; no dynamic brake unit; electronic reverse; diesel horn; operating headlights; operating couplers. This complicated and attractive paint scheme marks the new CN system freight colors, applying now to the old Grand Trunk Western lines. Lionel listed this as the GP-38-2, but it doesn't have the brake unit. **150 180**

	Exc	Mt

18840 U.S. ARMY: 1995, GP-7 diesel; glossy black body; white lettering; number on cab is "1821" in white; lighted numberboards also have "1821"; dual Type III can motors in four-wheel plastic trucks; stamped-metal frame with white edge; illuminated cab; headlights both ends; electronic reverse; diesel horn; operating couplers. **115 145**

18841 WESTERN MARYLAND: 1995, GP-20 diesel; red and white body, divided about in half with white on upper sides; black roof; black-painted short hood roof and side grills—a new touch for these diesels; black roadname lettering and number, which is "27" on cab; "27" in illuminated numberboards; "WM" wind decal on ends; dual Type III can motors in four-wheel plastic trucks; stamped-metal frame painted red; illuminated cab; headlights both ends; electronic reverse; diesel horn; operating couplers. This handsome engine headed the 11749 Western Maryland service station set for 1995, pulling a unit train of six WM quad hoppers. **130 160**

18844 NACIONALES DE MEXICO: 1995, GP-38-2 diesel; announced in the 1995 Stocking Stuffer catalog but never made. The bright blue and red of this engine might have been interesting to see, and it would have been one of the very few Lionel pieces named for railroads outside the U.S. or Canada. **Not Manufactured**

33000 LIONEL LINES: 1988–90, Railscope GP-9; gray and dark blue cab; white lettering and "3000"; (Note: previous Guide incorrectly reported number as "3300") red, white, and blue Lionel logo; twin Type III can motors. This revolutionary locomotive has a miniature video transmitter inside the cab that projects an "engineer's-eye" view to a television set. The photo image is sent by electronic pulse through the rails, then through an RF modulator (disguised as a stack of lumber) to the antenna terminals of a television. The result is a sharp black-and-white picture of the engineer's view, just as if the operator were inside the locomotive. Can be used with any television, although a Lionel TV is available separately (see 33002 entry in our companion Accessories volume, *Greenberg's Guide to Lionel Trains 1970–1997, Accessories*). This unit was initially a hit, but operators soon found that the batteries powering the camera in the locomotive ran down quickly, prompting much creative electronics jury-rigging to overcome the problem. Despite that, this engine remains a milestone in the growing partnership between Lionel trains and modern microelectronics. **200 250**

33004 NEW YORK CENTRAL: 1990, Railscope GP-9. Announced for 1990, but never made. **Not Manufactured**

33005 UNION PACIFIC: 1990, Railscope GP-9. Announced for 1990, but never made. **Not Manufactured**

52035 YORKRAIL TCA: 1994, GP-9 shell only; uncataloged; see 52037. **— 40**

52037 YORKRAIL TCA: 1994, GP-9 diesel; uncataloged special from the Train Collectors Association; yellow body; black top ⅓ of sides and roof; blue YORKRAIL logo on sides with small steam engine image in black; number on cab is "1754"; dual Type III can motors in plastic GP trucks; stamped-metal frame; separate grab-irons on nose; illuminated; electronic reverse; diesel horn; operating headlights; operating couplers. This is a special produced only for the TCA in conjunction with its 1994 Convention at York, Pennsylvania. Also note: the TCA produced a matching shell unit, cataloged by Lionel as 52035, with the number "1750", but with no frame, motor, or trucks. **125 150**

THE GENERAL ELECTRIC U36

The first Fundimensions diesel locomotive not patterned after any postwar design was the U36B, issued in 1974. Except for its not-quite-scale length, Fundimensions' "U-boat" was an accurate representation of the rugged General Electric prototype. The Seaboard Coast Line was the primary owner of the U36B engine type, which stands for "U"(universal), "36" (-hundred horsepower), and "B" (four-wheel trucks). The first Lionel models were the aptly numbered 1776 Seaboard Bicentennial locomotive and the 8470 Chessie System at the head of Fundimensions' Grand National freight set. Both these locomotives became very popular.

As a class, the U-boats offer more detailing than their GP counterparts and are slightly higher priced. The massive appearance of the U36s made them favorites of some Fundimensions collectors. In 1987 Lionel produced a new Santa Fe U36B (18801) with a twin can-motor configuration for the Traditional Series.

The "U" series was eventually replaced on the real railroads by the Dash 7 series, and then by the popular Dash 8 in 1988. This appears to be the case in Lioneville as well. There was a gap in U36 production from 1982 to 1987; and since the Santa Fe in 1987, no further U36 engines have appeared.

U36 LISTING

	Exc	Mt

18801 SANTA FE: 1987, powered U36B; Type II body; blue and yellow Santa Fe freight color scheme; yellow "Santa Fe" and blue "8801" on cab; black stamped-metal frame (same as the GPs); cab headlight only; twin can Type III motors mounted in trucks; electronic three-position reverse unit; operating couplers. To date this remains the only U36 engine made in the recent (five-digit) Modern Era. **80** **110**

GENERAL MOTOTRS' ELECTRO-MOTIVE DIVISION SPECIAL DUTY (SD) DIESELS

Lionel's models of the SDs can be divided into two major groups—the smaller GP-sized models (13-inch-long frames), consisting of SD-9s, SD-18s, SD-28s, and SD-38s. The other group is the "large" SDs—the scale length monsters in the SD-40, -50, -60, and -70 series.

The essential difference between Lionel's smaller SD models and the GP is the presence of the large six-wheel die-cast trucks on the SDs. The Electro-Motive Division made these locomotives beginning in the early 1950s in parallel with their GPs. The extra drive wheels in the trucks enabled the Special Duty engines to perform more heavy mainline passenger and freight duties than the GPs. In the 1960s and 1970s, GM slowly upgraded the GP series for freight and yard duties, but its main emphasis moved to the huge SDs, which dominate the rail lines today, using powers ranging from 4000 to 6000 horsepower!

In fact, Lionel's smaller SDs are virtually the same shell, railings, and frame as the GP, the frame being changed just slightly for a smaller fuel tank to accommodate the larger trucks. Lionel thus got maximum use out of its tooling.

Small SDs (SD-9, SD-18, SD-20, SD-28, and SD-38)

Typically, when Fundimensions introduced a new feature, it used that feature throughout a wide range of its line to help amortize the cost of the tooling. That is certainly true of the handsome six-wheeled solid die-cast trucks in current use on the SD and Dash 8/9 diesels. In 1978 Fundimensions placed the newly designed trucks under a Milwaukee GP-20 cab, rearranged the roof fans a bit, and changed the model to the SD-18.

For a period in the early 1980s, Lionel was experimenting with various GP and SD designs, some of which haven't been repeated since. It ultimately settled on the SD-9 and SD-18 (high and low nose) for its mid-range six-wheel diesels, and the SD-40 for the larger end.

After the SD-18 made its debut, Lionel made various minor changes to the basic cab to create alternate SDs. They used virtually the same GP-9 cab on the six-wheel trucks and called it the SD-9. The first of these was Fundimensions' 8063 Seaboard from 1980. Rearrangement of the roof a little more—three larger fans shrouds to the rear, the dynamic brake further forward, and moving the horn to the cab roof—resulted in an "SD-28." The first of these was a red and gray Burlington model in 1981. It has not been a frequent visitor to the Lionel line, however—only one (the 18834 C&O) has been made in the modern era period covered in this volume.

The GP-20 cab was also used unchanged on top of the six-wheel trucks, and designated an "SD-20" for a Conrail piece in 1997's Service Station set—the one and only time it has appeared.

Lionel made two odd "SD-24s" in the early 1980s, notable for their flat and angled cab roofs. Other GPs and SDs have rounded cab roofs (with the exception of the GP-38). The SD-24 model has not been repeated since.

In a final bit of experimentation, Lionel placed its GP-38 body on the six-wheel trucks and called it an "SD-38." This happened for a Bessemer & Lake Erie engine made in 1995 for J.C. Penney and its special engine series. This item is quite hard to find.

Actually, only a few small SD units have been made since

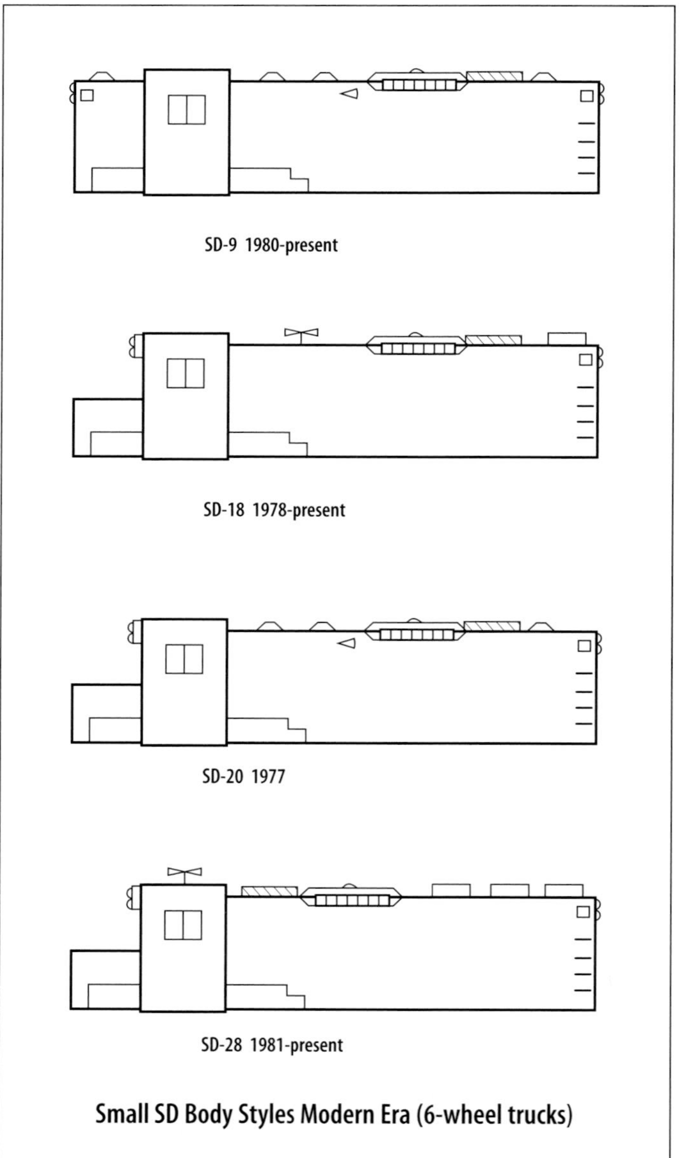

Small SD Body Styles Modern Era (6-wheel trucks)

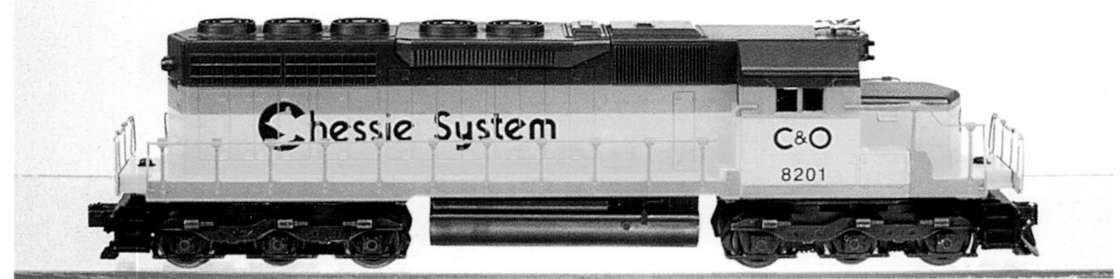

18201 C&O Chessie System SD-40

1987, and most of those were SD-9s and SD-18s. The demand for larger scale locomotives has propelled Lionel in the last decade more to the larger SD designs, while the smaller ones share the middle range of the line with the still-popular GPs. Since 1997, only one small SD unit has been made—the aforementioned Conrail model. Figure 4-5 depicts the principal styles of the small SDs since 1987.

Although these locomotives will run on O27 track, they are far better runners on the wider-radius O gauge trackage, where their long wheelbase shows to better advantage.

In terms of power, the small SD engines are usually found with a single larger vertical Type III Pittman can motor. The engines from the Fundimensions period had used the less-powerful Type II integral-motor-truck design. In 1996 and subsequent years, Lionel returned to the Type II motor, but with the larger field and armature motors previously used for the SD-40s.

Large SDs: SD-40, -50, -60, and -70

In 1982 Fundimensions introduced a spectacular new modern era diesel, a model of the brutish but attractive SD-40. Lionel's model of this locomotive is scale length (16¼ inches long frame end to frame end). Scale O gauge model railroaders have even purchased the body shell and trucks to adapt to their own operational requirements. It was first produced in 1982 in bright Santa Fe blue and yellow freight colors. Since then, successive years have seen this locomotive issued in a new paint scheme. The first models were produced only in single-motor configuration, using an extensively modified version of the Type II integral truck/motor drive. Many collectors found this hard to understand, since the locomotive was so large it would easily accommodate an extra motor.

The SD-40s produced after 1984 corrected the single-motor oversight. A big, blue Conrail SD-40 (18200) headed another limited-edition set for 1987. This model was slightly improved by the addition of reinforcing collars for the screw holes where the body fastens to the frame—cracks had developed in earlier models. Lionel eventually produced dummy SD-40 units to create some truly impressive double-headed train sets.

The SD-40 has been greeted with considerable acclaim by collectors because of its massive size and attractive design. It has many fine body details, including a realistic snowplow attachment on the front truck, and real chain link segments on the front and rear railings. Of course, as the 1990s progressed many of Lionel's new electronic gadgets were added to the SD-40s (and its later cousins).

The year 1994 saw another brand new SD model in Conrail colors. This was the SD-60M, a nice scale replica of EMD's latest 3800-horsepower locomotive, which is competing with the Dash 8s for freight dollars on modern railways in the U.S. Conrail is EMD's main customer, so it was logical that Lionel's first model of the SD-60M was in Conrail blue. The basic frame resembles the SD-40, but the body shell is entirely different. The cab and nose are larger, with four individual side windows. A flashing strobe was added to the cab roof. Yet another body style, based on the SD-60, but with a revised roof fan arrangement, appeared with the Rio Grande 18221-222 in 1995. Lionel called it the SD-50. So far the Rio Grandes are the only examples.

As popular as the big SDs are, there remains one operating restriction: their overhang will not clear O27 switches. This is also true of the scale Hudsons, TrainMasters, Dash 8s and 9s, the long aluminum passenger cars, and other longer rolling stock.

It is a little too soon to tell which of the big SD locomotives will become scarcer than others. Prices for the earlier units without the TrainMaster electronics have moderated a bit, but the Rio Grande and Milwaukee Road pairs from 1995, with RailSounds, have maintained their value.

SD LISTINGS

Exc Mt

18200 CONRAIL: 1987, powered SD-40; bright blue body; white Conrail wheel logo, striping, and lettering; "8200" on cab; blue side rails and white end rails; blue frame and blue-painted handrails; lighted cab; front and rear headlights; two modified Type II motors; three-position reverse; MagneTraction; electronic horn; operating couplers at both ends. Came with 11700 Conrail Limited set.

(A) As described. **250 325**

(B) Factory Error. Front marker boards read "8555"; rear marker boards read correct "18200" D. Finneyfrock Collection. **NRS**

18201 C&O CHESSIE SYSTEM: 1988, powered SD-40; yellow, vermilion, and dark blue cab; vermilion-painted side and end rails; dark blue Chessie cat logo and lettering; "8201" on cab; lighted

18209 CP Rail SD-40 (non-powered)

Exc Mt

cab; two headlights; six-wheel trucks; two modified Type II motors; three-position E-unit; MagneTraction; electronic horn; operating couplers at both ends. Headed 11705 Chessie System unit train. **250 325**

18202 ERIE-LACKAWANNA: 1989, dummy SD-40; uncataloged; gray cab; maroon and yellow striping; yellow lettering; yellow-painted frame; "8459" on cab; illuminated cab and headlight; die-cast trucks; matches 8458 from 1984. First dummy SD-40 produced. From 1989 Holiday Collection.

(A) As described. **130 165**

(B) Factory Error. Missing number and "Radio Equipped" on one side. R. Weidinger Collection. **NRS**

18203 CP RAIL: 1989, powered SD-40; red-painted gray plastic body; white "8203" on cab; large white "CP Rail" on main body; white and black CP Multimark logo at rear; diagonal red and white stripe on front; black and white stripe on rear; headlights at both ends; lighted cab interior and number boards; dual modified Type II motors in die-cast six-wheel trucks; three-position reverse; MagneTraction; electronic horn; snowplow attachment on front. This handsome engine headed the unique CP Rail freight set of 1989. A dummy unit was made in 1992.

(A) As described. **230 270**

(B) Factory Error. No graphics on either side of loco. G. Carpenter Collection. **NRS**

18204 CHESSIE SYSTEM: 1990, dummy SD-40; uncataloged; "8204" on cab; illuminated cab and headlight; metal frame and railings; die-cast trucks; matches 18201. From 1990 Stocking Stuffer package. **150 175**

18208 BURLINGTON NORTHERN: 1991, dummy SD-40; uncataloged; green body; black top ⅓ of sides and roof; white BN logo on cab and number, which is "8586"; green and white nose safety stripe; illuminated cab and numberboards; operating headlights; die-cast frame and trucks; released as a match to the 8585 BN SD-40 from 1985. Shown in the 1991 Stocking Stuffer brochure. **140 170**

18209 CP RAIL: 1992, dummy SD-40; uncataloged; decoration matches 18203 above, except number is "8209"; operating headlights; die-cast trucks; snowplow fitted to front. Intended as an add-on to the CP Rail freight set from 1989. **160 190**

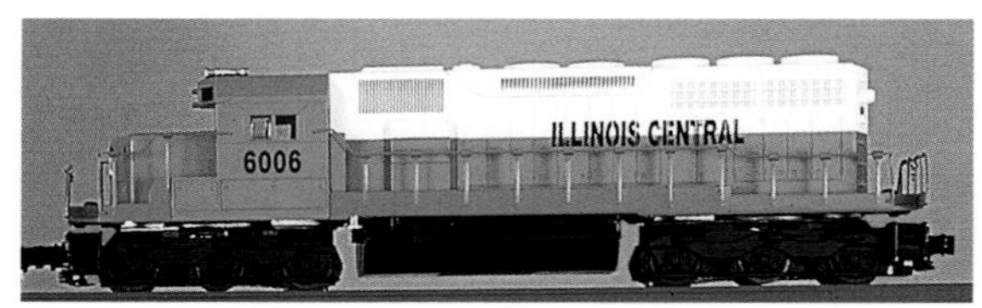

18210 ILLINOIS CENTRAL: 1993, powered SD-40; orange cab, nose, and lower half of sides; white top half of long hood and roof; black "ILINOIS CENTRAL" straddles orange/white divide; number on cab and numberboards is "6006"' black and white I-beam logo on nose; orange frame and handrails; two modified Type II motors; die-cast six-wheel trucks with MagneTraction; three-position E-unit; electronic diesel horn; operating headlights; die-cast operating couplers. A matching IC extended vision caboose (19716) appeared in the catalog, and a second powered SD-40 was made in 1994. **240 275**

18216 CONRAIL: 1994, SD-60M diesel; new model for Lionel; large new-design cab 16½ inches long; blue cab and frame with railings painted blue; white "CONRAIL QUALITY" and wheel logo on long hood; "CONRAIL QUALITY" also in white on nose; number on cab and in numberboards is "5500"; dual Type II modified AC motors on die-cast six-wheel trucks; new truck design, which is more detailed than those of an SD-40; MagneTraction; new die-cast metal frame with white edge line; railings have small chain sections at front and rear; underbody tank and details are similar to the SD-40; illuminated cab; operating headlights; ditch lights on front snowplow fitting (new features for the SD-model); flashing strobe on cab roof (also new); "Liontech" reverse unit; diesel RailSounds II; operating couplers. Lionel was in the process of developing TrainMaster Command Control at this point—had it been fully available, Lionel would have undoubtedly installed it in this engine. **350 400**

18217 ILLINOIS CENTRAL: 1994, powered SD-40; matches 18210 above; two Type II modified motors; same features as 18210 except number is "6007"; has new "Liontech" reverse unit, enabling two powered engines to be used in the same train without locking out the E-units. This is one of the first Lionel locomotives fitted with this new electronic reverse. **240 275**

18223 Milwaukee Road SD-40

	Exc	Mt

18221 DENVER & RIO GRANDE: 1995, powered SD-50 diesel; new model for Lionel; design based on the SD-60, but slightly redesigned cab and roof fan arrangement; glossy black-painted body; yellow-orange Rio Grande script at center of long hood; yellow and black safety striping on each end; number in yellow on cab is "5512" and in lighted numberboards; dual Type II modified AC motors on die-cast six-wheel trucks; MagneTraction; metal frame with yellow edge line; illuminated cab; operating headlights; ditch lights on front snowplow fitting; "Liontech" reverse unit; TrainMaster Command Control; RailSounds II; operating couplers. This is the first SD model equipped with TrainMaster Command. This and its companion 18222 remain the only SD-50s in Lionel's line to date. **375 450**

18222 DENVER & RIO GRANDE: 1995, powered SD-50 diesel; matches 18221 except number is "5517"; this unit is not Command-equipped, and has an electronic diesel horn, not RailSounds. Other details and features match 18221. **300 350**

18223 MILWAUKEE ROAD: 1995, powered SD-40; orange and black body, divided approximately in half, with black upper portion and roof; black lettering on orange section; red and white Milwaukee Road herald on cab; number is "154" in white on sides and in lighted numberboards; illuminated cab and headlights; die-cast metal frame; two modified Type II AC motors in die-cast six-wheel trucks; MagneTraction; "Liontech" electronic reverse unit; ditch lights in front snowplow attachment; RailSounds II; operating couplers. Released in tandem with 18224 below, but available separately. This engine was not made with the TrainMaster unit, though Lionel apparently planned to do so. But its Milwaukee colors made it a popular set nonetheless. A matching caboose was illustrated with the two engines. **— 375**

18224 MILWAUKEE ROAD: 1995, powered SD-40; same design as 18223, except number is "155" and this unit has an electronic diesel horn in place of RailSounds. Other features match 18223. **— 325**

18552 DULUTH, MISSABE & IRON RANGE: see 18813.

18555 CHICAGO & ILLINOIS MIDLAND: see 18823.

18806 NEW HAVEN: 1989, powered SD-18; dark Brunswick green body; orange-painted cab; orange "N" above white "H"; white "8806" on cab; illuminated cab and numberboards without numbers; headlights at both ends; stamped-metal frame and railings; single modified Type III can motor mounted upright in a six-wheel truck—a new scheme for the can motor, which is used here for the first time in an SD-series diesel; traction tires on drive wheels; three-position electronic reverse unit.

(A) As described. **110 130**

(B) Factory Error. No number on cab. R. Kaptur and J. Trelford Collections. **NRS**

18808 ATLANTIC COAST LINE: 1990, powered SD-18; black body; white lettering and "8808" on cab; two yellow stripes on side from cab to rear; illuminated headlights, cab and number boards without numbers; stamped-metal frame and railings painted yellow; single modified Type III can motor in six-wheel trucks; three-position electronic reverse; horn. Catalog incorrectly shows "8806" on cab. **100 125**

18810 CSX: 1990, powered SD-18; light gray body; blue cab roof, lettering, "8810" on cab, and CSX nose decal; stamped-metal frame and railings painted a matching gray; lighted cab, headlights and number boards without numbers; single modified Type III can motor; blue-painted six-wheel trucks; three-position electronic reverse; horn. Came as part of top-of-the-line 11717 CSX Freight Traditional Series set in 1990. **110 140**

18811 ALASKA: 1991, powered SD-9; dark blue and yellow Alaska paint scheme; blue main body; yellow cab nose and rear; yellow "ALASKA" and "8811" below cab window; "ARR" decal at rear; red, white, and blue nose decal; illuminated cab and number plates with numbers; headlights at both ends; electronic diesel horn; separate grab-irons on nose (a new detail for SD diesels); single modified Type III can motor in black six-wheel die-cast trucks; three-position electronic reverse unit; two operating couplers. Cataloged with a Type I (Pullmor) motor, but made with the Type III vertical can motor. Illustrated with a matching 16523 caboose. **120 160**

18813 DULUTH, MISSABE & IRON RANGE: 1990, powered SD-18; uncataloged; maroon-tuscan body; yellow stripe along length of body; yellow safety striping on frame; yellow lettering and "8813" on cab; green "D M" logo on lower front; headlights at both ends; illuminated cab and number boards; stamped-metal frame and railings; six-wheel die-cast trucks; modified Type III

Exc Mt

can motor; three-position electronic reverse unit. Special edition for J.C. Penney in its continuing engine series. Reportedly less than 3,000 made. Catalog number of engine together with Plexiglas display case and board is 18552. **175 200**

18823 CHICAGO & ILLINOIS MIDLAND: 1992, SD-9 diesel; uncataloged special for Sears; medium green body; red and white "lightning" stripe design runs around entire body; white lettering "C&IM"; "52" in white on cab and in lighted numberboards; stamped-metal frame and railings; single vertical Type III can motor; die-cast six-wheel trucks; three-position electronic reverse; diesel horn; operating headlights and lighted cab; operating couplers. This engine was shown only in the 1992 Sears Wishbook, along with a matching set of three C&IM Standard O boxcars and an extended vision caboose. It came with a display base and Plexiglas cover—together these were cataloged as 18555. The set of cars and caboose is cataloged as 18556. **150 175**

18824 MONTANA RAIL LINK: 1993, SD-9 diesel; blue body; black upper third of sides and roof' white lettering and "600" on cab and in lighted numberboards; white diagonal stripes on long hood "Montana RAIL LINK" on cab side in red and white; operating headlights and lighted cab; stamped-metal frame and railings; single modified Type III can motor in die-cast six-wheel trucks; three-position electronic reverse; diesel horn; operating couplers. Shown with a matching extended vision caboose in the catalog. **120 150**

18834 CHESAPEAKE & OHIO: 1994, SD-28 diesel; dark blue body; yellow roadname on long hood; yellow "C&O for Progress" logo on cab and in blue on nose; yellow nose front; no number on cab, but "8834" appears in lighted numberboards; stamped-metal frame and railings; single modified Type III can motor in die-cast six-wheel trucks; three-position electronic reverse; diesel horn; operating headlights and lighted cab; operating couplers. Headed the 11743 Chesapeake & Ohio freight set, the top-of-the-line Traditional set from 1994. This is also the only SD-28 made in the Lionel LTI/LLC period covered in this book, and the first since 1983. **125 150**

18842 BESSEMER & LAKE ERIE: 1995, SD-38 diesel; uncataloged special for J.C. Penney as part of its continuing special engine series; new design model for Lionel, created by placing the GP-38 body on the six-wheel trucks of the SD-series; orange body; black roof; white lettering and number, which is "868"; B&LE "I-beam" logo on cab; electronic horn; modified Type III can motor in die-cast six-wheel trucks; stamped-metal frame and railings; three-position electronic reverse; headlights; illuminated cab; operating couplers. Came with display base and Plexiglas cover, as did all the J.C. Penney models. It is also the only SD-38 model made by Lionel to date. Somewhat hard to find. Reportedly less than 1500 made. **— 325**

THE NW-2 SWITCHERS

For a very long time, from their initial production in the 1950s on into the '70s, the Lionel Corporation and Fundimensions had difficulty in identifying this unique General Motors Electro-Motive Division 1000-horsepower diesel switcher. It was often referred to as an SW-1, though the body in reality is an NW-2, a close cousin. Regardless of what they are called, these distinctive engines have not often been popular with collectors, even though some of them have become quite scarce. They are, however, popular with operators. The development of the switcher, first introduced by postwar Lionel in 1949, parallels that of the Alco—it underwent a cheapening process in 1955 by removing the Magne-Traction and stamping the frame rather than casting it. And like the small Alcos and the more modern RS-3s, this workhorse diesel gets little respect. Some of those hobbyists may not know what they're missing!

The modern era series began in 1970 with the 8010 Santa Fe switcher in blue and yellow—most of the early switchers followed the line of the cheaper postwar models.

Like most other locomotives, the NW-2 underwent a series of minor changes to the shell casting in the 1970s, as shown in our previous edition, *Greenberg's guide to Lionel Trains, 1970–1991*. These involved a series of changes to the side doors and the maintenance ladder between the first and second doors from the front. By 1989 it had settled down to the "Type VI."

Fundimensions initially limited its use of NW-2 switchers to the bottom-of-the-line sets, and only a few of these locomotives are truly scarce. There was a gap in production after 1984. Then, in 1989–90, Lionel introduced new models of the NW-2, now the body style VI, with many upgraded features—die-cast frame, die-cast trucks, a ringing bell, MagneTraction and wire handrails. The radio wheel on the top reappeared. Most important was the replacement of the can motor with the robust Type I Pullmor motor. None of these amenities had been seen on the NW-2 since 1955. And for the first time, an NW-2 switcher was at the head of a Collector set (the 18501 Western Maryland).

Unhappily, perhaps due to complaints about the higher prices of these units, there was another brief gap as Lionel

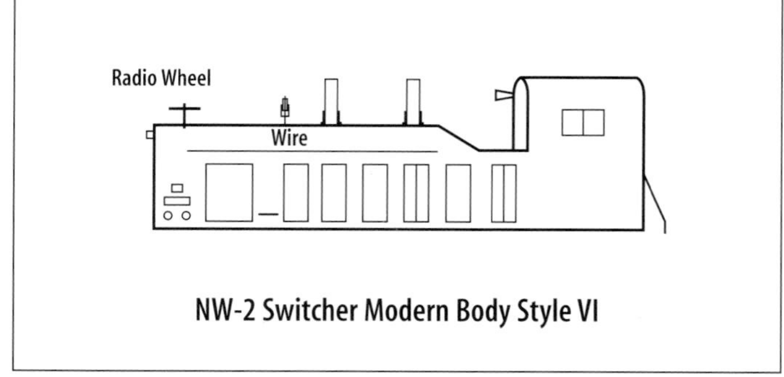

NW-2 Switcher Modern Body Style VI

18921 and 18928 C&NW NW-2 "cow" and "calf"

reverted to the less expensive can-motored version. It released quite a few during the period between 1993 and 1996.

The NW-2 switchers have no cab lighting, the illumination consisting simply of a nose headlight. The reason for this is that the cab is generally filled with the motor. The engines do have two operating couplers, however.

In 1995 and 1996, Lionel LTI created an interesting "calf"-unit add-on for the NW-2, somewhat like a B (booster) unit for the larger diesel styles.

Like the Alcos and RS-3s, most of the NW-2 switchers are relatively easy to acquire at good prices. Two of the more interesting ones are a colorful Georgia Power NW-2 heading an uncataloged set of the same name, and the black Bethlehem Steel engine that pulled the 1999 Service Station special set. The Navy and Coast Guard versions pulled two of Lionel's more popular Traditional Line sets of the decade.

This switcher is definitely a great specialization area for the beginning collector.

NW-2 SWITCHER LISTINGS

Exc Mt

18501 WESTERN MARYLAND: 1989, NW-2 yard switcher; dark gray Type VI body; cream top, lettering, number, and logo; Western Maryland wing logo on front reading "Fast Freight Line"; "8501" on cab; operating headlights at both ends, dioded to function in the direction of travel; running lights on front. This engine resurrects deluxe features not seen on the NW-2 since the postwar 6250 in 1955: Type I motor with Magne-Traction, die-cast frame and trucks, ringing bell, three-position E-unit and wire handrails. Good runner. First modern era NW-2 switcher to head a Collector set, the separate-sale Western Maryland Fallen Flags no. 4. **200 230**

18503 SOUTHERN PACIFIC: 1990, NW-2 yard switcher; Type VI body painted medium gray; white lettering; "8503" on cab; red stripe on chassis walkway edge; red-painted nose and lower cab rear; two operating headlights, dioded for direction of travel; running lights; electronic bell; die-cast frame and trucks; MagneTraction; Type I motor; three-position reverse; wire handrails. Engine continues the "deluxe" series of NW-2s started by the 18501. Cataloged with RailSounds circuitry, but

Exc Mt

not produced that way. Came with matching 19707 Southern Pacific searchlight caboose. **220 250**

18917 SOO: 1993, NW-2 yard switcher; red Type VI body; white lettering and number; Type III can motor in plastic trucks; stamped-metal chassis; not lighted; working headlight and running lights; three-position electronic reverse. Came as part of set no. 11741, the Northwest Express, and not boxed individually. **60 80**

18918 BOSTON & MAINE: 1993, NW-2 yard switcher; blue Type VI body; large white lettering and number, which is "8918" on cab; Type III can motor in plastic trucks; stamped-metal chassis; not lighted; working headlight and running lights; three-position electronic reverse; electronic diesel horn. A matching calf unit was added later. **75 90**

18920 FRISCO: 1994, NW-2 yard switcher; black Type VI body; yellow "FRISCO" lettering and number, which is "254" on cab; Type III can motor in plastic trucks; stamped-metal chassis; not lighted; working headlight and running lights; three-position electronic reverse; electronic diesel horn. A matching caboose was offered in the catalog. **75 90**

18921 CHICAGO & NORTH WESTERN: 1994, NW-2 yard switcher; yellow Type VI body with dark green roof; green "1017" on cab; red, green, and white CNW heralds on cab; Type III can motor in plastic trucks; stamped-metal chassis; not lighted; working headlight and running lights; three-position electronic reverse; electronic diesel horn. A matching "calf" unit was released later. **75 90**

18927 U.S. NAVY: 1995, NW-2 yard switcher; yellow Type VI body; black lettering; number is "65-00637" on cab; Type III can motor in plastic trucks; stamped-metal chassis; not lighted;

working headlight and running lights, which in this case are orange; three-position electronic reverse. Came as part of set no. 11745, the U.S. Navy set, and not boxed individually. The set was one of Lionel's more popular Traditional Line sets. A matching calf unit is available. **75 90**

18928 CHICAGO & NORTH WESTERN: 1995, unpowered "calf" unit for NW-2 switchers; first release of this new design; decor matches 18921 above; CNW herald, but no number on body; stamped-metal frame; operating light at rear; wire handrails; operating couplers. Hobbyists were lukewarm to this strange-looking new design. It uses the same frame and trucks as the NW-2, and the die is the same as the NW-2 but without the cab. Real railroads used these "calves" to add more pulling power to the "mother" switcher engine. **40 45**

18929 BOSTON & MAINE: 1995, unpowered "calf" unit for NW-2 switcher; first release of this new design; decor matches 18918 above; no number on body; stamped-metal frame; operating light at rear; wire handrails; operating couplers. **40 45**

18931 CHRYSLER MOPAR: 1994, NW-2 yard switcher; uncataloged; specially made for Chrysler Mopar products set; blue Type VI body; large white "Mopar" and Chrysler star logo on sides; number is "1818" in white on cab; Type III can motor in plastic trucks; stamped-metal chassis; not lighted; working headlight and running lights; three-position electronic reverse. Came as part of special 11818 Chrysler Mopar set. Not boxed individually. **70 90**

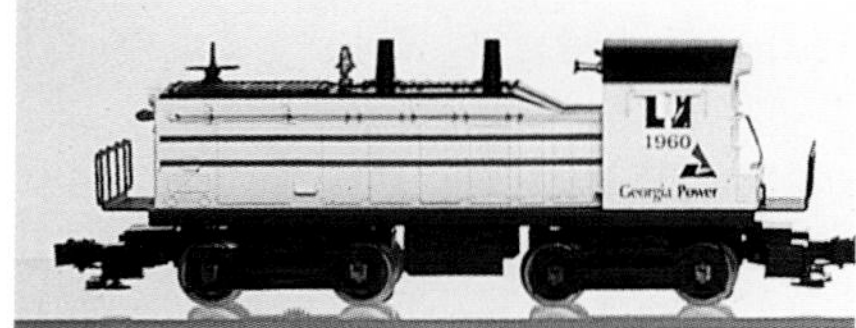

18943 GEORGIA POWER: 1995, NW-2 yard switcher; uncataloged; white Type VI body with black roof; brown stripes on sides; number in black is "1960"; brown and black "Georgia Power" and triangle insignia on cab; Type III can motor in plastic trucks; stamped-metal chassis; not lighted; headlight and running lights; three-position electronic reverse. Not individually boxed. This engine headed one of the most popular of all of Lionel's uncataloged sets, the 11819 Georgia Power set, made initially for employees of the Georgia Power Company. It also attracted a following of Olympics memorabilia collectors, because the boxcar also commemorated the upcoming 1996 Atlanta Olympic Games. Somewhat hard to find. **— 170**

THE FAIRBANKS MORSE (FM) TRAINMASTER

The long and elegant Fairbanks Morse TrainMaster is a legendary locomotive on the real railroads and in the world of Lionel. There were never very many made, either in the Lionel Corporation's long postwar period, or in Fundimensions' ownership after 1970. Therefore collectors have come to appreciate the subtle variations and handsome coloring of the locomotives that did appear. It was not until 1979 that Fundimensions revived the legend, after 13 years had passed since the last postwar Virginian model was made. Collectors, by then wary of some of the new company's efforts at cost-cutting, were anxious to see if justice would be done to the time-honored classic. Indeed, it was—the Fundimensions FM TrainMaster was a nearly exact duplicate of the postwar Lionel model, with all the premium features—two big Pullmor motors, six-wheel die-cast trucks, metal underbody fuel tank, and MagneTraction. The first "modern" model was a remake of the 1950s Virginian. There followed at discrete intervals new roadnames like Southern Pacific, Wabash, Jersey Central, and Santa Fe. All were good sellers, especially the "Black Widow Southern Pacific and the Wabash "Bluebird," a special for J.C. Penney that is now a true classic collectible.

True to form, the new Lionel management (LTI and LLC) have not made many of these engines either. In 1988 Lionel issued the 18301 Southern model with a matching scale high-cupola wood-sided caboose. In mid-decade the company came out with Pennsylvania and Reading versions, two names never produced previously. There was another gap in production until 1999 when, its new electronics in hand, Lionel revived two of the postwar favorites as part of its lucrative "Postwar Celebration Series"—the Jersey Central and Erie Lackawanna, both with TrainMaster Command Control and the other advanced wizardry.

All of the FM TrainMaster locomotives are desirable pieces, partially because only a few different models exist. Operationally, with two Pullmor motors and MagneTraction, they can only be out-pulled by the die-cast GG-1 electrics. As of yet, there have been no major variations in the body style, the heavy-duty stamped-metal frame or the six-wheel die-cast trucks of these engines. The FMs have an unusual truck that, with its blind driver on the innermost wheel, gives it an unbalanced look when viewed from the side. The only variations have occurred inside, where the mechanical E-unit gave way to the electronic reversing unit. Sounds, TrainMaster Command, and directional lighting were eventually added inside the ample shell. Oddly enough, none of these engines, postwar or later, have had any cab lighting, just headlights.

18301 Southern FM TrainMaster

FM TRAINMASTER LISTINGS

Exc Mt

18301 SOUTHERN: 1988, dual-motored Fairbanks-Morse TrainMaster; green cab; silver-painted lower sides and ends; white stripe at roofline; gold lettering and numbers; "8301" on cab; electronic diesel horn; stamped-metal frame and black railings; die-cast six-wheel trucks; operating headlights at both ends; two Type I Pullmor motors; MagneTraction; three-position reverse unit; operating couplers **270 300**

18307 PENNSYLVANIA: 1994, dual-motored Fairbanks-Morse TrainMaster; Brunswick green body; gold lettering and numbers; "8699" on cab and numberboards; electronic diesel horn; stamped-metal frame and black railings; die-cast six-wheel trucks; operating headlights at both ends; antenna on roof mounted with stanchions—a nice upgrade; two Type I Pullmor motors; MagneTraction; three-position "Liontech" reverse unit—this is the first FM so equipped; operating couplers. The red and white "FM" decals were included separately with this engine in case the user wished to apply them—the prototype Pennsy did not have them. **275 325**

18309 READING: 1993, dual-motored Fairbanks-Morse TrainMaster; dark green cab; gold lettering and numbers; "863" on cab and numberboards; electronic diesel horn; stamped-metal frame and black railings; die-cast six-wheel trucks; operating headlights at both ends; two Type I Pullmor motors; MagneTraction; three-position reverse unit; operating couplers. The red and white "FM" decals were included separately with this engine in case the user wished to apply them—the prototype Reading did not have them. This was first FM engine made after a five-year gap—it is not clear why it is numbered after the Pennsylvania model, yet was made before. The body colors of the two engines are virtually identical. **275 325**

THE GENERAL ELECTRIC DASH 8 DIESELS

During its 90-year history, Lionel occasionally was first, or nearly first, to issue models of popular new prototype engines. The best example was the speed Lionel exhibited in bringing out its O gauge version of the Union Pacific streamlined M-10000 in 1934, only a few months after the real thing crossed the country for the first time.

But the cost of the tooling also meant that other popular engines, such as the RS-3, were not modeled until decades after they first appeared on real railroads. And once created, the tooling for Lionel's models tended to be used for many years, often long after the prototype rolling stock had disappeared. New F-3s roll along Lionel layouts today, more than 20 years after they disappeared from America's railroads.

Happily, in the case of the General Electric Dash 8, Lionel was quick on the draw after GE created the huge 4000-horsepower prototype in the mid-1980s. Lionel has not only developed a scale-length new body style, but also a new six-wheel truck frame similar to, but not the same as, the one used on the SD-40. The first ones off the line came in 1989 (the 18205 Union Pacific) and 1990 (the 18206 Santa Fe), just a few short years after the real engines arrived. They are thus entirely creations of the new Lionel (LTI and LLC). They also demonstrate how the modern company still pursues modeling the railroad workhorses of the present day. These 16-inch-long engines are outfitted with two heavy-duty modified Type II motors (an AC winding integral to the motor truck). Lionel has lately come to call this motor "Pullmor" as well. This book refers to the separate Type I motor as "Pullmor"—since it is separable from the trucks. However, the new modified Type II motor-truck, with its larger number of windings, is nearly as powerful as the Type I, and is AC in design as well, so Lionel has adopted the

18309 Reading FM TrainMaster

18205 Union Pacific Dash 8-40C

Exc	Mt

advertising advantage of calling them both "Pullmor." These modified Type II motors had first appeared on the SD-40s in 1982. Sometimes the reader can distinguish Lionel's intention when they refer to it as an "open frame" AC motor.

The Dash 8s have come in both a "B" model (four-wheel trucks) and "C" models (six-wheel). The real ones come both ways as well. Their length restricts their operation to O31 track—they will not navigate the O27 switch machines.

Despite some initial quality-control problems with the first releases, the Dash 8s and Dash 9s have proved to be good sellers and now have taken over the lead in many of the top-of-the-line Collector/Heritage diesel sets from the GPs and U36s.

One significant innovation introduced with the Dash 8s occurred in 1994 when Lionel brought out two Norfolk Southern and two CSX powered units—intended to be run together. This was made possible by the newly developed "Liontech" electronic reverse unit, which differed from earlier circuits (and the mechanical "E-unit"), by resetting to forward after a momentary power interruption. It avoided the sometimes-difficult process of "synchronizing" the reverse units on two engines to enable them to run together. These sets were the first dual-powered engines Lionel had ever made. Previous matching engine sets had included only one powered unit—the others were dummy. Obviously this innovation, given that the Dash 8s have two powerful motors, would enable double-headed engines to pull trains of immense lengths!

The GE Dash series from Lionel has also added some very nice detailing not often seen on other engines.

All of them have MagneTraction, three-position reverse units, operating couplers at both ends, headlights at both ends, and a flashing warning light on the cab roof.

But other features were innovations for this engine design—a detailed chain link on the end railings, ditch lights on the front trucks (added in 1995), and a snowplow piece on the front. These new details eventually came to be used on other diesels too.

Oh, yes—and an engineer figure or two in the cab!

DASH 8 and DASH 9 LISTINGS

Exc	Mt

18205 UNION PACIFIC: 1989, Dash 8-40C diesel; yellow body; gray roof; red numbers and lettering; gray metal handrails and frame with red stripe along frame edge; lighted number boards reading "9100"; cab lights, headlights and a flashing warning light on the cab roof; black six-wheel die-cast trucks, similar to, but not exactly the same as, those on the SD-40s; dual modified Type II motors; MagneTraction; three-position reverse unit; electronic horn; operating couplers at both ends. The "9100" number, which is prototypical, marked one of the first times Lionel had departed from its "8XXX" numbering scheme on the engines. Realistic numbers were to become the norm for most of Lionel's premium engines in the 1990s. First in the new-style locomotives modeled after the popular GE prototype Dash 8-40C. Union Pacific was the first road to purchase the Dash 8-40C from GE. There were some reported problems with easily burnt-out armatures on this engine, as well as complaints that the trucks should have been painted gray as on the prototype. There are unconfirmed reports of gray-painted trucks as well. Reader comments requested. **225** **275**

18206 SANTA FE: 1990, Dash 8-40B diesel; yellow- and blue-painted cab body; yellow frame, handrails, and large "Santa Fe" on cab side; blue Santa Fe nose logo; "8206" on cab; cab lights, headlights, and a flashing warning light on the cab roof; no horn—the RailSounds for the set were included in the boxcar; dual modified Type II motors; MagneTraction; three-position reverse unit; operating couplers at both ends. Second in the new series of top-of-the-line diesels. This engine differs from its 1989 Union Pacific predecessor in that it has new four-wheel truck frames modeled more precisely after the "Floating Bolster" prototype. Came with 11713 Santa Fe Dash 8 set. **250** **300**

18207 NORFOLK SOUTHERN: 1992, Dash 8-40C diesel; black body; white NS wind logo on sides; white horse insignia on ends; "8689" on cab; cab lights, headlights and flashing warning light on the cab roof; electronic horn; dual modified Type II motors; MagneTraction; three-position electronic reverse unit (one of its first appearances); die-cast six-wheel trucks; die-cast frame with chain links on railings; snowplow; operating couplers at both ends; engineer figure. Good runner. Headed the 11718 Norfolk Southern unit train, the top-of-the line Collector set in 1992. A matching unit was added in 1994. Note: the catalog lists this as "18689", as does its box, but the official catalog number assigned by Lionel is 18207. The 18200s were the series designated for the higher-end diesels, whereas the 18600s were all small steam engines. **275** **325**

18211 SUSQUEHANNA: 1993, Dash 8-40B diesel; yellow and black body; black lower section of sides and ends; black lettering and "NYSW 4002" on cab; circle-S logo on nose; interior lighting; headlights; illuminated numberboards; flashing

18211 Susquehanna Dash 8-40E

Exc Mt

warning light on cab roof; electronic horn; dual modified Type II motors; MagneTraction; three-position electronic reverse unit; die-cast four-wheel trucks; die-cast frame with chain links on railings; frame has yellow hazard striping (shown solid in catalog); snowplow; operating couplers at both ends; engineer figure. A matching bay window caboose was released with this piece. A second engine appeared in 1994. **250 300**

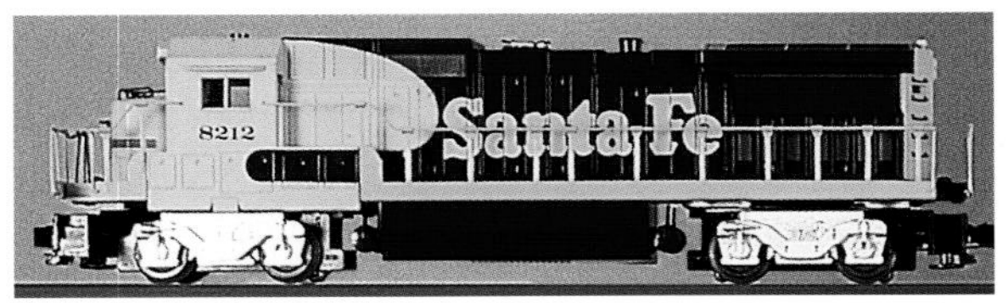

18212 SANTA FE: 1993, Dash 8-40B non-powered unit; description identical to 18206 above, except number on cab is "8212". Intended as an add-on for the 11713 Santa Fe Dash 8 set. Shown in the 1993 Stocking Stuffers catalog. **140 175**

18213 NORFOLK SOUTHERN: 1994, Dash 8-40C diesel; description matches 18207 above, except number on cab is "8688". This engine is one of the first equipped with the "Liontech" electronic reverse circuit, a modified version of the previous model which enables two powered engines to be run together on the same track and even in the same train, without trying to "synchronize" the E-units. The two engines (18207-13) mark the first time Lionel produced two matching powered engines. **250 300**

18214 CSX: 1994, Dash 8-40C diesel; gray body; blue cab and lower portion of sides; yellow nose; "CSX" in large block lettering in blue on sides and on nose; number in yellow in cab is "7500"; interior lighting; headlights; illuminated numberboards; flashing warning light on cab roof; electronic horn; dual modified Type II motors; MagneTraction; Liontech electronic reverse unit; die-cast six-wheel trucks; die-cast frame painted gray with yellow stripe on edge; chain links on railings; snowplow; operating couplers at both ends; engineer figure. Issued as a set with the powered 18215 unit below, but available individually. These engines were popular with CSX enthusiasts. The 1994 Spring release catalog showed the engines without the yellow stripe on the frame sides—the 1994 main catalog shows them correctly—and as they were made. **275 325**

18215 CSX: 1994, Dash 8-40C diesel; description matches 18214 above, except number is "7643". Intended as a set with 18214, but available individually. **275 325**

18218 SUSQUEHANNA: 1994, Dash 8-40B diesel; description matches 18211 previous, except number on cab is "4003". Includes "Liontech" electronic reverse to enable it to be run with the 18211 engine. **230 280**

18219 CHICAGO & NORTH WESTERN: 1995, Dash 8-40C diesel; yellow body; Brunswick green cab and roof; red, black, and white CNW logo on cab and nose; number is "8501" in black on side and in white on cab side; interior lighting; headlights; illuminated

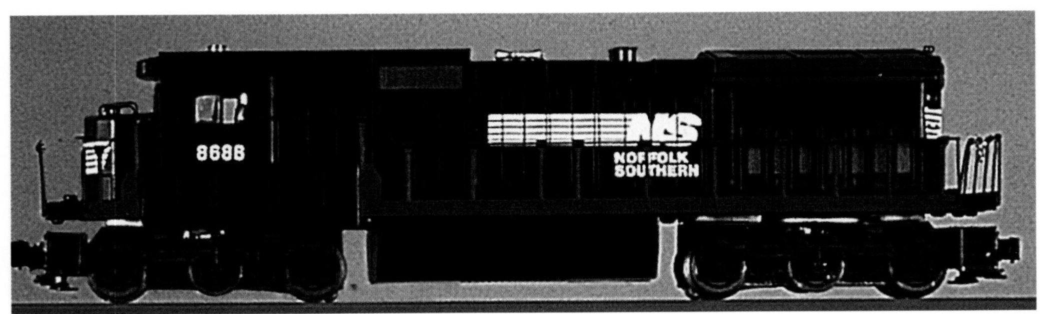

18213 Norfolk Southern Dash 8-40C

18907 Rock Island GE 44-ton switcher

Exc Mt

numberboards; flashing warning light on cab roof; dual modified Type II motors; MagneTraction; Liontech electronic reverse unit; die-cast six-wheel trucks; die-cast frame painted gray and yellow, with chain links on railings; railings also gray; snowplow; operating couplers at both ends; engineer figure; RailSounds II—first Dash 8 with this feature; operating ditch lights in the front truck—also the first Dash 8 with this new feature. Intended as a set with 18220 below. The latter engine does not have RailSounds, but has the older electronic horn. — 400

18220 CHICAGO & NORTH WESTERN: 1995, Dash 8-40C diesel; same description as 18219 above, except number is "8502"; this engine does not have RailSounds but does have an electronic horn; intended as a set with 18220. — 325

18689: see 18207.

GE 44-TON SWITCHERS

In 1992 Lionel reintroduced another old postwar favorite (well, perhaps not that favored)—the ungainly 44-ton center-cab diesel switcher. The story of the day goes that the union contract of 1937 forced railroads to have two operators in engines weighing more than 45 tons. GE thus made these 44-ton yard engines to avoid the payroll costs of the additional man.

This odd engine stands as the only piece Lionel makes that is oversized! At 11 inches, it is about 20 to 30 percent over-scale to the real thing, which looks even boxier than Lionel's model.

The modern version has two Type III can motors in a sturdy stamped-metal frame, and it pulls surprisingly well. It even includes headlights and a diesel horn.

The postwar company made these engines in five roadnames, and only from 1956 through 1959. It was an attempt to create an inexpensive switcher for the low-end market, but something better than the very small Vulcan switchers. The resultant piece was in fact longer than the short Alco models. The attempt wasn't successful, though, because most hobbyists and dealers felt the engine was unattractive.

Apparently Lionel Fundimensions did not feel enough interest in this switcher existed to spend time resurrecting it, and Lionel LTI did not do so until five years into their administration. Only two of them were made during the period covered in this book. Neither of them repeat the postwar roadnames. They haven't been especially successful in the modern era, either. But that may make at least the modern ones a good target for inexpensive collecting. Perhaps the underrated 44-tonner will make a comeback.

GE 44-TON SWITCHER LISTINGS

Exc Mt

18905 PENNSYLVANIA: 1992, GE 44-ton switcher; first remake of the postwar 44-ton switcher since 1959; dark green body; yellow roadname on side of frame; number on cab is "9312" in yellow; stamped-metal chassis painted green; dual Type III can motors, one in each four-wheel truck; three-position electronic reverse; electronic diesel horn; headlight; interior illumination. Postwar Lionel did not make a Pennsylvania model of this engine. 100 130

18907 ROCK ISLAND: 1993, GE 44-ton switcher; bright red body; white stripe along frame edge; white "371" and Rock Island shield on cab; red-painted stamped-metal frame; handrails; dual Type III can motors, one in each four-wheel plastic truck; three-position electronic reverse; electronic diesel horn; headlight; interior illumination. One of the very few Rock Island items made by modern Lionel. 90 120

CHAPTER 5

Electric Engines

Before we describe Lionel's production of electrics, a note on terminology is necessary. In prototype railroading, an electric engine is referred to as a "motor" because it receives its power from overhead wires and does not generate power internally as do steam and diesel locomotives. But in model railroading terms, anything that is powered and can pull a train is considered a "locomotive," whether it is a model steam, diesel, or electric engine. Obviously, all Lionel's engines actually operate on third-rail power, and not steam- or diesel-fuel-generated power.

Lionel has made four major types of electric engines during its postwar and modern eras.

EP-5 ELECTRICS

The first of the electrics to emerge from the miniature erecting shops of Fundimensions after the 1970 changeover was the "double-end" EP-5 rectifier electric. Fundimensions and the old Lionel had referred to this engine as "Little Joe," but that is an error. The real "Little Joe" was a quite different locomotive purchased by the Milwaukee Road and the Chicago South Shore & South Bend Railroad. The name came about because these South Shore locomotives were originally intended for Russian export during World War II; hence, the name "Little Joe" after Joseph Stalin. The real Little Joe had a dual-ended cab similar to the EP-5, but was larger and heavier, had a different wheel configuration, and a different-shaped cab front. The EP-5, on the other hand, was an electric made for the New Haven Railroad by General Electric. Famous for its rapid acceleration, it consequently earned the nickname "The Jet."

Except for its length and its four-wheel trucks (six-wheel types were used on the real thing), Lionel's model of the EP-5 was quite accurate. The two pantographs on Fundimensions' models were modifications of those of the postwar era. Instead of the fragile coil springs of the postwar models, Fundimensions incorporated a strip of spring steel to create upward pressure, thereby enabling these engines to maintain better contact on overhead catenary wires. Some postwar engines have been refitted with Fundimensions pantographs for this reason. But the steel strip can be fragile, too, with a tendency to snap under excessive loads.

The first modern EP-5, issued in 1975, was an 8551 Pennsylvania tuscan with gold striping and lettering. A 1976 model was an 8558 Milwaukee Road locomotive in maroon, orange, and black. In 1977 an attractive Great Northern EP-5 (8762) was made in dark green and orange. A special EP-5 (8272) was made for J.C. Penney in 1982. This engine had Pennsylvania colors and markings like its 8551 predecessor, but the nose and sides were bright gold with tuscan lettering. These early Fundimensions engines unfortunately did not feature Magne-Traction, an omission that has been corrected on all the EP-5s made since 1988. In 1988 another Great Northern model was made, this time with MagneTraction and a horn.

The EP-5 is a fine runner that looks good with either freight or passenger consists. The modern EP-5s are relatively common.

EP-5 LISTINGS

Exc Mt

18302 GREAT NORTHERN: 1988, GE EP-5 electric; orange and dark green cab; yellow striping, numbering, and lettering; red, white, and green Great Northern goat logos on sides and nose; "8302" on cab; single Type I motor; electronic horn; headlights at both ends; pantographs that can be wired for actual operation; three-position E-unit; operating couplers. Part of Great Northern Fallen Flags no. 3 set, whose components were sold separately. Similar to 8762 model of 1977, but includes MagneTraction and horn. Has the distinction of being the third (regular) issue of this engine with this road name, including the postwar 2358. It is not clear why Lionel did this, but may explain the sluggish sales of its Fallen Flags no. 3 set. **200 275**

18302 Great Northern GE EP-5

Exc Mt

18311 DISNEY: 1994, GE EP-5 electric; white body; red roof and nose roofs; black lettering with "Mickey Mouse Express" logo toward each end; multicolor Mickey, Minnie, and Daisy graphics on sides; single Type I motor with MagneTraction; electronic horn; headlights and illuminated number boards (reading "8311") at both ends; pantographs that can be wired for actual operation; three-position reverse unit; operating couplers. One of a continuing series of specials with Disney themes made by Lionel. Intended as a match for the Disney hi-cube boxcars and especially for the 19723 Disney extended vision caboose. **200 250**

GG-1 ELECTRICS

Although the EP-5s are fine electrics, collectors were really waiting for the "crème de la crème" of all the electrics—the famous Pennsylvania GG-1. The prototype, an amazing machine, had a service life of nearly 50 years. Even today, its Raymond Loewy–designed lines look fresh and contemporary.

In 1977 patience had its reward. Fundimensions put out a tuscan 8753 GG-1 that had the original die-cast body, two motors, and MagneTraction. The overall end-result was good, but a few minor flaws needed correcting. Collectors claimed that the nylon gearing did not hold up very well in this locomotive, and the body casting was rougher than it should have been. In 1978 Fundimensions issued an all-black GG-1 in Penn Central markings (8850). This locomotive was an operational and cosmetic improvement over its predecessor, but collectors did not like its paint scheme. It was a slow seller.

Only one other GG-1 (a PRR in Brunswick green-gold from 1981) was produced in the remainder of the Fundimensions era up to 1986. For 1987 Lionel produced another Pennsylvania GG-1 (18300) in a new bronze color with bluish-black striping and a matching N5C caboose to power the previously produced bullion cars. This combination formed a unique "money train." Like all the GG-1 locomotives except the Penn Central, the 1987 model was a hot seller, despite the fact that its unusual color scheme produced howls of dismay from some traditionalists. The 1989 model (18303) saw a prototypical Amtrak paint scheme applied to the GG-1, though the line edges were again somewhat rough and imprecise.

Since the GG-1 was primarily a Pennsylvania Railroad locomotive (Amtrak and Penn Central obtained theirs from the PRR), Lionel must have felt constrained to this roadname when producing its expensive GG-1 trains. All three made by Lionel LTI in the 1990s have been in that roadname.

All GG-1s are solid die-cast bodies, powered by two Type I Pullmor motors with MagneTraction, which helps explain their heft, pulling capacity, and price! The modern era GG-1 locomotives are highly prized by collectors and operators alike. These massive (seven-pound!) engines will out-pull any other locomotive, except perhaps the Fairbanks-Morse TrainMaster, because all 12 wheels are drivers.

GG-1 LISTINGS

Exc Mt

18300 PENNSYLVANIA: 1987, dual-motored GG-1 electric; bronze-painted die-cast body; black striping and lettering; red keystones on sides and ends; "8300" on cab; two Type I motors with MagneTraction; lights at both ends; headlights at both ends; pantographs which can be wired for actual overhead catenary operation; operating couplers. Offered with matching Pennsylvania N5C porthole caboose sold separately. Intended to pull train of various Lionel bullion cars issued in previous years.

(A) As described. **350 450**

(B) Probable prototype. Differs from production piece with: darker gold (bronze) paint; keystones lighter red; front, rear keystones have "18300", not "8300" as on production model; darker and thicker stripes; "PENNSYLVANIA" lettering larger than production model; casting is flawed, with window frames slightly concaved. This is clearly the prototype used for the 1987 catalog photos. J. Stalma collection. **NRS**

18303 AMTRAK: 1989, dual-motored GG-1 electric; flat-silver-painted body; black lettering and numbers; "8303" on cab; blue stripes running the length of the body; red nose; casting and paint have rough edges; two Type I motors with MagneTraction; headlights at both ends; pantographs which can be wired for actual overhead catenary operation; three-position E-unit; operating couplers. Part of Amtrak passenger set with six separate-sale, long aluminum cars. Though not Lionel's best paint effort, this engine sold reasonably well due to the Amtrak colors and the popular aluminum cars. **300 375**

18308 PENNSYLVANIA: 1992, dual-motored GG-1 electric; bright silver-painted body, black roof; red stripe; black lettering and number, which is "4866"; red and white PRR keystone at center of sides; red keystones on ends; two Type I motors with MagneTraction; headlights and running lights at both ends; pantographs which can be wired for actual overhead catenary operation; mechanical three-position E-unit; operating couplers. The engine's non-standard paint design caused some initial complaints. It was used, however, by the PRR. **300 375**

18305 Lackawanna MU car set

MULTIPLE UNIT (M.U.) COMMUTER CARS

The predecessors to the diesel-powered Budd cars were the electrically powered Multiple Unit commuter cars. Built in the 1920s and 1930s, these elegant long passenger cars serviced the electrified commuter routes of the northeast United States before World War II. They reduced the turnaround time and pollution associated with steam-powered trains in the crowded urban areas. After the war, diesel-powered units like the Budd cars took over commuter duties.

Lionel had never modeled these handsome motorized trains until 1991, when two MU commuter cars appeared in Lackawanna colors. The cars were roughly modeled on the heavyweight Madison-type passenger cars released the same year, but are distinguished by their overhead pantographs, which can be wired to actually operate the train. The main bodies are, however, noticeably different from the heavyweights in terms of rivet arrangement, window arrangement, and vestibule detail. The roof piece on the passenger cars is modified to accommodate the pantograph and headlight units at each end. At 15 inches long, they are close to scale. The Lionel Multiple Unit cars have some fine detailing: three individual chains on the doors at each end, cow-catcher pilot, red marker lights, die-cast trucks, interior illumination, and constant-voltage headlights.

These cars, along with the new long Madison cars, were obviously Lionel's response to increasing competitive pressure toward longer scale-detailed passenger cars.

MULTIPLE UNIT COMMUTER CAR LISTINGS

Exc Mt

18304 LACKAWANNA: 1991, powered/dummy Multiple Unit commuter two-car set; new Lionel model of electrically powered passenger cars used on commuter lines in the 1920s, '30s, and '40s; body based roughly on long Madison-style heavyweight cars also produced in 1991; dark gray-green car body; gold lettering; black roof piece; "2401" on powered coach unit; "2402" on dummy coach unit; twin Type III can motors, each riding in a dedicated four-wheel die-cast truck; pantograph on powered unit can be wired for overhead operation; electronic three-position reverse unit; directional headlights with constant voltage; each car illuminated with window silhouettes; red marker lights; three blackened door chains; two operating couplers on each car. Powered/dummy unit sold together as a set, not individually.

(A) As described **375 425**

(B) Factory error. Missing trailing "A" in "LACKAWANNA" on dummy unit. R. Belesky Collection. **NRS**

18305 LACKAWANNA: 1992, non-powered Multiple Unit commuter car set; add-on for 18304 set above, to produce a four-car train; description matches 18304 cars above, except numbers for these are "2400" for the (new design) combine car, and "2403" for the coach. Coach has pantograph, while the combine car does not. Both cars have illuminated window silhouettes and directional lighting. Pieces are sold together only as a set. These cars are also often found together with the 18394 pieces above as a four-car train. **200 275**

18306 PENNSYLVANIA: 1993, powered/dummy Multiple Unit commuter car set; tuscan car body; gold lettering and roadname; black roof; "4574" on powered combine; "483" on dummy coach unit; twin Type III can motors, each riding in a dedicated four-wheel die-cast truck; electronic three-position reverse unit; directional headlights with constant voltage; each car illuminated with window silhouettes; red marker lights; door chains; cow catcher on powered car; two operating couplers on each car. Powered/dummy unit sold together as a set, not individually. Announced in 1992, the set wasn't released until 1993. **325 400**

18310 PENNSYLVANIA: 1993, non-powered Multiple Unit commuter car set; two coach cars; add-on for 18306 set above, to produce a four-car train; description matches 18306 cars above, except numbers for these are "484" for and "485". Coaches have pantographs even though non-powered. Cars have illuminated window silhouettes and directional lighting. Pieces are sold together, only as a set. **225 275**

CHAPTER 6

Motorized Units

One of the more fascinating areas of production in the postwar era was that of the "motorized unit," little specialty self-propelled cars that buzzed around layouts of the period. These tiny powered units, delightful to watch in action, are often eagerly sought by collectors. Since they were relatively sparsely produced in the postwar era, and very few were made after the early 1960s, it was only natural that modern collectors had become curious about any possible reissue of them.

Perhaps because of the complicated gearing inside, Fundimensions did not begin to revive them until 1982. At that time, the company issued an attractive 8264 snowplow in Canadian Pacific maroon and gray markings. After that, each year saw more of these little novelties. In 1983 an 8368 Vulcan 2-4-2 engine was produced in blue and yellow Alaska markings as a light-duty switcher with two operating couplers. In 1984 a Pennsylvania fire car (8379) was produced, complete with hose reels and rotating fireman, just like the original. Other units performed other complicated tasks.

Lionel has gotten great mileage out of the stocky little cabs it uses on many of the motorized units. It was created initially for the Army, Navy, and Minuteman switchers in the postwar years. In the modern era it has served as the basic body for snowplows (straight and rotary) and the Vulcan (2-4-2) switchers. A similar but even smaller and stockier plastic body is used for gas turbine diesel (0-4-0) switchers. These units provide great opportunities for the beginning collector to acquire powered engines inexpensively, but keep in mind that they are meant for light yard-switching or stand-alone duty. Typically, a motorized unit can pull only two to three cars, at most. Recently, Lionel has placed them at the front of a few low-cost Traditional Line sets. The Vulcan (2-4-2) switchers have a large smokestack and at least one operating coupler, whereas the gas turbine diesel switchers have neither of these extra features. The turbine uses the same four-wheel truck/sideframe design as the NW-2 switchers. In the Fundimensions era it was a DC-only piece, but Lionel LTI upgraded it with a rectifier to be AC- or DC-capable.

The year 1987 saw the modern remake of Lionel's famous little Birney trolley of the mid-1950s in the form of a bright orange and blue Lionelville 8690. Delayed in production for almost two years, this little trolley represented significant advances in operation over its ancestor. It used a spur-gear drive instead of the old crosscut-gear system, so it ran much more quietly and efficiently. The new trolley's body casting was more detailed, with headlight lenses and open step-work. Silhouette figures filled all the windows, including a conductor figure at the end windows. It ran so efficiently that sometimes the reversing slide rebounded too far and the trolley froze in neutral when it hit a bumper. When allowed to run slowly at low voltage, this problem does not occur. In 1988 a two-tone green 18404 San Francisco version appeared. More trolleys followed in the 1990s, with several of them in Christmas themes. Two recent ones were packaged as full sets with transformer, track, two bumpers, and the occasional building accessory. In the 1990s Lionel added directional headlights to it. In 1995 with the 11809 Village trolley, the company redesigned the roof piece to feature lighted clerestory windows and removed the sometimes-troublesome reversing power pole. It also substituted an electronic reversing switch for the mechanical slide, which was subject to friction-induced hang-ups that would leave the trolley in neutral. We should mention that at the same time, the company cheapened the motor and frame considerably. The Type II integral motor was replaced with a small can motor, and the frame was changed to plastic from die-cast. The whole thing was noticeably lighter. Also, the roller pickups were removed in favor of a less-efficient sliding-shoe copper strap that simply slides along the track. The changes to the trolley permitted a lower sales price, but operators should beware of the limitations in using such a feather-light unit.

The popular operating burro crane was revived in 1988, 1989, and 1990. This incredibly complex little device—complete with actual controls—allows the operator to use the crane and hook to pick up trackside structures or debris. With a work caboose or gondola in tow, this intricate crane provides lots of operating enjoyment. However, perhaps because of the glut at that time, no more burro cranes have been made since.

Another exciting revival occurred in 1987—the 18401 Lionel handcar. The original Lionel handcar of the mid-1960s burned out very easily, but Lionel redesigned its drive system this time around—with the modern can motor providing much greater reliability. Unfortunately, the modern version retains the undesirable sliding-shoe power pickup on the frame—there appears to be no way Lionel could add the roller pickup to this miniature piece. The 1987 model was listed as part of the Traditional Series and had a very reasonable price. Santa Claus versions were produced in 1988 (18403) and 1989 (18408), followed by many more handcars in a variety of cartoon character themes. Several of these have become hot sellers. Even in our age of microelectronics, it's hard to see how Lionel ever got any kind of motor inside that handcar! In fact it is too small to put a reverse unit in. Perhaps someday soon Lionel will put numbers on the handcars so we can keep better track of them!

The mid-90s saw the rerelease of two other postwar favorites which, for whatever reason, Fundimensions had declined to remake. One is the fun no. 50 gang car (no. 18417 in its modern reincarnation), which automatically changes direction when its rubber bumpers strike an end-of-track obstacle, just like the Birney trolleys. In this case, a gang of three men ride on the car, and one flips direction when the car reverses itself. Like the trolley and the track maintenance car, which use the same frames, the gang car sports the reliable Pullmor motor, visible in all its glory right on top of the car.

In 1995 Lionel came out with another postwar-favorite that hadn't been seen on O gauge rails for more than 30 years. This was the 18423 "On-Track" step van, which looked like an everyday delivery truck riding on the rails. It was accompanied in the catalog by the 18424 pickup truck using the same frame and can-motor power. The two pieces were reminiscent of the postwar no. 68 executive inspection car, which performed in the same way, but had the body of a 1955 station wagon. The real railroads use vehicles of this type to travel around the right-of-way inspecting for damage, blockages, debris, or gaps in the rails, calling in repair crews before the big trains encountered the problem. Many more were made in the years following 1995, including a station wagon crew car in 1996 that looked much like the 1955 Desoto. The frames of these units are lightweight, with the small can motor mounted transversely like that of the handcars. They have a sliding-shoe pickup rather than a roller pickup. The pilot and trailing trucks are a thin metal design. These light units are not meant to pull anything and have considerable trouble negotiating grades. A traction tire is usually supplied to help.

The wheels and frame arrangement of the original no. 68 were slightly different than the modern versions.

The power for all these units varies across the board. The early trolleys and Vulcan diesels (snowplows, tampers, etc.) use a cut-down version of the Type II integral motor/truck, which is geared slower than a road diesel. One of the unsung achievements of modern Lionel is its rearrangement of the gearing in many of these pieces for smoother operation. The only significant operating problem has come when a softer nylon gear, which strips easily, is used for the main drive gear on the armature shaft. The 0-4-0 gas turbines and the handcars use a form of the Type III can motor with the rectifier circuit, meaning they operate on AC or DC. This can motor was added to later versions of the Birney trolleys in the mid-1990s, as part of their cost-reducing modifications. The handcars, newer trolleys and inspection vehicles, which all use the same frame, have the sliding-shoe power pickup strap, not a roller pickup.

Oddly enough, the gang car and track maintenance cars use the Type I Pullmor motor, visible on top of the metal frames.

The larger Budd RDC cars, which are discussed at the end of this chapter, use the premium Type I motor. These powered passenger cars could not correctly be categorized as diesel engines or passenger cars, and so are listed here.

MOTORIZED UNIT LISTINGS

Exc Mt

11809 VILLAGE TROLLEY: 1995–97, Birney-style trolley; four-wheel light tan body; red roof is a new piece with clerestory windows and no reversing power pole; red script "Village Trolley Co." lettering on sides with red and green holly logos; gold snowflake background; number is "109" on sides and in number board; illuminated with colored silhouettes including operators and Santa; ends printed "EASTBOUND" and "WESTBOUND"; directional headlights; Type III can motor mounted transversely in the plastic frame; sliding-shoe pickup; no BLT date. This item came in a set with 12 O27 track pieces, two bumpers, and a transformer. The number is assigned both to the set and to the trolley. Listed in the 1995 Stocking Stuffer catalog. Price for entire set. This trolley differs from its predecessors in several ways—it is much lighter with the plastic frame and can motor; the roof was redesigned to eliminate the power pole; and the reverse unit changed from a sliding metal piece to an electronic switch that is depressed when the bumper hits the end of track. **— 90**

18400 SANTA FE: 1987, 2-4-2 Vulcan rotary snowplow; brown-red oxide body; yellow snowplow fan with brown spiral stripe; yellow Santa Fe cross logo; yellow "8400" on cab; black frame and railings; three-position E-unit; operating coupler at rear. **150 190**

18401 LIONEL: 1987, handcar; bright orange body with no number; black push handles; two blue men with flesh-painted faces; no reverse; DC can motor with rectifier for AC operation; newer spur drive motor; sliding-shoe pickup; partially exposed gearwork. Advertised in catalog with remote-control reverse, but not made that way. The unit was made two ways: the early run had a darker orange body and no metal weights. The later run was a lighter color and included a traction weight in the center. E. Frei comment.

(A) First run: dark orange body, no weight. **35 45**

(B) Second run: light orange body. Traction weight added. **40 50**

18402 LIONEL LINES: 1988, operating burro crane; black die-cast frame; yellow cab; red lettering; light gray boom; supplied with

Exc Mt

controller that has three levers for switching from self-propulsion to rotating cab, raising or lowering the hook, and reversing the function of both levers. Essentially a revival of the 3360 unit of the mid-1950s. This has always been a cleverly designed and interesting operating unit, although its complexity makes it susceptible to breakdown. **75 100**

18403 SANTA CLAUS: 1988, handcar; green body; figures of Mr. and Mrs. Claus dressed in traditional attire; black hand pump; no lettering on car; DC can motor with rectifier for AC operation; sliding-shoe pickup. **35 40**

18404 SAN FRANCISCO: 1988, Birney-style trolley; four-wheel green body; dark olive green roof; yellow lettering; black plastic bumper covers; "8404" on cab window insert; illuminated with window silhouettes; reversing power pole; Type II integral motor truck; improved spur-gear drive; "BLT 1-88"; mechanically identical to the 8690 Lionelville, from 1986–87. The bump reverse may rebound and stall if the unit is operated too fast at too high a voltage. **95 120**

18405 SANTA FE: 1989, operating burro crane; black die-cast base; light gray cab (pictured as dark gray in catalog); white lettering, number and logo on cab and black boom; "BUILT BY / LIONEL" embossed into cab body at lower rear. See 18402 for description of operating modes. **75 90**

18406 LIONEL: 1989, 1991, motorized track maintenance car; unpainted dark red plastic body; white lettering, number and Lionel circle logo; dark gray motor cover; black frame; medium gray superstructure (pictured as white in catalog); bumper reverse mechanism; red- and white-striped sign reading "DANGER" on one side and "SAFETY / FIRST" on the other; olive-painted man on superstructure. Reissue of no. 69 postwar model. **65 80**

Exc Mt

18407 SNOOPY & WOODSTOCK: 1990–91, handcar; blue body; no lettering on car; white and black Snoopy standing on a box; yellow Woodstock figure resting on the hand pump; DC can motor with rectifier for AC operation; sliding-shoe pickup. **40 55**

18408 SANTA CLAUS: 1989, handcar; similar to 18403 released in 1988, except handcar body is light gray and pump handle is green; no lettering on car; DC can motor with rectifier for AC operation. It is not clear why Lionel produced a near-duplicate car rather than re-cataloging the 18403. **30 40**

18410 PENNSYLVANIA: 1990, operating burro crane; black die-cast frame with Brunswick green body; PRR keystone logo in red and white on cab; gold "Burro" and "18410" on cab door; black boom with gold "PENNSYLVANIA". See 18402 for description of operating modes. **90 110**

18411 CANADIAN PACIFIC: 1990, motorized firefighting car; silver body; white number, script lettering and base unit; maroon generator and hose reel; dark blue bumpers with white safety stripes; blue fireman with white-painted face; gold decorative bell; flashing warning light; bump reverse mechanism; "BLT 1-90". Includes outriggers and two feet of hose that winds with a ratchet crank. **80 100**

18412 UNION PACIFIC: 1991, motorized firefighting car. Announced in Lionel's 1991 Book 1 catalog, but not manufactured. **Not Made**

18413 CHARLIE BROWN & LUCY: 1991, handcar; light blue handcar body; no lettering or number on car; Charlie Brown in red and black; Lucy in yellow dress; DC can motor with rectifier for AC operation; sliding-shoe pickup **40 50**

18416 BUGS BUNNY & DAFFY DUCK: 1992, handcar; dark pink handcar body; Bugs Bunny in gray and white; Daffy in black and yellow; no lettering or number on frame; sliding-shoe pickup;

Exc Mt

DC can motor with rectifier for AC operation. As one of the earlier Warner Bros. character pieces from Lionel, this car was in demand and is now somewhat harder to find than most handcars. **85** **110**

18417 LIONEL: 1993, gang car; first Lionel rerelease of the postwar no. 50 gang car; black plastic frame similar to one on the motorized track maintenance car supports yellow superstructure with three black-painted workmen and a Type I Pullmor motor mounted on top of the frame behind the superstructure; unit reverses direction, and one workman rotates, when car strikes bumper; black "LIONEL" lettering and circle-L logo with "18417"; two fixed seated men in addition to the rotating one. The box label says two men pivot, but only one does. The curious thing about this car is not so much the action, which is similar to the Birney trolleys, but that the huge Pullmor motor can be supported on the tiny frame. **70** **90**

18419 LIONELVILLE: 1994, Birney-style trolley; four-wheel red body; gray roof; yellow lettering "LIONELVILLE" and "8419"; number also on illuminated number board insert; black plastic bumper covers; illuminated with silhouettes; reversing power pole; Type II integral motor truck; "BLT 1-94". See other mechanical notes under the 18404 entry. The catalog incorrectly states the trolley has a "DC motor." **75** **100**

18421 SYLVESTER & TWEETY: 1994, handcar; orange handcar body; Sylvester in black and white; Tweety in yellow and orange; no lettering or number on frame; DC can motor with rectifier for AC operation; sliding-shoe pickup. It is not clear why this handcar created less interest than the Bugs and Daffy car from two years before. **50** **60**

18422 SANTA & SNOWMAN: 1994, handcar; green handcar body; no lettering or number on car; Santa and bag in usual red and white; snowman with red scarf and black hat; DC can motor with rectifier for AC operation; sliding-shoe pickup. Shown in the 1994 Stocking Stuffers catalog. **35** **45**

18423 LIONEL ON-TRACK STEP VAN: 1995, on-track inspection vehicle; first release of inspection-type on-track vehicle similar to the 68 postwar favorite, but with a modern truck body; orange truck body with operating headlights and taillights; black "LIONEL TRACK TESTING EQUIPMENT" and Circle-L logo; body rides on a two-axle frame powered by a Type III can motor with rectifier, but no reverse unit; sliding-shoe pickup; the frame on this piece is basically the same as that of the handcar, but with a pilot and trailing axle added for stability; the added wheels are of very thin construction; the tires of the truck body fall between the drive wheels and the extension axles, giving the illusion that the truck is actually riding on the rails; the frame differs considerably from the original 68, where there were no drive wheels directly under the car body. But the functioning of the unit is the same, and this was the first appearance of this type of motorized unit since the 68 in 1961. Note LCCA made a reverse-color version of this unit in 1996 (52108). **40** **45**

18424 LIONEL ON-TRACK PICKUP TRUCK: 1995, on-track inspection vehicle; blue pickup truck body with operating headlights and taillights; black Circle-L logo (catalog pictures it orange, but it was made black); body rides on a two-axle frame powered by a Type III can motor with rectifier; no reverse unit; sliding-shoe pickup. Note LCCA made a reverse color version of this unit in 1996 (52107). See other comments under 18423. **40** **45**

18425 GOOFY & PLUTO: 1995, handcar; bright yellow handcar body; no lettering on frame; Goofy in blue and orange with yellow hat, pumping the handcrank alone while a smiling Pluto relaxes at the front of the car; DC can motor with rectifier for AC operation; sliding-shoe pickup. **40** **45**

Exc	Mt

18426 SANTA & SNOWMAN: 1995, handcar; dark red handcar body; no lettering or number on car; Santa and bag in usual red and white; snowman with red scarf and black hat; DC can motor with rectifier for AC operation; sliding-shoe pickup. Shown in the 1995 Stocking Stuffers catalog. This piece is identical to 18422 above except for the car body color. **40** **50**

18900 PENNSYLVANIA: 1988–89, 0-4-0 gas turbine; tuscan cab; gold lettering and number; gold stripe along lower flange of cab; "8900" on cab; black plastic truck frame with DC-only motor; white PRR logo on cab rear; front headlight; decorative bell; two-position forward/reverse switch; fixed couplers; "BLT 1-88". Part of 1989 Midnight Shift set 11708, but released first in an uncataloged Toys "R" Us set (also 11708) in 1988. **30** **40**

18910 CSX: 1993, 0-4-0 gas turbine switcher; unpainted blue cab; yellow "8910" and "CSX" lettering; plastic truck frame with DC can motor includes rectifier for AC operation; front headlight; decorative bell; decorative ladder; three-position electronic reverse; fixed couplers. One of three similar gas turbine switchers offered in 1993 as an inexpensive locomotive for small layouts. Still, the units boasted some upgrades since the previous switchers made by Fundimensions—notably the AC-DC operation and the three-position electronic reverse unit. The small cabs do not lend themselves to any more electronic gadgetry. With the traction tires, they are good runners. **35** **40**

18911 UNION PACIFIC: 1993, 0-4-0 gas turbine switcher; unpainted yellow cab; red "8911" and "UNION PACIFIC" lettering; plastic truck frame with DC can motor includes rectifier for AC operation; front headlight; decorative bell; decorative ladder; three-position electronic reverse; two fixed couplers. One of three similar gas turbine switchers offered in 1993. See other comments under 18910 above. **35** **40**

18912 AMTRAK: 1993, 0-4-0 gas turbine switcher; unpainted gray cab; blue "8912" and "AMTRAK" lettering; plastic truck frame with DC can motor includes rectifier for AC operation; front headlight; decorative bell; decorative ladder; three-position electronic reverse; fixed couplers. One of three similar gas turbine switchers offered in 1993. See comments under 18910 above. **35** **40**

Exc	Mt

18924 ILLINOIS CENTRAL: 1994–95, 0-4-0 gas turbine switcher; orange cab; black "8924" and "ILLINOIS CENTRAL" lettering, rather poorly applied; plastic truck frame with DC can motor includes rectifier for AC operation; front headlight; decorative bell; decorative ladder; three-position electronic reverse; fixed couplers. See other comments under 18910 above. **35** **40**

18925 DENVER & RIO GRANDE: 1994–95, 0-4-0 gas turbine switcher; black cab; orange "8925" and "DENVER & RIO GRANDE" lettering; plastic truck frame with DC can motor includes rectifier for AC operation; front headlight; decorative bell; decorative ladder; three-position electronic reverse; fixed couplers. See other comments under 18910 above. **35** **40**

18926 READING: 1994–95, 0-4-0 gas turbine switcher; green cab; white "8926" and "READING" lettering; plastic truck frame with DC can motor includes rectifier for AC operation; front headlight; decorative bell; decorative ladder; three-position electronic reverse; fixed couplers. See other comments under 18910 above. **35** **40**

18930 CRAYOLA: 1994–95, 0-4-0 gas turbine switcher; bright unpainted yellow plastic cab; green "Crayola" lettering; no number; green-painted plastic truck frame with DC can motor includes rectifier for AC operation; front headlight; decorative bell; decorative ladder; three-position electronic reverse; non-operating couplers. See other comments under 18910 above. This piece headed the 11813 Crayola set, which was uncataloged in 1994, but cataloged in 1995. **30** **35**

18508 and 18507 Canadian National Budd cars

THE BUDD CARS

In the early 1950s, railroads began to demand self-propelled passenger railcars for light rail service where their lines were not electrified. The Budd Company responded with an all-aluminum self-contained passenger car powered by two 275-horsepower diesel engines. These cars, formally named "Rail Diesel Cars" (RDCs), came to be known popularly as the "Budd Cars," after the company that manufactured them, and were very popular in short commuter service. They could still be seen in service on some Eastern lines into the late 1980s.

By 1956 postwar Lionel had released its own version of the Budd Car in Baltimore & Ohio markings. Though typically shorter than scale, these railcars were good sellers.

A long period followed during which no more of these attractive cars appeared. Then in 1977 Fundimensions introduced a Service Station Special set which was completely different from its predecessors: the firm had finally rereleased the handsome Budd diesel railcars in their original Baltimore & Ohio markings. The set had a powered baggage car and two dummy passenger coaches. The only minor disappointment with these items is that they do not have a horn as their postwar brethren did. Soon afterward, Fundimensions issued a powered passenger coach and a dummy baggage car. In 1978 Fundimensions issued another set, this time in colorful Amtrak markings. Again a long delay followed until Lionel LTI came out with a new set in Canadian National markings in 1992. The CN used Budd Cars in and around Montreal. These new units had MagneTraction, unlike the earlier Fundimensions models, but still lack the electronic horn. The CN set remains the only Budd set made in the Lionel LTI/LLC era.

The Budd railcars were very attractive, and they ran well because of the premium Type I separate motor and power truck. The silver paint on the modern cars is brighter than that of the Lionel originals and should have better wear characteristics.

BUDD CAR LISTINGS

Exc Mt

18506 CANADIAN NATIONAL: 1992, Budd Cars; set of two. See descriptions under 18507, 18508. Price for set. **250 300**

Exc Mt

18507 CANADIAN NATIONAL: 1992, non-powered Budd Car baggage unit; description matches 18508 following, except unit is non-powered, and number is "D203". Price for single unit, though it is not normally found for sale alone. Came as part of set 18506 with the powered coach (see next entry). **80 100**

18508 CANADIAN NATIONAL: 1992, Budd Car; powered coach unit; silver body; black lettering and number plate, which is "D202"; "Budd RDC" logo in black and red on plate at front side; vestibule ends decorated in CN green and yellow with red maple leaf on doors; detailed chains on vestibule doors; decorative horn; illuminated with window inserts; single Type I Pullmor motor with MagneTraction; three-position E-unit; die-cast trucks; operating couplers. Came as part of set 18506 with non-powered baggage car—see previous entries. Price for single unit, though not normally found alone. A follow-up set of two non-powered units was produced in 1993. These Budd Cars were the first ones made since 1980's Amtrak set from Fundimensions, and so far remain the only Budd Cars made by Lionel LTI or LLC. **175 220**

18510 CANADIAN NATIONAL: 1993, non-powered Budd Car coach; description matches 18508 above, except unit is not powered; number plate reads "D200". Price for single unit, though not normally found that way. Came as part of two-car set, no. 18512, with next entry. **90 120**

18511 CANADIAN NATIONAL: 1993, non-powered Budd Car coach; matches 18510 above, except number plate reads "D250". Price for single unit, though not normally found that way. Came as part of two-car set, no. 18512, with previous entry. **90 120**

18512 CANADIAN NATIONAL: 1993, set of two Budd Cars. See previous two entries. Price for set. **200 250**

CHAPTER 7

Automobile Carriers

The auto carrier is a modest and often overlooked member of Lionel's freight car line. There has never been exceptional collector interest in these cars, yet they continue to sell moderately well and provide a colorful alternative to long trains of boxcars or hoppers. The auto carriers, especially the new enclosed style introduced in 1990, represent a very affordable group of cars any level of collector can aspire to assemble on a budget. The cars have four desirable characteristics: affordable prices—as yet none of them is exceptionally rare or exorbitantly expensive; availability—none is very difficult to find, though some will prove a challenge; manageable quantity—a small number have been made in the modern era, relative to boxcars or flatcars; and accuracy—the enclosed long auto carrier is a superb model of the thousands of such cars to be seen everywhere on America's railroads today. The modern era auto carriers (both styles) even feature one other interesting attribute—they are not "remakes" of earlier postwar Lionel pieces. The postwar company never made auto carriers of this kind—their cars consisted only of flatcars with autos on top.

During the MPC/Fundimensions period prior to 1986, Lionel's versions of this piece consisted of the open-sided two- and three-tier model, which was a 14-inch flatcar surmounted by one or two "carrier" assemblies. Nine different models were made by MPC, with many variations of a few of them. However, the design of these cars (long, thin, high center of gravity, excess play in the wheelsets) caused them operational problems, such as tipping over on tight curves. After the changeover to LTI, the new firm made only one of this type of carrier for a long period: the 16208 Pennsylvania—which, oddly enough, was the only auto carrier of its type to actually come with autos. This unit featured a new wheelset mount that eliminated the tipping problem. Nine years later another single-level auto carrier car was made as a special for the LCAC (Lionel Collectors Association of Canada).

Partly as a result of these problems (and consequent disappointing sales) with the open auto carrier, and partly to follow the evolution of the real railroads toward enclosed auto carriers, Lionel in 1990 introduced an entirely new model to its production line. The new design features a cover for the top tier, screened sides, and sliding double doors at both ends. Rail lines had switched to this 89-foot-long type of auto carrier in the 1980s to better protect the cargo from vandalism, debris, and overgrown foliage along the right-of-way. Lionel's model is not longer or higher than the previous open style, but is about ½ inch wider and much heavier, making it a more stable freight car. Although somewhat foreshortened, it is nevertheless an excellent model of the prototype. Nor is it an easy model to manufacture, consisting of at least 33 individual parts, according to auto carrier expert Dick Johnson.

The main body of the car usually consists of unpainted plastic molded in the primary road color, with gray plastic side screens and either a silver or white-painted roof. The doors and ladders are provided loose in an envelope.

The first of the new style enclosed carriers was the 16214 Rio Grande in 1990. LOTS quickly picked up on the interest in the new car to release a special CSX version as its annual convention car in 1991. This is one of the hardest of the auto carriers to find; it also includes Standard O sprung trucks. From then until 1994, Lionel cataloged at least one auto carrier each year. The 16229 EL version came in a nice Erie Lackawanna Freight, which appeared in the 1991 Stocking Stuffers catalog. The special Chrysler Mopar set from 1994 included the 16260 Mopar version, and the ongoing Artrain series came out with a Conrail auto carrier in 1993. These last are not easy to find, but show up occasionally on for-sale lists, and are still reasonably priced. Most of the enclosed auto carriers have come on ASF trucks, though the more recent ones have graduated to the die-cast or Standard O trucks—and none have come with automobiles.

AUTOMOBILE CARRIER LISTINGS

Exc Mt

16208 PENNSYLVANIA: 1989, three-tier open-style auto carrier; tuscan body; white lettering; white PRR keystone logo on upper boards only; yellow "TRAILER TRAIN" across bottom of lower

16208 Pennsylvania auto carrier

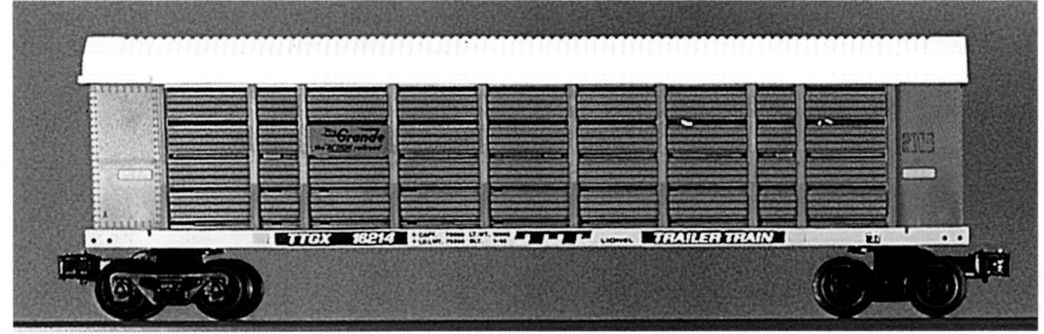

16214 Rio Grande two-tier auto carrier

	Exc	Mt

carrier; Type IIC or IID Symington-Wayne trucks fastened with metal rivets; "BLT 1-89"; new-style box; packaged with six HO scale die-cast autos (O will not fit); the only modern era auto carrier issued with autos. Autos are red, white, blue, silver, and black—three Chevrolet Corvettes and three Buick LeSabres. The Buicks have "LeSarre" misspelled on the bottom. **35 55**

16214 RIO GRANDE: 1990, two-tier enclosed auto carrier with screened sides and sliding double doors at both ends; painted white cover; orange plastic side supports, ends, ladders and doors; unpainted gray screened sides; mustard yellow "TRAILER TRAIN" flatcar with black and white lettering; black "RIO GRANDE" logo on boards; white, yellow, and black data on car ends; new-style ASF ride-control trucks with strong arm couplers fastened with metal rivets; "BLT 1-90". This was the first of Lionel's modern enclosed auto carriers.

(A) As described. **25 35**

(B) Factory error. No flatcar lettering on one side. W. Fuller Collection. **NRS**

16215 CONRAIL: 1990–91, two-tier enclosed auto carrier; screened sides, double doors at both ends; painted white cover; tuscan plastic side supports, ends, ladders, and doors; unpainted gray screened sides; yellow "TRAILER TRAIN" flatcar with black and white lettering; yellow and black data on ends; ASF trucks; "BLT 1-90". Cataloged in 1990, this car was not released until early 1991. **30 35**

16217 BURLINGTON NORTHERN: 1992, two-tier enclosed auto carrier, mustard yellow flatcar body with "TRAILER TRAIN" lettering in black and white; silver screened sides, double doors at both ends, painted silver cover, green plastic side supports, ends, ladders, and doors; green BN nameplate; ASF trucks; "BLT 1-92". **30 35**

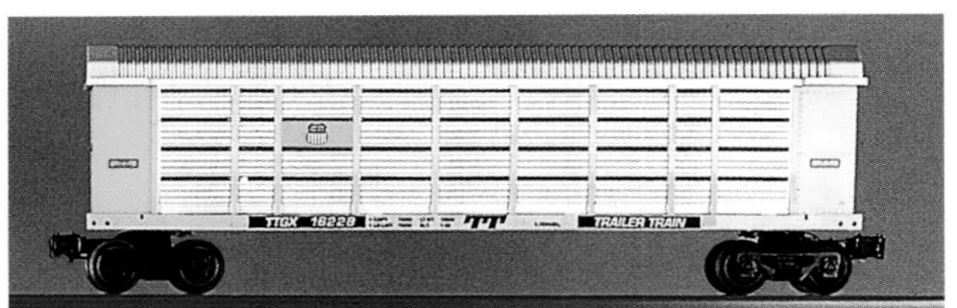

16228 UNION PACIFIC: 1992, two-tier enclosed auto carrier, screened sides, double doors at both ends, silver cover, yellow plastic side supports, ends, ladders and doors; unpainted light gray screened sides; red, white, and blue UP shield on marker plate in third row of screens; tan flatcar with black lettering and number; frame color is a different color than the main body; ASF trucks; "BLT 1-92". **30 35**

16229 ERIE-LACKAWANNA: 1991, uncataloged, two-tier enclosed auto carrier; double doors at both ends; white cover, yellow plastic side supports, ends, ladders, and doors, unpainted gray screened sides, maroon and white diamond "E" herald on nameplate; yellow flatcar frame with black and white "TRAILER TRAIN" lettering; ASF trucks; "BLT 1-91". This car came with the Erie-Lackawanna Freight set announced in the 1991 Stocking Stuffers brochure. **40 50**

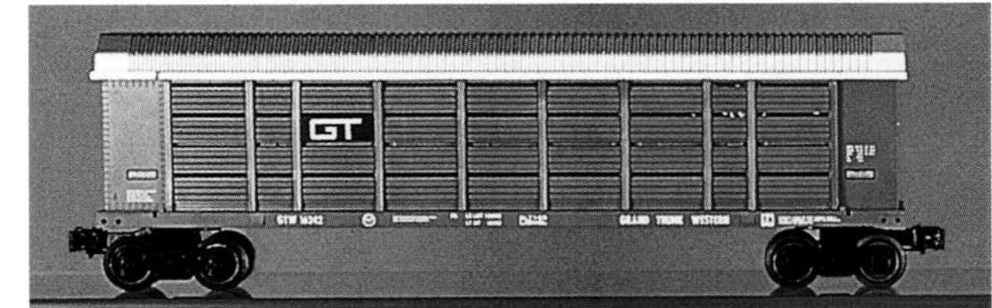

16242 GRAND TRUNK WESTERN: 1993, two-tier enclosed auto carrier; double doors at both ends; silver cover; light blue plastic side supports, ends, ladders, doors, and car frame, blue screened sides; white lettering and number on frame; white "GT" logo on darker blue marker plate on third row of slats; ASF trucks; "BLT 1-93". **35 40**

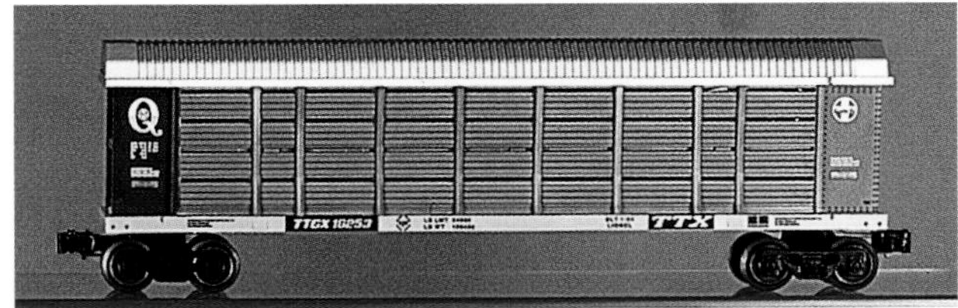

16253 SANTA FE: 1994, two-tier enclosed auto carrier, screened sides, double doors at both ends, silver cover, tuscan plastic side supports, ends, ladders, and doors, unpainted gray screened sides; mustard yellow car frame with black and white lettering; white Santa Fe "Q" logo to upper left and white cross herald to right; ASF trucks; "BLT 1-94". **30 35**

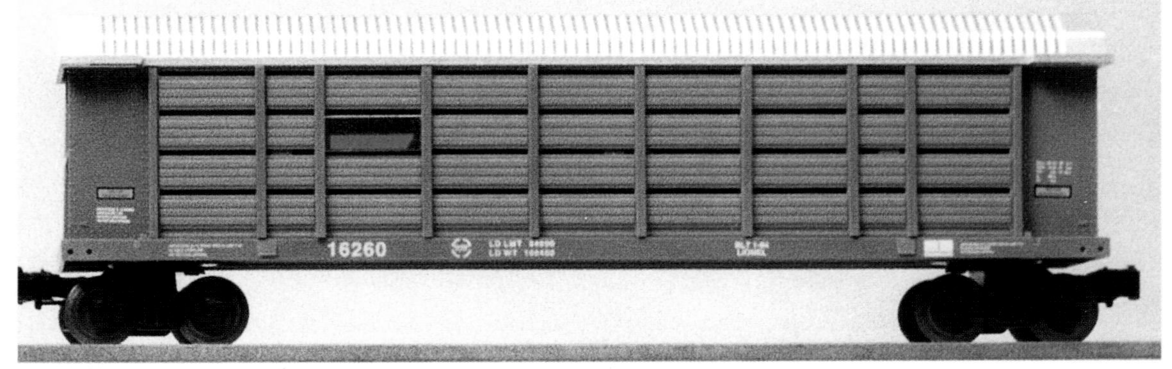

16260 Chrysler mopar two-tier auto carrier

	Exc	Mt

16260 CHRYSLER MOPAR: 1994, 1996, uncataloged, two-tier enclosed auto carrier, screened sides, double doors at both ends, silver cover, blue plastic side supports, ends, ladders, and doors, red and blue "MOPAR EXPRESS" on marker plate; white lettering on flatcar; ASF trucks; "BLT 1-94". Part of uncataloged 11818 Chrysler Mopar set. Unlike an earlier (1988) Chrysler set, this one included, logically enough, an auto carrier! Variation B appeared in the 11933 Dodge set from 1996, with a Dodge Motorsports nameplate.

	Exc	Mt
(A) Mopar version.	50	60
(B) Dodge version, in set 11933.	—	70

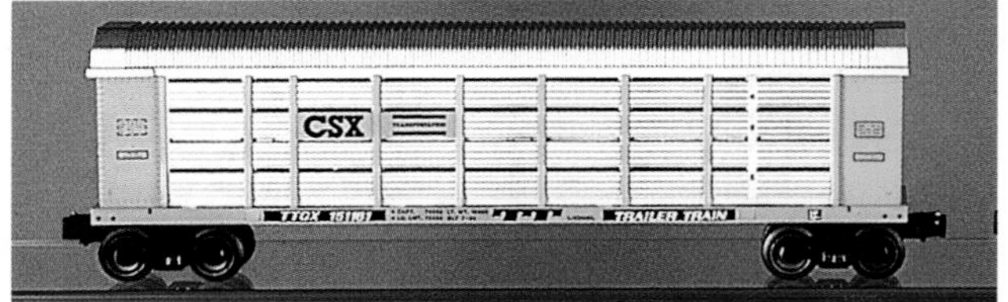

17890 CSX: 1991, uncataloged, two-tier enclosed auto carrier, 12th annual LOTS convention car released for 1991 Dayton convention; yellow flatcar body; silver-painted side slats and roof; white ends on roof; yellow side posts, ends, ladders, and doors; sliding double doors at each end; "CSX Transportation" in black on plate insert; white "TRAILER TRAIN and "TTGX 151161" on flatcar; small LOTS notation to upper right side; Standard O trucks—first auto carrier so equipped; "17890" is on box only, not on the car; "BLT 7-91"; 1350 made. Type VI box. Moderately hard to find. **90** **110**

52024 CONRAIL: 1993, uncataloged, two-tier enclosed auto carrier, 1993 Artrain special car; double doors at both ends; white cover, tuscan plastic side supports, ends, ladders, and doors; unpainted gray screened sides; white nameplate with "Artrain" in black; yellow flatcar frame with black lettering and Conrail logo; Standard O trucks; "BLT 1-93". Part of the continuing Artrain series. The car includes large Artrain endplates in addition to the normal nameplate. Limited run of 500. Moderately hard to find. **90** **110**

CHAPTER 8

Boxcars and Stock Cars

Ask a Lionel collector about his specialty, and chances are that person will tell you about some form or class of boxcar. The boxcar family has been the most prevalent style of freight car in Lionel's line since 1900, just as on the real railroads.

It is not hard to see why. In the first place, boxcars are fixed in the public mind as the "typical" rolling stock. A glance at any movie featuring railroads will usually reveal an abundance of boxcars. Great American railroad literature portrays courageous crewmen or unwitting passengers desperately battling the elements or their enemies in—or sometimes atop—the boxcars. Another important reason for the popularity of boxcars is practical: Color and graphics sell toy trains, and what better place to put your most colorful advertising than on the flat sides of a boxcar?

The many types of boxcars outsell all other types of tinplate rolling stock, combined. They have been absolutely crucial to the success of Lionel as a train manufacturer. The popularity of the boxcar to the train collectors and operators shows no signs of letting up even now as Lionel moves into its second century of train-making.

The only real trouble in collecting them lies in their sheer numbers and variety. Type or series collectors face a major challenge in acquiring all of a particular number series just because of the overwhelming quantity. The frenzy began in the postwar years with the famous 6464-series of "classic" boxcars. Thirty individual models of these cars were made, along with an almost endless list of variations within each. Fundimensions followed suit starting in 1970 with their 9200-, 9700-, and 9400-series boxcars. Lionel LTI and LLC have continued the tradition with classic boxcars in the 19200 and other five-digit series. Throw in the smaller boxcars, the stock cars, wood-sided boxcars, bunk and tool cars, the bullion-aquarium cars, and the Standard O cars, and the total very quickly becomes staggering.

Variation collectors have even more problems, because some of these cars have numbers of distinct variations in the body styles or molds, the frames, doors, colors, and so on. To make matters worse, some of the individual variations are very rare and nearly impossible to find. That, however, provides the "thrill of the chase" for dedicated collectors.

There has always been controversy about variation collecting. Why bother with variations if it is almost impossible to get them all? Some believe variations should not be stressed, while variation collectors naturally disagree. The resolution lies with individual interest. A hobbyist should have the opportunity to observe what interests him. Our Guides, as always, will strive to list as many of the pertinent details of a car as possible, including variations, since they may be of interest to varied groups of collectors. Many people are particularly curious about boxcar variations because of the heritage of research on the venerated postwar 6464 boxcars. Dr. Charles Weber, a noted expert on the 6464 cars, states it succinctly: "Whether one collects these variations or not, it is still interesting for many of us to learn about them. If a given collector isn't interested, that's his business, but many of us are. That's why they make chocolate and vanilla!"

We should also mention that variations of these trains come to light over long periods of time. On occasion an unknown variation will be discovered on a postwar piece even now. You are reading the story of the most recent Lionel production in this guide, meaning the number of confirmed variations is still relatively low. The reduced number of variations (relative to earlier decades) is also a result of improved quality control at Lionel and the more controllable manufacturing techniques used today.

So what good advice can be offered to the starting boxcar collector? The 19200-series of cars would probably be the best place to commence, if one is most inclined to the classic boxcar style. These cars are still readily available for the most part and, especially in the lower part of the series, still affordable. The latter half of the series includes the reissue 6464 car packs, in which exact duplicates of the original postwar cars were released in groups of three. These cars, individually or in the packs, command premium prices today, primarily because of the exceptional value and scarcity of the originals from the 1950s and '60s. On the other hand, they are a good way to acquire models of those postwar classics, without paying the exceptional prices that Like New/Excellent copies of the original 6464s now command.

One other good point about the 19200 series is the reintroduction of the fine rivet detail on the Type X boxcar body most often used for the 19200 cars. That is, these cars feature rivet detail on the sides not seen since the initial 6464-type cars made in the early 1950s. The first of the modern cars to use the new Type X body was the 19228 Cotton Belt. This was made possible by the pad printing technology in use now. The nicer of the boxcars in this series use the die-cast Standard O sprung trucks.

There are other values and satisfactions to be had in other types of boxcar collecting. For example, the bullion and aquarium cars, though individually expensive, are few enough that a full collection can be attained easily and on a budget. The same applies to the handsome bunk and tool car series. Modern Lionel has de-emphasized the shorter O27 boxcars in recent years, with the ever-increasing demand for scale and accuracy. But sharp-eyed collectors can still acquire the nice 6454-type short boxcars for very reasonable prices. They add fine color and class to the inexpensive O27 segment of Lionel's line. A few of them, such as ones supplied as specials for uncataloged sets, are sufficiently scarce now to yield a collecting challenge.

The Standard O boxcars, for those with somewhat deeper pockets, can be a good addition to the other Standard O freight cars on larger layouts.

The long stock cars are another good area to consider. Some believe them to be among the best-looking rolling stock produced by Lionel.

There are versions of the long and short classic boxcars, as well as the long and short stock cars, that are made as operating pieces. One will find bobbing animals peering out the sides or roofs, opening doors revealing men carrying loads, fish swimming around inside, or the famous horse and cattle cars that launch their vibrating cargo down trackside ramps and receive them back again. These have all been popular Lionel trains for five decades, and the modern era is no exception.

One final point: within each group of boxcars there is a wide variety of subseries on which a collector may focus. For example, there are the Toy Fair or Seasons Greetings series of classic boxcars, the Lionel 90th anniversary cars, or the "I Love" series of state cars. This chapter will discuss each of them in turn in the appropriate major subsection.

This Guide will divide the mass of boxcars into major groups, with a discussion preceding each group that identifies the unique aspects and the subseries within each. The categories are organized by the major style of boxcar body differences. The operating cars of each style are included within the major groups in proper numerical order.

Our regular readers might notice that one well-known category of boxcar—the wood-sided boxcars—isn't shown in the above table. That's because Lionel hasn't made any since 1986. So the interesting sets of wood-sided boxcars from the 1970s—especially the Tobacco Road series and the Bicentennial set—will have to remain the most recent examples of this handsome boxcar. You will find them in our 1991 *Guide*.

BULLION AND AQUARIUM CARS

We'll start the chapter with two fun but highly unlikely boxcar types, which are almost the antithesis of the realistic, true-to-life classic boxcars.

The Fort Knox bullion car and the Traveling Aquarium car were two of the most beloved eccentric boxcars made by postwar Lionel. Both were met initially with derision by collectors, who were only to find later that the objects of their derision had become desirable collectors' items. These fanciful cars share another common trait—almost identical bodies that are boxcars only in name. The sides each have two clear plastic panels, "revealed" by imitation fold-up curtains molded into the plastic. There are eight access "hatches" on the roof and dime-size "ventilation grates" on the ends. In the case of the aquarium cars the grates are simply open. These car bodies actually challenge the classic boxcars with their level of detail—superb rivet patterns, ladders, grab rails, and reporting plates.

The center panel of the bullion car—between the large windows—is slightly different from that of the aquarium car. On the bullion (also known as "mint") cars one finds a large "safe door" with handle and combination lock molded in. The area on the aquarium car simply has the Lionel circle-L logo molded into it. The windows in both types of cars are a clear plastic piece, clear and flat in the mint cars, but presenting a "wavy" appearance in the aquarium cars.

One other exterior difference is the presence of a coin slot in the roof of the mint car. Apparently postwar Lionel thought some youngsters might use it as a piggybank.

BULLION CARS

Postwar Lionel made only one bullion car, the 6445 Fort Knox. Lionel Fundimensions reintroduced it in 1979 in a colorful Southern Pacific Limited set. The great success of that release prompted a quick succession of other mint cars in the early 1980s. Each was named for an existing or past U.S. mint, such as San Francisco, Denver, or Carson City. As time went on, Lionel had to reach for increasingly obscure mint locations for the car, and so production naturally slowed from its earlier pace. In 1987 the company spurred interest in the bullion car set with a gold-painted GG-1 and caboose—allowing operators to run a true "money train." There were seven regular-production mint cars made prior to 1986, and one special production model for the TCA. All the regular production cars featured the Standard O sprung trucks. The cars can come with either a gold or silver ingot load, which is a single piece inside the car. The ingot loads are easily available in the parts market, so any difference is not considered a variation of any value.

Perhaps as a result of the lack of available mint names, Lionel LTI made only two mint cars during the period covered by this volume. Nonetheless, with their sprung metal trucks and stamped-metal frames, the mint cars have a certain quality element to them. Despite the opinions of the "true-to-life" collectors, these colorful cars are so impossibly whimsical that they have developed an appeal all their own.

AQUARIUM CARS

Though similar externally to the mint car, the entrails of the aquarium cars are entirely different. The operating aquarium cars have fairly complex internal mechanisms. They wind a film painted with scenes of the underwater world around a set of spools to create the illusion of fish swimming in a tank as the car moves. Sometimes there is a background scene/insert so that it appears the fish are swimming in front of a fixed underwater setting. The aquarium car is lighted to improve the visibility of this intriguing display.

As with the mint car, postwar Lionel produced only one aquarium car in all of the postwar years, the 3435 from 1959–62. Fundimensions also produced only one—the 9308 reissue in 1981. The 9308 is a very hard item to obtain today, despite being cataloged all the way until 1984. Modern Lionel, perhaps sensing a greater interest in this unusual car, has far exceeded that output, though it did not start until 1995.

An important reason for the sudden increase in production was a significant change in the operating mechanism that Lionel LTI implemented in 1995 for its 16681 car. The previous two releases had a noisy operating motor to drive the spools. It was a small can motor mounted to a special metal frame that was unique to anything else in Lionel's line. As such it was especially costly to make. The new model in the 16681 employed a gear mechanism attached to the wheel axle to drive the spool without a motor. This much simpler design meant both reduced costs for Lionel and a consequently lower price to the buyer. There's always a catch, though—the simpler design meant the underwater scene would not move unless the car was in motion. This doesn't seem to have influenced interest significantly, and the newer models are much cheaper than the older motorized cars.

BULLION AND AQUARIUM CAR LISTINGS

Exc Mt

16681 ANIMATED AQUARIUM CAR: 1995, operating aquarium car; gold body; black lettering "LIONELVILLE UNDERSEA DISPLAY" at center; illuminated; gear mechanism attached to axle drives film with sea creatures and underwater scenes around spools inside car; mechanism differs from older aquarium car designs in not being motorized; ASF trucks. First new aquarium car issue since 1981. Inexpensive new action mechanism, similar to the one in the animated gondolas, was a major change from earlier models, and this car is less expensive as a result—desirable now, however, because of rekindled interest in aquarium cars. **70 90**

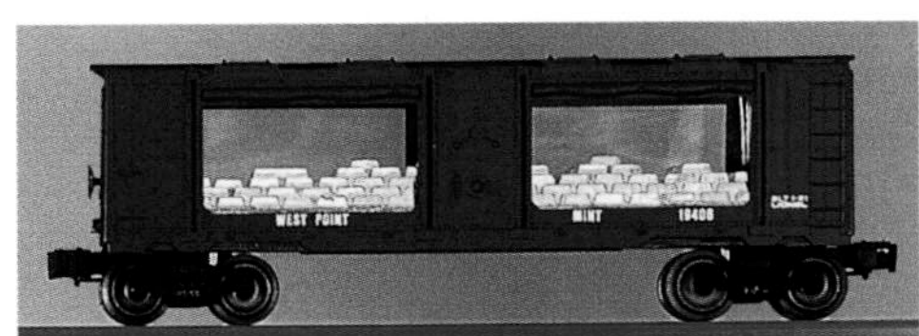

19406 WEST POINT MINT: 1991, bullion car; uncataloged; dark blue body; gold lettering and number; gold ingot load; coin slot; wavy-style windows were used here instead of the clear plastic types used previously; Standard O trucks; "BLT 1-91". Shown in the 1991 Stocking Stuffers brochure. **50 70**

Exc Mt

19419 CHARLOTTE MINT: 1993, bullion car; uncataloged; dark green body; silver lettering and number; catalog shows gold lettering; gold ingot load; coin slot; Standard O trucks; "BLT 1-93". Shown in the 1993 Stocking Stuffers brochure. **30 40**

BUNK AND TOOL CARS

In 1983 Lionel produced a surprise for collectors in the form of a totally new piece of rolling stock—the bunk car. In the real railroading world, bunk cars provide overnight housing to track gangs working on long-term repair jobs. Usually the bunk car was a converted boxcar, and Lionel followed the prototype quite well.

The Lionel bunk car uses the end and roof pieces from the wood-sided reefer series. The sides and bottom are traceable to the 9800-style reefer cars, but have been heavily modified. It retains the prominent underside air tanks from the reefers, but the wood slats have been turned vertically on the bunk car instead of horizontally as on the reefers. Four detailed windows were added, along with a small entrance door centered on the sides where the plug door was on the reefers. A third small ladder appeared next to the door, along with marker plates. Provision was made for small jewel lights on both sides of the car, and a hole was cut in the roof for a smokestack. The result of all these modifications was a car remarkably faithful to its prototype.

A healthy number of bunk cars appeared in the later 1980s, and the modern company has continued the sequence, a little more irregularly, into the 1990s. Some have come as part of uncataloged or limited-edition sets, and the later ones sport smoke units. All but the first few were illuminated, and like the lighted cabooses, the windows have a translucent plastic insert to diffuse the light. In 1990 Lionel upgraded the car with the nice 19656 Milwaukee Road—equipping it with a smoke unit and the handsome Standard O sprung metal trucks.

In 1986, during the company's ill-fated move to Mexico, Fundimensions created one last surprise for its faithful followers. A variation of the bunk car appeared in a B&O Freight set that year. Lionel called it a tool car. They had modified the sides of the bunk car by replacing the four square windows with two larger rectangular ones. New doors were molded into the car ends, while the marker lights and smokestack of the bunk car were eliminated. The entrance doors in the sides had cutouts punched so that the interior light would shine through, and the molded-in ladders were changed and rearranged.

These cars pose a difficult decorating challenge for the Lionel experts at the factory—the vertical wood slats make the lettering hard to apply and fuzzy to read.

Both the bunk and tool cars have met with warm reception from Lionel collectors. Uncataloged ones have been made for the

16801 Lionel Railroader Club bunk car

train clubs, including an extremely scarce pair for the Nassau Lionel Operating Engineers in 1991. Lionel also cleverly marketed matching pairs of bunk and tool cars in popular roadnames like Santa Fe, Jersey Central, and Amtrak.

All told, they are an excellent collecting choice for beginners and veterans alike.

BUNK AND TOOL CAR LISTINGS

Exc Mt

8391A LONG ISLAND: 1991, bunk car; uncataloged; third in a special series made for the Nassau Operating Engineers club in Levittown, New York; orange body; dark gray roof and ends; black LIRR lettering and "Dashing Dan" "Route of the Dashing Commuter" logo; illuminated; plastic arch-bar trucks; "BLT 6-91". Matches 8391B below—only 51 sets made. These matching cars are based on standard Lionel bunk/tool car bodies (using the 19654-5 Amtrak and 19652-3 Jersey Central) redecorated by PVP. The number is not the usual five-digit Lionel number because the cars were redecorated. The lettering on this car is somewhat hard to read. **— NRS**

8391B LONG ISLAND: 1991, tool car; uncataloged; matches 8391A—see details above. Sold in a set with 8391A. **— NRS**

16701 SOUTHERN: 1987, tool car; uncataloged; green sides; black roof and ends; gold Southern lettering and circular logo; unlighted, but has translucent window inserts; Standard O trucks. Part of 11704 Southern Freight Runner Service Station Special set. **50 65**

16702 AMTRAK: 1992, bunk car; uncataloged; orange body; light gray roof and ends; black lettering; illuminated; ASF trucks; "BLT 1-92". A near duplicate of the 19654 car from 1989. Part of 11723 Amtrak Work Train set. This car was initially listed in 1991 as part of the regularly cataloged 11723 Amtrak "Maintenance Train" set. However, the set was not made as shown there, but as described later in the 1992 Stocking Stuffer brochure—using the same number but now called the Amtrak "Work Train" set. The revised set had different rolling stock, all marked with 92 built dates. **30 35**

Exc Mt

16703 NEW YORK CENTRAL: 1992, tool car; gray body; black lettering; NYC oval logo to right side; illuminated with translucent window inserts; ASF trucks; "BLT 1-92". **35 40**

16801 LIONEL RAILROADER CLUB: 1988, bunk car; uncataloged; sixth annual special from the LRRC; dark blue-green body; yellow lettering; LRRC steam engine logo to right side; "INSIDE TRACK" logo to left; illuminated; Symington-Wayne trucks; "BLT 2-88". Came in Type VI box. **35 45**

16802 LIONEL RAILROADER CLUB: 1989, tool car; uncataloged; seventh annual special issue from the LRRC; dark blue-green body; yellow lettering; LRRC steam engine logo at right center; illuminated; plastic arch-bar trucks, a variation from earlier LRRC cars, which used Symington-Wayne trucks; "BLT 1-89". Came in Type VI box. Intended as a match for 16801. **40 50**

19651 AT & SF: 1987, tool car; medium gray body; black lettering; translucent window and door inserts; illuminated; plastic arch-bar trucks; "BLT 1-88". **25 30**

19652 JERSEY CENTRAL: 1988, bunk car; maroon body; white lettering, number, and Jersey Central Liberty logo; illuminated with translucent window inserts; plastic arch-bar trucks; "BLT 1-88". Matches 19653. Note that the red-maroon color of this car is difficult to capture accurately in photos. **20 25**

16802 Lionel Railroader Club tool car

Exc Mt

19653 JERSEY CENTRAL: 1988, tool car; maroon body; white lettering, number, and Jersey Central Liberty logo; illuminated with translucent window inserts; plastic arch-bar trucks; "BLT 1-88". Matches 19652. Note that the red-maroon color of this car is difficult to capture accurately in photos. **20 25**

19654 AMTRAK: 1989, bunk car; orange body; black lettering; illuminated with translucent window inserts; plastic arch-bar trucks; "BLT 1-89". Match for 19655. **25 30**

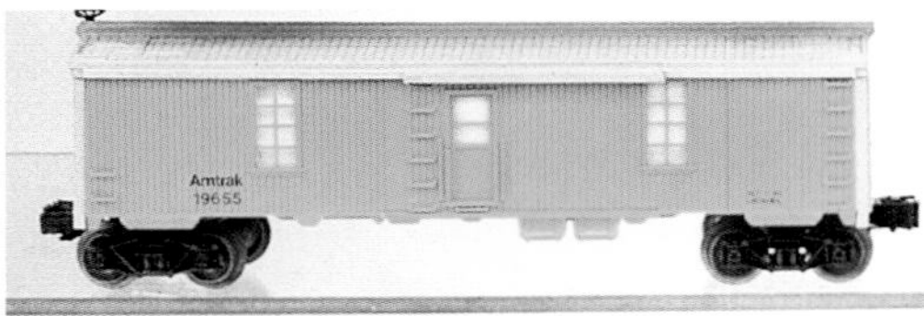

19655 AMTRAK: 1990–91, tool car; orange body; gray roof and ends; black lettering; illuminated with translucent window inserts; plastic arch-bar trucks; "BLT 1-90". Intended as a match for the 19654, but this car is a lighter orange than the 19654. **25 30**

19656 MILWAUKEE ROAD: 1990, bunk car with smoke; orange body; maroon roof and ends; black lettering and rectangular Milwaukee Road herald between two right-hand windows; illuminated with translucent window inserts; smoke unit—first bunk car so equipped; Standard O trucks—also the first bunk car so equipped—car underside slightly modified to accept these trucks; "BLT 1-90". This was among the first Lionel pieces to accomplish a power pickup on the Standard O sprung trucks—using a snap-on roller pickup and copper ground strip. **45 55**

19657 WABASH: 1992, bunk car with smoke; dark blue sides; gray roof; white lettering and Wabash flag to right side; illuminated with translucent window inserts; smoke unit; Standard O trucks; "BLT 1-92". Announced in the 1991 catalog but not made until 1992. **45 55**

19658 NORFOLK & WESTERN: 1991, tool car; green sides; silver roof and ends; white lettering; N&W circle logo on left side; illuminated with translucent window inserts; arch-bar trucks; "BLT 1-91." **25 30**

86009 CANADIAN NATIONAL GREAT LAKES REGION: 1986, bunk car; uncataloged; eighth annual commemorative car for the Lionel Collectors Association of Canada (LCAC); red sides; white lettering; LCAC circle logo; not lighted; plastic arch-bar trucks; "BUILT LCAC". This is a 5727 Marines bunk car stripped and redecorated by PVP/NBT (designator "706-1420"). 160 made. Difficult to find. **100 130**

CLASSIC (6464-STYLE) BOXCARS

Of all the many types of Lionel rolling stock, none is more venerated than the classic boxcar. The boxcar dominates the field of Lionel freight pieces, just as it does on the real railroads, and for more than 70 years it has formed the foundation of the Lionel hobby. Since World War II many millions of boxcars have been produced at Lionel's factories and are found in nearly every freight set Lionel has made.

For the purposes of this volume, the term "classic" is used to identify the standard 10¼-inch-long boxcar which traces its heritage to the revered 6464-series cars of the postwar era. The term also helps to differentiate it from the other boxcar types shown in the other subsections of this chapter, which use noticeably different bodies—the Standard O, Hi-Cube, bunk and tool, O27, stock, bullion/aquarium, and waffle-style cars. While these are all admittedly boxcars in the general sense, they are of a clearly separate ancestry from that of the 6464-type boxcars. Some in fact (the Standard O, Hi-Cube, bunk/tool, and waffle cars) have no postwar origin at all. They are boxcars of a strictly modern design, all appearing in the Lionel line after 1970.

The 6464 boxcars may well be the most studied and collectable model trains in Lionel's history. That intense interest carried through into the modern era as Fundimensions produced hundreds of classic-style boxcars, with many of them achieving a collector status rivaling that of the postwar cars. There are "9200"-series and "9400"-series and "9700"-series collectors of the Fundimensions cars, just as there are postwar 6464-series devotees. Lionel LTI and LLC have continued the tradition, with their boxcars from the "Famous Name" series.

There has been no indication that interest in boxcars is on the wane. In fact, the modern company continued to capitalize on the 6464 "mystique" by releasing remakes of the postwar cars, in three-packs, beginning in 1993. These sets have generated considerable interest, not the least because they enable modern collectors to obtain classic boxcars (they are decorated identically to the originals) without paying the exceptional premiums usually applied today to the 1950s versions. This has served to both allow modern operators to safely run these great boxcars on their layouts without subjecting their originals to the wear and tear, and to perhaps apply a little needed price restraint on the originals as well.

The number series in which the modern classic boxcars can be found are as follows:

16200-series	Boxcars (Traditional Line)
16600- and 16700-series	Operating boxcars (Traditional)
19200-series	Boxcars (Famous Name series)
19800-series	Operating boxcars
19900-series	Special Series classic boxcars
26200, 29200-series	Boxcars ("Classic" and "Heritage") (1997 and later)
52000- and 52100-series	Special production (clubs, etc.)

There are a few classic-type boxcars that do not fall into the group number sequences listed above. Those renegades are listed in numerical order within this subsection.

OPERATING BOXCARS

Many of the boxcars described here have operating mechanisms. There are a great variety of them. One major type, listed simply as an **operating boxcar,** has a plunger fixed to the metal frame of the boxcar chassis. When the plunger is activated by the magnet in an operating track, the side door opens to reveal a man apparently ready to unload something such as a box or a mailbag. The most recognized version of this car is the Post Office car, which began its career as the 9301 in 1972, and did not vanish from the line until 1985. Actually there are two types of figures used in these cars, one plain and one with a magnet to which the box or bag sticks. Depending on the strength of the magnet, it sometimes takes a good voltage to dislodge the sack from the man!

These operating boxcars are always a crowd-pleaser.

1987	19805	Santa Fe
1988	19809	Erie Lackawanna
1991	19816	Madison Hardware, uncataloged
1994	16679	U.S. Mail
1994	16687	U.S. Mail
1995	19821	Union Pacific

The **operating ice car** is another intriguing action piece. In this case the body is modified rather extensively to cut a hatch in the roof near one end. This hatch is spring loaded so that a plastic "ice" cube pushed onto it from a trackside icing station will fall into the car. The cubes are removed from the receiving bin inside the car via a large opening panel in the side. These cars are of course meant to be used with Lionel's operating ice station, which has a man on an elevated platform who sweeps the ice cubes into the car. It's meant to be reminiscent of the manner in which old-time boxcars were kept cool with ice cubes, prior to the days of air-conditioning. Although the ice cars are prototypically refrigerator cars, Lionel has based its ice car on the classic-boxcar body style, and so they are listed in this section of our book. There are actually no operating mechanisms or motors in the ice car itself—the motorized action occurs on the icing station. A unique feature of the ice cars is that they sport excellent rivet column details on the sides, like the best of the boxcars.

There was an unexplained drought in production of the operating ice car in the early modern era, even though it had been a popular postwar accessory. Only one, the 6700 PFE and its accompanying 2306 ice station, had been made during the whole Fundimensions period. Lionel LTI may have sensed a pent-up demand and released the 19803 Reading ice car in 1987, followed by quite a few others since then.

A new model of the icing station (12703) also appeared in 1988.

1987	19803	Reading
1988	19808	New York Central
1989	19813	Northern Pacific
1994	19817	Virginian
1994	19823	Burlington
1994	52067	Burlington (LOTS) uncataloged

The **operating milk car** is among the all-time action favorites of Lionel operators. The interior of the car has a mechanism as mechanically complex as anything Lionel puts inside its rolling stock. Weighted metal milk cans are stored on a ramp inside. They then drop down and are turned upright in front of a milkman figure. The man then pushes the can out onto a trackside platform and retreats back inside the car to retrieve the next can.

The milk car is a unique creation in the Lionel line. Logically, it should be listed as a refrigerator car, but Lionel's model is a hybrid. It has a roof similar to the wood-sided reefers but without a brakewheel and with a small hatch cut into it so the operator can reload the milk cans. The sides are very much boxcar style, with superb rivet detail like that on the best of the boxcars. The door unit is unique to the milk cars—a split design that opens quickly when the man pushes on them. Even the wheelsets on the milk cars are special—they use the sliding-shoe type of postwar bar-end trucks for power pickup from a UCS track. This allows it to be operated only when the UCS control button is pressed.

The milk car had not appeared at all in the modern era until the 9220 Borden car in 1983. The 19802 Carnation car followed in 1987. Given the long wait for production and the interest in the postwar cars, these pieces were good sellers and quite valuable now.

1987	19802	Carnation
1988	19810	Bosco
1994	19818	Dairymen's League
1994	52045	Penn Dutch (TCA) uncataloged

Yet another operating boxcar type is the **brakeman car.** This one was a surprise appearance in 1990 after an absence of 32 years from the Lionel catalogs. The little man rides on top here, but spends a lot of time on his stomach dodging telltales, which are placed ostensibly to warn him of an upcoming low overhang. The mechanism on the car is similar to that of the giraffe stock cars described later in this chapter—it includes a trip lever under the car activated by a mechanism fixed next to the track near the telltale poles. And as with the giraffe cars, the operator should be aware of its placement, since larger rolling stock can get tangled in the telltales and trackside trips. (Not to mention avoiding running the man under real low overhangs!) Two of these cars have been made in the 1990s: the 19811 Monon in 1990 and the 19815 Delaware & Hudson in 1992.

In the early 1990s, Lionel adapted its classic boxcar style (mainly using the less-expensive 9700 body mold) to reproduce the action it had previously used only on the short O27 boxcars—the **animated boxcar.** In this case a large hole—or two—was cut into the roof to allow the figure of an animal (or later, cartoon characters and other odd passengers like witches, aliens, and ostriches!) to rise up and down as the car rolls around the tracks. This is done with a simple gear and cam assembly attached to the wheel axles. The action of these cars is virtually identical to that of the shorter boxcars described later in this chapter.

There is another (so far unique) operating boxcar based on the design of the shorter O27 models. This is the **cop-and-hobo car.** Prior to the 1990s, this fascinating piece had used only the less expensive O27 boxcar as its basis. But in 1995 a new model, the 16705 C&O, converted the longer 9700-type regular boxcar to the use. In this case a spring-loaded platform extends above the car. On it a magnet keeps the figure of a cop—or a hobo—in place until the car runs under a bridge assembly, when the figure on the car runs up onto the bridge and pushes the other figure back onto the car. The action provides many hours of fun, but once again, placement of the bridge over the trains must be carefully chosen so as not to interfere with other things.

The car roof has two C-shaped slots cut into it to accommodate the platform. To date, the 16705 is the only long cop-and-hobo car made using the classic boxcar. There are two others that used the smaller O27 boxcar bodies.

In 1995 and 1996 the new Lionel LLC, hard on its program of rereleasing postwar classics, brought out the **missile-firing boxcar** (16710) and the red exploding boxcar (16719). The former car resembles the Electric Generator Car, but has a hinged split roof that opens and permits the missile launcher mechanism to rise up and fire the projectile. The exploding boxcar closely resembles the Classic boxcar, but with sealed doors and a pin down through the roof. Its sides and roof are in individual sections, which explode dramatically apart when the arming pin is removed and the car is struck by a missile. The energy for this is provided by a mousetrap-like spring-loaded mechanism inside. The exploding boxcar will be found in our companion Guide for the post-1996 period.

There are also an ever-expanding group of classic boxcars to which Lionel simply adds some of its electronic gadgetry to form another type of "operating" boxcar. One version includes a RailSounds circuit card inside, replaying digital recordings of such things as the chugs of a steam engine, whistles and horns, the rumble of the diesel motors, releasing brakes, and a myriad of other sounds. These have been popular items, allowing Lionel operators to activate the sounds as the train moves around the track, not just in a stationary trackside building. However, the cost of the new electronics is also reflected in the prices.

The boxcar body itself is otherwise standard.

Another category is the boxcars with End-of-Train Devices (abbreviated EOT, or sometimes ETD) mounted to the rear. These small LED-diode devices are very accurate simulations of the lights used on modern railroads to take the place of the caboose.

CLASSIC BOXCAR BODY STYLES

Lionel's modern era boxcar production is made up of five principal body types.

The body type designations go by a series of Roman numerals that were first devised for the postwar cars. **Types I through IV** refer to postwar production (see *Greenberg's Guide to Lionel Trains, 1945–1969*). The changes in the types revolved mostly around the progressive reduction in the number of rivets and rivet patterns found on the sides. **Types V through VIII** carried this process to its completion during the chaotic period of the early Fundimensions era (1970–72) as the rivets were almost entirely removed from the sides, leaving them completely smooth—a change made for the benefit of the decorating process. Some of the body types (there are subcategories within the earlier ones) also had variations in the door guides (see next section).

The first in our "current models," which is identified as **Type IX,** consists of smooth sides with a complete absence of rivet columns along the sides except at the extreme top and bottom. It has one end plate that reads "9700 / SERIES" and another reading "LIONEL". This car body first appeared in late 1972 and was the principal boxcar type made by Lionel for the next 19 years. By 1991 the decorating processes had advanced sufficiently to allow the company to restore the wonderful rivet detail and still apply intricate lettering and logos. The new pad printing and electrocal techniques enabled this change. The **Type Xa** body style debuted in 1991 on the 19228 Cotton Belt boxcar, and reversed more than 30 years of trends in reducing the molded detail on the cars. Full columns of rivets were restored to the sides of the boxcar. When Lionel released the 6464-type cars in the revived Girls' Set in 1991, it added metal door guides to the car and removed the "9700 SERIES" from the one end plate, leaving it blank. This was the **Type X** body style. Most of the classic boxcars in the 19200-series after this, including all of the 6464 three-packs, use this body style, with full rivets, metal chassis, metal door guides, and the Standard O sprung trucks—in other words, all the premium features.

Shortly after the new style appeared, around 1992–93, the company realized that its classic boxcars remained expensive to make and began an effort to create a cheaper model that retained the appeal of the 6464-style cars. It came up with a car that uses a plastic frame (previous boxcars of this type use a stamped sheet-metal chassis) into which the body snaps with no screws—and a side design that again had no rivets to interfere with the printing process. These changes were designed to reduce the assembly time—and hence cost—yet allow the company to use the popular 6464-type cars in even the lower-end sets. As such this new model began to supplant the short O27 boxcars in many sets. Lionel refers to it as a **"9700" style boxcar**—we will refer to it as the **Type XI** body type, because the original 9700-series boxcars Lionel made in the 1970s were actually different body molds than this. The endplates were entirely blank on the Type XI body. Lionel also changed the fully riveted body so that it too could use the plastic frame—by closing up the screw and tab holes on the ends and blanking out the end plates. This became the Type XII body style.

The differences in the five principal body types are described in the table below and in the accompanying figure.

	Rivet Columns	Chassis and Attachment	Endplates	Door Guides
Type IX 1972–	None*	Sheet metal w/ screw and tabs	1 "Lionel" 1 "9700"	Plastic/hooks
Type Xa 1991–	Full detail	Sheet metal w/ screw and tabs	1 "Lionel" 1 "9700"	Plastic/hooks
Type X 1991–	Full detail	Sheet metal w/ screw and tabs	1 "Lionel" 1 blank	Metal
Type XI 1993–	None*	Detailed plastic snap-in	Both blank	Plastic/ hooks
Type XII 1993–	Full detail	Detailed plastic snap-in	Both blank	Plastic/ hooks

* To be precise, there is one rivet at the bottom of each column and two at the top of each column of rivets on the side body. There are for all intents and purposes no rivet columns on these bodies, but these several individual rivets, which generally don't interfere with the decorating process, are visible on close examination.

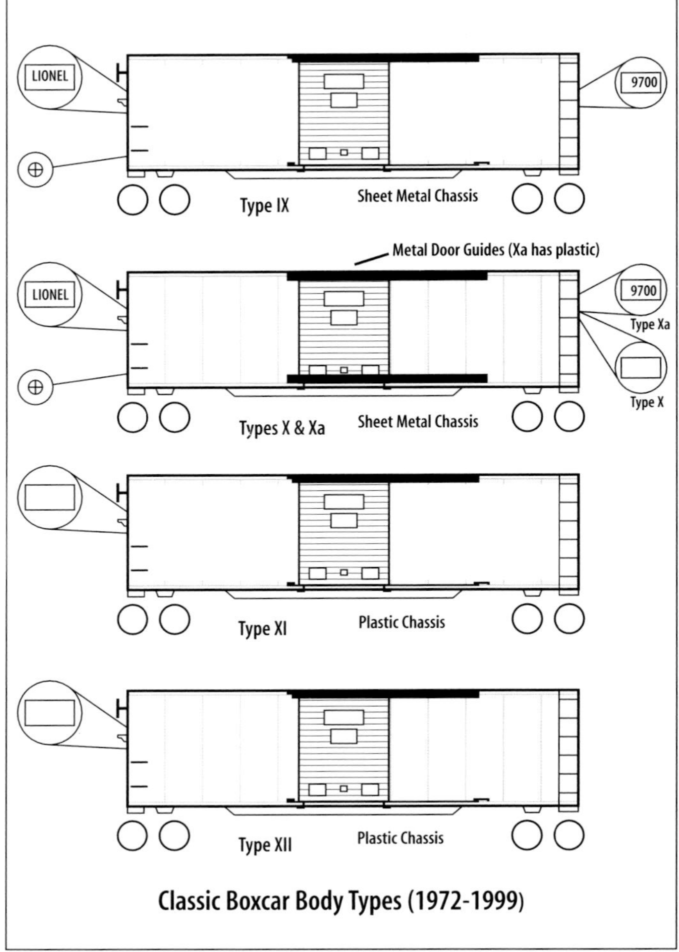

Classic Boxcar Body Types (1972-1999)

It should also be noted that some other Lionel guides do not acknowledge the modern-era body variations shown here. But the changes are very obvious!

In late 1999 Lionel designed a brand-new solid die-cast chassis for use on the Type X body. The chassis is heavier and has many molded-in details as compared to the older stamped-metal version. This should be considered yet another major body style

Note too that the above body descriptions are for the non-operating boxcars—the operating ones discussed earlier all involve some modification to the basic boxcar body. They could technically be called additional body styles, but we simply refer to them as a particular operating car variety.

DOOR GUIDES AND DOOR STYLE

Lionel uses three basic types of door guides in its classic boxcars. Type I features two metal guides at top and bottom, fastened to the car with rivets. This is the same as the postwar technique. It appears frequently today, most notably on the 6464-boxcar reissues. The Type II guides appeared only briefly in some of the early Fundimensions boxcars of the 1970s. They were simply plastic guides instead of metal, and they snapped into the same rivet holes. Type III is the common modern version; it uses a plastic top door guide, while the lower edge of the door has two plastic hook extensions that slide back and forth on a sill molded into the car body. The introduction of this guide in about 1972 corresponds to the change between the Type VII and VIII boxcar body styles, as described earlier. A nice feature about the operating boxcars (in which a man appears automatically when the door opens) is that the upper door guide on the car is metal.

After a turbulent period during the postwar years when many variations were produced, the boxcar doors themselves have settled into a single style during all of the modern era—a style that has five marker plates neatly aligned down the face of the door. These plates will sometimes have small print added to them in a very realistic fashion.

FRAME TYPES

Modern classic boxcars have two principal types of chassis (frames). The first is a simple stamped sheet-metal plate. It is attached to the car body by means of tabs at one end and a single (usually Phillips) screw through the other, which secures to a small metal tab. This sheet-metal frame has several minor variations, stamped with a 6464 number in one case and at other times simply with the Lionel address at Mt. Clemens or Chesterfield, Michigan. The electronics such as RailSounds or the End-of-Train light require a hole through the frame for the wires.

The second frame, a plastic one, appeared early in the 1990s. It was associated with the change to the Type XI and XII bodies and a general reduction in weight and cost to make the classic boxcars. This frame features a pattern of simulated crossed beams on the bottom. It secures to the main body simply by snapping in—no screws are involved. In recent years Lionel has sometimes taken to restoring weight to these cars by simply fastening a flat metal plate inside.

LEFT AND RIGHT SIDES

Several of these boxcars have a distinct "left" and "right" side, with graphics or lettering switching position (relative to the door or the brakewheel) when looked at from either side. Graphics often switch sides on double-door boxcars, with their off-center doors, depending on where the larger flat area is. Other classic boxcars, in particular the CP Rail with its black and white "Multimark" design, might have decoration oriented toward the brakewheel side.

BODY MOLD COLORS

The phrase "body mold" refers to the color of plastic used for the main boxcar body, whether painted or not. In the early Fundimensions years, Lionel used plastic in the form of solid pellets. Since it was hard to control the color, odd combinations sometimes resulted. A car painted brown might have been molded in orange plastic one time, and brown plastic another. To compound matters, the doors might have been molded in yet another color. Sometime in 1975–76 Fundimensions switched to a liquid plastic compound that was easier to color-control. So boxcars made after 1976 show far fewer variations in body mold and paint. To determine the body mold color, open the doors and observe the unpainted inside surfaces. In some cases, the body is entirely unpainted. This has occurred more often in recent years as the molding process became more quality-controlled.

A NOTE ON THE "AUTOMOBILE" DOUBLE-DOOR BOXCARS

Technically, the two-door automobile boxcars, also called "double-door" boxcars, are not "classic" boxcars at all. Though the basic body and frame are the same, there are important differences—namely, a wider door opening, longer metal door guides than those on the classic boxcars, and completely different split doors which feature fewer and thicker horizontal ribs, and only one marker plate. When Lionel made these cars in the postwar era (the 2458 and 6468 from 1947 through 1958), it did not classify them in the regular 6464 series. Modern Lionel has grouped them together, however, in the 9200-, 9700-, and 9400- numbers, as well as the five-digit 19200-series and others. Therefore they are reluctantly included in this section of the chapter.

These handsome double-door freight cars are modeled after a prototype used in the 1950s and 1960s to actually transport automobiles. Four could be loaded on ramps in a standard boxcar with sides modified for the larger opening. The Lionel model doors, considerably smaller than scale, enable their use on the 9700 standard body. In any event, the Lionel pieces seem to enjoy great popularity.

The early 1970s models of these cars featured full rivet detail on the sides, at a time when the classic boxcars were in the

16233	MKT	1992
16255	Wabash	1995
16256	Ford	1994u
16261	Union Pacific	1995
16623	MKT (Katy) with EOT	1991u
17882	B&O (LOTS)	1990u
19205	Great Northern	1988
19207	CP Rail	1988
19208	Southern	1988
19213	Spokane, Portland & Seattle	1989
19215	Union Pacific	1990
19230	Frisco w/ RailSounds	1991
19231	Tennessee, Alabama & Georgia	1991
19232	Rock Island	1991
19236	Nickel Plate Road	1992
19239	Toronto, Hamilton & Buffalo	1992
19240	Great Northern	1992
19251	Montana Rail Link	1993
19255	Erie	1993
19263	New York Central	1994

16241 Toys "R" Us boxcar

process of removing them. This nice detail disappeared in 1976. Fortunately, the full rivet detail returned with the TAG double-door boxcar made in 1991 and has graced these cars since then.

Many, if not all, of the double-door boxcars have distinct left and right sides, because of the off-center wider door opening.

There are also quite a few of the huge Standard O double-door boxcar models, which first appeared in 1991. They are listed in the Standard O boxcar section of this chapter.

For the type collector,we've provided a list of the regular O double-door boxcars created by modern Lionel from 1986 to 1995. They represent an eminently collectable group. Two other special releases were made for the train clubs in 1999, but overall the post-1995 production of automobile boxcars has dwindled.

SPECIAL SERIES CARS

There are various subsets and subseries of classic boxcars within the overall boxcar collection. Examples are the special identical car sets such as the 1990 Lionel 90th anniversary sets; the 6464-series remakes; the "I Love" series of state cars, which have appeared one each year; and the Season's Greetings and Toy Fair Car sets, also annual releases. Our Guide will have a brief introduction to these subseries at the appropriate point in the chapter.

CLASSIC BOXCAR LISTINGS

Exc Mt

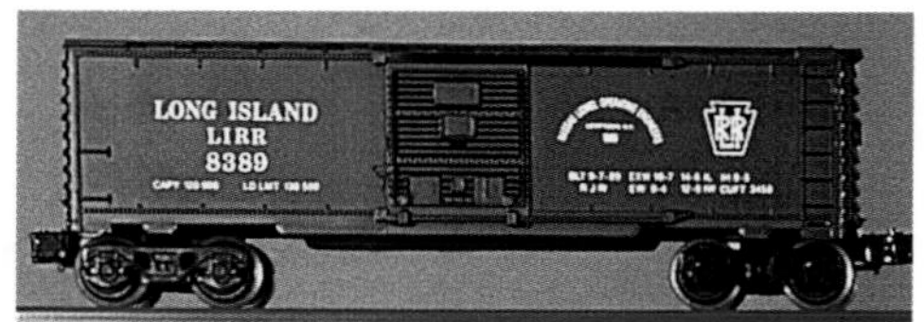

8389 LONG ISLAND RAILROAD: 1989, boxcar; uncataloged; first in an annual series of special cars made for the Nassau Lionel Operating Engineers (NLOE) club in Levittown, New York; tuscan body and doors; white lettering; black and white LIRR keystone; Symington-Wayne trucks; "BUILT 9-7-89"; 51 made. This is a standard Lionel classic boxcar redecorated by the Pleasant Valley Process Co. It was created using repainted 9620-series sports boxcars, which is why it has no Lionel catalog number. The number designates the year of the NLOE's founding (1983) and the year of production. Very hard to find. See also 52019. — **NRS**

Exc Mt

16206 DENVER & RIO GRANDE: 1989, boxcar; uncataloged; orange body; silver-painted doors; black roof; black lettering, number and logo; Standard O trucks; "BLT 1-89". Available only in the 11758 Desert King Service Station Special set. The car's number incorrectly implied it is a short O27 Traditional Line boxcar, but it is most definitely not. However, since the set was considered a Traditional Line set, the boxcar was numbered in this series. Initially this series was intended for the short (O27) boxcars, but as Lionel phased that line out, some later boxcars of the larger variety were assigned 16200 numbers. **50 60**

16232 CHESSIE SYSTEM: 1992–95, boxcar; blue body and doors; yellow lettering and Chessie cat logo to right side; "Chessie System" in yellow to upper left; ASF trucks; "BLT 1-92". This car appeared in the 11727 Coastal Limited set in 1992, and in the 11746 Seaboard Freight set in 1994. Both sets were available though uncataloged, the following years. The car comes in two body types, Type Xa with the full rivet detail and Type XI with the rivets removed and a plastic frame. One of the first examples of Lionel using the Type XI body—and one of the earliest cases of a "Classic"-style boxcar appearing in a lower-end Traditional Line set.

(A) Type Xa body, metal chassis. **25 30**

(B) Type XI body, plastic chassis **15 20**

16233 MISSOURI-KANSAS-TEXAS: 1992, double-door boxcar; yellow-orange body and doors; black lettering; large "M-K-T" to left side above number; "the Katy" in script to upper right; ASF trucks; "BLT 1-92". Part of 11728 High Plains Runner set. **20 30**

16234 AKRON, CANTON & YOUNGSTOWN: 1992, boxcar; yellow Type X body and doors; red lettering; large "ACY" to right side above "ROAD OF SERVICE"; "SERVING OHIO AND THE NATION" to upper left; Standard O trucks; "BLT 1-92". Part of the 1992 Service Station Special set, the 11733 Feather River. The car was shown with painted brown truck frames in the catalog, but was made with them as the regular unpainted black. **30 40**

16236 NEW YORK CENTRAL: 1992, boxcar; uncataloged; Type X body painted in classic red and gray Pacemaker scheme; red body and doors with gray lower portion of sides; white lettering and NYC oval herald at upper right; "Pacemaker" script to

	Exc	Mt

upper left; number underscored; Standard O trucks; "BLT 1-92". This car was made as a response to demand for a lower-cost alternative to the 16650 Pacemaker car with RailSounds made earlier in 1992. Without the electronics, this car was moderately priced. **35 40**

16237 RAILWAY EXPRESS AGENCY: 1992, boxcar; uncataloged; dark green Type Xa body with metal frame; gold lettering; REA diamond herald in red and white to upper right; Standard O trucks; "BLT 1-92". This car is a darker green than the 16649 REA car with RailSounds released earlier in the year and was made as a lower cost alternative without the RailSounds circuitry. **35 40**

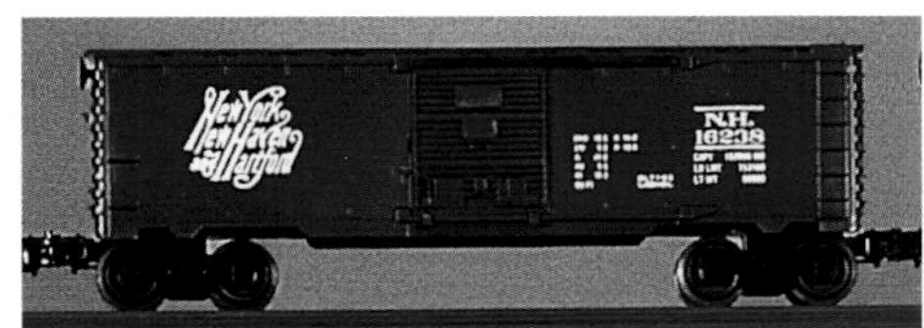

16238 NEW YORK, NEW HAVEN & HARTFORD: 1993–99, boxcar; green Type XI body; white lettering; "New York, New Haven and Hartford" in broad cursive script with text sharing large "N" and "H"; "NH" and number over-and underscored at center right; plastic underframe; ASF trucks; "BLT 1-93". Part of 11735 New York Central Flyer set, one of Lionel's most popular starter sets in the mid 1990s. It also appeared in the 16691 Rolling Stock Assortment set in 1994 and 1995, as well as the 11931 Chessie Flyer set in 1997, which was virtually identical to the NYC Flyer set except for the lettering on the caboose and tender. Lionel also placed it, somewhat incongruously, in the 11919 Docksider set in 1997, with a small bobber caboose and Docksider 0-4-0 steamer. In this consist the boxcar dominates the train. The set was designed to hit a very low-end price point for starter sets. Note that in the 1993 catalog this car was shown as brown, and in 1994 and subsequent ones, it appeared in its actual green. The engine also changes colors between those years, as does the flatcar! There is likely to be a brown prototype car. **15 20**

16239 UNION PACIFIC: 1993–95, boxcar; brown Type XI body; yellow lettering; "Be Specific- ship UNION PACIFIC" to right side; plastic chassis; ASF trucks; "BLT 1-93". Part of the 11736 Union Pacific Express set. No separate box. One of the earliest uses of the Type XI boxcar style. **15 20**

16241 TOYS "R" US: 1992–93, boxcar; uncataloged; white body and doors; Type IX mold; black lettering; multicolor TOYS "R" US and KIDS "R" US logos to left side; Geoffrey Giraffe image to right with "THE WORLD'S BIGGEST TOY STORE"; ASF trucks; no BLT date. Part of 11800 Toys "R" Us version of the Heavy Iron set, in which this boxcar replaces the regular 9339. The set is a Fundimensions carryover that was adapted for Toys "R" Us off and on since 1982. **50 60**

	Exc	Mt

16243 CONRAIL: 1993, boxcar; medium blue Type X body and doors; white lettering and Conrail wheel logo to right side; ASF trucks; "BLT 1-93". Part of 11740 Conrail Consolidated set, the top-of-the-line Traditional Line set in 1993. **30 40**

16244 DULUTH, SOUTH SHORE & ATLANTIC: 1993, boxcar; brown Type XII body and doors; white lettering; "THE SOUTH SHORE" in white outline to left side; "ROUTE SUPERIOR GATEWAY FOR SUPERIOR SERVICE" to right; "D.S.S.&A" and number over- and underscored to left side; plastic underframe; ASF trucks; "BLT 1-93". This is a first-ever use of this roadname for Lionel. **20 25**

16245 CONTADINA: 1993, boxcar; red Type XI body and doors; white "Contadina" to upper right; multicolor "Tomato Paste", farm scene to left side; dark blue number and built date; ASF trucks; "BLT 1-93". See also 52068. The electrocal decal of the farm scene on this car is poorly applied and has clouded the car sides around it. **20 25**

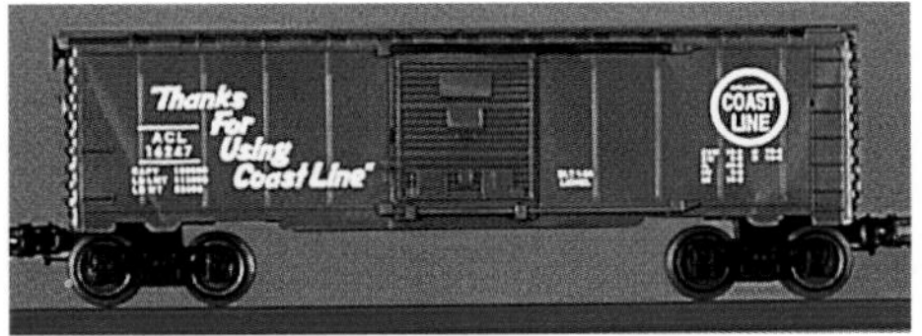

16247 ATLANTIC COAST LINE: 1994, boxcar; tuscan Type XII body and doors; white lettering; "Thanks For Using Coast Line" to left of doors; ACL circle logo to right; "ACL" and number over- and underscored to lower left; plastic frame; ASF trucks; "BLT 1-94". See also TTOS version of this car—the 52046. **20 25**

16248 BUDWEISER: 1993–94, boxcar; uncataloged; white type XI body; blue ends, roof, and doors; red and blue Budweiser label at left; blue and red lettering; "PROUD TO BE YOUR

Exc Mt

BUD" at right; ASF trucks; "BLT 9-93". Part of 11810 Budweiser set, available only from Anheuser Busch's gift catalog. **30 40**

16249 UNITED AUTO WORKERS: 1993, boxcar; uncataloged; dark blue body; Type IX mold; yellow lettering and number; "BUY AMERICAN" eagle herald to left side; UAW "UNION QUALITY" circle logo to right; ASF trucks; "BLT 1-93". Part of 11811 United Auto Workers Express set. **40 50**

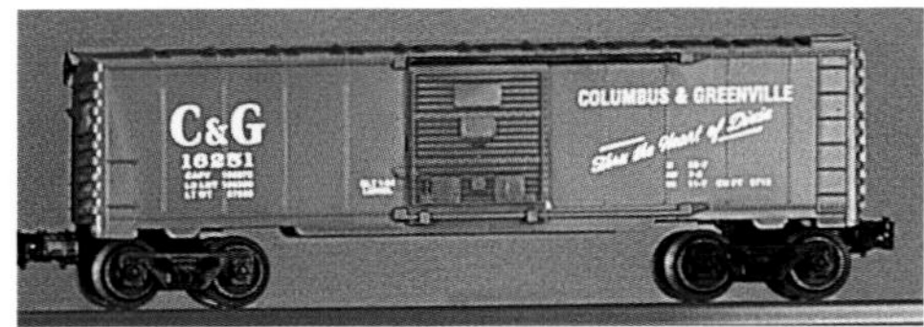

16251 COLUMBUS & GREENVILLE: 1994, boxcar; blue-green Type XII body and doors; white lettering; large "C&G" to left side; "Thru the Heart of Dixie" in slanted script to right side; plastic underframe; ASF trucks; "BLT 1-94". **20 25**

16252 U.S. NAVY: 1994–95, boxcar; white Type XI body and doors; black lettering "RAPID STRIKE ATTACK FORCE FLEET" to upper right; number on car is "USN 6106888" to left; ASF trucks; "BLT 1-94". Part of the popular 11745 U.S. Navy train set. **25 30**

16255 WABASH: 1995, double-door boxcar; brown body; white lettering; large "WABASH" to non-brakewheel side with "SERVING the Heart of America" just below; red Wabash flag inside white heart to upper brakewheel side, above "WAB" and number over- and underscored; plastic frame ASF trucks; "BLT 1-95". This car has distinct left and right sides. **20 25**

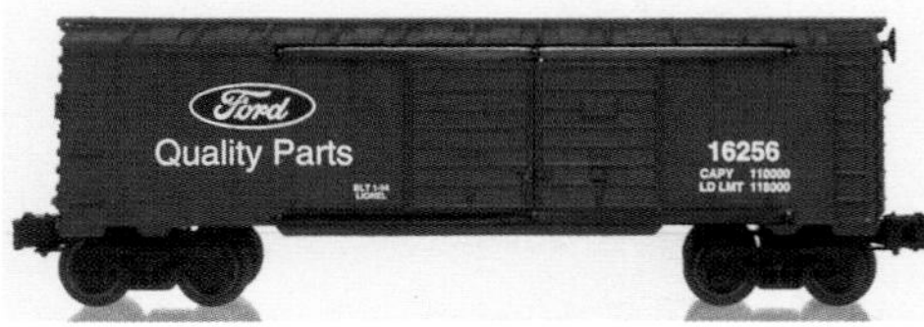

16256 FORD: 1994, double-door boxcar; uncataloged; brown body and doors; white lettering; blue and white Ford script logo inside oval to non-brakewheel side; ASF trucks; "BLT 1-94". Part of special 11814 Ford set made for the auto maker, and one of many Ford-related Lionel items made in the mid-1990s. **40 45**

16257 CRAYOLA: 1994–95, boxcar; white sides; yellow door; Type XI mold; orange roof and ends; car has no markings whatever on sides; ASF trucks; no BLT date. Part of the popular 11813 Crayola set, which appeared in a special Crayola brochure in 1994 and was cataloged regularly in 1995. The car has blank washable sides so children could use the crayons enclosed with the set to decorate the car themselves. **15 20**

16258 LEHIGH VALLEY: 1995, boxcar; green Type XII body; white lettering; "LV" diamond logo in black and white to right side; barcodes and data below; ASF trucks; "BLT 1-95". **20 25**

16259 CHRYSLER MOPAR: 1994, boxcar; uncataloged; chocolate brown body; Type XII mold with plastic chassis; yellow lettering; number over- and underscored; yellow, red, and blue Mopar oval logo to left side; reads "USE CHRYSLER ENGINEERED MOPAR PARTS AND ACCESSORIES"; ASF trucks; "BLT 1-94". Part of special 11818 Chrysler Mopar set. **— 40**

16261 UNION PACIFIC: 1995, double-door boxcar; reddish-brown body and doors; white lettering; UP shield in red, white, and blue; "SHIP AND TRAVEL THE AUTOMATED RAIL WAY" to front; metal door guides; ASF trucks; "BLT 95". This handsome car is part of the 11747 Lionel Lines steam set, the top-of-the-line Traditional set from 1995. It has a left and right side, with the shield appearing to the left side in one case and to the right on the other side. The other text is similarly displaced. **30 35**

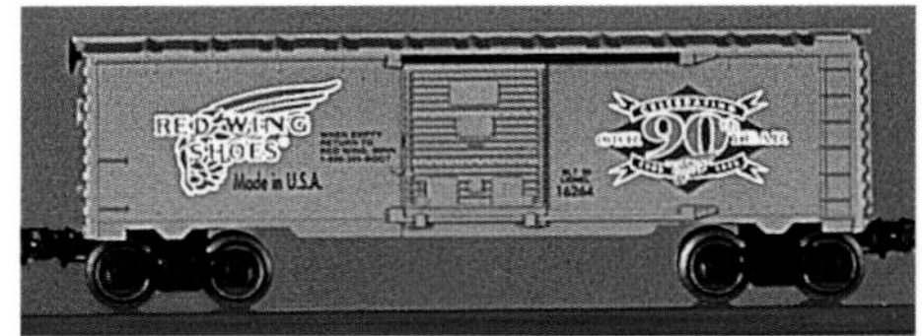

16264 RED WING SHOES: 1995, boxcar; light gray body and doors; Type XI mold; black lettering; red wing logo under "RED WING SHOES" with "Made in USA"; black, gold, silver, and red "CELEBRATING OUR 90th YEAR" herald to right side; ASF trucks; "BLT 95". Special car made for the anniversary of the shoe producer in Red Wing, Minnesota. Unusual because it was announced in the 1995 Stocking Stuffer catalog, as well as in the uncataloged 11820 Red Wing set. **25 30**

Exc Mt

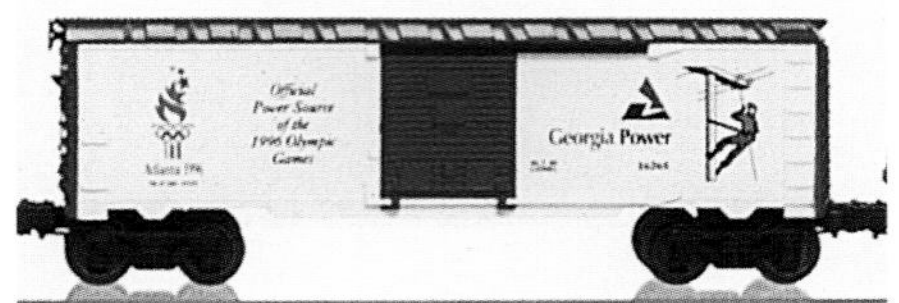

16265 GEORGIA POWER: 1995, boxcar; uncataloged; white sides; Type XI body; medium blue roof, ends, and doors; red and black lettering and graphics; Georgia Power triangle logo to right side with lineman working on pole; "We Sell Efficiency"; 1996 Atlanta Olympics symbol to left side with "Official Power Source of the 1996 Olympic Games"; ASF trucks; "BLT 95". Part of 11819 Georgia Power set, made especially for the Georgia Power Company. Reportedly 2,500 made. The set was popular and this boxcar particularly so because of the added interest in Olympic collectibles. Quite hard to find. — 175

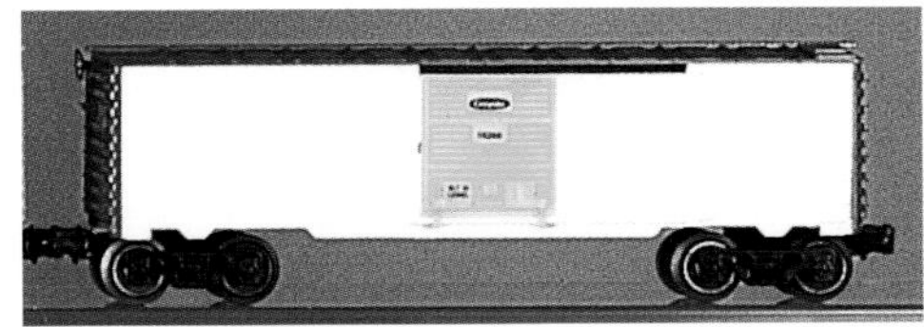

16266 CRAYOLA: 1995, boxcar; Type XI body; white sides; green roof and ends; no lettering on sides; door is slightly darker yellow than door on 16257 above; "Crayola" oval in black on upper door plate; number on center door plate; ASF trucks; "BLT 95" on lower left door plate. This car is an add-on to the 11813 Crayola set. Note similarity to 16257. This car also has blank washable sides so that "young engineer/artists," as the catalog refers to them, can decorate the car to suit. This car also differs from the 16257 by the roof-end color and the fact that there are small logos printed on the doorplates. 15 20

16267 SEARS ZENITH: 1995–96, boxcar; uncataloged; white body; black lettering; Type XI mold; car number is on the door; "SEARS Brand Central" in blue and red to left side; Zenith logo to lower right in red, above "The Quality Goes In Before The Name Goes On"; ASF trucks; "BLT 95" on door plate. Part of 11821 Sears Zenith set, available to customers who purchased Sears television products. Not individually boxed. — 40

16268 GM/AC DELCO: 1995, boxcar; uncataloged; dark blue Type XI body; red and blue United Delco circle logo to left, above "GM Parts for Your GM Car" in white; "UNITED DELCO" on white square to right side, highlighted in black; "GMUD" and number over- and underscored; ASF trucks; "BLT 95". Part of 11822 Chevrolet Bow Tie set. — 45

16600 AND 16700-SERIES OPERATING BOXCARS

Lionel assigned the 16600-series of numbers to its operating "Traditional Line" cars, of all types. Although technically these were of a less-expensive variety than their Classic brethren, some of the cars here are anything but. Here can be found boxcars with End-of-Train lights, RailSounds circuit boards, animated cars with bobbing figures poking through the roof, milk cars, ice cars (later in the '90s—see our companion guide), even remakes of the Space and Military-vintage missile and exploding boxcars.

16617 CHICAGO & NORTH WESTERN: 1989, boxcar with End-of-Train Device (EOT), an LED-blinking light in a small box intended (on prototype railroads) to replace the caboose; first Lionel car to include this device; Type IX mold; tuscan sides and roof; black ends; yellow EOT light; white lettering "ROUTE OF The Challengers" to right of doors; number under- and overscored; Symington-Wayne trucks; "BLT 1-89". 25 30

16622 CSX: 1990–91, boxcar with End-of-Train Device; dark blue body; yellow lettering and large "CSX" logo at upper right; ASF trucks; "BLT 1-90". 25 30

16623 MISSOURI, KANSAS, TEXAS: 1991, double-door boxcar with End-of-Train Device; orange body; brown roof; black lettering "M-K-T" and "Katy" script logo to left side; yellow EOT light; ASF trucks; "BLT 1-91". The catalog picture of this item is more yellow than the production orange piece. 25 30

16631 ROCK ISLAND: 1990–91, boxcar with Steam RailSounds; green body; gold lettering; red and yellow Rock Island shield herald to right of doors; RailSounds circuit board mounted inside body; ASF trucks; "BLT 1-90". The popularity of Lionel's electronic RailSounds technology prompted the company to begin placing it in boxcars and other rolling stock, as well as engines, beginning in 1990. It is, however, an expensive addition. Announced in 1990, but not released until early 1991. 120 150

16632 BURLINGTON NORTHERN: 1990, boxcar with diesel RailSounds; Type IX yellow body; silver roof; black lettering; large BN logo to upper right; RailSounds circuit board mounted inside body; ASF trucks; "BLT 1-90". 100 125

16639 BALTIMORE & OHIO: 1991, boxcar with steam RailSounds; Type IX silver body and door; black lettering; Capitol logo to

16686 Mickey Mouse & Big Bad Pete animated boxcar

Exc Mt

right of door; large "B&O" to left side; number underscored; RailSounds circuit board mounted inside; ASF trucks; "BLT 1-91". **120 140**

16640 RUTLAND: 1991, boxcar with diesel RailSounds; bright green and yellow Rutland paint scheme—green roof, ends, and lower portion of sides; yellow upper section; yellow doors; yellow and green contrasting lettering; green Rutland shield logo to right of door; number underscored; RailSounds circuit board mounted inside; ASF trucks; "BLT 1-91". **120 140**

16646 RAILBOX: 1992, boxcar with End-of-Train Device; yellow body; black doors; black lettering. Announced in 1992, but dropped from the line. **Not Made**

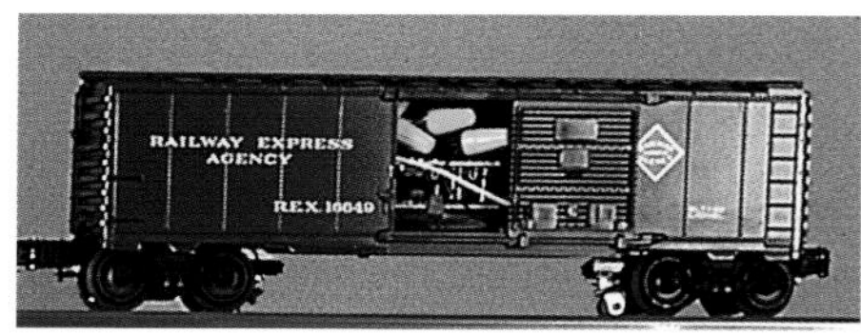

16649 RAILWAY EXPRESS AGENCY: 1992, boxcar with steam RailSounds; olive green Type Xa body and doors; yellow lettering; red and white REA diamond herald to upper right; RailSounds circuit board mounted inside; volume adjust; Standard O trucks; "BLT 1-92". Comes with sound activation button. The actual production piece was a lighter green than the olive-hue catalog picture. There was sufficient demand for this car—sans the RailSounds—that Lionel made a non-operating version of it later in 1992—the 16237. **120 150**

16650 NEW YORK CENTRAL: 1992, boxcar with diesel RailSounds; gray Type Xa body with red stripe on upper half of sides; white lettering and oval NYC logo to upper right; "Pacemaker" in script to upper left; number underscored; RailSounds circuit board mounted inside; volume adjust; metal

Exc Mt

frame; Standard O trucks; "BLT 1-92". Comes with sound activation button. There was sufficient demand for this car—sans the RailSounds—that Lionel made a non-operating version of it later in 1992—the 16236. **120 150**

16679 U.S. MAIL: 1994, operating boxcar; red, white, and blue-striped sides and doors; in that order from top to bottom; red roof and ends; white and black contrasting lettering; "UNITED STATES MAIL" in white to top left; "RAILWAY POST OFFICE" to right side with "POST OFFICE" in black on center white section; gray man appears with magnetically attached mailbag when underbody plunger is activated; ASF trucks; "BLT 1-94". Part of the 11743 C&O Freight set, Lionel's top-of-the-line Traditional set in 1994. **50 55**

16686 MICKEY MOUSE & BIG BAD PETE: 1995, animated boxcar; modified Type XII body with two holes cut in roof; plastic chassis; light brown body and doors; tan, white, and blue lettering; multicolor "MICKEY'S CATTLE MOOVER" electrocals on both sides; tan lettering; Mickey Mouse and Big Bad Pete cartoon characters bob up and down through roof as car moves; each figure is on cam-gear mechanism attached to wheel axles; ASF trucks; "BLT 95". Shown in the 1995 Stocking Stuffers catalog. **40 45**

16687 U.S. MAIL: 1994, operating boxcar; description identical to 16679 above, except for number. The lower blue stripe on this car is a shade darker than on the 16679. See other details under 16679. It is not clear why Lionel remade the identical car, except

Exc Mt

that it was a popular item and collectors disliked the fact that the 16679 was available only in the set. Accordingly, this car, offered for separate sale, is somewhat less scarce. **40 45**

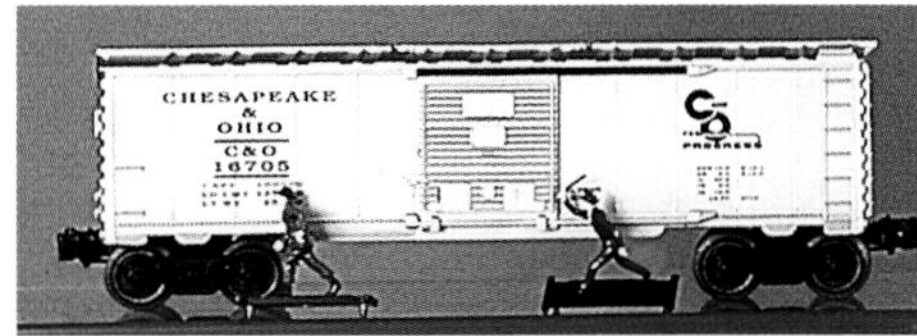

16705 CHESAPEAKE & OHIO: 1995, operating cop-and-hobo car; silver body; Type XII mold; black lettering; "C&O FOR PROGRESS" to right side; "C&O" and number over- and underscored to left; spring-loaded platform (not shown in photo) extends up from car top; supports cop or hobo figure magnetically held in place; light blue cop chases gray hobo from car to metal trestle (included separately); ASF trucks; "BLT 95". This is the first use of the long (9700 or 6464-type) boxcar for a cop-and-hobo action car. Previous ones used the short O27 cars. The platform does not look as tall or as long on this car as it does on the O27s, even though it is the same mechanism. **35 40**

16706 ANIMAL TRANSPORTATION SERVICE: 1995, operating giraffe car; orange Type XII body with plastic frame; blue "ATS" lettering over Africa map at right; "ANIMAL TRANSPORTATION SERVICE" to left side over ". . . with love and care, 'cross the nation" in dark blue; yellow and brown giraffe head bobs in and out of hole cut in roof as car moves; figure is attached to a cam-gear assembly mounted to the wheel axle; ASF trucks; "BLT 95". This is the first operating giraffe or animal car to use the longer 9700-type boxcar. Previous versions had used the O27 short boxcars—see that section of this chapter. **30 35**

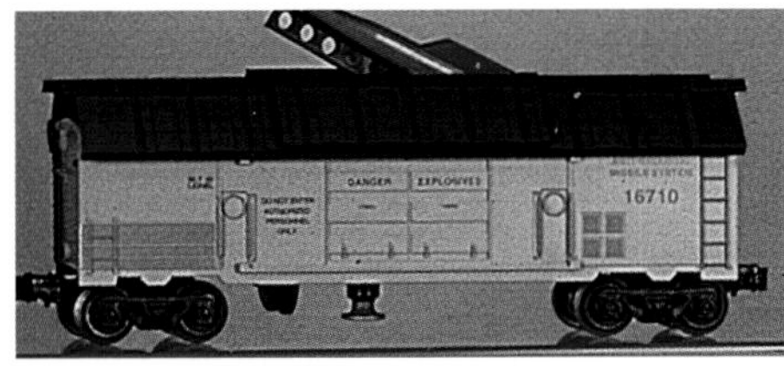

16710 US ARMY MISSILE LAUNCHING CAR: 1995, operating missile-firing boxcar; unique design with split roof permits missile launcher to rise up from inside and fire spring-loaded red missile; gray sides and ends, split green roof; red lettering "DO NOT ENTER—AUTHORIZED PERSONNEL ONLY" and "DANGER EXPLOSIVES"; green lettering "LAND-BASED BALLISTIC MISSILE SYSTEM"; metal chassis; ASF trucks; "BLT 95". This car is the first reissue of the postwar Lionel missile-firing Minuteman car (the 3665). The car body is unique to anything else in the Lionel line (the doors do not operate), though a similar body side is used on the GM Electro Motive Power car. The internal mechanism is also unique. It uses an air-hydraulic boot to raise the platform and a cam mechanism to fire the rocket (when the underbody plunger is activated by a UCS track). The catalog warns users that the car is "designed for use with Lionel-approved missiles, and not "foreign objects"! **40 50**

16806 TOYS "R" US: 1992; boxcar; uncataloged, white Type IX body; black lettering; Multicolor "TOYS "R" US" over "THE WORLD'S BIGGEST TOY STORE" to upper right; "Limited Edition 1992" logo to right side; ASF trucks; "BLT 1-92". Unlike other Toys "R" Us cars, this boxcar did not come in a set. It was available only through the stores. **35 40**

16808 TOYS "R" US: 1992–93, boxcar; uncataloged; special for the toy retailing giant; gray Type XII body and doors; blue roof and ends; black lettering; multicolor TOYS "R" US logo to upper right over "THE WORLD'S BIGGEST TOY STORE"; "1993 LIMITED EDITION" keystone logo to left side in green, yellow, and red; ASF trucks; "BLT 1-93". See other comments under 16806. Despite the date, the car was also available in 1992. **40 50**

17875 PORT HURON & DETROIT: 1989, boxcar; uncataloged; 10th annual special for the Lionel Operating Train Society (LOTS); dark blue body; silver roof; white lettering and number; white "PH-D" logo with red bar between "PH" and "D"; "ST. CLAIR BLUE WATER ROUTE"; number on car is "1289"; 17875 appears only on box; Standard O trucks; "BLT 7-15-89", the date of the LOTS national convention; 808 made; Type V box. **80 100**

	Exc	Mt

17882 BALTIMORE & OHIO: 1990, double-door boxcar with End-of-Train Device; uncataloged; 11th annual special for the Lionel Operating Train Society (LOTS); tuscan body; white lettering and B&O dome logo; number on car is "298011"; catalog number is on box; number under- and overscored; ASF trucks; "NEW 2-47". First train club car to sport an EOT; reissue of scarce 6468 postwar tuscan B&O automobile boxcar, which has the same "NEW 2-47" notation; 1216 made; Type V box. **75** **90**

17891 GRAND TRUNK/ARTRAIN: 1991, boxcar; uncataloged; annual special for the Artrain mobile art museum; third in the special series; blue Type Xa body; white lettering; large "GT" to brakewheel side; roadname and number to non-brakewheel side; red and white Artrain logo under GT; lettered for 20th anniversary of Artrain, 1971–1991; car has distinct sides, with the "GT" to the left in one case and the right on the other; Standard O trucks. Reportedly only 600 made. **80** **100**

19200-SERIES BOXCARS

With the change in ownership of Lionel in 1986 came a complete changeover of the numbering system used on the trains—a five-digit system replaced the old four-digit one. The classic boxcars, still carrying the "Famous Name" label applied to them by Fundimensions (and still bearing a "9700" end-plate!) were christened into a new 19200-series of numbers with a nice Tidewater Southern car in 1987. The long line of the "Famous Name" boxcars continues right through to the present day, now under the "29200" series.

These boxcars witnessed the return of the full-rivet detailing on the car sides when the Type Xa body appeared in 1991, and they were also among the first recipients of the ASF "strong-arm" wheel sets in 1990. The ASF trucks were the first new freight rolling stock trucks to have appeared in nearly 20 years.

The cars in this series are of the non-operating type. Operating ones using the same body style are found in the other sections of this chapter.

The scarcity of the 19200-series, which includes double-door automobile boxcars, varies widely. Some can be difficult to find today because of Lionel's penchant for cataloging them in only one year. During the postwar period and the early modern era, boxcars would be listed over several years' catalogs and made in several manufacturing runs. No more. Also, Lionel would often issue a boxcar only in sets (not for separate sale), which would force a collector to purchase an entire set to obtain the boxcar. So they are naturally more valuable and rare than the regular-issue ones. This is especially true for the higher-end collector sets like the Fallen Flags series, Service Station Specials, and most important, the uncataloged special releases for stores and businesses. The later ones with the sprung Standard O metal trucks are also more valuable than the ones with plastic trucks.

Of greatest interest within this series are the 6464 boxcar sets. Starting in 1993, Lionel put together a three-pack of cars that re-created the famous postwar cars, in the order they were originally released in the 1950s. They were given their original 6464 markings, as well as catalog numbers in the 19200s (later 29200s). With the scarcity of the originals—especially ones in good shape—this series was a hit from the get-go. The first release of three cars in 1993 is actually somewhat rare now because Lionel made them in fewer quantities, unsure of the initial response. The later sets are more available, but in general all these cars command a premium above the more run-of-the-mill boxcars. The advantage being that operator-collectors can run them safely on their layouts without causing wear-and-tear on the postwar originals. The new ones also have the modern features that the old ones don't—notably the Standard O trucks and the fast-angle wheels.

Lionel has mixed in some Hi-Cube boxcars into the 19200-numbers (see that subsection). There are also quite a few special classic boxcars found in the 52000-series.

For the most part, the interest in these boxcars stems from their attractive, bright, and prototypically correct graphics. They should all eventually achieve higher collector status just as their earlier 6464, 9700, and 9400 series cousins have done.

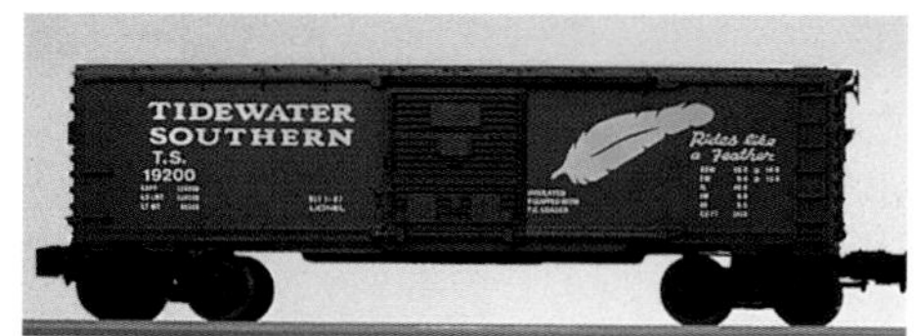

19200 TIDEWATER SOUTHERN: 1987, boxcar; tuscan body; Type IX mold; yellow lettering; yellow-orange feather logo with "Rides like a Feather" to right side; Symington-Wayne trucks; "BLT 1-87". This boxcar marks the beginning of the fourth major boxcar series of the modern era—successors to the 9200, 9400, and 9700-series boxcars. **15** **20**

19201 LANCASTER AND CHESTER: 1987, boxcar; blue lower sides and ends; white upper side; silver roof and ends; Type IX mold; contrasting blue and white lettering; L&C oval logo to right side; Symington-Wayne trucks; "BLT 1-87". A match for the 19310 L&C quad hopper released in 1989. Somewhat hard to find. **60** **75**

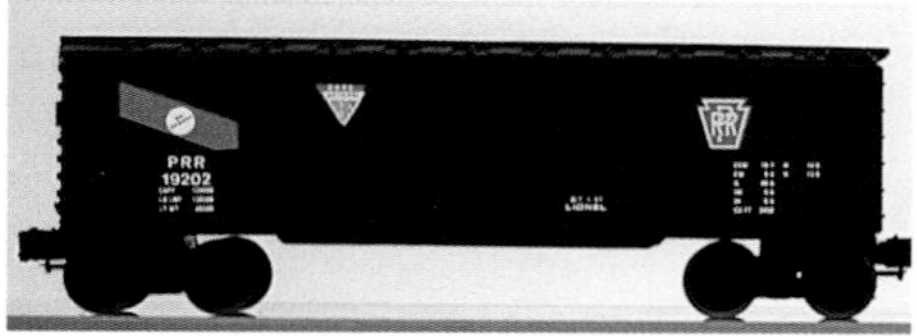

19202 PENNSYLVANIA: 1987, boxcar; dark flat Brunswick green body; white lettering; white and red banner logos to left; red

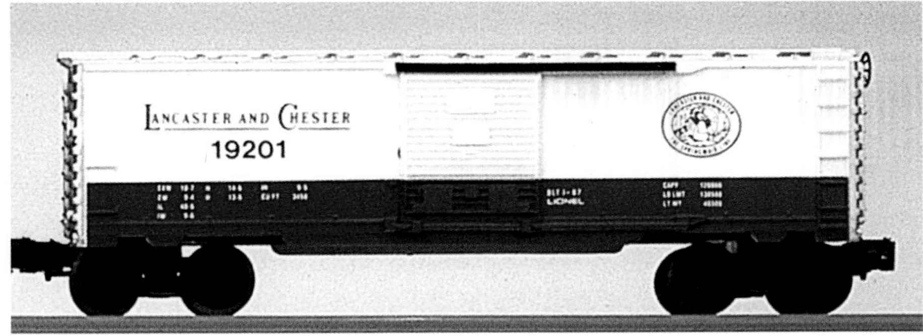

19201 Lancaster & Chester boxcar

	Exc	Mt

and white PRR keystone to right side; Type IX mold; Symington-Wayne trucks; "BLT 1-87". **35** **45**

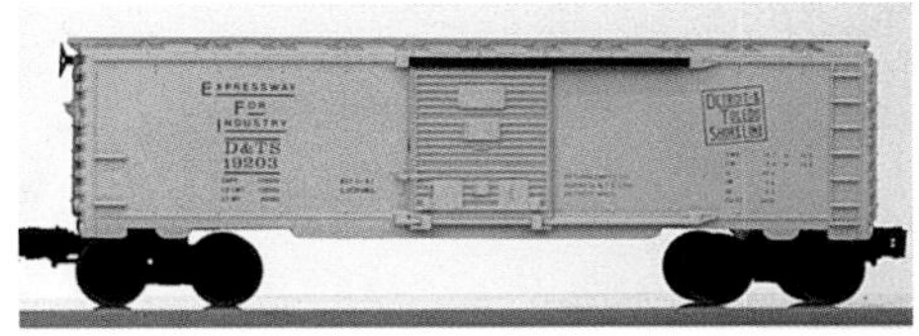

19203 DETROIT & TOLEDO SHORELINE: 1987, boxcar; yellow body; light red lettering; angled DT&S rectangle herald to right of doors in red; number under- and overscored; Type IX mold; Symington-Wayne trucks; "BLT 1-87". The light red lettering on this car can be hard to discern. **15** **20**

19204 MILWAUKEE ROAD: 1987, boxcar; brown body; Type IX mold; broad yellow stripe runs length of car through doors; contrasting yellow and brown lettering; red and white rectangular Milwaukee logo to right; Standard O trucks; "BLT 1-87". Part of Milwaukee Road Fallen Flags set no. 2, whose components were offered for separate sale only.

(A) As described. **30** **40**

(B) Factory error. Missing "MILWAUKEE ROAD" in brown on yellow stripe to left side. R. LaVoie collection. **60** **70**

19205 GREAT NORTHERN: 1988, double-door automobile boxcar; dark green roof and ends; orange sides and doors; dark green lettering; number under- and overscored; red and white circular

	Exc	Mt

goat logo to right side; Standard O trucks; "BLT 1-88". Part of Great Northern Fallen Flags set no. 3, whose components were offered for separate sale only. **30** **40**

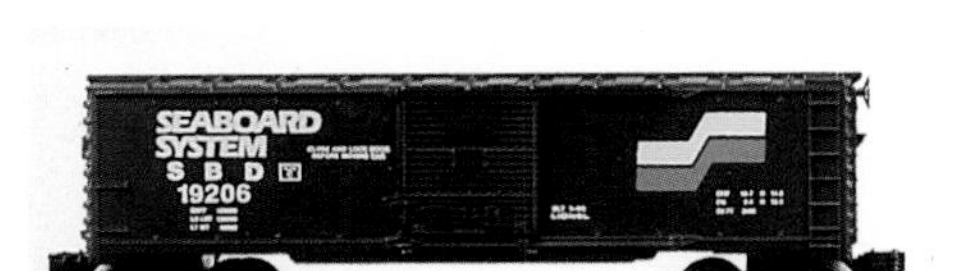

19206 SEABOARD SYSTEM: 1988, boxcar; black body and doors; Type IX mold; gold lettering; gold and red double-"SS" logo; Symington-Wayne trucks; "BLT 1-88". **15** **20**

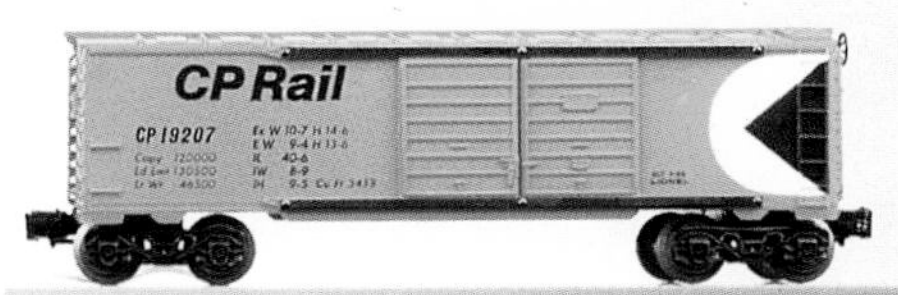

19207 CP RAIL: 1988, double-door automobile boxcar; bright burnt-orange body and doors; black lettering; black and white CP Rail logo at brakewheel end (note that this means the car has a distinct "left" and "right" side); Symington-Wayne trucks; "BLT 1-88". **15** **20**

19208 SOUTHERN: 1988, double-door automobile boxcar; tuscan body and doors; white lettering and DF logo to right side; Symington-Wayne trucks; "BLT 1-88".

(A) As described. **15** **20**

(B) Factory error, with one Symington-Wayne truck and one arch-bar truck. Appears to be legitimate error. M. DiMonda and W. Howell Collections. **—** **NRS**

Exc Mt

19209 FLORIDA EAST COAST: 1988, boxcar; dark blue body and doors; Type IX mold; yellow "Speedway" and "TO AMERICA'S PLAYGROUND" lettering; number under- and overscored; Symington-Wayne trucks; "BLT 1-88". **15 20**

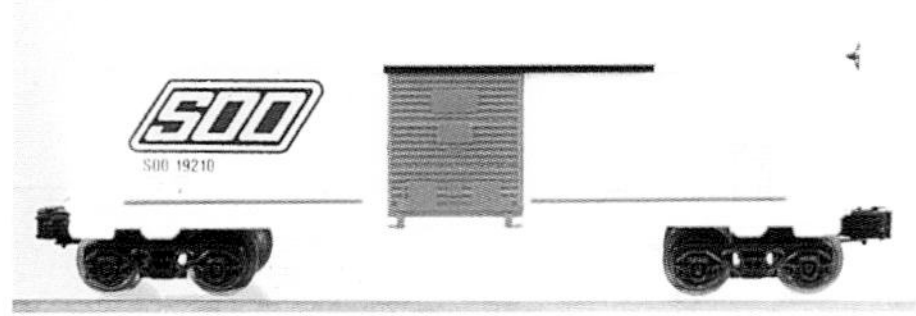

19210 SOO: 1989, boxcar; white body; red doors; red stripe along bottom; blue lettering; large "SOO" logo in blue and silver; Type IX mold; Symington-Wayne trucks; "BLT 1-89".

20 25

19211 VERMONT RAILWAY: 1989, boxcar; forest green body and doors; Type IX mold; white lettering, number and mountain logo; Symington-Wayne trucks; "BLT 1-89". **15 20**

19212 PENNSYLVANIA: 1989, boxcar; tuscan body and doors; Type IX mold; white lettering; PRR keystone in black and white to right of door; Symington-Wayne trucks; "BLT 1-89." **20 25**

19213 SPOKANE PORTLAND & SEATTLE: 1989, double-door automobile boxcar; tuscan body and doors; large "S.P.&S." logo in white; white lettering; Symington-Wayne trucks; "BLT 1-89". **20 25**

Exc Mt

19214 WESTERN MARYLAND: 1989, boxcar; brown body and doors; white lettering and WM logo; Type IX mold; Standard O trucks; "BLT 1-89". Part of Western Maryland Fallen Flags no. 4 set from 1989, whose components were offered only for separate sale. **25 35**

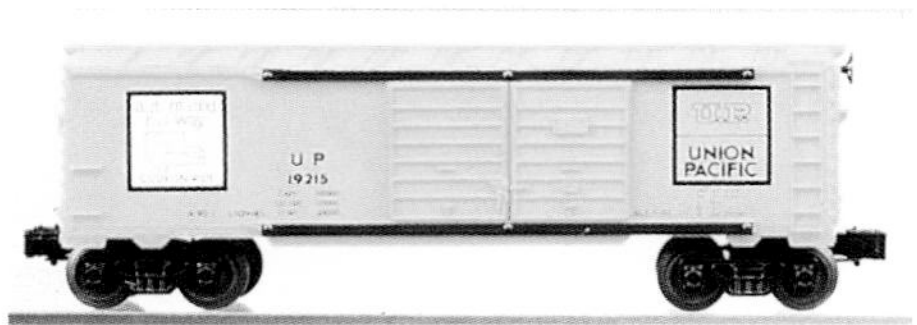

19215 UNION PACIFIC: 1990, double-door boxcar; yellow body and doors; black lettering and UP logo to one side of doors, with "U.P." in hollow outline letters; multicolor "automated rail way", "CUSHION RIDE" and map inside square black-outlined box; ASF trucks; "A-90-1" rather than BLT date. This car has a left and right side. The map is to the left of the door on one side and to the right of the door on the other side. **15 20**

19216 SANTA FE: 1990, boxcar; tuscan body and doors; Type IX mold; white and yellow lettering; large Santa Fe cross logo in white to left of doors; "Super Shock Control / A smoother ride" in white and yellow to right side; ASF trucks; "BLT 1-90". **15 20**

19217 BURLINGTON: 1990, boxcar; red body and doors; white lettering; "Burlington" in white to left side; black and white "Burlington Route" rectangle logo to right side; "EVERYWHERE WEST" under rectangle; number under- and overscored; Type IX mold; ASF trucks; "BLT 1-90". **15 20**

	Exc	Mt

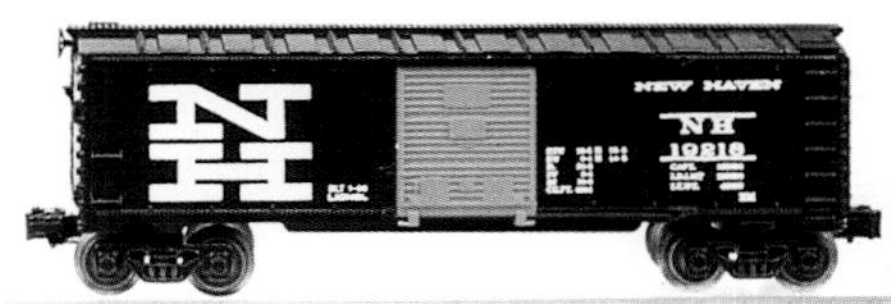

19218 NEW HAVEN: 1990, boxcar; black Type IX body; bright orange doors; white lettering; large white "N" over white "H" to left side; number under- and overscored; ASF trucks; "BLT 1-90". **15 20**

The 90th Anniversary Set

In 1990 Lionel celebrated its 90th birthday with a collector set of five matching boxcars depicting ten important events in the company's history. The set was headed by a GP-9 diesel and included a matching bay window caboose. Some buyers initially thought the images on the car were poorly done, but as it happened Lionel had applied an unusual antiquing process to the electrocals to blur the edges of the images. The catalog trumpeted the engine as having RailSounds in it, but the engineers could not fit the RailSounds circuit board into the GP, so they placed it in the 19219 boxcar.

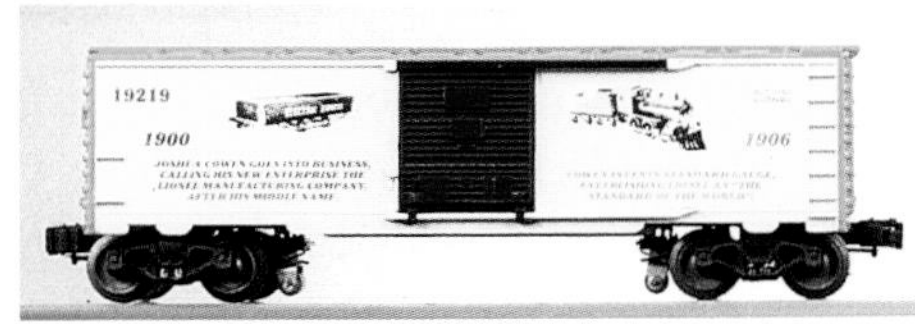

19219 LIONEL LINES: 1990, boxcar with diesel RailSounds; straw yellow sides; orange roof and ends; dark blue doors; Type IX mold; black lettering; antiqued multicolor electrocals and several lines of text depicting the founding of the company and the first gondola in 1900, and Standard gauge in 1906; doors are glued shut to deter tampering with the RailSounds circuitry; sounds are muffled because the speaker is face down on the frame; Standard O trucks; "BLT 1-90". This and the next four entries are part of the 11715 Lionel 90th anniversary set, which also included the 18502 GP-9 diesel and the 19708 bay window caboose. The car was also one of the first to use a power pickup on the Standard O sprung trucks. A spring-loaded roller pickup is snapped into the truck, and a copper wiper strip spans the two axles to complete the ground. **130 160**

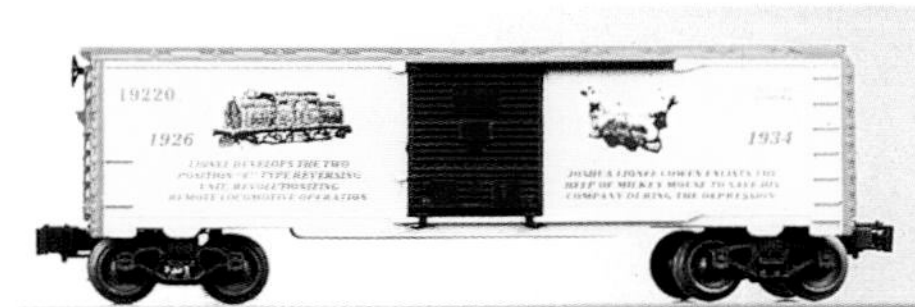

19220 LIONEL LINES: 1990, boxcar; electrocal images depict Lionel events in 1926 (E-unit development) and 1934 (Mickey Mouse handcar); otherwise matches 19219 above, except for number. Part of 11715 Lionel 90th anniversary set with 19219-19223. **25 35**

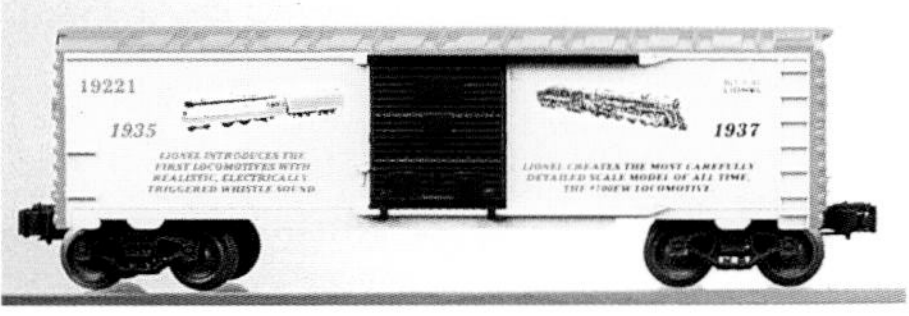

19221 LIONEL LINES: 1990, boxcar; images depict events at Lionel in 1935 (electrically activated whistles) and 1937 (the scale Hudson); otherwise matches 19219 above, except for number. Part of 11715 Lionel 90th anniversary set with 19219-19223. **25 35**

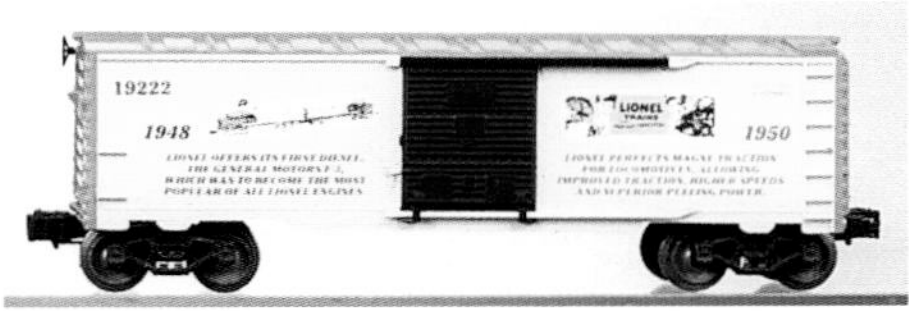

19222 LIONEL LINES: 1990, boxcar; images depict events at Lionel in 1948 (the F-3 diesel) and 1950 (MagneTraction); otherwise matches 19219 above, except for number. Part of 11715 Lionel 90th anniversary set with 19219-19223. **25 35**

19223 LIONEL LINES: 1990, boxcar; images depict events at Lionel in 1979 (reintroduction of American Flyer) and 1989 (RailSounds); otherwise matches 19219 above, except for number. Part of 11715 Lionel 90th anniversary set with 19219-19223. **25 35**

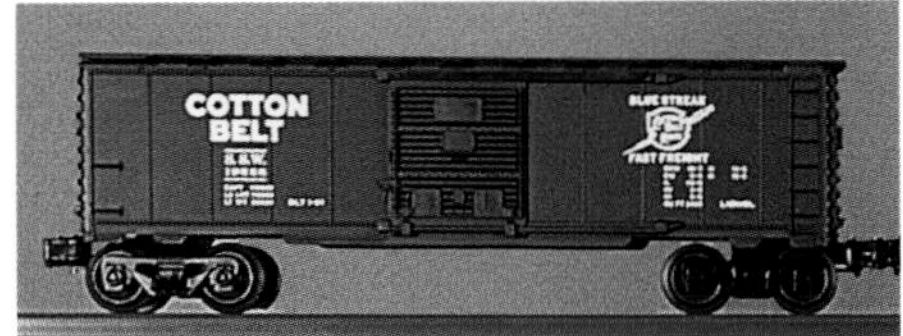

19228 COTTON BELT: 1991, boxcar; maroon-tuscan Type Xa body and doors; white lettering; blue and white lightning streak logo to right; number under- and overscored; metal frame; plastic door guides; ASF trucks; "BLT 1-91". This was the first boxcar to use the Type X (or Xa) body, which restores full rivet detail to the boxcar sides, since the 1950s. Prior to 1991, all modern Lionel's classic-style boxcars were of the Type IX type. The 19234 NYC Girls' set boxcar brought out the Type X body, which adds the metal door guides to the car.

Exc Mt

The 1993 release of the first 6464-series also used it, as did all the later such sets. **20 25**

19229 FRISCO: 1991, boxcar with diesel RailSounds; bright orange Type IX body and doors; silver roof; black lettering "Ship it on the Frisco!"; black and white shield logo to left side; diesel RailSounds circuit board inside with volume control; Standard O trucks; "BLT 1-91". Part of Frisco Fallen Flags set no. 5, whose components were only sold separately.

(A) As described. **100 125**

(B) Factory Error. Double stamping of "LD" and BLT data. W. Fuller Collection. **NRS**

19230 FRISCO: 1991, double-door automobile boxcar; red body and doors; white and black lettering, with pattern similar to 19229; Standard O trucks; "BLT 1-91". Part of Frisco Fallen Flags series no. 5, whose components were only sold separately. **25 35**

19231 TENNESSEE ALABAMA & GEORGIA: 1991, double-door automobile boxcar; royal blue body and doors; yellow lettering and TAG logo; excellent rivet details were restored to the sides of the double-door boxcars with this release; metal frame; ASF trucks; "BLT 1-91". **17 20**

19232 ROCK ISLAND: 1991, double-door boxcar; tuscan-maroon body and doors; white lettering and Rock Island shield; number under- and overscored; excellent rivet details; metal frame; ASF trucks; "BLT 1-91." **17 20**

19233 SOUTHERN PACIFIC: 1991, boxcar; dark green Type Xa body with added rivet detail; black ends; red and black lettering; "S" and "P" of roadname in larger red letters; sometimes difficult to see black lettering; circular red SP logo at upper left; ASF trucks; "BLT 1-91". **17 20**

19234 NEW YORK CENTRAL: 1991, boxcar; light blue ("robin's egg blue") body; Type X body mold with added rivet detail; canary yellow door; colors of body and doors are a reverse scheme from the 19235 Katy boxcar in this set; dark blue lettering; NYC oval logo at upper right; "Pacemaker FREIGHT SERVICE" at upper left; number underscored; metal frame and metal door guides; Standard O trucks; "BUILT BY LIONEL" (no date). Part of 11722 Girls' Train set, the modern revival of the famous 1957 Girls' Train. This was one of the earliest releases of the new Type X body—with metal door guides added. **65 80**

19235 KATY: 1991, boxcar; light (canary) yellow body; Type X body mold; light robin's egg blue door; colors are a reverse scheme from the 19234 car; black lettering "The Katy" in black script to upper right; Standard O trucks; "BLT 1-91". Part of 11722 Girls' Train set, the modern revival of the famous 1957 Girls' Train. **65 80**

19236 NICKEL PLATE ROAD: 1992, double-door boxcar; brown body; white lettering "Nickel Plate Road" script to upper left; "NKP" and number over- and underscored to right side; Standard O trucks; "BLT 1-92". Part of the Nickel Plate Fallen Flags series no. 6, whose components were all sold separately. **25 35**

19237 CHICAGO & ILLINOIS MIDLAND: 1992, boxcar; medium green Type Xa body; mustard yellow lettering; yellow C&IM diamond herald to upper right; large "C&IM" to upper left; number over- and underscored; ASF trucks; "BLT 1-92". C&IM was a popular road for Lionel in 1992—see also the Standard O boxcar section. **20 25**

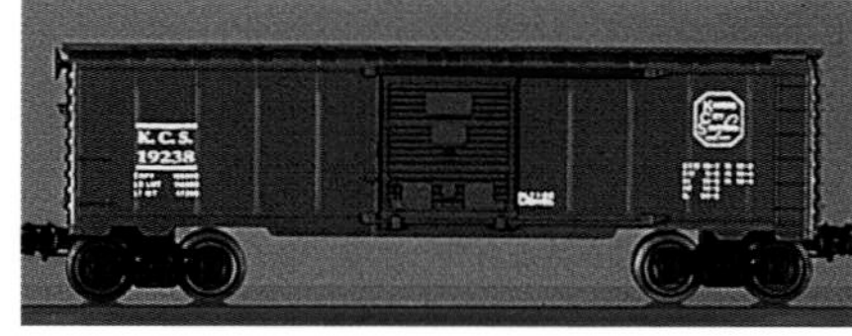

19238 KANSAS CITY SOUTHERN: 1992, boxcar; tuscan-maroon Type Xa body; white lettering; red and white KCS octagon logo to upper right; "K.C.S." and number over- and underscored to lower left; ASF trucks; "BLT 1-92". Kansas City Southern appeared on several other Lionel pieces in 1991 (a GP engine and an SP caboose), though it was never used before on any Lionel rolling stock. **18 25**

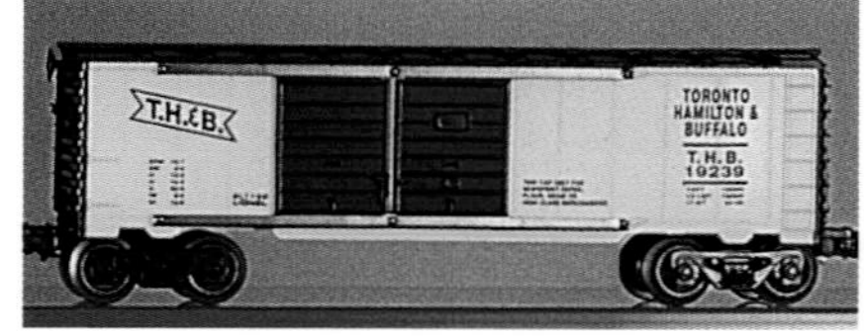

19239 TORONTO, HAMILTON & BUFFALO: 1992, double-door boxcar; yellow sides; black roof, ends and doors; black lettering; TH&B ribbon logo to brakewheel side; "T.H.B." and number over- and

Exc Mt

underscored to lower non-brakewheel side; added rivet details; metal frame; ASF trucks; "BLT 1-92". **15 20**

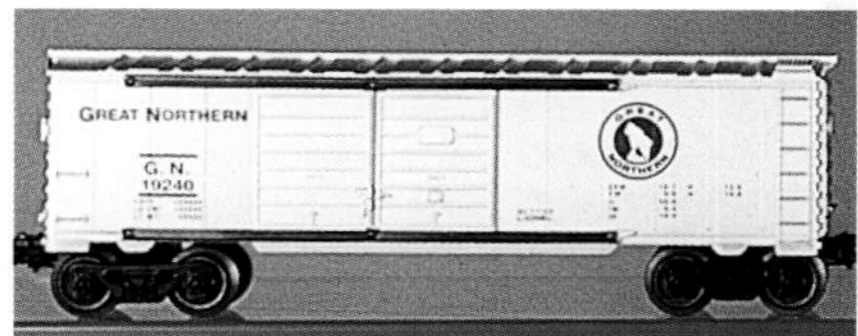

19240 GREAT NORTHERN: 1992, double-door boxcar; silver body and doors; dark green lettering; Great Northern goat logo to non-brakewheel side in black; "G.N." and number over- and underscored to lower brakewheel side; riveted body type; metal frame; ASF trucks; "BLT 1-92". **15 20**

19243 CLINCHFIELD: 1991, boxcar; uncataloged; forest green body; white lettering; "CLINCHFIELD" to upper right; large "C" to left side leading "Clinchfield Cushion Car"; for some reason Lionel used the number "9790" on this car; ASF trucks; "BLT 1-92". Part of 11726 Erie Lackawanna Freight set listed in the 1991 Stocking Stuffers brochure. **40 45**

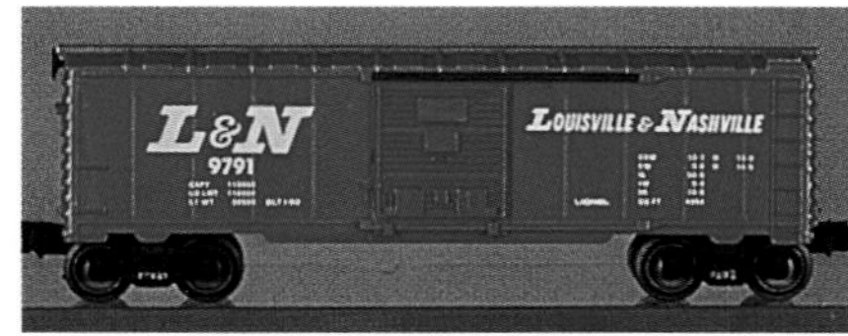

19244 LOUISVILLE & NASHVILLE: 1992, boxcar; medium blue Type Xa body and doors; yellow lettering; large "L&N" to left side; number on car is "9791", not 19244; Standard O trucks; "BLT 1-92". This car was part of the unique Louisville & Nashville set, which started out in the 1992 Book 2 catalog as a high-end Traditional Line set (no. 11729) with track, transformer, and a yellow Standard O caboose. It was not made that way, however. It was produced as shown in the 1992 Stocking Stuffers brochure—with no track or transformer, a red bay window caboose, and all the items sold separately. So the set as made didn't have a set number. **30 35**

The 6464-series Boxcar Sets

Beginning in 1993, Lionel created packaged sets of three boxcars, each reproducing the original 6464 pieces from the 1950s and 1960s. Having sung the praises of these true classics for 40 years, modern Lionel at last decided to remake them, with several modern features that were improvements on the originals—the sprung metal trucks and fast-angle wheels. And for this set Lionel LTI used its new Type X body, with nice all-metal door guides on the top and bottom, which had disappeared from the boxcars in the early '70s. Lionel-Fundimensions had made isolated attempts to re-create the 6464s with a few cars in the 9700 and 9400-series, but it was not until 1993 that Lionel LTI started the task in earnest. The three-packs of cars, with each one individually boxed, would remake the boxcars in the original order in which they were released, starting with the 6464-1 Western Pacific. One interesting fact about them is that none of them bear their assigned catalog number on the car body—all have only the original 6464-series numbers. The first set of three, designated by set no. 19247, is somewhat scarcer than the later ones because at first Lionel was cautious of the reaction to the new models and made them in fewer numbers. They shouldn't have worried—reaction was very positive, and all the subsequent series have been good sellers. This first group is now quite scarce and valuable. This first group is not shown in the catalog with the metal door guides, but the production pieces have them. Their appeal is an obvious one—the valuable originals can remain secure on the shelves or in their boxes, while the bright new remakes streak around the layouts!

19247 6464 SERIES, EDITION I: 1993, set of three boxcars; see 19248, 19249, and 19250 following. Price for set. **270 320**

19248 WESTERN PACIFIC: 1993, boxcar; silver Type X body and doors; dark blue lettering; "Rides like a Feather" to upper right above Lionel circle L logo; "W.P." and "6464" over- and underscored to lower left; metal door guides at top and bottom; Standard O trucks; "NEW 1-93". This is a reissue of the 6464-1 Western Pacific postwar boxcar from 1953. Part of a three-pack of 6464-series remakes produced in 1993, with 19249 and 19250 below. **90 110**

19249 GREAT NORTHERN: 1993, boxcar; orange Type X body and doors; white lettering; GN goat logo to upper right; Lionel Circle L to lower right; "G.N." and "6464" over- and underscored to lower left; metal door guides at top and bottom; Standard O trucks; "NEW 1-93". This is a reissue of the 6464-25 Great Northern postwar boxcar from 1953. Part of a three-pack of 6464-series remakes produced in 1993, with 19248 above and 19250 below. **90 110**

19250 MINNEAPOLIS & ST. LOUIS: 1993, boxcar; tuscan-maroon Type X body and doors; "THE PEORIA GATEWAY" to right side with Lionel Circle-L logo; "M&STL" and "6464" over- and underscored to lower left; metal door guides at top and bottom; Standard O trucks; "NEW 1-93". This is a reissue of the 6464-50 Minneapolis & St. Louis postwar boxcar from 1953. Part of a three-pack of 6464-series remakes produced in 1993, with 19248 and 19249 above. **85 100**

19251 MONTANA RAIL LINK: 1993, double-door boxcar; royal blue body and doors; white lettering; red "Montana" above "RAIL LINK" in white to non-brakewheel side; white diagonal stripe logo on opposite side; number on car is "10001"—catalog number does not appear; plastic frame—a downgrade from

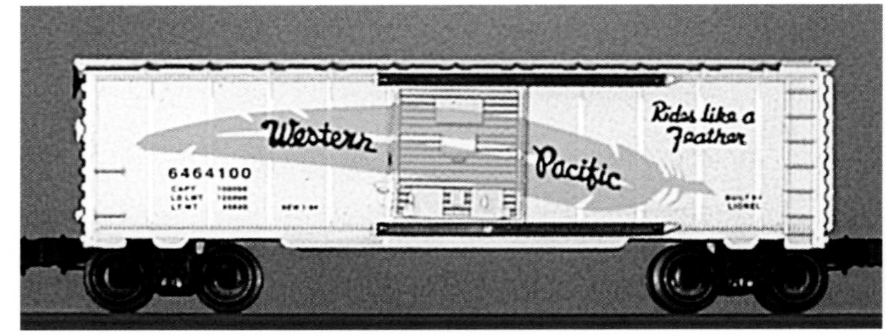

19259 Western Pacific boxcar

	Exc	Mt

earlier double-door boxcars; ASF trucks; "BLT 1-93". A nice match for the 18824 Montana Rail Link SD-9 diesel and 16541 caboose made earlier in 1993. **20 25**

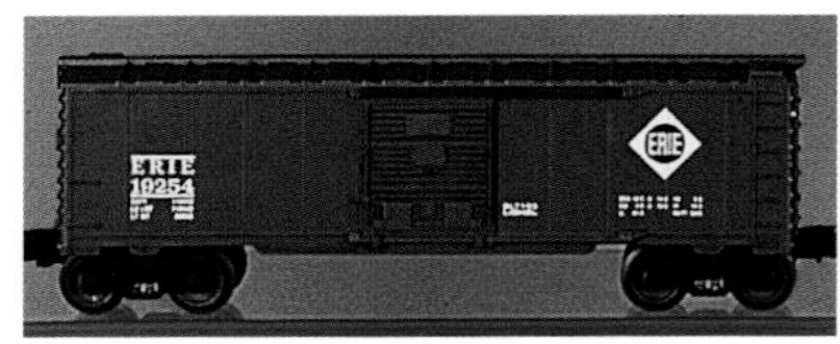

19254 ERIE: 1993, boxcar; tuscan Type Xa body and doors; white lettering; ERIE diamond logo in black and white to upper right; "ERIE" and number under- and overscored to lower left; Standard O trucks; "BLT 1-93". Part of Erie Fallen Flags set no. 7. **25 30**

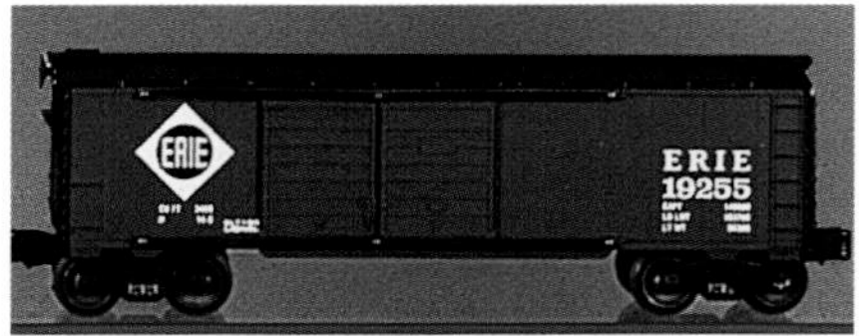

19255 ERIE: 1993, double-door boxcar; tuscan body and doors; black roof and ends; white lettering; large Erie diamond logo to brakewheel side; Standard O trucks; "BLT 1-93". Part of Erie Fallen Flags set no. 7. **25 30**

19257 6464 SERIES, EDITION II: 1994, set of three boxcars; see 19258, 19259, and 19260 following. Price for set. **140 160**

19258 ROCK ISLAND: 1994, boxcar; forest green Type X body and doors; gold lettering; "ROUTE OF THE ROCKETS" to upper left; Rock Island shield to upper right above Lionel circle-L logo; "R.I." and "6464" over- and underscored to center left; metal door guides at top and bottom; Standard O trucks; "NEW 1-94". This is a reissue of the 6464-75 Rock Island postwar boxcar from 1953. Part of the second edition of three 6464-series remakes produced in 1994, with 19259 and 19260 below. **40 50**

19259 WESTERN PACIFIC: 1994, boxcar; silver Type X body and doors; large yellow feather runs almost full length of body, and through the doors; black lettering; "Western Pacific" in black atop feather; "Rides like a feather" to upper right; number on car is "6464100" to left side; metal door guides at top and bottom; Standard O trucks; "NEW 1-94". This is a reissue of the 6464-100 Western Pacific postwar boxcar from 1954. Part of the second edition of three 6464-series remakes produced in 1994, with 19258 above and 19260 below. **50 60**

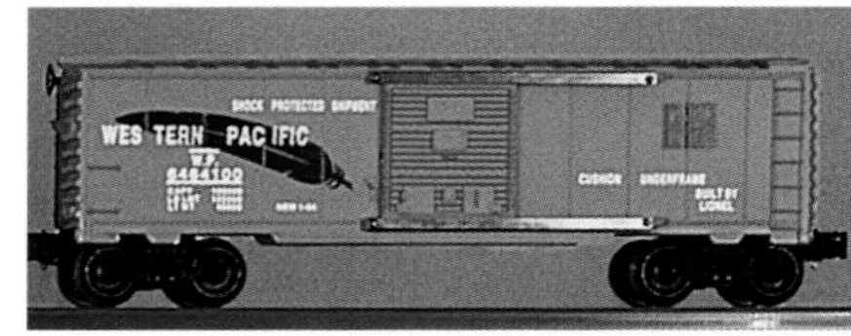

19260 WESTERN PACIFIC: 1994, boxcar; orange Type X body and doors; dark blue small feather (smaller than the 19259) at left side; WP feather route herald to upper right in blue; white lettering; "W.P." and number "6464100" over- and underscored at left; metal door guides at top and bottom; Standard O trucks; "NEW 1-94". This is a reissue of the 6464-100 orange small-feather variation of the Western Pacific postwar boxcar from 1954, which is a scarce and costly version. Now of course it is simply its own car! Part of the second edition of three 6464-series remakes produced in 1994, with 19258 and 19259 above. **50 60**

19263 NEW YORK CENTRAL: 1994, double-door boxcar; light blue-green sides and ends; black roof; white lettering; "NYC" above line and number to left side; black and white New York Central oval to right; metal door guides; plastic frame; Standard O trucks; "BLT 1-94." Part of the unique 11744 New Yorker Passenger/Freight set which served as the Service Station special for 1994. The set is unique because it is "mixed"—a freight set with two NYC passenger cars added. **35 40**

19266 6464 SERIES, EDITION III: 1995, set of three boxcars; see 19267, 19268, and 19269 following. Price for set. **110 125**

Exc Mt

19267 NEW YORK CENTRAL: 1995, boxcar; gray Type X body; red doors; red stripe on upper sides in classic "Pacemaker" paint scheme; white lettering "Pacemaker FREIGHT SERVICE" to upper left above "NYC" and number "6464125", which is underscored; NYC oval logo in white to upper right; metal door guides at top and bottom; Standard O trucks; "NEW 95". This is a reissue of the 6464-125 NYC postwar boxcar from 1954. Part of the third edition of three 6464-series remakes produced in 1995, with 19268 and 19269 below. **40 50**

19268 MISSOURI PACIFIC: 1995, boxcar; Type X body; blue sides with wide gray center stripe, which also runs through doors; gray roof and ends; yellow doors; white and black contrasting lettering; black "Eagle MERCHANDISE SERVICE" to right side on center stripe; Missouri Pacific Lines circle logo to left of door with "M.P." and "6464150" underscored; white capacity data; metal door guides at top and bottom; Standard O trucks; "NEW 95". This is a reissue of the 6464-150 Missouri Pacific postwar boxcar from 1954. Part of the third edition of three 6464-series remakes produced in 1995, with 19267 above and 19269 below. **40 50**

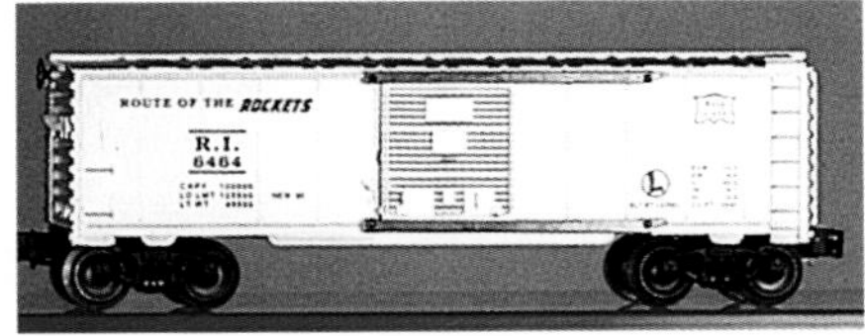

19269 ROCK ISLAND: 1995, boxcar; silver Type X body and doors; black lettering; "ROUTE OF THE ROCKETS" at top left; "R.I." and number "6464" over- and underscored at left; Rock Island shield above Lionel L at right side; metal door guides at top and bottom; Standard O trucks; "NEW 95". This is a reissue of the 6464-175 postwar Rock Island car. Note similarity, in both the postwar and modern eras, to the green Rock Island car made earlier (19258 in the modern case, 6464-75 in the postwar case). Part of the third edition of three 6464-series remakes produced in 1995, with 19267 and 19268 above. **40 45**

Exc Mt

19800 SERIES OPERATING BOXCARS

Many of Lionel's popular operating boxcars (those considered Collector Line or Heritage-series) are found in the 19800-series of numbers. This series also includes other types of cars, such as the gondolas, hoppers, smoking cabooses shown elsewhere in the book, as well as the operating stock and aquarium cars described in the other sections of this chapter. The "operating" classic-type boxcars listed below feature such long-time favorites as the plunger-operated man who pops out the door when the button is pressed; the milk cars that load milk cans onto a platform; the ice cars, which receive ice cubes from the Ice Station accessories; and the brakeman car, which sports a brave figure riding on top of the car who ducks as the warning telltales of an upcoming obstruction approach. Note also that some operating boxcars were also described under the 16600- and 16700-series earlier in the chapter.

19802 CARNATION MILK: 1987, operating milk car with platform; yellow sides; brown roof, ends and doors; red, yellow, and black Carnation Milk can logo and lettering; black ornate "UNION REFRIGERATOR TRANSIT CO." lettering; red and black capacity data and other lettering; white man pushes weighted milk cans out door onto platform; special sheet of decals included to decorate cans; platform has gray base and white railings; postwar die-cast bar-end trucks with sliding shoes for power pickup; "BLT 1-87". This car is a cross between a Lionel refrigerator car and a classic-style boxcar. It has detailed riveted sides like the boxcars, but a roof and end piece similar to the wood-sided reefers. The roof has a hatch for inserting the cans for storage on an interior ramp. Like the reefers, the car is also longer than the boxcars. The motor and activation mechanism inside are quite complex, with a ramp for storing the milk cans and levers to set them upright in front of the man before they are pushed out. Similar to Bosco operating milk car of postwar years, this item was a good seller. **85 110**

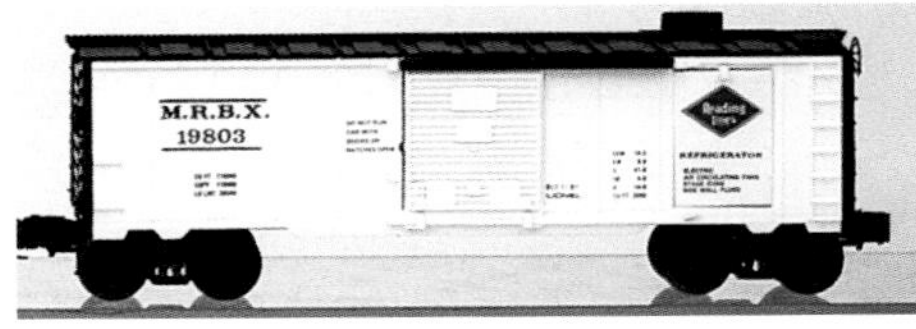

19803 READING LINES: 1987, ice car; white sides and doors; black roof and ends; body has excellent rivet detail; blue lettering and Reading diamond logo; "M.R.B.X." and number under- and overscored; roof hatch receives ice cubes—they are removed through a large door in the side of the car under the hatch; Standard O

	Exc	Mt

trucks; "BLT 1-87". Re-release of postwar ice car (6352) and its modern cousin, the 6700 from 1982. Meant to accompany the icing station accessories such as the modern 2306 and later models, on which a remotely activated man sweeps ice cubes onto the top of the ice car. **45** **55**

19805 SANTA FE: 1987, operating boxcar; red body; white Santa Fe lettering; red and white Santa fe cross logo; number under- and overscored; blue man appears when plunger is activated; Standard O trucks; "BLT 1-87". **30** **40**

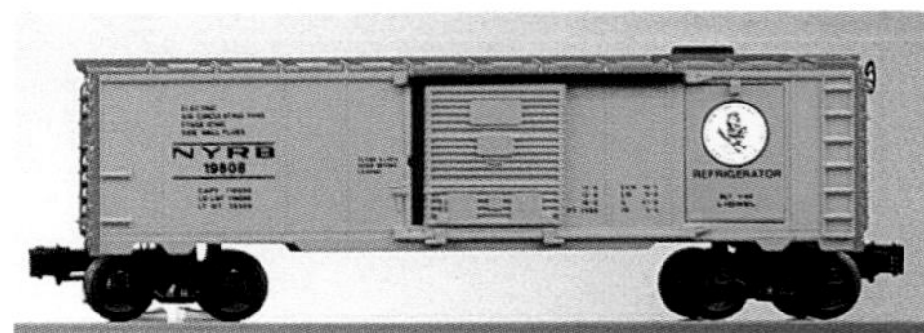

19808 NYRB: 1988, ice car; bright orange sides and doors; red roof and ends; number over- and underscored; NYRB is a part of the New York Central System; blue and white NYC "Early Bird" logo to right side; Standard O trucks; "BLT 1-88". **45** **55**

19809 ERIE LACKAWANNA: 1988, operating boxcar; reddish-brown body; white lettering, number and EL diamond logo; gray unpainted man tosses mail sack out of door when plunger is activated; Standard O trucks; "BLT 1-88". **30** **40**

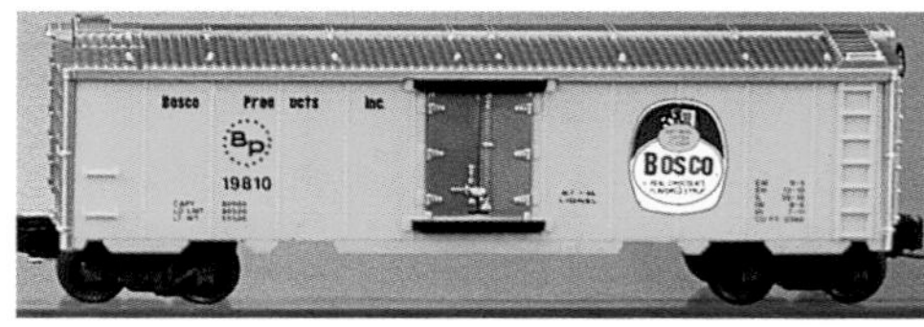

19810 BOSCO PRODUCTS: 1988, operating milk car with platform; bright yellow sides; silver-painted roof, ends, and doors; brown, white, red, and black Bosco electrocal; dark brown "Bosco Products Inc." lettering; gray and white platform; seven gray plastic milk cans with self-stick Bosco labels; postwar die-cast bar-end trucks with sliding shoes; "BLT 1-88". See 19802 for other details on this car. Reissue of postwar 3672. **100** **125**

	Exc	Mt

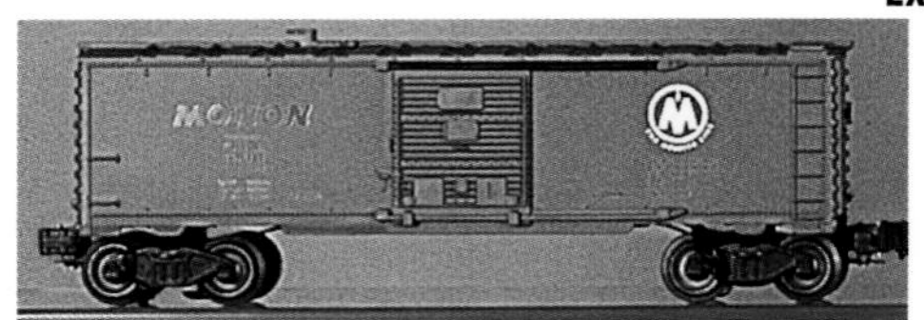

19811 MONON: 1990, operating brakeman car; gray body; red lettering; number under- and overscored; red and white circle-M "Hoosier Line" decal to right; latch mechanism under car causes blue man riding on top to duck as car approaches telltales; postwar-style die-cast bar-end trucks; "BLT 1-90". This is the first brakeman car issued since 1958. Set comes with two telltale poles and trackside mechanisms. **45** **55**

19813 NORTHERN PACIFIC: 1989, ice car; uncataloged; dark green body; black roof with ice hatch; gold lettering "NORTHERN PACIFIC" at top and "AMERICAN RAILWAY EXPRESS" to right side; round NP Monad herald in white, black, and red to left of doors; number is at both left and right sides; Standard O trucks; "BLT 1-89". Comes with 12-block ice load for operation with the 12703 Icing Station. Offered in 1989 Holiday Collection Flyer. **40** **50**

19815 DELAWARE & HUDSON: 1992, operating brakeman car; brown body and doors; white lettering; D&H circle logo in white to upper right; latch mechanism under car causes blue man riding on top to duck as car approaches telltales; postwar-style die-cast bar-end trucks; "BLT 1-92". Set comes with two telltale poles and trackside mechanisms. **45** **55**

19816 MADISON HARDWARE: 1992, operating boxcar; uncataloged; gray body with orange section on top two-thirds of sides; black and white contrasting lettering "MADISON HARDWARE CO. / LIONEL ELECTRIC TRAINS / Special Shipment" to left side; "Sales-Service-Since 1909" to right side around Lionel circle L; "FRAGILE" in black on door plate; number on car is 190991, the years in which the original Madison Hardware store operated in New York City; blue man appears carrying orange Lionel set box when underbody plunger activates; Standard O trucks; "BLT 1-92". This car was a special release for the reopening of Madison Hardware in Detroit, Michigan. Lionel

	Exc	Mt

owner Richard Kughn had bought the entire store (and its "priceless" stock) and brought it from its original location in downtown Manhattan, where it had been a fixture of Lionel trains parts and sales for many years. **140 160**

19817 VIRGINIAN: 1994, operating ice car; royal blue sides; silver roof and ends; ice hatch in roof; yellow lettering "VIRGINIAN" to upper right, in different panels on each side of car; "VGN" circle logo at left center; Standard O trucks; "BLT 1-94". Comes with 12-block ice load for operation with the Icing Station. A new icing station accessory, the 12847, was also made in 1994. **45 55**

19818 DAIRYMEN'S LEAGUE: 1994, operating milk car with platform; white sides and doors; dark blue roof and ends; blue Dairymen's League logos to both sides; large "MILK" lettering to lower right; catalog number not on car; gray and white platform; white man pushes seven gray plastic milk cans with self-stick labels onto platform when UCS track is activated; postwar die-cast bar-end trucks with sliding shoes; "BLT 1-94". See 19802 for other details on this car. **80 100**

19821 UNION PACIFIC: 1995, operating boxcar; medium gray body and doors; red stripes along upper and lower edges of sides; yellow lettering; "U.P." and "9146" over- and underscored to left; 19821 is not on car; "The Challenger" in red to right with "MERCHANDISE SERVICE" in yellow below; yellow "OVERNIGHT DELIVERY" in small letters on upper door plate; gray man tosses orange Lionel box out of door when underbody plunger is activated; Standard O trucks (catalog shows ASF trucks); "BLT 1-95". The catalog also shows this car as a lighter gray than it was actually made. **45 55**

19823 BURLINGTON NORTHERN: 1995, operating ice car; bright yellow sides; red roof with ice hatch; black lettering "BURLINGTON REFRIGERATOR EXPRESS" to left side; "WAY OF THE ZEPHYRS" just to right of door; red and black Burlington Route herald to far right; Standard O trucks; "BLT 94". Comes with 12-block ice load for operation with the Icing Station. This car is similar to the LOTS Burlington car made earlier in the year. The built date indicates it was planned for 1994, but not made till '95. **40 50**

19900 SPECIAL SERIES BOXCARS

Lionel set aside the 19900 series of numbers for special series cars, which so far have included the Toy Fair and Seasons Greetings/Christmas cars, as well as a group of cars in the "I Love"-state series. All are Classic boxcars in the 9700 and 19200 molds.

Collectors have coveted the annual Toy Fair cars since their initial appearance in 1973, even though Lionel itself didn't always go to the New York Toy Fair exhibition. This February expo is where many large toy manufacturers exhibit their wares planned for the upcoming year. The Toy Fair cars, which are never announced in any paper, continue to be in great demand and are almost always scarce limited editions. The Seasons Greetings cars have developed a collector following too. The early ones from the 1970s are quite scarce now. Most of the later ones were either cataloged regularly or made in sufficient quantity to make them still readily available at good prices. There are special items within this group that are harder to find, particularly the holiday cars given only to Lionel employees starting in 1991, and the Christmas cars that bear owner Richard Kughn's signature.

Since the company's Visitors Center opened in 1992, Lionel has produced several special Visitors Center boxcars, placed in the 19900-series as well. These are typically available only from the Visitors Center itself. There are also several Lionel Railroader Club (the company's own collectors club) cars found in this group.

The "I Love"-state series began somewhat unofficially with the 9475 Delaware & Hudson "I Love New York" car in 1984, though it wasn't labeled as part of a series then. A similar Michigan car, the 9486, followed in 1986. This one set the real idea in motion at Lionel, and the series began in earnest in 1987 with the 19901 I Love Virginia car. One state per year followed till 1995, when the pace picked up to two per year. Will there eventually be 50 cars? What about Puerto Rico? Does Lionel plan to be around that long? Stay tuned!

19900 TOY FAIR: 1987, boxcar; uncataloged; red body; silver roof and ends; red door; silver lettering; newly designed red, white, and blue "LIONEL" logo to right of door; WELCOME TO TOY FAIR 1987" to left side; "The Legend Lives On" to far right; Symington-Wayne trucks; "BLT 1-87". Annual boxcar marking the New York Toy Fair exposition. **90 110**

19901 I LOVE VIRGINIA: 1987, boxcar; yellow sides; blue roof and ends; pink "Virginia is for lovers" in script to upper right; blue lettering and "I LOVE VA" to upper left, with "LOVE" represented by a red heart; number under- and overscored; Symington-Wayne trucks; "BLT 1-87". First in the ongoing "I Love"-state series, though two earlier cars (the 9475 in 1984 and 9486 in 1986) followed the same theme. **30 40**

	Exc	Mt

19902 TOY FAIR: 1988, boxcar; uncataloged; silver sides; black roof, ends, and door; red, white, and blue "LIONEL" insignia to right side; black and gold Lionel circle L Large Scale decal to right side; "WELCOME TO TOY FAIR 1988" to left side; "THE LEGEND LIVES ON" to lower right; Symington-Wayne trucks; "BLT 1-88". Annual boxcar marking the New York Toy Fair exposition. **80 100**

19903 LIONEL CHRISTMAS: 1987, boxcar; uncataloged; white sides; dark green roof and ends; red doors; red, white, and blue Lionel insignia and circle L to upper right; red and green lettering to left side features bells and "Merry Christmas" in four languages; green number and built date; plastic arch-bar trucks; "BLT 1-87". Released as part of a special year-end package in 1987. Part of the ongoing annual Christmas boxcar series from Lionel. **40 50**

19904 LIONEL CHRISTMAS: 1988, boxcar; uncataloged; silver sides; red roof, doors and ends; red "Merry Christmas 1988" to left side; black and green lettering; mistletoe and Christmas tree electrocals; gold and black Lionel classics logo; red, white and blue Lionel insignia to upper right; Symington-Wayne trucks; "BLT 1-88". Part of the ongoing annual Christmas boxcar series from Lionel. **40 55**

19905 I LOVE CALIFORNIA: 1988, boxcar; medium blue sides; gold-painted roof and ends; gold "CALIFORNIA THE GOLDEN STATE" to upper right; white lettering and "I LOVE CA" to upper left, with "LOVE" represented by red heart; number under- and overscored; Symington-Wayne trucks; "BLT 1-88". Part of the "I Love"-state series. **20 25**

	Exc	Mt

19906 I LOVE PENNSYLVANIA: 1989, boxcar; maroon-wine colored body; white and gold lettering "I" and "PA" in white with red heart to upper left; "You've Got a Friend In Pennsylvania" in gold to right; number under- and overscored; Symington-Wayne trucks; "BLT 1-89". Part of the continuing "I Love"-state series.

(A) As described. **20 25**

(B) Factory error with red heart missing between "I" and "PA". D. Best Collection **NRS**

(C) With TCA overstamps—given to club officials in 1994 by President Bob Caplan. **NRS**

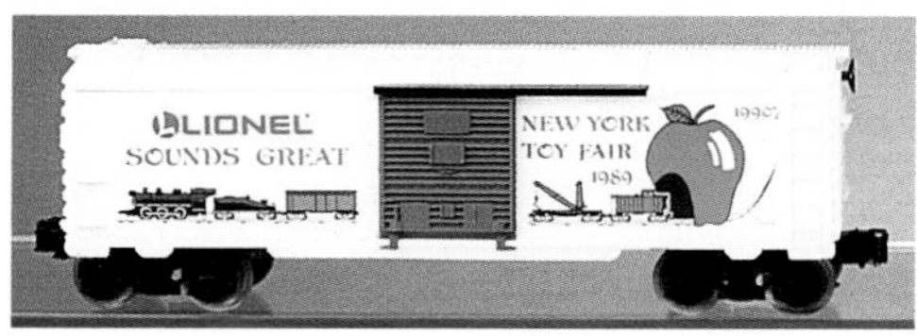

19907 TOY FAIR: 1989, boxcar; uncataloged; pale yellow body; dark green doors; green lettering; "NEW YORK TOY FAIR 1989" with large red and green apple decal to right side; "LIONEL SOUNDS GREAT" with train logo to left side; Symington-Wayne trucks; "BLT 1-89". Annual boxcar marking the New York Toy Fair exposition. **80 100**

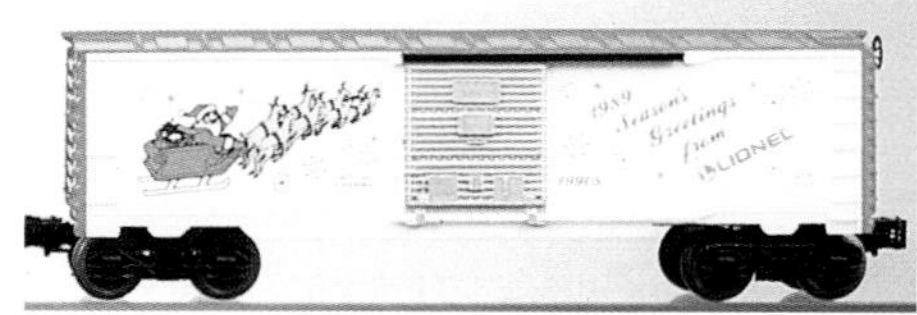

19908 SEASON'S GREETINGS: 1989, boxcar; uncataloged; white sides; orange roof and ends; silver doors; gold lettering; red and gold electrocal of Santa in sleigh at left side; red, blue, and gold "Season's Greetings from Lionel" to right side; blue snowflakes; Symington-Wayne trucks; "BLT 1-89". Part of the ongoing annual Christmas boxcar series from Lionel. Available from the 1989 Holiday Collection flyer. **35 45**

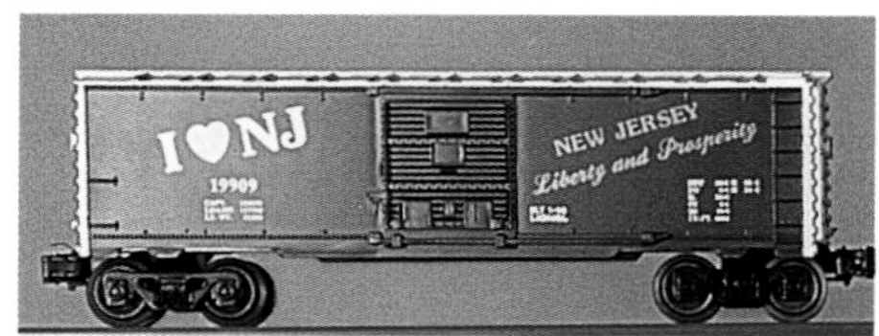

19909 I LOVE NEW JERSEY: 1990, boxcar; dark green body; gold roof and ends; white and gold lettering; "I" and "NJ" to left of

Exc Mt

door with red heart; "Liberty and Prosperity" in gold script to right side; ASF trucks; "BLT 1-90". Part of the continuing "I Love"-state series. **20 25**

19910 HAPPY HOLIDAYS: 1990, boxcar; uncataloged; white sides; gold roof and ends; green doors; green and gold lettering; "happy holidays 1990" in green on right side with red, white, and blue Lionel insignia; red, gold, yellow, and green candle and menorah to right side; ASF trucks; "BLT 1-90". Part of the ongoing annual Christmas boxcar series from Lionel. Shown in the 1990 Stocking Stuffers brochure. In 1990 for the first time, Lionel also released Large Scale, Standard Gauge, and American Flyer S gauge versions of the Season's Greetings cars, all decorated the same as this boxcar. **25 35**

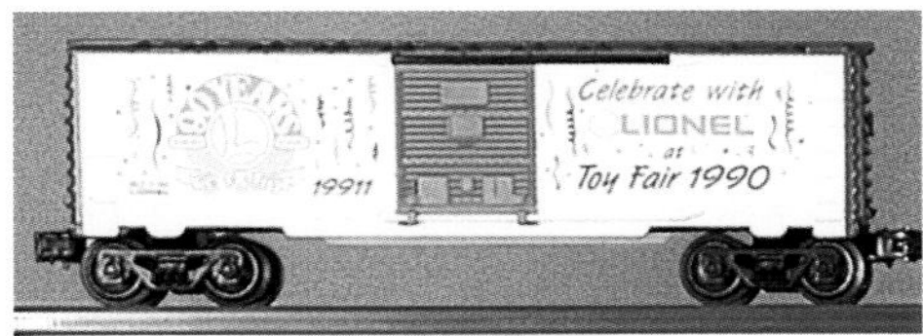

19911 TOY FAIR: 1990; boxcar, uncataloged; white sides; light blue roof and ends; red doors; red and blue lettering; car has extensive graphics in red, blue, and gold; gold 90th anniversary logo to left of door; "Celebrate with Lionel at Toy Fair 1990" to right side; ASF trucks; "BLT 1-90". Annual boxcar marking the New York Toy Fair exposition. **80 100**

19912 I LOVE OHIO: 1991, boxcar; white body; red roof and ends; white door; red and blue lettering; "With God All Things are Possible" in red script to right side; "I" and "OH" in blue with red heart to left side; number underscored; ASF trucks; "BLT 1-91". Part of the continuing "I Love"-state series. **20 25**

19913 SEASON'S GREETINGS: 1991, boxcar; uncataloged; white sides; red roof and ends; gold door; multicolor seasonal images including candy canes, nutcracker, rocking horse, etc., to left side; "Season's Greetings 1991" to right side in blue and green; Lionel circle L and name to lower right in red and blue; number in gold to upper right; ASF trucks; "BLT 1-91". As in 1990, this car was shown in the 1991 Stocking Stuffers brochure with S gauge and Classics (Standard gauge) cars decorated identically. Part of the ongoing Lionel Christmas car series.

(A) As described. **40 50**

(B) Special version for Lionel employees only, has owner Richard Kughn's signature in red, with "Thanks To A Great Team" (top car in photo). **250 300**

19914 TOY FAIR: 1991, boxcar; uncataloged; light tan body; brown doors; blue and red lettering "Welcome To Toy Fair 1991" to left, over red, white and blue Lionel logo; Multicolor "NEW DIRECTIONS" image to right with engine; ASF trucks; "BLT 1-91". Annual car for the Toy Fair expo. **80 100**

19915 I LOVE TEXAS: 1992, boxcar; blue sides and doors; green roof and ends; Type IX body; white lettering; "Friendship" in script to right side; "I" and "TEXAS" with red heart to left side; number underscored; ASF trucks; "BLT 1-92". Part of continuing "I Love"-state series. **20 25**

19916 CHRISTMAS CAR: 1992, boxcar; uncataloged; special available only to Lionel employees; white sides; red roof, ends, and doors; green handwritten "Merry Christmas / Happy New Year / 1992" to left; red and green Christmas wreath to right side; number and "BLT 1-92" in blue handwritten letters; Richard Kughn signature to lower left of doors. This car was designed by Lionel employee Bertha Collins and her granddaughter Laura. It was originally shown as the regular Christmas car in the 1992 Stocking Stuffer brochure, but was later made only for the employees while another car (the 19918) was made for the regular-release set. See additional comments under 19918. **250 300**

19917 TOY FAIR: 1992, boxcar; uncataloged; white sides and doors; black roof and ends; Type XI mold; black lettering; Lenny the Lion in outline form holding train; "1992 Lionel Toy Fair" in yellow; "PULLING TOGETHER TO BRING BACK THE MAGIC" with "MAGIC" in yellow; Lionel logo in red, white, and blue; ASF trucks; "BLT 1-92". Annual boxcar for the Toy Fair expo. **100 125**

19918 CHRISTMAS CAR: 1992, boxcar; uncataloged; white sides and doors; red roof and ends; red "Merry Christmas" to left side and "Seasons Greetings" to right; green and red leaf, flower and cardinal highlights; Standard O trucks; "BLT 1-92". Although this car was announced in the 1992 Stocking Stuffer brochure, it was not made as shown there. The item shown in the brochure was changed to 19916 and given out only to Lionel employees, whereas this piece was made as the 19918. This change was due, as described in a June 1992 letter from

Exc Mt

Lionel, to comments by customers and dealers that the ongoing Christmas car set should have a piece "more in keeping with the graphic designs of previous Christmas cars." The hand-designed car shown in the brochure was given only to Lionel's employees, and this more-traditional-design car was released as the next car in the series. **80 100**

19919 I LOVE MINNESOTA: 1993, boxcar; Type IX body; yellow sides; brown roof and ends; yellow doors; black lettering; "I" and "MINNESOTA" with red heart to upper right; blue lake design to left of door with "Land of 10,000 Lakes" lettering inside in white; ASF trucks; "BLT 1-93". Part of continuing "I Love"-state series. **25 30**

19920 LIONEL VISITORS CENTER: 1992, boxcar; uncataloged; Type IX body; tan colored sides; orange roof and ends; dark blue doors; black lettering; "LIONEL VISITORS CENTER to top left over red, white, and blue circle L logo; scissors cutting red ribbon to right side; "GRAND OPENING / FEBRUARY 19, 1992"; ASF trucks; no BLT date. This is a special made exclusively for sale at the newly opened Lionel Visitors Center in Chesterfield, Michigan. In future years the Visitors Center would make other special releases. **35 45**

19921 CHRISTMAS: 1993, boxcar; uncataloged; special for Lionel employees only; red body and doors; white lettering; white snow and ice trim on top of sides; "MERRY CHRISTMAS 1993" to left with number; "HAPPY NEW YEAR 1994" to right; green Christmas trees and snowman; car includes Richard Kughn's signature; ASF trucks; "BLT 1-93". Next in a series of holiday cars available only to Lionel's employees. **225 260**

19922 CHRISTMAS BOXCAR: 1993, boxcar; white sides; white doors; green roof and ends; Type XII body; red and green elf images to both sides of doors; "JOY TO THE WORLD" to left and "1993" to right side; green lettering; ASF trucks; "BLT 1-93". Shown in the 1993 Stocking Stuffers/1994 Spring release catalog. A matching S gauge car was also pictured later in that catalog. **40 45**

Exc Mt

19923 TOY FAIR: 1993, boxcar; uncataloged; white sides; Type IX mold; light blue roof, ends, and doors; black lettering; red and blue Lionel circle L and name at center right, between "WELCOME TO / TOY FAIR 1993"; "THE KEY TO YOUR SUCCESS" in black to left next to Authorized Value Added Dealer logo; ASF trucks; "BLT 1-93". Lionel had just introduced its Value Added Dealer program in 1993. **90 110**

19924 LIONEL RAILROADER CLUB: 1993, boxcar; uncataloged; silver Type XI body; dark blue roof, ends, and doors; blue and gold lettering; "LIONEL" with circle L and stylized "RRC" to left side; "1993 the INSIDE TRACK" and "1900–1999", "COUNTDOWN TO A CENTURY OF LIONEL" to right side; plastic chassis; ASF trucks; "BLT 1-94". Annual car for the Lionel Railroader Club (LRRC), which at this point was shifting its emphasis to the upcoming centennial of Lionel. Available only through the LRRC's newsletter, *The Inside Track.* **35 40**

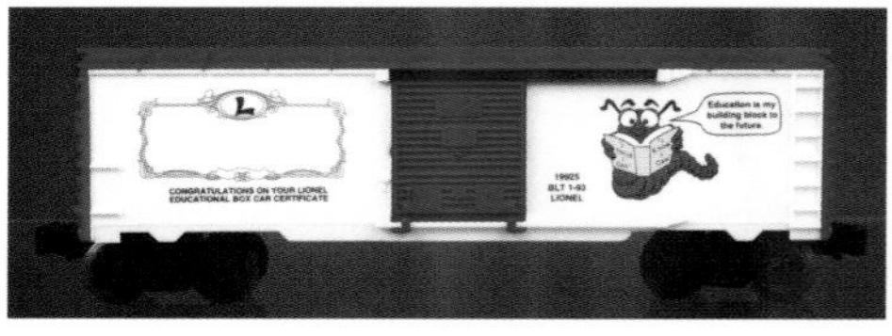

19925 LIONEL LEARNING CENTER: 1993, boxcar; uncataloged; white Type XI body; light blue roof, ends, and doors; light red scroll outline with Lionel L; bookworm to right in green and yellow, saying "Education is my building block to the future"; ASF trucks; "BLT 1-93". Gold plaques depicting completed courses were supplied to fit inside the scroll. Offered only to Lionel employees who completed certain in-house training courses. Very hard to find. **200 250**

19926 I LOVE NEVADA; 1994, boxcar; tuscan-maroon sides on Type XI body; silver roof and ends; silver lettering; "I" and "NEVADA" with red heart at upper left; "SILVER STATE"

	Exc	Mt

under pair of dice to right of doors; number over- and underscored to left side; ASF trucks; "BLT 1-94". Lionel billed this as the tenth in its "I Love"-state boxcar series. **20 25**

19927 LIONEL VISITORS CENTER: 1993, boxcar; uncataloged; tan-cream sides; blue roof and ends; orange door; black lettering; Lionel circle-L to center left; multicolor electrocal of trains exiting tunnels to right side; number on car is 1993; ASF trucks; no BLT date. Special exclusively for the Lionel Visitors Center. Second in the series. **30 35**

19928 CHRISTMAS: 1994, boxcar; uncataloged; special limited edition for Lionel employees only; white sides; Type XI body; red roof, ends, and doors; multicolor toy steam train electrocal to right side with gondola reading "TOYLAND" and smoke puffs spelling "LIONEL"; remainder of train to left side with Richard Kughn's signature in red; black number, and built date; Standard O trucks; "BLT 1-94". **200 250**

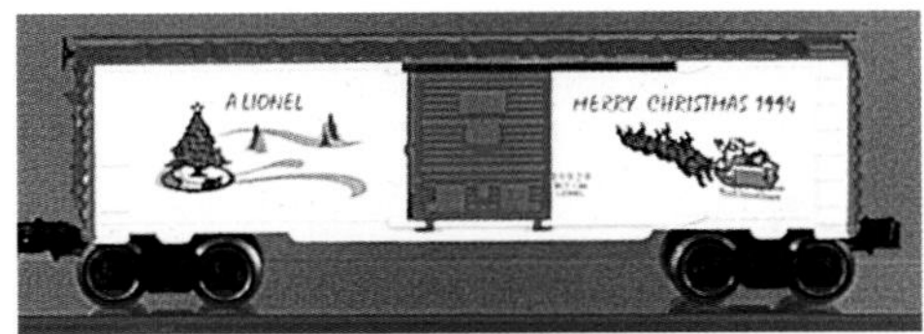

19929 MERRY CHRISTMAS: 1994, boxcar; white sides; red roof, ends, and doors; type XI mold; "A LIONEL MERRY CHRISTMAS 1994" in red across top of car; blue and green Christmas tree scene with trains to left; Santa and reindeer to right; ASF trucks; "BLT 1-94". Shown in the 1994 Stocking Stuffers/1995 Spring release catalog. A matching S gauge car was pictured. Part of Lionel's Season's Greetings car series. **35 40**

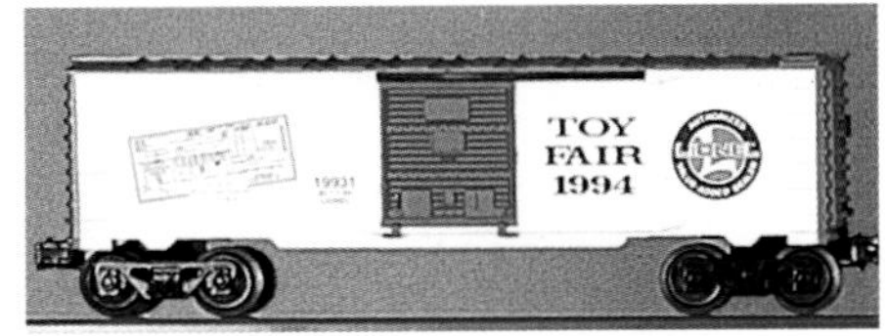

19931 TOY FAIR: 1994, boxcar; uncataloged; white sides; red roof, ends, and doors, Type IX mold; black lettering "TOY FAIR 1994"; "YOUR TICKET TO MODEL RAILROAD EXCITEMENT" to left with ticket image; "Authorized Lionel Value Added Dealer"; red, blue, black, and white Lionel logo to right side; ASF trucks; "BLT 1-94". One of a series of boxcars made for Toy Fair. **80 100**

19932 LIONEL VISITORS CENTER: 1994, boxcar; uncataloged; special exclusively for the Lionel Visitors Center; gray sides; black roof, ends, and doors; black lettering; red, white, and blue Lionel circle L to left over "1994"; multicolor city scene to right with Lionel trains and accessories; number not on car; ASF trucks; no BLT date. Third in the Visitors Center series. **35 40**

19933 I LOVE ILLINOIS: 1995, boxcar; Type XI body; light cream sides and doors; red roof and ends; orange "I" and "ILLINOIS" to upper left with red heart; black lettering; Lincoln image and "LAND OF LINCOLN" in black to right side, over silhouette map of Illinois; number over- and underscored to left center; ASF trucks; "BLT 1-95". Part of continuing "I-Love-state" series. **20 25**

19934 LIONEL VISITORS CENTER: 1995, boxcar; uncataloged; special exclusively for the Lionel Visitors Center; white sides; dark green roof, ends, and doors; black lettering; no number on car except "1995" "LIONEL TRAINS INC VISITORS CENTER" over "1995" to left; Michigan map; multicolor train scene electrocal to right; ASF trucks; "BLT 95". Fourth in the Visitors Center series. **30 40**

19937 TOY FAIR/DEALER PREVIEW: 1995, boxcar; uncataloged; Type IX mold; cream sides; brown roof, ends, and doors; brown and gold lettering; "LIONEL 1995 DEALER PREVIEW" to right side; electrocal of new CAB-1 TrainMaster hand-held controller to left side with "THE CONTROL IS IN YOUR HANDS"; ASF trucks; "BLT 95". This car is considered the next in the annual Toy Fair series, though Lionel did not attend the show in 1995, opting to conduct its own "Dealer Preview" in Michigan. **80 110**

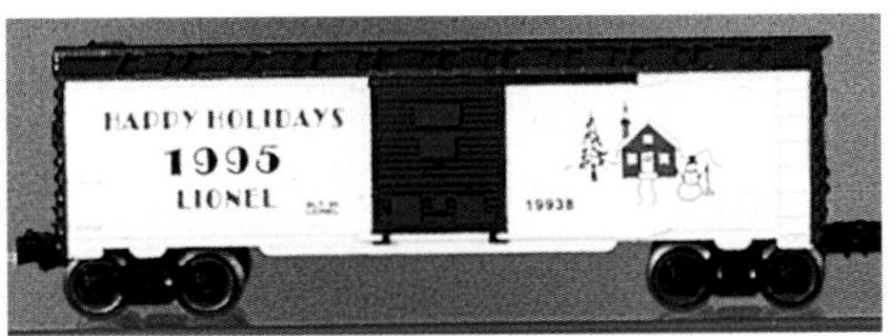

19938 HAPPY HOLIDAYS: 1995, boxcar; Type X body; white sides; green roof, ends, and doors; "HAPPY HOLIDAYS / 1995 / LIONEL" in red and green to left side; house, tree, and snowman scene to right side; ASF trucks; "BLT 95". This is the annual Lionel Seasons Greetings boxcar, shown in the 1995

Exc Mt

Stocking Stuffers catalog. Matching Large Scale and American Flyer cars were also available. **30 35**

19939 CHRISTMAS: 1995, boxcar; uncataloged; white sides; green roof, ends, and door; Type XII mold with rivet detail; green lettering and number; multicolor presents under tree with "1995" in red to right side; "Happy Holidays" script with presents to left side; Standard O trucks; "BUILT 95". Special for Lionel employees only—next in that series. **200 250**

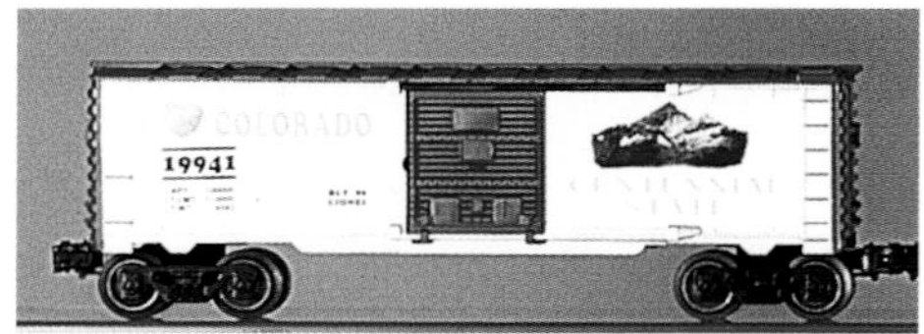

19941 I LOVE COLORADO: 1995, boxcar; Type XI body; silver sides; blue roof, ends, and doors; yellow "I" and "COLORADO" to upper left with red heart; yellow "CENTENNIAL STATE" to right side under black and white Rockies image; number over- and underscored; ASF trucks; "BLT 95". Part of continuing "I Love-state" series. **20 25**

19964 U.S. JCI SENATE: 1992, boxcar; uncataloged; made for the 20th anniversary of the JCI (Junior Chamber International) Senate; white boxcar body, Type XI mold; dark blue roof and door; "UNITED STATES JCI SENATE 1972–1992 20th Anniversary" to right side in blue; left side has blue shield logo with U.S. outline map; yellow wreaths and red banner; ASF trucks; "BLT 1-92". Less than 500 made. **80 110**

51401 PENNSYLVANIA: 1991, semi-scale boxcar; all-phenolic body; classic PRR tuscan paint scheme; white lettering and PRR shield to right side; "PENNSYLVANIA" and "100800" over- and underscored to left; detailed opening door with latch; stamped metal chassis with steps; metal door guides; Standard O trucks; "BLT 3-35". This unique boxcar was part of a four-car set made in 1991 to mark the scale freight cars originally made by Lionel in 1940. It is not of the classic boxcar style—though it closely resembles one. This car is made of the same dense phenolic plastic used on the heavyweight Madison passenger cars—both the 1940s and 1990s models. Hard to find. **120 160**

52000-SERIES SPECIAL PRODUCTION BOXCARS

Starting in 1992, Lionel assigned this series of numbers for its "special production" pieces, such as the cars made to order for train clubs like LCCA, TTOS, TCA, LOTS, and others as well as for individual one-time specials. All are consequently uncataloged, usually somewhat hard to find, and as a result will command extra premiums over regular-production cataloged pieces. Collectors will also find within their ranks some of the most unusual and nicely decorated of all the Lionel boxcars. The series includes all types of rolling stock, not just boxcars, so there are gaps in the numbers listed here.

Exc Mt

52009 WESTERN PACIFIC: 1993, boxcar; uncataloged; special for Sacramento Valley Division of the Toy Train Operating Society (TTOS); silver Type XII body with rivet detail and plastic chassis; black lettering; WP Feather River rectangle logo to right; small red feather to upper left with roadname; "WP" and "6464 1993" underscored to left side; Standard O trucks; "BLT 1-93" on door plate. This was one of several TTOS Western Pacific cars in the 1990s and is intended to closely resemble the venerable postwar 6464-100 original. Its release was planned to coincide with the new release of the first 6464-series three-packs, but there was some dissatisfaction with the plastic frame on this model. **55 70**

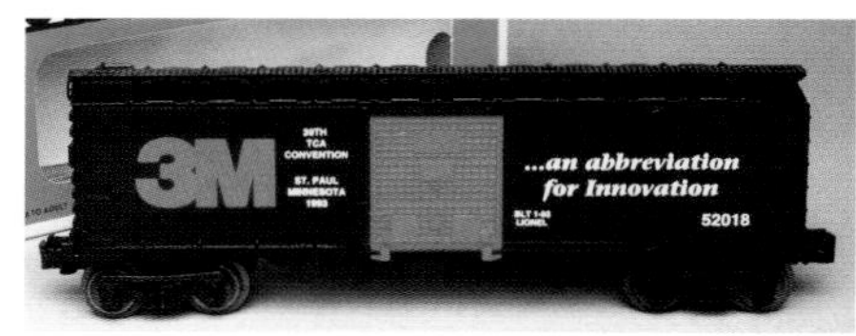

52018 TCA LAKES & PINES "3M": 1993, boxcar; uncataloged; glossy black XI body; red doors; white lettering; "3M" in red to left side, with ". . . an abbreviation for Innovation"; TCA 39th convention notation; ASF trucks; "BLT 1-93". Produced as a banquet special for the TCA's 39th Convention in St. Paul. Less than 200 made; extremely hard to find. **— 600**

52019 LONG ISLAND/NLOE: 1993, boxcar; uncataloged; 10th anniversary special for the Nassau Lionel Operating Engineers (NLOE); tuscan body; Type IX mold; white "LONG ISLAND" to left side over LIRR and "8393", signifying the ten years of the club's operations; NLOE logo with 10th anniversary banner to right of doors; red and white LIRR keystone to far right; ASF trucks; "BLT 6-93". Approx 425 made, on Lionel blanks decorated by PVP. Specialty collectors will note this car is nearly identical to the club's first boxcar produced in 1989 (the 8389), except that this one was made available to the general public, in a change from the usual NLOE practice. **50 65**

52022 UNION PACIFIC: 1993, boxcar; uncataloged; banquet special for the TTOS's 1993 convention; tuscan-brown Type IX body; yellow lettering; "Road of the Streamliners" to right side; roadname and "O.W.R.&N" with "652022" to center left, over- and underscored; TTOS Portland, Oregon, convention notation; ASF trucks; "BLT 8-93". Less than 100 made as banquet favors for the Convention. Very hard to find. **— 500**

52043 L.L. BEAN: 1994, boxcar; uncataloged; 1994 special for the New England Division of the Train Collectors Association

Exc Mt

(NETCA); medium blue body; Type X mold; red doors; red and white "L.L. BEAN" to upper right; white lettering; white stripe through center of body, but not doors; "AN OUTDOOR TRADITION SINCE 1912" to upper left with "NETCA" notation; number on car is "LLBX 1994"; Standard O trucks; no BLT date. This car used a set of blanks supplied by Lionel and decorated by the New England Car shops in Massachusetts. Part of a continuing series of NETCA annual cars. Prototypes of this car with darker blue body color and with yellow doors exist. Reportedly 300 made. **100 130**

52045 PENN DUTCH DAIRY: 1994, operating milk car; uncataloged; special for the TCA Toy Train Museum; red sides; black roof and ends; white doors; white lettering and number, which is "61052"; roadname in old German classic script to left side; Pennsylvania Dutch hex sign; "Our Products Are Wonderful Good". Car comes with the platform and milk cans, and decals for the cans. This car is the first in a group of cars with the Penn Dutch theme for TCA. It is a Lionel blank decorated by the New England Car Shops. Reportedly less than 200 made. **100 130**

52046 ATLANTIC COAST LINE: 1994, boxcar; uncataloged; special for TTOS; brown Type XII body; white lettering; ACL circle logo; ASF trucks; "BLT 1-94". This car is the same as the 16247 boxcar but with additional TTOS notations. **80 110**

52051 BALTIMORE & OHIO: 1995, boxcar; uncataloged; special for Toy Train Museum of the Train Collectors Association (TCA); silver Type X body; blue-green lower third of sides; silver and dark blue contrasting lettering; "BALTIMORE & OHIO" overscored to top left; "Sentinel" below in blue, with number "6464095"; yellow, white, green, and black Sentinel logo to right side; "THE NATIONAL TOY TRAIN MUSEUM" to right of door; metal door guides; Standard O trucks; "BLT 9-95". Part of a special series made for the TCA's museum. **50 60**

52052 TCA 40th ANNIVERSARY: 1994, boxcar; uncataloged; Further details requested. **— 130**

52053 CARAIL: 1994, boxcar; uncataloged; special for TTOS convention in Dearborn; white body; Type XII mold with plastic chassis; blue roof, ends, and doors; "Carail" stylized logo to right side; TTOS convention data to left; Standard O trucks; "BLT 1-94". Special for the TTOS Detroit show in 1994—unusual in that TTOS didn't usually produce specials available only at the convention. Many of these cars are available with Richard Kughn's signature. **75 90**

52054 CARAIL: 1994, boxcar; uncataloged; similar to 52053 above except with Richard Kughn signature and the red, white, and blue Lionel circle L in place of the TTOS convention data to the left side of the car. Extremely hard to find. Reportedly less than 100 made. **— NRS**

52057 WESTERN PACIFIC: 1995, boxcar; uncataloged; annual convention car for the Toy Train Operating Society (TTOS); Type X body; orange sides and doors; black roof and ends; large silver feather along length of sides and through doors; black lettering on feather "Western" to left side and "Pacific" to right; "Shock Protected Freight" to upper right; "WP" and "6464-1995" over- and underscored to left; orange lettering on brakewheel end denotes TTOS convention in Sacramento; metal door guides; Standard O trucks; "NEW 8-95". **65 70**

52058 SANTA FE: 1995, boxcar; uncataloged; special for TTOS Central California Division; brown Type X body with metal door guides and chassis; white lettering; "the Super Chief To California" at right; black and white Santa Fe cross logo to left; car has left and right sides, with "Santa Fe All the Way" and map on opposite side; number is "6464 1895" to commemorate 100 years of the Santa Fe in California; Standard O trucks; "BLT 1-95". **60 70**

52063 NEW YORK CENTRAL: 1995, boxcar; uncataloged special for TCA Museum; Type X body with metal frame and door guides; classic gray and red Pacemaker scheme; white lettering and NYC oval logo; number is "6464125", underscored; "National Toy Train Museum" notations to right side; Standard O trucks. Reportedly less than 300 made for the TCA's museum. Very hard to find. Both this piece and the 52064 below were offered by lottery to the TCA membership in 1995. **— 300**

52064 MISSOURI PACIFIC: 1995, boxcar; uncataloged; special for TCA Museum; gray type X body; blue stripes at top and bottom of sides; yellow door with gray central portion; black and white contrasting lettering; "National Toy Train Museum" notation to right; number is "6464150" underscored; Standard O trucks. Reportedly less than 300 made for the TCA museum. Very hard to find. **— 300**

Exc Mt

52067 BURLINGTON ROUTE: 1995, operating ice car; uncataloged; 16th annual Convention car for the Lionel Operating Train Society (LOTS); yellow sides; brown roof and ends; roof has hatch for operation with the Icing Station; detailed plastic undercarriage; black lettering "BURLINGTON REFRIGERATOR EXPRESS" to upper left; "B.R.D.X." and "50240" over- and underscored to center left; black, red, and white Burlington Route herald to far right; car has different left and right sides; one side has "Everywhere West" in script under the herald; other (non-hatch) side has "Way of the Zephyrs"; Standard O trucks; "BLT 95". Special "LOTS 95" ice cubes were included at the convention—add $15 to price for presence of the ice cubes. 1365 made. Lionel cataloged a nearly identical ice car later in 1995. (See 19823). **50 60**

52068 CONTADINA: 1994, boxcar; uncataloged; special for TTOS; same as 16245 except with TTOS notations and "Toy Train Parade". Made for the club's celebration at the California Railroad Museum in Sacramento in 1994. **— 70**

52070 KNOEBELS: 1995, boxcar; uncataloged; a first special made for the Pennsylvania amusement park; white sides; Type XI mold with plastic frame; green roof and ends; green lettering; "Knoebels Railway, Elysburg, PA" to right side; number and General-style engine to left side; ASF trucks; "BLT 95". First in a series of cars made for Knoebels. **50 60**

52075 UNITED AUTO WORKERS: 1995, boxcar; uncataloged; white body, Type XI mold; dark blue lettering; UAW wheel to upper right; sides feature photos of UAW officials; interlocking yellow and brown arms to left side with "SOLIDARITY FOREVER"; doorplates marked "UAW LOCAL 417" and "UNION MADE"; ASF trucks; "BLT 95". This item is not part of a set. **55 65**

Exc Mt

52082 LACKAWANNA: 1995, boxcar; uncataloged; medium blue-green Type IX body and doors; white lettering; "LACKAWANNA" in large block letters to upper left; "SNHS" and "1995" over- and underscored to center left; Steamtown engine logo to right side over "SCRANTON, PENNSYLVANIA"; ASF trucks; "BLT 7-95". This car was issued to mark the opening of the Steamtown National Historic Site in 1995. Available only at Steamtown. **70 90**

52096 DEPARTMENT 56–SNOW VILLAGE: 1995, boxcar; uncataloged; first special for Department 56; blue Type XI body; white lettering "The Original Snow Village" to upper left; "Department 56" to upper right; multicolor winter scenes on both sides; number on car is "9756", a number which oddly enough was skipped in the 9700-series of cars Lionel made in the 1970s; ASF trucks; "BLT 95" on door. Made exclusively for Department 56 through Allied Model Trains. Reportedly 5000 made. Department 56 creates lighted scale buildings and accessories with a Christmas theme. **— 100**

HI-CUBE BOXCARS

In 1976 Fundimensions added another all new boxcar to its growing roster of modern, prototypically correct rolling stock. This was the all-plastic "Hi-Cube" boxcar, derived from the full-scale 40-foot boxcar that is built 12 to 18 inches higher than the norm. Like the real thing, the Lionel Hi-Cubes had no catwalks on the roof. They also featured extensive riveting detail on the car sides. The new boxcar had large sliding doors fastened to rails by plastic hooks at both top and bottom. In addition, an all-new plastic frame was made for these cars. The Hi-Cube boxcar is about ½ inch longer than its Classic boxcar cousin, as well as ¼ inch taller.

The 1970s-era Hi-Cubes were made in two distinct series. One featured real railroad names. A first round starting in 1976 was repeated with a few more in 1982. Then in 1977 Lionel began its Mickey Mouse series, a group of colorful cars with Disney logos and characters. This set was yet another in a long series of collaborations between Lionel and Disney. The collectibility of both names meant this set was destined for success. Today the set (cars 9660 through 9672 plus the 8773 U36B engine and the 9183 caboose) is extremely scarce and hard to find intact. The 9667 Snow White car and the 9672 Mickey Mouse Birthday uncataloged car are each worth several hundred

Exc Mt

dollars alone. The value of the set continues to appreciate today.

For some reason, perhaps because of their operating characteristics, the Hi-Cube boxcars disappeared from Lionel's line after 1984. Lionel LTI brought it back in a revival of the Disney series, starting in the 1991 Stocking Stuffers brochure. This series used the heavier and steadier die-cast Standard O sprung trucks (the earlier set used plastic trucks) and was clearly an effort to capitalize on the success of the previous set as well as the attraction of Disney collectibles in general. Unsure of the reception, Lionel made the first two cars (19241 and 19242) in fewer numbers than the following ones. The reception was quite good, meaning the first two are hard to obtain now. The company made many more of the following cars, which it took to showing mainly in its late-year Stocking Stuffers catalogs, not in the regular catalogs. The notable feature of all these cars is the exceptionally detailed and many-colored electrocal graphics decorating each car.

Although the Hi-Cube boxcars are colorful and contemporary, operators should note that the rolling characteristics of the earlier Fundimensions models are poor. Because of their plastic frames and high center of gravity, they have a tendency to wobble or tip over unless weighted. This matter has been corrected recently by using die-cast wheelsets. Nonetheless, the cars show the real effort Lionel was making to add a contemporary flair to tinplate railroading.

Perhaps due to their somewhat toy-like appearance, these cars have not shown up often as part of the special offerings from the train clubs. However, one that did is a real corker—the 52077 TCA car from 1995. Only 125 of these were produced, and it is virtually impossible to find now.

HI-CUBE BOXCAR LISTINGS

Exc Mt

19241 MICKEY MOUSE: 1991, Hi-Cube boxcar; uncataloged; white sides; dark yellow roof, ends, and doors; black lettering and number; multicolor electrocal to left of door depicting evolution of Mickey Mouse character; Mickey "60 YEARS" banner to right of door; Standard O trucks—first use of the sprung trucks on a Hi-Cube boxcar in the modern era; "BLT 1-91". First Hi-Cube boxcar released since 1984. The company hinted in its description that the car would be the start of a "new Disney Commemorative train," an add-on to the Disney Hi-Cube set made in 1977–78. The heavy sprung trucks on this car improve its rolling characteristics substantially over earlier cars. Shown only in 1991 Stocking Stuffer brochure. Hard to find. Decals on the car can sometimes be found peeling. 125 150

19242 DONALD DUCK: 1991, Hi-Cube boxcar; uncataloged; white sides; red roof, ends, and doors; black lettering and number; multicolor electrocal to left of door depicting evolution of Donald Duck character; "HAPPY BIRTHDAY DONALD DUCK" banner to right of door; car intended to mark Donald's 50th birthday; Standard O trucks—first use of the sprung trucks on a Hi-Cube boxcar in the modern era; "BLT 1-91". An add-on to the Disney Hi-Cube set made in 1977–78. Shown only in 1991 Stocking Stuffer brochure. Hard to find. 125 150

19245 MICKEY'S WORLD TOUR: 1992, Hi-Cube boxcar, uncataloged; white sides; black roof, ends, and doors; black lettering and number; multicolor graphic of Goofy and Donald to left side; Mickey's World Tour circle logo to right side; Standard O trucks; "BLT 1-92". Part of new Disney Hi-Cube set that started with 19241. Shown in 1992 Stocking Stuffer brochure. 50 60

19246 DISNEY WORLD 20th ANNIVERSARY: 1992, Hi-Cube boxcar; uncataloged; white sides, red roof, ends, and doors; black, blue, red, and gold lettering; Mickey graphic to left of door with Disney World 20th anniversary herald; 20th anniversary logo to right of door; Standard O trucks; "BLT 1-92". Part of new Disney Hi-Cube set that started with 19241. Shown in 1992 Stocking Stuffer brochure. 60 75

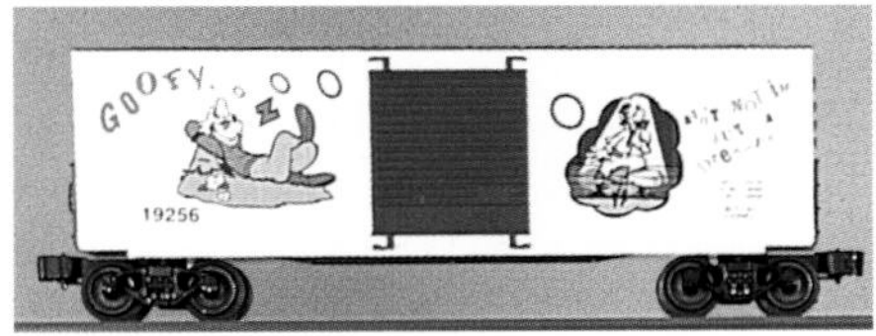

19256 GOOFY: 1993, Hi-Cube boxcar; white sides; blue roof, ends, and doors; black lettering and number; multicolor graphics—lounging Goofy to left side of door; "ain't nothin' but a Dreamer!" image to right side; Standard O trucks; "BLT 1-93". Part of new Disney Hi-Cube set that started with 19241. This is the first one of that set shown in the regular catalog. 35 45

19261 PERILS OF MICKEY I: 1993, Hi-Cube boxcar; uncataloged; white sides; purple roof, ends, and doors; red and blue lettering and number; multicolor cartoon images of various scenes with Mickey Mouse; different scenes on each side of car; Standard O trucks; "BLT 1-93". Part of the modern Disney Hi-Cube set beginning with 19241, but Lionel billed it as the start of a "sub-series" of "Perils of Mickey" cars. Scenes are from the "Mickey Mouse in the Mail Pilot" episode. Shown in the 1993 Stocking Stuffer catalog. 30 40

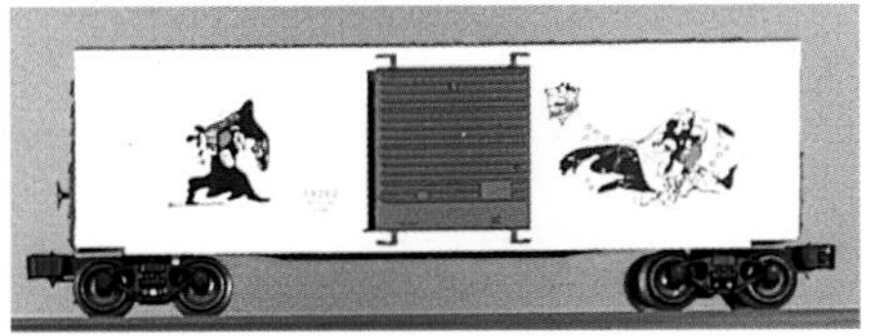

19262 PERILS OF MICKEY II: 1993, Hi-Cube boxcar; uncataloged; white sides; green roof, ends, and doors; green lettering and number; multicolor cartoon images of various scenes with Mickey Mouse; different scenes on each side of car; Standard O trucks; "BLT 1-93". Part of the modern Disney Hi-Cube set

52077 Great Northern Hi-Cube boxcar

Exc Mt

beginning with 19241, but Lionel billed it also as the second of a "subseries" of "Perils of Mickey" cars. Scenes are from the "Mickey Mouse Outwits the Phantom Blot" episode. Shown in the 1993 Stocking Stuffer catalog. **30 40**

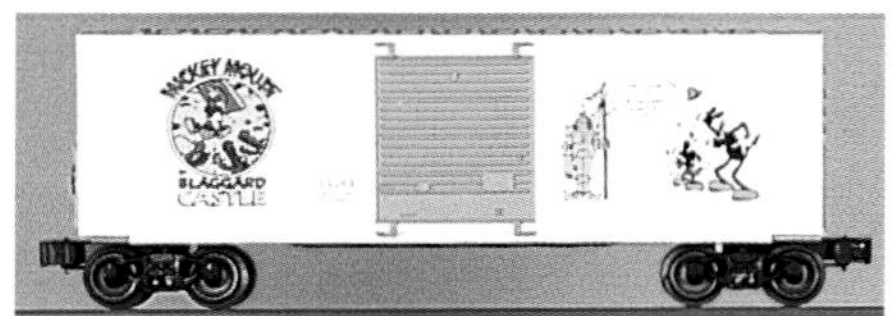

19264 PERILS OF MICKEY III: 1994, Hi-Cube boxcar; white sides; orange roof, ends, and doors; blue lettering and number; multicolor cartoon images of various scenes with Mickey Mouse; different scenes on each side of car; Standard O trucks; "BLT 1-94". Part of the modern Disney Hi-Cube set beginning with 19241, and third of a "subseries" of "Perils of Mickey" cars. **30 40**

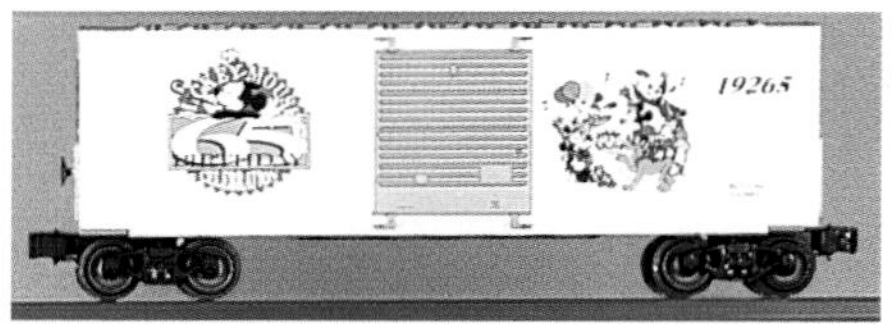

19265 MICKEY'S 65th BIRTHDAY: 1994, Hi-Cube boxcar; uncataloged; white sides; gold roof, ends, and doors; black lettering and number, which on this car is prominent to the upper right; multicolor Mickey Mouse birthday images on both sides of door; Standard O trucks; "BLT 1-94". Part of the modern Disney Hi-Cube set beginning with 19241. Shown in 1994 Stocking Stuffers catalog. **45 50**

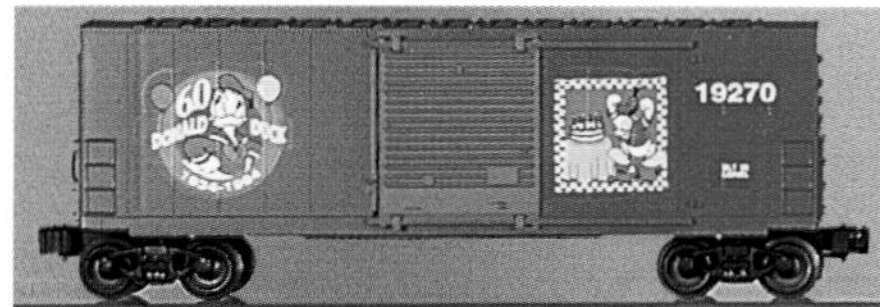

19270 DONALD DUCK 60th BIRTHDAY: 1995, Hi-Cube boxcar; uncataloged; medium blue body; red doors; white lettering and number; multicolor Donald Duck birthday image; different scenes on both sides of car; Standard O trucks; "BLT 95". This is the first of the recent Disney series of Hi-Cubes that did not have white sides, and roof/ends/doors of the same color. Part of the modern Disney Hi-Cube set beginning with 19241. Shown in 1995 Stocking Stuffers catalog. **35 45**

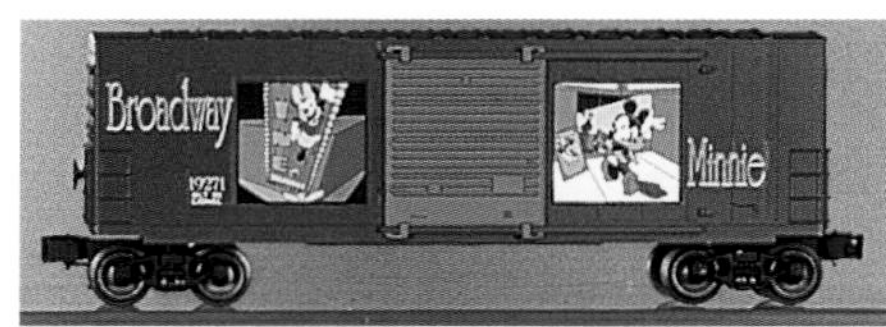

19271 MINNIE MOUSE: 1995, Hi-Cube boxcar; uncataloged; purple body; green doors; yellow lettering and number; multicolor Minnie cartoon images; "Broadway Minnie" in blue and yellow; different scenes on both sides of car; Standard O trucks; "BLT 95". Part of the modern Disney Hi-Cube set beginning with 19241. Shown in 1995 Stocking Stuffers catalog. **40 50**

52077 GREAT NORTHERN: 1995, Hi-Cube boxcar; uncataloged; special for the banquet at the 1995 Train Collectors Association Convention in Seattle; sponsored by the Pacific Northwest Division of TCA; blue body; white lettering; goat logo in white to right side; "9695"; Standard O trucks; "BLT 6-95". Reportedly only 125 made. Very hard to find. **— 400**

O27 SHORT BOXCARS

As mentioned earlier in this volume, the term "O27" denotes adjectives such as "short" or "inexpensive" or a minimum of special features. It derives from the "O27" track Lionel made, and still makes, originally for its lower-cost starter sets. This track is lower in height and made with less material than the regular (O31) tubular track. It is less costly yet performs essentially the same function. The term as applied to the rolling stock also implies smaller and less costly, but performing the same function. In the case of the boxcars, this subsection will feature the smaller "O27" boxcars, as distinguished from their larger "Classic" and "Standard O" cousins described in the other sections.

We should mention for completeness that there are also a few short stock cars in the Lionel line, of about the same length and height as the boxcars described here. The short stock cars are grouped with the other stock cars in their own subsection.

The short O27 boxcars look somewhat silly next to the Standard O boxcars or any of the larger items described in this chapter, but they are not really intended to be run in the same trains. For the most part, they should be in trains of like size, such as the short single dome tankers, two-bay hoppers, short gondolas, or SP cabooses. In fact, a set of these small colorful boxcars will look quite good behind some of Lionel's smaller Alco FA-units, NW-2 switchers, or 4-4-2 steamers.

From the earliest postwar days, Lionel has created shorter, inexpensive boxcars for its starter sets and special promotions. These little boxcars comprise one of the more neglected areas of toy train collecting, since they lack the glamour of their larger relatives, and so are often spurned by the hi-rail and scale collectors. Yet some are quite hard to find. They represent a real opportunity for the beginning collector to obtain rare cars at as-yet-reasonable prices. There are even a few gems-in-the-rough.

Many of the short O27 boxcars have come in the lower-end Traditional Line sets. Occasional stragglers will be found for separate-sale, especially the operating boxcars. Others may be found in inexpensive "rolling stock assortments." An important subcategory belongs to the uncataloged specials made for stores and businesses such as Mopar, True Value Hardware, Ace Hardware, and Toys "R" Us. In fact, there have been more than a dozen Toys "R" Us special boxcars made since the first one in 1975, resulting in an active collecting fraternity for these cars alone. A similar interest exists in the several True Value and Ace Hardware cars. These special cars would often appear as replacements for the regular-issue boxcars in otherwise standard Traditional Line sets—a kind of individualization of the set on behalf of the store.

The short O27 boxcars come in two major body styles, with operating and non-operating varieties within each. The first major style is the "fixed-door" or "plug-door" type, which traces its heritage from the 6014 postwar model. It is only 8½ inches long. This **"6014-style"** has non-operating doors molded into the car body. It is thus quite a bit less expensive to make than other boxcars with movable doors. The modern car is essentially the same as the postwar original except that it has a molded plastic bottom chassis rather than the stamped-metal frame used on the postwar pieces. This car was one of the first out of the docks when Lionel-Fundimensions took over production from the postwar company in 1970. It appeared then as the 9040 Wheaties car. Many others followed thereafter through the 1980s. For the detail-oriented, we will add that the body style on the 6014-type boxcars is known as "Type V." Types I through IV are of postwar heritage and are described in *Greenberg's Guide to Lionel Trains, 1945–1969, Volume I.* The progressive types outline a continuing process of rivet removal (to provide greater stamping area) paralleling that of the larger boxcars. The postwar "carryover" Type IV continued the process but was used only on two of the earliest releases in the modern era (the 9040 Wheaties and the 9041 Hershey's in the 1970s). Since 1973, all of the 6014-type boxcars have used the Type V style—which removed the rivets entirely, leaving completely smooth sides—and so our listings in this book will not reference the body type. Another point of interest—many Fundimensions models of this car included only one operating coupler, with the other a dummy. This cost-cutting practice persisted into the 1980s. Since 1986, though (the coverage period of this volume), both couplers have been operating ones.

There is a unique operating version of this car, also tracing to a postwar heritage—the cop-and-hobo car. On this one a spring-loaded platform towers high over the boxcar. On the platform can be found a plastic cop or hobo figure, held magnetically in place. The car passes under a low-clearance bridge as the figures chase each other on and off the bridge and the car platform. Operators of this car must of course be wary of the placement of the bridge (larger rolling stock tend to bang into it) as well as where they run the cop and hobo car (the poor cops and hobos tend to whack, unceremoniously, into tunnel portals!). Despite these limitations, Lionel LTI produced two models of the car—the 16614 Reading in 1989 and the 16624 New Haven in 1990–91, and a planned Great Northern car in 1991—before turning its attention elsewhere. In 1995 the company changed to the larger boxcar for its next release of the cop-and-hobo car—the 16705.

In 1984 Lionel Fundimensions carried the obscure O27 boxcar up a notch when it re-created the 9¼-inch-long **"6454-style"** boxcar, the second of the major boxcar body types in this section. The first example appeared in Chessie colors (the 7910) and was contemporary with an operating model (7912) made for Toys "R" Us. This handsome boxcar is basically a miniature version of the popular 6464-series classic boxcar, with opening doors, metal door guides, brakewheel, and full rivet detail. It adds a wonderful touch of class to the O27 train outfits. In fact, in single photos, it is sometimes difficult to distinguish the O27 and the O gauge classic boxcars. The easiest way is to note that the shorter ones have somewhat more rectangular doors and only one prominent marker plate. The doors on the classic boxcars have four large marker plates.

Again, there are both operating and non-operating 6454-style boxcars, with the former having a hole cut in the roof for a bobbing head or figure, such as Geoffrey Giraffe (for Toys "R" Us), a circus elephant, or Goofy. The figure will snap in and out of the car when a trackside trip mechanism activates the lever under the chassis, usually as a telltale pole gives the figure "warning" of an upcoming low overhang.

As Lionel pressed toward realism and scale railroading in the 1990s, the production of the short O27 boxcars has languished. Even the lower-end Traditional Line sets in recent years have used the Classic-type boxcars or similar types rather than the shorter ones. This transition was complete around 1994, and no small boxcars have been made since.

The small boxcars will be found in the 16200-series of numbers, while the operating models appear in the 16600-series.

027 SHORT BOXCAR LISTINGS

Exc Mt

16200 ROCK ISLAND: 1987–88, short boxcar, 6014-style, red body; white lettering and logo; plastic arch-bar trucks. Part of Rail Blazer set 11701. **10 12**

16201 WABASH: 1988–91, short boxcar, 6014-style; dark blue body; white lettering and numbers; white Wabash flag emblem; Symington-Wayne trucks; "BLT 1-88". Part of 11703 Iron Horse freight set. Models from the 1991 set have the ASF trucks. **10 12**

16203 KEY AMERICA: 1987, short boxcar; 6014-style; uncataloged; gray body, black lettering; "Key America Dealer" to left of door; names of appliance manufacturers to right side; Symington-Wayne trucks. Part of special 11754 Key America set, which was the same concept and design as the Hawthorne set from the same year. See following entry. Somewhat hard to find. **60 80**

16204 HAWTHORNE: 1987, short boxcar, 6014-style; uncataloged; special for the Hawthorne Home Appliances and Electronics store; white body; black lettering "Hawthorne / Competitive Prices Plus" to left of doors; "Plus" in red script; appliance manufacturers' logos in black to right of doors; Symington-Wayne trucks; "BLT 1-87". From special Hawthorne Home Appliances promotional set (no. 11756), with the 8902 ACL engine and caboose. Somewhat hard to find. **70 90**

16205 MOPAR: 1987–88, short boxcar; 6014-style; uncataloged; gray body; red, white, and blue lettering; three blue stripes; catalog number not on car; "1987" is the only number; Symington-Wayne trucks; "BLT 1-87". Part of 11757 Mopar Express, a special promotional set for Chrysler in 1987 and 1988. **50 60**

16207 TRUE VALUE: 1988, short boxcar; 6014-style; uncataloged; light blue body; dark blue lettering; red "True Value" script logo to right of doors; gold 40th anniversary logo to left; Symington-Wayne trucks; "BLT 1-88". Part of special True Value version (set no. 11762) of the Cannonball Express, in which this car replaced the usual 7925 Erie-Lackawanna car. This car and set were intended to celebrate True Value's 40th anniversary. The set was repeated in 1989 but with a new True Value car, the 16219. **50 65**

Exc Mt

16209 DISNEY MAGIC: 1988, short boxcar; 6014-style; uncataloged; white body; blue and red lettering; Disney Magic logo to right of doors in blue and lavender; "LIONEL" and circle-L to left of doors in red; Symington-Wayne trucks; "BLT 1-88". Came in a special Sears version of the Iron Horse Freight, in which this car replaced the 16201 Wabash car. Set number is 11764. Somewhat difficult to find. **75 100**

16211 HAWTHORNE: 1988, short boxcar; 6014-style; uncataloged; virtually same description as 16204 above, except appliance logos are rearranged, and car carries "BLT 1-88" date. Came as part of 1988 Hawthorne special set 11756, whose contents, other than the boxcar, were the same as the 1987 set (see also 16204). **50 75**

16213 SHOPRITE: 1988, short boxcar; 6014-style; uncataloged; yellow body; red and black lettering; "Shoprite / Does It Right" to left of doors; red and black circular Shoprite logo to right side; Symington-Wayne trucks; "BLT 1-88". Came in special Shoprite version (set no. 11767) of the Freight Flyer, in which this car replaced the 9001 Conrail car. This was a first special for the Shoprite food store chain. Reportedly 1100 made. **50 70**

16219 TRUE VALUE: 1989, short boxcar, 6454-style; uncataloged; yellow body, red script "True Value" to right side; black and red hammer logo to left side; other lettering in black and white; note upgrade to 6454-type operating-door boxcar, the first use of this body on the True Value series; Symington-Wayne trucks; "BLT 1-89". Came in special (set no. 11762) version of the Cannonball Express set, in which this car replaced the 7925 Erie-Lackawanna boxcar. **55 75**

Exc Mt

16220 ACE HARDWARE: 1989, short boxcar; 6014-style; uncataloged; white body; black lettering; large red "ACE" logo to right, with "Hardware" in black underneath; "LIONEL" and circle-L logo in black to left side; catalog number is not on the car; Symington-Wayne trucks; "BLT 1-89". Part of 11774 special Ace Hardware version of the Cannonball Express, in which this car replaced the 7925 Erie Lackawanna car. An unusual feature of this car (as compared to most other store specials) is the prominence with which the "LIONEL" logo is displayed. **50 65**

16221 MACY'S: 1989, short boxcar, 6014-style; uncataloged; white body; blue and red lettering; "macy's" to left in blue; "PARADE OF TOYS" to right in red with "TOYS" on blue block background; catalog number is not on the car; Symington-Wayne trucks; "BLT 1-89". Came in special 11772 Macy's version of the Freight Flyer set, in which this car replaced the 9001 Conrail car. Reportedly less than 500 made. Hard to find. **60 80**

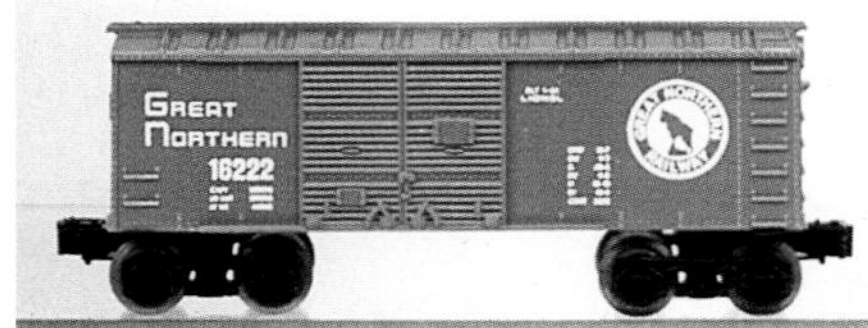

16222 GREAT NORTHERN: 1990–91, short boxcar; 6014-style; light blue body; white lettering; GN goat logo in white to right of doors; Symington-Wayne trucks; "BLT 1-89". Part of 16999 rolling stock assortment, which was cataloged in 1990, but available in 1991 also. **10 15**

16224 TRUE VALUE: 1990, short boxcar; 6454-style; uncataloged; white body; black lettering; black Lawn Chief logo to right of door; red True Value logo on left side; "ASK US!" in large black letters; ASF trucks; "BLT 1-90". Came in special 11781 True Value version of the Cannonball Express set, in which this car replaced the 7925 Erie Lackawanna boxcar. Lawn Chief is a lawn products subsidiary of True Value. Note that this is the third special True Value car in three years. **45 65**

16226 UNION PACIFIC: 1990, short boxcar; 6014-style; uncataloged; yellow body; black lettering and UP shield; "Ship and Travel the Automated Rail Way"; Symington-Wayne trucks. No individual box. Part of 11785 UP COSTCO set, made for the retail chain. Most set boxes are misspelled "COSCO". **25 35**

16227 SANTA FE: 1991, short boxcar 6014-style; red body; white lettering and cross logo; "Ship and Travel SANTA FE—all the way"; ASF trucks; "BLT 1-91". Part of 11720 Santa Fe special set. One of the very few regularly cataloged short boxcars in the 1990s. **15 20**

16250 SANTA FE: 1993–94, short boxcar, 6014-style; yellow body; blue lettering and Santa Fe cross logo to left side; "Ship and Travel / SANTA FE / all the way" to right side; ASF trucks; "BLT 1-93". This car is pictured only in a tiny photo in the 1994 catalog, but was apparently also available in 1993, as part of the 16692 Rolling Stock Assortment with three other O27-style cars. This car was one of the last O27 boxcars made by Lionel. **8 10**

16614 READING: 1989, short operating cop-and-hobo boxcar; 6014-style body; yellow sides; green roof and ends; green lettering; Reading Lines yellow and green diamond to right of doors; green extension platform; platform is spring-loaded inside car so that it slides correctly into bridge (supplied) constructed over track; blue cop chases (pushes) gray hobo on and off bridge; Symington-Wayne trucks. Came with special large display box. **30 35**

16624 NEW HAVEN: 1990–91, short operating cop-and-hobo boxcar; 6014-style; orange body and extension platform; white lettering; black "N" over white "H"; light blue cop chases black hobo on and off fixed gray metal bridge; number under- and overscored; ASF trucks; "BLT 1-90". Came with special large display box. **30 35**

16629 LIONELVILLE: 1990–91, short operating elephant boxcar; 6454-style white body with working doors; red lettering; clown electrocal in red, orange, and black to right side; elephant image to left; red "ANIMAL CAR" reading vertically immediately to right of door; track trip mechanism similar to the giraffe cars causes dark gray elephant figure protruding from top of car to duck under telltales; ASF trucks; "BLT 1-90". Part of popular 11716 Lionelville Circus Special set. **35 45**

16633 GREAT NORTHERN: 1991, short operating cop-and-hobo boxcar. Announced in Lionel's Book 1 catalog but not made. **Not Manufactured**

Exc Mt

16641 TOYS "R" US: 1990–91, short operating giraffe car; uncataloged; 6454-style; "TOYS "R" US" and "KIDS "R" US" lettering in multicolors to left of door; "GEOFFREY CAR" in blue to right of doors; Geoffrey giraffe image in engineer's cap to far right; operating giraffe figure is orange with brown spots; track trip mechanism and telltale pole included; ASF trucks; "BLT 1-90". Part of 11783 special Toys "R" Us version of the Heavy Iron set, in which this car was substituted for the GN boxcar. This same scheme had been applied for Toys "R" Us, with other boxcars, through the 1980s. **50 75**

16642 GOOFY: 1991, short operating boxcar; 6454-style; pale green-yellow body; multicolor Goofy electrocals; black lettering; blue, green, and yellow Goofy figure pops out of car roof; track trip mechanism and telltale pole included; ASF trucks; "BLT 1-91". Part of 11721 Mickey's World Tour set. **40 50**

STANDARD O BOXCARS

Lionel has maintained a steady momentum toward scale model railroading during the last 25 years. Nothing exemplifies this more than the handsome Standard O series of boxcars and rolling stock. "Standard O" is a phrase intended to designate near-scale length and dimensions, in conjunction with full car body detail and prototype decoration schemes. The booming market in scale-appearing rolling stock, even on Lionel's three-rail tubular track, forced Fundimensions' strong entry into the field in 1973. That is when it issued a remarkable group of box and refrigerator cars that were the first pieces equipped with the superb Standard O sprung trucks. The name Lionel gave to the car series was applied as well to the new trucks. The cars were not big sellers in their first years, possibly because of a lack of scale engines or other equipment to match. However, with the new scale Hudsons and large diesels such as the SD-40s, the situation has changed, and the Standard O series has gained new interest. So much so in fact that one of the train clubs, the Lionel Collectors Club of America, designated the 1990s as a "Standard O decade," during which all of its annual convention car specials would be of the Standard O variety. The period since Lionel LTI took over from Fundimensions has seen a greater variety of Standard O releases, including the wood-sided cabooses and a wonderful new series of Standard O tank cars.

Standard O boxcars are distinguished most easily from their illustrious Classic (6464) style relatives by a separate roof catwalk. They are also longer (just slightly—10¾ inches versus 10¼ inches) and somewhat taller than the Classic boxcars. The doors on the Standard boxcars are taller and thinner (relative to the body) and include fewer marker plates than the doors on the Classic boxcars. The pre-1998 Standard O boxcars sported a nicely detailed plastic underframe, as opposed to the stamped metal frame of the 6464-style boxcars. After 1998 Lionel LLC converted to a heavy metal frame, in a series it calls "heavyweights."

In its continuing effort to keep up with trends on the modern railroads. Lionel LTI introduced a major new large boxcar style in 1991. These were the large 50-foot ribbed double-door boxcars and were close to scale length at a hair less than 13 inches long. The most striking feature, aside from the length, was a new and very realistic body with heavy rib detail on the sides and entirely new roof and end designs. The ends bear an embossed "7200 series" on the marker plates, apparently a reference to the (1)7200 numbers to which they were assigned. The double doors of these cars open wide, as do those of the smaller automobile boxcars. The doors, of course, are also brand-new designs. Interestingly, there are two small marker plates on one of the doors and none on the other door. The plastic underframe of this car is similar in detail to the Standard O frame, but proportionately longer. The prominent ribs on the cars make for interesting challenges when Lionel prints the graphics. The first of these huge cars was the 17203 Cotton Belt in 1991.

The availability of the Standard O cars (boxcars and other types) varies considerably. Common cars such as the cataloged 17207 and 17209 are easy to acquire at good prices. On the other hand, cars in the top collector sets, as well as the many special issue train club cars, can be very difficult to find. Lionel has also added interesting features to these boxcars, such as lights and RailSounds, which serve to increase the value and cost.

Since Lionel's five-digit numbering scheme began in 1986, most of the regular-issue Standard O boxcars, including the new double-door ribbed ones, have been found in the 17200-series, which was dedicated to them. So far the trend continues, since few enough have been made so that the series is not exhausted—though for some reason in 1999 the company placed a few in the 29200-series. Special issue and train club Standard O cars can be found in the 52000-series of numbers. As with many other types of rolling stock, the catalog number may or may not be found on a given piece, though it is usually on the box.

STANDARD O BOXCAR LISTINGS

Exc Mt

17200 CANADIAN PACIFIC: 1989, Standard O boxcar; silver sides and doors; black roof and ends; red lettering; CP beaver logo in orange, white, and black to right of doors; Standard O trucks; "BLT 1-89". Part of 11710 CP Rail set. **60 70**

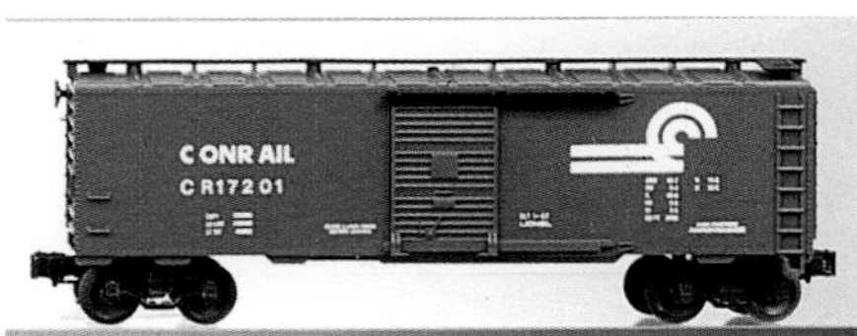

17201 CONRAIL: 1987, Standard O boxcar; tuscan body and doors; white lettering and Conrail "wheel" logo"; black catwalk; Standard O trucks; "BLT 1-87". Part of 11700 Conrail Limited set. **55 65**

	Exc	Mt

17202 SANTA FE: 1990, Standard O boxcar with diesel RailSounds; tuscan body; white and yellow lettering; "SHIP AND TRAVEL Santa Fe / all the way" in white to right of doors; black and white Santa Fe cross logo to left of doors; Standard O trucks with power pickup; "BLT 1-90". This is the first Standard O boxcar to include RailSounds. Part of 11713 Santa Fe Dash 8 set. Catalog indicates this car was to have an EOT light, with the 17302 reefer having RailSounds, but in production these features were switched. The door of this car is sealed to deter tampering with the RailSounds circuitry. **90 110**

17203 COTTON BELT: 1991, Standard O 50-foot double-door boxcar; entirely new highly detailed automobile (double-door) boxcar style for the Standard O line; 13 inches long; sides feature heavy ribbed supports and new door design; tuscan body and doors; white and yellow lettering "COTTON BELT" and "HYDRA-CUSHION"; detail lettering on the doors; Standard O trucks; "BLT 1-91".

(A) As described. **40 45**

(B) Factory Error. Two B-style doors (no plates), not usual A- and B-styles. Lettering is present anyway. S. Compatello collection. **NRS**

17204 MISSOURI PACIFIC: 1991, Standard O 50-foot double-door boxcar; new body style for the Standard O series; ribbed sides; 13 inches long; gray body with blue stripes on the upper and lower thirds of the sides; yellow doors with gray central stripe; black and white lettering "Eagle MERCHANDISE SERVICE"; number under- and overscored; Standard O trucks; "BLT 1-91".

(A) As described. **35 40**

(B) Factory Error. Missing white lettering, both sides. S. Compatello and T. Caron Collections. **NRS**

17207 CHICAGO & ILLINOIS MIDLAND: 1992, Standard O 50-foot double-door boxcar; green body; white "C&IM" lettering to left of doors; number under- and overscored; red stripe runs length of sides about ⅓ down from top; black and yellow C&IM diamond herald to right of doors; Standard O trucks; "BLT 1-92". See also 17210. **35 40**

17208 UNION PACIFIC: 1992, Standard O 50-foot double-door boxcar; yellow body; silver roof and ends; red, white, and blue UP shield to left side; multicolor "automated railway / CUSHION RIDE" map logo to right side; black lettering; Standard O trucks; "BLT 1-92". **35 45**

17209 BALTIMORE & OHIO: 1993, Standard O 50-foot double door boxcar; tuscan-maroon body; white lettering; "AUTOMOBILE" and Capitol Dome logo to left side; name and "296000" under- and overscored to right; Standard O trucks; "BLT 1-93". **35 40**

17210 CHICAGO & ILLINOIS MIDLAND: 1992, Standard O 50-foot double-door boxcar; uncataloged; green body; white "C&IM" lettering to left of doors; number under- and overscored; number on car is "16021"; red stripe runs length of sides about ⅓ down from top; black and yellow C&IM diamond herald to right of doors; Standard O trucks; "BLT 1-92". This car and the two following entries are virtual repeats of the 17207 C&IM car above, except for the number. They were made as a special set of three cars and caboose for sale in the Sears 1992 Wish Book catalog. The set (Lionel no. 18556) was sold at Sears as no. 49N95231. See also extended vision caboose no. 19718. Sears also offered a separate matching C&IM SD-9 engine that year. See 18823. **35 45**

17211 CHICAGO & ILLINOIS MIDLAND: 1992, Standard O 50-foot double-door boxcar; uncataloged; same as 17210 above except for number; number on car is "16022". See other details under 17210. Part of 18556 Sears C&IM set.

(A) As described. **35 45**

(B) Factory Error. Missing diamond herald one side. A. DeAmbrosis Collection. **NRS**

17212 CHICAGO & ILLINOIS MIDLAND: 1992, Standard O 50-foot double-door boxcar; uncataloged; same as 17210 above except for number; number on car is "16023". See other details under 17210. Part of 18556 Sears C&IM set. **35 45**

17213 SUSQUEHANNA: 1993, Standard O boxcar; green body; white lettering; large "SUSQUEHANNA" to left side with "NYSW" and "501"; white, red, and yellow Susie-Q figure to right side and "SHIP WITH SUSIE-Q"; Standard O trucks; "BLT 1-93". **35 40**

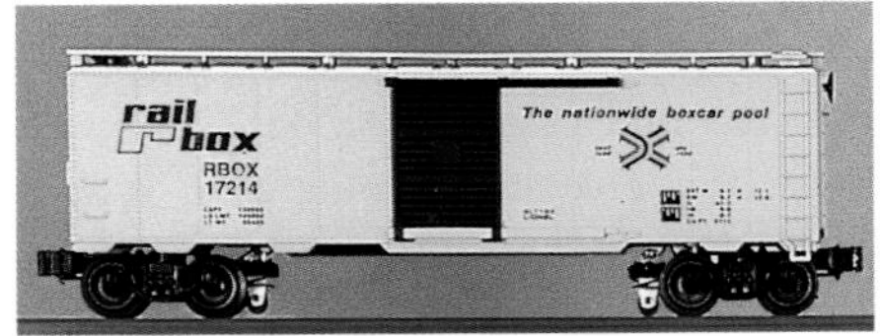

17214 RAILBOX: 1993, Standard O boxcar with diesel RailSounds; yellow body; silver roof and catwalk; black doors; black lettering; red and blue Railbox "X" logo to right side with "The nationwide boxcar pool" to upper right; diesel RailSounds circuitry inside; volume adjust; Standard O trucks; "BLT 1-93". The number of this car is listed as 16654 in the catalog. **120 140**

Exc Mt

17216 PENNSYLVANIA: 1994, Standard O 50-foot double-door boxcar; tuscan body and doors; white lettering; black and white PRR keystone to left of door; number on car is "60155"; Standard O trucks; "BLT 1-94". **40 50**

17217 STATE OF MAINE/NEW HAVEN: 1995, Standard O boxcar; blue body, roof and ends; white middle third of sides; red lower third; black and white lettering; "STATE OF MAINE" in white on upper blue section; "PRODUCTS" in white on red segment; "NEW HAVEN" in black at center with NYNH&H script logo to right; number on car is "45003"; "NH" and number over- and underscored to left; Standard O trucks; "BLT 1-95". Match for 17218 below. **35 45**

17218 STATE OF MAINE/BANGOR & AROOSTOOK: 1995, Standard O boxcar; blue body, roof, and ends; white middle third of sides; red lower third; black and white lettering; "STATE OF MAINE" in white on upper blue section; "PRODUCTS" in white on red segment; "BANGOR AND AROOSTOOK" in black at center; number on car is "2184"; "BAR" and number over- and underscored to left; Standard O trucks; "BLT 1-95". Match for 17217 above. **35 45**

17219 TASMANIAN DEVIL: 1995, Standard O boxcar; white sides; dark blue roof, ends and doors; black lettering and number; multicolor Tasmanian Devil images to left and right; large "TAZ" to left of door in red and orange; "HAPPY 40th BIRTHDAY / WILD THING" to right side; Standard O trucks; "BLT 95". Shown in the 1995 Stocking Stuffers catalog. **40 50**

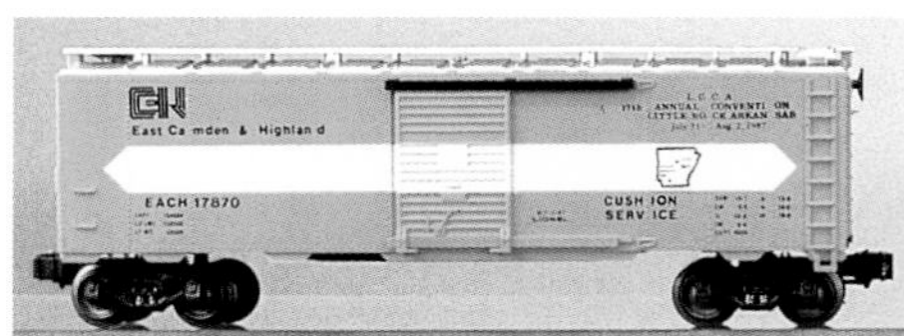

17870 EAST CAMDEN & HIGHLAND: 1987, Standard O boxcar; uncataloged; annual convention car for the Lionel Collectors Club of America (LCCA); orange body; cream stripe across sides and door; silver-painted roof and catwalk; black lettering and logo; black Arkansas map at right center; Little Rock convention notation at upper right; Standard O trucks; "BLT 1-87". 2,500 made. The first Standard O car commissioned by LCCA. **60 75**

Exc Mt

17876 COLUMBIA NEWBERRY AND LAURENS: 1989, Standard O boxcar; uncataloged; annual convention car for the LCCA; maroon body; white lettering; Columbia, South Carolina, convention notation in white; number under- and overscored; Standard O trucks; "BLT 1-89". 2650 made. The CNL was a subsidiary of the Atlantic Coast Line. **60 70**

17884 COLUMBUS & DAYTON: 1990, Standard O boxcar; special for the Toy Train Operating Society's (TTOS) national convention in Columbus, Ohio; light gray body; maroon lettering "Guaranteed Prompt Delivery"; Standard O trucks; "BLT 1-90". 1600 made. The decoration scheme on this car is easily the plainest of any of the TTOS convention cars. This car was ordered by TTOS when the originally planned 1990 convention car, a C&O boxcar with EOT device, was not ordered in sufficient quantity. Note: there were several other TTOS convention cars from other manufacturers in 1990, as well as in later years. **50 65**

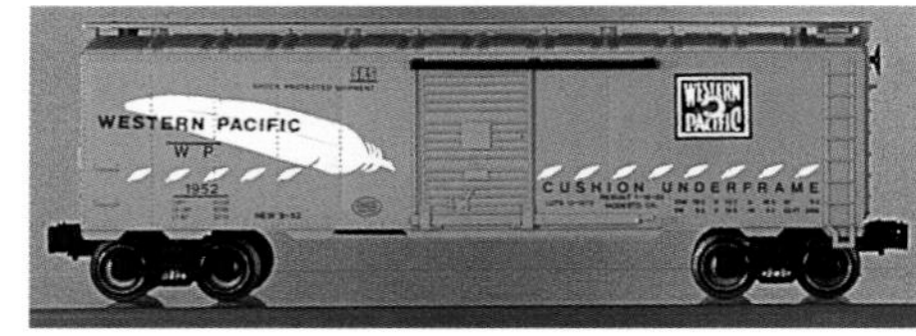

19960 WESTERN PACIFIC: 1992, Standard O boxcar; uncataloged; 13th annual special for the Lionel Operating Train Society's (LOTS) 1992 convention in Modesto, California; orange body and doors; silver feather to left side; WP Feather River Route herald in red, white, and black to right side; small silver feathers in a line across lower portion of body; black lettering; "WP" and "1952" over- and underscored to left; Standard O trucks; "REBUILT 7-18-92", the date of the convention. 1272 made, which is noted in the reporting data. Somewhat hard to find. **80 100**

52010 WEYERHAEUSER: 1993, Standard O 50-foot double-door boxcar; uncataloged; convention car marking the Toy Train Operating Society's (TTOS) 1993 Convention in Portland, Ore.; forest green body and doors; white lettering; "Weyerhaeuser" and triangle logo to left side; white lettering on both doors; Portland notation to lower right; number on car is "838593" and is underscored; Standard O trucks; "NEW 8-93".

(A) As described. **— 70**

(B) Factory error. Yellow load data missing on one side, double stamped on other. A. Kulischenko collection. **— NRS**

STOCK CARS

One of the most popular Lionel boxcar styles is the stock (or "livestock") car, first introduced by postwar Lionel in 1949 as the Armour operating cattle car. The wide horizontal wood slats and angle supports in the sides of the stock cars distinguish them from any other type of rolling stock in the line. They come in long and short, as well as operating and non-operating types. The operating ones feature some unusual and fun action concepts. The small stock cars include animated horses or outlaws (or elephants or cartoon characters) that bob in and out of the sides on hairsprings. Another version uses an ingenious trip mechanism to cause a giraffe (or other character assortment!) to duck and raise its head from the top of the car. This causes some operating limits to be imposed on the train layouts, of course. The car uses a telltale pole and trackside cam for operation, meaning that larger engines or rolling stock could run into them if not judiciously placed. And operators should beware of running the giraffe under low bridges or tunnel portals!

Some of the cartoon characters and other figures rub against the side of the hole when bobbing up through the roof. This can happen with the 16662 Bugs Bunny/Yosemite Sam car. It will sometimes be enough to prevent operation. The situation can often be remedied by bending the tab holding the figure toward the center of the car.

The giraffe car had a long run in the postwar era—the 3376 from 1960 through 1969. Fundimensions and modern Lionel have made frequent use of this popular car in the years since.

The poultry dispatch car is a unique model long stock car, with wider slats and a painted film on the inside illuminated by interior lights. One version is an operating one, with a man and broom appearing when the remote-control button is pushed, appearing to sweep out feathers from the car. This one is irreverently known as the "chicken sweeper" car. Despite the strange-looking chickens peering from the side, the poultry dispatch cars are perennial favorites.

The other type of long operating stock car is the cattle (or horse) car, which has been revived several times since 1970. It's safe to say they continue to provide endless hours of fun for kids and grown-up kids. The sight is a familiar one to Lionel fans of every age: the car comes with a trackside corral and eight animals—horses or cattle. A vibrating motor inside the car, and on the corral track, causes the horses to move along the channel inside the car (or corral) in an endless loop. It is forever a challenge to park the cars just right in front of the corrals so that the trap doors on the cars line up with the corral tracks, and the animals can come in and out properly. Lionel did recently improve the horse and cattle design by using a felt pad on the bottom of the figures rather than the small rubber fingers used earlier, which often as not had the animal going in circles instead of the intended path.

The long cars exist in four main body types. The operating poultry and cattle cars were described. Two other styles are non-operating. They are handsome models that appear most often in the Collector Line sets. The two styles differ in having a split (two-piece) door, or a single piece door. The former was the prevalent stock car through all of the postwar period and the early modern era. The latter first showed up on the 19519 Frisco stock car in 1991. Two other attractive statistics about the long stock cars: they are a half inch longer than the classic boxcars, making them appear more true-to-scale; and they have a heavy stamped-metal frame.

Another unique stock car model has appeared late in the modern era. A long phenolic-body semi-scale car in Chesapeake & Ohio markings was made in 1992 as a complement to a four-car set of freight pieces from 1991. It had many upscale features such as a metal brakewheel, metal door guides and door latches, nice underbody details, and of course the Standard O trucks. Otherwise it had about the same length and appearance as the Collector-style long stock cars. The semi-scale set was listed as a commemorative for the original semi-scale freight cars prewar Lionel made in 1940 to go with their just-released Hudson. The original 1940 set is considered by many collectors to be the best example of O gauge rolling stock ever made. The modern (and prewar) stock car, as a result of its metal and heavy phenolic construction, commands a premium price. It was not until 1999 that Lionel repeated this exceptional item—as a four-piece stock car pack in Rio Grande markings. In the interim the company somehow reduced its manufacturing costs, because the 1999 price of the four-pack would have bought only two of the C&O cars from 1992! This set was typical of several of the trends implemented by Lionel LLC in the 1990s; multi-car freight sets, prototypical accuracy, and a return to heavy die-cast or phenolic rolling stock reminiscent of the late prewar and early postwar heyday of O gauge railroading.

The short (a.k.a. "O27") stock cars come in three varieties. The two operating types were described before—they come in styles with side cutouts or top cutouts (as with the giraffe car). Ironically, some of these short operating stock cars have appreciated dramatically in value in the 1990s. Later in the LTI period, Lionel modified the top-cutout stock car (the giraffe car) so that two figures could operate on hairsprings like the side models. This reduced cost by eliminating the trip mechanism, plate, and telltales poles used earlier, but at a sacrifice of the crisp, sharp movement of the figures.

There is a non-operating small stock car that appeared only once in the period covered by this volume—the 16130 Southern Pacific. Between 1970 and 1986 Lionel-Fundimensions had made several non-operating short stock cars placed in the very low-end starter sets.

As to the number sequences, the short cars are found in the 16000-series, with 16100s designating the non-operating ones, and the 16600 and 16700 the operating versions. Other operating car types are also found in both series of numbers. The long cars are found in the 19500-series (non-operating) and 19800 (operating). The semi-scale cars (all types) are in their own sequence.

STOCK CAR LISTINGS

16110 SEARS CIRCUS: 1989, short-body operating horse transport car; uncataloged; orange body; white lettering "CIRCUS ANIMALS" and "1989"; no other number on car; two white horses bob in and out of sides on hairspring mechanism as car moves;

	Exc	Mt

Symington-Wayne trucks; "BLT 1-89". Part of uncataloged 11770 Sears Circus set. **25** **35**

16121 CHICAGO & NORTH WESTERN: 1992, long stock car; dark green body, yellow stripe on upper third of sides; single-door model; door is solid green, though it was shown as a split two-tone model in the 1992 catalog; yellow lettering; Standard O trucks; "BLT 1-92". Part of 11733 Feather River Service Station set, whose components were sold separately. **75** **90**

16125 VIRGINIAN: 1993, long stock car; white body with single door; black lettering; "VGN" circle logo to right of door; ASF trucks; "BLT 1-93". **25** **30**

16130 SOUTHERN PACIFIC: 1993–94, short stock car; non-operating; brown body; yellow lettering "LIONEL RANCH" and circle L to upper right; ASF trucks; "BLT 1-93". Part of the 16692 Rolling Stock Assortment. Available but uncataloged in 1993, this car and the assortment are shown only in a small unfocused picture in the 1994 catalog. It shows a short car with holes in the sides (as if for horses), but was not made that way. **10** **12**

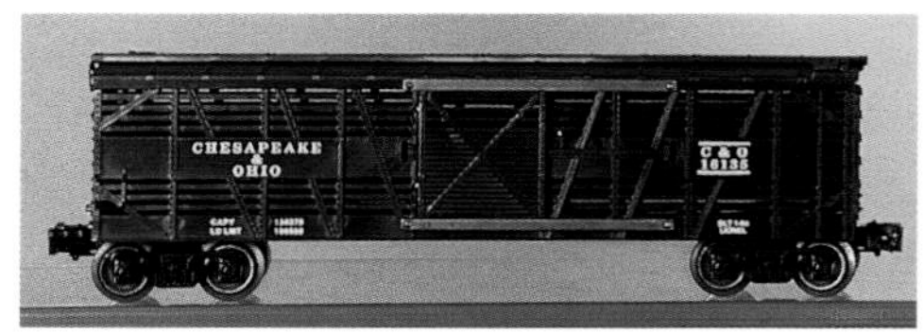

16135 CHESAPEAKE & OHIO: 1994, long stock car; black body and single door; yellow lettering; "C&O" and number over- and underscored to right side; ASF trucks; "BLT 1-94". Part of 11743 Chesapeake & Ohio Freight set, the top-of-the-line Traditional Line set in 1994. **30** **35**

16141 ERIE: 1995, long stock car; brown body with single door; white lettering and number; white Erie diamond logo to right side; ASF trucks; "BLT 95". Part of 11747 Lionel Lines Steam set, top-of-the-line for 1995. **30** **35**

16603 DETROIT ZOO: 1987, short-body operating giraffe stock car; tuscan-painted body; white lettering and Lionel lion logo; yellow giraffe with brown spots; includes cam, track plate, pole, and telltale fringes; Symington-Wayne trucks; "BLT 1-87".

(A) One operating coupler. **40** **50**

(B) Two operating couplers. **40** **50**

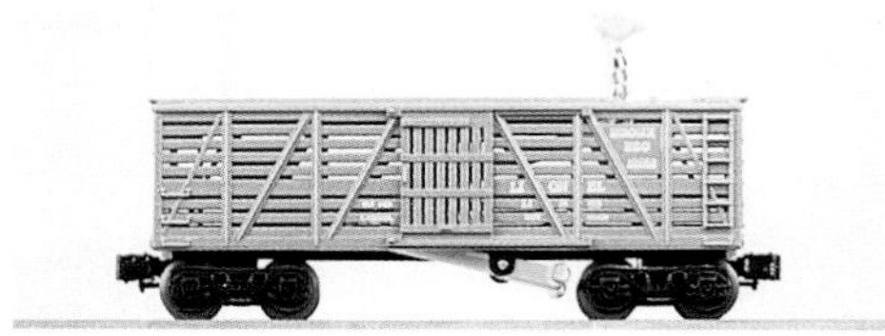

16605 BRONX ZOO: 1988, short-body operating giraffe stock car; blue body; yellow lettering and number; "LIONEL LINES" to right of door; yellow giraffe with brown spots; includes cam, track plate, pole, and telltale fringes; Symington-Wayne trucks; "BLT 1-88". A near direct remake of the postwar 3376-3386 models. **40** **45**

16630 SOUTHERN PACIFIC: 1990–91, short-body operating outlaw stock car; yellow body; black lettering "LIONEL RANCH" on right side; black outlaw and white sheriff move in and out of car sides as it moves; plastic arch-bar trucks; "BLT 1-90". Part of 11714 Badlands Express set. **25** **30**

16638 LIONELVILLE CIRCUS: 1991, short operating stock car; red body; white lettering; "KEEP HANDS AWAY FROM THE ANIMALS"; lion, tiger, seal, and zebra figures bob in and out of car sides on hairsprings; ASF trucks; "BLT 1-91". Add-on for the 11716 Lionelville Circus set. **60** **75**

16651 CIRCUS CLOWNS: 1992, short operating clown (giraffe) car; red body; black lettering and number, with "clowns, clowns, clowns" in script to upper right; red and green clowns bob up and down as car moves; levers with clowns use hairspring mechanism similar to the side-action stock cars described above, not the trip mechanism with telltale poles used on earlier giraffe cars; ASF trucks; "BLT 1-92". The simpler mechanism means the car is slightly less expensive than the other giraffe cars. **35** **40**

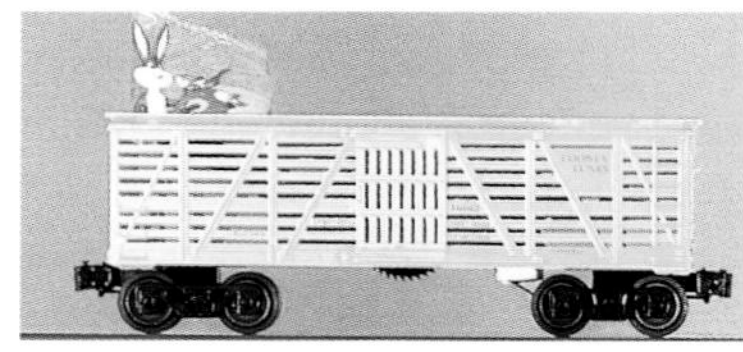

16662 BUGS BUNNY & YOSEMITE SAM: 1993–94, short operating stock car; unpainted yellow body; red lettering; "LOONEY TUNES" to upper right; Bugs and Yosemite Sam bob up and down through roof when car is in motion; ASF trucks; "BLT 1-93". See notes about bobbing figures in introduction. See also 16690. **30** **35**

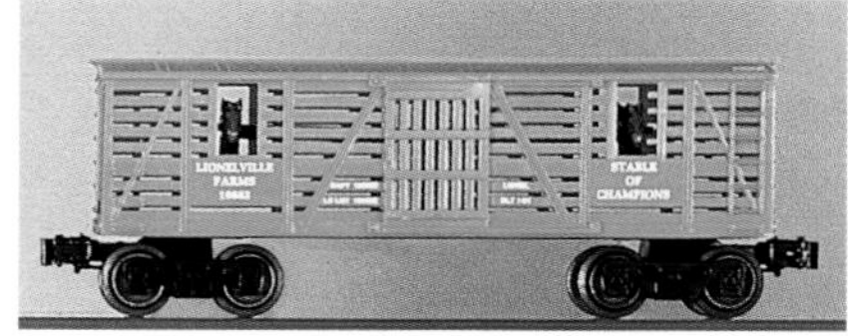

16682 LIONELVILLE FARMS HORSE CAR: 1994, short operating stock car; red-orange body; white lettering; "STABLE OF CHAMPIONS" to right side; black and white horses bob in and out of sides while car is in motion using hairspring mechanism; ASF trucks. "BLT 1-94". **25** **30**

16683 LOS ANGELES ZOO ELEPHANT CAR: 1994, short operating stock car; yellow body; black lettering and number; "LOS ANGELES ZOO" to upper right; gray elephant ducks inside car when acti-

	Exc	Mt

vated by track mechanism; comes with telltale pole, track plate and trip mechanism; ASF trucks; "BLT 1-94." **30** **35**

16690 BUGS BUNNY & YOSEMITE SAM: 1994, short operating stock car; uncataloged; unpainted orange body; dark blue lettering; "LOONEY TUNES" to upper right; Bugs and Yosemite Sam bob up and down through roof when car is in motion; ASF trucks; "BLT 1-94". An alternate-color version of the 16662 car. Listed in the 1994 Stocking Stuffers catalog. **30** **35**

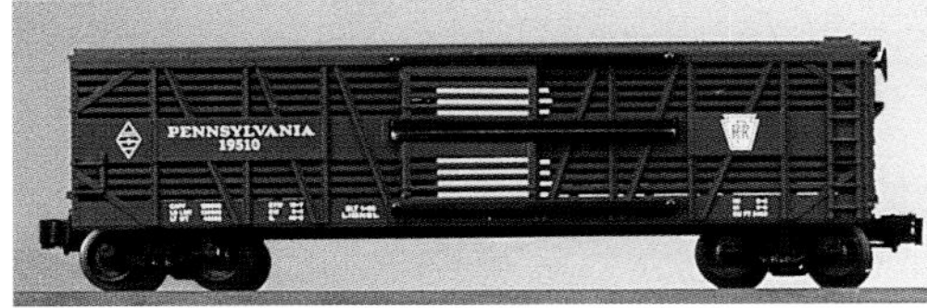

19510 PENNSYLVANIA: 1989, long stock car; uncataloged; tuscan body and split two-tier doors; white lettering and keystone logo to right side; gold FARR Series 5 diamond insignia at left; Standard O trucks; "BLT 1-89". Issued in a year-end 1989 holiday collection to supplement the Famous American Railroad Series no. 5 set from 1984. There are reports of this car being packaged in two different lengths of the Type V collector's box. **25** **35**

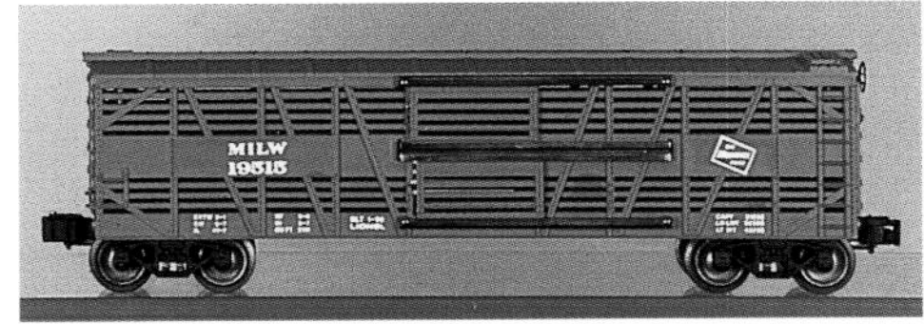

19515 MILWAUKEE ROAD: 1990, long stock car; uncataloged; red-brown body and split two-tier doors; white lettering; white and red Milwaukee rectangle herald to right of doors; Standard O trucks; "BLT 1-90". Offered in 1990 Stocking Stuffers catalog as a supplement to the 1987 Milwaukee Fallen Flags no. 2 set. **30** **35**

19519 FRISCO: 1991, long stock car; maroon body; single door—a change from previous stock car body styles; white lettering and Frisco logo to right of door; Standard O trucks; "BLT 1-91". Part of the Frisco Fallen Flags no. 5 set from 1991, whose components were all sold separately. **30** **35**

	Exc	Mt

19530 ROCK ISLAND: 1992, long stock car; uncataloged; tuscan body; tuscan single door; white lettering and Rock Island shield to right side; Standard O trucks; "BLT 1-92". Shown in the 1992 Stocking Stuffers brochure. **35** **40**

19800 CIRCLE L RANCH: 1988, operating cattle car and corral; tan sides; light gray roof and ends; black lettering "RAILWAY EXPRESS AGENCY"; "CIRCLE L RANCH" to left with "L" as the Lionel version; "TEXAS LONGHORNS" to right; postwar-style bar-end trucks (necessary because sliding shoe is needed to operate vibrator motor in the car); comes with medium orange and white cattle corral and eight brown cattle; postwar rubber fingers removed from cattle undersides and replaced with felt pad for better operation; "BLT 1-88". When remote-control track button is pressed, ramps on car sides drop down to the corral, and cattle move by vibration out of car, around the corral, and back into car. Similar in operation to postwar 3356 and modern horse car models. **95** **120**

19801 POULTRY DISPATCH: 1987, long poultry-style stock car; flat red body; red doors; black lettering; two lights inside illuminate celluloid strips of chickens on way to market; Symington-Wayne trucks; "BLT 1-87". Non-operating reissue of 6434 of postwar years and 9221 modern model. Operating model (see 9221 in Fundimensions Guide) includes man attached to magnetic plunger under car, similar to the operating boxcars. **40** **60**

19819 POULTRY DISPATCH: 1994, long poultry-style stock car with operating workman; red body; gray doors; black lettering and number; gray man with broom appears when plunger under car is activated by remote track section; two lights inside illuminate celluloid strips of chickens on way to market; Standard O trucks; "BLT 1-94". Reissue of 6434 of postwar years and 9221 modern model. Part of 11744 New Yorker Passenger/Freight set, which was the 1994 Service Station set. Note the catalog picture of the car does not show the operating magnetic plunger under the car. **55** **65**

Exc Mt

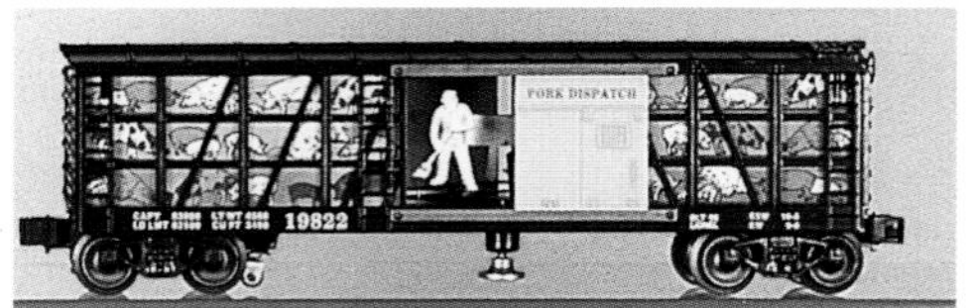

19822 PORK DISPATCH: 1995, long poultry-style stock car with operating workman; black body; yellow doors with black "PORK DISPATCH" lettering; yellow lettering and number; gray man with broom appears when plunger under car is activated by remote track section; two lights inside illuminated celluloid strips of pigs on way to market; Standard O trucks; "BLT 1-95". Note earlier models of this car transported chickens—this one carries pigs! **45 55**

51402 CHESAPEAKE AND OHIO: 1992, semi-scale long phenolic stock car; brown phenolic body; white lettering "C&O" and "95250" under- and overscored to left side; body has detailed door latch mechanism and metal underframe; same length and height as the long stock car, but slightly different detail; Standard O trucks; no built date. This car was intended as an add-on to the 1991 four-car release commemorating the prewar set of semi-scale freight cars made as a match for the original 700E Hudson from 1939. Hard to find. **200 250**

WAFFLE-SIDE BOXCARS

Lionel LTI tried a new tack in its boxcar repertoire in 1995. That year it introduced another new boxcar style known as the "waffle-side" models. They are almost identical in size and shape to the classic boxcars, but have an interesting and complex checkerboard pattern of raised and lowered sections on the sides. That must prove as challenging to the decorating process as the ribbed double-door boxcar sides described in the previous section. The ends, roof, and doors are also of a new design—the entire piece being a close representation of the waffle-side boxcars found on today's railroads. It is yet another example of modern Lionel's advance toward prototypical correctness. The new boxcars are an inexpensive line item for Lionel, since they have a plastic underframe that snaps into the body using no screws, and the four models released to date all have the plastic ASF trucks. The prominent brakewheel at one end is metal, however.

The first of the new series was the 15000 Rio Grande in 1995. Lionel even assigned a separate number series for the cars. This may have been a premature step—the company seems to have overanticipated interest in the cars. They made four through 1995 and 1996, but collector interest never materialized, perhaps because of the smaller size or the plastic construction. Production stopped with these four. Even though the last two were made in 1996, we are including them in this volume so that the full set is listed together.

Interestingly, then, these boxcars might make for a good collector opportunity—they are as yet inexpensive, available, and few in number, the perfect recipe for future appreciation!

WAFFLE-SIDE BOXCAR LISTINGS

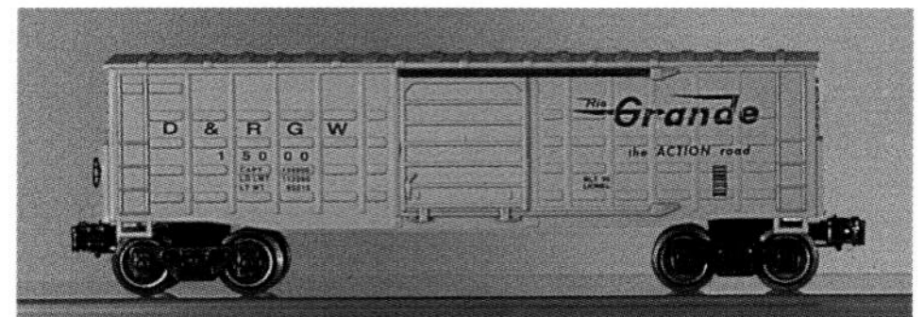

Exc Mt

15000 RIO GRANDE: 1995, waffle-side boxcar; new boxcar style introduced by Lionel with this piece in 1995; body includes checkerboard pattern of raised segments on the sides; orange body, black lettering; "D&RGW" to left side; "Rio Grande / the ACTION road" to right side; new black plastic underframe which snaps into body shell with no screws; ASF trucks; "BLT 95". Catalog says "BLT 1-95" This is the first waffle-side boxcar in the Lionel line and also opened a new number series. **— 25**

15001 SEABOARD: 1995, waffle-side boxcar; part of the new release of this style in 1995; brown body; white lettering; Seaboard Railroad heart-in-circle herald to right side; "THE ROUTE OF COURTEOUS SERVICE" to left side; "SEABOARD" and number to lower left—catalog shows this over- and underscored, but the car isn't made that way; ASF trucks; "BLT 95". **— 25**

15002 CHESAPEAKE & OHIO: 1996, waffle-side boxcar; dark blue body and doors; yellow lettering and Chessie cat logo to right side; "C&O" in large letters to left side; ASF trucks; "BLT 96". **— 25**

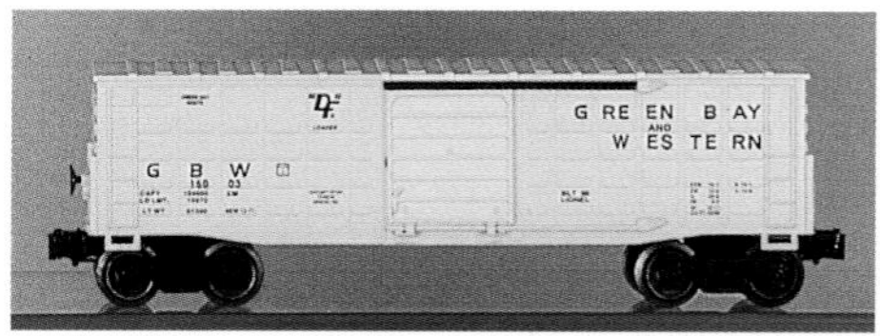

15003 GREEN BAY & WESTERN: 1996, waffle-side boxcar; yellow body and doors; black lettering and number; "DF" insignia to upper left of door; ASF trucks; "BLT 96". This is the last waffle-side car produced to date. **— 25**

CHAPTER 9

Cabooses

The irony about Lionel's cabooses is that just as the company was beginning to produce its most detailed and magnificent models—some of the best ever seen in tinplate—the real railroads began to phase them out on American rails!

The caboose is a car steeped in nostalgia. Few more cherished images of railroading exist than the one of a train crew enjoying breakfast cooked over a coal stove in the cramped way car at the end of a long freight. For most of us, a freight train without a caboose is unthinkable.

However, "efficiency" is the byword of the modern world. The caboose complicates switching assignments. Its need has been significantly reduced by the use of the inexpensive detachable signal devices for the last car of a train. Crews are much more comfortable in the commodious air-conditioned cabs of the modern diesel locomotives. Real railroaders do not feel quite as romantically attached to the caboose—veterans will be quick to tell you that these cars were not all cozy little houses on rails. Unless the caboose was quite modern, it was drafty in winter despite the heat of the stove, and nearly unbearable in the summer swelter. So today's cabooses have become highly specialized or, increasingly, nonexistent.

Lionel finally bowed to the trend in 1990, when it issued a Santa Fe freight set with an End-of-Train light fixed to the refrigerator car. It was the first freight set the firm had ever made without a caboose.

But fortunately, we model railroaders can set the terms of our own model worlds, and tinplate railroading still demands cabooses for its trains, regardless of romance, or the environment endured by their imaginary occupants. Modern Lionel has led the way by producing an astonishing variety of the popular caboose. There are nine major styles of cabooses in Lionel's modern line (see the accompanying diagram) with subvariations existing in some of the styles. Some are modeled after their postwar predecessors, like the N5C porthole caboose, the Southern Pacific–style small caboose, and the bay-window caboose. Others, like the extended vision caboose and the magnificent Standard O wood-sided and steel-sided types, are unique to the new breed of Lionel's train makers.

There are a sufficient number and variety of these colorful pieces that we have broken them into individual subsections. We will include an introductory section for each type to guide you through them and describe the individual variations within each. Within each category the pieces are organized by catalog number. The catalog number may or may not appear on the car itself. The categories are shown in the accompanying table.

Category	Pages
Bay window cabooses	127-130
Extended vision cabooses	130-133
N5C (Pennsy) porthole cabooses	133-134
Southern Pacific (SP)-type cabooses	134-139
Standard O wood-sided and steel-sided cabooses	139-143
Work, transfer, and bobber cabooses	143-145

BAY WINDOW CABOOSES

Lionel's postwar model of the bay window caboose was issued in only two regular production varieties—Lionel Lines and Erie, which was the first of the real railroads to use the bay window style of caboose. In the modern period Erie has been featured frequently on these cabooses.

In contrast, Fundimensions, which revived this caboose beginning in 1976, went on a run of more than 30 different roadnames on this handsome piece between then and 1986. During this time it became the dominant caboose in the Fundimensions lineup. The modern company has continued regular production of the bay window up to the present day, though it has been somewhat overshadowed by the extended vision and Standard O cabooses.

Fundimensions' original intent was to limit the bay window caboose to special sets, but demand became so acute that it soon entered regular cataloged production. In the '70s, Lionel went through some interesting controversies involving matching the colors of the caboose to the locomotives with which they often came—even though the real railroads had no such practice. Still the demand for this quality item continued to grow.

The reasons for the popularity are not hard to understand. Its construction is excellent. The modern version retained the stamped-metal chassis of the postwar cabooses, and the metal ladder trim adds an authentic touch. The lighting system—all these cabooses are lighted—is a little curious, but effective. A clear plastic insert is placed inside the body—all the way around the interior walls—which functions as "glass" for the windows. Molded as part of this insert are clear plastic fiber-optic rods that reach from the lightbulb in the center to the small red marker lights on the rear sides. The light bulb is a 12-volt plug-in clear lamp like those used in many automotive applications. The windows in the caboose's central bay are blocked with black paper, so as to hinder the glare of the bulb and redirect the light to the windows on the main body of the caboose. This paper is sometimes missing.

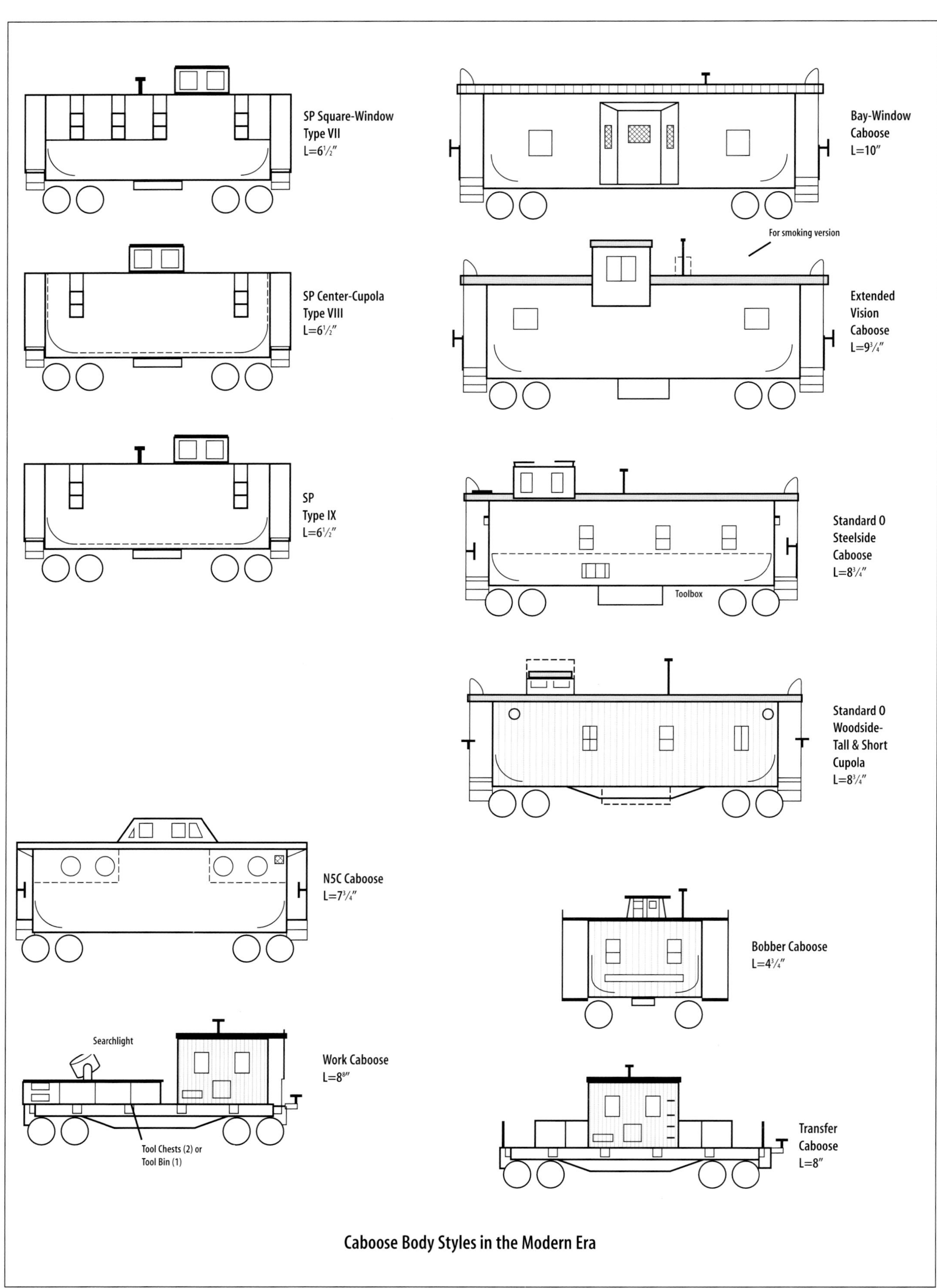
SP Square-Window
Type VII
L=6½″
Bay-Window
Caboose
L=10″
For smoking version
SP Center-Cupola
Type VIII
L=6½″
Extended
Vision
Caboose
L=9¾″
SP
Type IX
L=6½″
Standard O
Steelside
Caboose
L=8¾″
Toolbox
Standard O
Woodside-
Tall & Short
Cupola
L=8¾″
N5C Caboose
L=7¾″
Bobber Caboose
L=4¾″
Searchlight
Work Caboose
L=8″
Tool Chests (2) or
Tool Bin (1)
Transfer
Caboose
L=8″

Caboose Body Styles in the Modern Era

There have been minor changes to the body of the caboose through the modern era. Sometime around 1980, the body was altered to eliminate the lines of rivets running from the edges of the windows down to the bottom of the caboose side. This was done, presumably, to increase the graphics area on the car. The earlier style, identical to the postwar body, might be termed the "Type I." Type II, sans the vertical rivet lines, prevailed after 1980. Since all the cabooses in this volume utilize the Type II body, the distinction is not mentioned in the listings. Then around 1990, other mechanical changes were made: a brass insert was added to the holes where screw(s) attach the body to the frame—this is a wise addition that helps reduce the stresses creating cracks in the plastic when the screw is tightened on. Another change was to eliminate the "tab and single screw" method of mounting the body to the frame, in favor of two screws. This occurred around the same time. In 1996 Lionel changed the underbody frame to add tank details and toolboxes. All versions of this caboose have operating couplers at both ends.

The wheelsets have come in a variety of plastic or die-cast styles. Most of the more recent cabooses sport the nice die-cast O27 passenger trucks.

One last strange fact about bay window cabooses: with all their style, none have ever been equipped with smoke units, though there is plenty of interior room. Perhaps we can look forward to such an addition in the future.

BAY WINDOW CABOOSE LISTINGS

Exc Mt

16506 SANTA FE: 1988, bay window caboose; blue body and roof; yellow ends; yellow Santa Fe lettering and cross logo; illuminated; Symington-Wayne trucks; "BLT 1-88". Identical to the 9317 model made in 1979 except for the number. **30 35**

16510 NEW HAVEN: 1989, bay window caboose; tuscan body; black roof and end platforms; black and white lettering; serifed black "N" over white "H" to right side; illuminated; Symington-Wayne trucks; "BLT 1-89". **25 30**

Exc Mt

16517 ATLANTIC COAST LINE: 1990, bay window caboose; red body and roof; black frame and platforms; white lettering; illuminated; ASF trucks; "BLT 1-90". Issued in tandem with the 18808 ACL SD-18 diesel. **25 30**

16518 CHESSIE SYSTEM: 1990, bay window caboose; orange body; silver roof; yellow end platforms; black lettering and Chessie logo to left of window; illuminated; ASF trucks; "BLT 1-90". Part of 11717 CSX Freight set. **35 45**

16525 DELAWARE & HUDSON: 1991, bay window caboose; orange sides and ends; black roof; white lettering; illuminated; die-cast O27 passenger trucks; "BLT 1-91". Part of 11719 Coastal Freight Service Station set from 1991. **35 45**

16533 CHICAGO & NORTH WESTERN: 1992, bay window caboose; red body; yellow end platforms; yellow lettering; red, white and black CNW herald to left of bay window; illuminated; ASF trucks; "BLT 1-92". Released as a match for the 18816 C&NW GP-38 diesel. **30 40**

16535 ERIE LACKAWANNA: 1991, bay window caboose; uncataloged; maroon body; gray stripe with yellow highlights through center window section; yellow lettering; yellow "E" diamond logo below window; illuminated; ASF trucks. Part of 11726 E-L freight set in the 1991 Stocking Stuffers brochure. **35 45**

16538 LOUISVILLE & NASHVILLE: 1992, bay window caboose; uncataloged; red body; yellow end platforms; yellow lettering "1041" to left of window, "L&N" script to right; L&N circle logo on bay window; illuminated; O27 die-cast passenger trucks. Part of Louisville & Nashville set (components sold separately) shown in the 1992 Stocking Stuffers brochure. This caboose was the actual production piece for this set—it replaced a yellow steel-sided caboose shown in the 1992 Book 2 catalog. The yellow caboose was never made. **35 45**

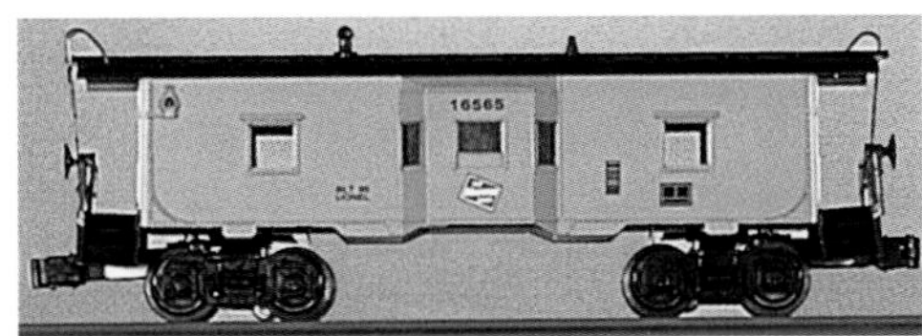

16565 MILWAUKEE ROAD: 1995, bay window caboose; orange body; black roof; yellow ends; black lettering; red and white Milwaukee Road rectangle on bay window; illuminated; O27 die-cast passenger trucks; "BLT 95". Made as a companion to the 18223 and 18224 Milwaukee Road SD-40s. **55 65**

Exc	Mt

16804 LIONEL RAILROADER CLUB: 1991, bay window caboose; uncataloged; ninth annual special issue from the LRRC; red body; gold-painted bay window; dark gray roof; white lettering; red LRRC steam engine logo on bay window; "INSIDE TRACK" logo to left; illuminated; ASF trucks; "BLT 1-91". A match for the 18818 Lionel Railroader Club GP-38 engine made in 1992, and has become a desirable piece. **40 50**

19708 LIONEL LINES 90th ANNIVERSARY: 1990, bay window caboose; straw/light yellow sides; dark blue bay window; orange roof; gold lettering and 90th anniversary logo; "AND THE LEGEND LIVES ON", "1990" on bay window; number not on car; illuminated; die-cast O27 passenger trucks; "BLT 1-90". Part of 11715 Lionel 90th anniversary set. **50 60**

19717 SUSQUEHANNA: 1993, bay window caboose; yellow body; black roof; black lettering; "NYSW" and S-circle logo on bay window; "SUSQUEHANNA" to lower left of car; illuminated; O27 die-cast passenger trucks; "BLT 1-93". Released as a companion to the 18211 Susquehanna Dash 8-40B, which was identically decorated. **45 55**

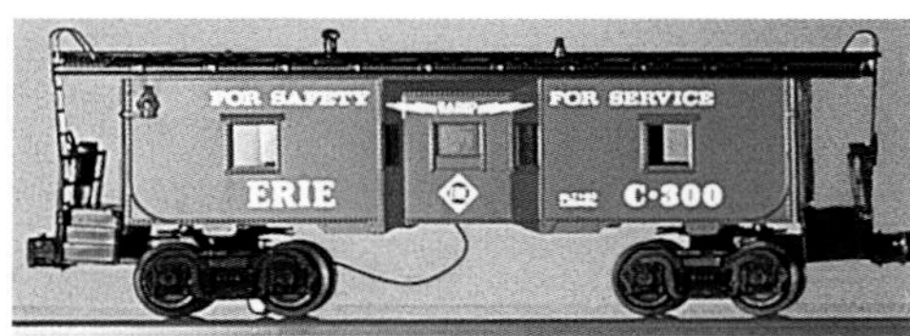

19719 ERIE: 1993, bay window caboose; red body; black roof; white lettering; "ERIE" and "C-300" to lower left and right of window, respectively; "FOR SAFETY" and "FOR SERVICE" above windows; "RADIO EQUIPPED" lightning bolts and black and white Erie diamond logo on bay window; illuminated; O27 die-cast passenger trucks; "BLT 1-93". Part of Erie Fallen Flags set no. 7, whose components were sold separately. **50 60**

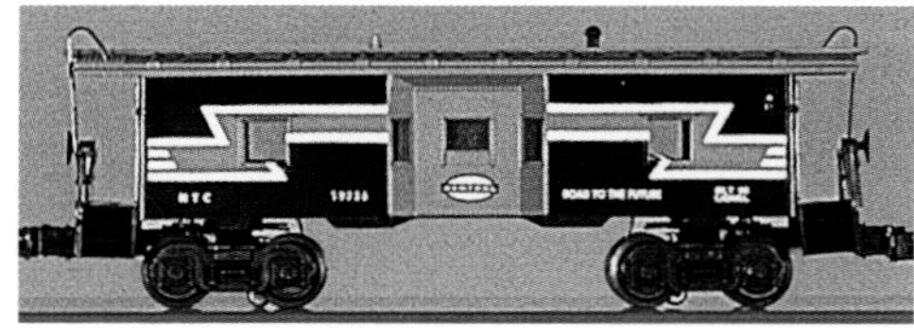

19726 NEW YORK CENTRAL: 1995, bay window caboose; uncataloged; black body; gray roof and bay window; white lettering; two-tone gray NYC lightning bolt design on sides; O27 die-cast passenger trucks; "BLT 95". This car is a somewhat hard-to-find add-on to the unique 11744 New York Central Service Station set from 1994, which had a mixed passenger-freight consist. The set was well received. **60 75**

52020 LONG ISLAND: 1993, bay window caboose; uncataloged; special for the 10th anniversary of the Nassau Lionel Operating Engineers (NLOE); gray plastic body with orange-painted sides; dark gray roof and platforms; black lettering; number is "8393"; "LONG ISLAND" at top; "Route of the Dashing Commuter" logo; illuminated; O27 die-cast passenger trucks; "BLT 6-93". This piece was a Lionel blank redecorated by NLOE and PVP. Reportedly only 66 made. It is intended as a match for the NLOE's 10 anniversary LIRR RS-3 diesel (see 52007). **80 120**

52036 TRAIN COLLECTORS ASSOCIATION: 1994, bay window caboose; uncataloged; 1994 convention car, and special for TCA's 40th anniversary; orange body; black roof; black stripe through center with silver highlights; black lettering "40th NATIONAL CONVENTION" to lower left; TCA circle logo in black on bay window; "1954–1994" to lower right; 52036 is not on the car; illuminated; ASF trucks; "BLT 1-94". Caboose matches the 40th anniversary F-3 ABA engine set released the previous year. **50 60**

EXTENDED VISION CABOOSES

In 1982 Fundimensions issued a fine Collector train set in Norfolk & Western markings known as the Continental Limited. The handsome maroon SD-24 and the rolling stock were all high quality. But the surprise was the caboose, which was unlike anything ever seen in tinplate. The extended vision caboose is a large near-scale-length, square-window cupola caboose, which on the real railroads illustrates the state-of-the-art in caboose construction. Many collectors regard it as among the finest tinplate cabooses ever produced.

The Lionel extended vision caboose has a stamped-metal frame with a black plastic battery box and brake cylinder piece attached to the frame by means of a channel. All of them are equipped with the O27 passenger-style or the arch-bar die-cast trucks. The frame is the same length as the bay-window caboose frame, and both cabooses use the same black plastic end platform piece with railings, brakewheels, ladders, and steps.

The sides, ends, and roof are molded in a single piece with a large hole in the roof. A separate molded cupola piece is snapped onto the roof atop this hole; it is secured by projections in the body shell on the sides. The cupola extends beyond the sidewalls of the caboose, and the windows allow the crew to observe not only along the top of the train but along the sides as well. Sometimes this removable cupola, especially if it has lettering on it, can cause problems if installed improperly. This happened with the 6905 Nickel Plate caboose from 1983. But since the top can easily be removed and reinstalled in the correct position, such events are not considered variations or factory errors.

The sides of the extended vision cabooses are absolutely smooth except for molded grab-rails near the platform, two large square windows per side, and molded signal lamps at both ends. Inside the car a clear plastic insert, similar to the one in the bay window caboose, has four plastic rods extending out to each corner from near the center lightbulb to provide illumination for the marker lights. All of these cabooses have interior illumination from this bulb, powered by a roller pickup on one truck. Later cabooses, after about 1993, added a second roller pickup to ensure constant illumination, and also to power the smoke units.

Because of their handsome scale appearance and the fact that nearly all have been limited-edition items, most of these cabooses command substantial price premiums. They often come as matches for the large modern diesels such as the Dash-8s and the SD-40s. And unlike those made in the Fundimensions era, many of the extended vision cabooses described in this volume include the added touch of a smoke unit, something yet to be added to the bay window cabooses. As always with smoke units, users should be careful to keep an eye on voltages, and keep the car moving, so as not to overheat the smoke mechanism.

EXTENDED VISION CABOOSE LISTINGS

Exc Mt

16541 MONTANA RAIL LINK: 1993, smoking extended vision caboose; blue body; silver main and cupola roofs; white lettering, including "MRL 10131" on front of cupola—first time lettering has been placed on that surface; "Montana RAIL LINK" in red and white at center of body; number is "10131"; 16541 does not appear; illuminated; die-cast arch-bar trucks; "BLT 1-93". Made as a companion to the 18824 Montana Rail Link SD-9 diesel. Montana Rail Link is a regional agricultural carrier formed in the 1980s. **60 75**

Exc Mt

16554 GRAND TRUNK: 1994, smoking extended vision caboose; red-orange body; black main and cupola roofs; white lettering "GT" in large script below cupola; number on car is "79052", 16554 does not appear; illuminated; die-cast arch-bar trucks; "BLT 1-94". Released with the 18836 Grand Trunk Western GP-38 diesel. **50 60**

19700 C&O CHESSIE SYSTEM: 1988, extended vision caboose; yellow sides; dark blue main and cupola roofs; dark blue lettering and Chessie cat logo; "C&O 19700" on cupola; O27 die-cast passenger trucks; "BLT 1-88". Cataloged with large vermilion stripe on lower half of caboose sides, but production pieces lack this stripe and are solid yellow. Part of 11705 Chessie System Unit Train set. **65 75**

19703 GREAT NORTHERN: 1988, extended vision caboose; red body; black main and cupola roofs; white lettering; red, white, and black goat logo at center; "WHAT'S YOUR SAFETY SCORE TODAY?" below this; illuminated; die-cast arch-bar trucks; "BLT 1-88". Part of Great Northern Fallen Flags set no. 3, whose components were all sold separately.

(A) As described. **50 65**

(B) Factory error. No goat inside circle. D. Aurand collection. **NRS**

19704 WESTERN MARYLAND: 1989, smoking extended vision caboose; red body and cupola; black main and cupola roofs;

	Exc	Mt

white lettering and stripes; illuminated; die-cast arch-bar trucks; "BLT 1-89". Part of Western Maryland Fallen Flags set no. 4, whose components were all sold separately. This was one of the first extended vision cabooses with a smoke unit—most extended vision cabooses hereafter have them. **55 65**

19705 CP RAIL: 1989, smoking extended vision caboose; yellow body; black roof; white and black lettering; white and black CP Rail logo at rear; illuminated; die-cast arch-bar trucks; "BLT 1-89". Available only in the 11710 CP Rail set. **50 60**

19706 UNION PACIFIC: 1989, smoking extended vision caboose; yellow body; red main and cupola roofs; red lettering; red "P" (not "UP") on cupola; black and white "End of Train, / but Safety / Rolls On" decal; bar code decal; number is "9706" dropping the "1"; illuminated; die-cast arch-bar trucks; "BLT 1-89". Issued as a match for the 18205 UP Dash-8 diesel.

(A) As described. **55 65**

(B) Factory error. No red "UNION PACIFIC" lettering on one side. W. Fuller observation. **NRS**

19710 FRISCO: 1991, smoking extended vision caboose; red body; black and white lettering and Frisco shield logo; "Ship it on the Frisco!"; bar code decal; illuminated; die-cast arch-bar trucks; "BLT 1-91". Part of Frisco Fallen Flags set no. 5, whose components were all sold separately. **55 65**

19711 NORFOLK SOUTHERN: 1992, smoking extended vision caboose; red body; gray main and cupola roofs; white lettering and NS stripe logo at center of body; illuminated; die-cast arch-bar trucks; "BLT 1-92". Part of 11718 Norfolk Southern Dash 8-40C Unit Train set. **60 70**

19715 DULUTH, MISSABE & IRON RANGE: 1992, extended vision caboose, uncataloged; yellow body; brown-maroon main and cupola roofs; circular "SAFETY FIRST" logo under cupola; number on car is "C-217"; illuminated; no smoke unit; die-cast arch-bar trucks; "BLT "1-93". A special for J.C. Penney, intended as a match for the 18813 DM&IR SD-18 made in 1990. Penney advertised that "up to 2000" would be produced. **55 65**

	Exc	Mt

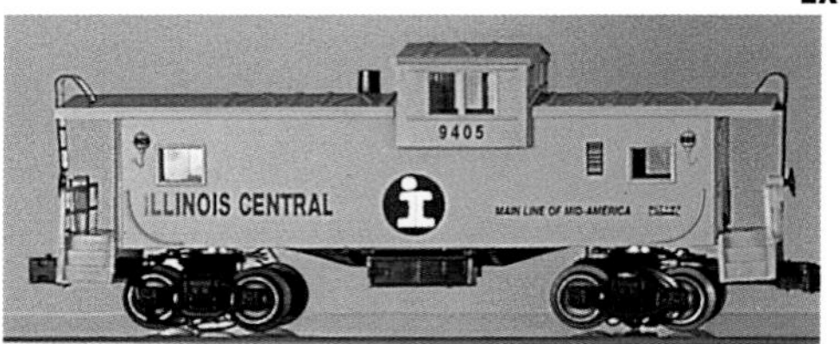

19716 ILLINOIS CENTRAL: 1993, smoking extended vision caboose; orange body; black lettering; black and white "I-beam" logo at lower center; "9405" is number (on cupola), 19716 is not on car; "MAIN LINE OF MID-AMERICA" in black to lower right; illuminated; die-cast arch-bar trucks; "BLT 1-93". Issued as a companion to the 18210 Illinois Central SD-40 diesel. **60 70**

19718 CHICAGO & ILLINOIS MIDLAND: 1992, extended vision caboose; uncataloged; green body; white lettering and number "74"; catalog number is not on car; yellow, black and white "Chicago & Illinois Midland" diamond logo at center of caboose; no other lettering except built date; illuminated; no smoke unit; die-cast arch-bar trucks; "BLT 1-92". Part of Sears exclusive C&IM set, which featured a matching SD-9 diesel and three green Standard O boxcars. Sears set number is 49N95231—shown only in the 1992 Sears Wish Book catalog. Lionel listed this set as no. 18556. **50 60**

19720 SOO LINE: 1993, extended vision caboose; white body with large "SOO" in black letters across center; red cupola; bar code; no other lettering on car except number and BLT date; illuminated; does not include a smoke unit; die-cast arch-bar trucks; "BLT 1-93". Part of 11738 Soo Line Service Station special set for 1993. **50 60**

19721 GULF, MOBILE & OHIO: 1993, extended vision caboose; uncataloged; special made for J.C. Penney to go with GM&O RS-3 diesel released the year before; red body; black main and cupola roofs; white lettering and GM&O wing logo on cupola side; illuminated; no smoke unit; number on car is "2956"; die-cast arch-bar trucks; "BLT 1-93". **60 75**

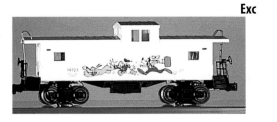

Exc Mt

19723 DISNEY: 1994, extended vision caboose; white body; red main and cupola roofs; black lettering and number; multicolor graphics of Disney characters on both sides; no smoke unit; illuminated; die-cast arch-bar trucks; "BLT 1-94". Released as a companion to the 18311 Disney electric engine, and intended to go with various Disney boxcars released in the years around 1994. — 50

19724 M-K-T: 1994, extended vision caboose; uncataloged; special made for JC Penney to match the 18558 MKT GP-7 diesel also made that year; green body; black main and cupola roofs; yellow lettering with large "MKT" at center; number on car is "125"; "RADIO EQUIPPED" on cupola sides; illuminated; no smoke unit; die-cast arch-bar trucks; "BLT 1-94".

45 55

19807 PENNSYLVANIA: 1988, smoking extended vision caboose; tuscan body and roof; gold lettering and number; number under- and overscored; "CENTRAL REGION" under number; illuminated; die-cast arch-bar trucks; "BLT 1-88". Caboose is numbered in the 19800-series because it was considered an "operating car" but not released as part of a set. Other cabooses of the type, all in sets, were in the 19700-series. 50 60

N5C PORTHOLE CABOOSES

Until the late 1980s, the N5C "Porthole" caboose was one of the mainstays of Lionel's postwar and modern era production, along with the Southern Pacific (SP) type. In real life the N5C, with its distinctive nautical "porthole" windows in the side, was used only by the Pennsylvania Railroad. That didn't stop Lionel-Fundimensions from issuing the caboose in dozens of roadnames and colors. It didn't stop Lionel in the postwar era either, when Virginian and Lehigh Valley cabooses were made. The attractive lighting and design have always kept it a favorite for operators and collectors.

Starting with Lionel LTI and continuing today, the company's emphasis has shifted away from the N5C to the extended vision and Standard O cabooses. This might be a reaction to increasing collector demand for prototypical "correctness," such that only Pennsylvania Railroad markings could be used with it. N5Cs appear occasionally in the more whimsical sets which make no claim toward real-life accuracy. For example, one came in a special Lionel Circus set. Another was a bronze caboose made as a match for a bronze GG1 pulling Lionel's set of fanciful "mint" cars. And another was a remake of the robin's-egg blue caboose from the infamous Girl's Train.

The continuing popularity of the Pennsy as a roadname for the trains gives Lionel plenty of opportunities to match accurate versions of this caboose with the many Pennsylvania locomotives made in recent years. This is true for the 19727 and 51702. Most of the modern lineup of these cabooses dates from the 1970s.

Lionel did upgrade the design of this caboose as Lionel LTI took over production from Fundimensions. It changed the trucks, which had previously been plastic, to the die-cast arch-bar or O27 passenger trucks, a step that improved both the appearance and the operation—the heavier weight being steadier on turns and switches. Later in the '90s the die-cast modular trucks were used.

The modern N5C uses the same stamped-metal frame and plastic end pieces (which have the platform, steps, ladder, and railings molded into one unit) as its postwar ancestors did. The removable brakewheels provided for both ends can be installed facing toward the car or away from it. An opaque white plastic insert in the top of the N5C shell serves to diffuse the interior light to an elegant warm "glow" from each window. Once in a while this insert will not be positioned properly and the jeweled red marker lights cannot be installed on the rear corners. The marker lights, while attractive, are also one of the caboose's problems—they have a tendency to get caught on the box when the caboose is put back inside.

In terms of the development of the caboose body, we should mention that all the cabooses in this volume are of the "Type III" variety. This type is missing a large horizontal ridge along the body below the windows that was present on the earlier two types. Type I is the postwar carryover that featured considerable numbers of rivets on the body sides. It was used on only one Fundimensions model—the 9160 in 1971. Type II appeared from 1971 through 1977, and reduced the number of rivets in order to improve the graphics application and stamping. Type III debuted in 1977 and is in use through the present. Readers are referred to a sketch detailing these varieties in the previous version of this Guide, *Greenberg's Guide to Lionel, 1970–1991, Volume I.*

One unique piece is worth mentioning—the 51702 all-metal "N-8" scale caboose made in 1992. Its shape resembles the N5C, but it has two square side windows rather than the four round ones in the regular N5C. This unique item, which included new design end platforms and roof handrails, is a one-of-a-kind so far, so it is listed here among its closest relatives. The N-8 even included a smoke unit, which none of the N5Cs so far have had. The N-8 is related to the semi-scale die-cast freight cars also released in 1992.

The availability and pricing of the N5C cabooses are highly variable today. The small number produced since 1986 makes them a good candidate for a collection on a modest budget, and their handsome looks make for bright additions to any rolling stock.

N5C CABOOSE LISTINGS

Exc Mt

16504 SOUTHERN: 1987, N5C caboose; uncataloged; red sides; yellow ends and railings; black roof and cupola; yellow Southern lettering and circle logo; illuminated; die cast arch-bar trucks; "BLT 1-87". Part of Southern Freight Runner Service Station special set, shown only in a special flyer in 1987. **35 45**

16522 LIONELVILLE CIRCUS: 1990-91, N5C caboose; yellow sides; red roof and ends; orange, gold and white tiger electrocal in center; black lettering "CHILLS" and "THRILLS"; illuminated; ASF trucks; "BLT 1-90". Part of 11716 Lionelville Circus Special. **25 35**

19701 MILWAUKEE ROAD: 1987, N5C caboose; dull orange sides and ends; black roof and cupola; red and white rectangular Milwaukee Road logo; black lettering; illuminated; die-cast arch-bar trucks; "BLT 1-87". Part of Milwaukee Road Fallen Flags set no. 2, whose components were all sold separately. **40 50**

19702 PENNSYLVANIA: 1987, N5C caboose; bronze-painted body; purplish-black lettering and number; red and black PRR keystone at center; illuminated; die cast arch-bar trucks; "BLT 1-87". Made as a match for the 18300 bronze Pennsylvania GG-1. **45 55**

19712 PENNSYLVANIA: 1991, N5C caboose; light blue body; white lettering; "N5c" in small letters to the front; number under- and overscored; illuminated; die-cast arch-bar trucks; "BLT 1-91". Remake of postwar 6427-500 caboose from the 1957 Girl's Set. The modern car came in a modern set, the 11722 Girl's Train in 1991. **55 65**

51702 PENNSYLVANIA: 1992, N-8 smoking caboose; fully die-cast brass body; entirely new caboose body made of metal, in keeping with Lionel's move to die-cast scale pieces in 1992–93 (see also the other semi-scale freight cars in the 51000-series of numbers); red body; gray roof and cupola; white lettering; red and white PRR keystone at center of sides; number on car is

Exc Mt

"478039"; "CENTRAL REGION" under number; yellow handrails and other trim; red metal end platforms; wire handrails and stanchions on roof, all are new designs for Lionel; illuminated; smoke unit with on-off switch; die-cast arch-bar trucks; "BLT 7-50". This unique caboose is not technically an N5C—it has two square windows on each side rather than four round porthole windows. However, its shape and size otherwise are similar to the N5C, and it is listed here. The N-8 is about an inch longer than regular plastic N5Cs, and the detail, metal, and other features on this piece are reflected in its price. Made as a match for the 18010 S-2 turbine. **300 350**

SOUTHERN PACIFIC SQUARE-WINDOW CABOOSES

The square-window (and square cupola) Southern Pacific-style box caboose has appeared in more Lionel sets and catalogs since World War II than any other type of caboose, and almost more than all the other types of cabooses combined. This little car goes by many names, including "square-window" (even though other cabooses also have square windows) and "square cupola" (even though other cabooses also have square cupolas). It developed those monikers in the postwar years, before the extended vision and Standard O models were around, to differentiate it from the other principal caboose made in those years, the N5C, which had round windows and a rounded cupola. We will refer to it as the Southern Pacific (SP)-type, after the railroad that pioneered its use. Interestingly, neither postwar nor modern Lionel actually made the caboose in Southern Pacific colors very often, preferring to decorate this inexpensive car in a myriad of other roadnames, including many which never used the style.

The SP is practically the definition of the term "O27," used by Lionel hobbyists to refer to the smaller-than-scale low-cost pieces found mostly in the company's starter sets. It contrasts to "O" and "Standard-O", which are longer and larger. At 6½ inches, the tiny SP is one of the smallest pieces Lionel makes, only just longer than an ore car. It is dwarfed by most of Lionel's rolling stock, looking most at home with the short boxcars, 1-dome tankers, ore cars, and 2-bay short hoppers.

The first postwar SP caboose appeared in 1947, and the years between 1948 and 1969 were dominated by (what else?) the Lionel Lines. A few models bore a small "SP" designation alone or above the roadname. Many were not lettered at all and came in the most inexpensive sets.

The body of the caboose has progressed through quite a few die changes over the years. Types I through IV appeared in the postwar years, along with some subvariations. Modern Lionel did not use any of these types after 1970 to our knowledge.

Fundimensions made some substantial changes to the SP caboose when it took over production in 1970. Several of the most important differences between the postwar and modern SP cabooses are in the chart on the next page.

The development of the separate end piece for this caboose was an interesting and unexpected innovation by the fledgling Fundimensions. It incorporated the steps, which had before been molded as part of the main body, and the railings into one unit. It looks nicer than the postwar end piece because the

Postwar	Modern Era
Steps molded as part of body piece	Steps part of separate end piece
Sheet metal frame w/ bent-up railing	Plastic frame, separate end and railing piece—railings extend to roof
No horizontal bar in windows	Horizontal bar in windows
Short cupola body only	Short and tall cupolas
Taller, thin smokestack	Short smokestack
Greater rivet detail	Less rivet detail

railings were extended all the way to the roof. Fundimensions also started the use of two types of cupolas, tall and short, something the postwar company never tried. Modern Lionel would have more fun mixing and matching cupolas on this and other cabooses as time went on. A nifty feature about the end railing piece is that sometimes it will be painted to match the roof or lettering color. Normally it is a molded black plastic.

The Type V body of the caboose (used only on a small number of pieces in the early 1970s) can be recognized most easily by the continuous horizontal ridge at the center of the body running from front to back just below the windows. In a noticeable change from postwar, this caboose introduced a tall cupola structure. Type VI followed quickly and persisted through 1980. The main difference between Type VI and Type V is that the horizontal ridge is broken under the cupola. It used tall cupolas as well.

Type VII appeared first in 1972, and its production overlapped that of the Type VI for a while. It differs from Type V and VI most noticeably in its return to the postwar-style low cupola. It has persisted as the main style of this caboose up to the present.

There are other less significant differences between these three styles, involving the rivets, the catwalk, the window frames, and the lower body edge. The interested reader is referred to a detailed sketch and discussion in the previous edition of this guide, *Greenberg's Guide to Lionel Trains, 1970–1991, Volume I.*

In 1995 Lionel LTI introduced a new style of this old warhorse car in which the cupola was moved to the center, not to the rear as it had been earlier. This was accomplished by making the roof a separate piece from the main body. The process also reduced the number of side windows from four to two, presumably to enable more graphics area, and added more detail to the underframe—a larger air tank and a nice toolbox detail. The new die also had beefed-up rivet patterns, and the windows set out from the sides noticeably more than on Type VII. Lionel and some catalogers refer to this as a "center cupola" model, but it is really just a variation of the basic SP body, and we will list it in this section as the **Type VIII center cupola.** Interestingly, Lionel used it for only five items in 1995–96 and has not used it since.

A **Type IX** variation in the body appeared sometime around 1994–95, where the two-window sides are used, and with the underframe from the type VIII, but with the cupola back toward the rear as it had been earlier.

The postwar model used a sheet metal frame, while most modern production uses a plastic frame, into which the body snaps—with no screws used. The modern plastic frame nevertheless had much more molded detail than the flat postwar sheet metal. The early Fundimensions pieces were unlighted, while most (not all) of the post-1986 pieces shown in our book are illuminated.

SP cabooses have been the mainstay of Lionel's starter sets and inexpensive production from the first year they were made more than 50 years ago. They are easy and inexpensive additions to a collection of Lionel's lower-end diesel and steam engines, with which Lionel often shows them in the catalogs. They rarely appear for separate sale, and the ones in the regular sets will not have individual boxes. The SP cabooses have also come in a few rolling stock assortments. Consistent with the low-cost goal, some Fundimensions and even early modern-era cabooses of this type only sported one operating coupler. We identify this fact in certain of the listings. Similarly, these cabooses most often use the plastic wheelsets, but occasionally a deluxe one is found with die-cast metal ones. This does make a noticeable operational difference on these lightweight cars—the heavier trucks help them stay on the track on curves and bumps.

One interesting difference between the SP cabooses and most other rolling stock described in this book is the lack of "special production" train club versions. While occasional uncataloged pieces have been made for special low-cost sets such as Ford, Sears, or Anheuser Busch, the train clubs have yet to produce an SP caboose as a convention or other special-event car. Generally, the clubs have avoided using cabooses as convention specials, and in particular the SP, which is too small and toy-like to meet the higher standards of the collectors. This may actually make things better for the SP caboose aficionados who are out there!

The most desirable of the SP-style cabooses are the ones from uncataloged sets like those just mentioned, though none can be considered truly rare. A very few from the higher-end Traditional Line cataloged sets, such as the 1995 Western Maryland Service Station set and the Georgia Power set the same year, attract some attention. Still, an excellent and colorful collection of SP cabooses can be built on a very moderate budget without great effort.

The numbering convention for SP cabooses was remarkably consistent up to 1996—all of them were in the 16500-series of numbers.

SP CABOOSE LISTINGS

Exc **Mt**

16501 LEHIGH VALLEY: 1987, SP caboose; yellow Type VII body; silver roof; black frame and end rails; black lettering; "ROUTE OF THE BLACK DIAMOND" illuminated; Symington-Wayne trucks; "BLT 1-87". Part of 11702 Black Diamond set.
20 **25**

Exc Mt

16505 WABASH: 1988–91, SP caboose; red Type VII body; white lettering, logo and numbers; not lighted; Symington-Wayne trucks; one operating coupler. Part of 11703 Iron Horse freight set. It is also found with ASF trucks, in the 1991 version of the set. **10 15**

16507 MOPAR EXPRESS: 1987–88, SP caboose; uncataloged; dark red Type VII body; black frame, platform and end railings; white lettering "ME 1987" and "MOPAR EXPRESS"; white stripes at bottom of sides; Mopar logo at lower center; catalog number not on car; not lighted; Symington-Wayne trucks; "BLT 1-87". From 11757 Mopar sets made for Chrysler. **35 45**

16508 LIONEL LINES: 1989, SP caboose; uncataloged; orange Type VII body; black lettering; large black circle L Lionel logo under cupola; parallel black stripes run length of car above and below name; number on car is "6508"; not lighted; Symington-Wayne trucks; no built date. Part of 11771 Microracers Special set made for K-Mart in 1989. **15 20**

16509 DENVER & RIO GRANDE: 1989, SP caboose; uncataloged; yellow Type VII body; black stripes; black lettering and logo; illuminated; die-cast arch-bar trucks; "BLT 1-89". Part of 11758 Denver & Rio Grande "Desert King" Service Station set in 1989. **25 30**

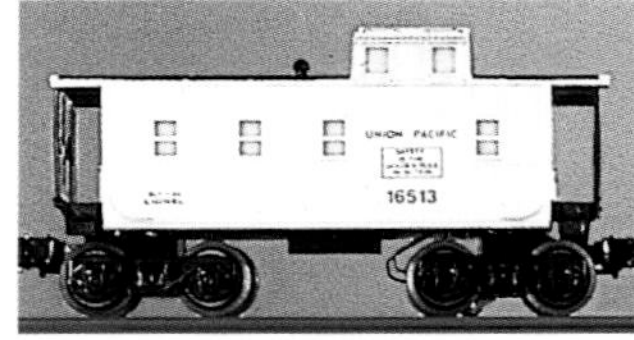

16513 UNION PACIFIC: 1989, SP caboose; silver Type VII body; black roof, platforms, and railings; red lettering "Safety is the Golden Rule in Action"; illuminated; Symington-Wayne trucks; "BLT 1-89." **15 25**

16515 LIONEL LINES: 1989, SP caboose; light blue-gray Type VII body; dark blue roof, platform, and railings; white lettering; red, white, and blue Lionel circle L logo under cupola; illuminated; Symington-Wayne trucks; "BLT 1-89". Intended to go with the 33000 Lionel Railscope engine. **20 30**

Exc Mt

16516 LEHIGH VALLEY: 1990, SP caboose; red Type VII body; black frame and end platforms; white lettering and number with "A" in front of "16516"; black and white "LV" diamond logo; bar code to left; illuminated; ASF trucks; "BLT 1-90". Designed to match 18807 Lehigh Valley RS-3 diesel. **20 25**

16520 SEARS CIRCUS: 1989, SP caboose; uncataloged; red body; white lettering "WELCOME TO THE SHOW" and yellow tiger electrocal under cupola; catalog number not on car; not lighted; Symington-Wayne trucks; "BLT 1-89" in yellow. Part of special 11770 Sears Circus Train set. **25 30**

16521 PENNSYLVANIA: 1990–91, SP caboose; tuscan Type VII body; white lettering; white PRR keystone; not lighted; Symington-Wayne trucks; "BLT 1-89", but issued in 1990 as part of the 16999 rolling stock assortment. It is likely this caboose was planned for a 1989 set that wasn't made. **10 15**

16523 ALASKA: 1991, SP caboose; blue Type VII body; yellow main and cupola roofs; yellow lettering and Eskimo figure; illuminated; ASF trucks; "BLT 1-91". Similar to postwar 6027. Intended as a match for the 18811 Alaska SD-9 diesel issued in 1991. **30 40**

16524 ANHEUSER-BUSCH: 1989, SP caboose; uncataloged; red Type VII body; white lettering; white eagle-A logo; no number on car; not lighted; Symington-Wayne trucks; "BLT 1-89". Part of uncataloged set No. 11775, the Anheuser-Busch beer set, available only through a 1989 Anheuser Busch gift catalog. **35 45**

16526 KANSAS CITY SOUTHERN: 1991, SP caboose; brown-tuscan Type VII body; white lettering; octagonal KCS logo in white under cupola; illuminated; ASF trucks; "BLT 1-91". Cataloged as a match for the 18812 KCS GP-38 diesel. **20 25**

16528 UNION PACIFIC: 1990–91, SP caboose; uncataloged; red

Exc Mt

Type VII body; white lettering and UP shield; number on car is "6528"; Symington-Wayne trucks; part of 11785 Union Pacific Costco set. Note that Lionel misspelled the store's name as "COSCO" on the set box. **20 25**

16529 ATSF: 1991, SP caboose; red Type VII body; white lettering; not lighted; number on the car is misprinted "16829"; ASF trucks; "BLT 1-91". Part of 11720 Santa Fe Special set (not to be confused with the 1996 set of the same name). The cataloged number for the piece is 16529, despite the number printed on the car. H. Hogue comment. **10 15**

16530 MICKEY'S WORLD TOUR '92: 1991, SP caboose; red Type VII body; yellow lettering; the number on the car is "16830" (catalog shows "1001"); multicolor Mickey's World Tour shield logo under cupola; not lighted; ASF trucks; "BLT 1-91". Part of 11721 Mickey's World Tour set. One of many Disney-oriented train pieces made by Lionel in the 1990s. Like the previous entry, this car was misnumbered (its true catalog number is 16530), with the confusion compounded by the 1991 catalog showing "1001" on it! **15 20**

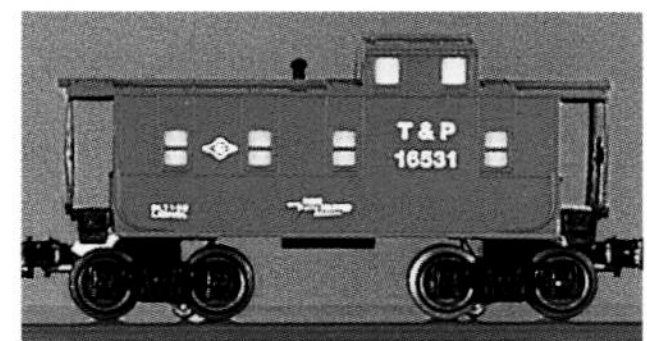

16531 TEXAS & PACIFIC: 1992, SP caboose; red Type VII body, white lettering; "T&P 16531" centered below cupola; small T&P logo between two front windows; illuminated; ASF trucks; "BLT 1-92". Released as a match for the 18623 T&P steam locomotive. **20 25**

16534 DELAWARE & HUDSON: 1992, SP caboose; red body; white lettering; white D&H circle logo under cupola with "The Bridge Line to New England and Canada"; "D&H Co." and number under second and third window; illuminated; ASF trucks; "BLT 1-92". Released in tandem with 18626 D&H steam locomotive. **20 25**

16536 CHESSIE SYSTEM: 1992, 94–99, SP caboose; yellow Type VII body; blue lettering; C&O and number below cupola; "Chessie System" in light blue with "C" as the Chessie Cat symbol, centered along bottom sides; not lighted; ASF trucks; "BLT 1-92". Part of 11727 Coastal Limited set in 1992, and the 11746 Seaboard Freight in 1994. It later appeared in entirely different colors (variation B) in the 1997 Chessie Flyer set, no. 11931.

(A) As described (yellow Type VII four-window body) in sets no. 11727 and no. 11746. **20 25**

(B) 97-99. Red Type IX (two-window) body, with white lettering. Same number. Otherwise same as (A). Came in Chessie Flyer set no. 11931. **20 25**

Exc Mt

16537 KATY (M-K-T): 1992–93, SP caboose; red Type VII body; yellow lettering and KATY logo centered under cupola; illuminated; ASF trucks; "BLT 1-92". Part of 11728 High Plains Runner set. Also came in the uncataloged version of the Heavy Iron set (no. 11800) made for Toys "R" Us in 1993, and which featured the 16241 Toys "R" Us boxcar. **20 25**

16543 NEW YORK CENTRAL: 1993–99, SP caboose; red body; white lettering; large NYC logo under cupola; number not on car; not lighted; ASF trucks; "BLT 1-93". Part of 11735 New York Central Flyer set, a set which served as the basis for Lionel's Traditional (starter) line in the 1990s. In 1998 this caboose changed style to the Type IX, with two windows. The number and set number remained the same. Interestingly, in 1998 the caboose is shown in two different ways in the two catalogs—once with the oval logo toward the front of the car and later with it centered under the cupola.

(A) Type VII four-window. **15 20**

(B) 1998–99 Type IX two-window style. **— 20**

16544 UNION PACIFIC: 1993–95, SP caboose; light gray body; yellow lettering; large UP shield in yellow below cupola; illuminated; ASF trucks; "BLT 1-93". Part of 11736 Union Pacific Express set.

(A) Type VII four windows. **25 30**

(B) Type XI two windows, 1994–95. **25 30**

16546 CLINCHFIELD: 1993, SP caboose; red type VII body; black main and cupola roofs; white lettering "CRR" and number at lower center; illuminated; ASF trucks; "BLT 1-93". Released in tandem with 18821 Clinchfield GP-38-2 diesel. **25 30**

16547 HAPPY HOLIDAYS: 1993–94, SP caboose; red body; gold lettering "Happy Holidays" in script to lower front; multicolor bell and ribbon electrocal below cupola; illuminated; ASF trucks; "BLT 1-93". Intended as a match for the 18827 Christmas RS-3.

(A) Type VII four-window model. **35 40**

(B) Type IX two-window style, 1994. **35 40**

16548 CONRAIL: 1993, SP caboose; blue Type VII body; black roof and cupola; white lettering and Conrail wheel logo; number in white at top of car below cupola; illuminated; ASF trucks; "BLT 1-93". Part of 11740 Conrail Consolidated set. **25 35**

	Exc	Mt

16551 ANHEUSER-BUSCH: 1993–94, SP caboose; uncataloged; red body; white lettering "Anheuser Busch, Inc" in script on lower side; A-eagle insignia under cupola; number in black toward front; illuminated; ASF trucks; "BLT 1-93". Part of special 11810 Budweiser set made for the beer giant in 1993–94. Available only through the Anheuser-Busch gift catalog.

	Exc	Mt
(A) Type VII four-window.	30	35
(B) Type IX two-window body, 1994.	30	35

16553 UNITED AUTO WORKERS: 1993, SP caboose; uncataloged; yellow Type VII body; black lettering; UAW wheel emblem under cupola; "SOLIDARITY" in large black letters under this; not lighted; ASF trucks; "BLT 1-93". Part of 11811 set made for the UAW. **35 40**

16555 CHESAPEAKE & OHIO: 1994, SP caboose; yellow Type VII body; black main and cupola roofs; dark blue lettering "C&O FOR PROGRESS" below cupola; illuminated; ASF trucks; "BLT 1-94". Part of 11743 Chesapeake & Ohio Freight set. **25 30**

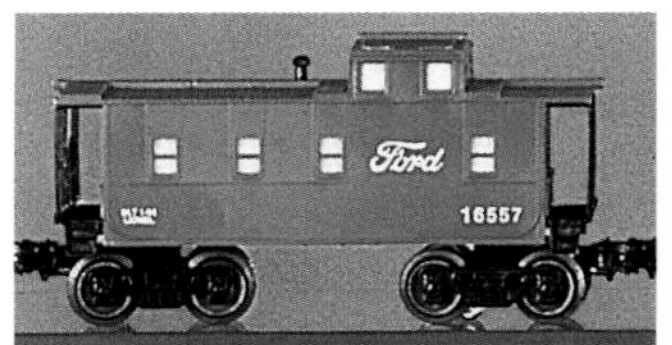

16557 FORD: 1994, SP caboose; uncataloged; red Type VII body; white lettering with "Ford" in script below cupola; illuminated; ASF trucks; "BLT 1-94". Part of 11814 Ford set. **20 25**

	Exc	Mt

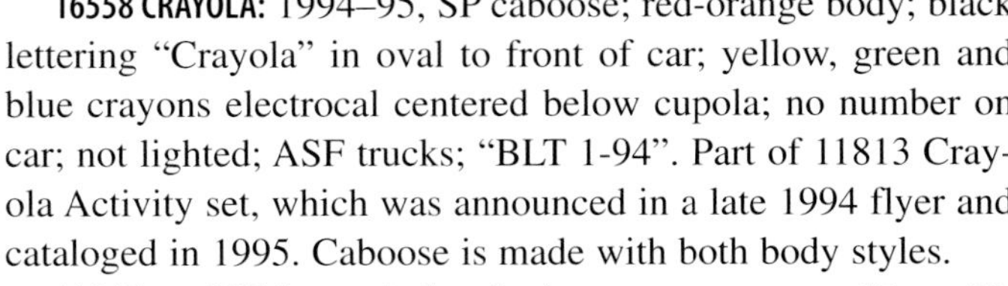

16558 CRAYOLA: 1994–95, SP caboose; red-orange body; black lettering "Crayola" in oval to front of car; yellow, green and blue crayons electrocal centered below cupola; no number on car; not lighted; ASF trucks; "BLT 1-94". Part of 11813 Crayola Activity set, which was announced in a late 1994 flyer and cataloged in 1995. Caboose is made with both body styles.

	Exc	Mt
(A) Type VII four-window body.	15	20
(B) Type IX two-windows.	15	20

16559 SEABOARD: 1995, SP caboose; red-orange type VIII body with center cupola, first issue of this new style caboose; sides have two windows instead of previous four; underbody also has more details than previous Type VII—air tank and tool box; white lettering "SEABOARD" overscored just under cupola; Seaboard circle logo centered; "5658" underscored below circle; "HOLD TIGHT TILL FOOTING'S RIGHT" to lower rear; illuminated; ASF trucks; "BLT 95". This is the first appearance of the Type VIII center cupola caboose. Issued in tandem with the 18838 Seaboard RS-3. **30 35**

16560 CHRYSLER MOPAR: 1994, SP caboose; uncataloged; red Type IX body; white lettering; "Mopar" at center; Chrysler logo in blue and white; number over- and underscored; illuminated; ASF trucks; "BLT 1-94". This piece, which is part of the 11818 Mopar set from 1994, is also one of the earliest SP cabooses to sport the Type IX two-window body style. **25 30**

16561 UNION PACIFIC: 1995, SP caboose; Type VIII center cupola; yellow body; brown cupola and roof piece; red lettering "UNION PACIFIC" at upper center; number is "25766";

Exc Mt

illuminated; ASF trucks; "BLT 95". Released with the 18640 Union Pacific steam loco. **30 35**

16562 READING: 1995, SP caboose; Type VIII center cupola; pale yellow body with green lower section; green roof; yellow and green contrasting lettering; "16562" in green centered on body; "READING" and other data on lower green portion; illuminated; ASF trucks; "BLT 95". Released in tandem with the 18639 Reading locomotive. **30 35**

16563 LIONEL LINES: 1995, SP caboose; red Type IX body; white lettering; large Lionel circle L logo at center; no number on car; illuminated; ASF trucks; "BLT 95". Part of 11747 Lionel Lines Steam set, the top-of-the-line ready-to-run set in the 1995 line. This is the first cataloged appearance of the Type IX caboose, which used the same two-window main body and detailed underframe as the Type VIII center-cupola style, but with a revised roof piece placing the cupola back toward the rear of the caboose. **25 30**

16564 WESTERN MARYLAND: 1995, SP caboose; Type VIII center cupola; white body with red lower third; black roof; black and white reverse lettering; "WM" stripe logo with number at upper center; ribbon herald and barcode in black at lower center; illuminated; die-cast arch-bar trucks (Lionel mistakenly calls them leaf-spring in the catalog, but the leaf-spring is a slightly different kind of truck); "BLT 95". Part of 11749 Western Maryland Service station set from 1995, but packaged individually. The catalog also incorrectly listed this caboose's number as 16544. **35 40**

16566 UNITED STATES ARMY: 1995, SP caboose, gray Type IX body; white lettering; number on car is "USA 907"; yellow end pieces and railings; illuminated; ASF trucks; "BLT 95". Advertised as a match for the US Army GP-7 released earlier in 1995. Shown in the '95 Stocking Stuffer/'96 Spring Release catalog. **25 30**

Exc Mt

16571 GEORGIA POWER: 1995, SP caboose; uncataloged; white Type IX body; black roof; brown stripes along lower portion of body; black and red Georgia Power lettering at center with black and red lightning triangle symbol; "52789" is the number on the caboose; illuminated; ASF trucks; "BLT 95". Part of 11819 Georgia Power set. Reportedly 2,500 made. **50 60**

16575 SEARS ZENITH: 1995–96, SP caboose; uncataloged; red two-window type IX body; white "Zenith Express" herald; other lettering and number in white; "Brand Central" in red, white, and blue to left side; ASF trucks; "BLT 95". Part of 11821 Sears Zenith set, which was the first of three starter sets released by Sears and Zenith in quick succession in 1995–96. **35 45**

16578 LIONEL LINES: 1995, SP caboose; uncataloged; yellow type VII body; red lettering; ASF trucks; no BLT date. This piece is part of the unusual 11906 Lionel Factory Selection Special set, which apparently was an effort by Lionel to sell off excess stock. Yet this caboose, and the completely unmarked 4-4-2 Columbia engine pulling it, appear nowhere else. **20 25**

16579 GM/AC DELCO: 1995, SP caboose; uncataloged; medium red Type IX body with two windows; number in black lettering; white rectangular herald reads "BASEBALL, HOT DOGS, APPLE PIE AND CHEVROLET" with the classic Chevy car emblem; ASF trucks; "BLT 95". Part of 11822 GM/AC Delco set, distributed to GM and AC Delco dealers and employees. **25 35**

16829: **see 16529.**

16830: **see 16530.**

52050 SCHUYLKILL HAVEN BOROUGH DAY: 1994, SP caboose; uncataloged; "1994" is the number on the caboose. Further details needed. Reader comments invited. **— 50**

STANDARD O CABOOSES

Wood-Sided

In the late 1930s, the Lionel Corporation introduced a beautifully executed scale model wood-sided caboose to accompany its new Hudson and the fine scale switchers of the period. Collectors have always regarded this caboose with awe and respect, for it is a superb model. They paid large sums for any surviving examples because they did not have a modern version available to them—until, that is, in 1986.

That year Lionel produced two magnificent reproductions of

the wood-sided caboose as part of an extremely limited direct-mail offer. The sides and roofs were expertly wood-scribed, metal ladders were used, handsome marker lights decorated the sides, and there were the same detailed square windows and cupolas as on the prewar piece. The 1986 cabooses also featured a brand-new type of metal wheelset—the die-cast arch-bar trucks. Unlike the Standard O trucks, they were easily adaptable for roller pickups, and these cabooses were indeed lighted.

One model, the 6907, was an exceedingly handsome New York Central slightly dressed up over its antique predecessor. This caboose had dark brown coloring offset by the black roofs. The other release was plain brown, but had the same body detail and was a match for the 8606 Boston & Albany Hudson, with which it was associated in the direct-mail offer.

To be sure, some of the fine detail work on the prewar version had to be sacrificed on the modern models because of prohibitive cost. But collectors were nonetheless very happy with the design, and these cabooses, along with most of the models that followed, have been in short supply and command a considerable price premium. These cabooses have normally been referred to as "Standard O" by Lionel, and are considered "semi-scale," with everything except the coupler and wheel flanges being of scale size. An interesting point is that they are not as massive or long as many of the other "Standard O" freight cars, nor even as long as the bay window or extended vision cabooses described in this chapter, hinting that they may not truly be "full scale." But that is simply an illusion—the real cabooses are somewhat short as well.

The frame of the wood-sided caboose is plastic, albeit well detailed, and the main body snaps into it, with no screws involved. The frame here includes the steps and platform molded as part of it—most other cabooses have a separate end piece. The railings and brakewheel are also snap-in pieces. The ladders are sheet metal. Another nice detail is the wire handrail along the underside. Like the other large cabooses, this one includes a clear plastic insert within the body to "distribute" (via fiber-optics) the light evenly to the side windows and marker lights. The cupola is a snap-in piece with its own clear plastic insert.

Lionel fans were in for more treats as the years progressed. In 1987 another New York Central wood-sided caboose was produced to match the gray New York Central Hudson. It also reduced the marker lights from four to two, helping the remaining ones illuminate better.

The first variation appeared in 1987 for the Conrail Limited set. Since Lionel used a "plug-in" design for the cupola, all it did was design a new high-window cupola, plug it into the roof piece and presto, a new high-cupola caboose was born. This one came in bright Conrail blue with white lettering, and it was a scale dead-ringer for the old Canadian National wooden cabooses of the early 1900s. Conrail actually gave a few of these ancient cabooses a new paint job and used them in its early years.

During the intervening years, Lionel has made wood-sided cabooses with both variations of cupolas, and all were well received.

Steel-Sided

In late 1990 Lionel issued a major revision to the Standard O wood-sided caboose. Although the new one retained the size and form of the wood-sided version, there are important body style differences. The first is that the steel-sided model has no wood slats on the sides and roof. It is in fact a smooth-side (steel-plate) caboose with exquisite rivet detail matching anything since the 6464 boxcars. And the new cabooses included smoke units and a flashing rear warning light similar to the End-of-Train light on the boxcars. The action of the smoke unit was improved by adding a piston/cam device to the wheel axle so that smoke puffs are synchronized to the wheel speed. Lionel advises, however, that the caboose should be kept moving or the smoke unit may burn out.

Other more subtle differences exist between the steel-sided and wood-sided cabooses. The window pattern is altered. The cupola is different—Lionel seems to enjoy altering the cupolas on its cabooses! The door at the rear has a different shape. There is nice grab-handle detail near the doors on the front and back of the steel-sided model. An opening toolbox was placed on the underside. The grab-rails on the side are individual pieces on the steel-sided model (they are molded in on the wood-sided), though this feature was matched on the wood-sided models produced later in the '90s. The marker lights were removed from the steel-sided version. In 1992, Lionel upgraded the wood-sided caboose to add the toolbox and the separate grab irons, and later added a smoke unit to a few of them.

Two steel-sided cabooses were introduced in 1990, including yet another New York Central version—this one in the famous gray-and-red Pacemaker paint scheme. This decor is popular with collectors, and the same can be said for this caboose.

In 1991 a Chessie model came out as a match for the 18011 Chessie T-1 engine.

We should mention the unique 51701 New York Central semi-scale caboose made in 1991. This one-of-a-kind model attempted to re-create the superb detail of the die-cast freight cars made by Lionel in the prewar era. The body was an all-metal zinc cast piece, and had deluxe features, like three-color marker lights. It was intended as a match for the 51000-series semi-scale freight cars made to commemorate the die-cast scale cars made by Lionel in 1940. Both the prewar and modern sets were billed as wonderful matches for the Hudsons, which they indeed are.

The 51701 is a unique item, being entirely metal. But since it resembles the other Standard O cabooses, we include it in this section.

The Standard O caboose is so important to the Lionel line that the company has devoted an entire series of numbers to it—the 17600s. There have been a few special production models of the caboose (most notably LCCA's 1990 Denver & Rio Grande Western) which can be found in other number groups. Most have been released individually or in association with engines, but there are exceptions.

To date, all of the Standard O cabooses have proved popular. Most have been made as matches for Lionel's best locomotives, another factor adding to their popularity. Lionel started production with a flair for the first four or five years, then there was an unexplained gap in production between 1992 and 1995. A slight upgrade for the wood-sided model marked the resumption of production that year.

Their cost and desirability make assembling a complete collection a challenge—those who endeavor to do so should be willing to devote time and much cash to the effort. We should note, however, that prices have eased slightly for some items since the last edition.

STANDARD O CABOOSE LISTINGS

Exc Mt

16538 L&N/FAMILY LINES: 1992, Standard O steel-sided caboose with smoke; yellow body; black lettering. This unusual piece was cataloged in 1992 with the 11729 Louisville & Nashville Express set. However, the caboose was never made and the set was retooled entirely, featuring a red bay window caboose instead. The revised set, as produced, is shown in the 1992 Stocking Stuffers brochure. See also 16538 in the bay window section of this chapter. This caboose would have been unique in the Standard O line had it been made—the only Standard O caboose to appear in a "Traditional Line" (not Collector Line) set. This point, and the associated cost, may have been a reason Lionel decided not to produce it. **Not Manufactured**

16539 WESTERN PACIFIC: 1992, Standard O steel-sided caboose; light gray body; tall cupola; orange stripe runs full length of sides through windows; black lettering "WP" and "539" under- and overscored at lower center; black, red, and white Western Pacific "Feather River" herald under cupola; cam operated smoke unit; opening toolbox; illuminated; flashing rear LED warning light; die-cast arch-bar trucks; "BLT 1-92". Part of 11733 Feather River Service Station set. It is not clear why this caboose is numbered as it is, while the other Standard O pieces are in the 17600-series. **60 70**

17600 NEW YORK CENTRAL: 1987, Standard O wood-sided caboose; uncataloged; light brown body and roof; low cupola; white lettering and number; black ladder, end rails and cupola roof rails; marker lights only at rear instead of at all four corners as on previous two models released in 1986; illuminated; die-cast arch-bar trucks; "BLT 1-87". Sold as a match for the 18002 gunmetal New York Central Hudson in the 1987 year-end "Happy Lionel Holidays!" brochure.

(A) As described. **50 65**

(B) Factory Error. No lettering one side. S. Compatello collection. **— NRS**

Exc Mt

17601 SOUTHERN: 1988, Standard O wood-sided caboose; red body; high cupola; black main and cupola roofs; yellow lettering and SR circular logo; illuminated; die-cast arch-bar trucks; "BLT 1-88". Made to complement the 18301 Southern F-M diesel.

(A) As described. **50 65**

(B) Factory error. No lettering one side. J. Freeman collection. **NRS**

17602 CONRAIL: 1987, Standard O wood-sided caboose; bright blue body; high cupola; white striping, lettering and Conrail logo; black main and cupola roof; first Standard O caboose to use a high-window cupola; marker lights only at rear; illuminated; die-cast arch-bar trucks; "BLT 1-87". Part of Conrail Limited set 11700. Somewhat hard to find. **80 100**

17603 ROCK ISLAND: 1988, Standard O wood-sided caboose; dark maroon body (shown as tuscan brown in the catalog); high cupola; black trim pieces; white number and Rock Island shield logo; illuminated; die-cast arch-bar trucks "BLT 1-88". Complement to the 18001 Rock Island Northern from 1987. **35 50**

17604 LACKAWANNA: 1988, Standard O wood-sided caboose; low cupola; dark brown body; black trim pieces; white lettering and logo; illuminated; die-cast arch-bar trucks; "BLT 1-88". A match for the 18003 Lackawanna Northern locomotive. **50 60**

Exc Mt

17605 READING: 1989, Standard O wood-sided caboose; red body and cupola; low cupola; black main and cupola roofs; white lettering; yellow-painted railings on end platforms and cupola roof; illuminated; die-cast arch-bar trucks; "BLT 1-89". Issued to accompany the 18004 Reading steam locomotive. **45 55**

17606 NEW YORK CENTRAL: 1990, Standard O steel-sided caboose; gray body with broad red stripe at top of sides; catalog pictures it as black, but actually made in red and gray Pacemaker scheme; red high cupola; black main and cupola roofs and end platforms; white lettering; catalog shows "17006" on car but it is actually numbered "17606"; number underscored; opening toolbox; illuminated; flashing rear warning light similar to End-of-Train lights on boxcars; light is a light-emitting diode; cam-operated smoke unit; Lionel advises caboose should be kept moving or smoke unit will burn out; die-cast arch-bar trucks; "BLT 1-90". First Standard O caboose with a smoke unit. New body style includes fine rivet and catwalk detail and separate grab-rails. **65 75**

17607 READING: 1990, Standard O steel-sided caboose; tuscan body and high cupola; black trim pieces and platforms; white lettering; opening toolbox; illuminated; cam-operated smoke unit; Lionel advises caboose should be kept moving to avoid smoke-unit burnout; flashing rear LED warning light; die-cast arch-bar trucks; "BLT 1-90." **55 65**

17608 C&O CHESSIE SYSTEM: 1991, Standard O steel-sided caboose; tuscan-red body with high cupola; black trim and platforms; white "C AND O FOR PROGRESS" lettering; opening toolbox; illuminated; cam-operated smoke unit; flashing rear LED warning light; die-cast arch-bar trucks; "BLT 1-91". Intended as a match for the 18011 Chessie T-1 steam locomotive. **65 80**

Exc Mt

17610 WABASH: 1991, Standard O steel-sided caboose; medium red body and high cupola; black trim and platforms; white lettering; opening toolbox; illuminated; cam-operated smoke unit; flashing rear LED warning light; die-cast arch-bar trucks; "BLT 1-91". **60 70**

17611 NEW YORK CENTRAL: 1990–91, Standard O wood-sided caboose; brown body and high cupola; white lettering "C.C.C. & St. L / 6003" with large black and white NYC oval in center; illuminated; die-cast arch-bar trucks; "BLT 1-90". This caboose was originally planned to be an Ontario & Western, as it was pictured in the 1990 Stocking Stuffers brochure with the 18009 Mohawk locomotive. When collector pressure forced a road name change on the Mohawk back to New York Central, the caboose was changed as well. As a result it was the fourth Standard O caboose lettered for the NYC, out of only 12 produced up to that time. Regularly cataloged in 1991. **60 70**

17612 NICKEL PLATE ROAD: 1992, Standard O steel-sided caboose; light brown body; white "Nickel Plate Road" script and number centered on sides; opening toolbox; illuminated; cam-operated smoke unit; flashing rear LED warning light; die-cast arch-bar trucks; "BLT 1-92". Came only in the Nickel Plate Fallen Flags set no. 6, whose components were all sold separately. **60 70**

17613 SOUTHERN: 1992, Standard O steel-sided caboose; light brown body; white "Southern" lettering, circle logo and "7613" centered on sides; opening toolbox; illuminated; cam-operated smoke unit; flashing rear LED warning light; die-cast arch-bar trucks; "BLT 1-92". Released in combination with the 18018 Southern Mikado locomotive. **60 70**

17615 NORTHERN PACIFIC: 1992, Standard O wood-sided caboose; maroon-medium brown body; high cupola; black trim pieces; black, white, and red Northern Pacific Monad logo at center, over "Main Street of the Northwest" script in white; "N.P." and number to lower front; illuminated; cam-operated smoke unit, first time the wood-sided caboose included one; opening toolbox—also a first for this type of caboose; die-cast arch-bar trucks, which are pictured painted maroon in the catalog; "BLT 1-92". This upgraded wood-sided caboose was

	Exc	Mt

offered as a companion to the beautiful 18016 Northern Pacific Northern steam engine. **60 70**

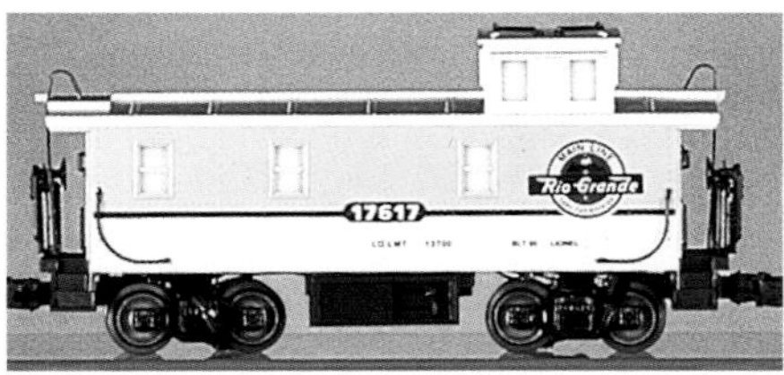

17617 DENVER & RIO GRANDE: 1995, Standard O steel-sided caboose; yellow body with silver lower third highlighted by black stripe; high cupola; silver roof; black trim pieces; blue, white, and black "Rio Grande-Main Line" herald below cupola; white number in small black oval at center of sides; black lettering on lower portion of body; illuminated; no smoke unit; opening toolbox; flashing rear LED warning light; die-cast arch-bar trucks; "BLT 95". The bright coloring of this caboose contrasts with the brown/red coloring of most other Standard O cabooses. As a result this one is somewhat harder to find. A good match for the Rio Grande PA-1s and SD-50s made in the mid '90s. **75 90**

17618 FRISCO: 1995, Standard O wood-sided caboose; medium maroon-brown body; tall cupola with one window; black and white lettering; Frisco shield below cupola; "SL-SF" and number over- and underscored below shield; black trim pieces; this caboose includes separate side grab-rail pieces, unlike earlier models on which these were molded details; no smoke unit; illuminated; die-cast arch-bar trucks; "BLT 95". Billed as a complement to the Frisco Mikado engine made in 1993. Shown in the 1995 Stocking Stuffers/1996 Spring release catalog. **65 75**

17880 DENVER & RIO GRANDE WESTERN: 1990, Standard O wood-sided caboose; uncataloged; annual LCCA convention car; black body; white lettering; white Ft. Collins, Colorado, convention notation at lower front; white "Royal Gorge Route Scenic Line" logo under cupola; high cupola; illuminated; die-cast arch-bar trucks; "BLT 1-90". 2,785 made. Came in Type V box. Intended as a match for the LCCA special 18090 Rio Grande 4-6-2 steam engine also made in 1990. **70 80**

51701 NEW YORK CENTRAL: 1991, semi-scale caboose; die-cast zinc body painted maroon-tuscan; white NYC lettering and 19400 number centered on sides; detailed handrails and end platforms; metal brakewheels; illuminated; three-color marker lanterns; die-cast arch-bar trucks; no built date. This is not precisely a Standard O caboose, though it closely resembles them. An exact replica of the 1940 semi-scale caboose produced to go with the original 700E Hudson. Released with other semi-scale freight cars (a hopper, boxcar, and tanker) in conjunction with the modern 1-700E Hudson reproduced in 1991. The modern caboose, like the original, is made entirely of die-cast zinc. Somewhat hard to find. **125 150**

52047 COTTON BELT: 1994, Standard O wood-sided caboose with smoke; uncataloged; special for the Toy Train Operating Society's (TTOS) Southwest Division; brown body; black main and cupola roofs; tall cupola; white lettering; Cotton Belt Route logo under cupola; "StLSW" at upper center and "TTOS SW Div/Cal-Stewart 93" under number; number on car is "1921"; illuminated; cam-operated smoke unit; die-cast arch-bar trucks; "BLT 6-48". This is a special car made by TTOS for its semi-annual Cal-Stewart meet in California. **75 85**

88011 CANADIAN NATIONAL: 1988, Standard O wood-sided caboose; uncataloged; 10th annual commemorative car for the Lionel Collectors Association of Canada (LCAC); orange body; white lettering; high cupola; green CNR maple leaf logo with "Serves All Canada"; LCAC circle logo on rear of body; illuminated; die-cast arch-bar trucks; "BUILT 11-88 LCAC". These are blank 17600-series Lionel bodies decorated by PVP. Reportedly 200 produced. Difficult to find. **— 200**

WORK, TRANSFER, AND BOBBER CABOOSES

This last subsection of cabooses is a kind of catch-all category that covers the remainder of Lionel's line, the smaller and less-expensive cabooses found mostly in the Traditional (later Classic) Line and the starter sets. This description is not all-inclusive, because some models, particularly of the work caboose, have been extensively upgraded with deluxe features such as die-cast trucks, interior lighting, and sometimes a searchlight, which bring them more into the Collector Line category.

These small cabooses have the advantages of being inexpensive for Lionel to produce, lightweight and easily packaged in any kind of set. The work and transfer cabooses use a standard Type II short flatcar, and so can be made quickly by snapping the simple superstructures onto leftover flatcar bodies.

Also, despite their recent origin, these cabooses have an old-time look about them that looks great at the end of a string of woodside boxcars and reefers.

Work Caboose

Postwar Lionel issued many work cabooses, mostly variations on a Delaware, Lackawanna & Western road name, which modern Lionel has only repeated once (in 1987). The modern work cabooses have four principal variations: one with two tool chests on the flatcar forward of the cab; a second with a single large bin in place of the tool chests; a two-tool chest model with a small metal searchlight mounted between them (in this case on a fully die-cast flatcar); and last a model with a single (larger) searchlight mounted on the car in front of the cab. The light is similar to those on the searchlight cars, and because it is larger, the two tool chests are omitted.

Fundimensions production of the work caboose began almost immediately after the transition—with the 9021 Santa Fe in 1970. Quite a few work cabooses were to appear in the following years. A Santa Fe work caboose from 1986 even included sprung Standard O trucks, perhaps a bit of overkill for the small and simple car.

Most times, these cabooses do not attract a great deal of collector attention. However, in 1989 this changed with the 19709 Pennsylvania. It was made as a companion for the popular B-6 switcher and marked a host of impressive upgrades for the lowly work caboose. It came in a handsome tuscan color with die-cast trucks and included the first smoke unit and interior illumination ever used on a work caboose. It even introduced a new detailed flatcar (the Type IV short version, as described in the flatcar chapter), and had metal brakewheels on raised posts. The next year Lionel followed up by adding an old-fashioned pivoting searchlight between the two tool chests. This was the 19707 Southern Pacific, and is a revival of the 2420 and 6420 postwar searchlight cabooses. It is a good-looking match for the 18503 Southern Pacific NW-2 switcher. Both pieces illustrated Lionel LTI's trend toward improved quality and nostalgic revivals of the old-time favorites. They were the first work cabooses numbered in the Collector series.

In the latter part of the 90s, Lionel took to releasing quite a few work cabooses in a "Fire and Rescue" theme. They looked terrific in sets like the Navy, Coast Guard, and Fire Response.

Transfer Caboose

In 1981 a new type of caboose emerged, based on the work caboose but with interesting differences. It was a type never made by the postwar company. The first was the 6420 Reading from the Reading Yard King set. It used a Type II short flatcar but with the square cab, or "shanty," in the center of the car, not at the rear as with the work caboose. This was the "transfer" caboose, which Lionel also sometimes refers to as a "maintenance" caboose. Nicely detailed pipe railings are mounted to either side of the shanty on the flatcar. The shanty is based on that of the transfer caboose, but has a different roof piece. Note that the shanty actually has a "left" and "right" side, with the ladder on one side, but not the other. After five or six appeared in the early 80s, Lionel has made only two transfer cabooses since 1986. One of them, the 16519 Rock Island, was the first of the transfer cabooses to have interior illumination installed.

Bobber Caboose

The four-wheeled bobber caboose was first made for the Kickapoo Valley & Northern set in 1972. It was an all-plastic car, completely new with Fundimensions production. Though it looks tiny, it is surprisingly faithful to the prototype, which can be found on the Strasburg Railroad in Pennsylvania, among other places. It is one of the few four-wheel cars in Lionel's repertoire and has almost no metal parts in its construction. Obviously the bobber caboose is only found in the most inexpensive of Lionel's sets, or occasionally as companions to the very small plastic steam engines like the Dockside switchers. These whimsical, rather cute cabooses are interesting additions to a collection, though at their rock-bottom price levels, they attract little serious attention.

Lionel's work, transfer, and bobber cabooses have until recently been cataloged in the 16500-series for the basic Traditional Line pieces, and in the 19700-series for the more deluxe Collector-type work cabooses. Like the small SP cabooses, no special production (uncataloged) work or transfer cabooses have yet been made for the train clubs.

WORK, TRANSFER, AND BOBBER CABOOSE LISTINGS

Exc **Mt**

16500 ROCK ISLAND: 1987–88, bobber caboose; bright red body; white lettering; gray frame, end rails, and stack; four plastic wheels; no number on car; one dummy coupler; no built date. Part of 11701 Rail Blazer set. **10** **15**

16503 NEW YORK CENTRAL: 1987, transfer caboose; black flatcar body and railings; white lettering on flatcar; medium gray cab with black number and black with gray "NYC" logo at center; Symington-Wayne trucks; "BLT 1-87". **15** **20**

16511 PENNSYLVANIA: 1988–89, bobber caboose; tuscan body; gold lettering, frame and railings; four plastic wheels; one dummy coupler. Part of 11708 Midnight Flyer set in 1989 and uncataloged 11708 Toys "R" Us Pennsy set (same components) the year before. **10** **15**

	Exc	Mt

16519 ROCK ISLAND: 1990, transfer caboose; black flatcar body; blue shanty with white Rock Island shield; white lettering on flatcar; illuminated with opaque window insert (first lighted transfer caboose); ASF trucks; "BLT 1-90". Intended to accompany the 18610 0-4-0 Rock Island switcher. **15 20**

16527 WESTERN PACIFIC: 1992, work caboose; intended as a match for the 18621 Western Pacific small steam engine, but both the caboose and engine were dropped from the 1992 line. **Not Manufactured**

16549 SOO LINE: 1993, work caboose; black flatcar body; white number on car; red cab and single bin; white "SOO" on cab; illuminated; ASF trucks; "BLT 1-93". No individual box. Part of 11741 Northwest Express set. **25 30**

16550 US NAVY: 1994–95, work caboose with searchlight; gray flatcar body; black lettering on car; yellow cab with "USN" and number; searchlight with black hood mounted on car front; illuminated cab; ASF trucks; "BLT 1-94". A part of the successful 11745 U.S. Navy Train set. Note that the catalog pictures this piece with a "16650" number, but it was made as the 16550. **20 25**

16552 FRISCO: 1994, work caboose with searchlight; black flatcar body; yellow lettering and number on car; yellow cab with black Frisco shield; searchlight with black hood on car front (no tool chests or bin); searchlight is the same as on the searchlight cars, not the small model used on several other work cabooses; illuminated cab; ASF trucks; "BLT 1-94". Made as a match for the 18920 Frisco NW-2 switcher. **30 35**

16645 AMTRAK: 1992, work caboose with searchlight; uncataloged; black flatcar body; silver cab; black "19816" and red and blue Amtrak arrow logo on cab; white flatcar lettering; illuminated; operating searchlight (no tool chests or bin); searchlight is of the same type as on the searchlight cars; light has black hood; ASF trucks; "BLT 1-92". Part of 11723 Amtrak Work Train set. The caboose has an unusual number because it is in sequence with the other cars in the set. The caboose was cataloged initially in the 1991 Book 2 as a light gray flatcar with orange cab, in a set called the "Amtrak Maintenance Train." But the company decided not to make the set as shown there. Instead it reappeared as the Amtrak Work Train in the 1992 Stocking Stuffer brochure, with all new rolling stock, and this caboose, which had drastically changed its colors. **30 40**

19707 SOUTHERN PACIFIC: 1990, work caboose with searchlight; light gray flatcar body made of die-cast metal; medium red cab and tool chests; yellow railings front and rear; white lettering on cab and flatcar; illuminated; opaque window insert; smoke unit; small operating searchlight on pivot between tool chests; searchlight has old-style metal housing, not the same hood as on the searchlight cars; brakewheels on raised posts; die-cast arch-bar trucks; "BLT 1-90". This is a remake of the postwar 6420 except for the roadname. Issued as a match for the 18503 Southern Pacific NW-2 switcher. **85 95**

19709 PENNSYLVANIA: 1989, 1991, work caboose; maroon-tuscan cab and tool chests; black roof; new die-cast metal black flatcar body; gold lettering on cab and frame; metal handrails; brakewheels on raised posts; smoke unit; illuminated; die-cast arch-bar trucks; "BLT 1-89". Issued as a match for the 18000 scale B-6 switcher. This car marks several impressive firsts in the work caboose series. **60 75**

19714 NEW YORK CENTRAL: 1992, work caboose with searchlight; blue-green die-cast flatcar body; matching cab and tool chests; white lettering flatcar; NYC oval logo in black and white on cab; illuminated; opaque window insert; smoke unit; small operating searchlight on pivot between tool chests; searchlight has old-style metal housing, not the same hood as on the searchlight cars; brakewheels on raised posts; die-cast arch-bar trucks; "BLT 1-90". **80 100**

CHAPTER 10

Crane and Derrick Cars

Crane cars have been staples on Lionel layouts since before World War II, and few operating cars more typify Lionel's trademark action philosophy. Modern Lionel has carried on the tradition, including a fascinating and confusing 6560 crane car, which transitioned the turbulent period in 1969–70 when the postwar Lionel Corporation was relinquishing its train line to the fledgling MPC/ Fundimensions management. The early Fundimensions period, with its emphasis on cost efficiency, did not see new crane cars. But after 1979, Lionel tried to offer at least one crane car every year. A number of excellent crane cars were released in the 1980s, and the current Lionel LTI/LLC period has followed suit.

Unlike most other pieces of Lionel's rolling stock, there are no major variations in the crane car, either in its car frame, cab, boom, or mechanism, all of which remain essentially the same as the postwar crane car. In the 1980s some of the cars sported the sprung Standard O trucks, but since the 1986 Kughn era began, most have featured the die-cast six-wheel trucks. All the crane cars since 1986 have been at the high end of the rolling stock line, either in Collector or high-end Traditional Line sets, or as single releases. In the 1990s, Lionel frequently offered crane cars and matching flatcars or gondolas to go with popular sets or locomotives that had been released earlier.

The derrick car is a sort of baby crane car without the cab. It is modeled after the postwar 6670 and has a standard long flatcar (6511-2 style) as its base, with the derrick assembly riveted to the car. The derrick is collapsible and snaps into position when raised. It operates with a hand crank and swivels. In the modern era, the outrigger mechanism used on some postwar versions has been omitted. This car, which made its first appearance in the post-1986 period in the Black Diamond Lehigh Valley set of 1987, represents a sort of "poor man's crane car," allowing Lionel to include an action car in some of its lower-end sets, while keeping its costs down.

In all, Lionel's modern crane cars are a colorful consist and most of them are desirable pieces. The fact that there are relatively few, yet most are readily available, makes them a good group to collect on a modest budget. They add an element of realism and play value to any layout, especially when combined with work cabooses and gondolas.

CRANE AND DERRICK CAR LISTINGS

Exc **Mt**

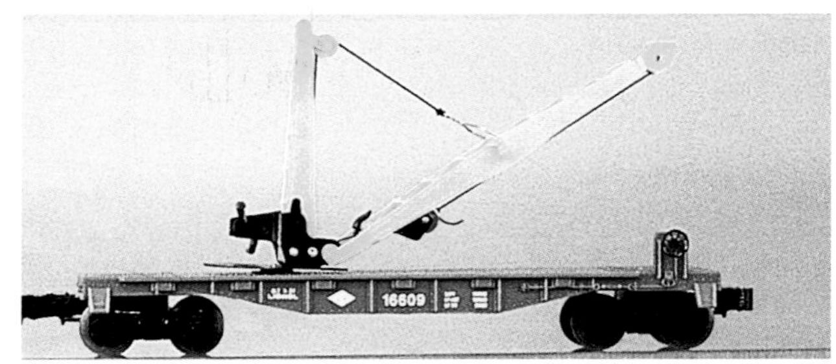

16609 LEHIGH VALLEY: 1987, derrick car; green flatcar body; white lettering and diamond logo; yellow derrick; Symington-Wayne trucks. Part of Black Diamond set 11702, one of the nicer Traditional Line sets released in Lionel Trains, Inc.'s first year. **25** **35**

16644 AMTRAK: 1992, crane car; gray frame; orange cab; black boom; black number and "Amtrak" on cab; white lettering on frame; ASF trucks (used because the car came in a Traditional Line set); "BLT 1-92". Part of the 11723 Amtrak Maintenance Train set. This set was originally cataloged in 1991 but was not made that year. Instead it was delayed until 1992, when it appeared in the 1992 Stocking Stuffers brochure with an entirely different freight consist than the 1991 catalog showed. **40** **45**

16653 WESTERN PACIFIC: 1992, crane car, black frame and cab, gray cab roof and boom; white lettering; black, white, and orange Western Pacific herald at rear of cab; die-cast six-wheel trucks (catalog pictures this item with Standard O trucks); "BLT 1-92". Part of the 11733 Feather River Service Station set. **50** **60**

16658 ERIE-LACKAWANNA: 1993, crane car, maroon car frame and cab; black cab roof; silver boom; yellow lettering on frame;

19402 Great Northern crane car

	Exc	Mt

white "E" logo on cab rear; die-cast six-wheel trucks; "BLT 1-93". Matches 16373 E-L flatcar, with both cars intended as add-ons to the Erie Fallen Flags set no. 7 also released that year. **60** **70**

16684 US NAVY: 1994–95, crane car; bright yellow car frame and cab; gray cab roof and boom; black lettering; "BUCYRUS ERIE" and "USN" on cab; "US NAVY" printed on boom; ASF trucks (car is part of a Traditional Line set); "BLT 1-94". Part of popular 11745 U.S. Navy train. No individual box. **35** **40**

16709 NEW YORK CENTRAL: 1995, derrick car; black flatcar; gray boom; white lettering on flatcar; ASF trucks; "BLT 95". First derrick car produced by Lionel since 1987. **25** **30**

19402 GREAT NORTHERN: 1988, crane car; black frame and boom; bright orange cab; dark green "GN" lettering on cab; red, white, and green goat logo; die-cast six-wheel trucks. Part of Fallen Flag set no. 3, all of whose components were for separate sale. **50** **60**

19405 SOUTHERN: 1991, crane car; green cab and frame; silver boom; silver cab roof; yellow lettering and SR logo on cab; SR circle logo on boom; die-cast six-wheel trucks; "BLT 1-91". Intended as a match for 11704 Southern Freight Runner Service Station Special set or the Southern Famous American Railroad set no. 4. Somewhat hard to find. **60** **80**

	Exc	Mt

19412 FRISCO: 1992, crane car; black frame and cab; silver boom; yellow lettering on frame and cab; yellow "FRISCO" herald at rear of cab; die-cast six-wheel trucks; "BLT 1-92". Released as an add-on to the 18504 Frisco Fallen Flags set no. 5 from the year before. **55** **65**

52008 TCA LIONEL LINES: 1993, crane car; uncataloged; black car frame; light gray cab; black boom; white lettering on car frame; number on car is "X1993", 52008 not on car; "LIONEL LINES" and "BUCYRUS ERIE" in black on cab side; notations for 39th TCA Convention in St. Paul, Minnesota, on rear of cab; six-wheel die-cast trucks; no built date except "X1993". 1993 TCA National Convention Car. Interestingly, other than the number and convention notation, Lionel's 19834 crane car released in 1997 is identical. **60** **75**

CHAPTER 11

Flatcars

During the postwar years, the Lionel Corporation made the flatcar its most versatile freight carrier. Flatcars were used to haul just about everything under the sun, from submarines and helicopters to transformers and Christmas trees. If the load could not be put on the flatcar directly, Lionel saw to it that the car was adapted to the purpose. Some cars were fitted with bulkheads to hold pipes, wood, or gas containers. A "depressed-center" car was created to carry taller loads, like the transformer, under low-slung layout overpasses. Other flatcars were fitted with fences or stakes. Still others had chocks to hold large machinery or autos in place. One model has a ramp superstructure holding barrels. Another has an operating platform that can be raised and lowered an inch or so. Track rails were carried as a load or fitted directly to the car so that lighted "radioactive waste containers" could be carried. Now and then just a plain old flatcar would appear, with no load at all. The list goes on and on.

In the modern era, Lionel's successor firms continue the tradition of including a flatcar of one sort or another in a large percentage of its sets. Numbers of different cars were cataloged every year. For a while in the Fundimensions era prior to 1986 flatcars were not featured quite as prominently, while the makers explored other rolling stock more suited to the colorful graphics. But the reliable old flatcar, notably in its incarnation as a carrier for trailers, made a comeback in the era of Lionel LTI.

It is with its use as a base for the Trailers-on-Flat-Cars (TOFCs) that the flatcar has seen its most extensive application in modern Lionel's freight line. There are such a large variety of these cars that our Guide breaks them out into a chapter of their own. This category will also find several of the most sought-after and valuable of the flatcars. Our book includes both the TOFCs (the flatcar) and TTUXs (the spine car) in that section.

Not only are there numerous flatcars in the conventional sense, but this versatile model has served as the basis for other varieties of rolling stock—including all the searchlight cars, the derrick cars (see the crane car chapter), and the work and transfer styles of caboose.

Lionel's use of the flatcar in the modern era has given an up-to-date realistic look to the freight line as well as to serve as a "do-it-all" platform to carry as many and sundry loads as imaginative minds could devise. "Variety is the spice of life" could serve as the motto for the Lionel flatcar fleet. Most flatcars are relatively inexpensive and available, and so constitute a broad opportunity for specialty collecting, although the sheer number of the cars poses a daunting challenge. An almost infinite variety of subsets of cars can be collected—for example, depressed-center cars, or cars with construction vehicles, or TV-radar cars, or barrel cars, or even the cars made for the fun "Invasion Earth!" series with Warner Brothers cartoon characters. Some uncataloged and other special production flatcars will prove quite hard to find.

The numbering scheme for flatcars is haphazard. Most of the lower-cost (Traditional or Classic Line) cars are found in the 16300-series (along with several other types of cars). This series was quickly used up and the cars after 1994 are found in the 16900-series. "Action" flats such as the track maintenance, boat cars, radar cars, and the like, were numbered in the 16600 series. But with all of Lionel's action cars this series too quickly ran out and was extended into the 16700- and 16900-series. Standard O flatcars are found in the 17500 series. A few Collector-level cars are found in the 19400-series. Recent years have found flatcars in the 20000- and 30000-series of numbers, with the numbers of products rising rapidly. There are a few special pieces in the 52000-series, though the train clubs generally shy away from flatcars as special pieces. There are exceptions.

Lionel confused the situation after 1996 by decorating its rolling stock with numbers relating back to the postwar models from the 1940s and 1950s. They were so caught up in this nostalgia that several cars are decorated with the same number (6424 and 6411, for example) and in some cases the catalog number (which is how this book is organized) is not shown in the catalog itself! Some of the catalogs in these years were also using artists' renditions rather than actual photos, reminiscent of the way 1950s Lionel did things. This was a clever marketing scheme, but it made things hard for collectors and historians to pinpoint required details!

The accompanying figure describes the various flatcar body types to be found in modern era production. Each is described briefly in the following sections. Three of the cars illustrated were introduced after 1996, and so the car listings will appear in our follow-up volume for post-1996 production. We will include a brief description of them below, however, for completeness.

Two other types of short flatcars are not shown in the figure (not produced since 1986), but described below for reference. Also the "raised-center" car (a.k.a. the "Allis Chalmers") is not shown—only one model was made since 1986—and our photo of it does it full justice. With all 15 styles of flatcar—if one counts the TTUX style shown in the next chapter—it's obvious that modern Lionel has been busy designing and creating new cars. Nine are completely new models since 1970, while the rest are carryovers from the postwar period, though the modern company made a few changes to the short Type IV. We should mention that there was another type of car—a four-wheel version of the short flatcar—that appeared only once in the Fundimensions era: the "Timberline" set in 1978. But since it has not been repeated since 1986, we don't include it here. The reader is referred to the 9019 entry in the previous guide *(Greenberg's Guide to Lionel Trains, 1970–1991, Volume I)* for more details. The body, sans trucks, was translated as is into the Type II short flatcar described here.

LONG FLATCARS

Long flatcars come in two nearly identical types, molds developed in the postwar era when this style of flatcar was a dominant member of the Lionel freight car line. Fundimensions-MPC introduced the modern flatcar in 1971 with the long 9121 Louisville & Nashville car carrying a bulldozer and scraper, using it precisely as the old Lionel Corporation had done. The L&N car stayed in the line off and on for eight years. The cars can also have bulkheads, which come in two varieties. One, which can be considered the "newer" of the two, having appeared first in 1973, is a rather unsteady solid plastic piece that usually fits into the holes at the extreme ends of the car. It has a tapered section at its top. The other bulkhead first showed up on modern cars on the 16333 Frisco in 1991, but it had been used on several postwar cars, notably the 6467. For some reason Fundimensions never used it. This bulkhead is more versatile and substantial than the thinner tapered one. It has an open frame that can be installed anywhere along the flatcar body, fitting into the stake holes. An angled structure extending forward permits this bulkhead to be stronger and steadier than its solid predecessor. It is used strictly on the long flatcars. It also features a nice metal brakewheel. Removable plastic stakes also show up on the long and short flatcars, as well as the Standard O kind, whether or not a load is included. Since these parts are easily removed and replaced, collectors should note which entries in this book list them as included in original production. The presence of bulkheads and stakes on cars that originally did not have them should not be made into a case for a variation. Of course, hobbyists can purchase bulkheads and stakes from parts dealers.

The long Lionel flatcar body is 10 inches long, and 11 inches coupler to coupler.

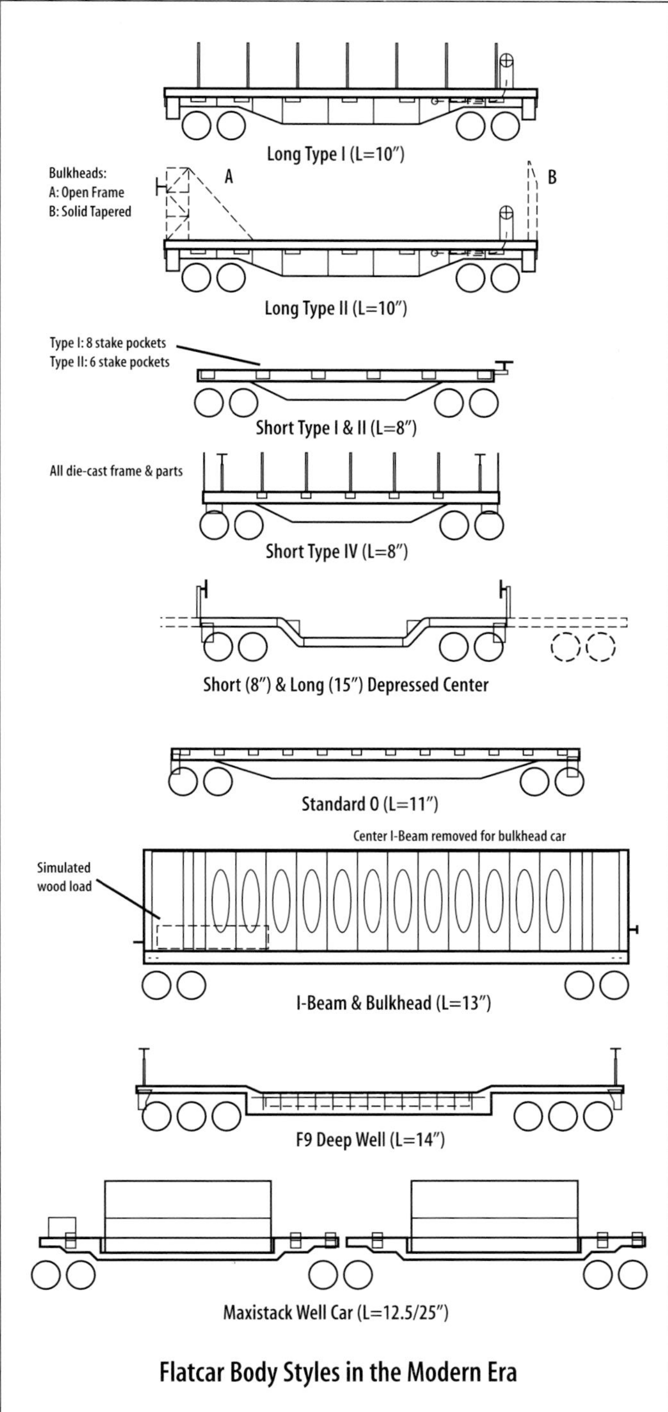

Flatcar Body Styles in the Modern Era

LONG TYPE I (or 6424-type) is recognized by the 6424-11 mold number on its underside and the prominent protruding vertical stiffeners found on the tapered beams that run the length of the car under the deck. The number 6424 refers to the postwar flatcar with autos on which it first appeared. The "protrusions" visible from the side are actually additional stiffeners present on the insides of the tapered beams. They are not on the Type II mold, and so the line of the tapered beam appears smooth on the Type II. There is another difference between the two molds. Type I has larger clumps of excess plastic present at the intersections of the deck support beams. This is visible only by examining the undersides.

There are other variations in both Type I and II molds having to do with stake holes and other cutouts for various superstructures or items mounted to the deck. Some of these are postwar in origin and others are modern variations.

The Type I body has appeared on a large number of modern-era products. It is the basis for all the regular-length Trailers-on-Flatcars (TOFCs—see separate chapter) except those which use the Standard O car base. It is also the basis for all the barrel ramp cars made since 1987.

The barrel ramp cars are based on the postwar 6343 car, which appeared only in 1961. The superstructure used on the barrel ramps is the same one used atop the buildings on the 342-345 culvert loader accessories. We should mention that the odd 16325 Microracers car did not actually include barrels on the ramp; rather it had four small "Microracer" race cars.

LONG TYPE II (or 6511-type) is recognized by the 6511-1 or -2 mold number on its underside and does not have the prominent protruding vertical stiffeners on the tapered beams as does Type I. The number 6511 refers to the postwar flatcar with pipes on which it first appeared.

This car has been used in the modern era for an increasing variety of applications. One was for the revival of the track maintenance hydraulic platform cars starting in 1987. None have been made since 1990.

The Type II car is also used for a version of the Lionel searchlight cars, in which a superstructure similar to that of the Track Maintenance cars is affixed atop the car to support the searchlight. And it has supported the derrick cranes on the derrick cars, as described in that chapter.

Lionel LTI devoted attention to the Type II long flatcar as a basis for carrying a dizzying variety of loads.

SHORT FLATCARS

Lionel's short flatcars—8 inches in length as compared to the 10 inches of the long style—have not been a major part of Lionel's line since the 1970s. The modern short cars are found principally in four types. Lionel has not used the first style since 1980, though it was quite prevalent earlier. Type II began to appear in the low-cost sets about then and continued through the early years of Lionel LTI (the late 1980s) and still appears now on work cabooses. But its use has been phased down considerably from what it was in the early 1980s. A third style was used only for General-type small flatcars. This model has also not appeared since 1986, we do not include it in this volume, but refer the reader to *Greenberg's Guide to Lionel Trains, 1970–1991, Volume I* for more details.

These cars are referred to by many collectors as "O27" to designate their smaller and less-expensive character, and can be distinguished from the longer flatcars by another obvious feature: a lack of vertical stiffeners on the underside tapered beams. The types of short cars differ in the number of stake holes/pockets they have, but none have the same number as the long flatcar.

SHORT TYPE I (or 9020-type) was the first car out of the block when MPC Lionel started operations in 1970. It was a new design, as compared to the old stamped-metal postwar version. As introduced first on the 9020 Union Pacific that year, it had a wood-scribed deck on top and bottom, and 16 plastic stakes that fit into molded holes around the perimeter. The 9020, which came in countless inexpensive sets in Fundimensions' early years, may well be the most plentiful car made in the modern era. Other later versions came with loads or sometimes with the solid-tapered bulkheads described under the long flatcar heading.

The short Type I car gave way to Type II around 1980.

SHORT TYPE II (or 9325-type) started life as a strange four-wheel car in 1978's Timberline set, then graduated to full Lionel-ship with the 9325 Norfolk & Western the next year. Its distinguishing features are six prominent stake hole pockets in each side (long flatcars have seven, Type I has eight, Type III has none, and Type IV has five), as well as a complete lack of steps. All the other long and short flatcar styles have at least one step. The deep stake pockets are also used to support fences, which were never used on the Type I short car. There is a minor difference with Type I in the thicker lip on this car's underside beam. Otherwise, it has the same nice wood-grained floor and upward-facing brakewheels as the Type I car. It appeared in several Fundimensions sets after its debut as 9325 ("9325" is molded into the deck bottom). It can be found with fences and crate loads or horses corralled for transport.

However, relatively few have been made since 1986. Of these, the 16352 cruise missile-carrying car was a surprisingly popular item and is now somewhat scarce. This car is used as the base for Lionel's transfer and work cabooses—see those subheadings in the Caboose chapter.

SHORT TYPE I (or 9020-type) was the first car out of the block when MPC Lionel started operations in 1970. It was a new design, as compared to the old stamped-metal postwar version. As introduced first on the 9020 Union Pacific that year, it had a wood-scribed deck on top and bottom, and 16 plastic stakes that fit into molded holes around the perimeter. The 9020, which came in countless inexpensive sets in Fundimensions' early years, may well be the most plentiful car made in the modern era. Other later versions came with loads or sometimes with the solid-tapered bulkheads described under the long flatcar heading.

The short Type I car gave way to Type II around 1980.

SHORT TYPE II (or 9325-type) started life as a strange four-wheel car in 1978's Timberline set, then graduated to full Lionel-ship with the 9325 Norfolk & Western the next year. Its distinguishing features are six prominent stake hole pockets in each side (long flatcars have seven, Type I has eight, Type III has none, and Type IV has five), as well as a complete lack of steps. All the other long and short flatcar styles have at least one step. The deep stake pockets are also used to support fences, which were never used on the Type I short car. There is a minor difference with Type I in the thicker lip on this car's underside beam. Otherwise, it has the same nice wood-grained floor and upward-facing brakewheels as the Type I car. It appeared in several Fundimensions sets after its debut as 9325 ("9325" is molded into the deck bottom). It can be found with fences and crate loads or horses corralled for transport.

However, relatively few have been made since 1986. Of these, the 16352 cruise missile-carrying car was a surprisingly popular item and is now somewhat scarce.

This car is used as the base for Lionel's transfer and work cabooses—see those subheadings in the Caboose chapter.

SHORT TYPE III (General style), is a unique variation of the car with wire supports under the deck where the tapered beams are on Type I and II. It has no brakewheel or stake pockets and is found most often with fences. The piece (mold number 1877) was styled for the 19th-century sets pulled by the old time General wood steam engines. This style has not appeared in the modern era from 1987 on. It last appeared in an uncataloged General set in 1986 made for American Express. It is not shown in the preceding figure.

SHORT TYPE IV (6411-style) is a re-creation of the postwar 6411 car brought out anew by Lionel LLC in 1996, 45 years after its last sighting. It had in fact appeared first as a work caboose (the 19709 PRR) in 1989. But it was not until 1996 that Lionel LLC produced it as a flatcar. The modern car even has the nice fitted metal handrails at the ends, which were a noted feature in the early postwar cars. Given the car's all-metal body, it should be no wonder that Lionel Fundimensions did not expend the cash to produce it. In that sense today's Lionel is taking a chance, and we shall see whether their gamble will continue in future years. In fact, much of their product in 1996 marked a return to die-cast metal bodies and features—a reversal of nearly fifty years of trends to plastic construction. The new model, which has the wire handrails, two post-mounted metal brakewheels, and metal stakes along with the metal frame, was a radical departure in this direction for such a lowly candidate as the short flatcar.

DEPRESSED-CENTER FLATCARS

These wonderful freight cars have been carried forward virtually unchanged from the postwar period, in which they were favorites of Lionel modelers everywhere. The extra half-inch which the center section drops down allows Lionel to carry a variety of tall cargo that might otherwise bang unceremoniously into low overhangs, bridges, or tunnel entrances. The restricted length of the center platform (3½ inches) does somewhat restrict the cargo loads, but has only slightly restrained Lionel from installing a dizzying variety of loads on it. Depressed-center cars have appeared most often with transformers and cable reels.

There are two major types of depressed-center cars—short (8 inches) and long (15 inches), with the short style being far more prevalent.

SHORT DEPRESSED-CENTER

This car was resurrected in 1989 after a long run in the postwar era. It was not manufactured during the Fundimensions period, but has made a strong comeback in the 1990s, both as a flatcar with load and as a base for the depressed-center searchlight cars. It is now one of Lionel's premier flatcar models. The car has a post-mounted brakewheel at each end. Of all the flatcar types, only this car and the new short die-cast car have metal steps. This bent sheet-metal piece is installed on the car underside just above the truck, swaged in place by melting a plastic plug molded in for the purpose. Metal steps, of course, were prevalent on many types of postwar rolling stock.

LONG DEPRESSED-CENTER

This is a die-cast extra-long flatcar reminiscent of the 6418 car that first appeared in 1957. It has rarely been used in the modern era, showing up as the 9233 transformer-carrier in 1980 and the 6509 girder-carrier in 1981. The car body has a longer center section (at 5 inches compared to 3½ for its smaller brother), but sports two brakewheels on posts like the small one does. This magnificent 15-inch monster doesn't appear more often for both financial and logistical reasons. It is an all-die-cast car and features four die-cast wheelsets. The difficulty of painting and decorating a die-cast body tends to drive manufacturing costs up. The cars are also difficult to use on smaller layouts with tighter track radii and so suffer from a certain resistance from operators of smaller pikes.

Still, they look wonderful in a long consist with Standard O cars on a long straightaway.

RAISED-CENTER FLATCARS (ALLIS CHALMERS)

A unique flatcar was designed specially for the 6519 Allis Chalmers nuclear reactor core carrier in 1958. It had a thick center section raised about a half inch from the flatcar ends. This raised center portion was hogged out substantially to carry the nuclear condenser, and so the cargo rides "through" the car rather than on it, secured by snap tabs and wire cables. This car has appeared very rarely.

It was rereleased as the 9232 car in the Fundimensions era, and as the 16349 Allis Chalmers in 1992, the period covered by this volume. It has not been used for any other modern era cars, but did appear twice in the postwar era as a missile-firing car and a Mercury capsule car.

There is only one modern model of this car so it is not shown in the figure, but is pictured at the top of the 16349 entry.

The raised brakewheel posts on these cars, from any era, are fragile and easily broken off. Collectors should take care to assure the brakewheels are intact when purchasing an excellent or better-condition car.

STANDARD O FLATCARS

These flatcars were created in the mid 1970s, beginning with the 9823 Santa Fe, and were intended to match the new Standard O boxcars, gondolas, reefers, and wood-sided cabooses appearing in Lionel's line at that time. Like all the cars in the series, these flatcars have realistic details, such as excellent wood-beam scribing on the deck surface, 12 stake pockets along each edge, and, of course, die-cast sprung Standard O trucks. For some reason, brakewheels are not included with this type of flatcar. At 11 inches, it is among the longest of the flatcars, but fortunately not so long that it can't be used on layouts with tighter curves. Early in the modern era, it most often appeared alone with stakes or with logs secured by chains. But in later years it has served as a platform for die-cast vehicles and construction equipment, as well as for longer trailers on some TOFCs, as can be seen in the TOFC chapter.

Standard O flatcars were initially not as warmly received as other types of Standard O stock, such as the ACF hoppers. After a few releases in the late 1980s, five years passed before Lionel LTI came out with a new one in 1994. Most notable of these cars during the modern period would have to be the series of three Western Maryland flatcars with logs, 17512-14, released in 1996 as a complement to the Western Maryland Shay.

I-BEAM

A super-long new style of flatcar appeared in the 1992 Lionel catalog. It was a phenomenal 20 inches long, and the prominent feature was a huge I-beam that ran vertically down the center of the car between two nicely detailed end bulkheads. The I-beam also had a multitude of large oval cutouts ("lightening holes") that are used on the real cars to reduce weight. New-style simulated plywood pallets were specially created for this car, which could neatly carry 24 of them with 12 (three stacks of four) on each side of the I-beam. The model was a superb re-creation of the real railroad prototype in service today. Unfortunately, the customer response to such a huge car (it would have to run only on O72 track in order not to impact switch machines) was lukewarm, since most hobbyists had a mixture of long and short rolling stock. Lionel responded by canceling the extra-long models and retooling the dies for a shorter (13-inch) car, which eventually reached production. The first released model was the 16371 Burlington.

The Toy Train Operating Society produced a very scarce version of the Union Pacific car (see 52084) in 1995.

Following a large diesel such as a Dash 8 or SD-40, these cars would make a truly impressive unit train!

Though not (technically) a part of the Standard O line, the I-beam flatcars are nonetheless longer than any other type of flatcar (except the long depressed-center), and all to date have carried the sprung Standard O trucks.

MAXISTACK "DEEP WELL" CAR

The Maxistack car has proved a very popular operating model of the real-world container carrier found all around the nation's railroads today. As an intermodal carrier, it can be used with Lionel's intermodal cranes. Its containers can be used as trailers for tractor-trailer sets, fitted with the undercarriage accessory. And with its articulated center truck, the Maxistack can be used on even smaller model railroad pikes, although the overhang on O27 track is substantial, and Lionel doesn't recommend its use with O27 switches. These multiple uses explain the car's popularity to date. The first of these 25-inch-long pieces released was the 16360 Norfolk & Western in 1993.

These cars are often confused as TOFC or TTUX cars (see the next chapter), but they are not, technically, because the containers are not on wheels—at least until the operator puts them there!

LOADS

As will be seen from our detailed listings, the loads carried by Lionel's flatcars, just as in the real world, vary all over the spectrum. Collectors should take note of our listings to verify that the proper load is actually with the car being purchased, since loads are easily changed and lost. Another point of interest—when Lionel contracted with Ertl and Corgi to carry some of their beautiful die-cast vehicles and construction equipment on the flatcars, Lionel found that with time the wheels on the models would react with the flatcar top, causing it to dissolve or distort or worse, fuse to the wheels of the vehicles. Lionel expert Lou Bohn explains that this occurs because the wheels of the models are "plasticized" polyvinyl chloride (PVC), while the flatcar top is "non-plasticized." "Plasticizer migration" will eventually occur between the two. Lou states that the same thing occurred with Lionel's handcar figures in the postwar years. Apparently not learning the postwar lesson in time, Lionel realized the problem too late for some of the 1995 production. Thereafter (1996 and later), Lionel installed a clear protective shield between the car surface and the tires. Buyers of flatcars with Ertl vehicles should check for the presence of this shield, or at least verify that the load hasn't been fused to the car. Shields can be obtained from Lionel.

FLATCAR LISTINGS

Exc Mt

16300 ROCK ISLAND: 1987–88, short flatcar with crate load; red type II body; white lettering "ROCK ISLAND"; black fencing, gray crate load; plastic arch-bar trucks; "BLT 1-87". Part of 11701 Rail Blazer set. **8 10**

16301 LIONEL: 1987, barrel ramp car; dark blue Long Type I flatcar body; yellow lettering and number; white superstructure (same structure as was used on the postwar culvert loader and unloader accessories); eight varnished wood barrels; Symington-Wayne trucks; no "BLT" date. This was Lionel's first reissue of the postwar 6343 barrel ramp car. **15 20**

16306 SANTA FE: 1988, barrel ramp car; red Long Type I flatcar body and superstructure; white lettering; white Santa Fe cross logo on ramp; eight varnished wood barrels; Symington-Wayne trucks. "BLT 1-88". **10 15**

16315 PENNSYLVANIA: 1988–89, flatcar with crate load; brown-maroon short Type II body; white lettering; black fences and 20-piece crate load; Symington-Wayne trucks; "BLT 1-88". Part of uncataloged 11708 Toys "R" Us Pennsy set in 1988, and the cataloged 11708 Midnight Shift set in 1989. **8 10**

16317 PENNSYLVANIA: 1989, barrel ramp car; tuscan Long Type I flatcar body and superstructure; gold lettering and number; PRR keystone logo in gold on ramp; eight varnished wood barrels; Symington-Wayne trucks; "BLT 1-89." **15 20**

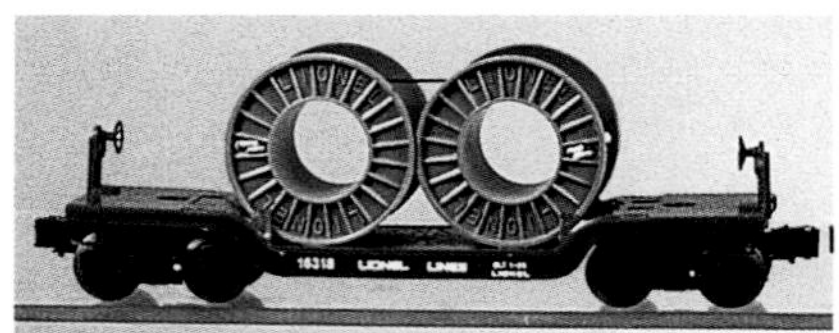

16318 LIONEL LINES: 1989, depressed-center flatcar; maroon body; white lettering; brakewheels on raised posts at each end; two gray cable reels embossed "LIONEL" with wire cable; reels held to car by elastic cord; Symington-Wayne trucks; "BLT 1-89". First reissue of postwar depressed-center flatcar (postwar

	Exc	Mt

car with reels was the 6561); this style of flatcar is also used for the depressed-center searchlight cars. **20** **25**

16320 GREAT NORTHERN: 1990, barrel ramp car; green long Type I flatcar body; yellow lettering and number; orange ramp structure with circular GN goat logo in green; eight varnished wood barrels; ASF trucks; "BLT 1-90". **15** **20**

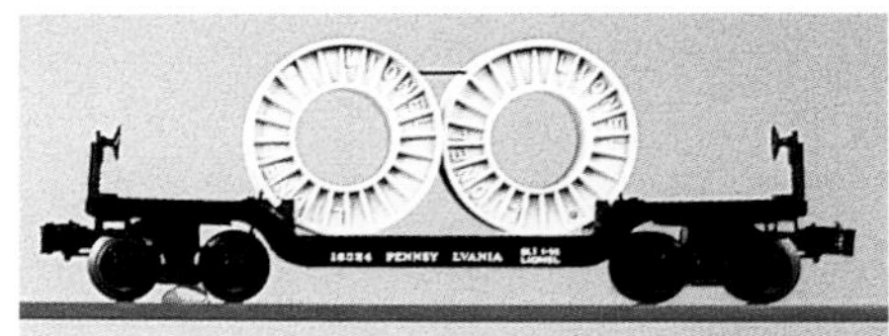

16324 PENNSYLVANIA: 1990, depressed-center flatcar with cable reels; black body; white lettering; two tan cable reels embossed "LIONEL"; ASF trucks; "BLT 1-90". **20** **25**

16325 MICRORACERS: 1989, barrel ramp car; uncataloged; unusual application of barrel ramp car to carry four small "Microracer" autos—red, yellow, green, and blue; red unpainted plastic long Type I flatcar body and barrel ramp; white lettering; large black and white sign reading "MICRO-RACERS EXHIBITION" affixed to ramp; comes with a black canister, labeled with racing flags and "MICRORACERS OIL", affixed to the car at the end of the ramp; Symington-Wayne trucks; "BLT 1-89." Part of uncataloged 11771 Microracers set available only through K-Mart. **25** **35**

16326 SANTA FE: 1991, depressed-center flatcar; light gray body; white lettering; two blue cable reels embossed "LIONEL" with wire cable; ASF trucks; "BLT 1-91". **20** **25**

16329 SOUTHERN PACIFIC: 1990–91, flatcar with fences; short Type II brown body; white lettering; tan fences (catalog shows them as white); two horses, Type V plastic arch-bar trucks; "BLT 1-90". Part of 11714 Badlands Express set. **15** **20**

16331 SOUTHERN: 1991, barrel ramp car. Announced in 1991 Book 1 catalog, but not manufactured. **Not Manufactured**

16332 LIONEL LINES: 1991, depressed-center flatcar with transformer; light blue body; white lettering with "TRANSFORMER CAR" in white on the upper levels of the car sides; gray transformer with four white insulators and sign reading "DANGER / 1,000,000 / VOLTS"; ASF trucks; "BLT 1-91." Reissue of postwar 6461 transformer car in new colors. **25** **30**

16333 FRISCO: 1991, flatcar with bulkheads and lumber load; long Type II tuscan body; white lettering and Frisco shield logo; two bulkheads; eight plastic stakes; three simulated plywood lumber pallets with ends realistically painted red; pallets mounted to car via small plastic pins; ASF trucks; "BLT 1-91". Sold separately, this is a good match for the Frisco Fallen Flags set no. 5 also released in 1991. This is the first modern reissue of the 6467 long flatcar with bulkheads, which are of an open-frame type, unlike the solid wall type used on previous flatcars. The open bulkheads include brakewheels. **25** **30**

16340 AMTRAK: 1991, long flatcar with stakes; This car was announced in the 11723 Amtrak Maintenance Train set in the regular 1991 catalog, but never made. Instead the set was heavily modified and produced as shown (and listed as the Amtrak "Work Train") in the 1992 Stocking Stuffers brochure. The flatcar in the production set was the 16370, which carried rails. **Not Manufactured**

16341 NEW YORK CENTRAL: 1992, depressed-center flatcar with transformer; tuscan flatcar body with white lettering; gray transformer; sign on side in white lettering reads "DANGER / 10,000,000 AMPS"; white insulators on transformer; two brakewheels on posts at car ends; ASF trucks; "BLT 1-92". Note the differences in the sign on this car versus the 16332 described above. **25** **30**

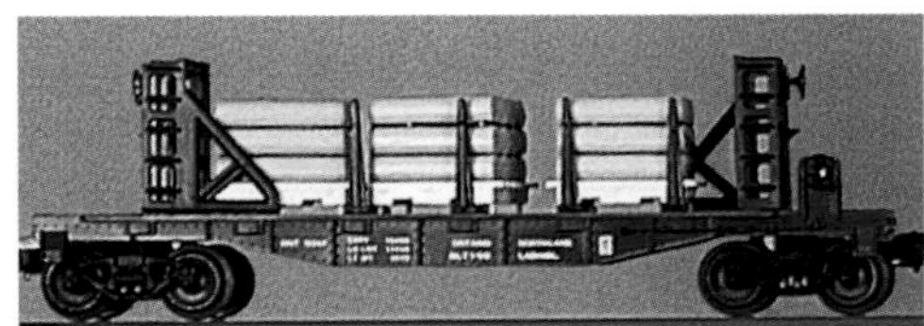

16347 ONTARIO NORTHLAND: 1992, flatcar with bulkheads and pulpwood load; long type II flatcar body in dark green; white lettering; black plastic open-frame bulkheads with brakewheels; eight stakes; three simulated pallets of wood similar to those on the 16333, except this car carries short "logs" of pulp wood rather than plywood; Standard O trucks; "BLT 1-92". **30** **35**

16348 LIONEL-ERIE: 1992, flatcar with liquefied gas tank; tuscan Type II long flatcar body; white lettering and number; plastic

Exc Mt

open-frame bulkheads with brakewheels at car ends; silver-painted tank with black lettering "Lionel" stylized to left; "LIQUEFIED GASES / LIQUEFIED HYDROGEN" and car number on tank to right side, with diamond Erie logo; tank is cardboard with thin metal end caps; ASF trucks; "BLT 1-92". Note that car number is on both tank and flatcar on this piece. The car is a reissue of the postwar 6469. **30 35**

16349 ALLIS-CHALMERS: 1992, raised-center flatcar with reactor-condenser core; dark blue car body; orange-yellow lettering and number; "ANOTHER PRODUCT OF ALLIS-CHALMERS"; "AC" in diamond logo to left and right sides; gray nuclear reactor core structure held to car with wires; raised brakewheels on posts at both ends of car (not installed in photo); ASF trucks; "BLT 1-92". A reissue of the popular 6519 postwar Allis-Chalmers car from 1960, this car also did well in sales. The postwar car body was orange, as was a Fundimensions version in 1980. And like those pieces, the raised brakewheels are both a unique feature and one that is easily damaged. The catalog shows only one brakewheel, but the released cars have two. Excellent and mint prices for this car must include intact brakewheels. **35 45**

16350 CP RAIL: 1991, flatcar with bulkheads and lumber load; uncataloged; long Type II red flatcar body; white lettering; two open-frame bulkheads with brakewheels; eight black plastic stakes; three lumber pallets with red-painted ends; pallets install into car top via pins; ASF trucks; "BLT 1-91." Part of 11726 Erie Lackawanna Freight set offered in the 1991 Stocking Stuffers brochure. **25 30**

16351 U.S. NAVY: 1992, flatcar with submarine; light gray Type II long flatcar body; white lettering and number; black operating submarine with "UNITED STATES NAVY" in white; submarine can operate in water via rubber-band drive mechanism preloaded by rotating nose piece; sub held to flatcar with a wire bracket; Standard O trucks; "BLT 1-92". This car, a reissue of the postwar 3830, was popular when released (as with the 16352 following); it is more difficult to find than other flatcars. **45 55**

16352 U.S. MILITARY: 1992, short flatcar with Cruise missile; short Type II red flatcar with white lettering and number; blue Cruise missile held to flatcar with two brackets; missile has deployable wings; box includes decal set, which should be intact for mint price; ASF trucks; "BLT 1-92". Though unrealistic, this car proved popular and is somewhat hard to find. **50 60**

16356 MKT: 1992–93, depressed-center flatcar with cable reels; red body; white lettering and number; two black cable reels embossed "LIONEL" held in place with flexible bungee; ASF trucks; "BLT 1-92". Part of 11728 High Plains Runner set and a later Toys "R" Us uncataloged set. **20 25**

16360 NORFOLK & WESTERN: 1993, Maxistack articulated deep well car with containers; first of a new style of articulated flatcar designed to model the Maxistack type of well car used on real railroads to carry intermodal containers; car uses the same design end pieces and shoulder screws as used on the TTUX flatcars first made in 1990 to allow other cars to be added on to the set, using the extra wheelset included, or to be run as a unit with only three wheelsets—the center one supporting the ends of both cars; red flatcar body; white "Maxi-Stack" lettering and numbers; cars are numbered individually 16361 and 16362; boxed together in a single box numbered 16360; each car has two silver Norfolk & Western containers; large "NW" at one end in black, "NWZ 203195" over- and underscored; ASF trucks (four wheelsets included in set—only three used for the assembled car); "BLT 1-93." Despite being articulated, the car is still long enough that it cannot negotiate O27 switches; O31 is the minimum radius it can handle. The containers used on this car can be fitted with undercarriages for use as a tractor-trailer, just as the real-world containers can; also intended for use with the Intermodal crane. Note that many other containers produced as separate accessories can fit on this car, but the original set comes with four silver NW containers. **55 65**

16361 NORFOLK & WESTERN: 1993, Maxistack container car; see description under 16360 above.

16362 NORFOLK & WESTERN: 1993, Maxistack container car; see description under 16360 above.

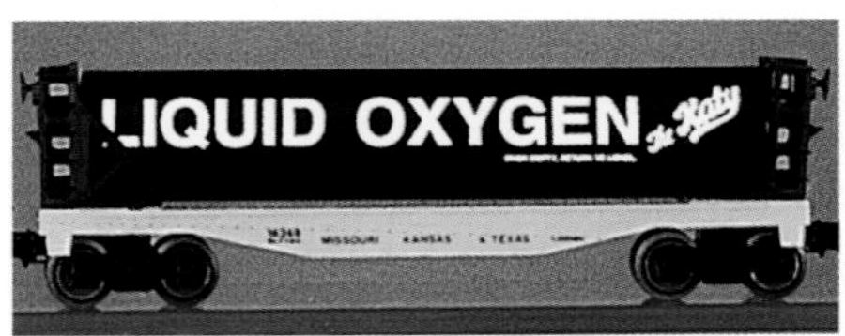

16368 MISSOURI, KANSAS & TEXAS: 1993, flatcar with tank; yellow Type II long flatcar body; black lettering and number on flatcar; two open-frame bulkheads with brakewheels at ends of car; black tank with large white "LIQUID OXYGEN" lettering

Exc Mt

at center and "The Katy" in script to right side; tank is cardboard with thin metal end caps; ASF trucks; "BLT 1-93". **25 30**

16369 AMTRAK: 1992, flatcar with wheel racks; uncataloged; black type I long flatcar body; white lettering and number on car; two orange wheel rack carriers mounted to top of car; eight sets of metal wheels and axles included; ASF trucks; "BLT 1-92". Part of the 11723 Amtrak Work Train set shown only in the 1992 Stocking Stuffers brochure. The wheel racks Lionel uses for this car are unique—resembling I-beams laid on their sides. Racks are secured to the car through the stake pockets. The first modern re-creation of the postwar 6262 wheel-carrying car. See comments on the 16643 in Chapter 15. **25 30**

16370 AMTRAK: 1992, flatcar with rails; uncataloged; black type II long flatcar body; white lettering and number; six black plastic stakes; 12 Lionel track rails, all 6 inches long; two orange retainer brackets secure rails to car top; ASF trucks; "BLT 1-92". Part of the 11723 Amtrak Work Train set only in the 1992 Stocking Stuffers brochure. See comments under 16340. The brochure captions incorrectly list this car as 16730, but the photo and production cars are properly labeled 16370. **25 30**

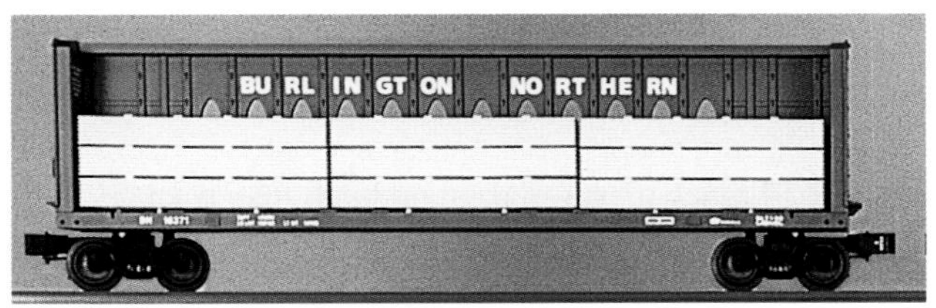

16371 BURLINGTON NORTHERN: 1992, I-beam flatcar with wood load; uncataloged; entirely new 13-inch-long flatcar style with detailed center beam ("I-beam") and ends; center beam features 12 large oval cutouts; green body; white lettering with "BURLINGTON NORTHERN" on the center beam above the cutouts; white lettering and number on flatcar; car includes end lettering; 24-piece simulated plywood pallets with ends painted red; pallets stack to each other and to car with pegs; Standard O trucks; "BLT 1-92". This is Lionel's first release of an entirely new model of modern flatcar that faithfully reproduces the full-size prototype. The company had unsuccessfully tried an even longer (20-inch) version of this car earlier in 1992, but the reception was not warm, so this car was substituted. Shown only in the 1992 Stocking Stuffers brochure. **40 50**

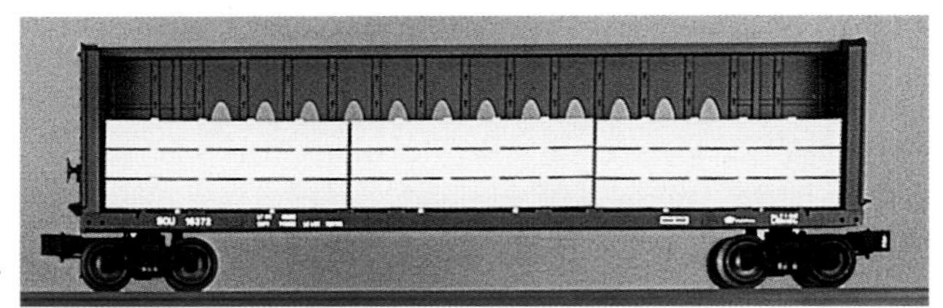

16372 SOUTHERN: 1992, I-beam flatcar with wood load; uncataloged; brown body; white lettering "SOU" and number on flatcar; car includes end lettering; 24-piece simulated plywood pallets with ends painted red; pallets stack to each other and to car with pegs; Standard O trucks; "BLT 1-92". See comments under 16371 for more details. The company had unsuccessfully tried a longer (20-inch) version of this car earlier in 1992, but the reception was not warm, so this car was substituted. Only in the 1992 Stocking Stuffers brochure. **30 35**

16373 ERIE LACKAWANNA: 1993, flatcar with stakes; maroon-brown long Type II body; yellow lettering and number; 14 black plastic stakes; no load; ASF trucks; "BLT 1-93" printed in two places on each side. Shown as a companion to the 16658 Erie crane car also released in 1993. At this stage, Lionel was regularly releasing crane car/flatcar combinations of this sort. Both cars intended as add-ons to the Erie Fallen Flags set from 1993. **20 25**

16375 NEW YORK CENTRAL: 1993–99, flatcar with stakes; long yellow Type II body; black lettering and number; sometimes came with red crate load (note that Lionel also offered this load as an accessory—12838); ten plastic stakes; two open-frame bulkheads with brakewheels mounted at ends of car; ASF trucks; "BLT 1-93". Part of 11735 New York Central Flyer set, and the later 11931 Chessie Flyer set, which was nearly identical. No individual box. This car was initially shown in the 1993 catalog as a dark green car, but was made in yellow. The engine and boxcar in the set also changed color from the versions shown in 1993. The car and sets are among the longer-running Lionel pieces in recent years. In later catalogs Lionel, in the midst of its nostalgia phase, referred to the car as a "6424" in honor of the postwar flatcars, though that number does not appear on this piece. **15 20**

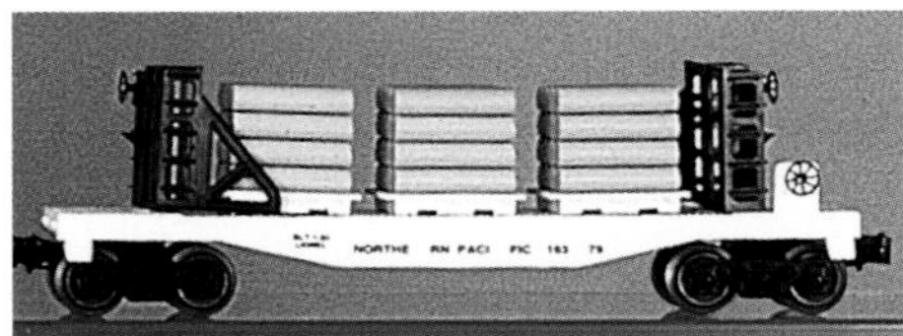

16379 NORTHERN PACIFIC: 1993, flatcar with bulkheads and pulpwood load; long Type II flatcar body in white; black lettering and number; two black plastic open-frame bulkheads with brakewheels; eight stakes; three simulated pallets of pulpwood logs; ASF trucks; "BLT 1-93". **20 25**

16380 UNION PACIFIC: 1993, I-beam flatcar with wood load; 13-inch-long yellow plastic body; red lettering; car has end lettering; 24-piece simulated plywood pallets with ends painted red; pallets stack to each other and to car with pegs; Standard O trucks; "BLT 1-93". See other comments under 16371. A version of this car was made for the Toy Train Operating Society in 1995. See 52084.

(A) As described. **30 35**

(B) Factory error. Lettering missing on one side. J. Trelford Collection. **— NRS**

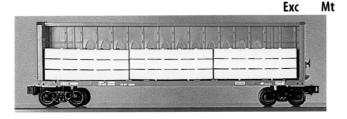

Exc Mt

16381 CSXT: 1993, I-beam flatcar with wood load; 13-inch-long red plastic body; white lettering; car has end lettering; 24-piece simulated plywood pallets with ends painted red; pallets stack to each other and to car with pegs; Standard O trucks; "BLT 1-93". See other comments under 16371. **30 35**

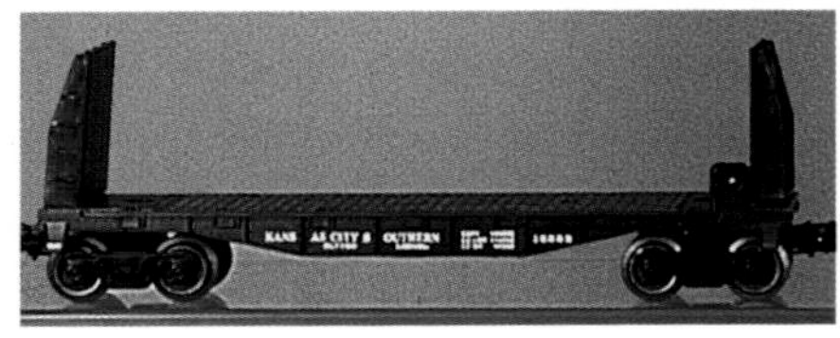

16382 KANSAS CITY SOUTHERN: 1993, flatcar with bulkheads; black long Type II flatcar body; white lettering and number; two plastic bulkheads at car ends; bulkheads are of the tapered solid-wall type; no load with car; ASF trucks; "BLT 1-93." **20 25**

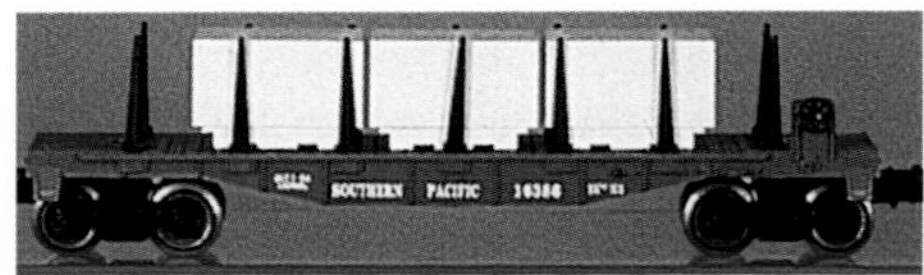

16386 SOUTHERN PACIFIC: 1994, flatcar with lumber load; long Type II brown flatcar body; white lettering; 14 black plastic stakes; three lumber pallets with red-painted ends; pallets install into car top via pins; note: car does not include bulkheads; ASF trucks; "BLT 1-94." **20 25**

16389 PENNSYLVANIA: 1994, flatcar with wheel racks; tuscan-brown type II long flatcar body; white lettering and number on car; two black plastic wheel rack carriers mounted to top of car; eight sets of metal wheels and axles included; ASF trucks; "BLT 1-94". See other comments under 16369. **25 30**

16390 LIONEL WATER CAR: 1994, flatcar with water tank; gray plastic long Type II flatcar body; black lettering and number on car "LIONELVILLE FIRE RESCUE"; black single-dome tank mounted to car (a first for modern Lionel)—tank is exactly like the single-dome tank cars (see tank car chapter) and includes metal walkway platform and ladder; wire handrails not included, however; white "WATER" lettering on tank to left and right; the tank is attached to the flatcar with a single screw, and the car is modified to permit the ladder to protrude; yellow plastic pump generator similar to ones found on searchlight cars fixed to one end of car (not shown in photo); ASF trucks; "BLT 1-94". Intended to go with the 16660 Lionel Fire car. **30 35**

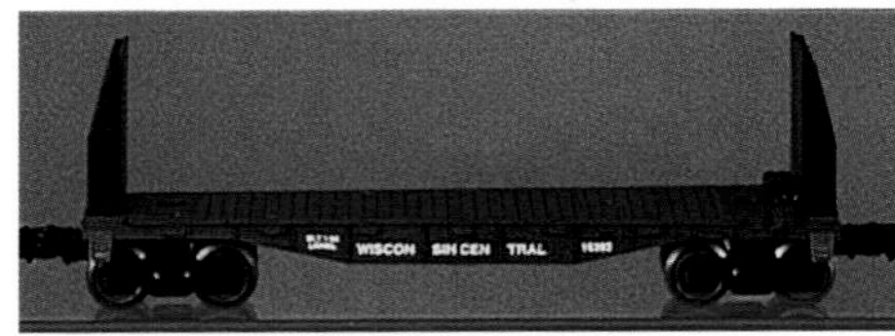

16393 WISCONSIN CENTRAL: 1994, flatcar with bulkheads; maroon Type II long flatcar body; yellow lettering; two black plastic bulkheads at car ends; bulkheads are the tapered solid-wall type; 14 black plastic stakes; no load; ASF trucks; "BLT 1-94". One of three flatcars of this type made by Lionel in 1994. **15 20**

16394 CENTRAL VERMONT: 1994, flatcar with bulkheads; light green Type II long flatcar body; yellow lettering; two black plastic bulkheads at car ends; bulkheads are the tapered solid-wall type; 14 black plastic stakes; no load; ASF trucks; "BLT 1-94". Sold separately and as part of the 11906 "Factory Selection" set. **15 20**

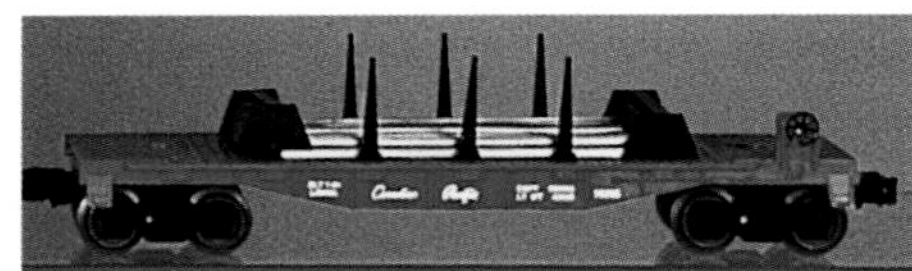

16395 CANADIAN PACIFIC: 1994, flatcar with rails; red type II long flatcar body; white lettering and number; "Canadian Pacific" in script; six stakes; six Lionel track rails all 6 inches long; two black retainer brackets secure rails to car top; ASF trucks; "BLT 1-94". **20 25**

16396 ALASKA: 1994, flatcar with bulkheads; dark blue long Type II flatcar body; yellow lettering and number; two plastic bulkheads at car ends; bulkheads are of the tapered solid-wall type; 14 black plastic stakes; no load with car; ASF trucks; "BLT 1-94." **20 25**

Exc Mt

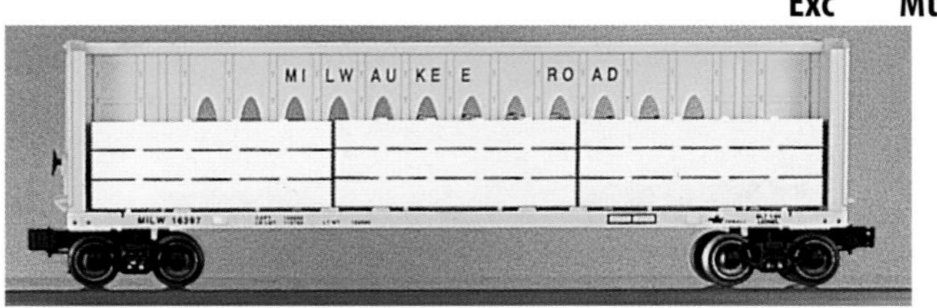

16397 MILWAUKEE ROAD: 1994, I-beam flatcar with wood load; 13-inch-long yellow plastic body; black lettering with "MILWAUKEE ROAD" on center beam above oval holes; black lettering and number on car frame; car has end lettering; 24-piece simulated plywood pallets with ends painted red; pallets stack to each other and to car with pegs; Standard O trucks; "BLT 1-94". See other comments under 16371. **35 40**

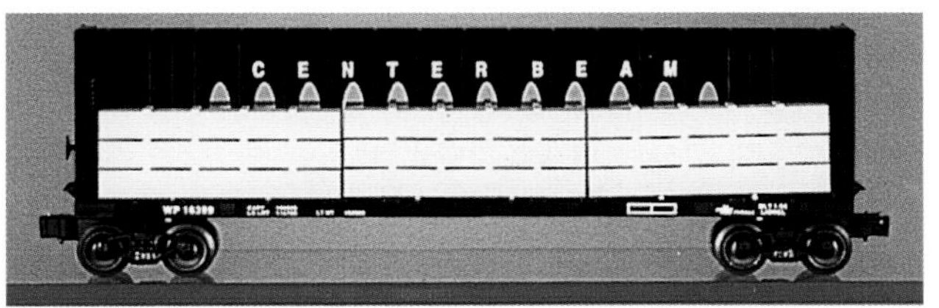

16399 WESTERN PACIFIC: 1994, I-beam flatcar with wood load; 13-inch-long black plastic body; white "WP" and number on car frame; white lettering with "CENTER BEAM" on I-beam above oval holes; car has end lettering; 24-piece simulated plywood pallets with ends painted red; pallets stack to each other and to car with pegs; Standard O trucks; "BLT 1-94". See other comments under 16371. **35 40**

16610 LIONEL: 1987–88, Track Maintenance flatcar; long Type II gray body; black lettering and number; bright blue two-deck superstructure with white lettering; two yellow men, one on each deck; hand-operated crank raises and lowers platform about one inch; Symington-Wayne trucks; no "BLT" date. This is modern Lionel's first remake of the postwar 6812 track maintenance car.

(A) As described. **15 25**

(B) Factory Error. Incomplete heat-stamped lettering on one side of superstructure. C. Whiting collection. **NRS**

16618 SANTA FE: 1989, track maintenance flatcar; long Type II red body; white lettering; gray superstructure with black "TRACK MAINTENANCE" lettering; two yellow men; hand-operated crank raises and lowers platform; Symington-Wayne trucks; "BLT 1-89". **15 25**

16620 CHESAPEAKE & OHIO: 1990–91, track maintenance flatcar; long Type II black body; white C&O lettering; translucent unpainted yellow superstructure with black lettering "TRACK MAINTENANCE" (lettering not pictured in catalog); two blue men; hand-operated crank raises and lowers platform; ASF trucks; "BLT 1-90". Some collectors did not like the toy-like appearance of the unpainted yellow plastic. **15 25**

16635 CP RAIL: 1991, track maintenance flatcar. Announced in Lionel's 1991 Book 1 catalog, but not manufactured. One of several 1991 flatcars that did not reach production. **Not Manufactured**

16652 LIONEL RADAR: 1992, flatcar with operating radar antenna; green Type II long flatcar body; white lettering; number on car is "6652", not 16652; large light gray plastic superstructure; one blue seated man at radar console; rotating radar antenna turns as car moves via gear mechanism fixed to one truck; antenna is black plastic; fixed white plastic cone antenna behind man; detailed black dial graphics on side of structure; color circular control panel decal; control panel and entire superstructure illuminated via a grain-of-wheat bulb mounted into flatcar body; power pickup on one truck; ASF trucks; "BLT 1-92". This action piece is a remake of the postwar 3540. **30 40**

16660 LIONEL FIRE CAR: 1993–94, flatcar with extension ladder; reissue of popular 3512 fire car from 1959; bright yellow long Type I flatcar body and matching large superstructure; black lettering and number on flatcar; black logo with "LADDER CO. 1993" on raised support near front of car; seated blue man with nozzle rotates as car moves via gear mechanism on one truck; black metal extension ladder can be raised and lowered and extended with hand cranks on base; ladder base rotates manually; two other metal ladders attached to car sides; flashing red warning light at rear of car powered by roller pickup; simulated bell; three metal hose nozzles included; ASF trucks; "BLT 1-93". One of the most action-filled of all Lionel's rolling stock products. The fire car was popular in the 1950s and remains popular today with this new incarnation. The catalog suggests a good fire-fighting scene by combining this car with the Lionel water car (16390) and Burning Switch Tower (12768). See also 16688. **40 45**

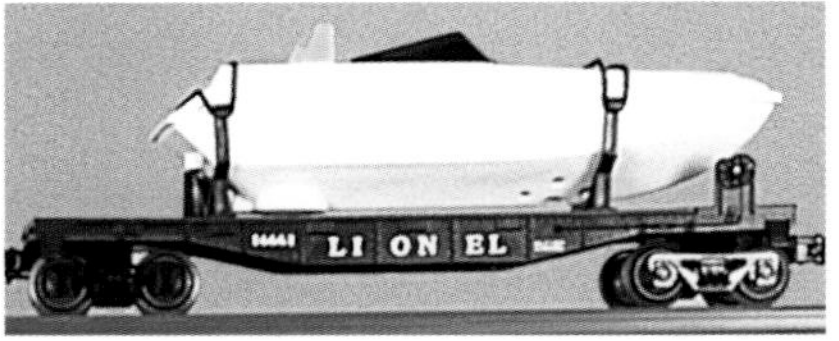

16661 LIONEL BOAT CAR: 1993, flatcar with operating boat; black long type II flatcar body; white lettering and number on car; white plastic unmarked boat secured to car with brackets; boat will operate in water with two AA-cell batteries (not included) which fit under the yellow plastic seat section; boat has a special buoyancy switch that turns it on when it's placed in water; reissue of 6501 in postwar; ASF trucks; "BLT 1-93". In fact the postwar boat was not electrically powered—but operated with a baking soda tablet, which reacted with water to produce an air-bubble "thrust." Like any battery-powered device, the batteries on the modern version should be removed from the boat when not in use. **30 35**

16666 LIONEL TOXIC WASTE CAR: 1993–94, flatcar with toxic waste containers; long type I yellow-orange body; red lettering on flatcar "LIONEL REMOVAL SERVICE"; two simulated toxic waste containers on flatcar; black containers with white lettering "DANGER TOXIC WASTE"; containers are illuminated via bulbs mounted to flatcar and roller pickup on one truck; ASF trucks; "BLT 1-93". This car is a reissue of the 6805 postwar car and Fundimensions' copies of it, the 9234 and 9389. This car differs, however, from the earlier models in that it does not have two track rails running the length of the flatcar, even though the containers retain the rail-shaped cutouts at the bottom, which were needed for the rails. **25 35**

16670 LIONEL TV: 1993–94, flatcar with operating TV platform; black Type II long flatcar body; white lettering "LIONEL" and number on flatcar; large white plastic superstructure; two blue seated men; one on rotating camera which turns as car moves; second man seated in front of control panel near a floodlight box; camera and floodlight box are gray plastic; detailed black dial graphics on side of structure similar to 16652; color circular control panel decal in front of lower man features the Lionel diner; control panel and entire superstructure illuminated via a grain-of-wheat bulb mounted into flatcar body; power pickup on one truck; other truck has gear mechanism to rotate camera platform; ASF trucks; "BLT 1-93". **20 25**

16677 NATO: 1994, flatcar with operating submarine; black Type II long flatcar body; white lettering and number; operating black submarine with gold lettering "HMS 2024" on conning tower; depth lines at front; submarine operates in water via a rubber-band drive preloaded by turning the separate nose piece; submarine held to car by a wire bracket; ASF trucks; "BLT 1-94". **35 40**

16680 LIONEL CHERRY PICKER: 1994, flatcar with cherry picker ladder; blue long Type I flatcar body; white lettering and number; "LIONELVILLE MAINTENANCE CREW CAR"; gray plastic ladder support with black metal extension ladder; ladder base rotates manually and ladder can be raised and extended with hand cranks; base, ladder, and mechanism are the same as on the fire car (16660); dark gray plastic housing snapped onto ladder end includes yellow-painted man who can be rotated out of the housing with a lever; housing pivots freely to remain vertical regardless of ladder angle; housing not shown in our photo; ASF trucks; "BLT 1-94". This car is the first reissue (Fundimensions did not make it) of the Lionel 6512 cherry picker car from 1963. The postwar car was part of the military and space–themed pieces from that time, and the figure then was an astronaut. There may be variations of this piece relative to the color the man is painted or to the housing he rides in. **25 30**

16688 LIONEL FIRE CAR: 1994, flatcar with extension ladder; bright red long Type I flatcar body and matching large superstructure; yellow lettering and number on flatcar; yellow logo with "LADDER CO. 1994" on raised support near front of car; seated blue man with nozzle rotates as car moves via gear mechanism on one truck; black metal extension ladder can be raised and lowered and extended with hand cranks on base; ladder base rotates manually; two other metal ladders attached to car sides; flashing red warning light at rear of car powered by roller pickup; simulated bell; three metal hose nozzles included; ASF trucks; "BLT 1-94". This car is identical to the 16660 from the year before except for colors. This one is slightly more in demand than the 16660 because the red color is an exact replica of the postwar 3512, a car hard to find in good condition today. See other comments under 16660. **55 65**

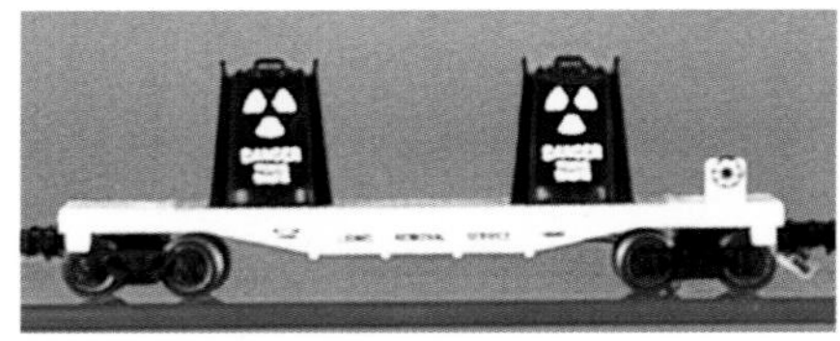

16689 LIONEL TOXIC WASTE CAR: 1994, flatcar with toxic waste containers; long Type I translucent white body; red lettering on

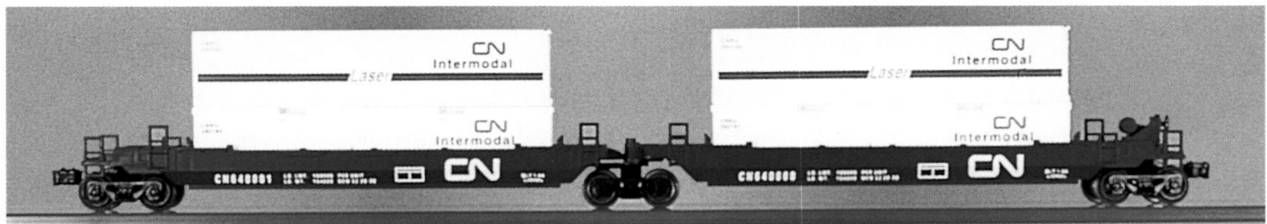

16912 Canadian National Maxistack

Exc Mt

flatcar "LIONEL REMOVAL SERVICE"; two simulated toxic waste containers on flatcar; black containers with white lettering "DANGER TOXIC WASTE"; containers are illuminated via bulbs mounted to flatcar and roller pickup on one truck; ASF trucks; "BLT 1-94". This car is virtually identical to the 16666 above, except for the flatcar color. See other comments under 16666. **30 35**

16704 LIONEL TV: 1994, flatcar with operating TV platform; yellow Type II long flatcar body; blue lettering "LIONEL" and number on flatcar; large light gray plastic superstructure; two blue seated men; one on rotating camera, which turns as car moves; second man seated in front of control panel near a floodlight box; camera and floodlight box are darker gray plastic; detailed black dial graphics on side of structure similar to 16652; color circular control panel decal in front of lower; control panel illuminated via a grain-of-wheat bulb mounted into flatcar body; power pickup on one truck; other truck has gear mechanism to rotate camera platform; ASF trucks; "BLT 1-94". This car differs only in colors from the 16670 version from 1993—the gray plastic structure here does not illuminate as completely as the white plastic on the earlier car; only the control panels light up. **30 35**

16708 CHICAGO & NORTH WESTERN: 1995, track maintenance car; long Type II yellow body; black lettering and number; black superstructure with no lettering; two blue men; hand-operated crank raises and lowers platform; ASF trucks; "BLT 1-95". **25 30**

16903 CANADIAN PACIFIC: 1994, flatcar with bulkheads and pulpwood load; long Type II flatcar body in gray; white lettering, number and "Canadian Pacific" in script; black plastic open-frame bulkheads with brakewheels; eight stakes; three simulated pallets of pulpwood logs; Standard O trucks; "BLT 1-94". Part of the 11744 New Yorker Service Station special set from 1994, an intriguing set that sported freight cars as well as passenger cars. **25 30**

Exc Mt

16907 LIONEL FARM EQUIPMENT: 1994, flatcar with tractors; long Type II flatcar body in gray plastic; black lettering "LIONEL FARM EQUIPMENT" and number on car; two black plastic wheel racks; similar to those used on the 16369; three die-cast farm tractors (made by Welly) carried instead of wheel-axle sets; tractors are red, black, and tan with detailed wheels; ASF trucks; "BLT 1-94". See other comments under 16369. **35 45**

16908 U.S. NAVY: 1994–95, flatcar with operating submarine; gray Type II long flatcar body; black lettering; number on car is "04039"—16908 does not appear; operating black submarine with white lettering "930"; submarine operates in water via a rubber-band drive preloaded by turning the separate nose piece; submarine held to car by a wire bracket; ASF trucks; "BLT 1-94". No individual box. Part of 11745 U.S. Navy Train, one of Lionel's more popular Traditional line sets in the modern era. **50 60**

16912 CANADIAN NATIONAL: 1994, Maxistack articulated deep well car with containers; second of a new style of articulated flatcar designed to model the Maxistack type of well car used on real railroads to carry intermodal containers; see detailed description under 16360; blue flatcar body; white "CN" lettering and numbers; cars are numbered "CN640000" and "CN640001"; boxed together in a single box numbered 16912; each car has two white CN "Laser" containers; large "CN" at one end in red, over "Intermodal", blue and red "Laser" stripe across center of container; each container numbered "CNRU 280184" through "CNRU 280187" in black; containers have end logos and lettering; ASF trucks (four wheelsets included in set—only three used for the assembled car); "BLT 1-94." The containers used on this car can be fitted with undercarriages for use as a tractor-trailer, just as the real-world containers can; also intended for use with the intermodal crane. Note that many other containers produced as separate accessories can fit on this car, but the original set comes with these four CN containers. The upper containers on this car are white with silver roofs, while the lower ones are a cream color. **50 65**

16913 CN: 1994; see 16912 above.

16914 CN: 1994; see 16912 above.

16920 LIONEL: 1995, flatcar with construction block helicopter; unusual short flatcar with Lego-type pieces that assemble to make a helicopter; announced in 1995 stocking stuffers catalog but never produced. **Not Manufactured**

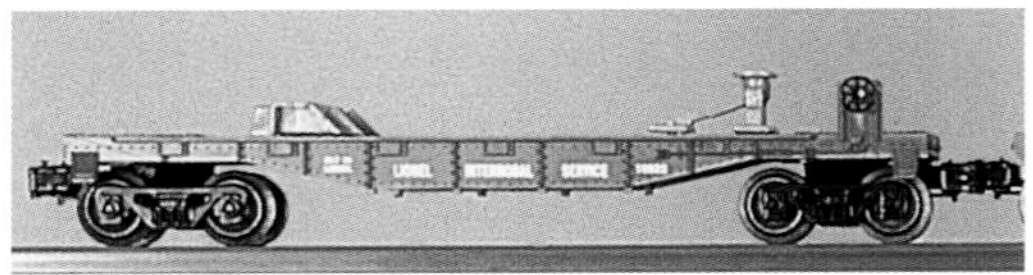

16923 LIONEL INTERMODAL SERVICE: 1995, flatcar with chocks; long Type I blue flatcar; white lettering and number; gray plastic chock and fifth wheel support; ASF trucks; "BLT 95". This is essentially a TOFC car without a trailer—it can be used to transport any of the other separate-sale trailers Lionel has offered. **20 25**

16927 NEW YORK CENTRAL: 1995, flatcar with short gondola; blue-green Type II long flatcar body; white "NYC" lettering and number; short black New York Central gondola load; gondola features NYC oval logo and capacity data; flatcar also carries two wheel-axle sets in front of the gondola; ASF trucks; "BLT 95". This unusual flatcar sports a pint-sized gondola of a style last seen in the 1972 Kickapoo Valley set made by Fundimensions. The tiny Kickapoo gondola had only two axles and four wheels, not the eight found on most Lionel rolling stock. **20 25**

16928 SOO LINE: 1995, flatcar with dump bin; short Type II flatcar; black body; white lettering and number; new-design brown plastic dump bin (manually operated) fixed to top; no lettering on bin; ASF trucks; "BLT 95". The pivoting manual dump bin on this car is a new-design mold for Lionel, and this piece is one of the few short flatcars released by Lionel in recent years. **15 20**

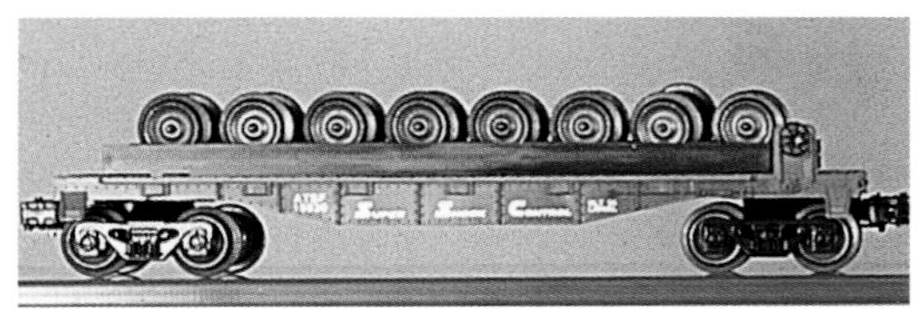

16930 SANTA FE: 1995, flatcar with wheel racks; dark red type II long flatcar body; white lettering "SUPER SHOCK CONTROL" and number on car; two black plastic wheel rack carriers mounted to top of car; eight sets of metal wheels and axles included; ASF trucks; "BLT 95". See other comments under 16369. **20 25**

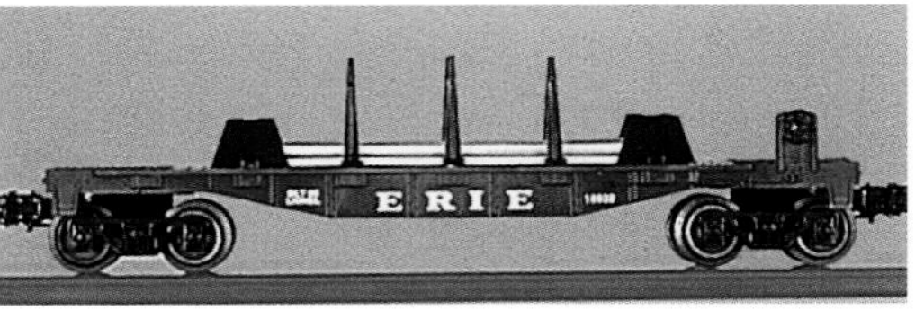

16932 ERIE: 1995, flatcar with rails; dark green type II long flatcar body; gold lettering "ERIE" and number; six plastic stakes; six Lionel track rails, all 6 inches long; two black retainer brackets secure rails to car top; ASF trucks; "BLT 95". **20 25**

16933 LIONEL LINES: 1995, flatcar with automobiles; Lionel-orange Type I long flatcar; blue lettering "LIONEL LINES" and number; red, white, and blue Lionel "L" decal in center; two black plastic wheel racks atop flatcar retain two blue 1950s-style sedans; sedans have black rubber tires, clear windshields, and silver bumpers; ASF trucks; "BLT 95". This car's orange and blue color scheme makes it a candidate as an add-on to the ongoing Lionel Lines freight set headed by the 8380 SD-28 diesel made by Fundimensions. **30 35**

16934 PENNSYLVANIA: 1995, flatcar with road grader; tuscan-brown Type I flatcar body; white lettering and number; mustard yellow die-cast Ertl road grader held in position by chocks; "CAT" grader can be removed to use on layout; grader features excellent detail and Lionel logos; ASF trucks; "BLT 95". This is the first of several collaborative efforts between Lionel and Ertl in recent years. The tires on the Ertl grader will sometimes react with the plastic on the flatcar top of this car—on later models Lionel installed a clear plastic shield between the load and the flatcar deck. Readers should check condition before buying the car. The early (1995) flats with Ertl vehicles are subject to this phenomenon ("plasticizer migration"), according to Lou Bohn. Shields are available from Lionel in two sizes. **35 40**

	Exc	Mt

16935 UNION PACIFIC: 1995, depressed-center flatcar with bulldozer; light gray depressed-center flatcar body; red lettering and number on car; mustard yellow die-cast Ertl bulldozer on center section; Lionel markings included on dozer, which is removable; ASF trucks; "BLT 95" and "LIONEL" lettered in red on the upper platforms of the car. This car is subject to the plastic migration between the wheels of the bulldozer and the flatcar, as mentioned under 16934 above. Buyers should check condition before purchasing. **40 45**

16936 SEA LAND: 1995, Maxistack articulated deep well car with containers; third of a new style of articulated flatcar designed to model the Maxistack type of well car used on real railroads to carry intermodal containers; see detailed description under 16360; red flatcar body; black and white "Sea Land" logos; white lettering and numbers; each car numbered individually "NYSW 16937" and "16938"; boxed together in a single box numbered 16936; each car has two silver SeaLand containers; "Sea Land" at center in black, with red, white, and black SL herald in center between words; ASF trucks (four wheelsets included in set—only three used for the assembled car); "BLT 95." The containers used on this car can be fitted with undercarriages for use as a tractor-trailer, just as the real-world containers can; also intended for use with the Intermodal crane. Note many other containers produced as separate accessories can fit on this car, but the original set comes with four Sea Land containers. **65 80**

16937 SEA LAND: 1995, Maxistack container car; see description under 16936 above.

16938 SEA LAND: 1995, Maxistack container car; see description under 16936 above.

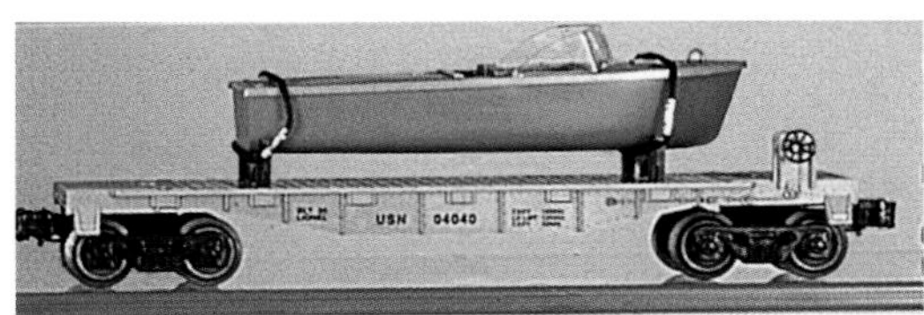

16939 U.S. NAVY: 1995, flatcar with boat; gray Type II long flatcar body; black lettering "USN"; number on car is "04040", not 16939; red and gray plastic boat secured to car with black brackets and flex rings; no lettering on boat; non-operating boat; ASF trucks; "BLT 95". Lionel billed this as an add-on to the 11745 U.S. Navy Train. **25 30**

	Exc	Mt

16944 GEORGIA POWER: 1995, depressed-center flatcar with transformer; uncataloged; gray flatcar body; black flatcar lettering with triangle logo and white Georgia Power lightning bolt triangle; black transformer with white GP triangle logo and insulators; number on car is "31348"; ASF trucks; "BLT 95". No individual box. Part of special 11819 Georgia Power set. **40 50**

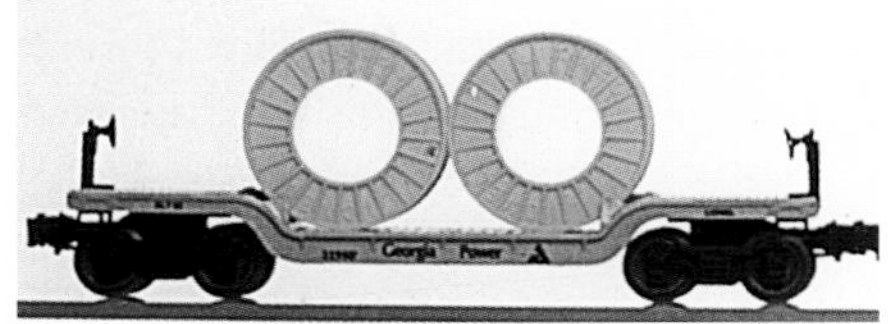

16945 GEORGIA POWER: 1995, depressed-center flatcar with cable reels; uncataloged; gray flatcar body; yellow-orange cable reels with wire; black flatcar lettering "Georgia Power" and triangle lightning bolt logo; car colors are deliberately identical to the postwar 6561; number on car is "31950"; ASF trucks; "BLT 95". No individual box. Part of special 11819 Georgia Power set. **40 50**

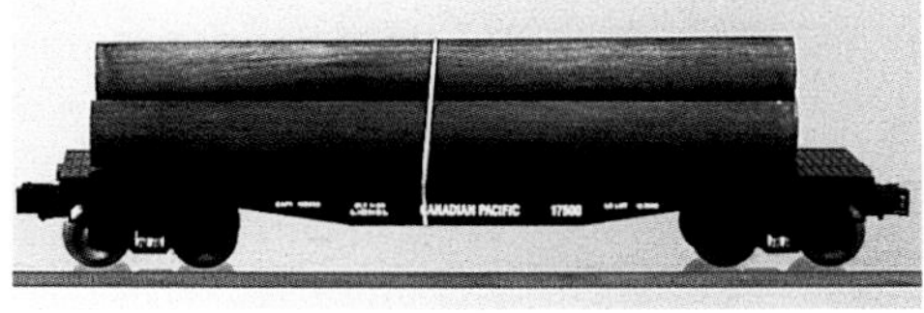

17500 CANADIAN PACIFIC: 1989, Standard O flatcar; black body; white lettering; supplied with 24 plastic stakes and three large dowel-logs restrained by chains; Standard O trucks; "BLT 1-89". Part of 11710 CP Rail Limited set. **45 50**

17501 CONRAIL: 1987, Standard O flatcar; brown body; white lettering and Conrail logo; 24 black plastic stakes; Standard O trucks; "BLT 1-87". Part of 11700 Conrail Limited set. **35 45**

17508 BURLINGTON: 1992, I-beam flatcar with wood load; new super-long (20-inch) flatcar design with perforated center beam and wood pallets. This car was announced in the 1992 Book 2 catalog but not made, apparently because its extreme length was too great a departure from Lionel's norms and would force modelers to run it only on O72 track. Its length would have caused it to hit the switch machine housings on smaller-radius switches. As a result, planned sales did not materialize. In response, Lionel released a smaller version (16371) in its 1992 Stocking Stuffer brochure. **Not Manufactured**

Exc Mt

17509 SOUTHERN: 1992, I-beam flatcar with wood load; never manufactured; see comments on 17508 above. Lionel released a smaller version as the 16372 in late 1992. **Not Manufactured**

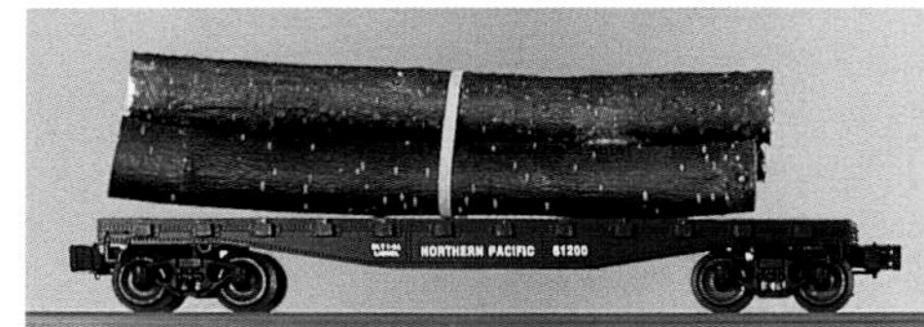

17510 NORTHERN PACIFIC: 1994, Standard O flatcar; black body; white lettering; number on car is "61200", 17510 does not appear; supplied with 24 plastic stakes and three large real-wood logs restrained by chains; Standard O trucks; "BLT 1-94". With this piece, the Standard O flatcar returned to Lionel's product line in 1994 after a five-year break. **35 40**

17515 NORFOLK SOUTHERN: 1995, Standard O flatcar with tractors; gray flatcar body; white lettering and NS logo on car; two gray and white die-cast metal diesel tractors which can be used separately with various trailers; tractors include Triple Crown logos on doors; three black chocks on car to hold tractors in place; Standard O trucks; "BLT 95". This is not really a "TOFC" flatcar, because it carries tractors, not trailers. Lionel billed it as a good complement to the 1992 Norfolk Southern set, which carried Triple Crown trailers. **50 60**

19409 SOUTHERN: 1991, flatcar with stakes; long Type I black body; white lettering; Standard O trucks; "BLT 1-91". This is the first use of the Standard O trucks on the long flatcar (versus Standard O) body. Pictured as a companion to the 19405 Southern crane car. **25 30**

Exc Mt

19413 FRISCO: 1992, flatcar with stakes; long Type II brown body; white lettering and number; 14 black plastic stakes; no load; Standard O trucks; "BLT 1-92". Pictured as a companion to the 19412 Frisco crane car. **20 25**

19414 UNION PACIFIC: 1992, flatcar with stakes; long Type II brown body; yellow lettering and "ROAD OF THE Streamliners" on car sides; 14 black plastic stakes; no load; Standard O trucks; "BLT 1-92". Part of 11733 Feather River Service Station Special set. **25 30**

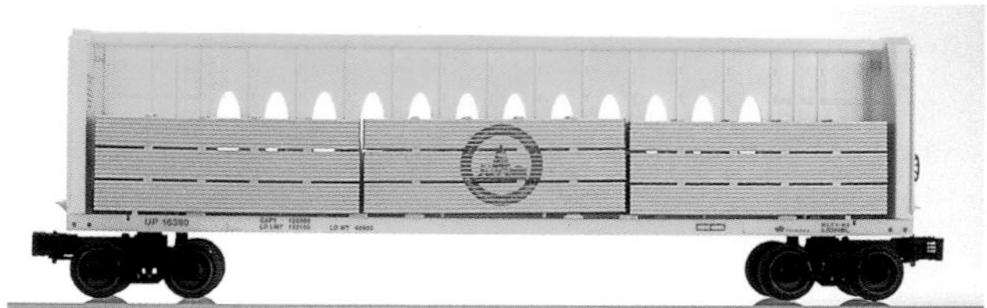

52084 UNION PACIFIC: 1995, I-beam flatcar with wood load; uncataloged; yellow plastic body; red lettering; car has end lettering; 24-piece simulated plywood pallets with ends painted red; pallets stack to each other and to car with pegs; car was specially made for banquet at TTOS's National Convention in Sacramento; it is identical to the 16380 car except for an added image of the California state capitol dome on the wood load; Standard O trucks. Very hard to find. **— 200**

CHAPTER 12

Flatcars with Trailers (TOFC) Trailer Train (TTUX) Cars

The growth of the flatcars with loads in the modern era has been paralleled by an explosive increase in production and interest in the trailers-on-flatcars (TOFCs) and their related intermodal carriers, the TTUX articulated flatcar with trailers, and the "Maxistack" style of well car, which is used to carry containers.

Modern Lionel, in its incarnations as Fundimensions, Lionel LTI and Lionel LLC, has far eclipsed the output of postwar Lionel in producing TOFC-style cars. Only a few were made during the late 1950s and early 1960s, all of them somewhat valuable today, even though each was not especially dynamic in decoration or coloring.

But right from the changeover in 1970, modern Lionel decided that this type of freight car was a winner and would occupy a prominent place in each year's freight line.

There are two major types of TOFCs made by modern Lionel. The first and most frequently encountered is the regular flatcar carrying one or two trailers. This style uses the 10-inch-long Type I flatcar mold as described in the flatcar chapter. Through 1988 Lionel produced these cars with two small vans. The vans/trailers came in two distinct types—the first (earlier) kind has one axle and rounded front ends. Only two of the models described in this volume—the 16303 Pennsylvania and 16311 Mopar—sport this van type. The later style, which debuted in 1988, has two sets of axles and wheels and squared-off front ends. Before 1975 Fundimensions had used a corrugated-side trailer similar to the ones found on the few postwar TOFC cars, but those quickly gave way to the smooth-side round-front variety which is better suited for graphics and decoration.

By 1988 Lionel was advancing toward more realistic prototypical trains, accessories and operations, and in that year came out with a new model flatcar with a long, detailed single van. The first specimen was the 16308 Burlington Northern. These trailers, expertly detailed with front pivot, rivets, chrome hubs, operating doors, and most especially a die-cast removable undercarriage, could also be used with the tractors Lionel was beginning to produce in those years. Like the real railroads, Lionel was acknowledging the importance of "intermodal" commerce, and the partnership it implied between the rail companies and trucking companies. In the case of the real railroads this partnership was an imperative to ensure the survival of rail transport. In Lionel land, the matter was not quite so urgent, but the company had to match the trends of the prototypical rail lines, to which it is naturally attached. It has done so quite enthusiastically. Nothing exemplified this more than the 1989 release of the spectacular Intermodal Crane, which could roam the rail yards and be used to lift trailers from the train cars to the highway trucks and back again. Many of the tractor-trailer sets Lionel has made in the past decade to go with these accessories and flatcars have been accurate and well decorated. The trailers can be divorced from the die-cast frame for use as an intermodal container, and vice versa. In the 1990s, Lionel even offered the frame (item no. 12852) as a separate accessory. All of this adds wonderful possibilities and play value to every layout.

Another "variation" of the trailer-on-flatcar is the version that uses the Standard O flatcar (11 inches long) rather than the Type I regular flatcar. Not many of these have been made, and all have come with the single long van. The most significant example in the modern period was the set of five identical Norfolk Southern cars made in 1992 as part of a very impressive Norfolk Southern unit train led by a massive NS Dash 8 40C diesel. Each car featured identical Triple Crown trailers.

Both the Standard O and regular O flatcars use similar plastic chock and fifth-wheel stanchion pieces that snap into the flatcar bodies through holes in the top.

The second major type of trailer car is the TTUX "Trailer Train," also known as a "spine car," introduced with the Sea Land set in 1990. It uses the same long vans as described above (exclusively), but Lionel created an ingenious and extremely accurate new articulated spine car in place of the flatcar. "Articulated" refers to the pivoting central wheelset, which essentially allows this huge car (or pair of cars) to "bend" in the middle. This entirely new mold is a narrow I-shaped center body (the "spine") flanked by trays that support the trailer tires. A fifth-wheel stanchion for the trailer is fitted at the other end of each car. These sets are supplied with an additional center pivot and wheelset (no couplers), which can be substituted for the end piece and allow more cars to be added, creating a unit train of any desired length. The task is accomplished with a unique brass shoulder screw and removable end platform pieces. The versions to date have come with a long van for each car. Each car is individually numbered, but they are meant to run as an articulated unit—21 inches long when assembled. Despite that, these cars can be run on the lower-radius tracks because of the central pivoting wheels. The car is certainly a unique milestone in Lionel's march to realism.

The Trailer Train (TTX) Corporation is a company that

leases rolling stock of this kind to the railroads—that is, the railroads do not actually own them. The four-letter codes designate cars and loads of different varieties. "TTHX", for example, designates a multipurpose flatcar. "TTUX" refers to a "single trailer/two axle" style. Since that lettering was on the first of Lionel's models of the cars, we use that code to refer to all of the articulated trailer cars made by Lionel in that style.

The Maxistack car might be considered a trailer-on-flatcar as well, except it is designed to carry intermodal containers. Such containers are used mainly in shipboard transport, but can be fitted with road wheels and stanchions to be pulled by a highway tractor-trailer. However, since the containers on Lionel's cars do not have wheels, we've included them in the flatcar section of the book.

In terms of numbering, Lionel once again has dumped these cars somewhat haphazardly into whatever number series was available. In the early years of the Lionel LTI era, a numbering scheme was followed to some extent. But as the numbers were used up, Lionel LLC opened new series and sometimes confused the matter by decorating the cars with postwar-era numbers, such as 6424, which the company has in fact used on multiple flatcars.

The 16300-series has some of the earlier "Traditional" inexpensive TOFCs, though a few of the uncataloged ones (like the 16311 Mopar) are anything but inexpensive. The few Standard O TOFC cars will be found in the 17500-series. Most of the uncataloged train club pieces are to be found in the 52000-series, which continues today. One notable exception to that is the 17871 special from the Toy Train Operating Society with Kodak and Xerox vans from 1987. This is one of the rarest of all TOFC flatcars. 19400-type numbers cover a few of the Collector-level cars, like the 19404 Western Maryland. The 16300-series has more recently given way to the 16900-series for the latest issues of the Traditional (a.k.a. Classic) TOFC cars.

All told, the TOFC flatcars are a dynamic area for specialty collectors. Some are readily available at good prices, while others are extremely rare and difficult to find. The last decade has found an increasing number of TOFC collectors, and they also have been a favorite of the Lionel train clubs, as demonstrated by the large number of them in the 52000-series of numbers at the end of this section. Those cars in particular, because of their very limited distribution, are the most difficult of all to obtain.

TOFC AND TTUX CAR LISTINGS

Exc Mt

16303 PENNSYLVANIA: 1987, TOFC flatcar; tuscan body; gold lettering and numbers; two tuscan round-front vans with gold lettering and keystone logo; Symington-Wayne trucks; "BLT 1-87". Lionel had difficulty with the initial run of this car, prompting collector complaints about the dull indistinct gold lettering set against the tuscan brown of the vans and car. It corrected the problem by triple-stamping the gold on later runs of the vans. The flatcars all have the dull lettering, however.

(A) Dull gold lettering on both flatcar and vans; early production run. **30 40**

(B) Same as (A) but vans have much brighter lettering; later production run. R. LaVoie comment. **30 40**

16307 NICKEL PLATE ROAD: 1988, TOFC flatcar; bright blue body with white lettering; two silver-painted trailers with blue logo and lettering; Symington-Wayne trucks; "BLT 1-88". The trailers are a new design; they have two axles each instead of one, and the front ends are squared off rather than rounded.

(A) As described. **25 30**

(B) Factory error. One trailer missing lettering both sides. C. O'Dell Collection. **NRS**

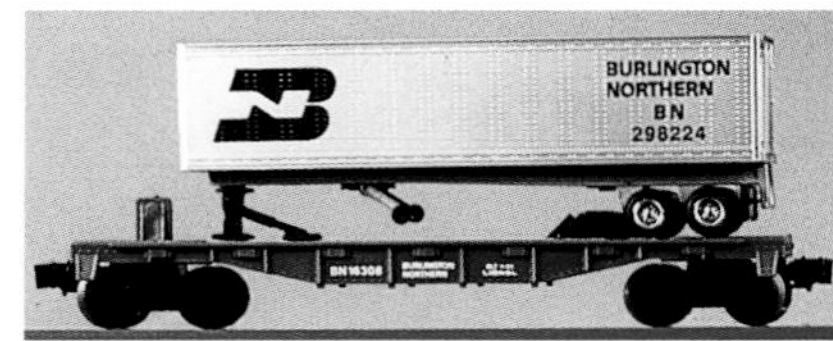

16308 BURLINGTON NORTHERN: 1989, TOFC flatcar; first regular production TOFC car with a single van; green body; white lettering and number; single new-design large trailer painted silver with green lettering and BN logo; van is numbered "298224" and has silver wheel hubs; new-type fifth-wheel stanchion fitted to flatcar—trailer does not have plastic prop wheels used on the smaller kind; Symington-Wayne trucks; "BLT 1-89". Same trailer design as the separate-sale 12725 Lionel and subsequent tractor-trailers. Most collectors felt the new trailer looks much more realistic than the two diminutive trailers offered up to this time. Scheduled for 1988, but not made until 1989. **35 45**

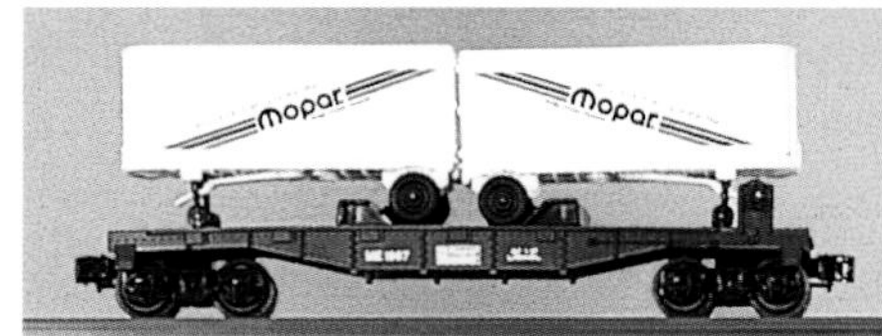

16311 MOPAR EXPRESS: 1987–88, TOFC flatcar; uncataloged; blue body; white lettering "ME 1987"; catalog number is not on car; two white trailers with red, blue, and black lettering "CHRYSLER MOTORS GENUINE PARTS / MOPAR"; blue

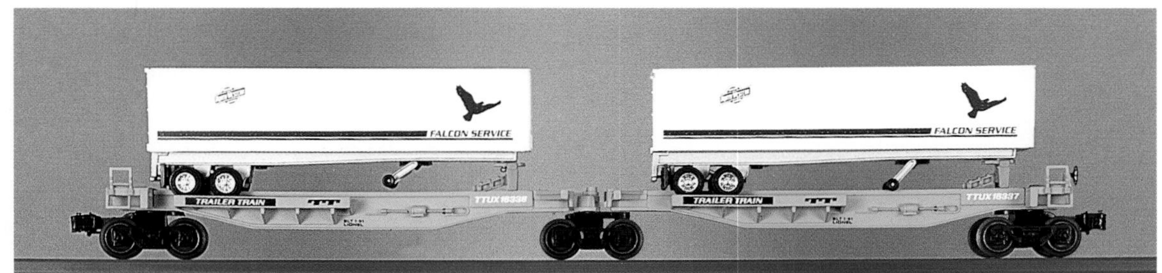

16334 Chicago & North Western TTUX cars

	Exc	Mt
stripes on vans; vans are the round front type with one axle; Symington-Wayne trucks; "BLT 1-87". Part of uncataloged 11757 Chrysler Mopar Express set. Hard to find.	90	110

16314 WABASH: 1989, TOFC flatcar; blue body; white lettering; two square-end trailers with two axles; trailers are a shade lighter blue than the flatcar; broad diagonal white stripe and red, white, and blue Wabash flag; white lettering and "Piggy-Back Service" logos on trailers; Symington-Wayne trucks; "BLT 1-89". **25 35**

16321 SEA LAND: 1990, TTUX articulated flatcar; see description for 16322 for details.

16322 SEA LAND: 1990, TTUX articulated flatcar; all-new Lionel flatcar body modeled after the TTUX Trailer Train cars common on American railroads; detailed narrow I-shaped center body painted mustard yellow; two trays flank the center beam to support trailer wheels; trailer front fits into orange plastic fifth-wheel stanchion; white and black "TRAILER TRAIN" and "TTUX 16322" lettering on flatcar; other car is labeled "16321"; one brakewheel on post on each car; long-style silver vans; black and red "Sea Land" lettering and "SL" logo on each van; vans made in Mexico; ASF trucks; "BLT 1-90" on one side of car only. The set of two cars comes assembled with three ASF trucks in a single box labeled "16322", resulting in an articulated car 21 inches long. A brass shoulder screw arrangement with removable end platform pieces and center triangular pivot pieces allows the user to add more cars by replacing the end truck with the extra center pivot and truck supplied in the box. Price for 16321/16322 set only. **60 75**

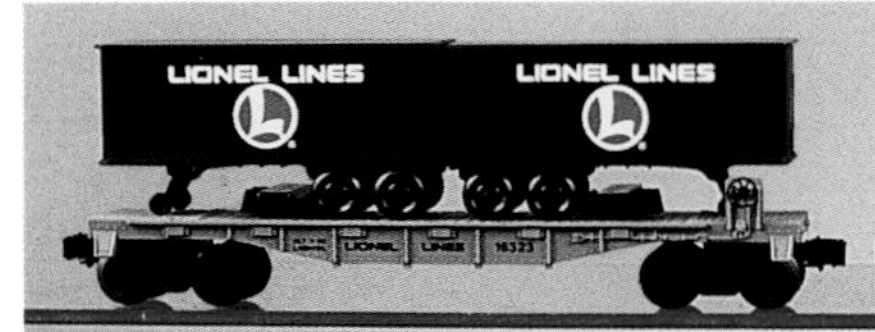

16323 LIONEL LINES: 1990, TOFC flatcar; light gray body with black lettering; two dark blue square-end trailers with white

	Exc	Mt
"LIONEL LINES" lettering and blue, orange and white circle L logo; ASF trucks; "BLT 1-90".		
(A) As described.	25	30
(B) Factory prototype. One normally-marked van. Other van is lighter blue with "LIONEL LINES" stamped in gold on one side and in white on the other; circle L logo missing from both sides. K. H. Miller Collection.	NRS	

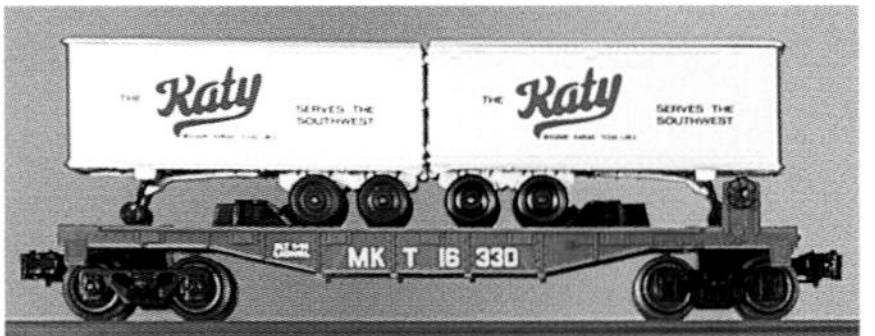

16330 MKT: 1991, TOFC flatcar; red body; white lettering; two silver and white square-end trailers with red and black lettering; "Katy" in red script; ASF trucks; "BLT 1-91". The number on this car is unusually large. **25 30**

16334 CHICAGO & NORTH WESTERN: set of two TTUX articulated cars; see 16338 below.

16335 NEW YORK CENTRAL: 1991, TOFC flatcar; black flatcar body with white lettering and NYC oval logo; single long gray and red van in Pacemaker paint scheme; van has silver roof and black frame; white NYC oval and white "Pacemaker / FREIGHT SERVICE" lettering on van; Standard O trucks; "BLT 1-91". Part of 11719 Coastal Freight Service Station special set. **60 75**

16337 CHICAGO & NORTH WESTERN: 1991, TTUX articulated flatcar; see description for 16338 for details.

16338 CHICAGO & NORTH WESTERN: 1991, TTUX articulated flatcar; mustard yellow spine flatcar; white and black flatcar lettering; cars are individually numbered "16337" and "16338"; white van(s) with black "FALCON SERVICE" and Falcon logo; red, white, and black CNW logo on vans; set comes with 16337 and 16338 assembled in a single box numbered 16334; extra wheelset for adding more cars; ASF trucks; "BLT 1-91". See 16322 listing for additional construction details. Second release of the new TTUX flatcar design. The 1991 catalog misprinted the number for the set (both cars) as "16634"—a number that was later used for a coal dump car. Price for 16337/16338 set only. **65 80**

16378 Toys "R" Us TOFC flatcar

Exc Mt

16345 SOUTHERN PACIFIC: 1992, TTUX articulated flatcar; mustard yellow spine flatcar; white and black flatcar lettering "TT" and "TRAILER TRAIN"; cars are individually numbered 16345 and 16346; cream-colored vans with yellow, black, and white Southern Pacific "Golden Pig Service" heralds at center of sides and on ends; vans have gray underframes and orange stripe with "SOUTHERN PACIFIC" repeated along lower edge; set comes with the two cars assembled in a single box, which is marked 16345; extra wheelset for adding more cars; ASF trucks; "BLT 1-92". See 16322 listing for additional details. Price for 16345/16346 set only. **60 75**

16346 SOUTHERN PACIFIC: 1992, TTUX articulated flatcar; see description for 16345 for details.

16357 LOUISVILLE & NASHVILLE: 1992, TOFC flatcar; tuscan brown flatcar body; white lettering, "L&N" logo, capacity data and bar code on flat car; single long van in gray with red "L&N" logo to right side; "PIGGYBACK SERVICE" to left side; van has end lettering; Standard O trucks; "BLT 1-92". Part of 11729 Louisville & Nashville Express set. The car and set are shown in two different ways in the regular 1992 catalog book 2 and the later 1992 Stocking Stuffers flyer. Initially shown with plastic ASF trucks, the car was actually released as shown in the Stocking Stuffer brochure—with Standard O trucks. The set itself was listed at first with track and transformer and a yellow Standard O steel-side caboose. The set as released was all sold separately, no track or transformer, and with a red-and-yellow bay window caboose! **30 40**

16363 SOUTHERN: 1993, TTUX articulated flatcar; mustard yellow spine flatcar; white and black flatcar lettering "TT" and "TRAILER TRAIN"; cars are individually numbered 16364 and 16365; box with both cars assembled together is marked 16363; silver-painted vans with large green and white "Southern Railway System" heralds at center of sides; vans have red detail data and end lettering; each van numbered sequentially "SOUZ 206500" and "SOUZ 206501"; set comes with the two cars assembled in a single box; extra wheelset for individual operation; ASF trucks; no BLT date; See 16322 listing for additional details. Price for set only. **55 70**

16364 SOUTHERN: 1993, TTUX flatcar; see 16363 for details.

16365 SOUTHERN: 1993, TTUX flatcar; see 16363 for details.

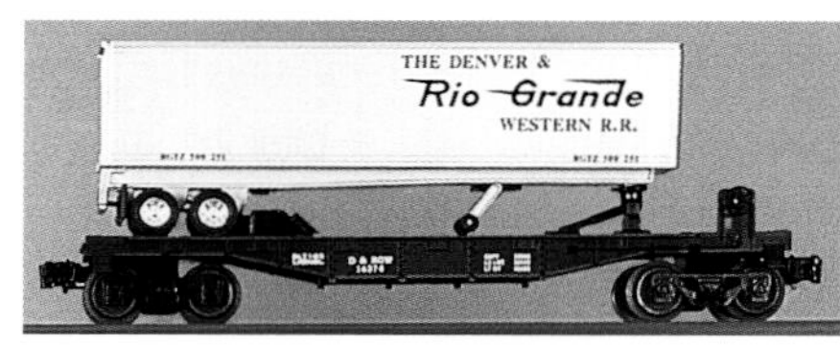

16374 DENVER & RIO GRANDE: 1993, TOFC flatcar; black flatcar body; white lettering and number; single long trailer painted silver with black "Rio Grande" logo; trailer has end lettering and logos; ASF trucks; "BLT 1-93". **25 35**

16376 UNION PACIFIC: 1993–95, TOFC flatcar; black body; yellow lettering and number; long open-top trailer with fences (a first for this type of car); trailer has red ends and floor, gray side fences; includes crate load; trailer can be used with other tractors, including matching red one that came with the set; ASF trucks; "BLT 93". Part of 11736 Union Pacific Express set. **25 30**

16378 TOYS "R" US: 1992–93, TOFC flatcar; uncataloged; black body; white lettering; single long van in white with Geoffrey Giraffe image and multicolor TOYS "R" US and KIDS "R" US logos; ASF trucks; "BLT 1-93". Part of special 11800 Toys "R" Us set. Somewhat hard to find. **80 110**

16383 CONRAIL: 1993, TOFC flatcar; tuscan body; white lettering, number and Conrail logo; single long white van with "CONRAIL MERCURY" in blue and gray; ASF trucks; "BLT

Exc Mt

1-93". Part of 11740 Conrail Consolidated set, the top-of-the line Traditional set in 1993. Set came with a matching Conrail tractor that can be used to pull the trailer. **50 65**

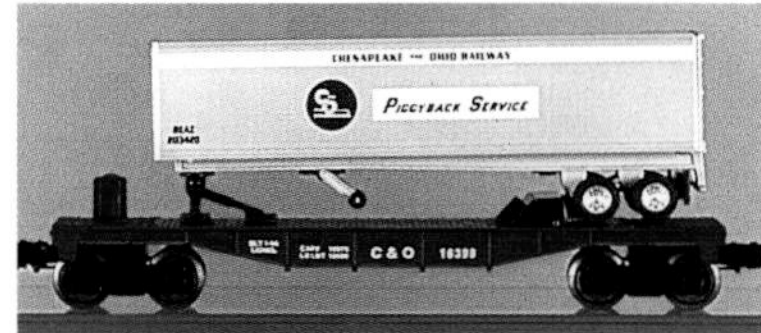

16398 CHESAPEAKE & OHIO: 1994, TOFC flatcar; dark blue body; yellow lettering; single long silver van with white stripe at top; "Piggyback Service" in black on white background on van sides; blue and yellow C&O logo on van sides and ends; van is numbered "283428" on sides and ends; ASF trucks; "BLT 1-94". Trailer can be used with tractor provided in the set. Part of 11743 Chesapeake & Ohio Freight set, top-of-the-line Traditional set from 1994. **60 70**

16904 NEW YORK CENTRAL: 1994, TTUX articulated flatcar; mustard yellow spine flatcar; white and black flatcar lettering "TT" and "TRAILER TRAIN"; cars are individually numbered 16905 and 16906; gray and red vans in classic NYC Pacemaker scheme; white lettering "Pacemaker Freight Service" to rear and NYC oval logo to front; set comes with the two cars assembled in a single box, which is numbered 16904; extra wheelset to add additional cars; ASF trucks; "BLT 1-94". See 16322 listing for additional details. Price for 16905/16906 set only. **55 65**

16905 NEW YORK CENTRAL: TTUX flatcar; see description for 16904 above.

16906 NEW YORK CENTRAL: TTUX flatcar; see description for 16904 above.

16910 MISSOURI PACIFIC: 1994, TOFC flatcar; medium blue flatcar body; white lettering on flatcar; single silver van; black lettering "Missouri Pacific Truck-Rail Service"; "M" and "P" in the name are in larger red letters; ASF trucks; "BLT 1-94". **25 30**

Exc Mt

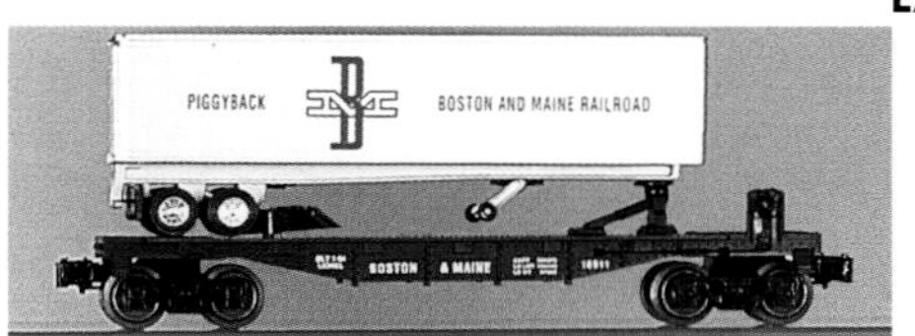

16911 BOSTON & MAINE: 1994, TOFC flatcar; black flatcar body; white lettering; single long silver van with blue lettering; large interlocking Boston & Maine logo on van; ASF trucks; "BLT 1-94".

(A) As described. **25 30**

(B) Trailer overstamped with NETCA logo. 102 exist. **— 120**

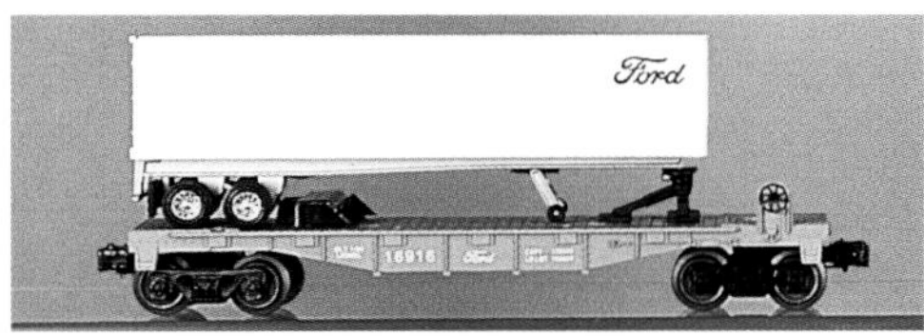

16916 FORD: 1994, TOFC flatcar; uncataloged; gray flatcar body; white lettering and number; single long white trailer with "Ford" in script to front; ASF trucks; "BLT 1-94". Part of special 11814 Ford set. One of numerous Ford-related rolling stock made by Lionel in 1993–95 period. **50 60**

16918 BUDWEISER: 1994, TOFC flatcar; uncataloged; intended as an add-on for the various Budweiser sets; never manufactured. **Not Manufactured**

16922 CHESAPEAKE & OHIO: 1995, TOFC flatcar; black flatcar body; white lettering; dark blue van with silver roof and yellow lower stripe and lettering "CHESAPEAKE & OHIO" across the top; C&O logo at center; "Ship and Go C&O"; trailer has yellow underframe; ASF trucks; "BLT 95". **25 30**

16925 NEW YORK CENTRAL: 1995, TOFC flatcar; black flatcar body; white "NYC" lettering and number; gray trailer with red lettering and red and white oval NYC logo at top center; logo is also on van ends; ASF trucks; "BLT 95". Lionel in 1995 dropped the month indicator from its built dates. Part of 11747 Lionel Lines Steam set, the premier ready-to-run set in the 1995 line. **55 70**

16926 FRISCO: 1995, TOFC flatcar; brown body; white lettering; two small square-end trailers; trailers silver with red and white lettering "Ship It On the Frisco" on diagonal white stripe; ASF trucks; "BLT 95". **30 35**

16953 REDWING SHOES: 1995, TOFC flatcar; uncataloged; red flatcar body; white lettering; number on car is "1905–95"; single white van with multicolor lettering; black stripe at bottom with "Shoemaker for America" in white and "Work Sport Steeltoe Leisure" in yellow; black lettering and red wing logo at center of sides, flanked by 90th anniversary diamond logos; wing

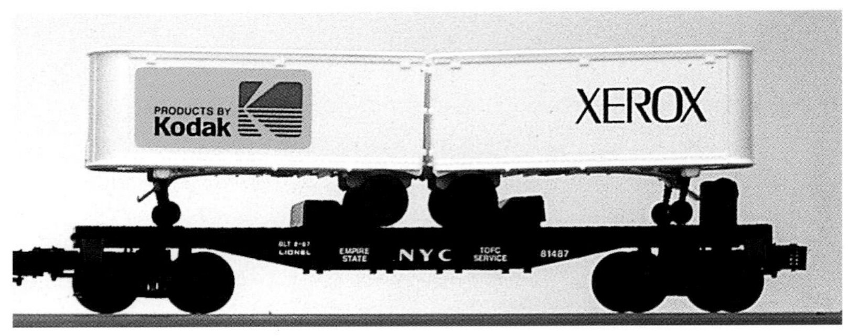

17871 New York Central TOFC flatcar

	Exc	Mt

logo also on front of van; additional black ad lettering on van and "T-4" designation at upper left; ASF trucks; "BUILT BY LIONEL" with no date. Sold individually and also part of the 11820 special Red Wing set produced for the Minnesota shoe manufacturer in 1995. **40 50**

16956 ZENITH: 1995–96, TOFC flatcar; uncataloged; black body; white lettering; single white van with red Zenith logo and black lettering; ASF trucks; "BLT 95". Part of Sears special Zenith set, no. 11821, which was offered as bonus to customers who bought wide-screen Zenith TVs. Reportedly less than 1500 made. **90 110**

16961 GM/AC DELCO: 1995, TOFC flatcar; uncataloged; medium gray flatcar body; black lettering and number on flatcar, with GM rectangle; single silver van with red, white and blue AC logo at rear, over "THE MARK OF EXCELLENCE" in black; "UNITED DELCO" herald at front and on front end; "GM PARTS FOR YOUR GM CAR" along bottom of van; "BLT 95"; ASF trucks. Part of special Chevrolet "Bow Tie" set no. 11822. The set featured a white tractor that could pull this trailer. **60 70**

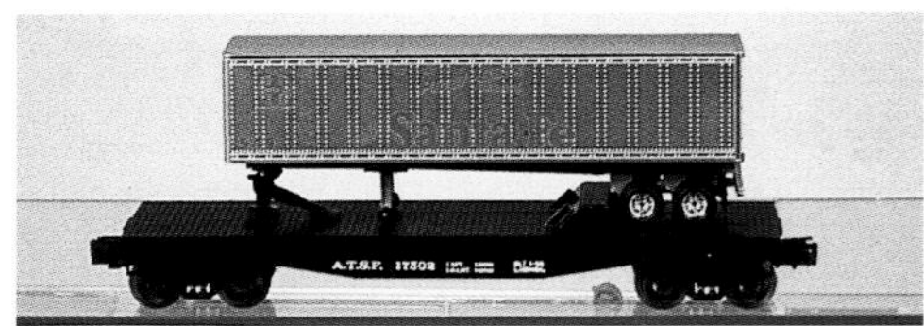

17502 SANTA FE: 1990, TOFC flatcar; Standard O flatcar body with single van; first TOFC car to use a Standard O car; black flatcar body with snap-in fifth-wheel stanchion and retention chock; white lettering on flatcar; silver-painted long van; red "Santa Fe" and cross logo on van; van numbered "549"; Standard O trucks; "BLT 1-90". Part of 11713 Santa Fe Dash 8 set. **65 75**

17503 NORFOLK SOUTHERN: 1992, TOFC flatcar; Standard O flatcar body with single van; gray flatcar body; white lettering and NS streak logo; single white van with "Triple Crown / Service" in large black letters to left; "i" in "Triple" is a series of three small red crowns; trailer has gray underframe and end lettering, including the Triple Crown logo; trailer is numbered "410000"; Standard O trucks; "BLT 1-92". Part of the 11718 Norfolk Southern Dash 8-40C unit train with the following four entries, all sequentially numbered. This was a popular Collector set for 1992. **60 70**

17504 NORFOLK SOUTHERN: 1992, TOFC flatcar with Triple Crown trailer. Identical to 17503 above except for flatcar number and trailer number, which is "410001". Part of 11718 Norfolk Southern unit train. **60 70**

17505 NORFOLK SOUTHERN: 1992, TOFC flatcar with Triple Crown trailer. Identical to 17503 above except for flatcar number and trailer number, which is "410002". Part of 11718 Norfolk Southern unit train. **60 70**

17506 NORFOLK SOUTHERN: 1992, TOFC flatcar with Triple Crown trailer. Identical to 17503 above except for flatcar number and trailer number, which is "410003". Part of 11718 Norfolk Southern unit train. **60 70**

17507 NORFOLK SOUTHERN: 1992, TOFC flatcar with Triple Crown trailer. Identical to 17503 above except for flatcar number and trailer number, which is "410004". Part of 11718 Norfolk Southern unit train. **60 70**

17871 NEW YORK CENTRAL: 1987, TOFC flatcar; uncataloged; special commemorative for the Toy Train Operating Society's 1987 National Convention in Rochester, New York; long Type I flatcar with Kodak and Xerox trailers; black flatcar with white lettering; car number is "81487"; catalog number is not on car; trailers are white and are the single-axle rounded-front style; red, yellow, and black Kodak insignia on one van; black "XEROX" in block letters on other van; Standard O trucks, "BLT 8-87". 876 made. Very hard to find. **300 350**

17887 CONRAIL: 1991, TOFC flatcar; uncataloged; Standard O flat with Armstrong van; special for LCCA. See listing for 17892.

17888 CONRAIL: 1991, TOFC flatcar; uncataloged; Standard O flat with Ford van; special for LCCA. See listing for 17892.

17889 SOUTHERN PACIFIC: 1991; TOFC flatcar; uncataloged; Standard O flatcar with Southern Pacific long van; special commemorative for the Toy Train Operating Society's 25th annual convention in Long Beach, California; brown flatcar body with white lettering; cream-colored van with black, yellow, white,

	Exc	Mt

and pink Southern Pacific "Golden Pig Service" logo on sides and one end; silver "25th ANNIVERSARY TOY TRAIN OPERATING SOCIETY" on orange strip along lower edge of van; "15791" is number on car; 17889 appears only on box; Standard O trucks; "BLT 1-91". **70 80**

17892 CONRAIL: 1991, TOFC flatcar set; uncataloged; special edition for the Lionel Collectors Club of America's 21st National Convention in Lancaster, Pennsylvania; set consists of dual Standard O flatcars, each with a long van; individual cars are numbered 17887 and 17888 and will sometimes be found for sale individually, but most often purchased as a set; this is the first time a train club commissioned a two-car set for its annual commemorative; tuscan Standard O flatcars with white lettering; two long-style trailers with multicolor logos; 17887 is the Armstrong floors van—white with blue stripe along lower edge and blue and red lettering; 17888 is the Ford New Holland van—white with red and blue stripes along lower edge; Ford logo at one end; both vans have silver underframes; Standard O trucks (both cars); "BLT 1-91" (both cars). Both cars originally came together in a mailer but each is also individually packed in a Type V box. Note that 17892 does not appear except on the outer mailer. Armstrong and Ford are well-known companies in the Lancaster area. The 1991 convention souvenir was an LCCA tractor (listed as no. 17895) that can be used to pull these trailers. Due to an oversight by Lionel, no LCCA convention data was printed on the van ends, as intended. These are the only LCCA cars lacking this information.

(A) Individual cars.	**60**	**70**
(B) Two-car set.	**110**	**140**

17895 CONRAIL: tractor; see 17892

19404 WESTERN MARYLAND: 1989, TOFC flatcar; deep red flatcar body; white lettering "TRAILER TRAIN" and "TT" logo; two square-end trailers painted silver with yellow "WESTERN MARYLAND" lettering; Standard O trucks; "BLT 1-89". Part of Western Maryland Fallen Flags set no. 4, whose components were all offered for separate sale. **30 40**

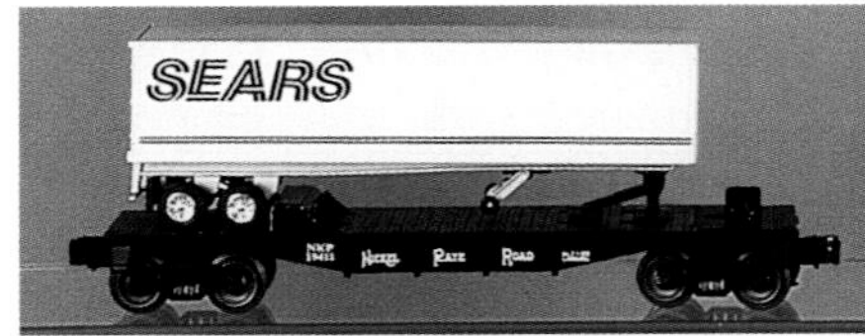

19411 NICKEL PLATE ROAD: 1992, TOFC flatcar; black flatcar body; white lettering; long single trailer painted off-white or cream with "SEARS" in brown; two brown stripes along lower side of trailer; Standard O trucks; "BLT 1-92". Part of Fallen Flags series no. 6, the Nickel Plate Road, whose components were all sold separately. **45 60**

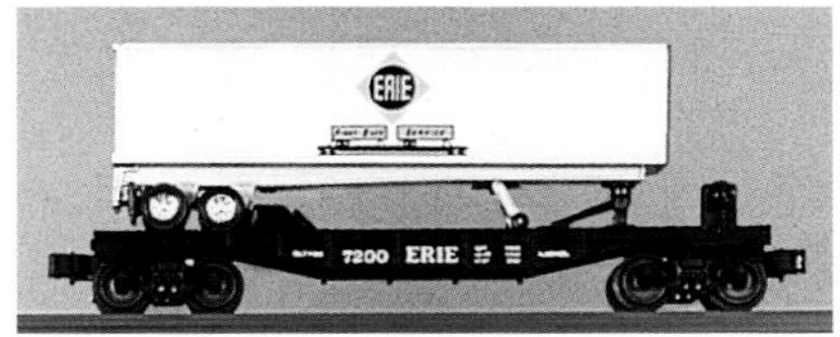

19415 ERIE: 1993, TOFC flatcar; black flatcar body; white lettering; number on car is "7200"; 19415 does not appear; silver-painted long single trailer with yellow and black Erie diamond logo on sides and ends; trailer numbered "70" on end; yellow and black "PIGGY-BACK SERVICE" logo showing two TOFC cars below diamond logo; Standard O trucks; "BLT "1-93". Part of Erie Fallen Flags set no. 7, whose components were sold separately. **30 40**

19416 ILLINOIS CENTRAL GULF: 1993, TTUX articulated flatcar; yellow spine flatcar; white and black flatcar lettering "TT" and "TRAILER TRAIN"; cars are individually numbered 19417 and 19418; box with both cars assembled together is marked 19416; silver-painted vans with black lettering "ILLINOIS CENTRAL GULF PIGGYBACK" highlighted in white; orange pig on roller skates; vans have Illinois Central I-beam logo on ends; each van is numbered "16416"; extra wheelset to add more cars; ASF trucks; "BLT 1-93"; See 16322 listing for additional details. Part of 11738 Soo Line Service Station Special set for 1993. Lionel by 1993 was hitting its stride in producing the TTUX spine cars. Price for set only. **75 95**

19417 ILLINOIS CENTRAL GULF: TTUX flatcar; see 19416 above for details.

19418 ILLINOIS CENTRAL GULF: TTUX flatcar; see 19416 above for details.

52000 DETROIT-TOLEDO TCA: 1992, TOFC flatcar; uncataloged; light blue flatcar body; silver lettering and number; stylized "DTC" on car and trailer; "1967–1992" also on both units; single long silver trailer with light blue lettering, denoting the 25th anniversary; TCA logo at front; ASF trucks; no BLT date. This car was a special made for the 25th anniversary of the TCA's Detroit Toledo Chapter in 1992; hard to find. **90 120**

52003 MEET ME IN ST. LOUIS: 1992, TOFC flatcar; uncataloged; banquet special car for the TCA 1992 convention in St. Louis; red flatcar body; white lettering; single long trailer lettered for "MOPAC" in white, with Ozark Division notations; Standard O trucks; "BLT 92". Reportedly 100 made. **400 500**

52013 NORFOLK SOUTHERN/ARTRAIN: 1992, TOFC flatcar; uncataloged; annual special for the Artrain traveling art museum; Standard O flatcar body; gray with white lettering; single long

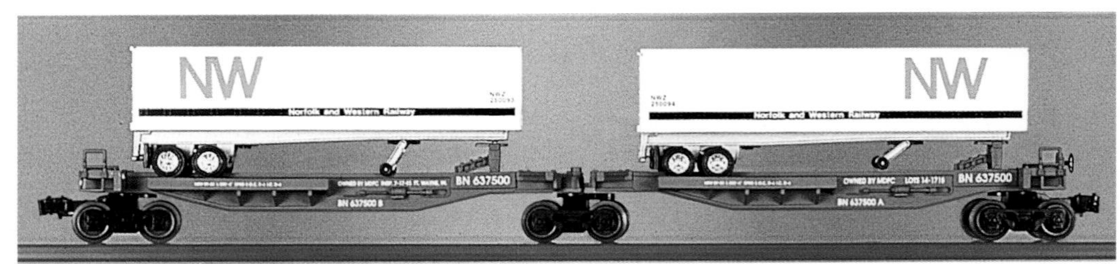

52014 Burlington Northern/NW TTUX flatcar

	Exc	Mt

white trailer with Artrain logo; Standard O trucks; reportedly fewer than 400 made. **150 250**

52014 BURLINGTON NORTHERN/NW: 1993, TTUX articulated flatcar; uncataloged; annual convention car for the Lionel Operating Train Society (LOTS); medium-green painted spine flatcar (first time this car was anything but mustard yellow); white lettering and BN insignias on flatcar with different lettering on each side of each car; cars are numbered 637500A and B; one long white NW van on each car; gray roofs; NW logos in orange are in different places on each van; black stripe near bottom of van with "NORFOLK & WESTERN RAILWAY" in white; vans have orange and red lettering on ends; one van numbered 250093, the other 250094; ASF trucks; "BLT 1-93". 1715 made. Somewhat hard to find. The first of Lionel's articulated flatcars produced for a train club—the LOTS 1993 convention in Fort Wayne, Ind. Also intended as a set with 52041 and 52042. **110 140**

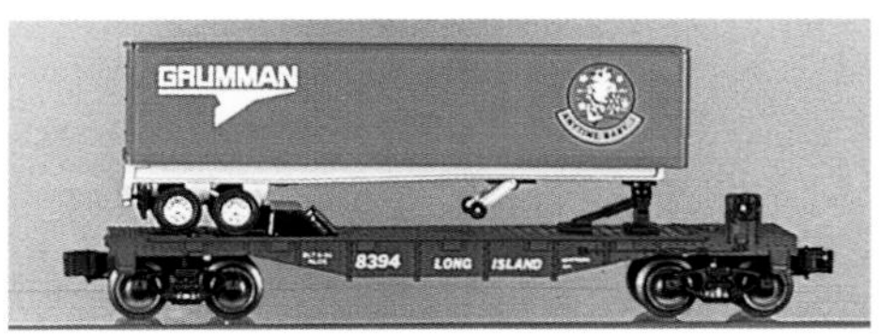

52026 LONG ISLAND/GRUMMAN: 1994, TOFC flatcar; uncataloged; annual special from the Nassau Lionel Operating Engineers (NLOE); dark gray flatcar body with "Long Island" lettering in white; number is "8394" designating the founding year of the club and year of production; single long van in medium blue; "GRUMMAN" logo in white to rear of van; black, white and brown "Tom Cat" insignia with the logo "ANYTIME BABY . . .", a reference to the aircraft builder's historical challenge to enemies of America; set came with a white tractor to pull the trailer; Standard O trucks; "BLT 6-94". Grumman is the major aerospace and defense contractor on Long Island. Hard to find. Reportedly 143 made. These cars are Lionel blanks decorated at PVP. This unit also came with a Grumman tractor, which was also made by Lionel and designated 52072. **250 350**

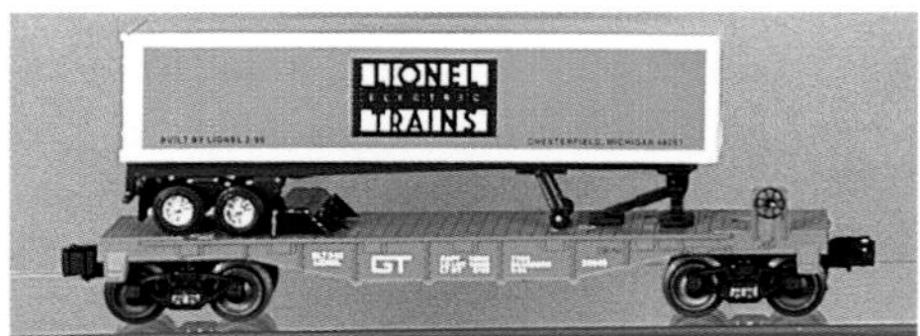

52040 GRAND TRUNK: 1995, TOFC flatcar; uncataloged; annual convention car for the Toy Train Operating Society's 1994 convention in Dearborn, Michigan; orange flatcar in individual box without the trailer; white GT logo and "TTOS / Dearborn / 8-94" lettering on flatcar; tractor and trailer are included in a separate individual box labeled 52033, with the flatcar box labeled 52034; both packed in a mailer labeled 52040; trailer is orange and cream with blue-painted undercarriage; large "Lionel Electric Trains" blue and orange rectangle logo at center of trailer; other blue lettering; "TTOS 1994" on rear doors; "TTOS Wolverine Division / Dearborn MI / 1994" on front of trailer in blue, with Michigan state silhouette in orange under the lettering; tractor with set is cream-colored with Lionel circle L logo on door; Standard O trucks; "BLT 2-95". Note that the car was released in 1995, though it marks the 1994 convention. The flatcar here has a catalog number 52034. **60 70**

52041 BURLINGTON NORTHERN/ CONRAIL MERCURY: 1994, TTUX articulated flatcar; uncataloged; annual convention car for the Lionel Operating Train Society (LOTS); medium-green painted spine flatcar; white lettering and BN insignias on flatcar with different lettering on each side of each car; cars are numbered 637500D and E; one long gray Conrail Mercury van on each car; blue and white lettering; vans have logos on ends; one van numbered "231093", the other "231094"; ASF trucks; "BLT 1-94". 1900 made. Car was a special for the LOTS 1994 convention in New Brunswick, New Jersey. It is also intended as a set with 52014 and 52042. **90 110**

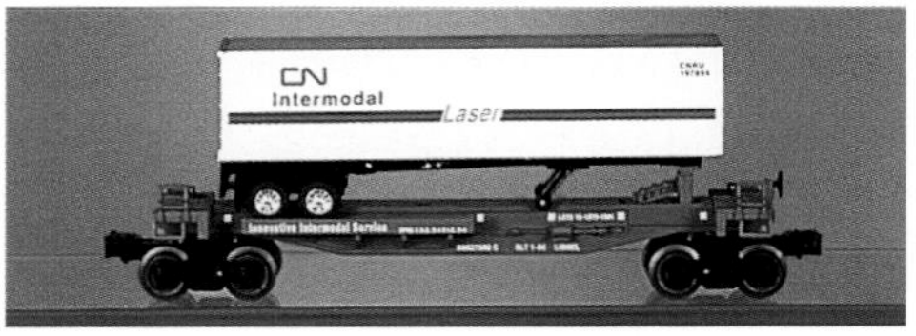

52042 BURLINGTON NORTHERN/CN: 1994, TTUX articulated (single) flatcar; uncataloged; 15th anniversary special for the Lionel Operating Train Society (LOTS); medium-green painted spine flatcar; white lettering and BN insignias on flatcar with different lettering on each side; car is numbered "637500C"; one long white Canadian National van with gray roof; "CN" in red to upper right; red and blue "LASER" beam stripe logo; van includes end lettering; van is numbered "197994"; van has black-painted undercarriage (all previous sets used a standard

Exc Mt

gray undercarriage); ASF trucks; "BLT 1-94". 1785 made. Car was made as an anniversary add-on, to produce a five-car articulated BN unit train, with 52014 and 52041. It is a single (versus double, as with previous TTUX sets) spine car with both trucks installed. It came in a full-length TTUX box, however. A tractor truck (no. 52048) was also produced as an accessory for the trailer. **60 75**

52048 CN: 1994; tractor; see 52042

52072 GRUMMAN: 1994; tractor; see 52026

52080 BOSTON & MAINE: 1995, TOFC flatcar; uncataloged; annual special from the New England Division of the TCA (NETCA), one of the most active of the TCA divisions in producing special cars; light blue flatcar with white "BM" logo and "NETCA 1995"; number on car is "91195"; matching blue long single van with yellow stripe near bottom; large white BM herald at right center; white "BOSTON AND MAINE RAILROAD—PIGGYBACK" lettering surrounding it; "NETCA 1995" at upper left; trailer is numbered 825 at lower center; Standard O trucks; no built date. Reportedly 298 made. These were Lionel-based cars redecorated for the NETCA by the New England Car Shops in Massachusetts. **100 125**

52083 EASTWOOD: 1995, TOFC flatcar with tanker; uncataloged; one of a continuing set of Lionel specials from the Eastwood Automobilia Co. in Malvern, Pennsylvania; tuscan flatcar with white "PENNSYLVANIA" lettering and number; new-type tanker trailer painted silver, also includes new-type die-cast undercarriage painted blue, which has a spare wheel bin; tanker has a red walkway fitted to the top; blue ladder at rear; large blue and white "Eastwood" logo to front of tanker and on tank end; "CHEMICALS FOR THE HOBBYIST" in white on red stripe across length of tank; additional advertising lettering in blue above and below red stripe; Standard O trucks; "BLT 9-95". This piece marks the first time a tanker was used on a Lionel TOFC car. Available only through the Eastwood catalogs. Reportedly 2500 made. **— 45**

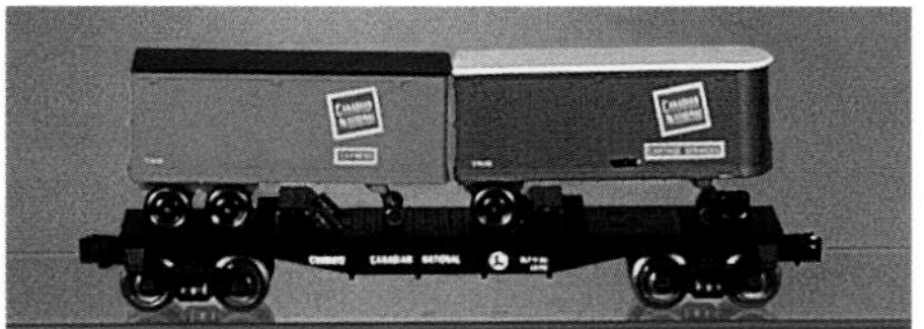

900013 CANADIAN NATIONAL: 1990, TOFC flatcar; uncataloged; annual commemorative for the Lionel Collectors Association of Canada (LCAC); black Type I flatcar body with white lettering; two short vans, one of each type (square-end and round-end); square-end double-axle van is in CN orange with black roof, lettered in gold and red "Express Services" with CN wafer logo; round-end single-axle van is CN green with white roof, lettered "Cartage Services" in gold and red with CN logo; LCAC circle herald is on flatcar and ends of vans; Standard O trucks; "BUILT 11-90 LCAC." Reportedly 375 made. These are Lionel-blank flatcars and vans redecorated by the Pleasant Valley Process Company. Hence the car carries no official Lionel catalog number. The marked number designates the year (1990) and the fact that the car is the 13th in a series of annual cars from the LCAC. Hard to find. **180 230**

CHAPTER 13

Gondolas

On real railroads, no piece of rolling stock takes as much abuse as the gondola car. Big loads of scrap steel, 55-gallon drums, machine parts, crushed automobiles, and other assorted refuse of our industrial society are routinely dropped into these decidedly unglamorous cars with nary a thought for the car's appearance or shape. One never sees gondolas in new condition, it seems. Instead, they are in various stages of abuse and decay—some have rusted sides, and some are dented beyond belief. But somehow all of them keep rolling on the rails and doing their jobs.

In a way, Lionel gondolas were subject to their own brand of abuse in the postwar period. Innumerable New York Central gondolas were made in black, red, green, and blue versions. Because they were meant to be loaded and played with, these cars probably took more abuse at the hands of young railroaders than any other cars. Look through a tinplate junk pile at a train show, and chances are that most of the junk cars are gondolas. Not only that, but the Lionel Corp. cheapened the cars as time went on, in the interest of cost savings. The postwar gondolas began with impressive metal frames and trucks and finished with absolutely bare undersides, plastic trucks, and cheap non-operating couplers.

In the modern era, Lionel has reversed that trend by bringing some style back to the lowly gondola car. Many of the newer ones come with the excellent Standard O sprung trucks. Some have been offered as separate-sale limited production items. Coal loads have been added, as well as scrap iron loads and handsome coil covers, designed to protect (theoretical) loads of iron or steel coils from the weather. New colors and rail markings have brightened the car considerably. Even the least expensive short gondolas have been made in brighter colors than their postwar predecessors.

There are five principal body styles used for the modern era gondolas (see accompanying figure).

SHORT GONDOLAS

Two of the styles are minor variations of the basic short gondola. This car, which traces its heritage back to the 6142 of the postwar era, comes in a version (Type I) with two steps on the left side and four on the right, with a large brakewheel and thin rims around the periphery of the mold. This type was a carryover of the postwar gondola. Sometime around 1977, the gondola mold was modified to create a version with three steps on each side and a smaller molded brakewheel. The new car also had a thicker, more pronounced edge rim. This was the Type II short gondola body. The short gondola has shown up only rarely in Lionel LTI production—it has recently been phased out of Lionel's line, even from the low-end Traditional Line sets.

Loads for the short gondolas have included round canisters or cable reels. We try to specify the original load in the listings for these cars, since they are easy to misplace or change around.

LONG GONDOLAS

By far the most abundant of Lionel's gondolas is the long style—at 9⁹⁄₁₆ inches it is some 20 percent longer than the short type. Its history goes all the way back to the 6462 New York Central from 1947. There are some differences from the postwar model. A few of the modern cars have molded brakewheels, while the postwar one included metal wheels or none at all. Recent gondolas from Lionel LLC have returned to the metal brakewheels. On the later postwar cars the bottom surface was smooth and devoid of all features. Fundimensions added girder and rivet detail that looks much better.

Close inspection of the bottom of the newer Lionel gondolas reveals a circle with the numbers "6462-2' and either a "1" or a "2" under the part number. This marking was the same as on the postwar cars. The "1" or the "2" refers to the side of the mold from which the car emerged after the plastic injection process. The mold for 6462-style gondolas is such that two cars were made at a time.

Loads for the long gondolas, like the short ones, have included cable reels and round canisters. One interesting feature readers will note in our long gondola listings: the presence (or absence) of under- and overscoring lines around the number and/or roadname abbreviation on the side of a car. This is especially noticeable on Lionel's gondolas and hoppers, and some boxcars have them, too. Sometimes a car might have variations where the top line, bottom line, or both, are missing. It was more an issue during the Fundimensions era, but less so during the Lionel LTI and LLC periods.

Since the Quaker City Limited set in 1979, most of Lionel's Collector-level sets have included a long gondola in colorful markings with Standard O sprung trucks. During the late 1980s, Lionel also introduced a wonderfully realistic coal load for the long gondola, which first appeared in the Great Northern and Western Maryland Fallen Flags sets. In the next Fallen Flags set—the Frisco from 1991—Lionel placed very detailed two-piece coil covers on the car for the first time. Many gondolas since then have included these covers, which also offer good surfaces for decoration. They proved so popular that Lionel offered them later for separate-sale in the accessory line.

A fun variation of the long gondola is the operating version, in which a cop and hobo chase each other around a set of molded crates inside the car. In the postwar (3444) model and the Fundimensions remake (9307) of this car, a vibrator motor

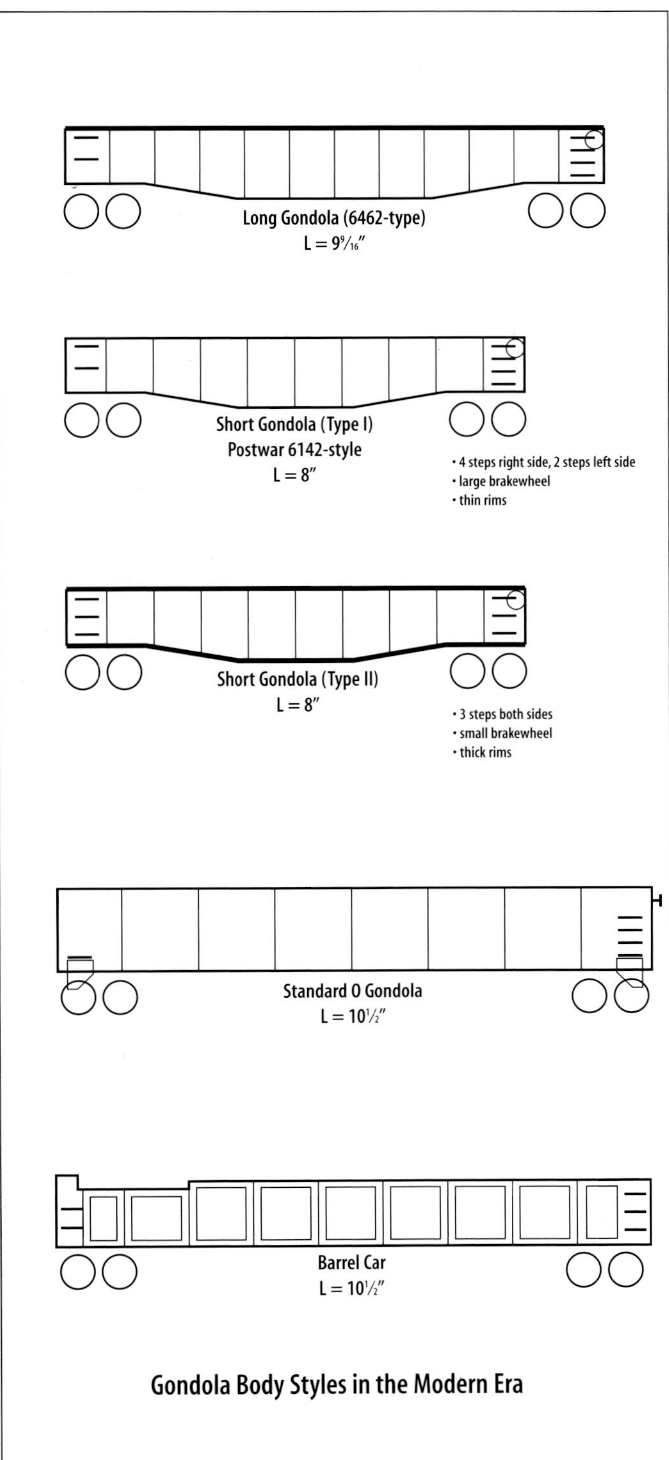

Gondola Body Styles in the Modern Era

could be activated to pull a length of film, to which the figures were attached, around two spools. All this was hidden under the crates. A simpler, less-expensive mechanism was devised by LTI for the 16628 Lionelville Circus car from 1990. Designers replaced the temperamental vibrator motor with a worm-gear shaft attached to the axle, which simply rotated the figures around as the car moved. This meant, of course, that the action would occur only when the car was in motion. But it did eliminate an expensive motor and power pickup. After only two appearances in the modern era, Lionel LTI apparently decided that this interesting car merited more attention, so two "Pinkerton" versions appeared in 1994 and 1995. The body of the car is otherwise identical to the regular long gondola.

STANDARD O GONDOLAS

Lionel Fundimensions stunned the O gauge world in 1973 with the release of its Standard O series, a step up from its previous shortened non-scale world into the arena of scale size and detailed models of real-world prototypes. The 9820 Wabash and 9821 Southern Pacific Standard O gondolas were among the first group of cars in the series. These cars measured 10½ inches long—almost an inch longer than the 6462-style gondolas. They featured wonderfully detailed coal loads and, best of all, the brand-new sprung-metal trucks. The trucks not only dramatically improved the car's ride and were highly realistic, but would become the backbone of Lionel's Collector train line for the rest of the century. Since the handsome Conrail set of 1987, which included the 17401 tuscan Conrail gondola, modern Lionel has been in the mode of releasing one or two Standard O gondolas, in sets or separately, every year. Following the lead of the long gondolas, some recent Standard O gondolas have sported coil covers, slightly larger than the ones used for the long gondolas.

OPERATING BARREL CARS

The last principal variation of the gondola is the operating barrel car, a reissue of the postwar favorite. The car body is unique from the other gondola types. Similar in length to Standard O cars, it has slightly raised panels on the body sides between the ribs, with one end cut down slightly for the ejector plate. A vibrator mechanism sends six wooden barrels up a chute built into the car. At the top of the chute, a workman kicks them off into a bin or the operating barrel ramp. The cars feature the older bar-end postwar trucks because they are the only kind equipped with the sliding shoe contacts needed for the car's operation. The first two barrel cars to appear in the modern era were the 9290 Union Pacific from 1983 and the 9225 Conrail in 1985. Oddly, Lionel Trains, Inc. did not produce any barrel cars during its run. Deciphering the numbering scheme for Lionel's gondolas is not simple, because other types of cars are often part of the number sequence. For the most part, the short ones can be found in the 16300-series, the long ones also in the 16300 sequence and later the 16900 numbers (Traditional Line) as well as the 19400-series (Collector Line). The Standard Os are found in the 17400 numbers. Operating (cop-and-hobo) cars have been placed in the 16600- and 16700-series with other types of operating cars. In recent years Lionel has drifted from the previous guideline and used numbers in the 26000- and 36000-series, so there's little telling where the next one will find itself. To confuse things more, the special gondolas produced for the train hobby clubs or other organizations are in the 52000-series!

Lionel's gondolas offer an excellent, if unglamorous, specialty area of collecting. They are colorful and, for the most part, available and inexpensive. The only drawback is that many come from sets and thus are not always for sale individually.

GONDOLA LISTINGS

Exc Mt

16304 RAIL BLAZER: 1987–88, short gondola; red or orange body; white numbering and lettering; two black cable reels; plastic arch-bar trucks; "BLT 1-87". Part of 11701 Rail Blazer set.

(A) 1988 production; red Type I body; two operating couplers. **5 6**

(B) 1987; orange Type I body; one dummy coupler. Probably earliest production—Lionel changed to red bodies in mid-production so car would match rest of set. **10 15**

(C) Same as (B), except Type II body. **8 10**

16309 WABASH: 1988–91, long gondola; medium brown body; white lettering and numbers; two unlettered white canisters; Symington-Wayne trucks; operating couplers. Part of 11703 Iron Horse Freight set. The 1991 set releases of this car have ASF trucks. **10 15**

16310 MOPAR EXPRESS: 1987–88, long gondola, uncataloged; tuscan body; white lettering; two canisters (only in 1987); 16310 does not appear on car—"1987" is the number on the car; Symington-Wayne trucks; "BLT 1-87". Came in 11757 Chrysler Mopar Express set. **30 35**

16313 PENNSYLVANIA: 1988–89, short gondola, green Type I body; white lettering and PRR logo; two black cable reels; Symington-Wayne trucks; "BLT 1-88". Part of uncataloged 11708 Toys "R" Us Pennsy set in 1988, which later became the cataloged 11708 Midnight Shift set in 1989. **10 15**

16327 THE BIG TOP: 1989, long gondola, uncataloged; yellow body; blue lettering "The Big Top"; 16327 is not on the car; two dark blue canisters labeled "Elephant Food" in white; Symington-Wayne trucks; "BLT 1-89". Part of uncataloged 11770 Sears Circus set. **20 25**

16328 NICKEL PLATE ROAD: 1990–91, long gondola; light gray body; yellow lettering; two black cable reels; Symington-Wayne trucks; "BLT 1-89". The yellow-on-gray lettering here can be hard to read. Came in the 16999 Rolling Stock assortment from 1990 and 1991. **10 15**

16336 UNION PACIFIC: 1990, short gondola, uncataloged; black body; yellow lettering and UP shield; two light gray canisters; number on car is "6336"; Symington-Wayne trucks. No individual box. Part of 11785 Union Pacific Express set produced for the Costco store chain in 1990, and also the uncataloged 11796 Union Pacific Express set (which was identical), issued to other retailers. On the set box, Lionel had misspelled the word as "Cosco". **20 25**

16339 MICKEY'S WORLD TOUR: 1991, long gondola; dark blue body; magenta lettering with large "1001" numerals over "Hello"s; two yellow canisters—one has Mickey saying "aloha", the other with a Swiss Chocolate logo; ASF trucks; "BLT 1-91". Not boxed individually. Part of 11721 Mickey's World Tour train set, one of many Disney-related trains produced by Lionel in recent years. **20 25**

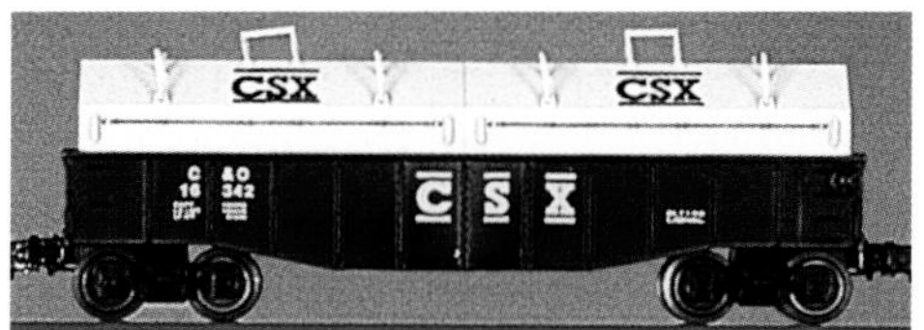

16342 CSX: 1992, long gondola with coil covers; black body with yellow lettering; "C", "S", and "X" under-and overscored in the center panels; light gray coil covers with blue "CSX" lettering; ASF trucks. "BLT 1-92". **20 25**

16343 BURLINGTON: 1992, long gondola with coil covers; red body with white lettering; black and white "Burlington Route" rectangle to right side; black coil covers with white lettering; ASF trucks. "BLT 1-92". **20 25**

16353 BOSTON & MAINE: 1991, long gondola with coil covers; uncataloged; orange body with black lettering; silver coil covers with no lettering; ASF trucks. Part of the 11726 Erie Lackawanna Freight set, which appeared only in the 1991 Stocking Stuffers brochure. **30 35**

16355 BURLINGTON: 1992–94, long gondola, red body with white lettering; ASF trucks, "BLT 1-92". Part of 11727 Coastal Limited set in 1992 and 1993, and the 11746 Seaboard Freight set in 1994, as well as a Rolling Stock Assortment, in which canisters were included. This is virtually the same car as the 16343 above except without the black logo and coil covers. **10 15**

16358 LOUISVILLE & NASHVILLE: 1992, long gondola with coil covers; gray body with white lettering; black coil covers with no lettering; Standard O trucks, "BLT 1-92" Part of 11729 L&N Express set. **25 30**

Exc Mt

16359 PACIFIC COAST: 1992, long gondola with coil covers; tuscan body with white lettering; gray coil covers with no lettering; Standard O trucks; "BLT 1-92". Part of 11733 Feather River Service Station set. This car was cataloged with its wheelsets painted brown but were made black. **30 35**

16367 CLINCHFIELD: 1993, long gondola with coil covers; black body with white lettering; gray coil covers with black Clinchfield circle logo and "CRR" over car number to left; ASF trucks; "BLT 1-93". **20 25**

16384 SOO LINE: 1993, long gondola with cable reels; white body with large red "SOO LINE" lettering; two black cable reels; ASF trucks; "BLT 1-93". Part of 11741 Northwest Express set. **15 20**

16387 KANSAS CITY SOUTHERN: 1994, long gondola with coil covers; black body, white lettering with thick "KCS" left of center; yellow coil covers with black lettering; ASF trucks; "BLT 1-94". One of several pieces made for the KCS short line in the 1990s, a railroad which was never before modeled by Lionel. **20 25**

16388 LEHIGH VALLEY: 1994, long gondola with canisters; tuscan body, white lettering and black "LV" logo to right of center; came with four orange canisters; ASF trucks; "BLT 1-94". **20 25**

16391 LIONEL LINES: 1993, long gondola; uncataloged; red body; white lettering; ASF trucks; "BLT 1-93". Part of special UAW set 11811. **20 30**

16392 WABASH: 1993–94, short gondola with canisters; dark red Type I body; white lettering; "WAB" and number under- and overscored; ASF trucks; "BLT 1-93". Uncataloged in 1993, this car was part of the 16692 O27 Rolling Stock Assortment in 1994. **8 10**

Exc Mt

16556 US NAVY: 1994–95, long gondola with canisters; black body, white lettering; two white canisters with white labeling "ROCKET FUEL"; ASF trucks; "BLT 1-94". Part of the very popular 11745 U.S. Navy train set. It is odd that this car is numbered as it is, with the 16500-series normally reserved for cabooses. The numbering may be accidental—Lionel also carried this on its books as 16909. **15 20**

16628 LIONELVILLE CIRCUS: 1990–91, operating gondola; cop and hobo car; bright blue body; yellow lettering "LAUGHTER" in large block letters on side panels; tan crate load with light blue lettering; ASF trucks; "BLT 1-90"; car motion causes green cop to chase white hobo carrying a brown sack around the crates. Lionel devised a simple non-electrical mechanism to activate the animation on this car using wheel motion only. A worm gear attached directly to the axle rotates a shaft connected to the cop and hobo figures. This assembly replaces the temperamental vibrator motor used earlier—the crates in the car still have a slot where the motor switch lever used to be. Paint detail on the figures is a marked improvement over the postwar and early Fundimensions era cars (such as the 9307)—both cop and hobo are highlighted with red and blue polka dots! Part of 11716 Lionelville Circus set. **40 50**

16674 PINKERTON: 1994, operating long gondola, cop-and-hobo car; red gondola body, white lettering; tan crate load with no lettering; car motion causes blue cop to chase gray hobo around the crates; ASF trucks; "BLT 1-94". See 16628 for operating description. **35 40**

16712 PINKERTON: 1995, operating long gondola; cop-and-hobo car; black gondola body, white lettering; tan crate load with no lettering; car motion causes blue cop to chase black, white, and green hobo around the crates; ASF trucks; "BLT 95". Identical to 16674 car except for the car body color, and the fact that the figures are painted. Lionel might have felt the black coloring improved the car's looks. See 16628 for operating description. **30 35**

16909: see 16556.

16915 LIONEL LINES: 1993–94, short gondola, uncataloged, green Type I body; black lettering; ASF trucks; "BLT 1-93". This is one of the very few short gondolas made by modern

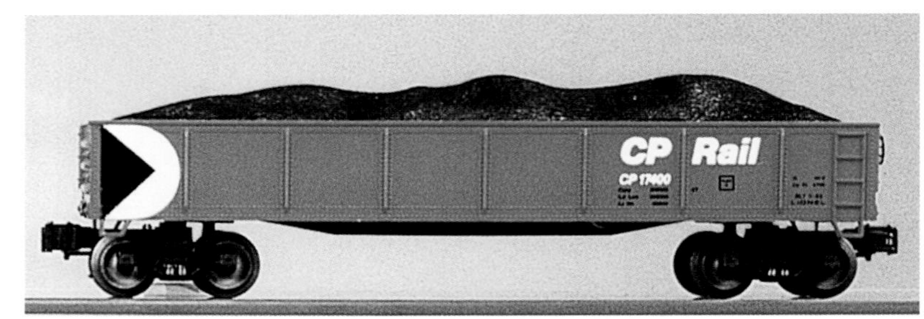

17400 CP Rail
Standard O gondola

	Exc	Mt

Lionel, and apparently was used to fill out some of the O27 rolling stock in various sets. **8 10**

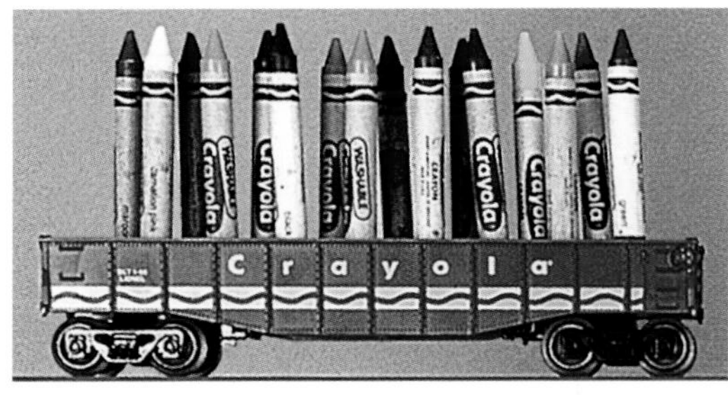

16917 CRAYOLA: 1994–95, long gondola, uncataloged in 1994; medium blue body; yellow "Crayola" lettering; yellow serpentine decor along length of car; no number on car; foam insert included to hold crayons that are supplied with the set; ASF trucks; "BLT 1-94". Part of 11813 Crayola Activity set, a popular low-cost set that featured a blank boxcar, which children could decorate using the crayons. Car and set appeared initially in a 1994 Crayola brochure, then in the 1995 regular catalog. **10 15**

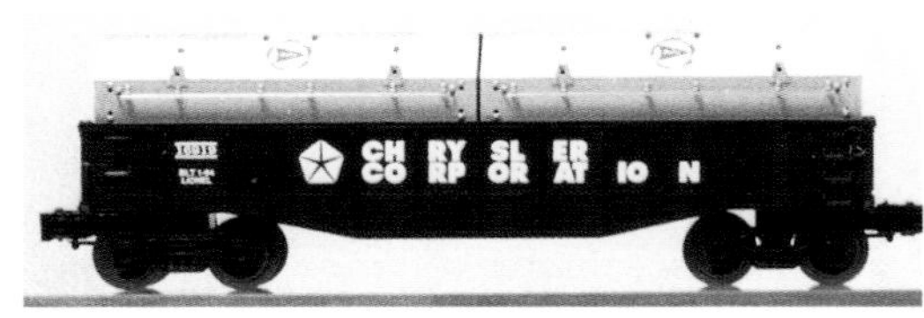

16919 CHRYSLER CORPORATION: 1994, 1996, long gondola with coil covers; uncataloged; black body; white lettering and Chrysler star; silver covers with red Mopar flag logo; ASF trucks; "BLT 1-94". Came in two sets:

(A) With 11818 Chrysler Mopar set, 1994. **35 40**

(B) With 11933 Dodge Motorsports set, with 3 unpainted white canisters, no covers, 1996. **35 40**

16929 BRITISH COLUMBIA RAILWAY: 1995, long gondola with cable reels; black body, white lettering; three gray cable reels; ASF trucks; "BLT 1-95." **20 25**

17400 CP RAIL: 1989, Standard O gondola; dark red body; white lettering "CP RAIL" to right; CP's "Multimark" logo in black and white on brakewheel side; simulated coal load; Standard O trucks; "BLT 1-89". Part of 11710 CP Rail set. It is not clear why this car is numbered ahead of the 17401 Conrail, which was made two years earlier. **50 55**

	Exc	Mt

17401 CONRAIL: 1987, Standard O gondola; brown-painted body; white lettering and "wheel" logo; simulated coal load; Standard O trucks; "BLT 1-87". Part of 11700 Conrail Limited set. **40 50**

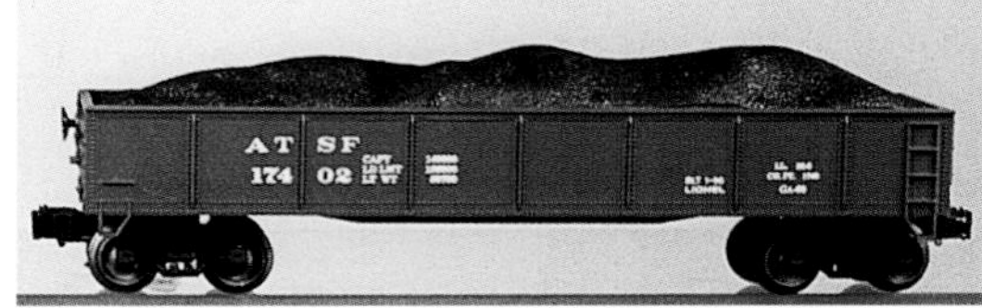

17402 ATSF: 1990, Standard O gondola; brown body; white lettering; simulated coal load; Standard O trucks; "BLT 1-90". Part of 11713 Santa Fe Dash 8 set.

(A) As described. **40 45**

(B) Factory error. Missing lettering on one side. W. Cunningham collection. **NRS**

17403 CHESSIE: 1993, Standard O gondola with coil covers; black body with yellow lettering and Chessie Cat logo in center; "B&O 371629" on left side; 17403 is not on car; black coil covers with yellow cat logo. Standard O trucks; "BLT 1-93". At this point Lionel was beginning to move its Standard O line to fully prototypical decor, which included removing its catalog number from the body. **35 40**

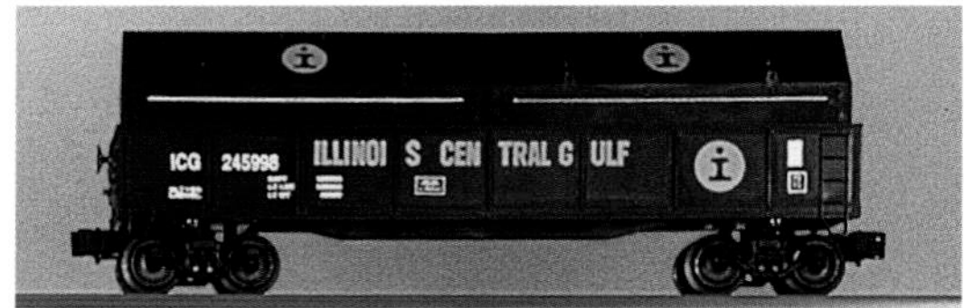

17404 ILLINOIS CENTRAL GULF: 1993, Standard O gondola with coil covers; black body with orange "ILLINOIS CENTRAL GULF" lettering and I-beam logo to right; white "ICG 245998" lettering

52004 Algoma Central long gondola

	Exc	Mt

to right; 17404 not on car; black coil covers with orange I-beam logo; Standard O trucks, "BLT 1-93." **35** **40**

17405 READING: 1994, Standard O gondola with coil covers; light yellow body with dark green lettering; "RDG 24876" to left of center; 17405 not on car; tuscan coil covers with white "Reading Lines" lettering; Standard O trucks, "BLT 1-94". **35** **40**

17406 PENNSYLVANIA: 1995, Standard O gondola with coil covers; tuscan body with white lettering and black and white PRR keystone; "PRR 385405" to left; lighter tuscan coil covers with black and white keystone logos; 17406 not on car; Standard O trucks, "BLT 95". **35** **40**

19400 MILWAUKEE ROAD: 1987, long gondola; brown body with two black cable reels; white lettering; red and white rectangular Milwaukee logo; under- and overscored number; Standard O trucks; "BLT 1-87". Part of Milwaukee Fallen Flags set no. 2, whose components were offered for separate-sale. **30** **40**

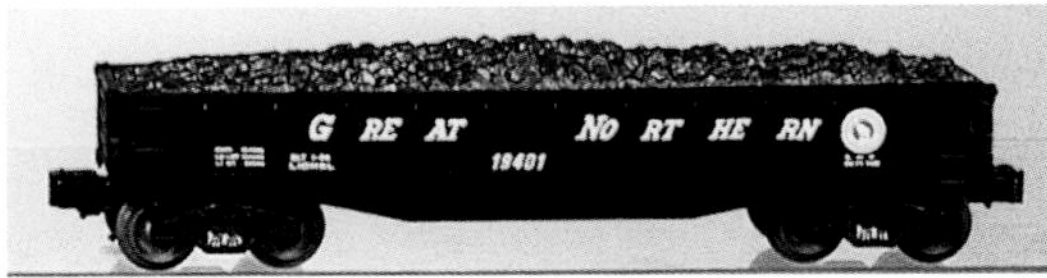

19401 GREAT NORTHERN: 1988, long gondola; black body; white slanted lettering; red and white circular goat logo; simulated coal load; Standard O trucks; "BLT 1-88"; Part of Fallen Flags set no. 3, whose components were all offered for separate-sale. **30** **35**

19403 WESTERN MARYLAND: 1989, long gondola; tuscan body; white lettering; simulated coal load; under- and overscored number; Standard O trucks; "BLT 1-89". Part of Fallen Flags set no. 4, whose components were all offered for separate-sale. **30** **35**

19408 FRISCO: 1991, long gondola; black body; white lettering; two new-style coil covers, decorated to match car—first gondola so equipped; Frisco shield on covers, with "SL / SF" and "19408" on lower edge of covers; metal brakewheel; Standard O trucks; "BLT 1-91". Part of Fallen Flags set no. 5, whose components were all offered for separate-sale. **35** **40**

19410 NEW YORK CENTRAL: 1991, long gondola; pink body; blue lettering and NYC oval logo; "N", "Y", and "C" in different panels on car side, each letter overscored; number under- and overscored; four unpainted white plastic canisters with black lettering; Standard O trucks; "BUILT BY LIONEL" and "NEW 1-91". An exact remake (except the number and trucks) of the pastel pink 6462 gondola from the 1957 Girls' set. The modern car came in the 1991 revival of the 11722 Girls' Train. **45** **50**

52004 ALGOMA CENTRAL: 1995, long gondola with coil covers; uncataloged; black body, white lettering, with black and white Algoma Central circular polar bear logo in center and LCAC "L" logo to right; black coil covers with white lettering "AC 9215" on one side and polar bear logo on the other; 52004 not on car; Standard O trucks; "NEW 11-92". This is the 15th in the series of "Comcars" for the Lionel Collectors Association of Canada (LCAC). "NEW 11-92" is misleading because the car

52016 Boston & Maine–NETCA long gondola

Exc Mt

was released in 1995, with LCAC about three years behind in its releases because of production difficulties. Hard to find. **90 110**

52016 BOSTON & MAINE–NETCA: 1993, long gondola with coil covers; uncataloged; silver body; black lettering; small NETCA notation; unmarked blue coil covers; ASF trucks; "BLT 1-93". One of a continuing set of desirable cars made for the New England Division of the TCA. Somewhat hard to find. **50 60**

52030 FORD: 1994, long gondola, uncataloged, black body, white lettering. "FDRX 4023" over- and underscored; 52030 is not on the car; ASF trucks, "BUILT 8-94". This was one of three special black-and-white Ford cars sold as a set (set was numbered 52028) for TTOS's annual convention in Dearborn, Michigan, in 1994. The other cars in the set were the 52029 tank car and the 52031 short hopper. No individual box. Usually sold with the set. **20 25**

52049 BURLINGTON NORTHERN ARTRAIN: 1994, long gondola with coil covers; uncataloged; green body, white lettering and logo; black coil covers with white Artrain logo and red striping; Standard O trucks; "BLT 1-94". 1994 installment of the special Artrain series. This is one of the few "special production" set of cars in the 52000-series that actually has the number on the car. **80 100**

CHAPTER 14

Hoppers

Of all the types of rolling stock in Lionel's train line, it is with the hopper cars that the most recent incarnations of the company, Lionel LTI and Lionel LLC, have struck out most impressively in new directions of modeling and style.

For nearly the entire Fundimensions era, from 1970 through 1985, Lionel had only two types of hopper cars in its line, both carryovers from the postwar era. The first was the short two-bay hopper, based on the prolific Lehigh Valley short hoppers made literally by the millions from the late 1940s through early '60s. The second type was the large, handsome 50-ton four-bay (Quad) hopper car, which first appeared in Norfolk & Western markings in 1954. The postwar company didn't bother making the hoppers in many other roadnames besides Lehigh Valley, and train operators seemed quite content with that, buying the cars by the caseful to produce "unit" trains of long lines of identical coal carriers resembling those pulled by the nation's leading coal-carrying railroad of that time.

Lionel-Fundimensions was similarly content to carry on with the traditional two types of hopper cars well into the 1980s, although they did produce far more roadnames on the cars than the postwar corporation. The cars were most often good sellers, fitting nicely into many Traditional and Collector Lines sets. They allowed Lionel (with its "billboard" advertising agreements) to place well-known brand names on the broad sides of the hoppers in bright color schemes, even if no such cars existed in the full-scale world. Through this period, though, the rising market force represented by collectors was beginning to push for new designs, claiming that people would buy only so many variations on the same car types. Still, the company had no reason to mess with a successful formula until the pressures of lower sales and competition in the late 1980s forced them to move more aggressively to modern railroad car styles and into the arena of scale modeling. Once prompted, they did so with gusto.

Lionel today has six distinct hopper cars to offer, from the old standby two-bay short hoppers to the foot-long 48-foot scale monsters. See accompanying figure..

ACF TWO- AND THREE-BAY CENTER-FLOW HOPPERS

In 1986 the company overturned tradition dramatically with a wonderful new near-scale model of the American Car & Foundry center-flow two-bay hoppers, which are seen everywhere on today's railroads. The interesting fact about this event was that Lionel's new cars were released uncataloged, in a special limited-edition flyer that also announced Lionel's popular B&A Hudson. As a result these first new ACF hoppers (the 6134 Burlington and the 6135 Chicago & North Western) are much in demand and hard to find now. This step also brought Lionel's hopper line into the Standard O realm, joining the boxcars, flatcars, and gondolas, which had seen Standard O versions for the prior 10 years.

Shortly thereafter, in 1988, Lionel LTI came out with a unit train in Chessie colors, and all the cars were stretched three-bay versions of the ACF hopper. The two-bay carbody is 8¾ inches long. Its three-bay brother is an impressive 10½ inches in length.

The advantage to using ACF hoppers is that they have allowed Lionel to decorate them in many other railroad names—roads that were not coal-carriers—because the ACF hopper is used to carry any kind of dry materials, from corn to grain to beans to powder cement. On real railroads, the round-sided ACF has been copied by other manufacturers since the patent expired. The rounded sides allow more cargo volume than the straight-sided hoppers.

Collector reaction to these two new releases was very favorable. The models have the wide chunky appearance of the real thing, with detailed roofs, hatches, and walk platforms, as well as excellent simulated ladder and ironwork on the ends. The bay covers on the bottom are also well detailed, if as yet nonfunctional. And of course the ACF hoppers ride on the sprung Standard O die-cast trucks. More important, however, was the affirmation that the company was listening to collector requests and the interests of railroad hobbyists to move their production into more modern arenas.

STANDARD O 48-FOOT RIBBED HOPPERS

The 1990s found Lionel plunging headlong toward scale modeling, and as if to punctuate their intentions, the company in 1991 came out with a near-scale model of the 48-foot ribbed-side, open-top three-bay hopper also common on U.S. railroads today. This wonderfully detailed hopper is even longer (11½ inches) than the quad hopper or the three-bay ACF hopper and is a great match for the ribbed 50-foot boxcars also introduced in 1991. The 48-foot (Standard O) hopper has superb rivet detail all around the side ribs, chassis and ends, and also has an excellent molded coal load with three distinct "piles" of coal. The car comes with manually operated bay doors at the bottom, which must be assembled by the user with a small pivot tab. There have been occasions when Lionel shipped the cars with the wrong complement of hatch doors. Three are of one type and the other three are a mirror image, so if a buyer receives six of the same type, he should contact Lionel for a correct set. Another nice touch is the metal brakewheel. In 1995 Lionel upgraded this excellent car by adding a nicely detailed roof piece (on the 17123 Cargill).

SHORT TWO-BAY HOPPERS (NON-OPERATING AND OPERATING)

Lionel has not neglected its veteran short and quad hoppers, even in recent years. The short two-bay hoppers are referred to by some hobbyists as "O27," denoting smaller size and lower cost. The car is only 8½ inches long, despite the efforts by some Lionel catalogers to claim it is longer and still turns up in many a starter train set. Users of this book should also be aware that several of the pre-1986 short hoppers, notably the 6137 Nickel Plate and the 6177 Reading, have turned up in rolling stock assortments as late as 1993.

Lionel LTI unveiled another interesting and classy "first" in 1995's 16418 C&NW short hopper—it included a coal load for the car, for the first time ever.

In 1981 the short hopper was modified to reproduce the operating hopper car of postwar years. A metal plate with hinged bin covers is attached to the bottom of the car and the square bin ports are punched out of the plastic. A plunger is attached to the plate. When pulled down by an electromagnet, it opens the bins and allows the coal to drain out of the car—most often into the tray of the 394 coal loader, which then carries it in a conveyor belt to another waiting hopper on an adjacent track. This nifty but usually messy operation was and is one of the most popular action sequences for many Lionel train fans.

A curiosity about the short operating hoppers is that both to date (the 19804 Wabash and the 19806 Pennsy) have been equipped with the Standard O sprung trucks, perhaps a bit of overkill for O27 short hoppers. There is one other curious difference between the operating and non-operating cars—the operating ones feature a metal brakewheel, while the plainer non-operating cars have a round molded plastic brakewheel, which is not, in truth, especially attractive.

QUAD HOPPERS

The 11-inch-long quad hopper, now a staple of the Lionel product line, has been issued in hundreds of roadnames and corporate names in the modern era. It has come at various times with and without hatched covers and with or without coal loads. The roofs on the covered ones have 12 hatches that actually open, but they are a bit fragile. Collectors should also beware of purported variations related to roof colors, since covers are very easy to change out.

The quad hoppers even today retain an odd plastic mold feature that was a source of much speculation: a drum-shaped projection at the center on the inside bottom of the car has been conjectured to be either a planned operating mechanism for opening the four hatches, or an accommodation for a radio receiver, such as was used for the electronic sets. Whatever the plan, this odd feature remains on the quad hoppers almost a half-century after the car was first introduced.

Postwar Lionel produced a huge number of quad hoppers, in a variety of body colors, lettered for the Lehigh Valley. Interestingly, modern Lionel has made only a very few hoppers in this road name (one of which was the lilac pastel car made for the reissue of the infamous Girls' set in 1991), preferring instead to apply its excellent graphics capabilities to other decorative possibilities. Lionel LTI and Lionel LLC have also apparently dropped further use of the "billboard" concept, a fact probably related to the increasing difficulty and cost of obtaining licenses. A few notable exceptions are the Ford cars from 1994 and pieces made for Cargill and Archer-Daniels-Midland. Most of the post-1986 hopper cars are decorated for existing and past railroads. The company has also produced several sets of "unit trains" with identically decorated hoppers differing only by one digit in their numbers. This has been an increasing trend in Lionel's freight cars of the 1990s. One of the company's earliest sets of unit trains involved five nice C&O yellow hoppers, the first three-bay versions of the ACF car. This set was 1988's Chessie System unit train. Another great example of this was a wonderful eight-car Western Maryland hopper set from 1995 and 1996.

DIE-CAST "SEMI-SCALE" QUAD HOPPERS

Lionel produced one other type of hopper, first seen as the 51501 B&O semi-scale quad hopper in 1991. This car, one of six cars in a set made in 1991–92, was part of a commemorative reminiscent of the semi-scale freight cars produced by prewar Lionel in 1940, in conjunction with the famous scale 700E Hudson. The modern 51501 is an all-metal freight car with superior detail. For most of the 1990s, this car remained a one of a kind. Then in 1998 Lionel embarked on a new program to produce large numbers of die-cast freight cars, apparently in response to collectors' demands. Although shorter in length (and height) than its plastic quad hopper cousin, the all-metal construction of this piece makes it many times heavier than the plastic hoppers, with a price tag to match.

In terms of value, there seem to be three levels of scarcity associated with the hopper cars. Most common are the regularly cataloged individual-sale cars with common roadnames. The next level would be those cars released only in Collector or limited-edition sets, such as the Chessie unit train or the Dupont cars. At the highest level are the club convention cars and the scarce uncataloged pieces produced in very small quantities. The Standard O cars, because of their size, will command a higher average cost as well.

The numbering systems for hoppers are somewhat varied: the 16400-series is used for the Traditional (or Classic) Line hoppers—usually the short and quad styles. The ACF and 48-foot Standard O hoppers are found in the 17000- and 17100-series; the Collector-level (or "Heritage") quad hoppers can be found in the 19300-series, the few operating hoppers (so far only the short kind) can be found in the 19800-series. There are some exceptions to these rules, mostly for the special-production train club cars, which are found all over the spectrum.

Collectors should also be aware that around 1995 Lionel took to decorating many of its pieces—particularly the higher-end and Standard O items—with prototypical numbers rather than catalog numbers. This practice had been in use by the train hobby clubs for quite a few years before that. It does, however, make things confusing with guides such as this, which are organized primarily by catalog number. We try to note in the listing when an item is marked with something other than its catalog number. Buyers should also note that, in general, the catalog number appears on the box end—when there is a box.

In all, the Lionel hoppers present an outstanding roster of rolling stock. Most of them are relatively easy to find, and a beginning collector can amass quite a few of them at reasonable prices. The popular hopper will certainly remain an integral part of thousands of Lionel layouts around the world.

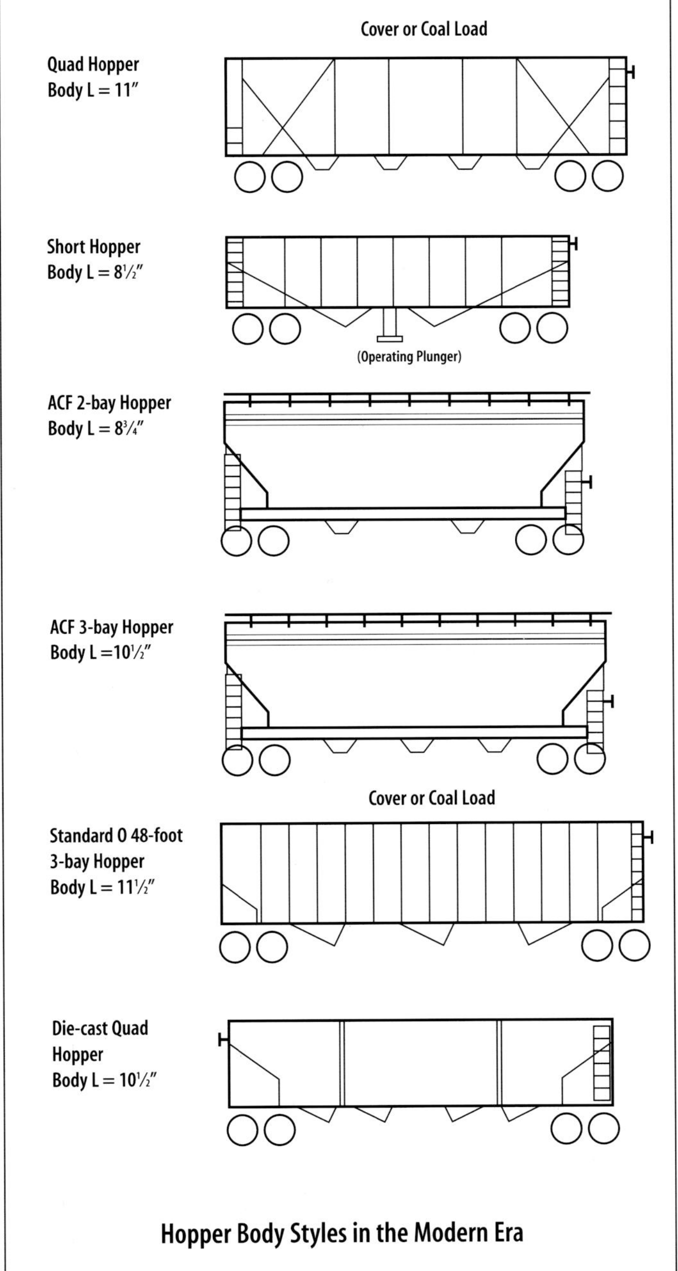

Hopper Body Styles in the Modern Era

HOPPER CAR LISTINGS

Exc Mt

8390 LONG ISLAND RAILROAD: 1990, covered quad hopper; uncataloged; second in a special series of cars by the Nassau Lionel Operating Engineers (NLOE) club in Levittown, New York; gray body; orange lettering; LI logo in orange circle to upper right; Symington-Wayne trucks; "BLT 2-90". 48 made, 45 with orange roofs, 3 with gray roofs, both shown here. This is a Lionel 19309 Seaboard quad hopper redecorated by the Pleasant Valley Process Co. The number refers to the founding year of the club (1983) and the year the car was made. — 120

8912 CANADA SOUTHERN: 1989, operating short hopper; uncataloged; 11th annual commemorative for the Lionel Collectors Association of Canada (LCAC); black body; white lettering, numbers and logos; LCAC circle logo to top left; Standard O trucks; "BUILT 11-89 LCAC". 265 made. This is a blank 19800-series Lionel O27 operating hopper decorated by the Pleasant Valley Process Co. PVP designator "305-1486". — 140

16400 PENNSYLVANIA: 1988–89, short hopper; gray body; black lettering, number and PRR keystone; Symington-Wayne trucks; "BLT 1-88". Part of 11708 Midnight Shift set in 1989 and an uncataloged Toys "R" Us version of the same set the year before. See 19806 for an operating version. 20 25

16402 SOUTHERN: 1987, quad hopper with coal load; uncataloged; gray body; black lettering and number; Standard O trucks; "BLT 1-87". Part of 11704 Southern Freight Runner Service Station set. 40 50

16406 CSX: 1990, quad hopper with black coal load; black body; yellow lettering; large "CSX" underscored at upper right; ASF trucks; "BLT 1-90". Part of 11717 CSX Freight set. 30 35

	Exc	Mt

16407 BOSTON & MAINE: 1991, covered quad hopper; gray body; black lettering and logo; Standard O trucks; "BLT 1-91". Part of 11719 Coastal Freight Service Station Special set. This was the first Service Station set from Lionel shown in the regular catalog. See also 52001. **30 40**

16408 UNION PACIFIC–COSTCO: 1990–91, short hopper; uncataloged; gray body; black lettering & UP shield; "6408" is the number on the car; Symington-Wayne trucks. No individual box. Part of 11785 Costco Union Pacific Express set from 1990, a specialty set derived from the regular-issue Nickel Plate Special, and made for the Costco wholesale outlet chain. It was also later part of the 11796 Union Pacific Express set (otherwise identical) made for other retailers. Lionel misspelled the name "Cosco" on the set box. **20 30**

16410 M-K-T: 1992–93, short hopper; dark green body; yellow lettering with large "MKT" to left-center; ASF trucks; "BLT 1-92". Part of 11728 High Plains Runner set and the uncataloged Toys "R" Us Heavy Iron set in 1993. **20 25**

16411 LOUISVILLE & NASHVILLE: 1992, quad hopper with coal load; black body; yellow lettering; large "L&N" to left side; Standard O trucks; "BLT 1-92". Part of 11729 Louisville & Nashville Express set, the top-of-the-line Traditional Line set in 1992. The car and set are shown in two different ways in the regular 1992 catalog book 2 and the later 1992 Stocking Stuffers flyer. Initially shown with a cover and plastic ASF trucks, the car was actually released as shown in the Stocking Stuffer brochure—with a coal load and Standard O trucks. The set itself was listed at first with track and transformer and a yellow Standard O steel-side caboose. The set as released was all sold separately, no track or transformer, and with red and yellow bay window caboose. **30 35**

16412 CHICAGO & NORTH WESTERN: 1994, covered quad hopper; dark red body; white lettering; white North Western logo at upper right; ASF trucks; "BLT 1-94". **20 25**

16413 CLINCHFIELD: 1994, quad hopper with coal load; black body; white lettering; ASF trucks; "BLT 1-94". See also 52059. **20 25**

	Exc	Mt

16414 CCC & STL: 1994, short hopper; black body; white lettering; New York Central oval logo to upper right; ASF trucks; "BLT 1-94". The catalog optimistically states the length of this car at 10 inches. Its body is in reality only 8½ inches long, a bit over 9 when counting the couplers. **15 20**

16416 DENVER & RIO GRANDE: 1995, covered quad hopper; black body; white lettering; "Rio Grande / the "ACTION" road" script to right side; ASF trucks; "BLT 95". Car was shown in the 1995 Spring release catalog with a coal load, but released with a cover, as shown in the regular 1995 catalog. **20 25**

16417 WABASH: 1995, quad hopper with coal load; black body; white lettering; white Wabash flag logo in upper right; "WAB" and number over- and underscored to upper left; ASF trucks; "BLT 1-95". Car was shown in the 1995 Spring release catalog with a cover, but released with a coal load, as shown in the regular 1995 catalog. **20 25**

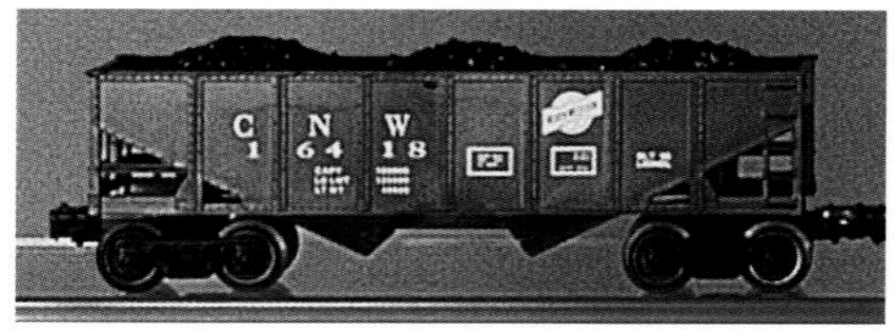

16418 CHICAGO & NORTH WESTERN: 1995, short hopper with coal load; dark green body; yellow lettering; yellow North Western herald to upper right; ASF trucks; "BLT 95". This car is notable because it is the first time—ever—that Lionel incorporated a simulated coal load into its short hopper. **20 25**

Lionel had been moving toward the concept of unit trains throughout the modern period, since Richard Kughn's LTI took over production in 1986. In 1995 the company produced an eye-catching Service Station set of identical quad hoppers in Western Maryland livery. Led by the 18841 GP-20 in red and black, the set featured four covered gray quad hoppers, each consecutively numbered (16424–16427), and two black quad hoppers with coal loads, also numbered in sequence. In 1996 the company followed up with a special two-car package of black hoppers to add to the set, creating a unit train with a grand total of eight quad hoppers. Even the caboose in this set was different—a new design center-cupola style. This Service Station Special set (11749) has been in considerable demand since its release.

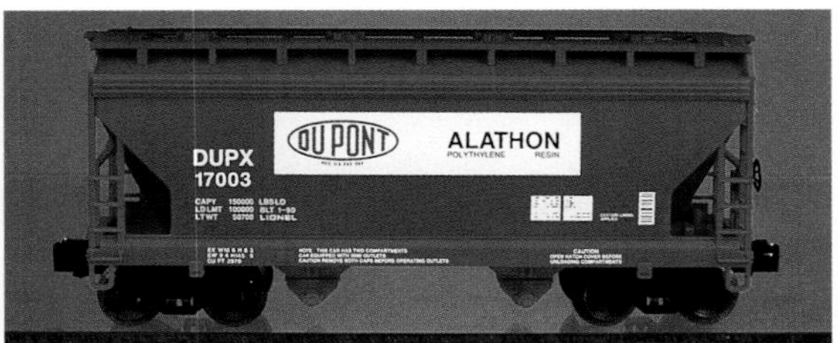

17003 DuPont Alathon ACF hopper variations A (left) and B

Exc Mt

16420 WESTERN MARYLAND: 1995, quad hopper with coal load; black body; white lettering; "WESTERN MARYLAND" with two sets of four horizontal lines across top; Standard O trucks; "BLT 95". This car was part of a set with the following seven entries—the 11749 Western Maryland Service Station set, a unit train that eventually totaled eight identically decorated Western Maryland hoppers, each consecutively numbered. **30 35**

16421 WESTERN MARYLAND: 1995, quad hopper with coal load; identical to 16420 above except for number. Part of 11749 Western Maryland Service Station unit train set. **30 35**

16422 WESTERN MARYLAND: 1995–96, quad hopper with coal load; identical to 16420 above except for number. Released in late 1995 as an add-on to the 11749 Western Maryland Service Station unit train set. Sold as a set only with 16423. This two-car pack (sold as item no. 16429) was listed in the 1995 Stocking Stuffers/1996 Spring releases catalog, but not in the regular 1996 catalogs. **30 35**

16423 WESTERN MARYLAND: 1995–96, quad hopper with coal load; identical to 16420 above except for number. Released in late 1995 as an add-on to the 11749 Western Maryland Service Station unit train set. Sold as a set only with 16422. This two-car pack (sold as item no. 16429) was listed in the 1995 Stocking Stuffers/1996 Spring releases catalog, but not in the regular 1996 catalogs. **30 35**

16424 WESTERN MARYLAND: 1995, covered quad hopper; gray body; black lettering; otherwise identical to 16420 above except for number. Part of 11749 Western Maryland Service Station unit train set. **30 35**

16425 WESTERN MARYLAND: 1995, covered quad hopper; gray body; black lettering; otherwise identical to 16420 above except for number. Part of 11749 Western Maryland Service Station unit train set. **30 35**

Exc Mt

16426 WESTERN MARYLAND: 1995, covered quad hopper; gray body; black lettering; otherwise identical to 16420 above except for number. Part of 11749 Western Maryland Service Station unit train set. **30 35**

16427 WESTERN MARYLAND: 1995, covered quad hopper; gray body; black lettering; otherwise identical to 16420 above except for number. Part of 11749 Western Maryland Service Station unit train set. **30 35**

16429: see 16422.

16430 GEORGIA POWER: 1995, quad hopper with coal load; uncataloged; blue-green body; white stripe at top of car with number "82947" and "WE SELL EFFICIENCY" in green; white Georgia Power Company logo at center of car with silhouette of Georgia state and "A Citizen Where Ever We Serve" slogan; ASF trucks; "BLT 95". Part of 11819 Georgia Power set, made especially for employees of the Georgia Power Company in 1995. Reportedly 2,500 made. The set has proven to be very popular. **— 90**

17000: see 17107.

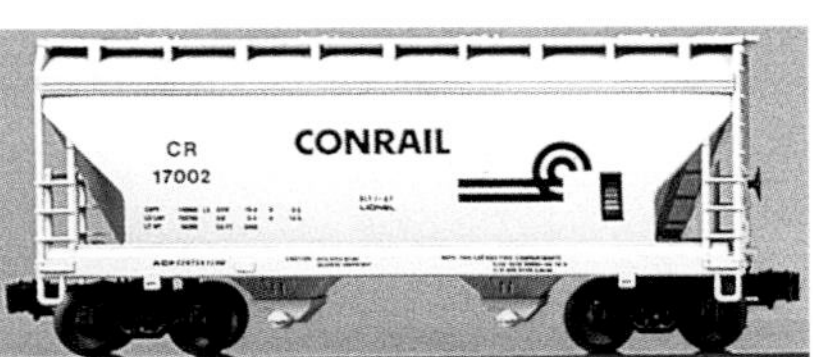

17002 CONRAIL: 1987, ACF two-bay center-flow hopper; light gray body; black lettering and logo; Standard O trucks; "BLT 1-87" with bar code. Part of 11700 Conrail Limited set. **65 80**

17003 DUPONT ALATHON: 1990, ACF two-bay center-flow hopper; medium red body; white lettering; large white rectangle at center with red DuPont logo and "ALATHON" in black;

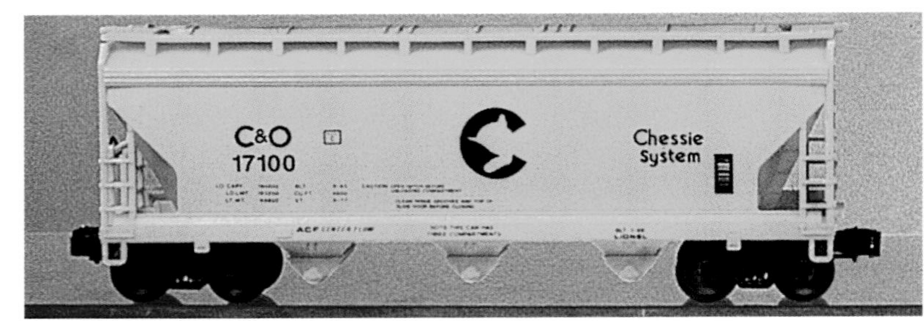

17100 C&O Chessie System ACF hopper

Exc Mt

Standard O trucks; "BLT 1-90". Came only with 11713 Santa Fe Dash 8 set. Original production had the word "POLYETHYLENE" under "ALATHON" spelled without the first "E". This can be seen on the prototype in the catalog. Lionel corrected this on most subsequent pieces by painting a black strip over the error and reprinting the correct word in white. This also resulted in some fun missed steps:

(A) "POLYETHYLENE". **70 80**

(B) "POLYTHYLENE". Rare variation. **NRS**

(C) Factory Error. One side "POLYETHYLENE", other side "POLYTHYLENE"! R. Feneran Collection. **NRS**

(D) Factory Error. One side "POLYETHYLENE", other side has no lettering on blank white stripe. R. Jorjorian Collection. **NRS**

17004 MKT: 1991, ACF two-bay center-flow hopper; dark green body; yellow lettering; large "MKT" at center; car also has end lettering; Standard O trucks; "BLT 1-91". **35 40**

17005 CARGILL: 1992, ACF two-bay center-flow hopper; cream–light tan colored body; brown lettering and Cargill teardrop logo in center; car includes end lettering; Standard O trucks; "BLT 1-92". **35 40**

17006 SOO LINE: 1993, ACF two-bay center-flow hopper; light gray body; black and green lettering; "SOO LINE" in large green letters in center; yellow wheat stalk logo at lower right; "A Soo Line Colormark Car" in script lettering at upper left; Standard O trucks; "BLT 1-93" on frame. Part of 11738 Soo Line Service Station Special set from 1993.

(A) As described. **50 60**

(B) Factory Error. Missing wheat stalk. H. Hickok Collection. **NRS**

17007 GREAT NORTHERN: 1994, ACF two-bay center-flow hopper; light gray body; black lettering; red, white, and black mountain goat circle logo to right; number on the car is "173872"; 17007 is not on the car; Standard O trucks; "BLT 1-94". **35 45**

17008 DENVER & RIO GRANDE: 1995, ACF two-bay center-flow hopper; light gray body; black lettering; "Rio Grande wind logo and "the ACTION road" underscored to right side; number on the car is "10009"; 17008 is not on the car; Standard O trucks; "BLT 95". Lionel billed this as a "great accompaniment" to the 18222 DRG SD-50 diesel also released in 1995. **30 40**

17100 C&O CHESSIE SYSTEM: 1988, ACF three-bay center-flow hopper; new "stretched" design based on the two-bay models introduced in 1986; bright yellow body; dark blue lettering and Chessie cat logo; Standard O trucks; "BLT 1-88" with bar code. Part of 11705 Chessie System unit train, which also included the following four cars. See also 17105 added later. This and the Burlington Northern Limited set from 1985 were Lionel's first real forays into the "unit" train concept. **45 55**

17107 DuPont Sclair ACF hopper

Exc Mt

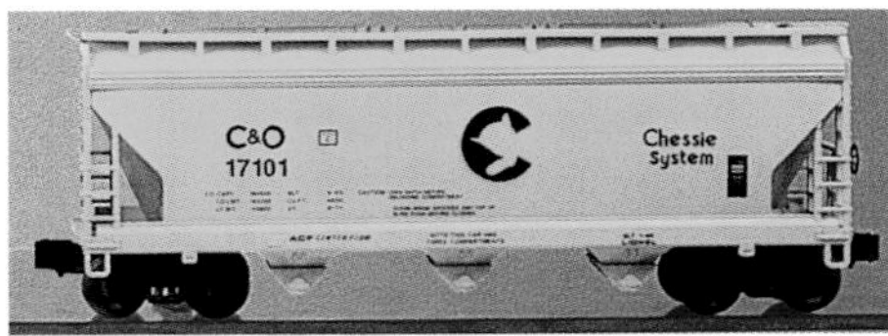

17101 C&O CHESSIE SYSTEM: 1988, ACF three-bay center-flow hopper; matches 17100 above. Part of 11705 Chessie System unit train. **45 55**

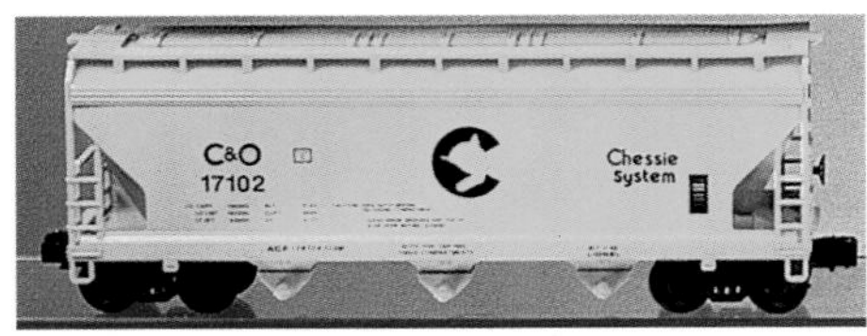

17102 C&O CHESSIE SYSTEM: 1988, ACF three-bay center-flow hopper; matches 17100 above. Part of 11705 Chessie System unit train. **45 55**

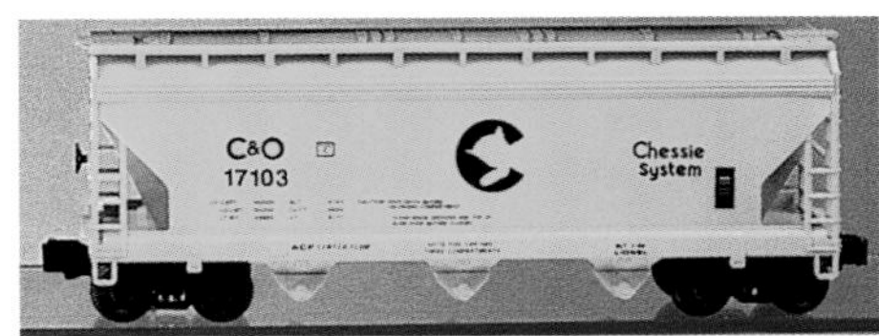

17103 C&O CHESSIE SYSTEM: 1988, ACF three-bay center-flow hopper; matches 17100 above. Part of 11705 Chessie System unit train. **45 55**

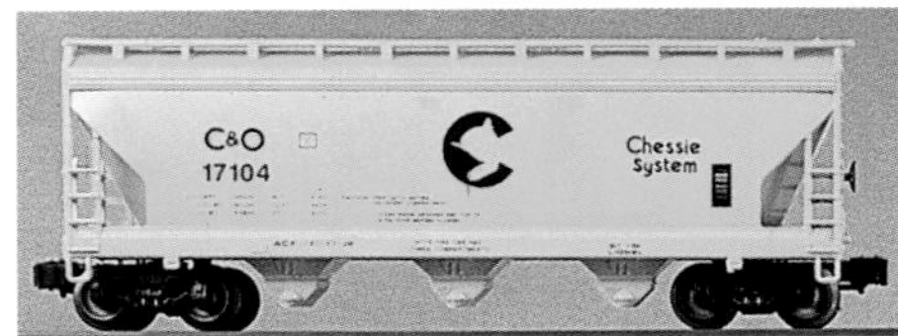

17104 C&O CHESSIE SYSTEM: 1988, ACF three-bay center-flow hopper; matches 17100 above. Part of 11705 Chessie System unit train. **45 55**

Exc Mt

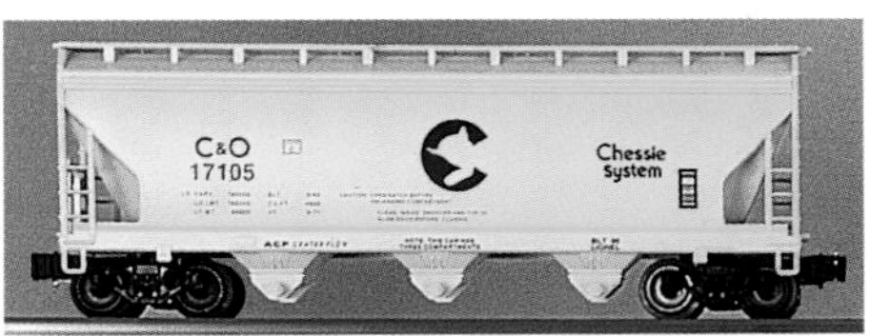

17105 C&O CHESSIE SYSTEM: 1995, ACF three-bay center-flow hopper; matches 17100 above; "BLT 95". Intended as an add-on to 1988's 11705 Chessie System unit train. See description under 17100. **40 50**

17107 DUPONT SCLAIR: 1989, ACF three-bay center-flow hopper; orange body; broad diagonal white stripe with black highlights; overstamped black lettering "sclair" and DUPONT POLYETHYLENE"; "DOCX 17107" to lower left; car was cataloged as 17000, but made as 17107; extensive decals with chemical data to right; Standard O trucks; "BLT 1-89". Came only with the 11710 CP Rail Freight set. The bright orange color of this car is a strange combination with the dark red of the other set components. **70 90**

17108 SANTA FE: 1990, ACF three-bay center-flow hopper; brown body; white lettering; large "Santa Fe" at center; extensive capacity, load, and operations data; Standard O trucks; "BLT 1-90". Available only with 11713 Santa Fe Dash 8 set. **60 70**

17109 NORFOLK & WESTERN: 1991, ACF three-bay center-flow hopper; gray body; black lettering with "NORFOLK AND WESTERN" spelled out; car also has end lettering; Standard O trucks; "BLT 1-91". **25 35**

Exc Mt

17110 UNION PACIFIC: 1991, 48-foot three-bay Standard O hopper with coal load; new design near-scale model of prototype 48-foot-long hoppers with ribbed sides; tuscan-maroon body; white lettering; detailed coal load; metal brakewheel; Standard O trucks; "BLT 1-91". Entirely new hopper car model produced by Lionel in response to hobbyists' interest in O scale modeling of modern prototypes. The heavily ribbed sides and detail of this 11½-inch-long car make it a good match for the ribbed Standard O boxcars also released starting in 1991. **30 40**

17111 READING: 1991, 48-foot three-bay Standard O hopper with coal load; new design near-scale model of prototype 48-foot-long hoppers with ribbed sides; black body; white lettering; detailed coal load; metal brakewheel; Standard O trucks; "BLT 1-91". See 17110 above for other notes on this model.
35 45

17112 ERIE LACKAWANNA: 1992, ACF three-bay center-flow hopper; gray body; black lettering; "E" diamond logo in black to right side; car includes end lettering; Standard O trucks; "BLT 1-92". **30 40**

17113 LEHIGH VALLEY: 1992–93, 48-foot three-bay Standard O hopper with coal load; ribbed sides; light gray body; black lettering; small red LV flag logo at center; detailed coal load; Standard O trucks; "BLT 1-92". See 17110 above for other notes. Planned for 1992 but delayed until '93. **40 50**

17114 PEABODY: 1992–93, 48-foot three-bay Standard O hopper with coal load; ribbed sides; bright yellow body with green lower portion and orange highlight stripe; black lettering; detailed coal load; Standard O trucks; "BLT 1-92". See 17110 above for other notes. Planned for 1992 but delayed until '93. The bright color scheme on this long hopper has made it a popular item, now somewhat hard to find. **50 60**

Exc Mt

17118 ARCHER DANIELS MIDLAND: 1993, ACF three-bay center-flow hopper; medium blue body; white lettering; blue and white ADM flame logo at center; black and white capacity data; number on the car is "60029"; car has end lettering; Standard O trucks; "BLT 1-93". **35 45**

17120 CSX: 1994, 48-foot three-bay Standard O hopper with coal load; ribbed sides; black body; yellow lettering "COKE EXPRESS" across top; "CSX" underscored at right; "295110" is the number on the car; 17120 is not on the car; detailed coal load; Standard O trucks; "BLT 1-94". See 17110 above for other notes on this model. **30 40**

17121 ILLINOIS CENTRAL GULF: 1994, 48-foot three-bay Standard O hopper with coal load; ribbed sides; orange body; black lettering; large black and white I-beam logo at right center; "72867" is the number on the car; 17121 is not on the car; detailed coal load; Standard O trucks; "BLT 1-94". See 17110 above for other notes on this model. **30 40**

17122 ROCK ISLAND: 1994, ACF three-bay center-flow hopper; light blue body; black and white lettering; "THE ROCK" in white to upper left; large black and white hexagon "R" logo to right side; "800200" is the number on the car; 17122 is not on the car; Standard O trucks; "BLT 1-94". **35 45**

Exc Mt

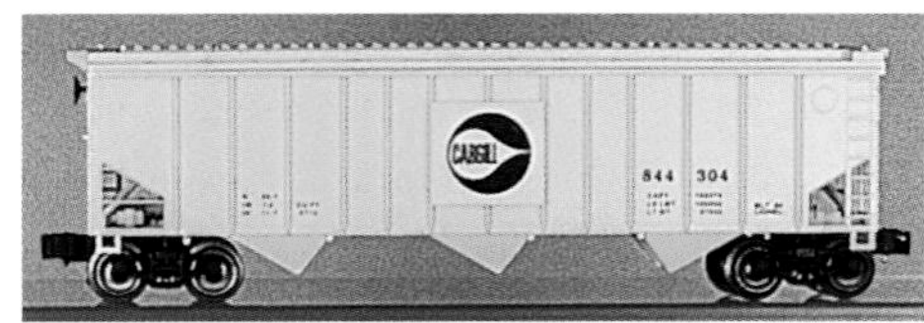

17123 CARGILL: 1995, 48-foot three-bay Standard O hopper with cover; ribbed sides; yellow body; black lettering; large black Cargill teardrop logo on new center nameplate; "844304" is the number on the car; 17123 is not on the car; new design detailed roof piece, a first for this car type; Standard O trucks; "BLT 95". Compare to 17005 ACF hopper. The catalog shows the nameplate to left of center. **35 45**

17124 ARCHER DANIELS MIDLAND: 1995, ACF three-bay center-flow hopper; gray body; black and white lettering; "ADM BioProducts" flame logo to right center; "50224" is the number on the car; 17124 is not on the car; Standard O trucks; "BLT 95". Car is a match with the 17118 ADM car from 1993. **35 45**

17125 GOODYEAR: 1995, ACF three-bay center-flow hopper; a gray and blue prototype is visible on page 68 of the 1995 catalog, but the car never reached production, probably because of licensing hurdles. **Not Manufactured**

19302 MILWAUKEE ROAD: 1987, quad hopper with coal load; yellow body; black lettering and "America's Resourceful Railroad" to upper right; Standard O trucks; "BLT 1-87". Part of Milwaukee Fallen Flags set no. 2, whose components were all sold separately. **35 40**

19303 LIONEL LINES: 1987, quad hopper with coal load; uncataloged; dark blue body with bright orange-painted sides; blue ends and bottom; red, white, and blue Lionel "L" logo to right side; dark blue lettering; Symington-Wayne trucks; "BLT 1-87". Part of a year-end package deal for 1987. Two shades of blue have been observed in the "L" decal—dark and light blue. It is not known which is scarcer. This car is considered part of the separate-sale "Lionel Lines" set, whose components have been issued over a long period beginning in 1982. **30 40**

19304 GREAT NORTHERN: 1988, covered quad hopper; light gray body and cover; black lettering; red and white circular "goat" logo to right side; Standard O trucks; "BLT 1-88". Part of Great Northern Fallen Flags set no. 3, whose components were all sold separately. **35 45**

19309 SEABOARD: 1989, covered quad hopper; very light gray body and cover; black lettering; Symington-Wayne trucks; "BLT 1-89". **20 25**

19310 LANCASTER & CHESTER: 1989, quad hopper with coal load; light blue body; white stripe at top; blue and white lettering; detailed oval L&C logo in center; Symington-Wayne trucks; "BLT 1-89". **25 30**

19311 SOUTHERN PACIFIC: 1990, covered quad hopper; light gray body; red lettering; "SOUTHERN PACIFIC" in large letters at right; red SP Lines circle logo to left; ASF trucks; "BLT 1-90". **20 25**

19312 READING: 1990, quad hopper with coal load; black body;

Exc Mt

white lettering; large "READING" at top center; red, white, and black Reading Lines logo at upper right; under- and over-scored number; ASF trucks; "BLT 1-90". This car has a somewhat higher price and scarcity than other regular-issue hoppers, since railfans would buy many of them to create realistic Reading coal trains. **25 35**

19316 WABASH: 1991, covered quad hopper; gray body; red lettering; large "WABASH" at top center; red, white, and blue Wabash flag logo at top right; under- and overscored number; ASF trucks; "BLT 1-91". **20 25**

19317 LEHIGH VALLEY: 1991, quad hopper with coal load; lilac (light purple) body; darker purple lettering; "LV" in diamond to right side; number under- and overscored; Standard O trucks; "BUILT BY LIONEL" with "NEW 1-91". Reissue of the postwar 6436-57, which was part of the Girls' set in 1957. The modern car was part of the 1991 reincarnation of that set—the 11722 Girls' Train. The original 6436-57 is, of course, extremely hard to find in good condition, as are all the components of the 1957 Girl's set. **50 65**

19318 NICKEL PLATE ROAD: 1992, quad hopper with coal load; black body; white lettering; Standard O trucks; "BLT 1-92". Part of the Nickel Plate Fallen Flags Series no. 6, whose components were all sold separately. **30 35**

19319 UNION PACIFIC: 1992, covered quad hopper; tuscan-brown body; white lettering; ASF trucks; "BLT 1-92". **20 25**

19324 ERIE: 1993, quad hopper with coal load; black body; white lettering; name and number over- and underscored at center; yellow "ERIE" diamond logo in yellow to upper right; Standard O trucks; "BLT 1-93". Part of Erie Fallen Flags Series no. 7, whose components were all sold separately. **30 35**

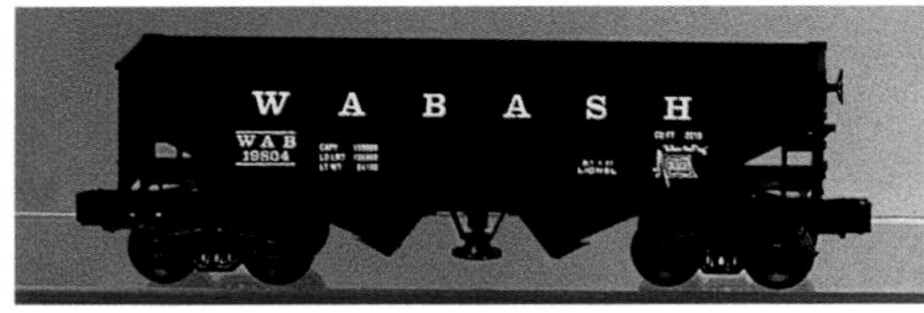

19804 WABASH: 1987, operating short hopper; black body;

Exc Mt

white/gray lettering and Wabash flag logo; number over-and underscored; magnetically activated plunger under car opens hinged covers on the hopper bays; Standard O trucks; "BLT 1-87". **35 40**

19806 PENNSYLVANIA: 1988, operating short hopper; light gray body; black lettering and keystone logo at upper right; magnetically activated plunger under car opens hinged covers on the hopper bays; Standard O trucks; "BLT 1-88". **35 45**

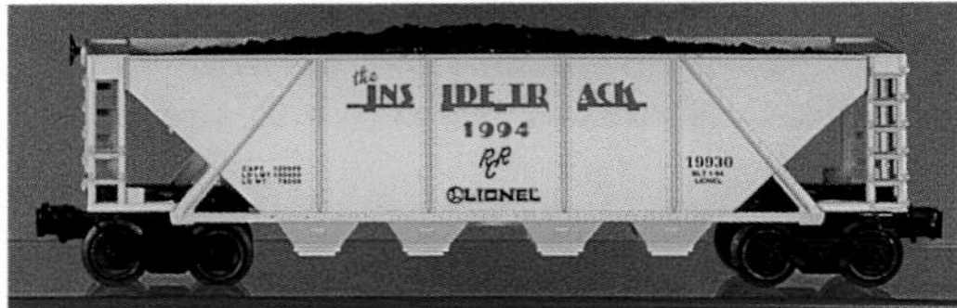

19930 LIONEL RAILROADER CLUB: 1994, quad hopper with coal load; uncataloged; mustard yellow body; red and black lettering; "the INSIDE TRACK / 1994" in red at upper center; black "RRC" and Lionel logos at lower center; ASF trucks; "BLT 1-94". Special annual car for the Lionel Railroader Club (LRRC), available only through the LRRC newsletter. **35 40**

19962 SOUTHERN PACIFIC: 1992, ACF three-bay center-flow hopper; uncataloged; gray body; black lettering; "496035" is the number on the car; "CAL STEWART 1992" on frame; Standard O trucks; "BLT 2-65"; car is a special to mark the 1992 Cal-Stewart meet of the TTOS's Southwest Division. **70 80**

19963 UNION EQUITY: 1992, ACF three-bay center-flow hopper; uncataloged; medium yellow body; dark green lettering; white, green, and yellow Union Equity hexagon logo to right side; TTOS 92 Convention logo to lower right; Standard O trucks; "BLT 8-92". Annual convention car for the Toy Train Operating Society (TTOS) to mark its 1992 Oklahoma convention. **50 60**

51501 BALTIMORE & OHIO: 1991, semi-scale all-metal quad hopper; part of a unique set of six semi-scale pieces offered in 1991–92, a rerelease of the famous scale rolling stock initially made in 1940 in conjunction with the original Lionel Hudson 700E made in 1939; black zinc die-cast body; white lettering; "B & O" and number over- and underscored to left side; "BALTIMORE & OHIO" to right; number on the car is "532000"; 51501 is in small letters lower on the car; four operating hinged and spring-loaded hopper bay doors (no mechanism to open them, however); Standard O trucks; "NEW 3-27". Difficult to find. Similar to the prewar company's plan, these modern versions of the semi-scale cars were released the year after the

	Exc	Mt

scale Hudson appeared (in this case the 1-700E in 1990). The originals were prewar Lionel's first attempt at true scale railroad models. **100 125**

52001 BOSTON & MAINE: 1992, quad hopper with coal load; uncataloged special for the New England Division of the TCA; gray body; black lettering; same as 16407 from 1991, except with coal load substituted for cover, and with added NETCA markings; Standard O trucks; "BLT 1-91". **50 75**

52023 D&TS: 1993, ACF two-bay center-flow hopper; uncataloged; gray body; black lettering; "EXPRESSWAY FOR INDUSTRY" underscored at center; red and white Detroit & Toledo Shore Line decal to right; considerable technical detail stamped on car in various places, including lower bay hatches; "2601" is number on the car, not 52023; Standard O trucks; "NEW 7-93". Annual convention car for the Lionel Collectors Club of America (LCCA) for their 1993 Dearborn convention. **45 55**

52031 FORD: 1994, short hopper; uncataloged; black body; white lettering and "Ford" in script at upper center; "FDRX 1458" under- and overscored on left side; 52031 is not on the car; ASF trucks; "BLT 8-94". Special car to mark the TTOS Dearborn convention in 1994. Part of a unique three-car O27 set with the 52030 gondola and the 52029 tank car, all identically decorated. Each car was individually boxed in a larger set box, which was cataloged as 52028. **30 35**

52038 SOUTHERN: 1994, 48-foot three-bay Standard O hopper with coal load; uncataloged; brown-tuscan body; ribbed sides; white lettering with "SOUTHERN" in large block letters; "Central of Georgia Div." notation to upper left; number on car is "360794" not 52038; Chattanooga convention notation on ends; Standard O trucks; no BLT date. Annual convention car for the LCCA, to mark their 1994 Tennessee show. **40 55**

52059 CLINCHFIELD: 1994, quad hopper with coal load; uncataloged; black body; white lettering; "16413" is the number on the car, which is the same as the virtually identical regular-release car from 1994; this special version has additional Eastern Division York meet notations; ASF trucks; "BLT 1-94; special for the banquet at the TCA's National Convention in York, which was sponsored by its Eastern Division. See also 16413. **110 130**

CHAPTER 15

Log and Coal Dump Cars

The Lionel modern era log dump car is modeled after the late postwar Lionel Corporation examples, particularly the 3361. It is an all-plastic car with an open-frame flatcar body (mold number 6362) and a central log cradle released by a spring-loaded plunger. A single brakewheel is mounted low on the frame at one end. When the magnet in an operating track pulls down the plunger, the cradle tilts and dumps its load into a waiting trackside bin. The early modern era cars (through 1987) featured wooden dowels representing the log loads on the car. Recently, Lionel used more realistic logs (actually, small branches!) on the cars, a trick that postwar Lionel applied on its log dump cars until 1962. The operating mechanism is simple and reliable enough, but the loose logs have a tendency to fall off the car at higher train speeds on curves, so the user must decide whether to run the trains, and tie down the logs, or operate the car with loose logs and risk unplanned off-loading! The car arrives with somewhat unsightly rubber bands or tie-wraps holding the logs to the cradle. Some more recent cars are supplied with nice chain-link wraps.

The "real" logs on later cars proved sufficiently popular that Lionel released them as an individual "accessory"—item no. 12740.

The log dump cars made by modern Lionel have come in a nice variety of roadnames. As a group they are very available and inexpensive, with the exception of the special Milwaukee Road car produced for LOTS in 1988. This car is rare.

The coal dump car is essentially a modified log dump car, with a tilting coal bin attached to the cradle and two snap-in bulkhead pieces, which include brakewheels, on the flatcar. There is no comparable postwar piece, since the Lionel Corporation principally used its die-cast metal coal dump cars. A significant operating problem, which Lionel has yet to fix, concerns the hinge on the side of the dump bin which opens to release the coal when the mechanism tilts. This hinge is made of fragile plastic and breaks easily. Users must handle this area carefully. Also, as with most of the coal-related cars and accessories Lionel has produced since prewar times, operators should take care to avoid an explosion of the coal all over their layouts. The plastic coal that Lionel supplies with these cars—and for separate-sale—is made of PVC plastic pellets, which tend to pick up static electricity and stick to everything, including the operator.

Both the log and coal dump cars come in special oversized boxes, since both come with loads and with a 2160-type trackside bin.

The modern coal dump cars do not, as a rule, interest collectors a great deal. The recent models bear little resemblance to, and do not operate as well as, the die-cast black postwar 3469. Thousands of 3469s can still be found, a fact that may explain the lukewarm reception the modern cars have received.

The numbering on these cars has been fairly consistent in the modern era—all within the 16600- and 16700-series, since they are considered operating cars. An exception was the special-issue LOTS car in 1988. Since the 16600- and 16700-series have been exhausted, future cars of this type will probably show up in the 36000-series.

The interest in the cars is variable, so Lionel has had to be cautious in its releases. A disproportionate number of coal and log dump cars have been announced but then not made because of lack of orders.

However, Lionel has produced a surprisingly large group of log and coal dump cars since 1987. Budget-minded collectors can put together a good set of these cars for a reasonable price, with Lionel releasing them on the average of one of each type per year.

LOG AND COAL DUMP CAR LISTINGS

Exc Mt

16600 ILLINOIS CENTRAL: 1988, coal dump car; black flatcar base with white lettering; orange dump bin and bulkheads; white I-beam logo on bin; trackside bin and simulated coal included; Symington-Wayne trucks. "BLT 1-88". Catalog hints at a brown body, but it was made black. **15 25**

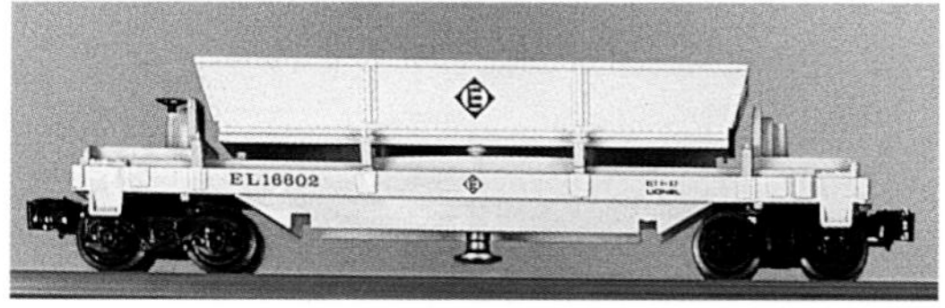

16602 ERIE LACKAWANNA: 1987, coal dump car; gray flatcar and bin; gray bulkheads; maroon lettering and diamond "E" logo; trackside bin and simulated coal included; Symington-Wayne trucks; "BLT 1-87". With this car, modern Lionel returned to outfitting its coal-dump car line with two operating couplers. From 1974 through 1987, all the coal and log dump cars had one dummy coupler. **15 25**

16604 NEW YORK CENTRAL: 1987, log dump car; black flatcar and cradle; white "N Y C" lettering and number; three stained

	Exc	Mt

dowels and 2160 trackside bin included; Symington-Wayne trucks; "BLT 1-87". Separate-sale item, but matches rolling stock in the 1502 Yard Chief set from 1985. **15** **25**

16607 SOUTHERN: 1987, coal dump car; uncataloged; black body and bulkheads; dark green dump bin; gold lettering on car body and gold Southern herald on bin; Standard O trucks, a first for this car; "BLT 1-87". Part of 11704 Southern Freight Runner Service Station Special set. The number on this car—and also on the box—was incorrectly printed as 16707, while Lionel carries it in its records as 16607. N. Bonadies and R. Wolf comment. **20** **30**

16611 SANTA FE: 1988, log dump car; blue flatcar body with white lettering; yellow log cradle (the only log dump car with a different-colored cradle); three realistic logs (for the first time on this car since 1962); trackside bin included; Symington-Wayne trucks; cataloged in 1988, but "BLT 1-89". **15** **25**

16612 SOO LINE: 1989, log dump car; light brown body and log cradle; white lettering "SOO LINE"; three real wood logs and dump bin; Symington-Wayne trucks; "BLT 1-89". **15** **25**

16613 MKT: 1989, coal dump car; black body and dump bin and bulkheads; white lettering; "The Katy" in script on bin; simulated coal and trackside bin included; Symington-Wayne trucks; "BLT 1-89". **15** **25**

16619 WABASH: 1990, coal dump car; dark gray body; brown bulkheads; brown bin with white Wabash flag; simulated coal and trackside bin included; ASF trucks; "BLT 1-90". **15** **25**

	Exc	Mt

16621 ALASKA: 1990, log dump car; translucent unpainted yellow body and cradle; black lettering "ALASKA RAILROAD" and round ARR logo; three real wood logs and trackside bin included; ASF trucks; "BLT 1-90". Some collectors disliked the "toy" appearance of the bright yellow plastic on this car, a result of Lionel skipping the paint step. **20** **25**

16627 CSX: 1990, log dump car; dark blue flatcar and log cradle; white lettering "CSX"; three real wood logs and trackside bin included; ASF trucks; "BLT 1-90". Part of 11717 CSX Freight set. **20** **25**

16634 WESTERN MARYLAND: 1991, coal dump car; brown body with white "WM" logo; red-orange coal bin with "WESTERN MARYLAND" in white; red-orange bulkheads; simulated coal load and trackside bin included; ASF trucks; "BLT 1-91". Can be added to the Western Maryland Fallen Flags no. 4 set; listed in the 1990 catalog but delayed until 1991. **25** **30**

16636 RIO GRANDE: 1991, log dump car; orange body and log cradle; black lettering "Rio Grande"; three real wood logs and trackside bin included; ASF trucks; "BLT 1-91". **20** **25**

16643 AMTRAK: 1991, coal dump car; cataloged with black body, white lettering, number and "Amtrak" logo; orange coal dump bin and bulkheads. Lionel called it a "ballast dump car" because there is no reason for Amtrak to haul coal around! Pictured in the 1991 catalog as part of the 11723 Amtrak Maintenance Train set. This set was not made until 1992, when it appeared in the 1992 Stocking Stuffers brochure. At that point Lionel must have realized the inconsistency, and replaced this car with a wheel-rack flatcar (16369) in the released set. **Not Manufactured**

16656 BURLINGTON: 1992, log dump car; uncataloged; green flatcar body; white lettering; green log cradle; three real wood logs and dump bin; ASF trucks; "BLT 1-92"; car appeared in the 1992 Stocking Stuffers brochure, where it is offered in an "Operating Car Assortment"—as catalog number 16695, with the 16657 Lehigh Valley coal dump car described below. **20** **25**

16657 LEHIGH VALLEY: 1992, coal dump car; uncataloged; dark gray flatcar body; white lettering; light gray bulkheads and coal bin with white "LEHIGH VALLEY" lettering; simulated coal and dump bin; ASF trucks; "BLT 1-92"; car appeared in the 1992 Stocking Stuffers brochure, where it is offered in an "Operating Car Assortment"—as catalog number 16695, with the 16656 Burlington log car described above. The car has been found disassembled in its box, because of poor packaging. **20** **25**

Exc Mt

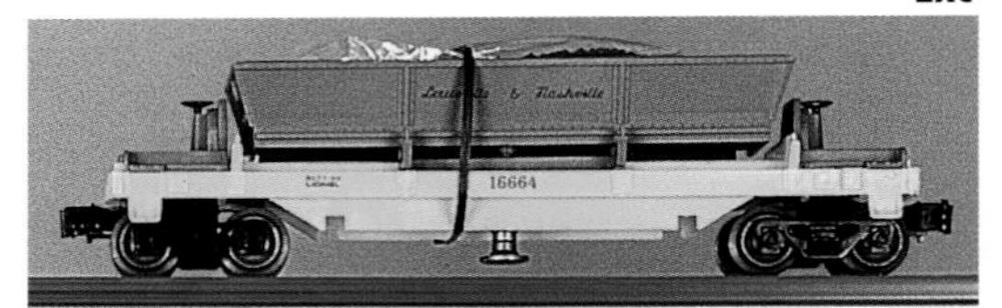

16664 LOUISVILLE & NASHVILLE: 1993, coal dump car; yellow body with red lettering; gray coal bin with script "Louisville & Nashville" in red; gray bulkheads; simulated coal load and trackside bin included; ASF trucks; "BLT 1-93". **25 30**

16665 MAINE CENTRAL: 1993, log dump car; green flatcar and log cradle; white lettering; three real wood logs and trackside bin included; ASF trucks; "BLT 1-93". **25 30**

16668 ONTARIO NORTHLAND: 1993, log dump car; green flatcar and log cradle; white lettering; three real wood logs and trackside bin included; ASF trucks; "BLT 1-93". No individual box. Part of 11741 Northwest Express set. **25 30**

16675 GREAT NORTHERN: 1994, log dump car; dark green flatcar and log cradle; orange lettering; three real wood logs and trackside bin included; ASF trucks; "BLT 1-94". **25 30**

16676 CHICAGO, BURLINGTON & QUINCY: 1994, coal dump car; gray body with dark red lettering "BURLINGTON ROUTE"; vivid red coal bin and bulkheads large white "CB&Q" lettering on bin; simulated coal load and trackside bin included; ASF trucks; "BLT 1-94". **25 30**

16707: see 16607.

16713 GREAT NORTHERN: 1995, log dump car; orange flatcar and log cradle; green lettering—a reverse-color version of its 16675 predecessor from the year before, but never manufactured.
Not Manufactured

Exc Mt

16714 CHICAGO, BURLINGTON & QUINCY: 1995, coal dump car; red body with white lettering—a reverse-color version of its 16676 predecessor from the year before, but never manufactured.
Not Manufactured

16928 SOO LINE: 1995, flatcar with coal bin. See Flatcar chapter.

17874 MILWAUKEE ROAD: 1988, log dump car; uncataloged; ninth annual LOTS Convention car; first car for LOTS produced entirely by Lionel; tuscan body and log cradle; white lettering; three real wood logs with chains and spring, similar to postwar 6361 log carrier; number on car is "59629"; 17874 is not on car or box; Standard O trucks (first LOTS car and first modern-era log dump car with them); "BLT 1-88"; came in Type V box; 519 made. Quite hard to find. **120 150**

CHAPTER 16

Ore Cars

The introduction of a new small hopper car style in 1984 was noteworthy in that it demonstrated modern Lionel's intent to move into new areas and designs with its freight cars, rather than simply standing pat with tools and dies inherited from the postwar corporation.

The stubby little ore car, which appeared that year in Soo and Penn Central colors, is remarkably similar to its full-size prototype and features a wealth of molded details on its body, exceeding that of most other Lionel cars.

Ore cars are much shorter than standard coal hopper cars, and for a good reason: ore is much heavier than coal. If a full-size hopper were fully loaded with ore, the weight would exceed its limits and destroy the car. Railroads sometimes used coal hoppers for ore service, but loaded them only about two-thirds full.

The Lionel ore car is a fine model of the real thing, very similar to the Atlas/Rivarossi scale O cars, which have been around for some time. Collectors have noted one aesthetic aspect of the Lionel cars, however: the bodies ride somewhat too high—proportionally—on their trucks, a fact that is visually exaggerated by the car's short length. The regular hoppers ride at the same height, but it is less obvious because of their length. The Lionel ore car is 6 inches long, sans couplers, compared to 8½ inches for the shortest hoppers, and more than 10 for the long quad hoppers

The majority of these cars have been produced since the corporate hand-over to Lionel Trains, Inc., in 1986. They have become a very important constituent of Lionel's freight line since then.

Ore cars have been brisk sellers for several very good reasons. They are inexpensive and prototypical and operators can buy whole fleets of them for unit trains. This has led to an increase in value of some of the cars, but most are still readily available, so they are still a good opportunity for beginners and experienced collectors alike. Lionel itself has recognized the unit train potential, offering several fleets of ore cars in sets in the 1990s, with each car individually numbered.

The early modern era ore cars came without loads, but recent ones have featured nice simulated ore loads in light and dark colors, and loads have been offered in the accessory line to add to the cars that didn't have them.

Several ore cars were made for the train clubs and are thus somewhat harder to find. Most notable is a wonderful series produced by the Gadsden Pacific Division, Inc., in support of their Toy Train Operating Museum in Tucson, Arizona. Each car is lettered for real mining companies in Arizona. An interesting twist here is that the series "appears" to start with an Anaconda car, which was TTOS's National Convention car in 1988. But in fact the Anaconda car—representing one of Arizona's largest mining concerns—is not part of the annual Museum series. Thereafter, the GP Division, a nonprofit group based in Tucson, began to sponsor its own set of ore cars, and has produced them since 1989 strictly as fundraisers for the museum. The organization is not affiliated with TTOS, though the confusion is understandable considering the name of the Museum (the TTOM), and the fact that TTOS has a GP Division, as well as the existence of the Anaconda car in the first place. Another interesting footnote about them is that the boxes in which the cars were released have labels misspelled "GASDEN"—without the first "D". In a few years, Lionel gave up fighting with the annoying spelling by just labeling them "GP series"!

ORE CAR LISTINGS

Exc Mt

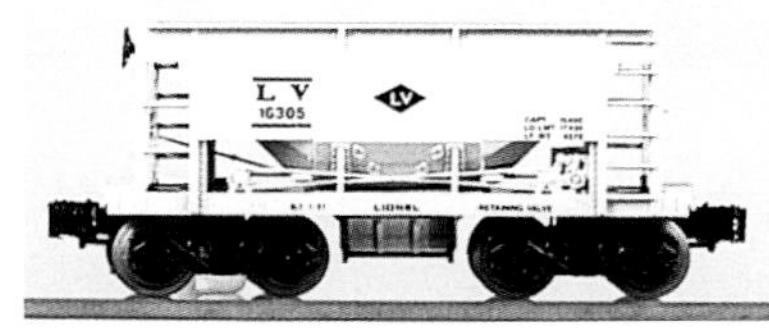

16305 LEHIGH VALLEY: 1987, ore car; gray body; black lettering and diamond logo; no load; Symington-Wayne trucks; "BLT 1-87". Came only in set 11702, the Black Diamond. Quite hard to find. **90 110**

16385 SOO LINE: 1993, ore car, gray body, black lettering; no load; ASF trucks; "BLT 1-93". Came only in set 11741, the Northwest Express. Somewhat hard to find. **55 65**

16800 LIONEL RAILROADER CLUB: 1986, ore car; uncataloged; fifth annual special issue from the Lionel Railroader Club (LRRC); yellow body; black lettering; steam engine logo at lower center; "SPECIAL EDITION / THE INSIDE TRACK" at lower left; no load; Symington-Wayne trucks; "BLT 10-86". The "Inside Track" is the LRRC's newsletter. This may have been one of the first Lionel cars numbered with five digits, and one of the first released in a Type VI box, though some models have also come in a Type V box. Somewhat harder to find than the other LRRC cars. **75 90**

Exc Mt

17872 ANACONDA: 1988, ore car; uncataloged; special commemorative for TTOS National Convention in Tucson, Arizona; reddish-brown body; no load; white lettering; frame reads "TTOS 88 / CONV CAR"; number on the car is "81988"; Symington-Wayne trucks; "BLT 1-88"; 1824 made. This car is often associated with the Gadsden-Pacific Division, Inc.'s series of annual "Museum" ore cars, but it is not in fact part of the series.

(A) As described. **70 90**

(B) Factory error. No lettering on one side. D. Mareck collection. **NRS**

17878 MAGMA: 1989, ore car; uncataloged; black body; white lettering; frame reads "GP 89 MUSEUM CAR"; light gray ore load; Symington-Wayne trucks; "BLT 1-89"; 1701 made. This is the first in the series of annual ore cars produced by the Gadsden Pacific Division, Inc., a nonprofit corporation in Arizona, as a fundraiser for its Toy Train Operating Museum in Tucson. This organization is not affiliated with the TTOS. **65 80**

17881 PHELPS-DODGE: 1990, ore car; uncataloged; light gray body; black lettering; white ore load; frame reads "GP 90 Museum Car"; ASF trucks; "BLT 1-90"; approx. 1500 made. Second in the GPD Museum series of ore cars. **40 50**

17886 CYPRUS: 1991, ore car; uncataloged; silver body; royal blue and black lettering; frame reads "GP 91 Museum Car"; white ore load; ASF trucks; "BLT 1-91". Third in the GPD Museum series. **40 50**

Exc Mt

19300 PENNSYLVANIA: 1987, ore car; tuscan body; white lettering; white PRR keystone logo; Symington-Wayne trucks; "BLT 1-87". **20 25**

19301 MILWAUKEE ROAD: 1987, ore car; red oxide–orange body; white lettering; no load; Symington-Wayne trucks; "BLT 1-87". Sold separately, this item is also frequently used with the Milwaukee Fallen Flags set no. 2. **20 25**

19305 B&O CHESSIE SYSTEM: 1988, ore car; black body; yellow lettering, number and Chessie cat logo; no load; Symington-Wayne trucks; no "BLT" date. **20 25**

19307 B. & L.E.: 1989, ore car (Bessemer & Lake Erie); light brown body; white lettering and Bessemer I-beam logo to right side; came with copper-colored simulated ore load—first ore car so equipped; Symington-Wayne trucks; "BLT 1-89". **15 20**

19308 GREAT NORTHERN: 1989, ore car; tuscan body; white lettering; copper-colored ore load; Symington-Wayne trucks; "BLT1-89".

(A) As described. **15 20**

(B) Factory error. No printing on one side. J. Lambert Collection. **NRS**

	Exc	Mt

19313 B&O: 1990–91, ore car; black body; white lettering; large "B & O" at center; light brown ore load; ASF trucks; "BLT 1-90". 15 20

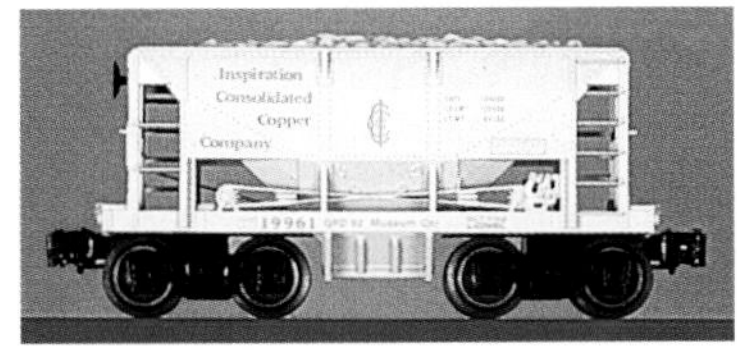

19315 AMTRAK: 1991, ore car; orange body; black lettering; gray ore load; ASF trucks; "BLT 1-91". Amtrak, principally a passenger line, does not use ore cars, though it has used versions of the two-bay hoppers for ballast maintenance. 20 25

19320 PENNSYLVANIA: 1992, ore car; tuscan body; white lettering; white PRR keystone logo; Standard O trucks; "BLT 1-92". This car is a virtual repeat of the 19300 from 1987, except that LTI installed a load and sprung metal trucks and brought the car into its Collector Line, as well as to a higher price point. 25 30

19321 B. & L.E.: 1992, ore car (Bessemer & Lake Erie); light brown body; white lettering and Bessemer I-beam logo to right side; Standard O trucks; "BLT 1-92". This car is a virtual repeat of the 19307 from 1989, except that LTI installed the sprung metal trucks and brought the car into its Collector Line. 25 30

19322 CHICAGO & NORTH WESTERN: 1993, ore car; tuscan body; white lettering; limestone ore load; ASF trucks; "BLT 1-93". 20 25

19323 DETROIT & MACKINAC: 1993, ore car; tuscan body; white lettering; maroon-colored gravel ore load; ASF trucks; "BLT 1-93". 20 25

19961 INSPIRATION CONSOLIDATED COPPER: 1992, ore car; uncataloged; light tan body; orange lettering; frame reads "GPD 92 Museum Car"; white ore load; ASF trucks; "BLT 1-92"; fourth in the GPD Museum series. The numbering of this car is unusual, since the 19900-series was generally reserved for particular series of boxcars, such as the "I Love" set and Christmas/Toy Fair cars. 35 45

52011 TUCSON, CORNELIA & GILA BEND: 1993, ore car; uncataloged; black body; yellow lettering; frame reads "GP 93 Museum Car"; white ore load; Standard O trucks, the first (and only) one in the GPD series to come with them; "BLT 1-93". Fifth in the GPD Museum series. 30 40

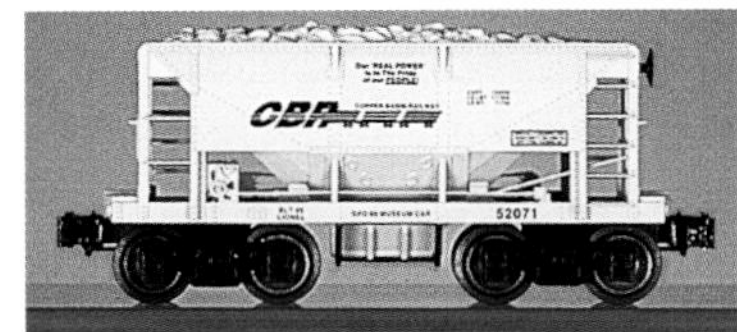

52027 PINTO VALLEY MINE: 1994, ore car; uncataloged; green body; white lettering; frame reads "GPD 94 Museum Car"; ore load; ASF trucks; "BLT 1-94". Sixth in the GPD Museum series. 30 35

52071 COPPER BASIN RAILWAY: 1995, ore car; uncataloged; gray body; white lettering; "Our REAL POWER is in the Pride of our PEOPLE!"; frame reads "GP 95 Museum Car"; white ore load; ASF trucks; "BLT 1-95". Seventh in the GPD Museum series. 35 40

CHAPTER 17

Passenger Cars

One of the real pleasures of tinplate railroading has always been to start up a train layout, turn off all the lights, and watch the action by night. If the layout were well-equipped, street and signal lights would shine, searchlights would beam onto the platform, and the locomotive would come flying around a curve, its headlight reflecting off the tracks. One could watch the locomotive speed past, followed by a long string of lighted passenger cars, possibly with small silhouettes of people in the windows.

Obviously, tinplate doth not live by freight cars alone. Passenger trains have been popular since the dawn of model railroading. The modern Lionel period at the end of the century has been no exception.

There are six major types of passenger cars made by modern Lionel, listed in approximate order of cost and complexity:

- Short streamlined O27 cars based on the postwar 2400-series
- Old-time passenger cars designated as General style
- Short versions of the Madison cars, which we call 9500-series
- Long, extruded-aluminum cars based on the postwar 2500-series
- Long heavyweight Pullman-style passenger cars similar to the late pre- and postwar Madison cars
- "Scale" heavyweight Pullman cars (1996 and later)

Each major style of car also has quite a subset of individual bodies, such as a standard coach, vista-dome cars (short and long varieties), diners, baggage cars, combine cars (passengers and baggage in the same car), and observation cars. Some sets had multiple coaches or vista dome cars, and the full collection could extend to impressive lengths.

The 9500-series short Madison cars, so named because of the number series in 1973 in which they first appeared, have recently come to be called "baby" Madisons as well, after the longer and scale-length Madison cars were resurrected in 1991.

"Madison" is the common name used by many Lionel hobbyists for this particular style of passenger coach. Some purists also call them "Irvington" cars, derived from the fact that the first cars of this type to appear in the late prewar years were named "Irvington," as were a good number of the postwar models. Lionel itself, however, called them "Madison."

All passenger cars, regardless of type, were part of, or were later additions to, passenger train sets, many of which have snappy names like the *Blue Comet,* the Southern Pacific *Daylight*, or the Burlington *Zephyr*. We have included brief descriptions of the sets and the common features and graphics on the cars of which they are made up.

SHORT (O27) STREAMLINED PASSENGER CARS

These cars, modeled on the old 2400-series of postwar years but without some of the detailing of the originals, were first reissued by Fundimensions in 1973 as part of the TCA's Bicentennial set. They had the same plastic wooden beam-style trucks as the earlier 9500-style cars (odd, since these were archaic trucks for cars of a modern design) and were illuminated. There wasn't a great emphasis on this type of car in the next ten years. After taking over in 1986, however, Lionel Trains, Inc., expanded this line considerably. In 1987 LTI made a handsome set of Pennsylvania 2400-series cars in authentic tuscan and black with gold lettering. To make sure that the lettering was bright and crisp, Lionel's factory workers stamped each side of every car three times, using the Tampo process. New Amtrak cars were made in 1988 as part of a Silver Spike set; and combines, baggage cars, and diners were made later for both sets.

In 1989 a six-car set of O27 passenger cars was made in two-tone New York Central gray. This set was popular despite some problems with the engine. Another O27 set in attractive forest green was released in 1990, this time lettered for the Northern Pacific. Still another set followed in 1991, decorated in the orange and brown of the Illinois Central.

Lionel's Great Lakes Express Service Station set from 1990 introduced the idea of roller pickups on both trucks—to improve the lighting in the cars and avoid the annoying flickering that the single-roller variety would encounter over the gaps at switches.

A great variety of individual body types are found in the O27 streamlined sets. They range from baggage cars (which were initially dark but began to be illuminated in 1991) to combine cars, to diner cars, to coaches, to observation cars, and two types of vista domes. The full-length vista dome made its appearance in 1995, and of course Lionel made good use of the opportunity to release full-domed add-ons to earlier sets, sometimes decades after they were first made.

Quite a few of these sets were released later in the 1990s. All can be found at reasonable prices today, and they are excellent choices for both the beginning and veteran collector.

GENERAL-STYLE PASSENGER CARS

This old-time car has rarely been used in the Lionel LTI/LLC periods, though it had been a staple in the Fundimensions period. They are faithful reproductions of the postwar issues. The 1988 Service Station set, the "Dry Gulch," features three of these cars in Virginia & Truckee markings. Another single baggage/combine car appeared in 1990's "Badlands" set, and TCA got into the act with a handsome General-style car issued for its 1990 Atlanta convention.

There are only two body types made for the General-style coaches, which explains why the sets released to date include only two or three cars. The two types are a standard coach and a baggage-coach combine car with large doors at each end.

9500-SERIES SHORT PASSENGER CARS

In 1973 Fundimensions began the production of its 9500-series passenger cars with the Milwaukee Special set. In this set, a 4-4-2 steam locomotive in Milwaukee Road markings pulled three orange Milwaukee passenger cars with maroon roofs and gold lettering. These cars were excellent models of the passenger coaches used during the 1920s on almost every American passenger railroad. They were lighted and highly detailed, with little vents in the clerestories, detailed closed vestibules, and translucent window inserts. A few sore points about the cars—from some traditionalists—were their length (it did not quite match the length of the classic pre- and postwar Madison cars) and their couplers. The couplers were non-operating and mounted directly onto the car bodies; if the track was not level or had rough spots, the cars could easily uncouple accidentally. Some operators went so far as to put twist-ties around the coupler knuckles to keep them together! If for any reason the coupler broke off and took the screw hole in the car with it, the operator was out of luck.

Other frustrating problems arose. At first, the firm found it had a problem with translucence of the plastic when the cars were lighted. If the cars were left unlined, the light would glow through the roofs and sides, creating an unsightly "blob" of light instead of the lighted window effect Lionel wanted. One early attempt to fix the problem involved painting the tops of the lightbulbs with heat-resistant silver paint. That did not work because it cut the light too much. To solve this problem as inexpensively as possible, Lionel designed a cardboard roof liner that would come down a little way over the sides inside the car and completely shade the roof. Overall, this fix worked well, except when the liner slid down to cover the windows, in which case the purchaser would have to laboriously pry open the roof pieces to push the liner back up to the roof. The liner eventually was extended down around the windows to avoid slipping. Overall, then, Lionel's 9500 passenger cars show four different schemes for shading the light in these cars, as follows (from Henry Edmunds):

- No cardboard roof liner present
- Unfinished plain cardboard liner
- White finished cardboard liner
- Unfinished yellow cardboard liner extending down the sides of the car with holes for the windows

Getting at the lightbulbs to change them was a horrendous problem never fully solved. The roof and translucent window pieces were made of one casting that snapped into the car bodies. At first, there were tabs on the car bottoms, but these actually had to be cut off to remove the roof. Later, the tabs were eliminated in favor of projections in the translucent window inserts, which snapped into the window frames. Even with this arrangement, getting the roofs off these cars has always been a job to tax the most patient of people.

Another less significant design quirk has led to several variation reports from collectors. The surface of the car body around the windows is inset from the surfaces above and below, making painting in this region more difficult (Lionel often paints the window strip a different color from the remaining body on the 9500-style cars). As a result, some cars have incomplete painting in this area.

The Milwaukee Special was followed during the next years by a *Broadway Limited* set with Pennsylvania cars in tuscan and black with gold lettering, and a *Capitol Limited* with Baltimore & Ohio cars in blue and gray with gold lettering. In 1976, full baggage cars were introduced. Diner cars were produced for all three sets in 1988 and 1989—12 years after the original production!

In 1977 the cars were finally changed to operating couplers. The next year, 1978, the *Blue Comet* set debuted with a significant improvement—die-cast six-wheel passenger trucks. Several changes were made to the casting of the car underside to accommodate these trucks, and unfortunately earlier cars cannot be retrofitted with them.

Despite the headaches, the "baby Madison" cars have been universally popular.

In 1986 Fundimensions released its last passenger set—six 9500-style Wabash cars in handsome dark blue and gray *Bluebird* colors pulled by a matching 4-6-2 Pacific steam engine. They were the first entries in the new "Fallen Flags" Series of special Collector sets, and remain the only passenger set in the Fallen Flags series. This particular set is still in demand today.

In the post-1986 era, modern Lionel has scaled down its production of these cars considerably, but has not abandoned them. Nice sets appeared in the mid-'90s in Chicago & North Western, Baltimore & Ohio, Norfolk & Western, and the always-popular New York Central two-tone gray. The latter came in a very well-received mixed freight passenger set in 1995.

There are five principal types of cars in the 9500-style Madison models—coaches, baggage cars, diners, combine cars, and observation cars. No vista domes exist. The diners were late additions, first appearing in 1987, and some of them are rather hard to find.

LONG EXTRUDED-ALUMINUM PASSENGER CARS

Nice as the Madison cars were, they were not the passenger cars everyone was waiting for early in the modern era, when the recovery of Lionel from its near-collapse in the 1960s was still in doubt. The wait for modern collectors ended in 1979 with the reissue of the big extruded-aluminum cars from the fabled *Congressional Limited* in beautiful Pennsylvania markings. Instead of the flat finish of the postwar issues, the new Lionel cars had a polished aluminum finish that looked great behind the Pennsylvania F-3 twin-motored diesels also produced that year. These cars were an outstanding success for Fundimensions, and it was inevitable that more would follow.

So it went for the next five years. A startling chrome Burlington *Zephyr* set was produced in 1981. One of the most breathtaking sets of all came the next year, when Fundimensions issued the "J"-class Norfolk & Western steam engine and six stunning aluminum *Powhatan Arrow* passenger cars painted deep maroon with black roofs and gold lettering and striping. Some collectors believe this set to be the most beautiful passenger set ever produced in tinplate. Unfortunately, the quality was reflected in the stiff price exacted for the cars, especially the diner, which was produced later in extremely limited quantities.

The follow-up to the *Powhatan Arrow* set was just as impressive. In 1982 Fundimensions produced a long-anticipated Southern Pacific *Daylight* set. Like the Norfolk & Western, the *Daylight* set has attracted a big following because of its beautiful red, orange, black, and silver color scheme.

By this time Fundimensions was really on a roll, producing set after beautiful set of these cars in colors and styles no postwar aluminum set could have hoped to match. In 1983 they changed the style of the cars. All of the previous aluminum cars had been made with fluted sides and roofs, just as their postwar predecessors were. With the New York Central cars of 1983, Fundimensions eliminated the scribing and produced the cars with smooth sides and roofs. Though they were very attractive, collectors soon voiced complaints about them. The smooth-sided cars would fingerprint very easily, and the paint on the cars would chip too easily, leaving unsightly aluminum marks through the paint. For many collectors the New York Central set represented a distinct decline in quality.

The next set, 1984's Union Pacific *Overland Limited,* sparked more complaints regarding poor color matching between the locomotives, doors, and the observation car. In addition, collectors complained that the red striping on the cars was very poorly applied, giving the smooth-sided cars a rather cheap look. Lionel was, in fact, having production problems at the time, with its ill-fated decision to move production to Mexico. It is unfortunate that such a fine set fell victim to the difficulties the factory was experiencing.

For 1985 Lionel rectified the error somewhat, but at the cost of repeating a successful formula until it wore out its welcome. That year saw the production of a smooth-sided set in brown and orange Illinois Central *City of New Orleans* colors. This time, at least, the quality was right; the colors looked very good and the set, pulled by a great-looking Illinois Central ABA trio, was impressive. So was the price. This was the sixth set issued as aluminum passenger cars pulled by F-3 premium diesels. The tremendous expense of these sets raised the question of how extensive the resources of modern era collectors really were.

Whether for that reason or because of the turmoil created by the management changeover, Lionel gave aluminum car collectors a brief rest. In 1989 a new set in Amtrak colors appeared, and this time the extruded bodies returned to the fluted side and roof designs of their pre-1983 predecessors. 1989 also saw the introduction of a new style body, the full-length vista dome, which looked much more realistic than the partial vista dome cars used earlier. In 1991 a new chrome Santa Fe set came out, 30 years after the last Santa Fe passenger cars disappeared from the postwar Lionel line. The new set marks several interesting firsts—the cars included the first use of silver-painted trucks, the F-3 diesels pulling the cars carried the first RailSounds electronics used in a passenger set, and the rear car was a very interesting brand new body style—a combination observation/vista dome design.

Lionel LTI followed up with one set every year thereafter: the Great Northern *Empire Builder* in 1992, the *California Zephyr* in 1993, a stunning Lackawanna set in 1994, and a re-issue of the *Powhatan Arrow,* this time on smooth-sided cars, in 1995.

Also making its debut in 1995 was a duplex roomette car, featuring simulated first-class accommodations. This brought the total of different aluminum carbodies to nine—baggage, combine, short and long vista dome, diner, coach, duplex, observation, and dome-observation. About that time Lionel also remodeled the observation cars on a few pieces (notably the cars in the TCA and NLOE special sets) to create an open chamber in the back, which was fitted with detailed furniture and sometimes a few passenger figures. Lionel called it a "Solarium" car.

As befits a top-of-the-line product, Lionel's long aluminum passenger cars contain the best features: illumination with silhouette window strips (except the baggage cars), heavy stamped-metal frames, and die-cast trucks with operating couplers. Of course, each set is pulled by the best of Lionel's massive steam and diesel engines. All extruded-aluminum passenger cars were available for separate-sale only, never in a set box. However, one operator caution: these cars, and several of the longer diesels, cannot negotiate O27 switches. Another caution is economic. The typical car will run buyers $100 and more, and when combined with the other set cars and the premium diesels usually matched to them, will set collectors back $1,000 or more.

These aluminum cars remain unfailingly popular among a wide range of Lionel hobbyists. Today, 50 years after their first appearance, they still make up some truly magnificent sets that illustrate the apex of tinplate achievement.

LONG HEAVYWEIGHT "MADISON" CARS

From 1973 through 1990 Lionel—if not all of its fans—had been content with the somewhat shortened versions of the famous Madison cars produced by the postwar company immediately before and after World War II. The story goes that the original dies for the cars had been lost, so that Lionel/Fundimensions was forced to create its own dies in 1973 in order to produce new passenger cars. The new ones, however, were 3 or 4 inches shorter than the originals. Still the modern company got great mileage out of their "baby Madison" passenger car sets, as we discussed above—many sets were produced, all quite successful.

But all through this period Lionel had been under competitive pressure from other manufacturers to produce longer, more scale-length versions of the heavyweight passenger cars, and collectors had been clamoring for a rerun of the original full-length Madison cars. They got their wish in 1991. Clearly, given the time needed to make new dies, Lionel must have been planning this event for some years.

The first modern set, in the same handsome tuscan colors as the 1940s versions, even included the Sager Place observation car that had been cataloged, but never made, in the early postwar era. The new cars were made in thick phenolic plastic, to simulate the heavy Bakelite plastic from which the originals were made, and which gave them their "heavyweight" nickname. Each car also had a detailed underbody mold with a prominent air tank. Unlike the smaller Madison sets, these models include operating doors. Later sets followed on the success of this first venture; trains in the bright colors of the Southern Pacific Daylight, the Pere Marquette, Wabash, and Pennsylvania were to follow. Thus far there have been only three car bodies made in this series—coaches and observation cars, with baggage cars following in 1993. Of course, vista-domes were never part of these classic-styled trains. A combine car may be in the future, though.

There is nothing in all of Lionel railroading quite like seeing a scale Hudson pulling a set of heavyweight Madison cars. Now, after a 50-year wait, modern Lionel hobbyists have new opportunities to witness this spectacle.

Overall, modern era Lionel has met the challenge of producing passenger cars extremely well. The beginning collector can secure quite a few passenger cars (aside from the longer Madison and aluminum ones) without severe damage to the wallet.

Passenger Car Numbering System

In the post-1986 five-digit era, Lionel decided to number its long extruded-aluminum cars (considered Collector pieces) in the 19100-series. The smaller O27 streamlined cars, the General-style coaches, and the short 9500-style Madison sets appear in the 16000-series. The 15100-series took over as the 16000-numbers ran out. Add-on diner cars made in the late 1980s for the 9500-series Madison sets have been given 19000-series numbers. Then that series began to be used for the long "heavyweight" Madison cars starting with the 19015-18 Lionel Lines cars.

Most passenger cars do not carry their catalog number. Only a very few carry a "BLT" date, as most freight cars do. These are usually the isolated coaches placed in mixed-freight trains.

All passenger cars have come in sets or have been issued as add-ons to sets.

A mention about uncataloged specials: Since most of the train clubs have shied away from passenger cars in their annual convention car series, there are relatively few uncataloged special passenger cars or sets. There are exceptions—for example, the TCA produced a distinctive set of orange and black long aluminum cars during the late 1990s.For the most part, though, the passenger cars and sets have been cataloged.

The number of distinct passenger sets has risen substantially in the post-1986 modern Lionel era, reflecting the customer's ongoing demand for these premium cars. Fundimensions produced about 22 sets in the period from 1970 through 1986. In contrast, Lionel LTI and LLC made more than 50 individual sets from 1987 to the end of the century, with an average of five or six cars per set. The number of individual cars is rising fast too, owing to the company's penchant for adding newly minted body styles onto older sets, trying to get maximum mileage out of them.

PASSENGER CAR LISTINGS

Exc Mt

The Virginia Train Collectors Set

Before the club disbanded in the mid-1990s the Virginia Train Collectors produced the last of their annual special cars as an O27 passenger set in 1992. A total of seven cars were made using Lionel blanks supplied to the VTC. The cars were decorated by PVP in the Norfolk & Western colors—tuscan-maroon with black roofs and gold lettering. Approximately 200 of each were made. As a result of being decorated outside the factory, the numbers on the cars are "7692-1" through "7692–7", which designates the year the club was founded and the year of production. The cars were collectively supplied to VTC under Lionel's catalog number 52002. There were plans to produce a matching engine but these did not materialize. The cars all ride on the O27 die-cast passenger trucks. These cars will generally be found for sale together.

7692-1 VTC: 1992, O27 baggage car; uncataloged; see description above. **35 45**

7692-2 VTC: 1992, O27 combine car; uncataloged; see description above. **35 45**

7692-3 VTC: 1992, O27 dining car; uncataloged; see description above. **35 45**

7692-4 VTC: 1992, O27 coach; uncataloged; see description above. **35 45**

7692-5 VTC: 1992, O27 vista dome car; uncataloged; see description above. **35 45**

7692-6 VTC: 1992, O27 coach; uncataloged; see description above. **35 45**

7692-7 VTC: 1992, O27 observation car; uncataloged; see description above. **35 45**

15100 AMTRAK: 1995–96, short O27 streamlined coach; matches 16095 entry, except car name is "DANBURY". Add-on for 11748 Amtrak passenger set. See set description preceding 16095 entry. **35 40**

The Pennsy Set

This set, which really has no name, consists of the 16000 through 16003 O27 short streamlined cars. It was the first appearance of this style since the Quicksilver Express in 1982, and the first foray of Richard Kughn's new Lionel Trains, Inc., into the world of passenger sets. Although not one of Lionel's better graphics efforts (the lettering is blurred and not well spaced or centered), the set sold reasonably well.

The first four cars (two coaches, a vista dome, and an observation) came out in 1987, followed by a 16009 combo in 1988, a 16022 baggage in 1989, and a 16031 diner in 1990. Finally, a full vista dome (16094) came out in 1995, for a (current!) total of

Exc Mt

eight. Each car is classic PRR tuscan with gold lettering and a black roof. All are illuminated with window silhouettes (although not shown that way in the 1987 catalog), and each has Type IV plastic wood-beam passenger trucks and operating couplers. The set (separate-sale only, no set box) was cataloged with the 18602 Pennsy 4-4-2 Columbia steam engine in 1987 and with a nice-looking pair of Pennsy Alco diesels in 1988 (18901-18902).

16000 PENNSYLVANIA: 1987–88, short streamlined O27 vista dome; revival of 2400-style cars not seen since "Quicksilver Express" cars of 1982; tuscan-painted body; gold lettering and number; black unpainted roof; illuminated; wood-beam four-wheel passenger trucks; operating couplers. Part of Pennsy passenger set, whose components were all sold separately. See set description above.

(A) As described. **20 25**

(B) Factory Error. No lettering one side. J. Nowaczyk collection. **NRS**

16001 PENNSYLVANIA: 1987–88, short streamlined O27 passenger coach; matches 16000. Part of Pennsy passenger set, whose components were all sold separately. See set description preceding 16000 entry. **20 25**

16002 PENNSYLVANIA: 1987–88, short streamlined O27 passenger coach; matches 16000. Part of Pennsy passenger set, whose components were all sold separately. See set description preceding 16000 entry. **20 25**

16003 PENNSYLVANIA: 1987–88, short streamlined O27 observation; does not have red marker lights on end; matches 16000. Part of Pennsy passenger set, whose components were all sold separately. See set description preceding 16000 entry. **20 25**

16009 PENNSYLVANIA: 1988, short streamlined O27 combine; made as an add-on for Pennsy passenger cars introduced in 1987; matches 16000. See set description preceding 16000 entry. **20 25**

The Virginia and Truckee "Dry Gulch" Service Station Special

The next three entries (16010 through 16012) comprise the unusual and handsome "Dry Gulch Line" Service Station Special set for 1988 (11706). The set came boxed with the 18702 General-style engine in black and gold. The General-style coaches are a golden yellow with a gray roof and green stripe above the windows. Each has white lettering and numbers (sometimes blurred and indistinct) and plastic Type V arch-bar trucks with operating couplers; each is illuminated with translucent window strips. Each car was also boxed within the set box. The set was similar to the Rock Island and B&O sets of the early 1980s. There are variations of the 16010 coach with small and large lettering above the windows.

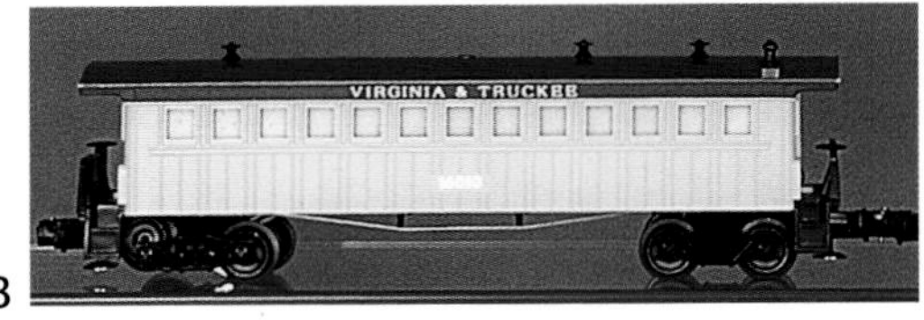

B

16010 VIRGINIA & TRUCKEE: 1988, General-style coach; uncataloged; yellow sides; gray roof; green stripe; white lettering; illuminated; plastic arch-bar trucks. Part of 11706 Dry Gulch Service Station Special set. See set description above.

(A) Small "VIRGINIA & TRUCKEE" lettering; gold-yellow sides; matches 16011 and 16012. M. Blacet collection. **35 40**

(B) Large lettering. Does not match other cars. Car color is straight yellow. J. Strock and B. Trigg Collections. **50 70**

16011 VIRGINIA & TRUCKEE: 1988, General-style coach; uncataloged; matches 16010. Part of 11706 Dry Gulch Service Station Special set. See set description preceding 16010 entry. **35 40**

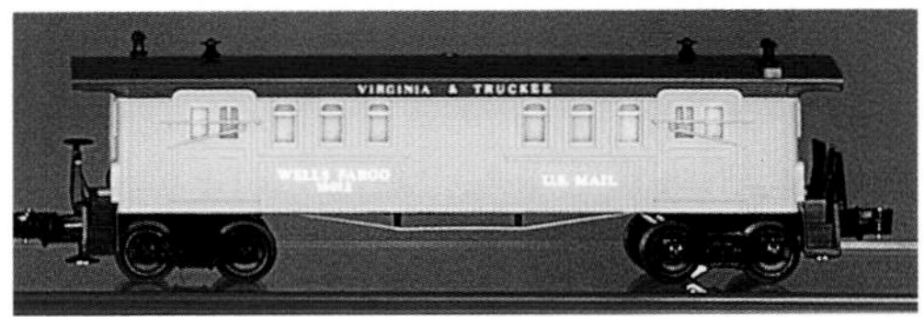

16012 VIRGINIA & TRUCKEE: 1988, General-style baggage/combine; uncataloged; "U.S. MAIL" and "WELLS FARGO"; matches 16010. Part of 11706 Dry Gulch Service Station Special set. See set description preceding 16010 entry. **35 40**

Amtrak Silver Spike

Following its first entry into the passenger field with the Pennsy set, LTI came out with an excellent boxed Traditional Line set (11707) in Amtrak colors called the "Silver Spike". The following three O27 streamlined cars made up the set along with the 8903-8904 Alco AA diesel combination. In this respect, it looked very similar to the *Lake Shore Limited* set from 1976, except the Silver Spike set has window silhouettes, and the red/blue arrow logo is not painted on a white background as it was on the earlier set. Each car is silver-painted with the red and blue Amtrak arrow strips around the windows. The cars have blue and white lettering, Type IV plastic wood-beam passenger trucks with operating couplers, and each is illuminated and has window silhouettes. Add-ons to the set were a 16023 coach in 1989, a 16033 baggage in 1990, and a 16048 diner car in 1992.

16018 New York Central short streamlined coach

	Exc	Mt

16013 AMTRAK: 1988–89, short streamlined O27 combine; silver-painted body; red, white, and blue Amtrak striping and logo; passenger silhouettes in windows; illuminated; plastic wood-beam passenger trucks; operating couplers. Part of 11707 Silver Spike passenger set. See set description above.

(A) As described **30 35**

(B) With added "Mopar Express" lettering. Special limited production for a Chrysler Mopar Express/Amtrak Silver Spike set. This set was available only via a direct mail sweepstakes through Chrysler in 1989. Very few made, extra markings added by Chrysler. S. Troski comment. **— NRS**

16014 AMTRAK: 1988–89, short streamlined O27 vista dome; matches 16013. Part of 11707 Silver Spike set. See set description preceding 16013 entry.

(A) As described. **30 35**

(B) Additional Mopar lettering. See 16103(B). **— NRS**

16015 AMTRAK: 1988–99, short streamlined O27 observation; matches 16013. Part of 11707 Silver Spike set. See set description preceding 16013 entry.

(A) As described. **30 35**

(B) Additional Mopar lettering. See 16103(B). **— NRS**

New York Central Passenger Set

By 1989 Lionel was in a groove in its production of the short O27 streamlined passenger cars. This set, like 1987's Pennsy, really has no name, and all components were offered for separate-sale only. It was a surprisingly good seller, with many New York Central fans hungry for reasonably priced trains. Instead of waiting for add-ons, Lionel this time released six cars at the same time (baggage, combo, two coaches, vista dome, and observation—16016 through 16021). Each is painted in the classic NYC two-tone gray with black roof and white lettering "NEW YORK CENTRAL" above the windows and name and numbers below. Each is illuminated with window silhouettes and has the Type IV plastic wood-beam passenger trucks with operating couplers. The only add-on to this set was the 16041 diner car from 1991. The set was cataloged with the 18606 Atlantic steam locomotive, which has had some operating problems. See the Steam Locomotive chapter for details.

Reader George Romich sent us an interesting note on this set. It seems it is a nearly exact match for a 1950s era Marx NYC passenger set, among the few Marx sets made with interior lighting. When Marx was in the train business it usually spent time remaking what Lionel produced. It is nice to see Lionel returning the favor!

16016 NEW YORK CENTRAL: 1989, short O27 streamlined baggage; gray body; light gray central stripe; black roof; white lettering; illuminated; plastic Type IV wood-beam passenger trucks; operating couplers. Part of separate-sale NYC passenger set. See set description above. **25 30**

16017 NEW YORK CENTRAL: 1989, short O27 streamlined combine car; "LAKE MICHIGAN"; matches 16016. Note silhouettes in baggage door! Part of separate-sale NYC passenger set. See set description preceding 16016 entry. **25 30**

16018 NEW YORK CENTRAL: 1989, short O27 streamlined coach; "CHICAGOLAND"; matches 16016. Part of separate-sale NYC passenger set. See set description preceding 16016 entry.

(A) As described. **25 30**

(B) Factory error. Missing light gray window stripe. R. LaVoie Collection. **NRS**

16019 NEW YORK CENTRAL: 1989, short O27 streamlined vista dome; "LASALLE"; matches 16016. Part of separate-sale NYC passenger set. See set description preceding 16016 entry. **25 30**

	Exc	Mt

16020 NEW YORK CENTRAL: 1989, short O27 streamlined coach; "KANKAKEE"; matches 16016. Part of separate-sale NYC passenger set. See set description preceding 16016 entry.

(A) As described. **25 30**

(B) Factory error. Missing lettering and numbers on one side. A. Broderdorf collection. **NRS**

16021 NEW YORK CENTRAL: 1989, short O27 streamlined observation; "FORT DEARBORN"; matches 16016. Part of separate-sale NYC passenger set. See set description preceding 16016 entry. **25 30**

16022 PENNSYLVANIA: 1989, short O27 streamlined baggage car; add-on to the Pennsy passenger set from 1897; matches 16000. See set description preceding 16000 entry. **25 30**

16023 AMTRAK: 1989, short O27 streamlined coach; add-on to the 11707 Amtrak "Silver Spike" set of 1988; matches 16013. See set description preceding 16013 entry.

(A) As described **20 25**

(B) Factory error. Missing numbers, both sides. R. Beaulieu collection. **NRS**

16024 NORTHERN PACIFIC: 1992, short O27 streamlined diner car; matches 16034. Add-on for 1991 Northern Pacific passenger set. See set description preceding 16034 entry. **30 40**

	Exc	Mt

Lionel Lines Great Lakes Express Service Station Set

This unique short O27 streamline passenger set was a big seller for LTI. It featured the following four passenger cars and, more impressively, a handsome light gray 18611 2-6-4 Atlantic Lionel Lines steam locomotive. Another unique item about the set is that the cars have Type VI die-cast O27 passenger trucks, not the plastic Type IV wood-beam trucks that had been used in previous modern era cars. Ironically, the original postwar 2400-series cars used these die-cast trucks, so Lionel has come full circle.

The Great Lakes Express cars are forest green with gray roofs, white lettering, yellow highlight stripes, and window trim. Only four cars were included, each lettered for cities in Michigan important to modern Lionel's operation. "LIONEL LINES" is above the windows and name and numbers below. All the cars are illuminated with window silhouettes. Another interesting fact about this set is that each car has two roller pickups, not just one as on earlier cars of the type. The second pickup tended to solve the annoying problem of flickering lights because the single-roller variety would run over gaps in the center rail at switches. This boxed Traditional Line set (all Service Station Specials are considered Traditional Line) carries a 11712 set number. As a Service Station set announced in a separate flyer, all these cars are considered uncataloged.

16027 LIONEL LINES: 1990, short O27 streamlined combo car; uncataloged; "MT. CLEMENS"; forest green body; gray roof; white lettering; yellow stripes and window frames; illuminated; window silhouettes; die-cast Type VI O27 passenger trucks with roller pickups on each truck; operating couplers. Part of the 11712 Great Lakes Express Service Station Special set. See set description above. **30 40**

16028 LIONEL LINES: 1990, short O27 streamlined coach; uncataloged; "DETROIT"; matches 16027. Part of Great Lakes Express Service Station Special set 11712. See set description preceding 16027 entry. **30 40**

16029 LIONEL LINES: 1990, short O27 streamlined coach; uncataloged; "LANSING"; matches 16027. Part of Great Lakes Express Service Station Special set 11712. See set description preceding 16027 entry. **30 40**

16030 LIONEL LINES: 1990, short O27 streamlined observation; uncataloged; "CHESTERFIELD"; matches 16027. Part of Great Lakes Express Service Station Special set 11712. See set description preceding 16027 entry. **30 40**

16031 PENNSYLVANIA: 1990, short O27 streamlined diner; add-on to Pennsy passenger set of 1987; matches 16000. See set description preceding 16000 entry. **25 30**

16033 AMTRAK: 1990, short O27 streamlined baggage car; illuminated; add-on to 11707 Silver Spike set of 1988; matches 16013. See set description preceding 16013 entry. **30 35**

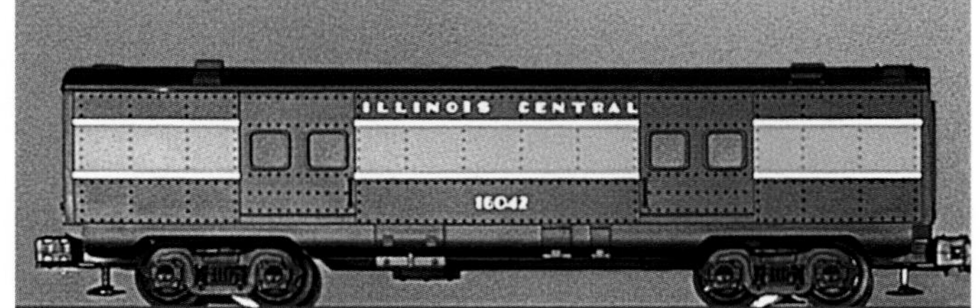

16042 Illinois Central short streamlined baggage car

Exc Mt

Northern Pacific Passenger Set

This is the fifth set in four years following the short O27 streamline passenger set formula, with which LTI had obviously become quite comfortable. Similar to the NYC set the year before, this no-name set of six cars (16034 through 16039) was released (separately) in 1990. The cars are intended to be pulled by the 18609 2-6-4 Northern Pacific steam locomotive offered the same year. An unusual feature is that none of these cars is named—only "NORTHERN PACIFIC" above the windows in white and the red and black Monad ("yin and yang") logo at the lower center.

The set cars are quite attractive: forest green upper body and roof, light (lime) green lower body, and white stripe between the two. Each car is illuminated with window silhouettes and has plastic versions of the O27 passenger truck—a new-style truck that was designated Type XIII. The set has been popular. It is the first time ever that Lionel has made a passenger set lettered for the Northern Pacific. The set was cataloged again in 1991. A diner (16024) was added in 1992.

16034 NORTHERN PACIFIC: 1990–91, short O27 streamlined baggage car; forest green body and roof; lime green lower body; white lettering and stripe; Monad logo; illuminated; plastic Type XIII O27 passenger trucks (a new style truck) with operating couplers. Part of separate-sale-only Northern Pacific passenger set. See set description above. **20 25**

16035 NORTHERN PACIFIC: 1990–91, short O27 streamlined combo car; matches 16034. Part of separate-sale only Northern Pacific passenger set. See set description preceding 16034 entry. **20 25**

16036 NORTHERN PACIFIC: 1990–91, short O27 streamlined coach; matches 16034. Part of separate-sale-only Northern Pacific passenger set. See set description preceding 16034 entry. **20 25**

16037 NORTHERN PACIFIC: 1990–91, short O27 streamlined vista dome; matches 16034. Part of separate-sale-only Northern Pacific passenger set. See set description preceding 16034 entry. **20 25**

16038 NORTHERN PACIFIC: 1990–91, short O27 streamlined coach; matches 16034. Part of separate-sale-only Northern Pacific passenger set. See set description preceding 16034 entry. **20 25**

Exc Mt

16039 NORTHERN PACIFIC: 1990–91, short O27 streamlined observation; matches 16034. Part of separate-sale-only Northern Pacific passenger set. See set description preceding 16034 entry. **20 25**

16040 SOUTHERN PACIFIC: 1990–91, General-style baggage/combo car; orange body; gray ends, roof and trim; white lettering "SOUTHERN PACIFIC" above windows; not illuminated; Type V plastic arch-bar trucks; "BLT 1-90". This is one of just a few Lionel passenger cars to carry a built date. It is also a rare case of a passenger car that did not come in a set with other similar cars. This car (Lionel called it a "payroll car") came in the 11714 "Badlands Express" set. **25 30**

16041 NEW YORK CENTRAL: 1991, short O27 streamlined diner car; add-on to NYC passenger set from 1989; matches 16016. See set description preceding 16016 entry. This add-on piece had two power roller pickups, unlike its earlier cousins. **35 45**

The Illinois Central Passenger Set

LTI continued its set formula for the short O27 streamlined passenger cars with this set released in 1991, the sixth such set in five years. The cars in this no-name set also have no names of their own, just "ILLINOIS CENTRAL" in yellow above the windows and numbers below. The set is intended to be pulled by the 18620 Illinois Central 2-6-2 steam locomotive also released in 1991. It is, in effect, the little brother of the F-3-powered Illinois Central *City of New Orleans* set made in 1985.

As before, the set is separate-sale only. Each car has a brown body with orange window stripe. The stripe is separated from the brown areas with yellow accent stripes. Each has yellow lettering, and all are illuminated with window silhouettes, including, for once, the baggage car—though it does not have silhouettes. The cars ride on the new Type XIII plastic O27 passenger trucks. A full vista dome car was released as an add-on in 1995.

16042 ILLINOIS CENTRAL: 1991, short O27 streamlined baggage car; brown body with orange central stripe; brown and orange areas separated by yellow accent stripes; yellow lettering "ILLINOIS CENTRAL" above windows and number centered below; illuminated (the first time a short O27 baggage car was so equipped); Type XIII plastic O27 passenger trucks. Part of separate-sale-only Illinois Central passenger set. See set description above. **25 30**

	Exc	Mt

16043 ILLINOIS CENTRAL: 1991, short O27 streamlined combo car; illuminated with window silhouettes; otherwise matches 16042. Part of separate-sale-only Illinois Central passenger set. See set description preceding 16042 entry. **25 30**

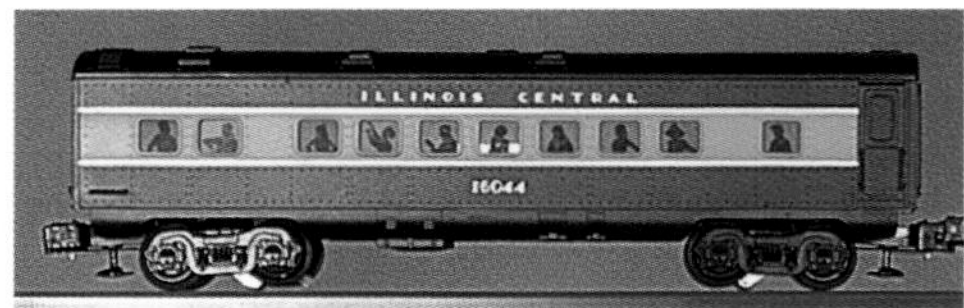

16044 ILLINOIS CENTRAL: 1991, short O27 streamlined coach; illuminated with window silhouettes; otherwise matches 16042. Part of separate-sale-only Illinois Central passenger set. See set description preceding 16042 entry. **25 30**

16045 ILLINOIS CENTRAL: 1991, short O27 streamlined vista dome car; illuminated with window silhouettes; otherwise matches 16042. Part of separate-sale-only Illinois Central passenger set. See set description preceding 16042 entry. **25 30**

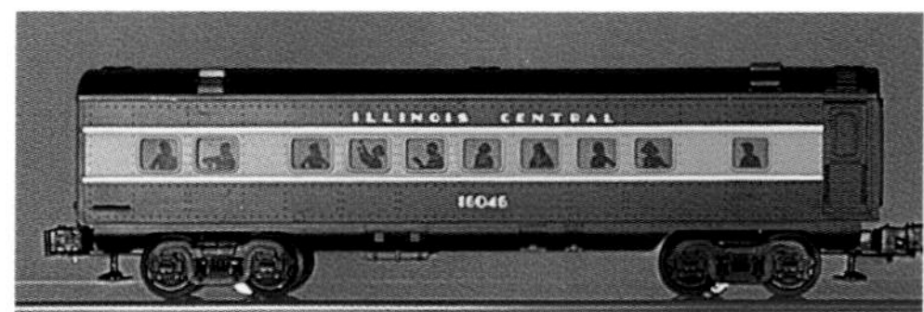

16046 ILLINOIS CENTRAL: 1991, short O27 streamlined coach; illuminated with window silhouettes; otherwise matches 16042. Part of separate-sale-only Illinois Central passenger set. See set description preceding 16042 entry. **25 30**

16047 ILLINOIS CENTRAL: 1991, short O27 streamlined observation car; illuminated with window silhouettes; otherwise matches 16042. Part of separate-sale-only Illinois Central passenger set. See set description preceding 16042 entry. **25 30**

	Exc	Mt

16048 AMTRAK: 1991–92, short O27 streamlined diner car; add-on to the 11707 Amtrak "Silver Spike" set of 1988; matches 16013. See set description preceding 16013 entry. This item was cataloged in 1991, but delayed until 1992. **30 35**

16049 ILLINOIS CENTRAL: 1992, short O27 streamlined diner car; add on to the Illinois Central passenger set released the year before. See set description preceding 16042 entry. **30 35**

Chicago & North Western Set

Lionel had not made a (full) set of the short 9500-style passenger cars since the 1986–87 appearance of the Wabash Fallen Flags set. In 1993 LTI decided to reintroduce the handsome cars with a roadname it had never before modeled in any passenger coaches—the Chicago & North Western. A beautiful five-car set in green and black covered a two-page spread in the catalog with the 18630 steam engine. Each was illuminated with the window silhouettes, had the die-cast six-wheel trucks, and was accented in gold lettering. The set was well-received at its release.

16050 CHICAGO & NORTH WESTERN: 1993, 9500-style baggage car; dark gray-green body; black roof; gold lettering; roadname at upper center and "6620" number at lower center; illuminated; die-cast six-wheel (Type VIII) trucks. Part of C&NW passenger set advertised to go with the 18630 steam locomotive produced the same year. **40 50**

16051 CHICAGO & NORTH WESTERN: 1993, 9500-style combine car; illuminated with window silhouettes; number is "6630"; otherwise matches 16050 above. See set description preceding 16050 entry. **40 50**

16052 CHICAGO & NORTH WESTERN: 1993, 9500-style coach; illuminated with window silhouettes; number is "6616"; name on car is "LAKE GENEVA"; otherwise matches 16050 above. See set description preceding 16050 entry. **40 50**

Exc Mt

16053 CHICAGO & NORTH WESTERN: 1993, 9500-style coach; illuminated with window silhouettes; number is "6602"; name on car is "EVANSTON"; otherwise matches 16050 above. See set description preceding 16050 entry. **40 50**

16054 CHICAGO & NORTH WESTERN: 1993, 9500-style observation car; illuminated with window silhouettes; number is "6603"; name on car is "MT. FARAKER"; otherwise matches 16050 above. See set description preceding 16050 entry. **40 50**

The Santa Fe Super Chief

As one of its lower-priced Traditional Line sets in 1993 and 1994, LTI made a three-car set (numbered 16058 through 60) of the O27 streamlined passenger cars in faux Santa Fe livery, pulled by the warbonnet Santa Fe Alco engine in a set dubbed the *Super Chief.* It was the latest in a long line of Lionel Santa Fe passenger sets. These cars closely resembled the 2442-2445 postwar O27 cars with their red stripe through the window section. The decoration was otherwise basic, with a black "SANTA FE" above the windows, and the car number and type (such as "PULLMAN" or "VISTA DOME") underneath. Farther back in the 1993 catalog, Lionel advertised an additional three cars for the set (16055-57), and a non-powered A unit for the engine. A full vista dome car would be added in 1995. Each car is illuminated and rides on the Type XIII plastic O27 passenger trucks.

16055 SANTA FE: 1993–94, short O27 streamlined coach; silver body; red stripe through window area; black lettering and number; illuminated with window silhouettes; Type XIII plastic O27 passenger trucks. One of three add-on Santa Fe *Super Chief* cars intended to go with the three-car 11739 *Super Chief* set, which included 16058-16060. See set description above. **25 35**

16056 SANTA FE: 1993–94, short O27 streamlined vista dome car; matches 16055 above. See set description preceding 16055 entry. **25 35**

Exc Mt

16057 SANTA FE: 1993–94, short O27 streamlined coach; matches 16055 above. See set description preceding 16055 entry. **25 35**

16058 SANTA FE: 1993–94, short O27 streamlined combine car; matches 16055 above. See set description preceding 16055 entry. **25 35**

16059 SANTA FE: 1993–94, short O27 streamlined vista dome car; matches 16055 above. See set description preceding 16055 entry. **25 35**

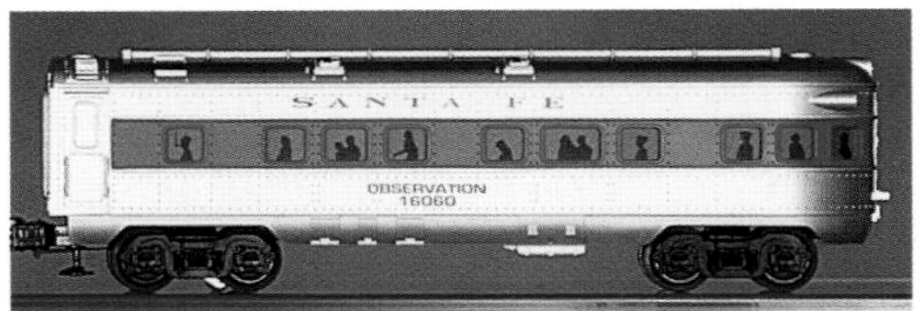

16060 SANTA FE: 1993–94, short O27 streamlined observation car; matches 16055 above. See set description preceding 16055 entry. **25 35**

The Norfolk & Western Set

The N&W's attractive maroon, gold, and black paint scheme has long been a favorite among model railroaders. This set from 1994 was no exception. The collection of five 9500-style short Madison cars followed on the success of the maroon long extruded-aluminum cars from the 1981 *Powhatan Arrow* set, a popular collector's choice. This was in any case the first use of the N&W roadname on the 9500-style cars, and so created yet another stunning set of "baby Madisons" to add to the string of many made by Lionel since 1973. Not only was it received well, but it inspired the company to rerelease the *Powhatan Arrow* itself again the following year. Each of these cars is a deep maroon with black roof, bright gold lettering, name, and numbers. Each rides on the six-wheel die-cast trucks, and all are illuminated.

The units go well with either the 18638 N&W steam locomotive listed in 1994, or with the 18040 streamline "J" made in 1995.

16061 NORFOLK & WESTERN: 1994, 9500-style baggage car; maroon body; black roof; gold lettering; number is "6061"; name is "PLUM RUN"; die-cast Type VIII six-wheel trucks; illuminated. Part of five-piece Norfolk & Western passenger car set, all sold separately. See set description above. **45 55**

16065 Norfolk & Western 9500-style observation car

	Exc	Mt

16062 NORFOLK & WESTERN: 1994, 9500-style combine car; illuminated; number is "6062"; name is "HIGH BRIDGE"; otherwise matches 16061 above. Part of five-piece Norfolk & Western passenger car set, for separate sale. See set description preceding 16061 entry. **45 55**

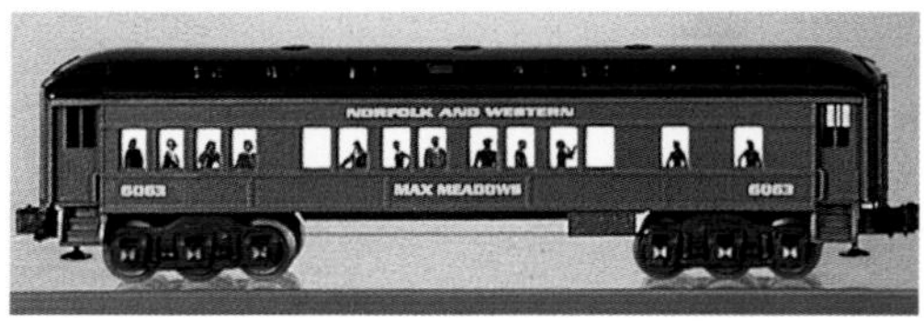

16063 NORFOLK & WESTERN: 1994, 9500-style coach; illuminated; number is "6063"; name is "MAX MEADOWS"; otherwise matches 16061 above. Part of five-piece Norfolk & Western passenger car set, for separate sale. See set description preceding 16061 entry. **45 55**

16064 NORFOLK & WESTERN: 1994, 9500-style coach; illuminated; number is "6064"; name is "HIGH HILL"; otherwise matches 16061 above. Part of five-piece Norfolk & Western passenger car set, for separate sale. See set description preceding 16061 entry. **45 55**

16065 NORFOLK & WESTERN: 1994, 9500-style observation car; illuminated; number is "6065"; name is "HANGING ROCK"; otherwise matches 16061 above. Part of five-piece Norfolk & Western passenger car set, for separate sale. See set description preceding 16061 entry. **45 55**

New York Central Passenger/Freight Set

Like the Norfolk & Western's scheme, the New York Central's two-tone gray "lightning flash" colors have been collector favorites since the 1940s. Lionel had already created sets of the long extruded-aluminum sets and the shorter O27 streamlined cars in the same gray scheme. Thus a Madison set could be expected as the next step. So when the unusual 1994 Service Station set appeared with both NYC freight and passenger cars pulled by a handsome NYC RS-3, Lionelers took close notice. The demand for the set and these unique cars proved such that the company shortly released a full set (four more) in its 1994 Stocking Stuffer catalog, as well as a terrific and unannounced bay window caboose to add to the set. The four-car set was also announced as a Service Station Special, meaning Lionel in 1995 actually had two Service Station sets. The following two cars were part of the initial 1994 set, while the add-on four car set is listed under 16087 through 16090. These are 9500-style short Madison cars riding on the six-wheel die-cast trucks. The bodies are medium gray with a darker gray stripe through the window area, and a black roof, which is a glossy black. There are white accent lines above and below the windows, and the lettering is white as well. Each is illuminated, with all except the baggage featuring window silhouettes. The cars have four-digit numbers, which are the catalog numbers minus the initial "1".

16066 NEW YORK CENTRAL: 1994, 9500-style combine car; gray body; darker gray stripe though window area; white highlight lines and lettering; "NEW YORK CENTRAL" centered above windows; car number is "6066" at front and rear; name is "ELKHART COUNTY"; illuminated with window silhouettes (silhouettes not shown in the catalog); Type VIII die-cast six-wheel trucks. This car is part of the 11744 New York Central Passenger Freight set, which was the 1994 Service Station Special, along with 16067. Four additional cars (16087-90) were released to match in 1995. Boxed individually as well as in set box. **50 60**

16067 NEW YORK CENTRAL: 1994, 9500-style coach; deco matches 16066 above, except number is "6067" and name is "SILVER LAKE". Part of 11744 New York Central Passenger/Freight set, the 1994 Service Station set. Boxed individually as well as in set box. See set description preceding 16066 entry. **50 60**

The Union Pacific Passenger Cars

Exc Mt

One of postwar Lionel's most memorable diesel locomotives was its anniversary 2023 Union Pacific Alco with a gray nose. In 1950 Lionel also produced a matching set of short streamlined passenger cars. This 1994 set of five was a re-creation of those classics, the only difference being that the modern set was lettered for "Union Pacific" rather than "Lionel Lines" as on the 1950 models. Each of the modern cars is a bright yellow with gray roof. Horizontal red lines accent the sides, and each window is outlined in red. The usual features were included—happily Lionel returned to its die-cast Type VI four-wheel passenger trucks after several forays with the plastic versions. Each car is illuminated with silhouetted figures in the coaches. Each is numbered with its own catalog number, except dropping the initial "1". Two cars were added later in 1994 for a total of seven. The set was intended as a match for the 18119 UP Alcos described elsewhere in the 1994 catalog.

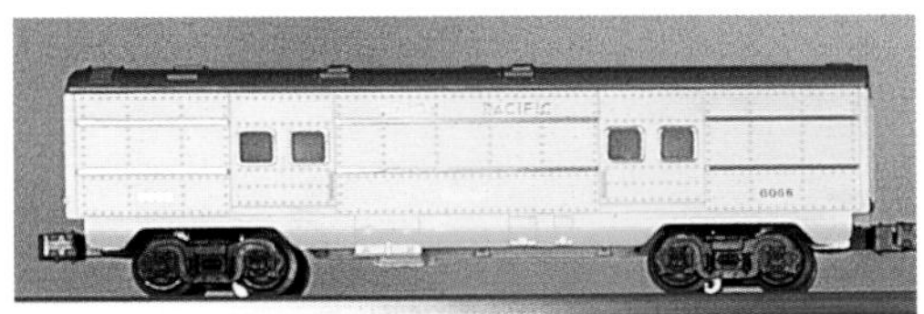

16068 UNION PACIFIC: 1994, short O27 streamlined baggage car; yellow body; gray roof; red lettering and accent lines around windows; number on car is "6068"; name at lower center is "ROMEO"; illuminated; die-cast Type VI passenger trucks. Part of Union Pacific set of passenger cars, sold separately. See set description above. **40 50**

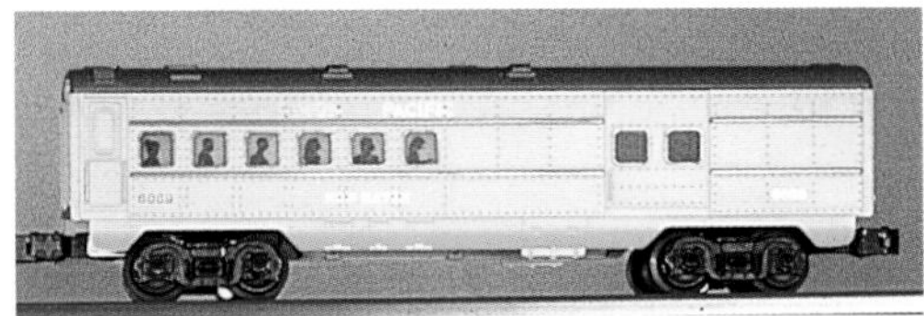

16069 UNION PACIFIC: 1994, short O27 streamlined combine car; number on car is "6069"; name at lower center is "NEW HAVEN"; otherwise matches 16068 above. Part of Union Pacific set of passenger cars, sold separately. See set description preceding 16068 entry. **40 50**

16070 UNION PACIFIC: 1994, short O27 streamlined coach; number on car is "6070"; name at lower center is "PLAINFIELD"; otherwise matches 16068 above. Part of Union Pacific set of passenger cars, sold separately. See set description preceding 16068 entry. **40 50**

Exc Mt

16071 UNION PACIFIC: 1994, short O27 streamlined diner car; number is "6071" and name is "NEW BALTIMORE"; otherwise matches 16068 above. Add-on for Union Pacific passenger set. See set description preceding 16068 entry. Shown in 1994 Stocking Stuffers catalog. **40 50**

16072 UNION PACIFIC: 1994, short O27 streamlined vista dome car; number on car is "6072"; name at lower center is "ST. CLAIR SHORES"; otherwise matches 16068 above. Part of Union Pacific set of passenger cars, sold separately. See set description preceding 16068 entry. **40 50**

16073 UNION PACIFIC: 1994, short O27 streamlined coach; number is "6073" and name is "WESTFIELD"; otherwise matches 16068 above. Add-on for Union Pacific passenger set. See set description preceding 16068 entry. Shown in 1994 Stocking Stuffers catalog. **40 50**

16074 UNION PACIFIC: 1994, short O27 streamlined observation car; number on car is "6074"; name at lower center is "LIVINGSTON"; otherwise matches 16068 above. Part of Union Pacific set of passenger cars, sold separately. See set description preceding 16068 entry. **40 50**

The Missouri Pacific Passenger Set

By 1995 Lionel had established a pattern of releasing mid-scale steam or diesel locomotives and separate sets of four or five of the short Madison or streamlined passenger cars to go with them. This colorful consist of blue and gray Missouri Pacific 9500-style short Madison cars fits the bill to a T and marks another passenger railway never previously used in the

Exc Mt

Lionel line. A rather standard Missouri Pacific GP-7 was shown on the page preceding these handsome cars, with everything for sale separately. Each car is a royal blue, with a gray area through the windows and yellow accent lines above and below the gray area. The roofs were gray and the lettering a silver-gray. The pieces, all illuminated, rode on the six-wheel die-cast trucks.

16075 MISSOURI PACIFIC: 1995, 9500-style baggage car; royal blue body; gray area through doors/windows highlighted with horizontal yellow stripes; light gray roof; silver-gray lettering; illuminated; car number is "6620" on lower center of body; Type VIII die-cast six-wheel trucks. Part of five-piece Missouri Pacific passenger car set. Sold separately. See set description above. **40 50**

16076 MISSOURI PACIFIC: 1995, 9500-style combine car; description matches 16075 above, except number is "6630". Part of five-piece Missouri Pacific passenger car set. Sold separately. See set description preceding 16075 entry. **40 50**

16077 MISSOURI PACIFIC: 1995, 9500-style coach; description matches 16075 above, except number is "6616". Part of five-piece Missouri Pacific passenger car set. Sold separately. See set description preceding 16075 entry. **40 50**

16078 MISSOURI PACIFIC: 1995, 9500-style coach; description matches 16075 above, except number is "7805". Part of five-piece Missouri Pacific passenger car set. Sold separately. See set description preceding 16075 entry. **40 50**

Exc Mt

16079 MISSOURI PACIFIC: 1995, 9500-style observation car; description matches 16075 above, except number is "6609". Part of five-piece Missouri Pacific passenger car set. Sold separately. See set description preceding 16075 entry. **40 50**

New Haven Passenger Set

The set formula continued along with this series—five streamlined silver, orange, and black O27-style cars to go with the New Haven Alcos released in 1994. Lionel might have planned the cars for 1994 when the engines came out, but perhaps realized the market had been strained with the number of passenger sets it was producing by then and delayed these until a year later. The set cars are a striking silver with a bright orange stripe through the window area, and black lettering and black roof. Each is illuminated, including the baggage car, which in 1994 began to be lighted in these sets. They have the plastic Type XIII O27 passenger trucks. A gap in the numbering of the cars in the set implied others would be released later. In fact, a new full-vista dome model appeared later in 1995.

16080 NEW HAVEN: 1995, short O27 streamlined baggage car; silver body; black roof; black lettering and numbers; orange stripe through window area; illuminated; number is "6080"; Type XIII plastic trucks. Part of five-car New Haven passenger set. See set description above. **30 35**

16081 NEW HAVEN: 1995, short O27 streamlined combine car; description matches 16080, except number is "6081". Part of five-car New Haven passenger set. See set description preceding 16080. **30 35**

16082 NEW HAVEN: 1995, short O27 streamlined coach; description matches 16080, except number is "6082". Part of five-car New Haven passenger set. See set description preceding 16080. **30 35**

16083 NEW HAVEN: 1995, short O27 streamlined vista dome car; description matches 16080, except number is "6083". Part of five-car New Haven passenger set. See set description preceding 16080. **30 35**

16084 NEW HAVEN: 1995, short O27 streamlined full vista dome car; matches 16080, except number is "6084". Add-on for the

Exc Mt

New Haven set. See set description preceding 16080. This is an all-new-style car body, with the vista-dome roof extending almost the full length of the car. First issue of this new model. **35 40**

16086 NEW HAVEN: 1995, short O27 streamlined observation car; description matches 16080, except number is "6086". Part of five-car New Haven passenger set. See set description preceding 16080. **30 35**

16087 NEW YORK CENTRAL: 1995, 9500-style baggage car; illuminated; decor matches 16066 above, except number is "6087"; car has no name. Part of 16091 New York Central Passenger Car set (with the following three entries), one of the 1995 Service Station sets, and intended as an supplement to the two cars in the 1994 NYC Service Station set. See set description preceding 16066 entry. **45 55**

16088 NEW YORK CENTRAL: 1995, 9500-style coach; illuminated; decor matches 16066 above, except number is "6088"; name on car is "LICKING RIVER". Part of 16091 New York Central Passenger Car set (which was 16087-16090), one of the 1995 Service Station sets, and intended as an supplement to the two cars in the 1994 NYC Service Station set. See set description preceding 16066 entry. **45 55**

16089 NEW YORK CENTRAL: 1995, 9500-style dining car; illuminated; decor matches 16066 above, except number is "6089"; name on car is "RIPPLING STREAM". Part of 16091 New York Central Passenger Car set (which was 16087-16090), one of the 1995 Service Station sets, and intended as an supplement to the two cars in the 1994 NYC Service Station set. See set description preceding 16066 entry. **45 55**

Exc Mt

16090 NEW YORK CENTRAL: 1995, 9500-style observation car; illuminated; decor matches 16066 above, except number is "6090"; name on car is "BABBLING BROOK". Part of 16091 New York Central Passenger Car set (which was 16087-16090), one of the 1995 Service Station sets, and intended as an supplement to the two cars in the 1994 NYC Service Station set. See set description preceding 16066 entry. **45 55**

16091 NEW YORK CENTRAL: four car set; see 16087-16090.

16092 SANTA FE: 1995, short O27 streamlined full vista dome car; illuminated; "PULLMAN" and "16092" below windows; description matches 16055. Add-on for Santa Fe Super Chief set from 1993–94. See set description preceding 16055 entry. This piece also matches the Warbonnet set from 1997–98. **35 40**

16093 ILLINOIS CENTRAL: 1995, short O27 streamlined full vista dome car; illuminated; otherwise matches 16042; see set description preceding 16042 for other details. Intended as an add-on for the 1991 Illinois Central O27 passenger set. **35 40**

16094 PENNSYLVANIA: 1995, short O27 streamlined full vista dome car; illuminated; otherwise matches 16000; see set description preceding 16000 for other details. Intended as an add-on for the 1987 "Pennsy" O27 passenger set. **35 40**

The Amtrak Passenger Set

Lionel gave this set the same generic name as its long extruded-aluminum set from 1989, but this one is made up of the less-costly O27 cars. Nonetheless it was one of the company's more successful starter sets. The set consisted of the following three cars, along with two more coaches and a vista dome sold as add-ons later in the catalog. One of the cars bears the "15100" number, as Lionel at this stage had run out of the 16000-series of numbers. The set was pulled by a matching Amtrak Alco (18936), with a non-powered A unit sold separately as well, creating a good-looking eight-piece train. The cars replicate modern Amtrak's familiar color scheme—the red, white, and blue strip through the windows, on a sharp silver

Exc Mt

body. Each is illuminated with the passenger silhouettes and rides on the plastic O27 passenger trucks. Unlike some other O27 sets, each car has its own name.

16095 AMTRAK: 1995–96, short O27 streamlined combine car; silver body; red, white, and blue stripes through window section; black "Amtrak" centered over windows; car name is "NEW SMYRNA"; illuminated; plastic Type XIII trucks. Part of 11748 Amtrak passenger set. See set description above. **30 35**

16096 AMTRAK: 1995–96, short O27 streamlined vista dome car; matches 16095 above, except car name is "SILVER DOME". Part of 11748 Amtrak passenger set. See set description preceding 16095. **30 35**

16097 AMTRAK: 1995–96, short O27 streamlined observation dome car; matches 16095 above, except car name is "LAKE WORTH". Part of 11748 Amtrak passenger set. See set description preceding 16095. **30 35**

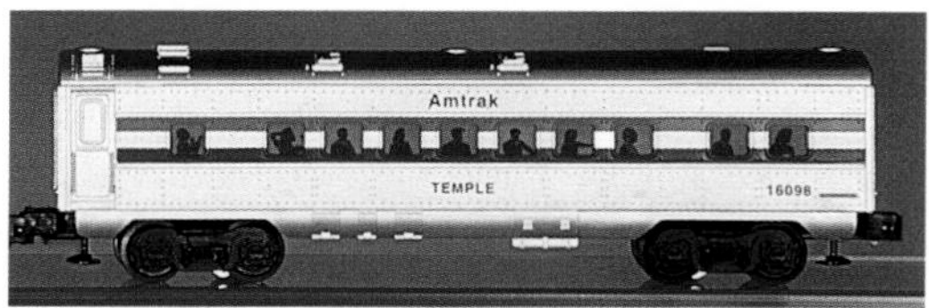

16098 AMTRAK: 1995–96, short O27 streamlined coach; matches 16095 above, except car name is "TEMPLE". Add-on for 11748 Amtrak passenger set. See set description preceding 16095. **30 35**

16099 AMTRAK: 1995–96, short O27 streamlined vista dome; matches 16095 above, except car name is "HIGH-DOME". Add-on for 11748 Amtrak passenger set. See set description preceding 16095. **30 35**

17879 VALLEY FORGE: 1989, 9500-style dining car; uncataloged special for the Train Collectors Association (TCA); Brunswick green body; black roof; gold stripes above and below windows; gold "PENNSYLVANIA LIMITED" above windows; "DINER" to upper right; "VALLEY FORGE, BY GEORGE" in gold at lower right; TCA logo to left side; illuminated with passenger silhouettes; "17879" is not on car, and the box is incorrectly labeled "19879"—Lionel's true catalog number for the piece is 17879; number on car is "1989"; six-wheel die-cast passenger trucks. Intended as an add-on to the TCA Passenger Special set released from 1980 to 1985. This was the TCA's 1989 national Convention car, marking the club's 1989 convention in Valley Forge. **60 80**

Exc Mt

17883 NEW GEORGIA RAILROAD: 1990, General-style coach; uncataloged; TCA 1990 National Convention car; gray body; light blue roof; red stripes highlighting windows; Confederate flag at lower center; black lettering "ATLANTA 1990" and "DIXIE DIVISION" along top; illuminated; TCA logo to left in red and white; Type IX die-cast arch-bar trucks; "BLT 1-90"; catalog number not on the car—"1990" is the visible number. Many, if not all, Lionel boxes for this car are misnumbered "17873" rather than "17883". **60 80**

19000 THE BLUE COMET: 1987, 9500-style diner car; uncataloged; "GIACOBINI"; made as a match for the 9536-40 *Blue Comet* passenger cars of 1978–79. Shown in the year-end Holiday package for 1987. When Lionel created the new diner model for the short Madison series in the late '80s, it released add-on diners for the other earlier sets as well—see the next four entries.

(A) As described. **75 85**

(B) Factory error. Cream stripe between windows does not cover fully down to sills. J. Riemersma collection. **NRS**

19001 SOUTHERN CRESCENT: 1987, 9500-style dining car; uncataloged; made as a match for 9530-9534 *Southern Crescent* passenger cars from 1977–78, including the older four-wheel trucks. Announced in 1987 year-end package. See *Southern Crescent* set description in the Lionel-Fundimensions Guide for 1991. **75 85**

19002 PENNSYLVANIA: 1988, 9500-style dining car; uncataloged; matches Pennsylvania *Broadway Limited* cars produced from 1974–76, except this car has Type IV wood-beam trucks with operating couplers. See *Broadway Limited* set description in the Lionel-Fundimensions Guide for 1991. Announced in a 1988 holiday brochure. **40 50**

19003 THE MILWAUKEE ROAD: 1988, 9500-style dining car; uncataloged; matches Milwaukee Special cars produced from 1973–76, except this car includes Type IV trucks with operating couplers. The colors are slightly darker than on the earlier set. See Milwaukee Special set description in the Lionel-Fundimensions Guide for 1991. Announced in 1988 holiday brochure. **40 50**

19010 BALTIMORE & OHIO: 1989, 9500-style dining car; uncataloged; matches B&O *Capitol Limited* set produced in 1975, except this car has operating couplers. See *Capitol Limited* set description in the Lionel-Fundimensions Guide for 1991. Appeared in late 1989 Holiday Collection brochure. **40 50**

Exc Mt

19011 LIONEL LINES: 1993, long Madison baggage car; add on for the 1991 heavyweight Lionel Lines set; new body style that was not included in the 1991 set; operating doors; finished floor piece inside; not illuminated; car number is "9011"; released in fewer quantities than the 1991 set, this piece is now difficult to find. See set description below. **200 275**

The Long Madison Cars

The following four cars comprised a long-awaited remake of the famous heavyweight "Madison" passenger car sets produced in 1941–42 and 1946–50. Lionel Trains, Inc., chose the 50th anniversary of their first appearance to unveil a brand new model of these classic passenger cars so prominent on the American railroads in the early part of this century.

The original prewar and postwar Lionel sets are near-legend in the Lionel hobby today, and finding them for sale now in good condition is a difficult proposition. This pent-up demand, as well as competitive pressures from other manufacturers to produce longer scale-length passenger cars, led Lionel finally to re-create the legend.

The modern Madison cars are about 3 inches longer (15 inches) than their short Madison cousins, which had served Lionel's passenger car demand so well from 1973 to 1987. The 1991 set (as well as the later ones) is made of a modern heavy phenolic plastic, simulating the "Bakelite" plastic from which the postwar cars were made and which made each of them a real "heavyweight." The new material is somewhat more flexible than Bakelite, and thus results in many fewer damaged cars during production and handling. Bakelite was a patented trade name for the plastic at the time, but the patent has since expired. Each car in this set is a handsome tuscan with white lettering and die-cast six-wheel trucks, adding still more to the weighty impression. The modern set does include some interesting differences: passenger silhouettes in the windows, spring-loaded swinging doors on a metal end piece, and most interestingly, the modern set has the Sager Place observation car, which was pictured but never made in the postwar era.

Each car rides on a stamped metal frame and is illuminated with two operating couplers. Each is named for a location significant to the history of the Lionel Corporation. They were sold separately, not in a set. The cars are pictured, as they often were in the postwar catalogs, right behind the scale New York Central Hudson. A baggage car was added in 1993, numbered ahead of these cars.

19015 LIONEL LINES: 1991, long Madison coach; new model of the long heavyweight passenger cars prominent on the real railroads in the 1920s and made originally by Lionel in the 1940s; tuscan-painted body 15 inches long and made of heavy phenolic plastic similar to the "Bakelite" plastic used to make the 1940s originals; white lettering "IRVINGTON"; "9015" is the number on the car; illuminated with window silhouettes; spring-loaded swinging doors; die-cast six-wheel trucks; two operating couplers. Remake of postwar 2625. Part of separate-sale Madison car set. See set description above. Irvington is the northern New Jersey town in which the Lionel Corporation factory was located. **100 130**

19016 LIONEL LINES: 1991, long Madison coach; car name is "MADISON" in white, "9016" the number on the car; otherwise matches 19015. Part of separate-sale Madison car set. See set description preceding 19015 entry. Madison is the New York City avenue on which Joshua Lionel Cowen's family lived, and which was the home of one of the most important Lionel dealers—Madison Hardware. **100 130**

19017 LIONEL LINES: 1991, long Madison coach; car name is "MANHATTAN" in white, "9017" the number on the car; otherwise matches 19015. Part of separate-sale Madison car set. See set description preceding 19015 entry. The original Lionel Corporation headquarters was located in Manhattan. **100 130**

19018 LIONEL LINES: 1991, long Madison observation; car name is "SAGER PLACE" in white, "9018" the number on the car; metal rear platform; illuminated drumhead; there is a coupler on the rear truck; otherwise matches 19015. Part of separate-sale Madison car set. See set description preceding 19015 entry. The original postwar Sager Place observation car (2626) was pictured in the 1946 advance catalog but was never made. Sager Place is the Irvington, New Jersey, street where the old Lionel factory was located. **120 150**

19019 SOUTHERN PACIFIC: 1993, long Madison baggage car; new body style with operating doors; not illuminated; car number is "9019"; otherwise decoration matches SP Daylight passenger cars (19023-26) made in 1992. See set description below. Shown in the 93 Stocking Stuffer catalog. **125 150**

The Southern Pacific Daylight Long Madison Cars

Following its success with the Lionel Lines cars, the company released another great set of the long "heavyweight" Madison cars, this time decorated in the bright red (or red-orange) and orange of the Southern Pacific's *Daylight* train. Like the previous set, each car was made of the heavy phenolic plastic and had metal end pieces with spring-loaded opening doors. In this case the doors were a bright orange. Each car has the die-cast six-wheel trucks under a stamped-metal frame, and is illuminated with window silhouettes. A new-model baggage car (not made with the Lionel Lines set) was added to the set in 1993, though numbered before the 1992 cars.

19023 SOUTHERN PACIFIC: 1992, long Madison coach; car name is "ARCATA BAY"; *Daylight* paint scheme to match SP *Daylight* loco released in 1991; dark orange sides, broad lighter orange stripe through center and windows; black roof; metal end piece with opening door painted orange; silver lettering with road name centered over windows and car name below; number on car is "9023"; six-wheel die-cast trucks; illuminated with window silhouettes. Part of four-car set with 19024-26. **110 140**

19041 Pere Marquette long Madison coach

Exc Mt

19024 SOUTHERN PACIFIC: 1992, long Madison coach; car name is "HALF MOON BAY"; number is "9024"; otherwise matches 19023. See set description preceding 19023 entry. **110 140**

19025 SOUTHERN PACIFIC: 1992, long Madison coach; car name is "DRAKES BAY"; number is "9025"; otherwise matches 19023. See set description preceding 19023 entry. **110 140**

19026 SOUTHERN PACIFIC: 1992, long Madison observation; car name is "SUNSET BAY"; number is "9026"; open metal rear platform with illuminated drumhead reading "SOUTHERN PACIFIC LINES" in blue, silver and gold; otherwise matches 19023. See set description preceding 19023 entry. **110 140**

The Reading Long Madison Cars

Lionel had planned a second four-car set of its newly minted "heavyweight" Madison cars for 1992, this one outfitted in the familiar green and yellow of the Reading Company. Unfortunately, as with other items of the somewhat ill-fated 1992 line, demand for this set did not materialize and it was never made. A pity, too, because it would have marked the first time ever that Lionel had modeled a Reading passenger set (many Reading freight cars exist)—despite the railroad's longtime visibility in Pennsylvania and the Northeast. The catalog cars had been designated 19027 and 19031 through 19033. Lionel finally corrected the oversight in 1996, albeit with a set of short O27 passenger cars.

19038 ADOLPHUS BUSCH: 1992–93, 9500-style observation car; uncataloged special made for the Anheuser Busch catalog. More details needed. Reader comments requested. **— 100**

The Pere Marquette Resort Special

The failure of the Reading Madison set did not deter Lionel. In the 1993 Book 2 catalog appeared a very similar four-car unit, this time decorated for the Pere Marquette, a regional rail service to northern Michigan's lakeside resorts. This too was a first-time Lionel production for this railway, in terms of passenger coaches. The by-now familiar heavy phenolic cars are decorated in brown and black, with gold lettering again prominent on the sides. A beautiful Berkshire 2-8-4 steam locomotive earlier in the catalog was a perfect match for the set. An interesting touch with the baggage car here is the inclusion of a wood-grained simulated floor inside the car.

Exc Mt

19039 PERE MARQUETTE: 1993, long Madison baggage car; brown body made of heavy phenolic plastic; black roof; gold lettering "PERE MARQUETTE" centered between operating doors; no number on car; illuminated; stamped metal frame with wood grain floor insert inside car; six-wheel die-cast O gauge passenger trucks. Part of four-car set called the Pere Marquette Resort Special, with following three entries. **60 80**

19040 PERE MARQUETTE: 1993, long Madison coach; illuminated; car number is "1115"; otherwise matches 18039 above. Part of Pere Marquette Resort Special. **60 80**

19041 PERE MARQUETTE: 1993, long Madison coach; illuminated; car number is "1116"; otherwise matches 18039 above. Part of Pere Marquette Resort Special. **60 80**

19042 PERE MARQUETTE: 1993, long Madison observation car; illuminated; metal rear platform with lighted drumhead; car number is "36"; additional lettering at lower center for "PARLOR CAR / BUFFET"; otherwise matches 18039 above. Part of Pere Marquette Resort Special. **60 80**

	Exc	Mt

Amtrak Passenger Set

Amtrak collectors were rewarded in 1989 with this magnificent set of seven long extruded-aluminum passenger cars. The set has several interesting firsts: it is the first passenger set, large or small, specifically designated to be pulled by a GG-1 (in this case the Amtrak 18303), and this set is the first to make use of the realistic full vista dome car. As it happens, the set also has a small vista dome car. The car bodies here mark Lionel's return to fluted sides on its long aluminum cars, and only the central window strip is decorated in the red, white, and blue Amtrak arrow scheme. Only six cars were cataloged in 1989—the full vista dome car was announced in a year-end holiday brochure. But as a separate-sale Collector set it did not matter—everything was released at essentially the same time. There is no lettering except a white "Amtrak" on the window strip and a separate plate with black four-digit numbers (the "1" is dropped from the numbers on the cars). All the cars are illuminated with window silhouettes (except the baggage car) and have the Type VII die-cast O gauge passenger trucks.

19100 AMTRAK: 1989, long extruded-aluminum double-door baggage car; unpainted polished aluminum with red, white, and blue Amtrak arrow window strip; "9100" number plate; illuminated; die-cast O gauge passenger trucks with operating couplers. Part of separate-sale Amtrak passenger set. See set description above. **90 110**

19101 AMTRAK: 1989, long extruded-aluminum combine car; "9101" number plate; illuminated with window silhouettes; otherwise matches 19100. Part of separate-sale Amtrak passenger set. See set description preceding 19100 entry. **90 110**

19102 AMTRAK: 1989, long extruded-aluminum coach; "9102" number plate; illuminated with window silhouettes; otherwise matches 19100. Part of separate-sale Amtrak passenger set. See set description preceding 19100 entry. **90 110**

19103 AMTRAK: 1989, long extruded-aluminum vista dome; "9103" number plate; illuminated with window silhouettes; otherwise matches 19100. Part of separate-sale Amtrak passenger set. See set description preceding 19100 entry. **90 110**

19104 AMTRAK: 1989, long extruded-aluminum dining car; "9104" number plate; illuminated with window silhouettes; otherwise matches 19100. Part of separate-sale Amtrak passenger set. See set description preceding 19100 entry. **90 110**

	Exc	Mt

19105 AMTRAK: 1989, long extruded-aluminum full vista dome car; uncataloged; illuminated; new body style for Lionel's long aluminum cars; features a vista dome nearly the entire length of the car, rather than about ⅓ the length as on regular vista domes; car also has an altered side window pattern and large vents on one side; "9105" number plate. Otherwise matches paint scheme of Amtrak passenger set. See set description preceding 19100 entry. Pictured in the 1989 holiday brochure. **100 120**

19106 AMTRAK: 1989, long extruded-aluminum observation car; "9106" number plate; illuminated with window silhouettes; otherwise matches 19100. Part of separate-sale Amtrak passenger set. See set description preceding 19100 entry. **90 110**

19107 SOUTHERN PACIFIC: 1990, long extruded-aluminum full vista dome car; uncataloged; illuminated; add-on for Southern Pacific Daylight set from 1982. See set description in the Lionel-Fundimensions Guide for 1991. Announced in the 1990 Stocking Stuffer brochure. **75 100**

19108 NORFOLK & WESTERN: 1991, long extruded-aluminum full vista dome car; uncataloged; add-on for the N&W Powhatan Arrow set released in 1981; maroon sides; gold lettering and striping; black roof; Powhatan Arrow nameplate; number on car is "576". Announced in the 1991 Stocking Stuffer brochure. See set description in the Lionel-Fundimensions Guide for 1991. **90 110**

A note on the full vista dome car from Lionel:

The full vista dome car (or "Big Dome") made its debut in Lionel Land in 1989, but the real railroads had used them since the 1950s. Some are still in use today. The Budd Company built 24 of them for the Santa Fe for use on the Super Chief and El Capitan. Budd made more of them for the Great Northern, and Southern Pacific built their own for the *Daylight* runs. Pullman Standard built big domes for the Milwaukee Road's *Hiawatha,* and these eventually landed with the Canadian National. The full dome cars today were purchased by Amtrak from the Santa Fe.

Lionel's car had some interesting differences from the other body styles of the aluminum series. This one had vents added to the sides on the door end, and there are fewer and smaller windows on the sides. Later on Lionel added a detailed insert under the dome, which showed seats and tables, and sometimes passenger figures. The tables have fiber-optic lights to simulate table lamps.

In its O gauge world, having invested in its new tooling for the car, Lionel began to release add-on full vista domes for many of its earlier long extruded-aluminum sets, the first of which was the 19107 Southern Pacific.

Santa Fe Passenger Set

Yet another stunning long extruded-aluminum passenger set appeared in the 1991 catalog, another set which exhibited LTI's penchant for introducing new features and variations. This set resurrected the famous Santa Fe F-3 diesels (18100 through 18102)—this time with RailSounds—which had proved such reliable favorites over the years. The passenger cars brought

19118 and 19119 Great Northern extruded-aluminum passenger cars

Exc Mt

back the big Santa Fe liners last seen in 1961. But modern Lionel solved the problems with the troublesome name strips of the earlier set by using simple nameplates attached directly to the car sides. Each car has a "SANTA FE" nameplate above the windows in black and a number nameplate in black below. The 1991 catalog showed the cars with their catalog numbers (less the "1"), but the production pieces had entirely different numbers—prototypically correct ones—and even two cars without numbers at all.

Three unusual features distinguish this set. First, the cars are a combination of the fluted and smooth-sided aluminum cars used earlier in the modern era. The sides are fluted while the roof is smooth. Second, Lionel has applied attractive silver paint to the sides of the Type VII die-cast O gauge trucks used for these cars. Earlier aluminum passenger cars had black-sided trucks. Lastly, LTI created yet another new body style—a combination vista-observation car.

Given these factors, and the popularity of the Santa Fe roadname with many collectors, this set proved a hit and is now somewhat harder to find than many other passenger sets.

The five separate-sale cars announced in 1991 (19109 through 19113) are all illuminated (except the baggage) with window silhouettes.

19109 SANTA FE: 1991, long extruded-aluminum double-door baggage car; unpainted polished aluminum body; fluted sides; smooth roof; no decoration other than "SANTA FE" nameplate in black lettering above the windows, with a small number plate (reading "3400") below the window; not illuminated, but all other cars in the set are; silver-painted die-cast O gauge passenger trucks with operating couplers. Part of separate-sale Santa Fe passenger set. See set description above. The 1991 catalog listed the number as "9109". **110 140**

19110 SANTA FE: 1991, long extruded-aluminum combo car; illuminated; "3500" number plate; otherwise matches 19109. Part of separate-sale Santa Fe passenger set. See set description preceding 19109 entry. **110 140**

19111 SANTA FE: 1991, long extruded-aluminum diner car; illuminated; "601" number plate; otherwise matches 19109. Part of separate-sale Santa Fe passenger set. See set description preceding 19109 entry. **110 140**

19112 SANTA FE: 1991, long extruded-aluminum coach; illuminated; car has no number, but is named "SQUAW VALLEY"; also has small "PULLMAN" nameplate; otherwise matches 19109. Part of separate-sale Santa Fe passenger set. See set description preceding 19109 entry. **110 140**

19113 SANTA FE: 1991, long extruded-aluminum vista-observation; illuminated; no number on car; name is "VISTA VALLEY"; has small "PULLMAN" nameplate; otherwise matches 19109. Part of separate-sale Santa Fe passenger set. See set description preceding 19109 entry. **120 150**

The Great Northern Empire Builder

For all its colorful passenger trains throughout the previous 50 years, Lionel had for some reason never before modeled one of the great passenger experiences ever—the Great Northern's *Empire Builder* run from Chicago to Seattle. Residents of the Great Plains along its route will well remember the striking green and orange streamliners, but Lionel-land had somehow missed out on the opportunity. That oversight was corrected in 1992 with a terrific consist of long aluminum cars in the green and orange livery, pulled by a matching set of Great Northern F3 A-B-A diesels (11724) with diesel RailSounds. Each passenger car in this set is dark green with orange stripes through the window area and on the lower portion of the body, highlighted in yellow. The set featured one of each of the types of car bodies, but not a long vista dome, which was certain to appear later (see 19183). The five cars made for the set are of the smooth-side variety (not fluted), and all have the Type VII O gauge trucks. All except the baggage car are illuminated with window silhouettes. Only two of the set cars have names. Full vista dome cars were released in 1998, though the "EMPIRE BUILDER" lettering on the latter two differed from the main set.

19116 GREAT NORTHERN: 1992, long extruded-aluminum double-door baggage car; dark green-painted body with wide orange stripes through center window section and along lower portion of sides; orange areas are highlighted by thin yellow stripes; yellow lettering with "EMPIRE BUILDER" centered over windows; roadname at upper front and rear of car; number on car is "1200"; die-cast O gauge passenger trucks. Part of separate-sale Great Northern *Empire Builder* set. **90 110**

Exc Mt

19117 GREAT NORTHERN: 1992, long extruded-aluminum combine car; illuminated; number on car is "1240" and car name is "CROSSLEY LAKE"; otherwise matches 19116 above. Part of Great Northern *Empire Builder* set. **90 110**

19118 GREAT NORTHERN: 1992, long extruded-aluminum coach; illuminated; number on car is "1212" and car has no name; otherwise matches 19116 above. Part of Great Northern *Empire Builder* set. **90 110**

19119 GREAT NORTHERN: 1992, long extruded-aluminum vista dome car; illuminated; number on car is "1322"; car has no name; otherwise matches 19116 above. Part of Great Northern *Empire Builder* set. **90 110**

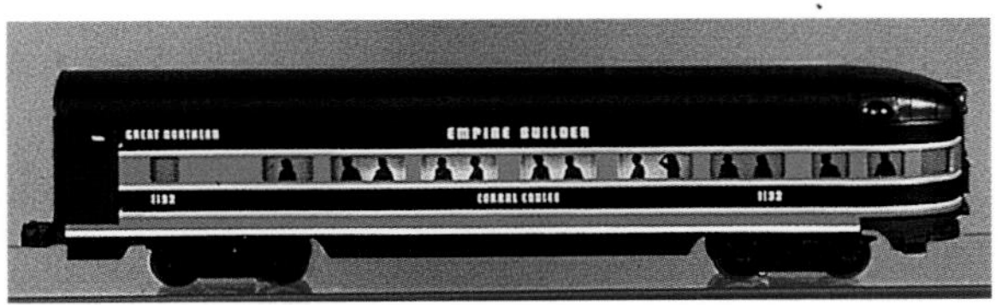

19120 GREAT NORTHERN: 1992, long extruded-aluminum observation car; illuminated; number on car is "1192"; car name is "CORRAL COWLEE"; otherwise matches 19116 above. Part of Great Northern *Empire Builder* set. **90 110**

19121 UNION PACIFIC: 1992, long extruded-aluminum vista dome car; uncataloged; gray and yellow-painted body with broad yellow section at center of sides; lettering and highlight lines in red; illuminated with window silhouettes; car number is "9121"; Type VII four-wheel die-cast trucks. This is an add-on for the UP *Overland Limited* set from 1984. See set description in the Lionel-Fundimensions Guide for 1991. Announced in the 1992 Stocking Stuffer brochure. **90 110**

The California Zephyr

The success of its bright aluminum Santa Fe long passenger cars in 1991 led the company to try again with another Zephyr train—this time the *California Zephyr*—in 1993. The chrome Burlington *Texas Zephyr* from 1980 was one of Fundimensions' most innovative. This choice proved to be another hit. The six-car set, designed to match the new Rio Grande PA-1 diesels, featured yet another new passenger car body—an offset vista dome car. This set had four vista dome cars, an unusual fact in itself, as well as a baggage car and the vista-observation car first seen in the Santa Fe set. But the vista domes here were different in that the dome was offset slightly toward the rear of the car, not centered as on earlier models. Lionel also rearranged the windows along the sides, and for the first time ever, installed a detailed interior piece with seats and tables, to be visible under the dome. Though other manufacturers had been doing this for some time in their passenger cars, this addition was a first for Lionel in its O gauge line. All the cars other than the baggage were illuminated and had silver-painted die-cast Type VII trucks.

19122 CALIFORNIA ZEPHYR: 1993, long extruded-aluminum baggage car; polished silver fluted body; "CALIFORNIA ZEPHYR" in black on nameplate between operating doors; "SILVER ANTELOPE" on another nameplate on lower center of sides; two small "D&RGW" nameplates to front and rear; silver-painted Type VII die-cast trucks. Part of six-piece *California Zephyr* set with next five entries. **100 125**

19123 CALIFORNIA ZEPHYR: 1993, long extruded-aluminum vista dome car; new roof piece with vista dome offset toward rear of body; polished silver fluted body; roof is also fluted; "CALIFORNIA ZEPHYR" in black on nameplate centered under dome; "SILVER BRONCO" on another nameplate on lower portion of sides centered under the one above; two small "D&RGW" nameplates to front and rear; no number on car; silver-painted Type VII die-cast trucks; illuminated with window silhouettes; newly tooled sides with rearranged windows relative to earlier long aluminum cars; new interior insert has tables and chairs visible through dome. Part of six-piece *California Zephyr* set. **100 125**

19124 CALIFORNIA ZEPHYR: 1993, long extruded-aluminum vista dome car; matches 19123 above except name on car is "SILVER COLT". Part of six-piece *California Zephyr* set. **100 125**

19125 CALIFORNIA ZEPHYR: 1993, long extruded-aluminum vista dome car; matches 19123 above except name on car is "SILVER MUSTANG". Part of six-piece *California Zephyr* set. **100 125**

19126 CALIFORNIA ZEPHYR: 1993, long extruded-aluminum vista dome car; matches 19123 above except name on car is "SILVER PONY". Part of six-piece *California Zephyr* set. **100 125**

19129 Illinois Central full vista dome car

Exc Mt

19127 CALIFORNIA ZEPHYR: 1993, long extruded-aluminum vista-observation car; matches 19123 above except name on car is "SILVER SKY". Car also has light rear drumhead with "California Zephyr". Part of six-piece *California Zephyr* set.
100 125

19128 SANTA FE: 1992, long extruded-aluminum full vista dome car; uncataloged; polished aluminum fluted body; illuminated; numberplate reads "507"; add-on to 1991 Santa Fe passenger set. See set description preceding 19109 entry. Announced in 1992 Stocking stuffer brochure. Somewhat hard to find.
150 200

19129 ILLINOIS CENTRAL: 1993, long extruded-aluminum full vista dome car; brown body; broad orange stripe with yellow highlights on lower portion of sides; yellow and black lettering; car number is "9129" on orange strip at front and rear; die-cast Type VII trucks; illuminated with window silhouettes. An addition to the Illinois Central *City of New Orleans* set from 1985. See set description in the Lionel-Fundimensions Guide for 1991. Shown in the 1993 Stocking Stuffer catalog. **80 100**

19130 LACKAWANNA: see 19131-34

The Lackawanna Set

This set continued Lionel's modern series of long aluminum passenger cars begun with the 1989 Amtrak. And as with the previous sets, it was designed to be pulled by the premium engines from the Collector line, in this case the Erie Lackawanna PA diesels from 1993. These cars are considered by some to be among the handsomest of Lionel's extruded-aluminum cars. They are a light gray with black roof pieces. The roof piece is fluted while the sides are smooth. The sides have a maroon stripe running through the window area and three yellow highlighting lines. The lettering is a matching maroon. The cars other than the baggage are illuminated with window silhouettes, and the observation car features a lighted

Exc Mt

drumhead. All ride on the die-cast four-wheel Type VII trucks. The first four cars were designated as set no. 19130, though each was available individually. It was shown this way in the 1993 Stocking stuffer catalog. By the time the 1994 catalog came out, a fifth car (the 19136 Utica) had been added, and the end of the year saw another piece (the 19135 Ithaca). An interesting note is the change from the prototypes in the 1993 Stocking Stuffer catalog, which showed the roadnames and car names in lower-case letters—and the observation car named "Philadelphia"—to the 1994 catalog, where the names are all upper case and the last car changed identity to "BALTSUROL CLUB"! And even that didn't stay—the production piece, as can be seen from our photo, reads simply "BALTUSROL"!

19131 LACKAWANNA: 1994, long extruded-aluminum baggage car; not illuminated; see set description above for details; car number is "2000". Part of five-car Lackawanna passenger set.
80 100

19132 LACKAWANNA: 1994, long extruded-aluminum diner car; illuminated with window silhouettes; see set description prior to 19131 entry for other details; car name is "BINGHAMTON" and number on car is "469". Part of five-car Lackawanna passenger set.
80 100

19133 LACKAWANNA: 1994, long extruded-aluminum coach; illuminated with window silhouettes; see set description prior to

Exc Mt

19131 entry for other details; car name is "BUFFALO" and number on car is "260". Part of five-car Lackawanna passenger set. **80 100**

19134 LACKAWANNA: 1994, long extruded-aluminum observation; illuminated with window silhouettes; see set description prior to 19131 entry for other details; illuminated rear drumhead; car name is "BALTUSROL" and number on car is "789". Part of five-car Lackawanna passenger set. Note the 1993 Stocking Stuffer catalog shows this car named "Philadelphia". It was changed to "BALTSUROL CLUB" for the 1994 catalog, but the actual piece reverses the "S" and the "U" in the name, and drops the "CLUB". **80 100**

19135 LACKAWANNA: 1994, long extruded-aluminum combine car; illuminated with window silhouettes; see set description prior to 19131 entry for further details; car name is "ITHACA", and number is "425". Add-on for the Lackawanna passenger set. Shown in the 1994 Stocking Stuffer catalog. **80 100**

19136 LACKAWANNA: 1994, long extruded-aluminum coach; illuminated with window silhouettes; see set description prior to 19131 entry for other details; car name is "UTICA" and number on car is "211". Part of five-car Lackawanna passenger set. This car did not appear in the initial announcement of the set in the 1993 Stocking Stuffer catalog, but was shown in the 1994 regular catalog. **80 100**

19137 NEW YORK CENTRAL: 1995, long extruded-aluminum "roomette" car; new design aluminum car body; two-tone gray body; black roof, white highlight lines and lettering; car name is "Dunkirk Harbor"; no number; illuminated with window silhouettes; Type VII die-cast O gauge trucks. This piece is

Exc Mt

intended as an add-on for the New York Central *Twentieth Century Limited* set from 1983–84. See set description in the Lionel-Fundimensions Guide for 1991. This car uses new tooling for the extruded-aluminum coaches—a rearranged window sequence with two higher windows simulating a first-class roomette rather than the "second class" coach. **— 110**

19138 SANTA FE: 1995, long extruded-aluminum "roomette" car; new design aluminum car body; description matches 19109, except car name is "INDIAN LAKE". This piece is intended as an add-on for the Santa Fe passenger set from 1991. See set description preceding the 19109 entry. This car uses the new body style introduced in 1995 with rearranged higher windows simulating a first-class roomette. **— 130**

19139 NORFOLK & WESTERN: 1995, long extruded baggage car; not illuminated; see set description prior to 19141 entry for other details; number on car is "577". Add-on for the Norfolk & Western passenger set made earlier in 1995. **90 115**

19140 NORFOLK & WESTERN: 1995, long extruded combine car; illuminated with window silhouettes; see set description prior to 19141 entry for other details; number on car is "494". Add-on for the Norfolk & Western passenger set made earlier in 1995. **90 115**

Norfolk & Western Powhatan Arrow

This 1995 set had its genesis in the success of the similar *Powhatan Arrow* set made by Fundimensions in 1981, which also featured the resurrection of the postwar N&W "J" locomotive. Both sets wore the spectacular maroon and black of the Norfolk & Western on the long aluminum cars. The 1995 set, like its predecessor, accompanied another release of the streamlined "J"—the 18040, with RailSounds. The cars in both sets are certainly among the most beautiful ever made by

Exc Mt

Lionel. The maroon sides are set off by gold striping and a black roof. The lettering is a matching gold, as is the distinctive *Powhatan Arrow* herald centered below the windows. The cars are all illuminated with window silhouettes, and the observation car features a lighted drumhead. All ride on the die-cast four-wheel Type VII trucks. The initial four-car set was different from the usual formula in that it featured a diner rather than a baggage car. Of course, a baggage car (and a combo, both numbered earlier than these items) would soon follow. A roomette car was released in 1996. The main difference between the 1995 set and the 1981 version—this one used smooth-sided cars, while the earlier one had fluted sides and roofs.

19141 NORFOLK & WESTERN: 1995, long extruded-aluminum diner car; illuminated with window silhouettes; see set description above for details; car number is "495". Part of four-car Norfolk & Western passenger set. **90 115**

19142 NORFOLK & WESTERN: 1995, long extruded-aluminum coach; illuminated with window silhouettes; see set description prior to 19141 entry for other details; number on car is "537". Part of four-car Norfolk & Western passenger set. **90 115**

19143 NORFOLK & WESTERN: 1995, long extruded-aluminum coach; illuminated with window silhouettes; see set description prior to 19141 entry for other details; number on car is "538". Part of four-car Norfolk & Western passenger set. **90 115**

19144 NORFOLK & WESTERN: 1995, long extruded-aluminum observation car; illuminated with window silhouettes; illuminated drumhead; see set description prior to 19141 entry for other details; number on car is "582". Part of four-car Norfolk & Western passenger set. **90 115**

19159: see 19141-19144.

51200-series Smithsonian 20th Century Set

In 1992 and 1993, Lionel tried a different tack in its production. That year it teamed up with the Smithsonian and a Michigan marketing company to sponsor two- and three-rail versions of the Dreyfuss Hudson engine (made of brass), as well as a set of O scale passenger cars to go with it. This program also created a group of three BR-50 European 2-10-0 steam engines for two-rail operation. The engines and cars were all made in extremely limited quantities, sold only to subscribers of the "Lionel Smithsonian Collection." The passenger cars were numbered in the 51200-series, made of brass, and named for actual cars used on the New York Central's *Twentieth Century Limited.* The names included cities such as "Detroit" and "Toledo", other locations and names, and numbers alone for the baggage and diner cars. Lionel limited the production to 500 units of each car. There were various models, including baggage cars, coaches, diners, and observation cars. Lionel offered them monthly to its Smithsonian Collection members, at $500 per. For whatever reason, perhaps price, perhaps an unsuccessful foray into two-rail (not an area where Lionel has been able to adequately compete), or perhaps complaints from its dealer network, this program ended in 1993 and has not been repeated.

Inasmuch as these are two-rail brass models, and produced in the Far East, we will not list them in detail, but will simply note the collective group numbers and typical price for each. The limited quantity of each makes them somewhat hard to find now, and when available, they are usually sold as a set.

51220 through 51245: LIONEL SMITHSONIAN COLLECTION: 1993–94, set of 26 brass two-rail passenger cars. Made to match the Lionel Smithsonian Dreyfuss Hudson engine. 500 of each piece exist. Hard to find. Usually sold as a set with the Hudson. Price listed is for any single item. **— 500**

52002: see 7692-1 through -7.

The TCA Annual Set

In 1995 the Train Collectors Association (TCA) began an alternative approach to their annual convention car series. In addition to several freight cars each year (of various makes and gauges), the club started what was to be an annual series of very nice extruded-aluminum Lionel O gauge passenger cars. The convention city would be named on the car sides, but otherwise the cars would be identically decorated. They were painted to match the special TCA 40th anniversary F-3 diesel engines released in 1993. Through 2001 there were seven cars, each a

	Exc	Mt

different body style and city name, all decorated in the TCA's striking orange and black theme. Each has a silver lower frame and end pieces. A lower side strip is in black, with the lettering of the convention city in silver. The window section in the center is a bright orange, and over the windows is "TRAIN COLLECTORS ASSOCIATION" in black. The roof piece is black also. There are silver accent stripes between the black and orange sections. The bodies on all the cars are of the smooth-side variety. The unique aspect of this set is that the first car—the Seattle observation car in 1995, was the first model of a new "solarium" observation car, wherein the entire rear of the car is open, covered in glass, and fitted with a detailed interior piece with seats and tables. The TCA cars are all illuminated (except the baggage car) and have window silhouettes. They are fitted with the four-wheel die-cast O gauge trucks. Since only one is produced per year, the 52000-series numbers that were assigned to them are rather widespread. Of course, since these are among the few special production train club passenger cars, all are uncataloged, and hence have the 52000-series numbers.

	Exc	Mt

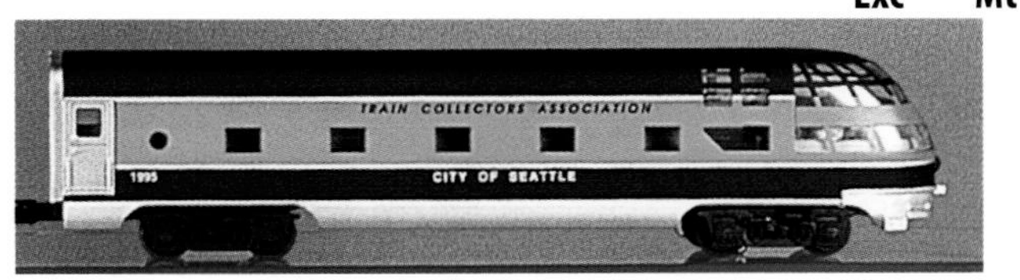

52062 TRAIN COLLECTORS ASSOCIATION: 1995, uncataloged; long extruded-aluminum "solarium" observation car; first in a series of annual aluminum passenger cars for the TCA; this is the club's Convention Car for 1995, marking the show in Seattle; it is also an entirely new Lionel aluminum car model—a "solarium" with glass-enclosed rear end, rather than rounded with a single door, as with previous observation cars; silver frame and ends; black lower side stripe with "CITY OF SEATTLE" in silver; orange window area with "TRAIN COLLECTORS ASSOCIATION" centered above in black; black roof; "1995" in silver at front of car; silver highlight lines; illuminated with window silhouettes; Type VII die-cast O gauge passenger trucks. See set description above. — **175**

CHAPTER 18

Refrigerator Cars

One of the mysteries about Lionel model railroading in the modern era is why train collectors have not paid more attention to the lowly refrigerator cars—also known as "reefers." They represent the creativity and ingenuity of Lionel at its best. Longer than their boxcar counterparts, reefers are made entirely of stout plastic pieces that are extremely well detailed.

Most important, reefers have given modern Lionel a chance to show off its capabilities with graphics, which are much more technically advanced than the postwar company could muster. Colorful electrocals grace the sides of these cars, advertising just about every conceivable product that can be grown, manufactured, or imagined. During the Lionel-Fundimensions period, the 9800-series of the refrigerator cars displayed a huge number of interesting and colorful items, including a few strange choices for refrigeration: Bazooka Bubble Gum, Cheerios, and Old Dutch Cleanser, among others! The situation was reminiscent of the late 19th century on American railroads, where for quite some time producers would hire out space on railroad boxcars to advertise their wares. It was not unusual for a boxcar on a New York Central train of those years to advertise Lydia Pinkham's Patented Vegetable Elixir while carrying machine tools! These were known more commonly as "billboard reefers," and the phrase has been most appropriate to apply to Lionel's equally peculiar refrigerator cars 100 or more years later.

Fundimensions produced some 130-plus wood-sided refrigerator cars from 1970–86, far more individual models than postwar Lionel had managed. Some of the more collectable and recognizable series of billboard reefers made by Fundimensions were: the Favorite Spirits series (which read somewhat like a Who's Who of the liquor industry); the Beer car series, for those inclined to lower-proof beverages; the Favorite Food series, which advertised places such as Taco Bell, Pizza Hut, and the now-defunct Arthur Treacher's; and a "Candy" series that hawked some of America's most mouth-watering snacks, such as Cracker Jack, Oreos, and Baby Ruth.

However, Lionel LTI and Lionel LLC have not made reefer cars at near the pace Fundimensions maintained. In the late 1980s Lionel LTI did start a new series of "Famous Inventor" reefers, and there were occasional forays into billboard reefers like Alka Seltzer and Green Giant. In 1995 Lionel created a handsome set of four Standard O cars with Tropicana colors. But in general, modern Lionel has produced far fewer refrigerator cars than Fundimensions did in its 16 years. The recent cars were not very brisk sellers, and headaches with obtaining licensing agreements at reasonable costs may have resulted in limited recent production.

The refrigerator cars, as a whole, represent a fine opportunity for collectors because most of them are still readily available, with some at real bargain prices. Only a few are scarce—mostly the ones in collector sets or uncataloged special production like the occasional car made for the collectors clubs. A set of Lionel reefers can look super in a long string behind one of the modern diesels.

In terms of numbering, modern Lionel has been relatively consistent in the sequences used: for the most part, the 19500-series is applied to the regular issue wood-sided and 9800-type reefers. Except in 1994–95 when for some reason reefers jumped to the 16100-series and other odd numbers. The Standard O varieties are found in the 17300-series of numbers. There are a few special-production reefers for the clubs and others which can be found in the 52000-series and other isolated places.

BODY STYLES

There are four principal body types used in the modern era refrigerator cars (see accompanying figure):

9800-STYLE REEFERS

This most common of Lionel's reefers is a 10½-inch-long all-plastic car, which can trace its roots back to the 6572 REA and 6672 Santa Fe reefers of the postwar era. But since postwar Lionel did not produce very many of these reefers, we refer to them as "9800-style," marking the great number of Fundimensions freight cars of this style that were given 9800-series numbers from 1973 to 1986. Actually, the connection to postwar is only a partial relation, because the modern version, as produced by Fundimensions, has side pieces with detailed wood scribing, as opposed to the postwar cars, which had smooth steel-plated and riveted sides like the 6464 boxcars. But the wonderfully detailed roof and end pieces were carried forward from postwar to modern production, as was the very distinctive chassis. The bottom of the 9800-style reefer distinguishes it the most from other boxcars and the other reefer types—the two prominent molded air tanks and motor details can't be mistaken. The car is actually almost ¾ inch longer than the classic 6464-type boxcars.

The 9800 reefer consists of two major elements—the roof-end piece in a single section, and the bottom and sides made in another single section. The two pieces attach at the end with screws. The sides on this car are very distinguishable from other types of rolling stock (except the bunk and tool cars, which sharp-eyed readers will note bear a close resemblance to the reefers), with vertically scribed slats and a plug door that must be pulled out via a very small tab before it can be slid to the side. This can present a problem if not done carefully, and the door guides (metal in the earliest Fundimensions production, but plastic in the rest of the modern period) can be easily popped off or broken.

The car also has a unique non-symmetrical aspect. It has a noticeable "left" and right" side that is clearly visible in our photos. On one side the ladder to the left of the door, near the car end, has two rungs, and on the opposite side this ladder has five rungs.

STANDARD O REEFERS

In 1973 Fundimensions introduced a line of full-scale box and refrigerator cars known as the Standard O series. They were the first cars equipped with the excellent Standard O sprung trucks, and this series of cars gave that name to the truck design. The release of the Standard O reefers was intermittent in the Fundimensions period (Standard O boxcars were much more prevalent), but Lionel LTI and Lionel LLC have given more significant emphasis to this product line. This was a logical consequence of having many other types of Standard O rolling stock available now, such as the ACF hoppers, long flatcars, and Unibody tank cars.

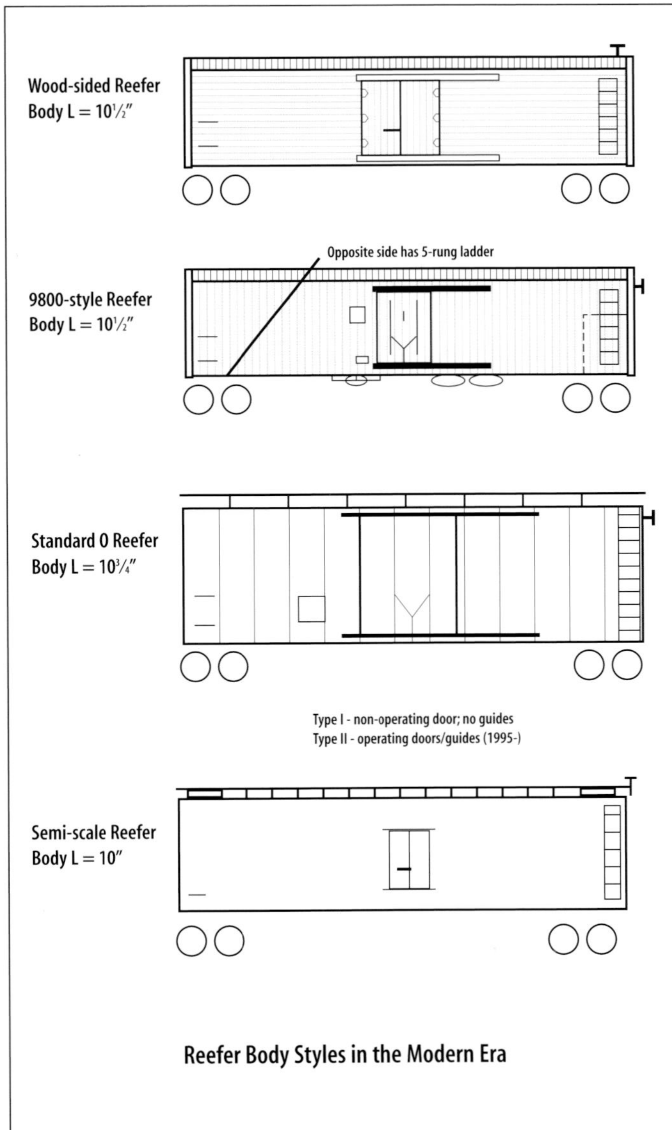

Reefer Body Styles in the Modern Era

As a completely new style, the Standard O reefer has no postwar predecessor as its smaller 9800-style cousin does. The big 10⅝-inch-long reefer can easily be distinguished by the distinctive, detailed catwalk on the top. There is an impressive amount of molded-in detail on the car, like access panels and the door latch mechanism. The Standard O style differs from the 9800 and wood-sided types in that it has a bottom chassis (with no sides), and the body of the car is molded in one piece (sides, ends, and roof together) like regular boxcars.

The car comes in two distinct types. The early version, Type I, featured a non-operating molded-in door. The bottom chassis and the main body snap together with tabs at the ends. No screws are used. This style prevailed from the initial release in 1973 until 1995. At that point Lionel modified the car heavily, introducing an operating plug door (like the 9800-series cars have) with prominent black plastic door guides. It also changed the attachment scheme, abandoning the two end tabs in favor of four screws at the corners of the car which install straight up from below. This is the Type II model and first shows up on a good-looking set of identical Tropicana reefers from 1995-96.

The 17302 Santa Fe Standard O reefer from 1990 marked a unique first for Lionel. It was the first Standard O car equipped with the new model of the end-of-train device (EOT) blinking light, which has been replacing cabooses on real railroads since the 1970s. As such it was at the end of the first Lionel freight set ever made without a caboose.

WOOD-SIDED REEFER

In 1980 and 1982 Fundimensions introduced a new series of refrigerator cars based on an old-time theme. The first series from 1980 was known as the "Turn of the Century" series, and featured realistic weathered paint schemes and old railroad names like Oppenheimer Sausage Casings, Dairymen's League, and the American Refrigerator Transit Co. Aside from the paint scheme, the news regarding this series was an entirely new side and bottom piece for the car. It had horizontal wood slat scribing on the sides, unlike the vertical scribing found on the 9800-series of reefers. It also had exceptionally detailed riveting on a handsome scribed undercarriage. The door was a new design too, with fine latch and hinge details. The door slides open smoothly like a boxcar's doors, not like the plug doors of the 9800 series. The new cars even rode on the sprung Standard O trucks. But probably because the weathered look was so dramatically non-Lionel, the Turn-of-the-Century cars didn't sell as well as hoped.

In 1982 the company upgraded the model somewhat further to what we now know as the wood-sided reefer. The 1980 cars had a roof-end piece that was the same design as the 9800-style reefers. In 1982 it was changed to a brand new design. The ends have vertical wood slats, and the roof is scribed across its width. Four ice hatches are present in the corners of the roof, and all the wood scribing was given a skillfully grained look. The wood-sided reefer, at 10¼ inches, is only just shorter than the 9800-type reefer. It attaches the roof piece to the bottom with a screw at each end that installs from below into deep-sunk wells. The brakewheel was moved from the end (where it is on the 9800-series) to the top of the car. Although true to the prototype, this particular feature can be annoying when the owner puts the car back in its box—the brakewheel invariably will catch on the box divider. In most current production the brakewheel is shipped taped to the bottom to prevent damage.

In 1987, after some so-so sales the previous three years, Lionel hinted it was ending the series with three five-digit reefers. This proved just a case of semantics, though, because the car reappeared the next year with two good-looking cars in a new "Famous Inventor" series. This set, which started with the 19506 Thomas Newcomen and 19507 Thomas Edison, continued through the next few years and a total of ten cars ending, appropriately enough, with the 19528 Joshua Lionel Cohen and the 19529 A.C. Gilbert in 1992. The series went through three different types of wheelsets (plastic arch-bar, Symington-Wayne, and ASF) during its run.

One interesting feature about this reefer style is that either its own doors or the doors from regular boxcars (the type that are on the 19200 and 6464-style) can be used interchangeably. In fact, the boxcar doors were used on the uncataloged Old Glory series of reefers in 1989.

SEMI-SCALE REEFERS

A unique "semi-scale" reefer (pioneered by the 51301 Lackawanna) was made in 1992 as part of a six-car set intended to go with Lionel's rerelease of the 700E Hudson—the 1-700E from 1990. The prewar company had created scale freight cars to go with the original 1939 Hudson. The 1991–92 cars, like their predecessors, were all metal or phenolic cars with an exceptional level of detail and rugged construction.

The majority of reefer cars in the post-1986 period have been of the wood-sided variety, with the 9800 plug-door type taking a secondary position.

Collectors should pay attention to the pictures and descriptions in this guide, because it is a simple matter to change the roof-end pieces on these cars to mix and match roof colors. As such, beware of anyone seeking to assert that a nonstandard roof color is a rare variation. The same advice applies to doors.

REFRIGERATOR CAR LISTINGS

Exc Mt

16131 TEXAS & PACIFIC: 1994, 9800-style reefer; mustard yellow body; black lettering; "DF" between wings to left of door; "HYDROFRAME-60" and TP diamond logo to right side; ASF trucks; "BLT 1-94". **20 25**

16133 SANTA FE: 1994, 9800-style reefer; light yellow sides and doors; black roof and ends; black lettering; large Santa Fe cross logo to left side; "Ship and Travel SANTA FE—all the way" to right side; ASF trucks; "BLT 1-94". **20 25**

16134 READING: 1994, 9800-style reefer; gray body and doors; black lettering; blue and white Reading logo to right of door; "MRBX" and number under- and overscored to left side; ASF trucks; "BLT 1-94". Car was offered for separate sale and as part of the 11906 Factory Selection set. **20 25**

16143 READING LINES: 1995, 9800-style reefer; orange sides and doors; dark brown roof and ends; black lettering; "MRBX" and number over- and underscored to left side; black and white Reading Lines electrocal to right of door; ASF trucks; "BLT 96". Came as part of 11747 Lionel Lines Steam set, the top-of-the-line Traditional set in 1995. **25 30**

16146 DAIRY DISPATCH: 1995, 9800-style reefer; orange sides and doors; red roof and ends; black lettering; "DSDX" and number over- and underscored to left side; "REFRIGERATOR" and extensive capacity data to right of door; ASF trucks; "BLT 96". **20 25**

16223 BUDWEISER: 1989, 9800-style billboard reefer; uncataloged; white body; red roof and ends; red and black lettering; large "BUDWEISER" logo to left; Eagle-A logo to right; "ANHEUSER-BUSCH / BEER CAR" around eagle; no number on the car; Symington-Wayne trucks; "BLT 1-89". Part of 11775 Anheuser-Busch special set. One of several Lionel specials made for Budweiser and Anheuser-Busch in the modern era. Somewhat hard to find. **60 70**

16235 REA EXPRESS: 1992, wood-sided reefer; dark green body and doors; black roof and ends; white lettering; black and white REA square-X logo to right of door; Standard O trucks; "BLT 1-92". Car was first shown in the 11729 Louisville & Nashville set in the 1992 Book 2 catalog, but the set was not produced as shown there, with track, transformer, and yellow cupola caboose. Instead, it was produced with all-separate-sale pieces as shown in the 1992 Stocking Stuffer brochure. **30 35**

17302 Santa Fe Standard O reefer with EOT

Exc Mt

16805 BUDWEISER MALT NUTRINE: 1991–92, wood-sided billboard reefer; uncataloged; light tan-cream sides; forest green roof, ends, and doors; red, brown, and blue "Anheuser Busch BEER CAR" and A-B eagle herald; number on car is "3285" over bottle logo; car has lettering on door; ASF trucks; "BLT 1-91". This special reefer was intended as an add-on to the Budweiser 11775 set from 1989. It was only available through the Anheuser-Busch gift catalog. **80 100**

16807 H.J. HEINZ: 1994, wood-sided billboard reefer; white sides; dark green roof and ends; black, green, and red lettering; "HEINZ PICKLE REFRIGERATOR LINE" above "317" to left side; 16807 not on the car; H.J. Heinz trademark in red and brown to left side; Standard O trucks; "BLT 1-93". Shown in the 1993 Stocking Stuffers/1994 Spring Release catalog. **30 35**

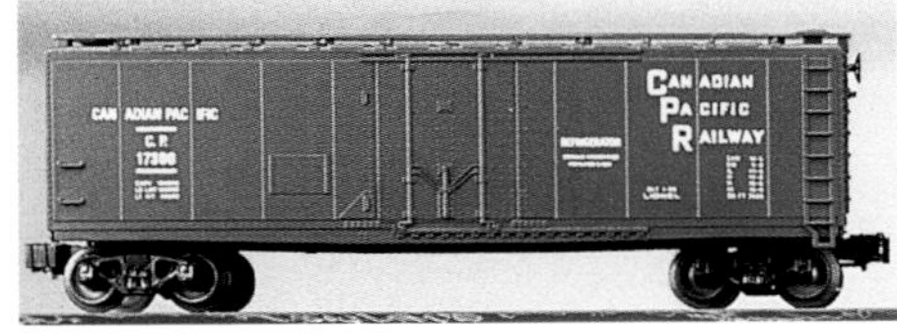

17300 CANADIAN PACIFIC RAILWAY: 1989; Standard O reefer; tuscan Type I body; white lettering; number over- and underscored; Standard O trucks; "BLT 1-89". Part of 11710 CP Rail set. **45 55**

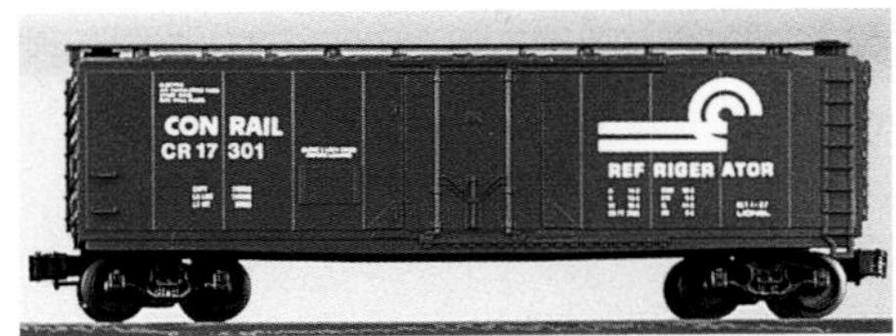

17301 CONRAIL: 1987, Standard O reefer; medium blue Type I body; white lettering and Conrail wheel logo; black catwalk; Standard O trucks; "BLT 1-87". Part of 11700 Conrail Limited set. **55 65**

17302 SANTA FE: 1990, Standard O reefer; yellow Type I body; black roof and ends; black lettering and large black cross logo; "Ship and Travel / SANTA Fe / all the way"; blinking yellow EOT light on brakewheel side powered from roller pickup snapped on one Standard O truck; "BLT 1-90". Came only in the 11713 Santa Fe Dash 8 set. See 17202 in the boxcar chapter for a related story. Catalog indicates this car has RailSounds, but it came with the EOT device instead. This is the first Standard O series car with an end-of-train (EOT) device, the first EOT in a set, the first Lionel freight set without a caboose, and one of the first cars for which a power pickup technique was devised for the Standard O trucks. **55 65**

17303 CHESAPEAKE & OHIO: 1993, Standard O reefer; yellow Type I body; white roof; black lettering; black "C & O for Progress" logo to right side; number on the car is "7890", not 17303; Standard O trucks; "BLT 1-93". **30 40**

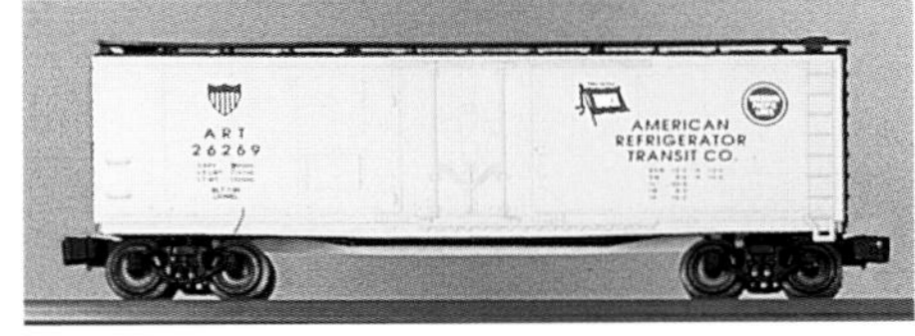

17304 WABASH: 1994, Standard O reefer; yellow Type I body; brown roof and ends; black lettering; red, white, and blue U.S. shield to left over "ART" and "26269" in black; 17304 is not on the car; Wabash flag logo in red, white and blue, and Missouri Pacific red sun logo to right of door, centered over "AMERICAN / REFRIGERATOR / TRANSIT CO."; Standard O trucks; "BLT 1-94". **35 45**

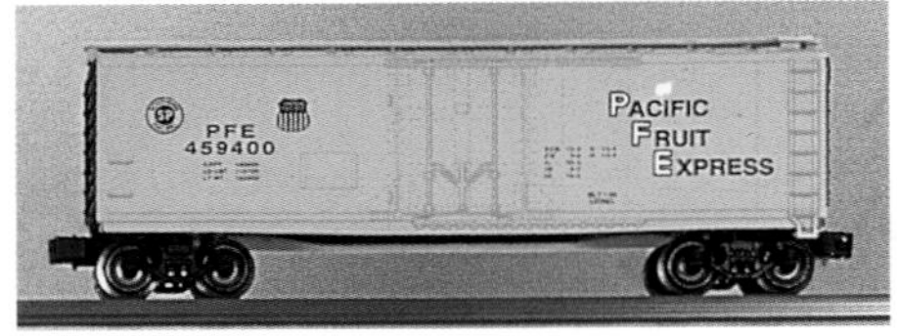

17305 PACIFIC FRUIT EXPRESS: 1994, Standard O reefer; orange Type I body and doors; black lettering; Union Pacific and Southern Pacific shields centered above "PFE" and "459400" to left side; "PACIFIC / FRUIT / EXPRESS" with P, F, and E in large white letters to right of door; 17305 does not appear on car; Standard O trucks; "BLT 1-94". Intended as a set with 17306. **35 40**

17306 PACIFIC FRUIT EXPRESS: 1994, Standard O reefer; identical to 17305 above, except number is "459401". Intended as a set with 17305. **35 40**

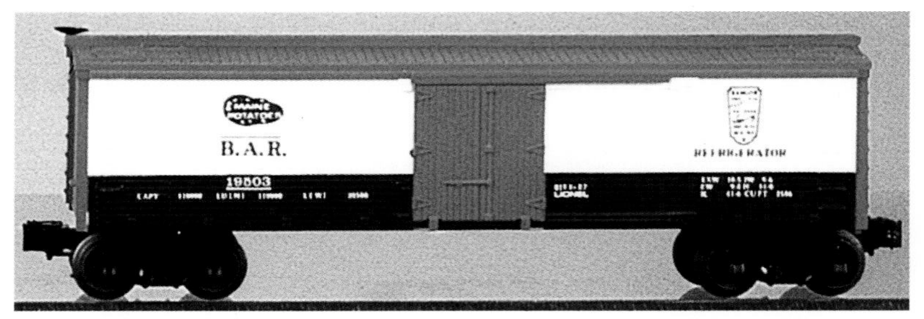

19503 Bangor & Aroostook wood-sided reefer

	Exc	Mt

17307 TROPICANA: 1995, Standard O reefer; orange Type II body and doors; sea blue-green lettering (sometimes hard to read); black and white capacity data block to far right; "Tropicana" in green and white to left of door; green, white, and orange logo of girl with oranges to near left of door; number on car is "TPIX 300"; 17307 does not appear; Standard O trucks; "BLT 95". First of a set of four identical Tropicana cars made in 1995–96, to represent, as Lionel had it, "the seemingly endless line of bright orange refrigerated cars carrying Tropicana orange juice north from Florida." These initial two cars were reasonably popular, prompting release of two supplemental cars in late 1995. This car is also the first appearance of the Type II Standard O reefer, which has an operating door. **40 45**

17308 TROPICANA: 1995, Standard O reefer; identical to 17307 above except number is "TPIX 301". Intended as a set with 17307 and 17309-10. See other comments on 17307. **40 45**

17309 TROPICANA: 1995, Standard O reefer; identical to 17307 above except number is "TPIX 302". Intended as a set with 17307 and 17308. See other comments on 17307. Shown in the 1995 Stocking Stuffers/1996 Spring Release catalog. **40 45**

17310 TROPICANA: 1995, Standard O reefer; identical to 17307 above except number is "TPIX 303". Intended as a set with 17307-9. See other comments on 17307. Shown in the 1995 Stocking Stuffers/1996 Spring Release catalog. **40 45**

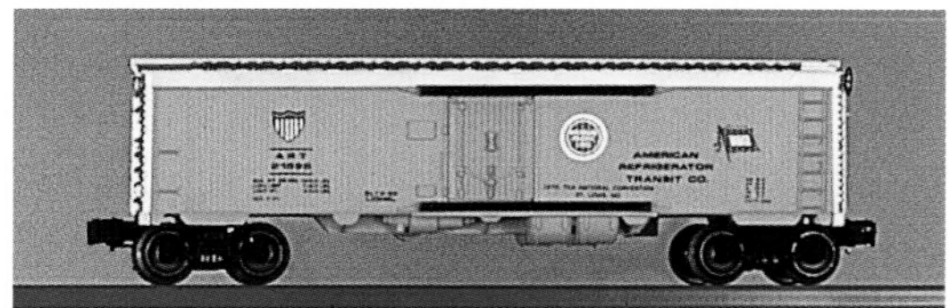

17898 WABASH: 1992, 9800-style reefer; uncataloged; annual convention car for the Train Collectors Association; orange sides; silver roof and ends; black lettering; full-color U.S. shield to left, above "ART / 21596"; 17898 is not on car; red Missouri Pacific sun logo and red, white, and blue Wabash flag herald to right of door, centered over "AMERICAN / REFRIGERATOR / TRANSIT CO."; Standard O trucks; "BLT 6-92". Car marks the 1992 TCA convention in St. Louis. The graphics on this car are similar to those on the 17304 released in 1994. **45 55**

19324: see 19524.

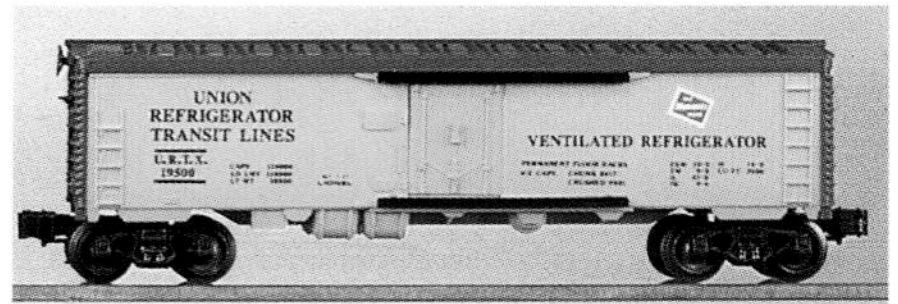

19500 MILWAUKEE ROAD: 1987, 9800-style reefer; yellow sides; brown roof and ends; black lettering; "UNION REFRIGERATOR TRANSIT LINES" to left side; number under- and overscored; red and white rectangular "MILWAUKEE ROAD" logo; Standard O trucks; "BLT 1-87". Part of Milwaukee Fallen Flags set no. 2, whose components were sold separately. **35 45**

19502 CHICAGO & NORTH WESTERN: 1987, wood-sided reefer; Brunswick green lower sides, doors, and roof; yellow upper sides; dark green lettering; "NORTH WESTERN REFRIGERATOR LINE" to left side; number under- and overscored; red, yellow, and green North Western (Chicago & North Western) logo; arch-bar trucks; "BLT 1-87". **30 40**

19503 BANGOR & AROOSTOOK: 1987, wood-sided reefer; dark blue lower sides; white upper sides; red roof, ends, and doors; contrasting blue and white lettering; Bangor & Aroostook logo to right; Maine potato in brown to left; "B.A.R." and number over- and underscored to left side; arch-bar trucks; "BLT 1-87". **30 35**

19508 Leonardo da Vinci wood-sided reefer

Exc Mt

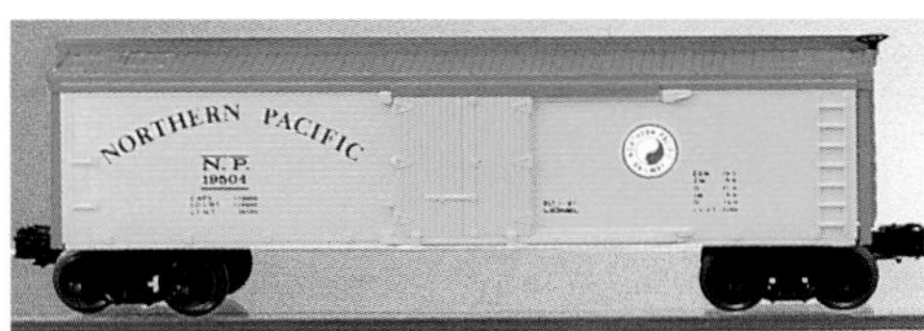

19504 NORTHERN PACIFIC: 1987, wood-sided reefer; yellow sides and doors; bright red-orange roof and ends; black lettering; number under- and overscored; red and white Monad decal logo; arch-bar trucks; "BLT 1-87". Some models have peeling decals. **25 30**

19505 GREAT NORTHERN: 1988, 9800-style reefer; green and orange Great Northern paint and striping scheme; green and white lettering; "EXPRESS REFRIGERATOR" on center green stripe to right side; Standard O trucks; "BLT 1-88". Part of Fallen Flags set no. 3, whose components were all sold separately. **45 55**

19506 THOMAS NEWCOMEN: 1988, wood-sided reefer; Famous Inventor series; white sides and doors; bright red roof and ends; black lettering and steam engine electrocal; "THOMAS NEWCOMEN / 1663–1729 / INVENTOR OF THE STEAM ENGINE" to left side; arch-bar trucks; "BLT 1-88". This is the first car of the "Famous Inventor" wood-sided reefer series that continued to 1992. **20 25**

19507 THOMAS EDISON: 1988, wood-sided reefer; Famous Inventor series; light tan sides and doors; dark brown roof and ends; black and white phonograph electrocal to right; black, white and flesh-color Edison figure to left; black, white, and gold electric lamp electrocal to right; text listing invention years for the phonograph (1877) and the electric lamp (1880); arch-bar trucks; "BLT 1-88". Released with 19506 as the first two cars in the Famous Inventor series. **20 25**

19508 LEONARDO DA VINCI: 1989, wood-sided reefer; Famous Inventor series; pale straw-yellow sides; gold roof and ends (catalog shows brown roof); black lettering; "LEONARDO DA VINCI / 1452–1519 / PAINTER-SCIENTIST / INVENTOR" to right of door; Mona Lisa electrocal to left; Symington-Wayne trucks; "BLT 1-89". **20 25**

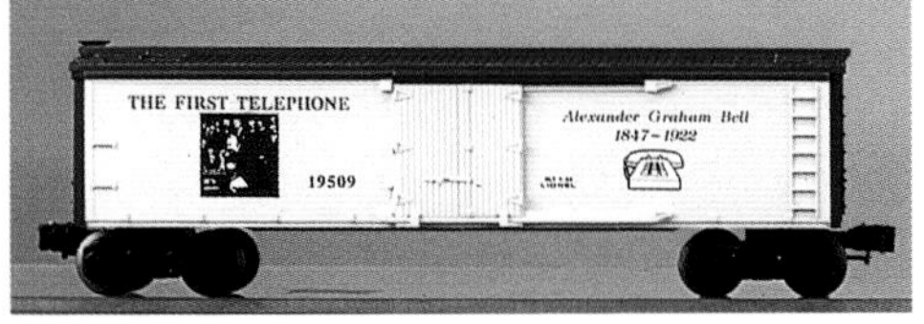

19509 ALEXANDER GRAHAM BELL: 1989, wood-sided reefer; Famous Inventor series; light blue sides; dark blue roof and ends; black lettering; "Alexander Graham Bell / 1847–1922" to right of door; electrocal of Bell with the first telephone to left side; Symington-Wayne trucks; "BLT 1-89". **20 25**

19511 WESTERN MARYLAND: 1989, 9800-style reefer; orange sides; brown roof; red ends; black lettering; large "WESTERN MARYLAND" in black across top of car with two sets of four horizontal lines; Standard O trucks; "BLT 1-89". Part of Western Maryland Fallen Flags Series no. 4, whose components were all sold separately. Very similar to 9818 reefer from 1980. **30 35**

19512 WRIGHT BROTHERS: 1990, wood-sided reefer; Famous Inventor series; light gray/off-white sides; green roof and ends; dark green lettering; "KITTY HAWK 1903" to right of door

	Exc	Mt

with Wright Flyer electrocal; "WILBUR WRIGHT / 1867–1912 / ORVILLE WRIGHT / 1871–1948" in black to left; ASF trucks; "BLT 1-90". **20 25**

19513 BEN FRANKLIN: 1990, wood-sided reefer; Famous Inventor series; tan sides; red roof and ends; black lettering; "BEN FRANKLIN / 1706–1790" at right; electrocal of Franklin to left; "INVENTOR-PUBLISHER-STATESMAN"; 1990 was the 200th anniversary of Franklin's death; ASF trucks; "BLT 1-90". **20 25**

A packaged set of three wood-sided reefers was an uncataloged Lionel release in late 1989. The three cars (19516-18) depicted significant events in U.S. history. They came together in a star-studded "Old Glory" set box, as set no. 19599. Note the sequence of the door colors. The doors used here were unique also, being 6464 boxcar-type doors rather than the usual reefer doors. This is the only time such doors were used on the wood-sided reefers. Though not shown in 1989, this set was cataloged in 1991.

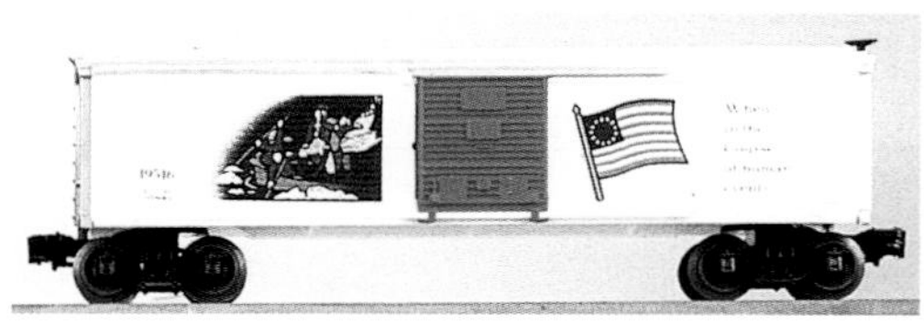

19516 GEORGE WASHINGTON: 1989, 1991, wood-sided reefer; Old Glory set; white sides; gray roof and ends; red boxcar-type door; electrocal of Washington crossing the Delaware at left; 13-star flag to right; blue lettering "When in the Course of human events . . . "; Type V plastic arch-bar trucks; "BLT 1-89". Part of three-car Old Glory set no. 19599, announced in a late 1989 flyer and cataloged in 1991. **15 20**

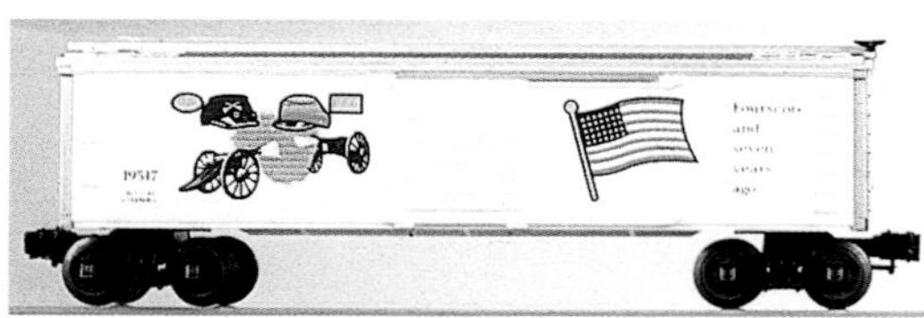

19517 CIVIL WAR: 1989, 1991, wood-sided reefer; Old Glory set; white sides; gray roof and ends; white boxcar-type door; electrocal of Union and Confederate caps and artillery to left; 35-star flag to right; blue lettering "Four score and seven years ago . . . "; Type V plastic arch-bar trucks; "BLT 1-89". Part of three-car Old Glory set no. 19599, announced in a late 1989 flyer, and cataloged in 1991. **15 20**

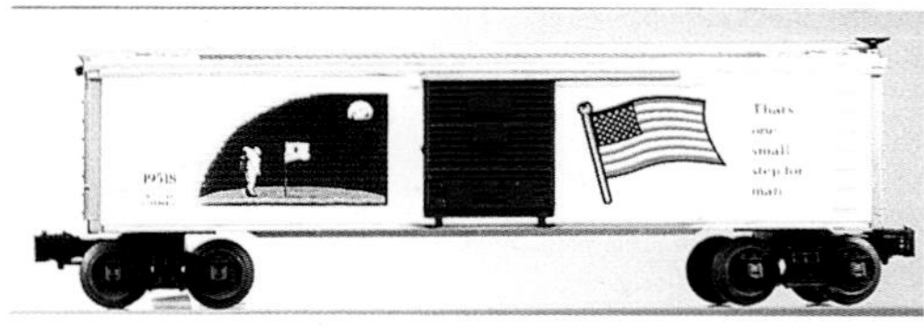

19518 MAN ON THE MOON: 1989, 1991, wood-sided reefer; Old Glory set; white sides; gray roof and ends; blue boxcar-type door; electrocal of Armstrong on the moon to left; 50-star flag to right; blue lettering "That's one small step for man . . . "; Type V plastic arch-bar trucks; "BLT 1-89". Part of three-car Old Glory set no. 19599, announced in a late 1989 flyer, and cataloged in 1991. **15 20**

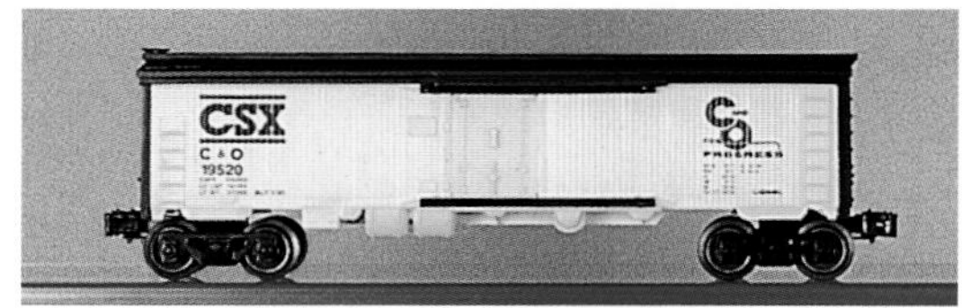

19520 CSX: 1991, 9800-style reefer; yellow sides; black roof and ends; black lettering; large "CSX" over- and underscored to left side; "C and O for Progress" logo to right; ASF trucks; "BLT 1-91". Lionel billed this as the "first time it had put CSX markings on a reefer." **20 25**

19522 GUGLIELMO MARCONI: 1991, wood-sided reefer; Famous Inventor series; silver sides; black roof, ends, and door; black lettering; "GUGLIELMO MARCONI / 1874–1937 / INVENTOR" to left side; "HIS WIRELESS TELEGRAPH SAVED LIVES AT SEA" to right with electrocal of ship avoiding iceberg using radio; ASF trucks; "BLT 1-91". **20 25**

19523 ROBERT GODDARD: 1991, wood-sided reefer; Famous Inventor series; white sides and door; red roof and ends, red lettering; "THE MAN BEHIND EVERY ROCKET THAT FLIES" with rocket electrocal to left side; "ROBERT GODDARD / 1882–1945 / ROCKET SCIENTIST" to right; ASF trucks; "BLT 1-91". **20 25**

19524 DELAWARE & HUDSON: 1991, 9800-style reefer; yellow body and roof; black ends; blue lettering and large D&H shield logo to right of door; Standard O trucks; "BLT 1-91". Part of 11719 Coastal freight Service Station Special set for 1991. The car number was incorrectly listed in the catalog as "19324". It should have been 19524. The 19324 number was used later for an Erie hopper. **25 30**

19525 ALKA SELTZER: 1991, wood-sided billboard reefer; uncataloged; light blue sides; dark blue roof and ends; dark blue lettering; electrocal of Speedy to left of door; red, white and blue Alka-Seltzer rectangle logo to right side; Standard O trucks; "BLT 1-91". Shown only in the 1991 Stocking Stuffers brochure. This is one of the more popular modern era wood-sided reefers. **40 45**

19526 GREEN GIANT: 1991, wood-sided billboard reefer; uncataloged; white sides; dark green roof and ends; black and green lettering; "ho.. ho.. ho.." and electrocal of the Giant to right of

Exc Mt

door; "Green Giant" in large light green letters to left; Standard O trucks; "BLT 1-91". Shown only in the 1991 Stocking Stuffers brochure. **30 40**

19527 NICKEL PLATE ROAD: 1992, 9800-style reefer; yellow body; tuscan-brown roof and ends; black lettering; "GARX" and number over- and underscored to left; Nickel Plate Road script to right; Standard O trucks; "BLT 1-92". Part of Nickel Plate Fallen Flags series no. 6, whose components were all sold separately. **30 35**

19528 JOSHUA LIONEL COHEN: 1992, wood-sided reefer; Famous Inventor series; orange sides; red roof, ends and doors; black lettering; "JOSHUA LIONEL COHEN / 1877–1965" to left of door; "STANDARD OF THE WORLD" with steam engine logo to right side; ASF trucks; "BLT 1-92". **30 40**

19529 A.C. GILBERT: 1992, wood-sided reefer; Famous Inventor series; yellow-cream sides and doors; dark blue roof and ends; dark blue lettering; image of Erector-set Ferris wheel to left of door; "A.C. GILBERT / 1884–1961 / ERECTOR SET INVENTOR / S GAUGE PIONEER" to right side; ASF trucks; "BLT 1-92". **25 35**

19531 RICE KRISPIES: 1992, wood-sided billboard reefer; uncataloged; white sides; medium blue roof, doors, and ends; red, blue, and black lettering "Kellogg's RICE KRISPIES" to left of door; multicolor electrocal of Snap, Crackle, and Pop to right side; Standard O trucks; "BLT 1-92". Shown only in the 1992 Stocking Stuffers brochure. **35 45**

19532 HORMEL: 1992, wood-sided billboard reefer; uncataloged; white sides; black roof and ends; green and black lettering; large "HORMEL / GOOD FOOD" sign which spans the center of the car, including the doors; number on the car is "901"; 19532 does not appear; Standard O trucks; "BLT 1-92". Shown only in the 1992 Stocking Stuffers brochure. **30 40**

19535 ERIE: 1993, 9800-style reefer; yellow sides; brown roof and ends; black lettering; black and white Erie diamond logo to right side; "URTX" and number over- and underscored to left; Standard O trucks; "BLT 1-93". Part of Erie Fallen Flags set no. 7 from 1993, whose components were all sold separately. **30 35**

19536 SOO LINE REA: 1993, wood-sided reefer; dark green body and doors; yellow lettering; red and white "RAILWAY

Exc Mt

EXPRESS AGENCY" diamond to right side; Soo Line "dollar" logo in yellow to left; Standard O trucks; "BLT 1-93". Part of 11738 Soo Line Service Station Special set from 1993. **30 35**

19537 KELLOGG'S: 1993, wood-sided billboard reefer; white body and doors; red roof and ends. Shown in the 1993 Stocking Stuffers/1994 Spring Release catalog, but the car was never made. **Not Manufactured**

19538 HORMEL: 1994, wood-sided billboard reefer; yellow sides and doors; tuscan-brown roof and ends; black lettering; "Dairy Brand Hams, Bacon, Lard" to right of door; "GEO. A HORMEL & CO." in arched letters to left side; number on car is "102"; 19538 does not appear; Standard O trucks; "BLT 1-94". Shown in the 1994 Stocking Stuffer/1995 Spring Release catalog. **30 35**

19539 HEINZ: 1994, wood-sided billboard reefer; white sides and doors, red roof and ends; black lettering; red "HEINZ 57" shield to left; red, black, and green Heinz "Pure Food Products" circle logo with pickle, to right of door; Standard O trucks; "BLT 1-94". Shown in the 1994 Stocking Stuffers/1995 Spring Releases catalog. **30 35**

19599 OLD GLORY SET: 1989, 1991, uncataloged in 1989; packaged set of three 9800 reefer cars, 19516, 19517, and 19518. See notes with 19516. Price includes set box. **45 55**

51301 LACKAWANNA: 1992, semi-scale reefer; part of a set of six cars in 1991–92 intended to re-create the famous detailed scale freight cars first made by Lionel in 1940; all-phenolic body with operating doors and door latch; metal frame; white sides and ends; tuscan-brown roof; black lettering; "7000" is the number on the car, not 51301; detailed capacity data to right side; Standard O trucks; "NEW 8-57". Very hard to find. **300 375**

52073 PACIFIC FRUIT EXPRESS: 1995, Standard O reefer; uncataloged; special for Southwest Division of the Toy Train Operating Society (TTOS); orange Type II body and doors; black ends; black lettering; Union Pacific and Southern Pacific

Exc Mt

shields centered above "PFE" and "459402" to left side; "PACIFIC / FRUIT / EXPRESS" with P, F, and E in large white letters to right of door; 52073 does not appear on car; small graphics for TTOS SW Cal Stewart; Standard O trucks; "BLT 95". This car is decorated identically to, and intended as an addition to, Lionel's 17305-6 PFE reefers from 1994, except for the black ends and operating doors. Note that the number is in sequence with the 17305-6 cars. The piece is a special for TTOS's Cal-Stewart train meet in Pasadena, and is part of a group of cars made for it in the 1990s. Another TTOS PFE car would follow in 1998. **55 65**

52074 IOWA BEEF PACKERS: 1995, Standard O reefer; uncataloged; annual convention car for the Lionel Collectors Club of America (LCCA); dark blue Type II body; black lettering; large "IBP" in yellow to upper right, with white brown and yellow cow-head logo; "IBPX and 197095" under- and overscored to left; 52074 does not appear; black lettering on car end for LCCA's 1995 convention in Des Moines; Standard O trucks; "NEW 7-95". **40 45**

Exc Mt

52097 CHESSIE SYSTEM: 1995, 9800-style reefer; uncataloged; annual special for the Artrain traveling art museum; medium yellow body; black lettering; "Chessie System" to upper right with the "C" as the Chessie cat logo; silver Artrain 25th anniversary graphic to left; "Artrain" in red and blue to lower left; no number on car; Standard O trucks; "BLT 95". **70 80**

87010 CANADIAN NATIONAL EXPRESS: 1987, wood-sided reefer; uncataloged; ninth annual commemorative car for the Lionel Collectors Association of Canada; green sides; black roof and ends; green doors; yellow lettering; yellow LCAC circle-L logo to right of doors; Standard O trucks; "BUILT LCAC". Reportedly 190 made. This was a Lionel-blank reefer decorated by the PVP. PVP designator "605-1464". **140 175**

CHAPTER 19

Searchlight Cars

The operating searchlight car ranks as one of Lionel's most recognizable and popular action cars, in this or any era.

There have been two types of searchlight cars used during the modern era by Lionel LTI and Lionel LLC. The first is patterned after the postwar 6822 "Night Crew" searchlight car, except that the rubber man of the postwar version was omitted. This car uses a standard flatcar body (long Type II, mold 6511-2—see the Flatcar chapter) with a superstructure attached that closely resembles the one used on the track maintenance cars. Instead of the extension platform used on the maintenance cars, a metal yoke with a bulb socket and plastic lens hood is placed on the superstructure, wired to a roller pickup on the trucks.

The second searchlight car type appeared in 1989, when LTI revived the depressed-center extension searchlight car last seen in 1959 on the 3650. This type uses a standard depressed-center flatcar with a plastic generator hood on one side and a removable searchlight on the other, held in place by a magnet. In the center is a cable reel with enough wire to allow the light to be placed up to four feet from the car.

The postwar company had a third type of searchlight car that was the same as the second style just discussed, except it included a noisy vibrator motor that permitted the searchlight hood to rotate. This is actually the most popular of the postwar searchlight cars (both other types require the light to be rotated manually). This model would seem an ideal candidate for modern Lionel to revive and retool, given the development of its quiet and smooth can motor, but it is yet to be seen if they will do so.

The first Fundimensions searchlight car enjoyed a long life—the tuscan 9302 Louisville & Nashville car, cataloged from 1973 through 1979, an eternity for a Lionel train. But through the 1970s and early '80s, only five other road names were released.

With the ownership change and new numbering system in 1987, LTI started issuing one or two searchlights each year. Many, like the Lehigh and 1989's Rio Grande, came only in sets and are somewhat hard to find. Even the company's own Lionel Railroader Club got into the act with a special issue. LTI revived the depressed-center extension searchlight car style in 1989, with the 16615 in Lionel Lines colors. 1993 was a big year for searchlight car enthusiasts—four were released that year.

The numbering system Lionel uses for the searchlight cars has been quite consistent during the modern era, unlike many other kinds of rolling stock. All the modern cars are numbered in the 16600- and 16700-series, except the Lionel Railroader Club car, which, as a special series, was given a 16800-range number.

Readers should note that in the 1990s Lionel re-created the searchlight caboose, another postwar favorite from the 1950s. These can be found in the caboose chapter. And about the same time they rereleased the unusual "Generator" boxcar, which includes a searchlight that plugs into the boxcar. Check the boxcar chapter for details.

So, until just a few years ago, the modern searchlight cars offered little incentive to collectors because there were only a few varieties, and most of them were quite numerous. The situation has changed, however. The recent cars are a handsome and collectable group.

Nor can one think of any layout as complete without the dramatic piercing of the night by the moving beam of the operating Lionel searchlight car.

SEARCHLIGHT CAR LISTINGS

Exc **Mt**

16601 CANADIAN NATIONAL: 1988, searchlight car; maroon flatcar body and light hood; light gray superstructure; white lettering; Symington-Wayne trucks; "BLT 1-88". **20** **25**

16606 SOUTHERN: 1987, searchlight car; green flatcar base; white lettering; gray superstructure; black searchlight hood; Symington-Wayne trucks; "BLT 1-87". Except for its trucks, this car matches the rolling stock in the 11704 Southern Freight Runner Service Station set, though it was not sold with the set.

(A) As described. **20** **25**

(B) 1988, special overstamp for the TCA Southern Division, with the circular Southern Division TCA logo overstamped on the superstructure. Additional marking was added by PVP (Code no. 705-1469). Less than 125 made. **30** **40**

16608 Lehigh Valley searchlight car

	Exc	Mt

16608 LEHIGH VALLEY: 1987, searchlight car; black flatcar body; white lettering; light gray superstructure; silver searchlight hood; Symington-Wayne trucks; "BLT 1-87". Came only in the 11702 Black Diamond set, the top-of-the-line Traditional Line set for 1987. Somewhat hard to find. **40 45**

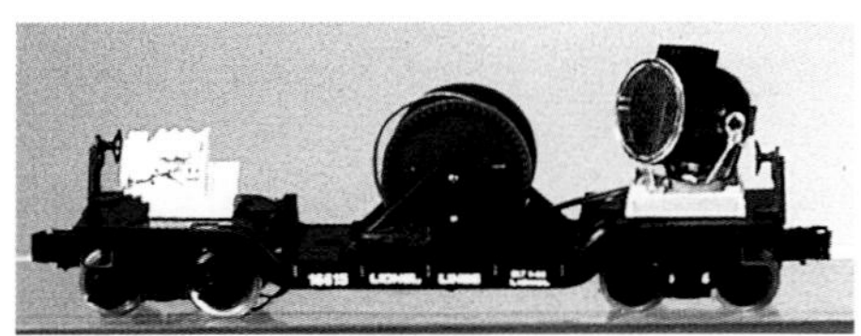

16615 LIONEL LINES: 1989, extension searchlight car; first in a series of new depressed-center searchlight cars—reissues of the postwar 3650—in which the light can be moved and repositioned up to four feet from the car; black short depressed center flatcar body; white lettering; light gray generator housing; black searchlight hood; green cable reel with hand crank to wind and unwind wire; Symington-Wayne trucks; "BLT 1-89". **25 35**

16616 RIO GRANDE:1989, searchlight car; uncataloged; pale yellow flatcar body; medium gray superstructure; black searchlight hood; black lettering; die-cast arch-bar trucks with unusual raised rivet holding trucks to body; "BLT 1-89". Part of the uncataloged 11758 Desert King Service Station set. **30 35**

16625 NEW YORK CENTRAL: 1990, extension searchlight car; light brown/tuscan depressed-center flatcar body; white lettering; orange generator housing; light gray searchlight hood with blue lens; light tan cable reel with wire and hand crank; ASF trucks; "BLT 1-90". **30 35**

16626 CSX:1990, searchlight car; dark green flatcar body and searchlight hood; yellow lettering; light gray superstructure; ASF trucks; "BLT 1-90". Came only in 11717 CSX freight set, the premier Traditional Line set for 1990.

(A) As described. **25 30**

(B) Factory error. Lettering missing from one side. J. Nowaczyk Collection. **NRS**

	Exc	Mt

16637 WESTERN PACIFIC: 1991, extension searchlight car; brown flatcar body; yellow lettering; light gray generator housing; black searchlight hood; orange cable reel with wire and hand crank; ASF trucks; "BLT 1-91". **30 35**

16659 UNION PACIFIC: 1993–95, searchlight car; unpainted red flatcar body; yellow lettering; yellow superstructure; black light hood; ASF trucks; "BLT 1-93". No individual box. Came only in 11736 Union Pacific Express set. **25 30**

16663 MISSOURI PACIFIC:1993, searchlight car; red flatcar body; white lettering; red searchlight hood; gray superstructure; ASF trucks; "BLT 1-93." **25 30**

16667 CONRAIL: 1993, searchlight car; blue body; white lettering; light gray superstructure; black light hood; ASF trucks; "BLT 1-93". Came only in 11740 Conrail Consolidated freight set, one of the nicer 1993 Traditional Line sets. No individual box. **30 35**

16669 SOO LINE: 1993, searchlight car; black body; white lettering; yellow superstructure; black light hood; ASF trucks; "BLT 1-93". No individual box. Came in 11741 Northwest Express set. **20 25**

16678 ROCK ISLAND: 1994, searchlight car; yellow body; black lettering; red superstructure; yellow searchlight hood; ASF trucks; "BLT 1-94". **25 30**

16625 New York Central extension searchlight car

	Exc	Mt

16685 ERIE: 1995, extension searchlight car; black depressed-center flatcar body; white lettering; "ERIE" in underscored white letters on lower deck; gray generator housing; black searchlight hood on a light yellow base, tan cable reel with wire and crank; ASF trucks; "BLT 95". **30** **35**

16711 PENNSYLVANIA: 1995, searchlight car; tuscan flatcar body; white lettering; yellow superstructure with keystone logo in tuscan; black searchlight hood; ASF trucks; "BLT 95". **30** **35**

	Exc	Mt

16803 LIONEL RAILROADER CLUB: 1990, searchlight car; uncataloged, eighth annual special issue from the Lionel Railroader Club; red flatcar body; white lettering; gray superstructure with red "SPECIAL EDITION" and "INSIDE TRACK" logo; black searchlight hood; ASF trucks; "BLT 5-90". Came in Type VI box. Somewhat hard to find. **30** **40**

CHAPTER 20

Tank and Vat Cars

Lionel has paid great attention to tank cars in its product lines over the years, in both the postwar and modern era. Though tankers are found much more often in industrialized areas of the nation than in the rural heartland, the tank cars on the Lionel Lines are staples of its freight trains, exceeded in quantity only by boxcars and hoppers. On real railroads today, the tank car is the second-highest revenue-producing piece of rolling stock, (after hoppers). Boxcars, though countless in number, produce less revenue for their owners than these freight cars.

By 1983, Lionel Fundimensions had re-released all of the four major types of tank cars used by the postwar Corporation (see accompanying figure). These are the long and short single-dome tank cars, with the short version not including a metal catwalk or ladder; the two-dome version; and the three-dome version. Typically the short single-dome car and the two-dome cars would be found in Lionel's lower-end Traditional line starter sets, while the longer cars were up in the Collector Line.

What was surprising was that until 1990, modern Lionel had not developed its own original versions of tank cars. On real railroads, tank cars exist in astonishing variety, and other scale-model firms have issued many more tank car styles than Lionel. The trend was broken in 1990 when Lionel Trains, Inc. at last announced a new tanker body style based on the GATX **"Unibody"** construction, in which tank, dome, and ends are cast in one piece. These wonderful models, which unlike their smaller brethren include no flatcar platform, are now considered Standard O cars, designed to go with the other scale rolling stock in that line as well as with the large engines such as the SD-40s. Thus far all Unibody tank cars have exhibited the same great details—metal ladders, detailed dome walkway, platforms with brakewheel and railings on the ends, placards (shipped separately in the box), and thin metal tension rods running the length of the car under the tank, to which the ladders are attached. Several of these new Unibody tank cars have appeared each year since then, and most have been good sellers. A few, like the LCCA's uncataloged NASA tank car, have commanded great interest.

The six types of tank cars in modern Lionel's line feature some interesting construction details and variations. The first **two-dome car** didn't appear in the modern era until 1983, and was a re-release of the inexpensive "Scout"-style tank car of the postwar years. In 1987 Lionel LTI upgraded this piece to the premium style with wire handrails—a resurrection of the popular 6465 Sunoco car of the early '50s. Since 1988, all the Lionel two-dome tankers have been of this upgraded variety, though only a small number have actually been made in recent years. The **three-dome car** has seen more production, and this particular model sports nice steam-valve details on the domes. The **long single-dome** tank car, with its trademark metal platform around the dome, is patterned after the postwar 6315, and has proved to be the predominant tanker style in the modern Lionel line. The smallest of the tank cars is the **short single-dome car** (tank length is only 6¾ inches), modeled after the postwar 6015. This car doesn't include the platform or ladder of its longer relative and is usually found in inexpensive sets or rolling stock assortments. Most catalogers refer to it as "O27" denoting its smaller size and lower cost.

The construction differences between the modern era Lionel cars and those made in the postwar era are more or less minor. The postwar cars had their brakewheels on a raised shaft; in modern production they are mounted directly on the frame without the shaft. The other noticeable difference, as with most modern trains, is the lettering and coloring, which is much brighter and crisper than on the postwar models, thanks to improved decorating technology available today.

Of the five types described so far, only the premium two-dome tank car sports a stamped metal frame, to which the tank is fastened with two screws. The long single-dome car (the one with the dome platform) and the three-dome cars, whose tanks are the same length, use the same open plastic frame. The tanks on these cars are fastened in place with just one screw in the center of the frame. This particular frame, though with nice details in the steps, pressurization tank, and rivets, was certainly a candidate for upgrade to die-cast, which did at last occur in 1991 with the release of the semi-scale Shell tank car. The shorter single-dome tank rides on a very inexpensive and thin plastic frame into which it snaps using molded plastic tabs. No screws are used, and with time the tabs can work loose, a situation for which operators should keep a sharp eye.

A unique all-metal tank car (the 51300 Shell) was produced in 1991 as part of a six-car "semi-scale" series to recall the 1940 release of a similar set of scale freight cars to go with the 700E scale Hudson. This single-dome all-die-cast tanker, with a body about the same size as the plastic one-dome car but with a die-cast metal frame a half-inch longer, is somewhat hard to find now, as are the other five cars in the set. It was a one-time product design until 1998, when Lionel came out with a fleet of die-cast tankers in Sinclair and Getty colors, packaged as sets.

It should also be noted that a few of the "four-digit tank cars"—that is, those produced before the 1987 changeover to ownership by LTI, when the numbering changed to five digits—show up in the post-1986 modern era either as part of carry-over sets or in a rolling stock assortment. One example is the blue 6312 Chessie tank car, part of the 1984 Fundimensions Chessie System set which was in an assortment as late as 1993. Details

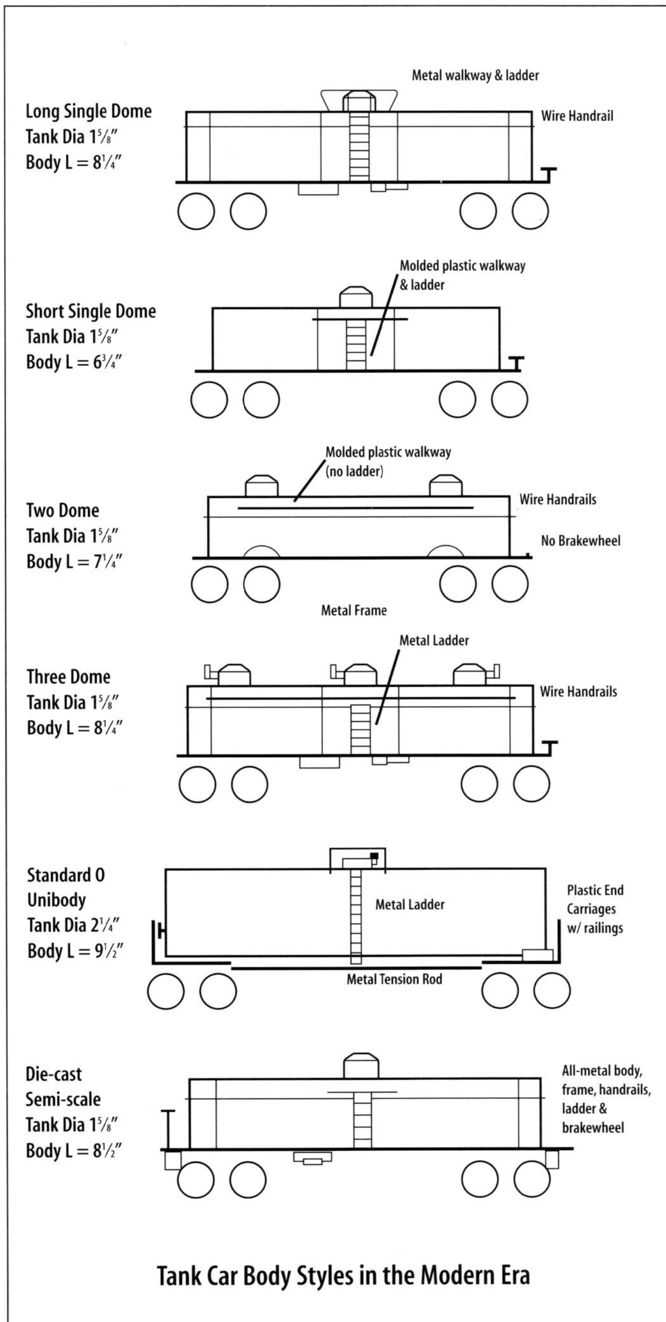

Tank Car Body Styles in the Modern Era

of these cars are listed in the 1970–1986 Greenberg Guides.

Although very few of the modern era Lionel tank cars can be considered rarities, they are certainly colorful, and a good collection can be built at relatively modest cost. Tank cars from Collector-level sets, such as the 16102 Southern, the 16105 D&RG and the tank cars from the 19600-series Fallen Flags sets will tend to show more appreciation because of their limited production. The same holds for the uncataloged cars such as the 16106 Mopar, 17885 Artrain, and the handsome tank cars made for many of the train clubs. These will be the hardest for the collector to find. The popular Unibody tankers can be expected to be in demand as well for some time to come. The die-cast tank cars are comparatively more expensive than the plastic cars, owing to the extra costs of the material and processing.

The numbering system for Lionel's modern tank cars is relatively straightforward: the 16100-series contains the regular-issue, less-expensive tank cars or ones released in Traditional (later "Classic") sets; the 17900-series designates the Standard O Unibody cars; and the 19600 series designates the Collector-level (or "Heritage" as Lionel began to call the line in 1996) tank cars found in the higher-end sets such as the Fallen Flags. These are principally the premium single-dome tank cars. The uncataloged train club cars can be found all over the spectrum, however, with many showing up in the 52000 series, which encompassed many types of special-production cars. The 17800 series was also briefly used for some special cars.

TANK CAR LISTINGS

Exc Mt

8392 see 17893

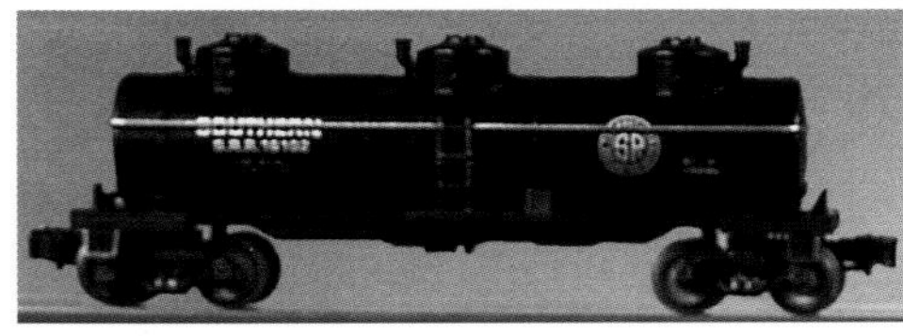

16102 SOUTHERN: 1987, three-dome tank car; uncataloged; dark green tank body; black plastic frame; gold lettering and Southern herald; chromed handrail; metal ladder; Standard O trucks; "BLT 1-87". Part of 11704 Southern Freight Runner Service Station Special set. **30 40**

16103 LEHIGH VALLEY: 1988, two-dome tank car; unpainted gray body; black lettering and number; red flag logo; stamped metal frame; Symington-Wayne trucks; "BLT 1-88". Separate-sale item, but matches 11702 Black Diamond set from 1987. This was the first time modern Lionel used wire handrails on the two-dome tank car. Revival of the premium 6465-style tank car not seen since the early '50s. **25 30**

16104 SANTA FE: 1989, two-dome tank car; black body; white lettering; bar code to right side; stamped metal frame; wire handrails; Symington-Wayne trucks; "BLT 1-89". **20 25**

16105 RIO GRANDE: 1989; three-dome tank car; uncataloged; silver-painted body; black lettering; black plastic frame; wire handrails; Standard O trucks; "BLT 1-89". Only in the 11758 Desert King Rio Grande Service Station Special set. **50 60**

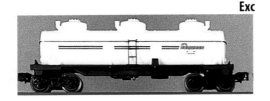

Exc Mt

16106 MOPAR EXPRESS: 1988, three-dome tank car; uncataloged; white body; red and blue lettering; blue stripes; black plastic frame; metal ladder; no number on car; Symington-Wayne trucks; "BLT 1-88". Offered only as part of uncataloged 11757 Mopar Express set in 1988. This set was the same as the Mopar set from 1987, except this car was added for 1988. Reportedly only 600 made. **75 100**

16107 SUNOCO: 1990, two-dome tank car; black body; white lettering; Sunoco yellow and red arrow decal logo to left; black stamped metal frame; wire handrails; ASF trucks; "BLT 1-90". Modern Lionel continued the tradition of including Sunoco tank cars in its line—postwar Sunoco tank cars were produced by the millions!

(A) As described. **20 25**

(B) Factory error, with no lettering on one side, but with decal. J. Czelusta collection. **NRS**

16108 RACING FUEL: 1989, short single-dome tank car; uncataloged; yellow body; black ends; black lettering "RACING FUEL"; number on the car is "6108"; black plastic frame; Symington-Wayne trucks; "BLT 1-89". Part of 11771 Microracers set made for K-Mart. The "G" in "RACING" is not exactly aligned vertically with the rest of the word. R. Walle comment. **15 20**

16109 BALTIMORE & OHIO: 1991, single-dome tank car; black body; white lettering and capitol dome logo; car has end lettering; number under- and overscored; metal dome walkway and ladders; wire handrails; black plastic frame; Standard O trucks; "BLT 1-91". Part of 11719 Coastal Freight Service Station Special set. This is the first Service Station Special to be cataloged—previous ones were uncataloged. **40 45**

16111 ALASKA: 1990–91, 1993–94, short single-dome tank car; unpainted white plastic body; dark blue or black lettering and Eskimo logo; black plastic frame; Symington-Wayne or ASF

Exc Mt

trucks; "BLT 1-89". Came with 16999 rolling stock assortment. All the pieces in this assortment say "BLT 1-89", but were issued in 1990 with Symington-Wayne trucks, while most regular issue rolling stock in 1990 had the new ASF strong-arm trucks. Lionel may have used this means to sell off excess Symington-Wayne trucks and Traditional Line pieces for a 1989 set that was never made. The car also appeared in the 16692 Rolling Stock assortment shown in the 1993 Stocking Stuffers/1994 Spring Releases catalog. Also note—the previous edition of this Guide erroneously reported this car with a metal frame. It has a plastic frame.

(A) Black lettering and logo. Letters are wider. S-W trucks. Early production. **25 30**

(B) Dark blue lettering and logo, letters thinner. ASF trucks. Later production. D. Record Collection. **20 25**

16112 DOWX: 1990, three-dome tank car; yellow body; blue lettering; Dow logo to right; wire handrails; metal ladders; plastic frame; ASF trucks; "BLT 1-90". Available only in 11717 CSX freight set. **30 35**

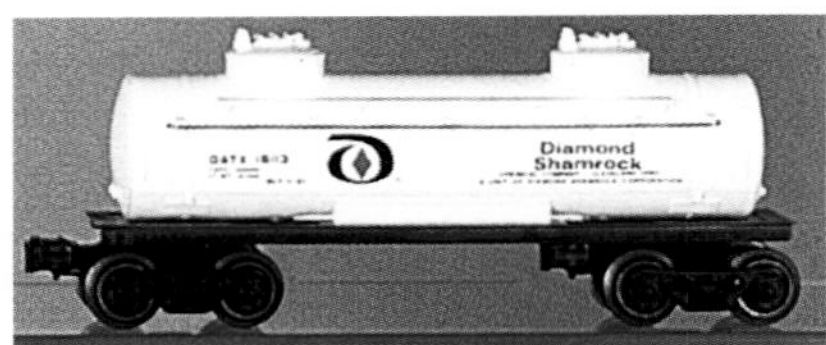

16113 DIAMOND SHAMROCK: 1991, two-dome tank car; white body; black lettering; black and red "d" logo; stamped metal frame; wire handrails; ASF trucks; "BLT 1-91". **20 25**

16114 HOOKER: 1991, short single-dome tank car; dark blue body; yellow lettering "HOOKER / NIAGARA FALLS, NY"; "GATX" and number over- and underscored; plastic frame; ASF trucks; "BLT 1-91". Part of 11720 Santa Fe Special set. **20 25**

16115 M-K-T: 1992, three-dome tank car; green body; yellow lettering, large "M-K-T" to left and "16115" to right; car includes end lettering; wire handrails, metal ladders; plastic frame; ASF trucks; "BLT 1-92". **20 25**

16116 U.S. ARMY: 1991, single-dome tank car; uncataloged; black body; white lettering; metal dome walkway and ladders; wire handrails; plastic frame; ASF trucks; "BLT 1-91". Part of 11726 Erie Lackawanna Freight set shown only in the 1991 Stocking Stuffers brochure. **40 50**

Exc Mt

16119 M-K-T: 1992–93, two-dome tank car; black body; yellow lettering; "KATY" shield logo in yellow to left side; stamped metal frame; wire handrails; ASF trucks; "BLT 1-92". Part of 11728 High Plains Runner set, and also the 11800 Toys "R" Us set in 1993. **15 20**

16123 UNION PACIFIC: 1993–95, three-dome tank car; yellow body; black lettering; UP shield logo to left; metal ladders; black plastic frame; ASF trucks; "BLT 1-93". Part of 11736 Union Pacific Express set. Also shown in the 16691 Rolling Stock assortment in 1995. **15 20**

16124 PENNSYLVANIA SALT: 1993, three-dome tank car; dark blue body; yellow lettering; overscored number and PRR shield to left; "Chemicals" in red script to right; yellow-painted wire handrails; metal ladders; black plastic frame; ASF trucks; "BLT 1-93". **20 25**

16126 JEFFERSON LAKE SULPHUR CO: 1993, three-dome tank car; yellow body; black lettering; over- and underscored "NATX 16126" to left; wire handrails; metal ladders; black plastic frame; ASF trucks; "BLT 1-93". Part of 11740 Conrail Consolidated set. **25 30**

16127 MOBIL: 1993, single-dome tank car; silver-painted body; red lettering; red, white, and blue "Mobil" to left side; red and white flying horse logo to right side; metal platform and ladders; wire handrails; black plastic frame; ASF trucks; "BLT 1-93". **25 30**

16128 ALASKA: 1994, single-dome tank car; silver-painted body; black lettering; metal platform and ladders; wire handrails; black plastic frame; ASF trucks; "BLT 1-94". **20 25**

16129 ALASKA: 1993–94, short single-dome tank car; black body; white lettering and Alaska Eskimo logo to left side; black plastic frame; ASF trucks; "BLT 1-93". Pictured in the 16692 Rolling Stock assortment in 1994, this car was also apparently available, though uncataloged, in 1993. A near-reverse-color cousin of the 16111. **15 20**

16132 DEEP ROCK: 1994, three-dome tank car; black body; yellow lettering, large "DEEP-ROCK" stretched letters in center; wire handrails, metal ladders; plastic frame; ASF trucks; "BLT 1-94". **25 30**

Exc Mt

16136 BALTIMORE & OHIO: 1994, single-dome tank car; black body; white lettering; B&O capitol dome logo to right; name and number under- and overscored to left side; metal platform and ladders; wire handrail; black plastic frame; ASF trucks; "BLT 1-94". Part of 11743 Chesapeake & Ohio Freight Set. **30 35**

16137 FORD: 1994, single-dome tank car; uncataloged; black body; white lettering; "Ford" in script to right side; "FDRX 12" over- and underscored to left; metal platform and ladders; wire handrail; black plastic frame; ASF trucks; "BLT 1-94". Part of 11814 Ford set. **30 35**

16138 GOODYEAR: 1995, single-dome tank car; black body; white lettering; white Goodyear logo to left side; car includes end lettering; metal platform and ladders; wire handrail; black plastic frame; ASF trucks; "BLT 95". **25 30**

16140 DOMINO SUGAR: 1995, single-dome tank car; light blue body with dark blue center section; black lettering; white and blue Domino sugar oval logo to right; Amstar Corporation insignia in black and white to left side; metal platform and ladders; wire handrail; black plastic frame; ASF trucks; "BLT 95". Note that this car is a nice match for the 9116 Domino Sugar hopper made by Fundimensions in 1974. **25 30**

16142 SANTA FE: 1995, single-dome tank car; gray and red body; black and white lettering; "GASOLINE" in white on red section of body and red band around lower part of dome; "UTLX 16142" in black to right side; gray-painted metal platform and

	Exc	Mt

ladders; wire handrail; black plastic frame; ASF trucks; "BLT 95". The red stripe at one end makes this an intriguingly handsome tank car and doesn't actually include the name "Santa Fe" on it. Part of the top-of-the-line Traditional set for 1995, the 11747 Lionel Lines Steam set. **30 35**

16144 SAN ANGELO: 1995, three-dome tank car; yellow body; black lettering; "SANX 16144" over- and underscored on left side; wire handrail, metal ladders; plastic frame; ASF trucks; "BLT 95". At this point in its catalogs, Lionel dropped the month designation in many of the "Built" dates on its pieces. **25 30**

16147 CLEARLY CANADIAN: 1994, short single-dome tank car; uncataloged; white body; blue and red lettering; number is not on the car; blue bottled water logo to left side; red maple leaf inside round "IMPORTED BOTTLED WATER" herald on car ends; black plastic frame; ASF trucks; no BLT date. This was a special promotional piece (less than 1000 reportedly made) to encourage stores to advertise the bottled water and other products from the Clearly Canadian Beverage Company. This promotion, carried out mostly in the Midwest, involved this car and raffle drawings for the regular-production New York Central Flyer freight set. **65 80**

16149 ZEP: 1995, short single-dome tank car; uncataloged; yellow body; dark blue lettering; "ZEP" oval logo to left side; "CLEAN ACROSS AMERICA" to right side; ASF trucks; "BLT 9-95". Reportedly 2500 made. Zep is a manufacturer of industrial cleaning products based in Atlanta. A 52141 Zep boxcar was made in 1997. **60 75**

17873 ASHLAND: 1988, three-dome tank car; uncataloged; 1988 convention car for the LCCA; black body; white lettering; red, white, blue and black Ashland Oil decal; white Lexington, Kentucky, convention notation; Standard O trucks; "BLT 1-88"; number and built date stamped on the plastic frame; Type V box. Some versions come with a special token available only at the convention. Add $30 to the value for the presence of the token. Two variations exist. The initial run was dull black. Later cars were oversprayed to help the Ashland decal stick to the paint. H. Overtoom comment.

	Exc	Mt
(A) Shiny black; 2396 made.	55	70
(B) Dull black; 924 made.	70	90

17877 KATY: 1989, single-dome tank car; uncataloged; 1989 convention car for the TTOS convention in Dallas; red body; gray plastic frame; black metal platform and ladders; wire handrails; yellow lettering "M-K-T / Missouri-Kansas-Texas" to right side; "Katy" in script to left; Standard O trucks; 17877 is not on the car, only on the box; "3739469" is the number on the car; "BLT 1-89"; 1425 made. This car replaced the planned Ewing Oil car as the 1989 convention car when Lorimar productions, owner of the television show Dallas, declined permission for the Ewing car to be manufactured. When the TTOS's designer of this car sent the initial artwork to Lionel, he scribbled a number on the car, thinking Lionel would insert its own catalog number. Instead, Lionel obediently decorated the car with the number he had written, which turned out to be his phone number! J.P. Neil comment. **60 75**

17885 ARTRAIN: 1990, single-dome tank car; uncataloged; bright medium blue body; white lettering and Artrain logo to left side; metal platform and ladders; wire handrails; Standard O trucks; "BLT 1-90". Artrain is a mobile art museum, based in Michigan, which transports art exhibits by train around the United States. This car could be obtained only via a 1990 fundraiser for Artrain, in which it was offered in return for a donation to the museum. Reportedly less than 1000 were made. This is the second Artrain car after the special 9486 Michigan 150th Anniversary car issued in the same fashion in 1986–87. Both cars are all-Lionel produced. Artrain has continued to release an annual car since 1990.

	Exc	Mt
(A) As described.	70	90
(B) Version with Richard Kughn signature.		130

17893 BAOX: 1993, single-dome tank car; annual commemorative car for the Lionel Collectors Club of Canada (LCAC); black body; white lettering; red and white "B/A" oil drop decal to right side (British American Oil Company Ltd., the Canadian subsidiary of Gulf Oil); "B.A.O.X. 914" over- and underscored to left; 17893 is only on the box, not on the car; metal dome walkway and ladder; wire handrail; black plastic frame; Standard O trucks; "BLT LCAC 11-91". This car was intended for release in 1991 (hence the 914 number—the 14th car in the LCAC series, set for 1991), but was delayed until 1993. Reportedly 450 made. **80 100**

17893 LONG ISLAND: 1992, single-dome tank car; uncataloged special for the Nassau Lionel Operating Engineers (NLOE) group in New York; black plastic mold painted dark gray; orange ends; black lettering "8392" designating the group's

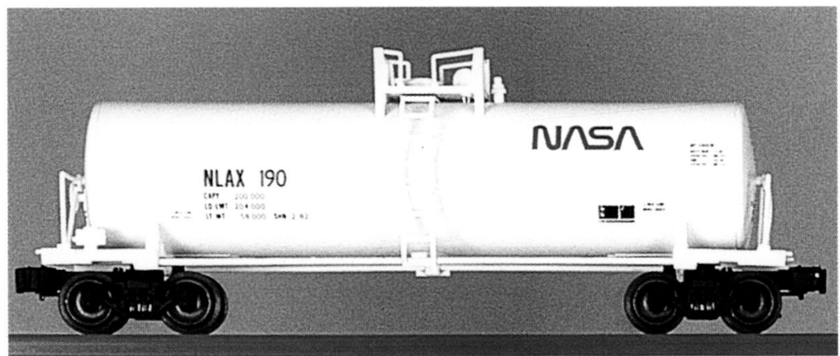

17899 single-dome Standard O Unibody tank car

Exc Mt

founding year and the year of release; LIRR keystone herald in red and white to right side; metal dome walkway and ladder; wire handrail; black plastic frame; Standard O trucks; "BLT 2-92". Reportedly only 55 made, this piece is a Lionel blank tank car decorated by PVP. It was however, given a Lionel catalog number—the same, interestingly, as the LCAC tank car above. Quite hard to find. **100 140**

17899 NASA: 1992, single-dome Standard O Unibody tank car; uncataloged; 1992 convention car for the LCCA's show in Orlando, Florida; white body; red and black lettering; red "NASA" worm logo to right side; "190" is the number on the car, 17899 is not on the car; car includes convention data on ends; railings, brakewheel, and red warning placard on plastic end platforms; plastic dome walkway and metal ladders; Standard O trucks; "BLT 1-92". This car is a close model of the NASA tank cars used to haul fuel and fluids at the Kennedy Space Center. **75 85**

17900 SANTA FE: 1990, single-dome Standard O Unibody tank car; first Standard O tank car released by Lionel; entirely new tank car model produced by LTI in late 1990; based on GATX (General American Transportation) Unibody design, where tank body, ends, and dome are a one-piece casting; black tank body with large white "Santa Fe" letters to left; bar code and chemical data to right; railings, brakewheel, and red warning placard on end platforms; detailed plastic dome walkway and metal ladders; detailed dome valves and hatch; underbody drain; metal tension rod connected between end carriages; Standard O trucks; "BLT 1-90". The tank on this piece is longer (9½ inches) and of larger diameter than any previous tank car. The car is also unique in that there is no full-length chassis frame—the tank ends rest on short platforms attached directly to the Standard O trucks, with the remainder of the tank unsupported. Two thin metal tension rods connect the two end carriages in order to maintain their spacing. Though this car was offered for separate sale only, it goes well with the Santa Fe Dash-8 set issued earlier in 1990. **40 50**

Exc Mt

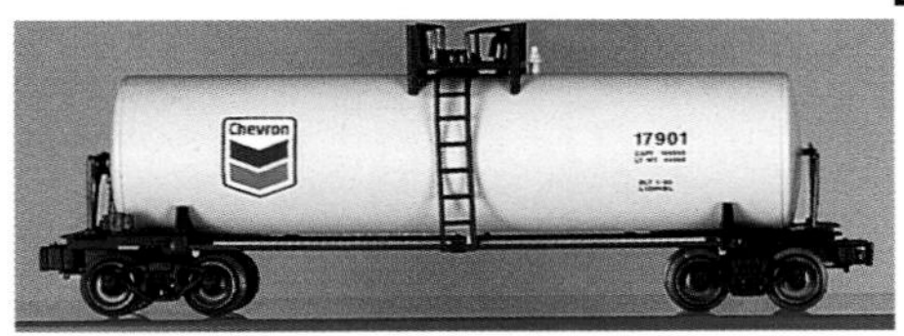

17901 CHEVRON: 1990, single-dome Standard O Unibody tank car; cream-light tan body; red, white, blue, and black Chevron logo to left; black lettering; railings, brakewheel, and warning placards on end platforms; plastic dome walkway; metal ladders; detailed dome valves and hatch; underbody drain; metal tension rods; Standard O trucks; "BLT 1-90". See 17900 for more background. **35 45**

17902 NEW JERSEY ZINC: 1991, single-dome Standard O Unibody tank car; white and blue body; blue lower portion of tank; blue and white lettering, "TiO_2 SLURRY" and "NJZ"; detailed capacity data; white-painted dome walkway; black metal ladder; railings, brakewheel, and warning placard on end platforms; detailed dome valves and hatch; underbody drain; metal tension rods; Standard O trucks; "BLT 1-91". See 17900 for more background.

(A) As described. **40 50**

(B) Factory error. "NJZ" on one side only. S. Chaney collection. **NRS**

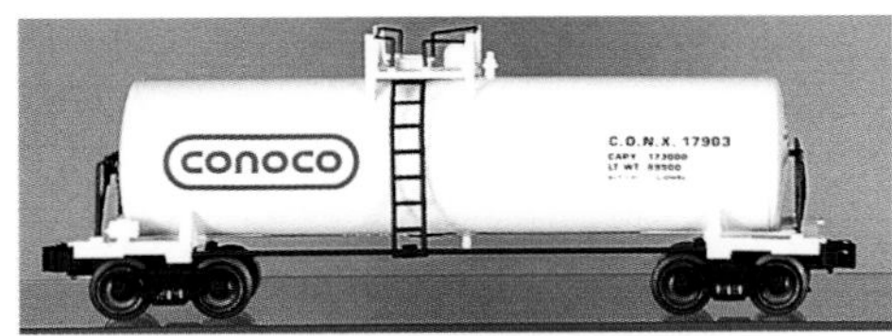

17903 CONOCO: 1991, single-dome Standard O Unibody tank car; white body; black lettering, large red "Conoco" logo to left; white-painted dome walkway; black metal ladder; railings, brakewheel, and warning placard on end platforms; detailed dome valves and hatch; underbody drain; metal tension rods; Standard O trucks; "BLT 1-91". See 17900 for more background. **40 50**

Exc Mt

17904 TEXACO: 1992, single-dome Standard O Unibody tank car; silver body; black lettering and Texaco "star" logo; star logo on ends; black dome walkway; metal ladders; black plastic end platforms with placards; metal brakewheel; metal tension rods; Standard O trucks; "BLT 1-92". See also 17900. **40 50**

17905 ARCHER DANIELS MIDLAND: 1992, single-dome Standard O Unibody tank car; black body; white and green lettering "ADM CORN SWEETENERS"; yellow "C" to left made up of corn kernels; black dome walkway; metal ladders; black plastic end platforms with placards; metal brakewheel; metal tension rods; Standard O trucks; "BLT 1-92". See also 17900. **40 50**

17906 SCM: 1993, single-dome Standard O Unibody tank car; white body with dark blue lower portion of tank; contrasting dark blue and white lettering; "TiONA" to right side; detailed capacity and text; "78286" is the number on the car; black dome walkway; metal ladders; black plastic end platforms with placards; metal brakewheel; metal tension rods; Standard O trucks; "BLT 1-93". See also 17900. **50 60**

17908 MARATHON: 1995, single-dome Standard O Unibody tank car; silver body; blue lettering; red and blue "M" logo to left side; black plastic dome walkway; metal ladder; railings, brakewheel, and warning placards on end platforms; metal tension rod; Standard O trucks; "BLT 1-95". **50 60**

19600 MILWAUKEE ROAD: 1987, single-dome tank car; dull orange-painted body; black lower third of tank; black dome cover and ends with white lettering; black lettering on tank body; red and white rectangular Milwaukee logo at right; black metal dome walkway and ladders; wire handrails; Standard O trucks; "BLT 1-87". Part of Milwaukee Fallen Flags set no. 2, whose components were all offered for separate sale. This is one of the first regular-issue tank cars to include end lettering, which became a common practice later. **45 55**

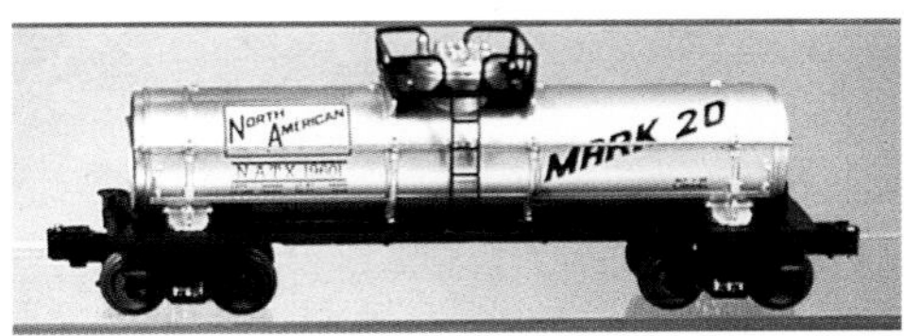

19601 NORTH AMERICAN: 1989, single-dome tank car; silver-painted body and dome; black "MARK 20"; black red and blue North American decal; number under- and overscored; black metal dome walkway and ladders; wire handrails; Standard O trucks; "BLT 1-89". Part of Western Maryland Fallen Flags Series no. 4, whose components were all offered separately. **35 45**

19602 JOHNSON: 1991, single-dome tank car; silver-painted body; red and black "Johnson" logo across middle; black lettering; plastic frame; black metal dome walkway and ladders; wire handrail; Standard O trucks; BLT "1-91". Part of Frisco Fallen Flags series no. 5, whose components were all sold separately. **30 40**

19603 GATX: 1992, single-dome tank car; black body; yellow lettering "GATX 19603" over- and underscored to left side; GATX triangle logo to right side; car includes end lettering; wire handrail; metal dome walkway and ladders; plastic frame; Standard O trucks; "BLT 1-92". Part of Nickel Plate Fallen Flags Series no. 6, whose components were all offered for separate sale. **35 45**

19604 GOODYEAR: 1993, single-dome tank car; black body; white lettering and Goodyear logo to left side; car includes detailed end lettering; wire handrail; metal dome walkway and ladders; plastic frame; Standard O trucks; "BLT 1-93". Part of 11738 Soo Line Service Station Special set. **35 45**

19605 HUDSON'S BAY: 1994, single-dome tank car; yellow body; black lettering "Hudson's Bay Oil and Gas"; stylized "H" flame

Exc Mt

logo in red to right side; wire handrail; metal dome walkway and ladders; plastic frame; Standard O trucks; "BLT 1-94". Part of 11744 New Yorker Passenger/Freight Station Special set, an intriguing set which included freight cars as well as two passenger coaches. **35 40**

19935 LIONEL RAILROADER CLUB: 1995, single-dome tank car; uncataloged; annual LRRC car; black body; gold lettering "LIONEL" and "L" circle logo to left side; "the INSIDE TRACK / 1995" to right side; 19935 is not on the car, a first for the Railroader Club series; wire handrail; metal dome walkway and ladders; plastic frame; ASF trucks; "BLT 95". **30 40**

38356 DOW CHEMICAL COMPANY: 1987, three-dome tank car; uncataloged; eighth annual LOTS Convention Car; this is a Lionel 6314 B&O three-dome tank car redecorated by PVP/NBT; sky blue tank body; dark blue lettering; yellow and black "DOW" logo; dark blue lettering and capacity data on car ends; yellow-painted wire handrails; number over- and underscored; PVP designator "705-1454"; Symington-Wayne trucks; 450 made. Type III box. Though not entirely a Lionel product, this car is included for completeness of the set. Hard to find. **90 120**

51300 SHELL: 1991, semi-scale single-dome tank car; part of a set of six scale freight cars released in 1991–92 to commemorate the detailed prewar semi-scale pieces made by Lionel in 1940 as rolling stock for the 700E Hudson—Lionel's first real entry into scale railroading; zinc die-cast body; black tank, no walkway; die-cast metal frame, ladder and handrails; white lettering with large "SHELL" to left; detailed capacity data to right side; "8124" is the main number on the car, 51300 appears in small letters to the lower right; brakewheel stanchion; Standard O trucks. As with the original 700E, these new cars go well with the modern Hudson, including the semi-scale 1-700E from 1990. After a seven-year wait, Lionel returned to the die-cast tank car model in force in 1998, releasing a total of 11 in the 26900-series. Somewhat hard to find. **100 130**

Exc Mt

52029 FORD: 1994, short single-dome tank car; uncataloged; part of a unique three-car O27 set of Ford cars released for TTOS's convention in Detroit in 1994; black tank body with white "Ford" script on right side; "FRDX 12" over- and underscored on left side; 52029 is not on car; black plastic frame; ASF trucks; "BLT 8-94." Came in an individual box in a three-pack with the 52031 short hopper and the 52030 gondola. **30 35**

52032 FORD: 1994, single-dome tank car; uncataloged; special for the Toy Train Operating Society in association with the organization's convention in Detroit; black body; white lettering; number on car is "FRDX 14"; black metal dome walkway and ladders; wire handrail; ASF trucks; "BLT 8-94". Car is similar to the 16137 Ford car produced the same year. This one includes a special "Welcome, Richard Kughn" signature in white. 1994 was a year in which Lionel produced several Ford-related pieces. 500 cars exist, initially available only through the TTOS at the Convention. **90 110**

VAT CARS

Lionel's vat cars are a curious but attractive creation. A metal frame is the basis for a low-slung open framework car with a roof supported by girder work on the sides and ends. Within this open framework are four round vats resting on the car base. The roof has simulated hatches atop each of the vats. The piece derives from the postwar 6475 Libby's car, first seen in 1963. The first modern vat car was the 9128 Heinz Pickle car from 1974. Lionel Fundimensions continued to release one every few years.

Lionel hit the jackpot in 1983 with a handsome vat car with bright Budweiser markings. This promotion was quite successful, and the company decided that other "billboard"-type vat cars for well-known brand names might be a good gamble and followed that one with cars labeled for Miller Lite and Dr. Pepper. Lionel LTI continued the idea with a unique beer train—the uncataloged Anheuser-Busch set from 1989, which was so popular that Lionel and the beer giant the next year released another handsome Anheuser vat car with the distinctive A-eagle logo on the vats.

Many of the other Lionel vat cars in the modern era have been released uncataloged, such as the Eastwood Automobilia vat car from 1995. As such these cars, given that only a few have come out in the post-1986 modern era, present an interesting and satisfying challenge to collectors, and one that will not hit the billfold too hard.

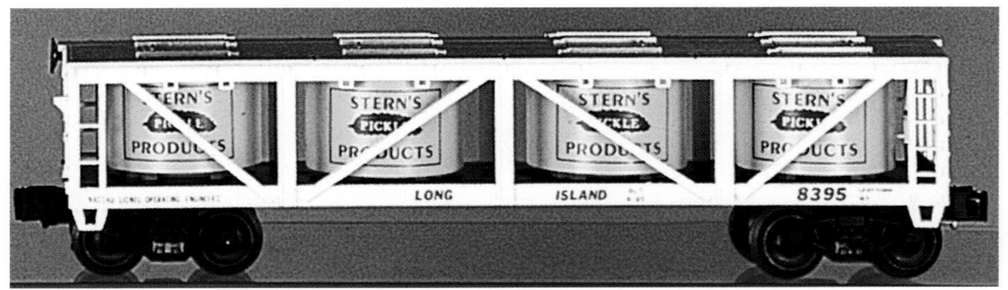

52061 Sterns Pickle/Long Island vat car

VAT CAR LISTINGS

Exc Mt

16225 BUDWEISER: 1990, vat car; uncataloged; dark gray frame; black roof; white lettering on car; white vats with gray wood-slat appearance; Anheuser A-eagle logo on each vat; ASF trucks; "BLT 1-90". Intended as an add-on to the uncataloged 11775 Budweiser set from 1989. Available only from an Anheuser-Busch catalog. Less than 2500 made.

(A) As described. **100 125**

(B) Factory error, with no lettering at all on the car body. S. Competello and S. Sloat Collections. This car is shown in the photo. **NRS**

19420 LIONEL LINES: 1994, vat car; orange frame, blue roof; blue lettering on frame; white vats with red, white, and blue Lionel Circle-L logo; ASF trucks; "BLT 1-94". With its Lionel orange-and-blue styling, this car is a logical add-on to the Lionel Lines freight set (headed by the 8380 SD-28 engine from 1983), to which Lionel occasionally adds new pieces. **25 30**

19421 HIRSCH BROTHERS: 1995, vat car; black body and roof; white lettering; black vats with "Hirsch" in script and labeling for "BEANS & PORK" on 2 vats, "CATSUP" on 2 vats, "MUSTARD" is shown on one of the vats in the catalog, but the car doesn't come with one; ASF trucks; "BLT 95". Hirsch Brothers is a manufacturer in Louisville, Ky. **25 30**

52044 EASTWOOD: 1995, vat car; uncataloged; one of a series of special Lionel cars produced for the Eastwood Automobilia company in Malvern, Pa.; dark blue frame; light gray roof; gold lettering on frame; black, red, light gray and medium gray vats with logos of various paints and coatings; Standard O trucks; "BLT 1-94". Available only through the Eastwood catalogs; 5000 made.

(A) As described. **35 40**

(B) Factory error. No lettering on frame. J. Pulvermacher Collection. **NRS**

52061 STERNS PICKLE/LONG ISLAND: 1995, vat car; uncataloged; one of a series of special cars produced by the Nassau Lionel Operating Engineers (NLOE) of Long Island; white body; silver roof; red lettering "LONG ISLAND" on frame; four yellow vats with red "STERN'S PRODUCTS" lettering and green pickle; number on the car is "8395", adhering to the NLOE's code of showing the founding year and the year of release; Standard O trucks; "BLT 6-95". Hard to find. Reportedly only 114 made. This was a Lionel blank decorated by PVP. **— 175**

Index

Number	Name	Type	Year	Page
16141	Erie	Stock car	95	124
16142	Santa Fe	1-d tank	95	235
16143	Reading	Reefer	95	222
16144	San Angelo	3-d tank	95	236
16146	Dairy Dispatch	Reefer	95	222
16147	Clearly Canadian	Sh 1-d tank	94u	236
16149	Zep	1-d tank	95u	236
16200	Rock Island	Short boxcar	87-88	118
16201	Wabash	Short boxcar	88-91	118
16203	Key America	Short boxcar	87u	118
16204	Hawthorne	Short boxcar	87u	118
16205	Mopar	Short boxcar	87-88u	118
16206	Denver & Rio Grande	Boxcar	89u	92
16207	True Value	Short boxcar	88u	118
16208	Pennsylvania	Auto carrier	89	80
16209	Disney Magic	Short boxcar	88u	118
16211	Hawthorne	Short boxcar	88u	118
16213	ShopRite	Short boxcar	88u	118
16214	Rio Grande	Auto carrier	90	81
16215	Conrail	Auto carrier	91	81
16217	Burlington Northern	Auto carrier	92	81
16219	True Value	Short boxcar	89u	118
16220	Ace Hardware	Short boxcar	89u	119
16221	Macy's	Short boxcar	89u	119
16222	Great Northern	Short boxcar	90-91	119
16223	Budweiser	Reefer	89u	222
16224	True Value	Short boxcar	90u	119
16225	Budweiser	Vat car	90u	240
16226	Union Pacific Costco	Short boxcar	90-91u	119
16227	Santa Fe	Short boxcar	91	119
16228	Union Pacific	Auto carrier	92	81
16229	Erie-Lackawanna	Auto carrier	91u	91
16232	Chessie System	Boxcar	92-95	92
16233	Missouri-Kansas-Texas	DD boxcar	92	92
16234	AC&Y	Boxcar	92	92
16235	REA Express	Woods. reefer	92	222
16236	New York Central	Boxcar	92u	92
16237	REA	Boxcar	92u	93
16238	New Haven	Boxcar	93-99	93
16239	Union Pacific	Boxcar	93-95	93
16241	Toys "R" Us	Boxcar	92-93u	93
16242	Grand Trunk Western	Auto carrier	93	81
16243	Conrail	Boxcar	93	93
16244	Duluth, South Shore	Boxcar	93	93
16245	Contadina	Boxcar	93	93
16247	Atlantic Coast Line	Boxcar	94	93
16248	Budweiser	Boxcar	93-94u	93
16249	United Auto Workers	Boxcar	93u	94
16250	Santa Fe	Short boxcar	93-94	11
16251	Columbus & Greenville	Boxcar	94	94
16252	U.S. Navy	Boxcar	94-95	94
16253	Santa Fe	Auto carrier	94	81
16255	Wabash	DD boxcar	95	94
16256	Ford	DD boxcar	94u	94
16257	Crayola	Boxcar	94-95	94
16258	Lehigh Valley	Boxcar	95	94
16259	Chrysler Mopar	Boxcar	94u	94
16260	Chrysler Mopar	Auto carrier	94u, 96u	82
16261	Union Pacific	DD boxcar	95	94
16264	Red Wing Shoes	Boxcar	95	94
16265	Georgia Power	Boxcar	95u	95
16266	Crayola	Boxcar	95	95
16267	Sears Zenith	Boxcar	95-96u	95
16268	GM/AC Delco	Boxcar	95u	95
16300	Rock Island	Short flatcar	87-88	152
16301	Lionel	Barrel ramp	87	152
16303	Pennsylvania	TOFC flatcar	87	164
16304	Rail Blazer	Sh gondola	87-88	174
16305	Lehigh Valley	Ore car	87	193
16306	Santa Fe	Barrel ramp	88	152
16307	Nickel Plate Road	TOFC flatcar	88	164
16308	Burlington Northern	TOFC flatcar	89	164
16309	Wabash	Gondola	88-91	174
16310	Mopar Express	Gondola	87-88u	174
16311	Mopar Express	TOFC flatcar	87-88u	164
16313	Pennsylvania	Sh gondola	88-89	174
16314	Wabash	TOFC flatcar	89	165
16315	Pennsylvania	Sh flat w/crates	88-89	152
16317	Pennsylvania	Barrel ramp	89	152
16318	Lionel Lines	Dep cntr flat	89	152
16320	Great Northern	Barrel ramp	90	153
16321	See 16322			165
16322	Sea Land	TTUX flatcar	90	165
16323	Lionel Lines	TOFC flatcar	90	165
16324	Pennsylvania	Dep cntr flat	90	153
16325	Microracers	Barrel ramp	89	153
16326	Santa Fe	Dep cntr flat	91	153
16327	The Big Top	Gondola	89u	174
16328	Nickel Plate Road	Gondola	90-91	174
16329	Southern Pacific	Short flat w/fences	90-91	153
16330	MKT	TOFC flatcar	91	165
16331	Southern	Barrel ramp	NM	153
16332	Lionel Lines	Dep cntr w/transf	91	152
16333	Frisco	Flat w/bulkhds	91	153
16334	See 16338			165
16335	New York Central	TOFC flatcar	91	165
16336	Union Pacific	Sh gondola	90u	174
16337	Chicago & North Western	TTUX flatcar	91	165
16338	Chicago & North Western	TTUX flatcar	91	165
16339	Mickey's World Tour	Gondola	91	174
16340	Amtrak	Flat w/stakes	NM	153
16341	New York Central	Dep cntr w/transf	92	153
16342	CSX	Gondola	92	174
16343	Burlington	Gondola	92	174
16345	Southern Pacific	TTUX flatcar	92	166
16346	Southern Pacific	TTUX flatcar	92	166
16347	Ontario Northland	Flat w/bulkhds	92	153
16348	Lionel-Erie	Flat w/tank	92	153
16349	Allis-Chalmers	Raised-cntr flat	92	154
16350	CP Rail	Flat w/bulkhds	91	154
16351	U.S. Navy	Flat w/submarine	92	154
16352	U.S. Military	Sh flat w/missile	92	154
16353	Boston & Maine	Gondola	91	174
16355	Burlington	Gondola	92-94	174
16356	MKT	Dep cntr flat	92	154
16357	Louisville & Nashville	TOFC flatcar	92	166
16358	Louisville & Nashville	Gondola	92	174
16359	Pacific Coast	Gondola	92	175
16360	Norfolk & Western	Maxistack	93	154
16361	Norfolk & Western	Maxistack	93	154
16362	Norfolk & Western	Maxistack	93	154
16363	See 16364-16365			166
16364	Southern	TTUX flatcar	93	166
16365	Southern	TTUX flatcar	93	166
16367	Clinchfield	Gondola	93	175
16368	MKT	Flat w/tank	93	154
16369	Amtrak	Flat w/wheels	92	155
16370	Amtrak	Flat w/rails	92	155
16371	Burlington Northern	I-beam flat	92	155
16372	Southern	I-beam flat	92	155
16373	Erie Lackawanna	Flat w/stakes	93	155
16374	Denver & Rio Grande	TOFC flatcar	93	166
16375	New York Central	Flat w/stakes	93-99	155
16376	Union Pacific	TOFC flatcar	93-95	166
16378	Toys "R" Us	TOFC flatcar	92-93u	166
16379	Northern Pacific	Flat w/bulkhds	93	155
16380	Union Pacific	I-beam flat	93	155
16381	CSXT	I-beam flat	93	156
16382	Kansas City Southern	Flat w/bulkhds	93	156
16383	Conrail	TOFC flatcar	93	166
16384	Soo Line	Gondola	93	175
16385	Soo Line	Ore car	93	193
16386	Southern Pacific	Flat w/lumber	94	156
16387	Kansas City Southern	Gondola	94	175
16388	Lehigh Valley	Gondola	94	175
16389	Pennsylvania	Flat w/wheels	94	156
16390	Lionel Water Car	Flat w/tank	94	156
16391	Lionel Lines	Gondola	93u	175
16392	Wabash	Sh gondola	93u, 94	175
16393	Wisconsin Central	Flat w/bulkhds	94	156
16394	Central Vermont	Flat w/bulkhds	94	156
16395	Canadian Pacific	Flat w/rails	94	156
16396	Alaska	Flat w/bulkhds	94	156
16397	Milwaukee Road	I-beam flat	94	157
16398	C&O	TOFC flatcar	93	167
16399	Western Pacific	I-beam flat	94	157
16400	Pennsylvania	Sh hopper	88-89	181
16402	Southern	Quad hopper	87u	181
16406	CSX	Quad hopper	90	181
16407	Boston & Maine	Quad hopper	91	182
16408	Union Pacific Costco	Sh hopper	90-91u	182
16410	MKT	Sh hopper	92-93	182
16411	Louisville & Nashville	Quad hopper	92	182
16412	Chicago & North Western	Quad hopper	94	182
16413	Clinchfield	Quad hopper	94	182
16414	CCC & StL	Sh hopper	94	182
16416	Denver & Rio Grande	Quad hopper	95	182
16417	Wabash	Quad hopper	95	182
16418	Chicago & North Western	Sh hopper	95	182
16420	Western Maryland	Quad hopper	95	183
16421	Western Maryland	Quad hopper	95	183
16422	Western Maryland	Quad hopper	95-96	183

Number	Name	Type	Year	Page
16423	Western Maryland	Quad hopper	95-96	183
16424	Western Maryland	Quad hopper	95	183
16425	Western Maryland	Quad hopper	95	183
16426	Western Maryland	Quad hopper	95	183
16427	Western Maryland	Quad hopper	95	183
16429	See 16422	Quad hopper set	95	183
16430	Georgia Power	Quad hopper	95u	183
16500	Rock Island	Bobber caboose	87-88	144
16501	Lehigh Valley	SP caboose	87	135
16503	New York Central	Transfer caboose	87	144
16504	Southern	N5C caboose	87u	134
16505	Wabash	SP caboose	88-91	136
16506	Santa Fe	Bay-W caboose	88	129
16507	Mopar Express	SP caboose	87-88u	136
16508	Lionel Lines	SP caboose	89u	136
16509	Denver & Rio Grande	SP caboose	89u	136
16510	New Haven	Bay-W caboose	89	129
16511	Pennsylvania	Bobber caboose	88-89	144
16513	Union Pacific	SP caboose	89	136
16515	Lionel Lines	SP caboose	89	136
16516	Lehigh Valley	SP caboose	90	136
16517	Atlantic Coast Line	Bay-W caboose	90	129
16518	Chessie System	Bay-W caboose	90	129
16519	Rock Island	Transfer caboose	90	145
16520	Sears Circus	SP caboose	89u	136
16521	Pennsylvania	SP caboose	90-91	136
16522	Lionelville Circus	N5C caboose	90-91	134
16523	Alaska	SP caboose	91	136
16524	Anheuser-Busch	SP caboose	89u	136
16525	Delaware & Hudson	Bay-W caboose	91	129
16526	Kansas City Southern	SP caboose	91	136
16527	Western Pacific	Work caboose	NM	145
16528	Union Pacific	SP caboose	90-91u	136
16529	AT&SF	SP caboose	91	137
16530	Mickey's World Tour	SP caboose	91	137
16531	Texas & Pacific	SP caboose	92	137
16533	C&NW	Bay-W caboose	92	129
16534	Delaware & Hudson	SP caboose	92	137
16535	Erie Lackawanna	Bay-W caboose	91u	129
16536	Chessie System	SP caboose	92,94-99	137
16537	Katy	SP caboose	92-93	137
16538	Louisville & Nashville	Bay-W caboose	92u	129, 141
16538	L&N Family Lines	Std O steel cab	NM	129
16539	Western Pacific	Std O steel cab	92	141
16541	Montana Rail Link	ExtV caboose	93	131
16543	New York Central	SP caboose	93-99	137
16544	Union Pacific	SP caboose	93-95	137
16546	Clinchfield	SP caboose	93	137
16547	Happy Holidays	SP caboose	93-94	137
16548	Conrail	SP caboose	93	137
16549	Soo Line	Work caboose	93	145
16550	U.S. Navy	Work caboose	94-95	145
16551	Anheuser-Busch	SP caboose	93-94u	138
16552	Frisco	Work caboose	94	145
16553	United Auto Workers	SP caboose	93u	138
16554	Grand Trunk	ExtV caboose	94	131
16555	Chesapeake & Ohio	SP caboose	94	138
16556	U.S. Navy	Gondola	94-95	175
16557	Ford	SP caboose	94u	138
16558	Crayola	SP caboose	94-95	138
16559	Seaboard	SP CC caboose	95	138
16560	Chrysler Mopar	SP caboose	94u	138
16561	Union Pacific	SP CC caboose	95	138
16562	Reading	SP CC caboose	95	139
16563	Lionel Lines	SP caboose	95	139
16564	Western Maryland	SP CC caboose	95	139
16565	Milwaukee Road	Bay-W caboose	95	129
16566	United States Army	SP caboose	95	139
16571	Georgia Power	SP caboose	95u	139
16575	Sears Zenith	SP caboose	95-96u	139
16578	Lionel Lines	SP caboose	95u	139
16579	GM/AC Delco	SP caboose	95u	139
16600	Illinois Central	Coal dump	88	190
16601	Canadian National	Searchlight	88	229
16602	Erie Lackawanna	Coal dump	87	190
16603	Detroit Zoo	Op short stock car	87	124
16604	New York Central	Log dump	87	190
16605	Bronx Zoo	Op short stock car	88	124
16606	Southern	Searchlight	87-88u	229
16607	Southern	Coal dump	87u	191
16608	Lehigh Valley	Searchlight	87	230
16609	Lehigh Valley	Derrick car	87	146
16610	Lionel	Track maint	87-88	157
16611	Santa Fe	Log dump	88	191
16612	Soo Line	Log dump	89	191
16613	MKT	Coal dump	89	191

Number	Name	Type	Year	Page
16614	Reading	Op short boxcar	89	119
16615	Lionel Lines	Ext searchlight	89	230
16616	Rio Grande	Searchlight	89u	230
16617	C&NW	Boxcar	89	95
16618	Santa Fe	Track maint	89	157
16619	Wabash	Coal dump	90	191
16620	Chesapeake & Ohio	Track maint	90-91	157
16621	Alaska	Log dump	90	191
16622	CSX	Boxcar	90-91	95
16623	Missouri-Kansas-Texas	DD boxcar	91	95
16624	New Haven	Op short boxcar	90-91	119
16625	New York Central	Ext searchlight	90	230
16626	CSX	Searchlight	90	230
16627	CSX	Log dump	90	191
16628	Lionelville Circus	Op gondola	90-91	175
16629	Lionelville	Op short boxcar	90-91	119
16630	Southern Pacific	Op short stock car	90-91	124
16631	Rock Island	Boxcar	90-91	95
16632	Burlington Northern	Boxcar	90	95
16633	Great Northern	Op short boxcar	NM	119
16634	Western Maryland	Coal dump	91	191
16635	CP Rail	Track maint	NM	157
16636	Rio Grande	Log dump	91	191
16637	Western Pacific	Ext searchlight	91	230
16638	Lionelville Circus	Op short stock car	91	124
16639	Baltimore & Ohio	Boxcar	91	95
16640	Rutland	Boxcar	91	96
16641	Toys "R" Us	Op short boxcar	90-91u	120
16642	Goofy	Op short boxcar	91	120
16643	Amtrak	Coal dump	NM	191
16644	Amtrak	Crane car	92	146
16645	Amtrak	Work caboose	92	145
16646	Railbox	Boxcar	NM	96
16649	REA	Boxcar	92	96
16650	New York Central	Boxcar	92	96
16651	Circus Clowns	Op short stock car	92	124
16652	Lionel Radar	Flat w/radar	92	157
16653	Western Pacific	Crane car	92	146
16655	RailSounds Tender	Tender only	93	40
16656	Burlington	Log dump	92	191
16657	Lehigh Valley	Coal dump	92	191
16658	Erie-Lackawanna	Crane car	93	146
16659	Union Pacific	Searchlight	93-95	230
16660	Lionel Fire Car	Flat w/ladder	93-94	157
16661	Lionel Boat Car	Flat w/boat	93	157
16662	Bugs Bunny/Yosemite	Op short stock car	93-94	124
16663	Missouri Pacific	Searchlight	93	230
16664	Louisville & Nashville	Coal dump	93	192
16665	Maine Central	Log dump	93	192
16666	Toxic Waste Car	Flat w/canisters	93-94	158
16667	Conrail	Searchlight	93	230
16668	Ontario Northland	Log dump	93	192
16669	Soo Line	Searchlight	93	230
16670	Lionel TV	Flat w/TV platform	93-94	158
16673	Steam Tender w/whistle	Tender only	94-97	40
16674	Pinkerton	Op gondola	94	175
16675	Great Northern	Log dump	94	192
16676	CB&Q	Coal dump	94	192
16677	NATO Submarine	Flat w/submarine	94	158
16678	Rock Island	Searchlight	94	230
16679	U.S. Mail	Op boxcar	94	96
16680	Lionel Cherry Picker	Flat w/ladder	94	158
16681	Lionelville Undersea	Aquarium car	95	85
16682	Lionelville Farms	Op short stock car	94	124
16683	Los Angeles Zoo	Op short stock car	94	124
16684	U.S. Navy	Crane car	94-95	147
16685	Erie	Ext searchlight	95	231
16686	Mickey & Big Bad Pete	Op boxcar	95	96
16687	U.S. Mail	Op boxcar	94	96
16688	Lionel Fire Car	Flat w/ladder	94	158
16689	Toxic Waste Car	Flat w/canisters	94	158
16690	Bugs Bunny/Yosemite	Op short stock car	94u	125
16701	Southern	Tool car	87u	86
16702	Amtrak	Bunk car	92u	86
16703	New York Central	Tool car	92	86
16704	Lionel TV	Flat w/TV platform	94	159
16705	Chesapeake & Ohio	Cop & Hobo boxcar	95	97
16706	Animal Transportation	Giraffe car	95	97
16707	See 16607			192
16708	C&NW	Track maint	95	159
16709	New York Central	Derrick car	95	147
16710	Missile Launching Car	Missile boxcar	95	97
16711	Pennsylvania	Searchlight	95	231
16712	Pinkerton	Op gondola	95	175
16713	Great Northern	Log dump	NM	192
16714	CB&Q	Coal dump	NM	192

Number	Name	Type	Year	Page
16800	Lionel Railroader Club	Ore car	86u	193
16801	Lionel Railroader Club	Bunk car	88u	86
16802	Lionel Railroader Club	Tool car	89u	86
16803	Lionel Railroader Club	Searchlight	90u	231
16804	Lionel Railroader Club	Bay-W caboose	91u	130
16805	Budweiser Malt Nutrine	Reefer	91-92u	223
16806	Toys "R" Us	Boxcar	92u	97
16807	H.J. Heinz	Woods. reefer	94	223
16808	Toys "R" Us	Boxcar	93u	97
16829	See 16529			139
16830	See 16530			139
16903	Canadian Pacific	Flat w/bulkhds	94	159
16904	New York Central	TTUX flatcar	94	167
16905	See 16904			167
16906	See 16904			167
16907	Lionel Farm Equipment	Flat w/tractors	94	159
16908	U.S. Navy	Flat w/submarine	94-95	159
16909	See 16556			175
16910	Missouri Pacific	TOFC flatcar	94	167
16911	Boston & Maine	TOFC flatcar	94	167
16912	Canadian National	Maxistack	94	159
16913	Canadian National	Maxistack	94	159
16914	Canadian National	Maxistack	94	159
16915	Lionel Lines	Sh gondola	93u	175
16916	Ford	TOFC flatcar	94	167
16917	Crayola	Gondola	94-95	176
16918	Budweiser	TOFC flatcar	NM	167
16919	Chrysler Corporation	Gondola	94u	176
16920	Lionel	Flat w/constr heli	NM	160
16922	C&O	TOFC flatcar	95	167
16923	Lionel Intermodal Serv	Flat w/chocks	95	160
16925	New York Central	TOFC flatcar	95	167
16926	Frisco	TOFC flatcar	95	167
16927	New York Central	Flat w/short gond	95	160
16928	Soo Line	Sh flat w/dump bin	95	160, 192
16929	British Columbia	Gondola	95	176
16930	Santa Fe	Flat w/wheels	95	160
16932	Erie	Flat w/rails	95	160
16933	Lionel Lines	Flat w/autos	95	160
16934	Pennsylvania	Flat w/road grader	95	160
16935	Union Pacific	Dep cntr w/bulldzr	95	161
16936	Sea Land	Maxistack	95	161
16937	Sea Land	Maxistack	95	161
16938	Sea Land	Maxistack	95	161
16939	U.S. Navy	Flat w/boat	95	161
16944	Georgia Power	Dep cntr w/transf	95u	161
16945	Georgia Power	Dep cntr w/reels	95u	161
16953	Redwing Shoes	TOFC flatcar	95u	167
16956	Zenith	TOFC flatcar	95u	168
16961	GM/AC Delco	TOFC flatcar	95u	168
17000	See 17107			183
17002	Conrail	ACF 2-b hopper	87	183
17003	DuPont Alathon	ACF 2-b hopper	90	183
17004	MKT	ACF 2-b hopper	91	184
17005	Cargill	ACF 2-b hopper	92	184
17006	Soo Line	ACF 2-b hopper	93	184
17007	Great Northern	ACF 2-b hopper	94	184
17008	Denver & Rio Grande	ACF 2-b hopper	95	184
17100	C&O Chessie	ACF 3-b hopper	88	184
17101	C&O Chessie	ACF 3-b hopper	88	185
17102	C&O Chessie	ACF 3-b hopper	88	185
17103	C&O Chessie	ACF 3-b hopper	88	185
17104	C&O Chessie	ACF 3-b hopper	88	185
17105	C&O Chessie	ACF 3-b hopper	95	185
17107	DuPont Sclair	ACF 3-b hopper	89	185
17108	Santa Fe	ACF 3-b hopper	90	185
17109	Norfolk & Western	ACF 3-b hopper	91	185
17110	Union Pacific	Std O hopper	91	186
17111	Reading	Std O hopper	91	186
17112	Erie-Lackawanna	ACF 3-b hopper	92	186
17113	Lehigh Valley	Std O hopper	92-93	186
17114	Peabody	Std O hopper	92-93	186
17118	Archer Daniels Midland	ACF 3-b hopper	93	186
17120	CSX	Std O hopper	94	186
17121	Illinois Central Gulf	Std O hopper	94	186
17122	Rock Island	ACF 3-b hopper	94	186
17123	Cargill	Std O hopper	95	187
17124	Archer Daniels Midland	ACF 3-b hopper	95	187
17125	Goodyear	ACF 3-b hopper	95	187
17200	Canadian Pacific	Std O boxcar	89	120
17201	Conrail	Std O boxcar	87	120
17202	Santa Fe	Std O boxcar	90	121
17203	Cotton Belt	Std O 50-ft boxcar	91	121
17204	Missouri Pacific	Std O 50-ft boxcar	91	121
17207	C&IM	Std O 50-ft boxcar	92	121
17208	Union Pacific	Std O 50-ft boxcar	92	121
17209	Baltimore & Ohio	Std O 50-ft boxcar	93	121
17210	C&IM	Std O 50-ft boxcar	92u	121
17211	C&IM	Std O 50-ft boxcar	92u	121
17212	C&IM	Std O 50-ft boxcar	92u	121
17213	Susquehanna	Std O boxcar	93	121
17214	Railbox	Std O boxcar	93	121
17216	Pennsylvania	Std O 50-ft boxcar	94	122
17217	State of Maine/NH	Std O boxcar	95	122
17218	State of Maine/B&A	Std O boxcar	95	122
17219	Tasmanian Devil	Std O boxcar	95	122
17300	Canadian Pacific	Std. O reefer	89	223
17301	Conrail	Std. O reefer	87	223
17302	Santa Fe	Std. O reefer	90	223
17303	Chesapeake & Ohio	Std. O reefer	93	223
17304	Wabash	Std. O reefer	94	223
17305	Pacific Fruit Express	Std. O reefer	94	223
17306	Pacific Fruit Express	Std. O reefer	94	223
17307	Tropicana	Std. O reefer	95	224
17308	Tropicana	Std. O reefer	95	224
17309	Tropicana	Std. O reefer	95	224
17310	Tropicana	Std. O reefer	95	224
17400	CP Rail	Std O gondola	89	176
17401	Conrail	Std O gondola	87	176
17402	AT&SF	Std O gondola	90	176
17403	Chessie	Std O gondola	93	176
17404	Illinois Central Gulf	Std O gondola	93	176
17405	Reading	Std O gondola	94	177
17406	Pennsylvania	Std O gondola	95	177
17500	Canadian Pacific	Std O flatcar	89	161
17501	Conrail	Std O flatcar	87	161
17502	Santa Fe	Std O TOFC flatcar	90	168
17503	Norfolk Southern	Std O TOFC flatcar	92	168
17504	Norfolk Southern	Std O TOFC flatcar	92	168
17505	Norfolk Southern	Std O TOFC flatcar	92	168
17506	Norfolk Southern	Std O TOFC flatcar	92	168
17507	Norfolk Southern	Std O TOFC flatcar	92	168
17508	Burlington	I-beam flat	NM	161
17509	Southern	I-beam flat	NM	162
17510	Northern Pacific	Std O flatcar	94	162
17515	Norfolk Southern	Std O flat w/tract	95	162
17600	New York Central	Std O wood cab	87u	141
17601	Southern	Std O wood cab	88	141
17602	Conrail	Std O wood cab	87	141
17603	Rock Island	Std O wood cab	88	141
17604	Lackawanna	Std O wood cab	88	141
17605	Reading	Std O wood cab	89	142
17606	New York Central	Std O steel cab	90	142
17607	Reading	Std O steel cab	90	142
17608	C&O Chessie System	Std O steel cab	91	142
17610	Wabash	Std O steel cab	91	142
17611	New York Central	Std O wood cab	90-91	142
17612	Nickel Plate Road	Std O steel cab	92	142
17613	Southern	Std O steel cab	92	142
17615	Northern Pacific	Std O wood cab	92	142
17617	Denver & Rio Grande	Std O steel cab	95	143
17618	Frisco	Std O wood cab	95	143
17870	East Camden & H. LCCA	Std O boxcar	87u	122
17871	New York Central TTOS	TOFC flatcar	87u	168
17872	Anaconda TTOS	Ore car	88u	194
17873	Ashland LCCA	3-d tank	88u	236
17874	Milwaukee Road LOTS	Log dump	88u	192
17875	Port Huron & Detroit LOTS	Boxcar	89u	97
17876	Columbia Newberry LCCA	Std O boxcar	89u	122
17877	Katy TTOS	1-d tank	89u	236
17878	Magma TTOM	Ore car	89u	194
17879	Valley Forge TCA	9500-style pass	89u	210
17880	D&RGW LCCA	Std O wood cab	90u	143
17881	Phelps Dodge TTOM	Ore car	90u	194
17882	Baltimore & Ohio LOTS	DD boxcar	90u	98
17883	New Georgia Railroad TCA	General-type pass	90u	210
17884	Columbus & Dayton TTOS	Std O boxcar	90u	122
17885	Artrain	1-d tank	90u	236
17886	Cyprus TTOM	Ore car	91u	194
17887	See 17892			168
17888	See 17892			168
17889	Southern Pacific TTOS	Std O TOFC flatcar	91u	168
17890	CSX LOTS	Auto carrier	91u	82
17891	Grand Trunk Artrain	Boxcar	91u	98
17892	Conrail LCCA	Std O TOFC set	91u	169
17893	BAOX LCAC	1-d tank	93u	236
17893	Long Island NLOE	1-d tank	92u	236
17895	See 17892			169
17898	Wabash TCA	Reefer	92u	224
17899	NASA LCCA	Std O tank	92u	237
17900	Santa Fe	Std O tank	90	237
17901	Chevron	Std O tank	90	237

Number	Name	Type	Year	Page
17902	New Jersey Zinc	Std O tank	91	237
17903	Conoco	Std O tank	91	237
17904	Texaco	Std O tank	92	238
17905	Archer Daniels Midland	Std O tank	92	238
17906	SCM	Std O tank	93	238
17908	Marathon	Std O tank	95	238
18000	Pennsylvania	B-6 0-6-0	89, 91	27
18001	Rock Island	Northern 4-8-4	87	27
18002	New York Central	Hudson 4-6-4	88	27
18003	Lackawanna	Northern 4-8-4	88	28
18004	Reading	Pacific 4-6-2	89	28
18005	New York Central	Hudson 4-6-4	90	28
18006	Reading	T-1 4-8-4	89	28
18007	Southern Pacific	J-Class 4-8-4	91	29
18008	Disneyland	General 4-4-0	90	39
18009	New York Central	Mohawk 4-8-2	90-91	29
18010	Pennsylvania	Turbine 6-8-6	91-92	29
18011	Chessie System	T-1 4-8-4	91	29
18013	See 18008			39
18014	Lionel Lines	Atlantic 2-6-4	91	29
18016	Northern Pacific	Northern 4-8-4	92	30
18018	Southern	Mikado 2-8-2	92	30
18022	Pere Marquette	Berkshire 2-8-4	93	30
18023	Western Maryland	Shay	92	30
18024	Texas & Pacific	Mohawk 4-8-2	92u	30
18025	See 18024			30
18026	New York Central Dreyfus	Hudson 4-6-4	92u	31
18027	New York Central Dreyfus	Hudson 4-6-4	92u	31
18028	Pennsylvania Smithsonian	Pacific 4-6-2	93u	31
18029	See 18027			31
18030	Frisco	Mikado 2-8-2	93u	31
18034	Santa Fe	Mikado 2-8-2	94	31
18040	Norfolk & Western	J-Class 4-8-4	95	31
18041	Boston & Albany		NM	32
18042	Boston & Albany	Hudson 4-6-4	95	32
18043	Chesapeake & Ohio	Streamline Hudson	95	32
18090	Denver & Rio Grande LCCA	Pacific 4-6-2	90u	32
18100	Santa Fe	F-3 A	91	45
18101	Santa Fe	F-3 B	91	45
18102	Santa Fe	F-3 Ad	91	45
18103	Santa Fe	F-3 B	91u	45
18104	Great Northern	F-3 A	92	45
18105	Great Northern	F-3 B	92	45
18106	Great Northern	F-3 Ad	92	45
18107	Rio Grande	Alco PA-1 A-B-A	92	48
18108	Great Northern	F-3 B	93	45
18109	Erie	Alco A	93	48
18110	Erie	Alco B	93	48
18111	Erie	Alco Ad	93	48
18112	TCA 40th Anniv	F-3 A	94	46
18113	TCA 40th Anniv	F-3 B	94	46
18114	TCA 40th Anniv	F-3 Ad	94	46
18115	Santa Fe	F-3 B	93	46
18116	Erie Lackawanna	Alco PA-1 A-A	93	48
18117	Santa Fe	F-3 A	93	46
18118	Santa Fe	F-3 Ad	93	46
18119	Union Pacific	Alco A	94	48
18120	Union Pacific	Alco Ad	94	49
18121	Santa Fe	F-3 B	94	46
18122	Santa Fe	F-3 B	95	46
18200	Conrail	SD-40	87	61
18201	C&O Chessie System	SD-40	88	61
18202	Erie-Lackawanna	SD-40d	89u	62
18203	CP Rail	SD-40	89	62
18204	C&O Chessie System	SD-40d	90u	62
18205	Union Pacific	Dash 8-40C	89	68
18206	Santa Fe	Dash 8-40B	90	68
18207	Norfolk Southern	Dash 8-40C	92	68
18208	Burlington Northern	SD-40d	91u	62
18209	CP Rail	SD-40d	92u	62
18210	Illinois Central	SD-40	93	62
18211	Susquehanna	Dash 8-40B	93	68
18212	Santa Fe	Dash 8-40Bd	93	69
18213	Norfolk Southern	Dash 8-40C	94	69
18214	CSX	Dash 8-40C	94	69
18215	CSX	Dash 8-40C	94	69
18216	Conrail	SD-60M	94	62
18217	Illinois Central	SD-40	94	62
18218	Susquehanna	Dash 8-40B	94	69
18219	Chicago & North Western	Dash 8-40C	95	69
18220	Chicago & North Western	Dash 8-40C	95	70
18221	Denver & Rio Grande	SD-50	95	63
18222	Denver & Rio Grande	SD-50	95	63
18223	Milwaukee Road	SD-40	95	63
18224	Milwaukee Road	SD-40	95	63
18300	Pennsylvania	GG-1	87	72

Number	Name	Type	Year	Page
18301	Southern	FM Trainmaster	88	67
18302	Great Northern	EP-5	88	71
18303	Amtrak	GG-1	89	72
18304	Lackawanna	M.U. Commuter	91	73
18305	Lackawanna	M.U. Commuter	92	73
18306	Pennsylvania	M.U. Commuter	93	73
18307	Pennsylvania	FM Trainmaster	94	67
18308	Pennsylvania	GG-1	92	72
18309	Reading	FM Trainmaster	93	67
18310	Pennsylvania	M.U. Commuter	93	73
18311	Disney	EP-5	94	72
18400	Santa Fe	2-4-2 Snowplow	87	75
18401	Lionel	Handcar	87	75
18402	Lionel Lines	Burro crane	88	75
18403	Santa Claus	Handcar	88	76
18404	San Francisco	Trolley	88	76
18405	Santa Fe	Burro crane	89	76
18406	Lionel	Motor. track maint	89-91	76
18407	Snoopy & Woodstock	Handcar	90-91	76
18408	Santa Claus	Handcar	89	76
18410	Pennsylvania	Burro crane	90	76
18411	Canadian Pacific	Fire-fighting car	90	76
18412	Union Pacific	Fire-fighting car	NM	76
18413	Charlie Brown & Lucy	Handcar	91	76
18416	Bugs Bunny & Daffy Duck	Handcar	92-93	76
18417	Lionel	Gang car	93	77
18419	Lionelville Electric	Trolley	94	77
18421	Sylvester & Tweety	Handcar	94	77
18422	Santa & Snowman	Handcar	94	77
18423	Lionel On-Track Step Van	On-track vehicle	95	77
18424	Lionel Pickup truck	On-track vehicle	95	77
18425	Goofy & Pluto	Handcar	95	77
18426	Santa & Snowman	Handcar	95	78
18500	Milwaukee Road	GP-9	87	55
18501	Western Maryland	NW-2	89	65
18502	Lionel Lines	GP-9	90	55
18503	Southern Pacific	NW-2	90	65
18504	Frisco	GP-7	91	56
18505	Nickel Plate Road	GP-7p&d	92	56
18506	Canadian National	Set of two	92	79
18507	Canadian National	Budd Car	92	79
18508	Canadian National	Budd Car	92	79
18510	Canadian National	Budd Car	93	79
18511	Canadian National	Budd Car	93	79
18512	Canadian National	Set of two	93	79
18513	New York Central	GP-7	94	56
18514	Missouri Pacific	GP-7	95	56
18550	Milwaukee JC Penney	GP-9	87u	56
18551	See 18809			51
18552	See 18813			63
18553	See 18817			56
18554	See 18822			51
18555	See 18823			63
18558	MKT	GP-7	94u	56
18600	Atlantic Coast Line	Columbia 4-4-2	87u	34
18601	Great Northern	Columbia 4-4-2	88	34
18602	Pennsylvania	Columbia 4-4-2	87	34
18604	Wabash	Columbia 4-4-2	88-91	34
18605	Mopar Express	Columbia 4-4-2	87-88	34
18606	New York Central	Atlantic 2-6-4	89	34
18607	Union Pacific	Atlantic 2-6-4	89	34
18608	Rio Grande	Atlantic 2-6-4	89u	34
18609	Northern Pacific	Atlantic 2-6-4	90	34
18610	Rock Island	1665 Switcher 0-4-0	90	34
18611	Lionel Lines	Atlantic 2-6-4	90u	35
18612	Chicago & North Western	Columbia 4-4-2	89	35
18613	Atlantic Coast Line	Columbia 4-4-2	89u	35
18614	Sears Circus Train	Columbia 4-4-2	89u	35
18615	Grand Trunk Western	Columbia 4-4-2	90	35
18616	Northern Pacific	Columbia 4-4-2	90u	35
18617	Adolphus III	Columbia 4-4-2	89u	35
18618	Baltimore & Ohio		NM	35
18620	Illinois Central	Atlantic 2-6-2	91	35
18621	Western Pacific		NM	35
18622	Union Pacific	Columbia 4-4-2	90-91u	35
18623	Texas & Pacific	Columbia 4-4-2	92	35
18625	Illinois Central	Columbia 4-4-2	91u	36
18626	Delaware & Hudson	Atlantic 2-6-2	92	36
18627	Chesapeake & Ohio	Columbia 4-4-2	92-99	36
18628	MKT	Columbia 4-4-2	92-93	36
18630	Chicago & North Western	Pacific 4-6-2	93	36
18632	New York Central	Columbia 4-4-2	93-99	36
18633	Union Pacific	Columbia 4-4-2	93-95	36
18633	Chesapeake & Ohio	Columbia 4-4-2	93-94	37
18635	AT&SF	Atlantic 2-6-4	93	37
18636	Baltimore & Ohio	Pacific 4-6-2	94	37

Number	Name	Type	Year	Page
18637	United Auto Workers	Columbia 4-4-2	93u	37
18638	Norfolk & Western	Atlantic 2-6-4	94	37
18639	Reading	Pacific 4-6-2	95	37
18640	Union Pacific	Pacific 4-6-2	95	38
18641	Ford	Columbia 4-4-2	94u	38
18642	Lionel Lines	Pacific 4-6-2	95	38
18689	See 18207			70
18700	Rock Island	Dockside 0-4-0	87-88	38
18702	Virginia & Truckee	General 4-4-0	88	39
18704	Lionel Lines	Porter 2-4-0	89u	38
18705	Neptune	Dockside 0-4-0	90-91	38
18706	AT&SF	Porter 2-4-0	91	38
18707	Mickey's World Tour	Porter 2-4-0	91	38
18709	Lionel Employee Learning	Dockside 0-4-0	92u	38
18710	Southern Pacific	Porter 2-4-0	93	39
18711	Southern	Porter 2-4-0	93	39
18712	Jersey Central	Porter 2-4-0	93	39
18713	Chessie System	Porter 2-4-0	94-95	39
18716	Lionelville Circus	General 4-4-0	90-91	40
18800	Lehigh Valley	GP-9	87	57
18801	Santa Fe	U36B	87	60
18802	Southern	GP-9	87u	57
18803	Santa Fe	RS-3	88	51
18804	Soo Line	RS-3	88	51
18805	Union Pacific	RS-3	89	51
18806	New Haven	SD-18	89	63
18807	Lehigh Valley	RS-3	90	51
18808	Atlantic Coast Line	SD-18	90	63
18809	Susquehanna	RS-3	89u	51
18810	CSX	SD-18	90	63
18811	Alaska	SD-9	91	63
18812	Kansas City Southern	GP-38	91	57
18813	Duluth, Missabe & Iron R	SD-18	90u	63
18814	Delaware & Hudson	RS-3	91	52
18815	Amtrak	RS-3	91-92	52
18816	Chicago & North Western	GP-38-2	92	57
18817	Union Pacific	GP-9	91u	57
18818	Lionel Railroader Club	GP-38	92u	57
18819	Louisville & Nashville	GP-38-2	92	57
18820	Western Pacific	GP-9	92	57
18821	Clinchfield	GP-38-2	93	58
18822	GM&O JC Penney	RS-3	92-93u	52
18823	C&IM	SD-9	92u	64
18824	Montana Rail Link	SD-9	93	64
18825	Soo	GP-38-2	93	58
18826	Conrail	GP-7	93	58
18827	Happy Holidays	RS-3	93	52
18830	Budweiser	GP-9	93-94u	58
18831	Southern Pacific	GP-20	94	58
18832	Pennsylvania	RSD-4	95	52
18833	Milwaukee Road	RS-3	94	52
18834	Chesapeake & Ohio	SD-28	94	64
18835	New York Central	RS-3	94	53
18836	Canadian National/GTW	GP-38-2	94	58
18837	Happy Holidays	RS-3	94	53
18838	Seaboard	RSC-3	95	53
18840	U.S. Army	GP-7	95	59
18841	Western Maryland	GP-20	95	59
18842	Bessemer & Lake Erie	SD-38	95u	64
18844	Nacionales De Mexico	GP-38	NM	59
18890	Union Pacific LOTS	RS-3	90u	53
18900	Pennsylvania	0-4-0 switcher	88-89	78
18901	Pennsylvania	Alco A	88	49
18902	Pennsylvania	Alco Ad	88	49
18903	Amtrak	Alco A	88	49
18904	Amtrak	Alco Ad	88	49
18905	Pennsylvania	44-ton	92	70
18906	Erie Lackawanna	RS-3	91u	53
18907	Rock Island	44-ton	93	70
18908	New York Central	Alco A	93	49
18909	New York Central	Alco Ad	93	49
18910	CSX	0-4-0 switcher	93	78
18911	Union Pacific	0-4-0 switcher	93	78
18912	Amtrak	0-4-0 switcher	93	78
18913	Santa Fe	Alco A	93-94	49
18915	Western Maryland	Alco A	93	50
18916	Western Maryland	Alco Ad	93	50
18917	Soo	NW-2	93	65
18918	Boston & Maine	NW-2	93	65
18919	Santa Fe	Alco Ad	93-94	50
18920	Frisco	NW-2	94	65
18921	Chicago & North Western	NW-2	94	65
18922	New Haven	Alco A	94	50
18923	New Haven	Alco Ad	94	50
18924	Illinois Central	0-4-0 switcher	94-95	78
18925	Denver & Rio Grande	0-4-0 switcher	94-95	78
18926	Reading	0-4-0 switcher	94-95	78
18927	U.S. Navy	NW-2	94-95	65
18928	Chicago & North Western	Calf unit, NW-2	95	66
18929	Boston & Maine	Calf unit, NW-2	95	66
18930	Crayola	0-4-0 switcher	94u-95	78
18931	Chrysler Mopar	NW-2	95u	66
18934	Reading	Alco A	95	50
18935	Reading	Alco Ad	95	50
18936	Amtrak	Alco A	95-96	50
18937	Amtrak	Alco Ad	95-96	50
18943	Georgia Power	NW-2	95u	66
19000	Blue Comet	9500-style pass	87u	210
19001	Southern Crescent	9500-style pass	87u	210
19002	Pennsylvania	9500-style pass	88u	210
19003	Milwaukee Road	9500-style pass	88u	210
19010	Baltimore & Ohio	9500-style pass	89u	210
19011	Lionel Lines	Long Madison pass	93	211
19015	Lionel Lines	Long Madison pass	91	211
19016	Lionel Lines	Long Madison pass	91	211
19017	Lionel Lines	Long Madison pass	91	211
19018	Lionel Lines	Long Madison pass	91	211
19019	Southern Pacific	Long Madison pass	93	211
19023	Southern Pacific	Long Madison pass	92	211
19024	Southern Pacific	Long Madison pass	92	212
19025	Southern Pacific	Long Madison pass	92	212
19026	Southern Pacific	Long Madison pass	92	212
19027	Reading	Long Madison pass	NM	212
19031	Reading	Long Madison pass	NM	212
19032	Reading	Long Madison pass	NM	212
19033	Reading	Long Madison pass	NM	212
19038	Adolphus Busch	9500-style pass	92-93u	212
19039	Pere Marquette	Long Madison pass	93	212
19040	Pere Marquette	Long Madison pass	93	212
19041	Pere Marquette	Long Madison pass	93	212
19042	Pere Marquette	Long Madison pass	93	212
19100	Amtrak	Long alum pass	89	213
19101	Amtrak	Long alum pass	89	213
19102	Amtrak	Long alum pass	89	213
19103	Amtrak	Long alum pass	89	213
19104	Amtrak	Long alum pass	89	213
19105	Amtrak	Long alum pass	89	213
19106	Amtrak	Long alum pass	89	213
19107	Southern Pacific	Long alum pass	90u	213
19108	Norfolk & Western	Long alum pass	91u	213
19109	Santa Fe	Long alum pass	91	214
19110	Santa Fe	Long alum pass	91	214
19111	Santa Fe	Long alum pass	91	214
19112	Santa Fe	Long alum pass	91	214
19113	Santa Fe	Long alum pass	91	214
19116	Great Northern	Long alum pass	92	214
19117	Great Northern	Long alum pass	92	215
19118	Great Northern	Long alum pass	92	215
19119	Great Northern	Long alum pass	92	215
19120	Great Northern	Long alum pass	92	215
19121	Union Pacific	Long alum pass	92u	215
19122	California Zephyr	Long alum pass	93	215
19123	California Zephyr	Long alum pass	93	215
19124	California Zephyr	Long alum pass	93	215
19125	California Zephyr	Long alum pass	93	215
19126	California Zephyr	Long alum pass	93	215
19127	California Zephyr	Long alum pass	93	216
19128	Santa Fe	Long alum pass	92u	216
19129	Illinois Central	Long alum pass	93	216
19130	Lackawanna	Set of four	94	216
19131	Lackawanna	Long alum pass	94	216
19132	Lackawanna	Long alum pass	94	216
19133	Lackawanna	Long alum pass	94	216
19134	Lackawanna	Long alum pass	94	217
19135	Lackawanna	Long alum pass	94	217
19136	Lackawanna	Long alum pass	94	217
19137	New York Central	Long alum pass	95	217
19138	Santa Fe	Long alum pass	95	217
19139	Norfolk & Western	Long alum pass	95	217
19140	Norfolk & Western	Long alum pass	95	217
19141	Norfolk & Western	Long alum pass	95	218
19142	Norfolk & Western	Long alum pass	95	218
19143	Norfolk & Western	Long alum pass	95	218
19144	Norfolk & Western	Long alum pass	95	218
19159	See 19141-19144			218
19200	Tidewater Southern	Boxcar	87	98
19201	Lancaster & Chester	Boxcar	87	98
19202	Pennsylvania	Boxcar	87	98
19203	D&TS	Boxcar	87	99
19204	Milwaukee Road	Boxcar	87	99
19205	Great Northern	DD boxcar	88	99
19206	Seaboard	Boxcar	88	99

Number	Name	Type	Year	Page
19719	Erie	Bay-W caboose	93	130
19720	Soo Line	ExtV caboose	93	132
19721	Gulf, Mobile & Ohio	ExtV caboose	93u	132
19723	Disney	ExtV caboose	94	133
19724	MKT	ExtV caboose	94u	133
19726	New York Central	Bay-W caboose	95u	130
19800	Circle L Ranch	Op cattle stock car	88	125
19801	Poultry Dispatch	Poultry car	87	125
19802	Carnation Milk	Milk car	87	105
19803	Reading Lines	Ice car	87	105
19804	Wabash	Op sh hopper	87	188
19805	Santa Fe	Op boxcar	87	106
19806	Pennsylvania	Op sh hopper	88	188
19807	Pennsylvania	ExtV caboose	88	133
19808	NYRB	Ice car	88	106
19809	Erie Lackawanna	Op boxcar	88	106
19810	Bosco	Milk car	88	106
19811	Monon	Brakeman car	90	106
19813	Northern Pacific	Ice car	89u	106
19815	Delaware & Hudson	Brakeman car	92	106
19816	Madison Hardware	Op boxcar	92u	106
19817	Virginian	Ice car	94	107
19818	Dairymen's League	Milk car	94	107
19819	Poultry Dispatch	Op poultry car	94	125
19820	RailSounds II Tender	Tender only	96	40
19821	Union Pacific	Op boxcar	95	107
19822	Pork Dispatch	Op poultry car	95	126
19823	Burlington Northern	Ice car	95	107
19900	Toy Fair 1987	Boxcar	87u	107
19901	I Love Virginia	Boxcar	87	107
19902	Toy Fair 1988	Boxcar	88u	108
19903	Lionel Christmas	Boxcar	87u	108
19904	Lionel Christmas	Boxcar	88u	108
19905	I Love California	Boxcar	88	108
19906	I Love Pennsylvania	Boxcar	89	108
19907	Toy Fair 1989	Boxcar	89u	108
19908	Season's Greetings	Boxcar	89u	108
19909	I Love New Jersey	Boxcar	90	108
19910	Happy Holidays	Boxcar	90u	109
19911	Toy Fair 1990	Boxcar	90u	109
19912	I Love Ohio	Boxcar	91	109
19913	Season's Greetings	Boxcar	91u	109
19914	Toy Fair 1991	Boxcar	91u	109
19915	I Love Texas	Boxcar	92	109
19916	Christmas	Boxcar	92u	109
19917	Toy Fair 1992	Boxcar	92u	109
19918	Christmas Car	Boxcar	92u	109
19919	I Love Minnesota	Boxcar	93	110
19920	Lionel Visitors Center	Boxcar	92u	110
19921	Christmas Employee	Boxcar	93u	110
19922	Christmas Boxcar	Boxcar	93	110
19923	Toy Fair 1993	Boxcar	93u	110
19924	Lionel Railroader Club	Boxcar	93u	110
19925	Lionel Learning Center	Boxcar	93u	110
19926	I Love Nevada	Boxcar	94	110
19927	Lionel Visitors Center	Boxcar	93u	111
19928	Christmas Employee	Boxcar	94u	111
19929	Merry Christmas	Boxcar	94	111
19930	Lionel Railroader Club	Quad hopper	94u	188
19931	Toy Fair 1994	Boxcar	94u	111
19932	Lionel Visitors Center	Boxcar	94u	111
19933	I Love Illinois	Boxcar	95	111
19934	Lionel Visitors Center	Boxcar	95u	111
19935	Lionel Railroader Club	1-d tank	95u	239
19937	Toy Fair/Dealer Preview	Boxcar	95u	111
19938	Happy Holidays	Boxcar	95	111
19939	Christmas Employee	Boxcar	95u	112
19941	I Love Colorado	Boxcar	95	112
19960	Western Pacific LOTS	Std O boxcar	92u	122
19961	Inspiration Consol TTOM	Ore car	92u	195
19962	Southern Pacific TTOS	Std O hopper	92u	188
19963	Union Equity TTOS	ACF 3-b hopper	92u	188
19964	U.S. JCI Senate	Boxcar	92u	112
33000	Lionel Lines Railscope	GP-9	88	59
33004	New York Central RS	GP-9	NM	59
33005	Union Pacific RS	GP-9	NM	59
38356	Dow Chemical LOTS	3-d tank	87u	239
51220-245	Smithsonian Collection	Brass pass		218
51300	Shell	Semi-sc tank	91	239
51301	Lackawanna	Semi-sc reefer	92	227
51401	Pennsylvania	Semi-sc boxcar	91	112
51402	Chesapeake & Ohio	Semi-sc stock car	92	126
51501	Baltimore & Ohio	Semi-sc Q hop.	91	188
51701	New York Central	Semi-sc caboose	91	143
51702	Pennsylvania	N8 diec caboose	92	134
52000	Detroit-Toledo TCA	TOFC flatcar	92u	169
52001	Boston & Maine NETCA	Quad hopper	92u	189
52002	See 7692-1 to -7			218
52003	Meet Me in St. Louis TCA	TOFC flatcar	92u	169
52004	Algoma Central LCAC	Gondola	95u	178
52005	Canadian National LCAC	F-3 B	93u	46
52007	Long Island NLOE	RS-3	92u	54
52008	Lionel Lines TCA	Crane car	93u	147
52009	Western Pacific TTOS	Boxcar	93u	112
52010	Weyerhaeuser TTOS	Std O boxcar	93u	122
52011	Tucson, Cornelia & GB	Ore car	93u	195
52013	Norfolk Southern Artrain	Std O TOFC flatcar	92u	169
52014	Burlington LOTS	TTUX flatcar	93u	170
52016	Boston & Maine NETCA	Gondola	93u	178
52018	3M TCA	Boxcar	93u	112
52019	Long Island NLOE	Boxcar	93u	112
52020	Long Island NLOE	Bay-W caboose	93u	130
52022	Union Pacific TTOS	Boxcar	93u	112
52023	D&TS LCCA	ACF 2-b hopper	93u	189
52024	Conrail Artrain	Auto carrier	93u	82
52026	LI/Grumman NLOE	TOFC flatcar	94u	170
52027	Pinto Valley Mine TTOM	Ore car	94u	195
52029	Ford TTOS	Sh 1-d tank	94u	239
52030	Ford TTOS	Gondola	94u	178
52031	Ford TTOS	Sh hopper	94u	189
52032	Ford TTOS	1-d tank	94u	239
52035	TCA Yorkrail	GP-9 shell	94u	59
52036	TCA 40th	Bay-W caboose	94u	130
52037	TCA Yorkrail	GP-9	94u	59
52038	Southern LCCA	Std O hopper	94u	189
52040	Grand Trunk TTOS	TOFC flatcar	95u	170
52041	Burlington Northern LOTS	TTUX flatcar	94u	170
52042	Burlington Northern LOTS	TTUX flatcar	94u	170
52043	L.L. Bean NETCA	Boxcar	94u	112
52044	Eastwood	Vat car	95u	240
52045	Penn Dutch Dairy TCA	Op milk car	94u	113
52046	ACL TTOS	Boxcar	94u	113
52047	Cotton Belt TTOS	Std O wood cab	94u	141
52048	See 52042			171
52049	Burlington Northern Artrain	Gondola	94u	178
52050	Schuylkill Haven	SP caboose	94u	139
52051	B&O TCA	Boxcar	95u	113
52052	TCA 40th Anniv	Boxcar	94u	113
52053	Carail TTOS	Boxcar	94u	113
52054	Carail	Boxcar	94u	113
52057	Western Pacific TTOS	Boxcar	95u	113
52058	Santa Fe TTOS	Boxcar	95u	113
52059	Clinchfield TCA	Quad hopper	94u	189
52060	VTC Tender w/whistle	Tender only	94u	40
52061	Sterns Pickle NLOE	Vat car	95u	240
52062	TCA City of Seattle	Long alum pass	95u	219
52063	New York Central TCA	Boxcar	95u	113
52064	Missouri Pacific TCA	Boxcar	95u	113
52067	Burlington Route LOTS	Op ice car	95u	114
52068	Contadina TTOS	Boxcar	94u	114
52070	Knoebels	Boxcar	95u	114
52071	Copper Basin TTOM	Ore car	95u	195
52072	See 52026			171
52073	Pacific Fruit Express TTOS	Std. O reefer	95u	227
52074	Iowa Beef Packers LCCA	Std. O reefer	95u	228
52075	United Auto Workers	Boxcar	95u	114
52077	Great Northern TCA	Hi-Cube boxcar	95u	116
52080	Boston & Maine NETCA	TOFC flatcar	95u	171
52082	Lackawanna Steamtown	Boxcar	95u	114
52083	Eastwood	TOFC flatcar	95u	171
52084	Union Pacific TTOS	I-beam flat	95u	162
52096	Department 56	Boxcar	95u	114
52097	Chessie System Artrain	Reefer	95u	228
86009	Canadian National LCAC	Bunk car	86u	87
87010	Canadian National LCAC	Woods. reefer	87u	228
88011	Canadian National LCAC	Std O wood cab	88u	143
900013	Canadian National LCAC	TOFC flatcar	90u	42